Lecture Notes in Computer Science 16589

The series Lecture Notes in Computer Science (LNCS), including its subseries Lecture Notes in Artificial Intelligence (LNAI) and Lecture Notes in Bioinformatics (LNBI), has established itself as a medium for the publication of new developments in computer science and information technology research, teaching, and education.

LNCS enjoys close cooperation with the computer science R & D community, the series counts many renowned academics among its volume editors and paper authors, and collaborates with prestigious societies. Its mission is to serve this international community by providing an invaluable service, mainly focused on the publication of conference and workshop proceedings and postproceedings. LNCS commenced publication in 1973.

Laura Bocchi · Burcu Kulahcioglu Ozkan
Editors

Formal Techniques for Distributed Objects, Components, and Systems

46th IFIP WG 6.1 International Conference, FORTE 2026
Held as Part of the 21st International Federated Conference on Distributed Computing Techniques, DisCoTec 2026
Urbino, Italy, June 8–12, 2026, Proceedings

Editors
Laura Bocchi
University of Kent
Canterbury, UK

Burcu Kulahcioglu Ozkan
Delft University of Technology
Delft, The Netherlands

ISSN 0302-9743 ISSN 1611-3349 (electronic)
Lecture Notes in Computer Science
ISBN 978-3-032-28186-9 ISBN 978-3-032-28187-6 (eBook)
https://doi.org/10.1007/978-3-032-28187-6

This Springer imprint is published by the registered company Springer Nature Switzerland AG
The registered company address is: Gewerbestrasse 11, 6330 Cham, Switzerland

Preface

This book constitutes the refereed proceedings of the 46th IFIP WG 6.1 International Conference on Formal Techniques for Distributed Objects, Components, and Systems, FORTE 2026, held in Urbino, Italy, as part of the 21th International Federated Conference on Distributed Computing Techniques, DisCoTec 2026, during June 8–12, 2026.

FORTE is a well-established forum for fundamental research on theory, models, tools, and applications for distributed systems. It solicits submissions focused on foundational aspects of distributed software systems, presenting approaches or tools to formally model, soundly implement, and rigorously validate these demanding but ever more necessary systems and applications. As our dependency on such software systems grows, also our responsibility as researchers grows to provide both trustworthy and usable solutions.

This year we received 27 submissions. Following a rigorous single-blind review process in which each submission received at least three reviews, the Program Committee accepted 12 regular papers, 2 tool papers, and 1 short paper.

We would like to thank the Program Committee members and all additional reviewers for their professional work and strong commitment to the success of FORTE 2026. We are grateful to the authors for thoughtfully addressing the reviewers' comments and suggestions during the preparation of their final papers.

As Program Chairs of FORTE 2026, we actively contributed to the selection of the keynote speaker and tutorial talk for FORTE. We are most grateful to Nathalie Bertrand for accepting our invitation to be the FORTE-related keynote speaker.

April 2026

Laura Bocchi
Burcu Kulahcioglu Ozkan

Organization

Program Committee

Ana Almeida Matos	Universidade de Lisboa, Portugal
Laura Bocchi	University of Kent, UK
Marco Carbone	IT University of Copenhagen, Denmark
Soham Chakraborty	TU Delft, the Netherlands
Matteo Cimini	University of Massachusetts Lowell, USA
Cezara Drăgoi	AWS/ENS, France
Wan Fokkink	Vrije Universiteit Amsterdam, the Netherlands
Adrian Francalanza	University of Malta, Malta
Simon Gay	University of Glasgow, UK
Elisa Gonzalez Boix	Vrije Universiteit Brussel, Belgium
Ping Hou	University of Oxford, UK
Leander Jehl	University of Stavanger, Norway
Jonas Kastberg Hinrichsen	Aarhus University, Denmark
Burcu Kulahcioglu Ozkan	Delft University of Technology, the Netherlands
Cosimo Laneve	University of Bologna, Italy
Diego Marmsoler	University of Exeter, UK
Hernan Melgratti	Universidad de Buenos Aires, Argentina
Claudio Antares Mezzina	Università di Urbino, Italy
Maurizio Murgia	Gran Sasso Science Institute, Italy
Rodrigo Otoni	Università della Svizzera italiana, Switzerland
Luca Padovani	Università di Bologna, Italy
Jovanka Pantovic	University of Novi Sad, Serbia
G. Michele Pinna	Università di Cagliari, Italy
Sanjiva Prasad	Indian Institute of Technology Delhi, India
Violet Ka I Pun	Western Norway University of Applied Sciences, Norway
Alceste Scalas	Technical University of Denmark, Denmark
Ana Sokolova	University of Salzburg, Austria
Peter Thiemann	Universität Freiburg, Germany
Bernardo Toninho	Instituto Superior Técnico and INESC-ID, Portugal
Emilio Tuosto	Gran Sasso Science Institute, Italy
German Vidal	VRAIN, Universitat Politècnica de València, Spain
Shoji Yuen	Nagoya University, Japan

Additional Reviewers

Cederquist, Jan
Inoue, Yusuke
Inverso, Omar
Mangla, Tarun
Zavattaro, Gianluigi

Contents

Regular Papers

Regular Papers

A Jacobi-Based Distributed Clock Synchronization Algorithm for Wide-Area Networks

Haoran Pang[1], Wei Zhang[1], and Yanwei Xu[2](✉)

[1] Tsinghua University, Beijing, China
phr22@mails.tsinghua.edu.cn, zhangwei.2020@tsinghua.org.cn
[2] Huawei Technologies Co., Ltd., Shenzhen, China
xuyanwei1@huawei.com

Abstract. Clock synchronization is essential for maintaining temporal consistency in distributed systems, particularly in large-scale and wide-area networks with asymmetric delays. Existing approaches broadly fall into two categories. Centralized optimization methods can achieve high accuracy but rely on global coordination and thus suffer from limited scalability. Distributed protocols improve scalability through local message exchanges; however, classical averaging-based schemes and more recent iterative methods such as the Classless Time Protocol (CTP) do not explicitly account for the correlation between round-trip times (RTTs) and clock offset, making them susceptible to delay asymmetry in wide-area environments. In this paper, we start from the loop-based formulation with RTT weighting (LERW) and, through an equivalence transformation, reformulate it into the node-space clock-based model with RTT weighting (CERW). From this model, we derive a Jacobi-type iterative scheme, yielding an RTT aware distributed clock synchronization algorithm. We further provide a convergence analysis of the iteration. In addition, spectral-radius analysis of the iteration matrix yields a principled reference-clock selection strategy for faster synchronization. Extensive simulations demonstrate that the proposed method achieves faster convergence, better scalability, and significantly lower synchronization errors than existing approaches.

Keywords: clock synchronization · distributed algorithm · reference clock selection

1 Introduction

Accurate clock synchronization is fundamental for maintaining temporal consistency, event ordering, and coordinated scheduling in distributed systems, and underpins many applications such as distributed logging, performance monitoring, and latency measurement. [12,13]. Widely deployed protocols such as the Network Time Protocol (NTP) [15] and the Precision Time Protocol (PTP) [1]

Published by Springer Nature Switzerland AG 2026
L. Bocchi and B. Kulahcioglu Ozkan (Eds.): FORTE 2026, LNCS 16589, pp. 3–19, 2026.
https://doi.org/10.1007/978-3-032-28187-6_1

estimate clock offsets through four-timestamp exchanges and are commonly used in both local and wide-area networks. As a result, a variety of synchronization protocols have been developed to improve accuracy and scalability under different deployment scenarios.

From a system design perspective, clock synchronization approaches can be broadly categorized into centralized and distributed paradigms. Centralized schemes aggregate measurements at a coordinator and solve a global optimization problem to compute clock corrections. Representative examples include HUYGENS [5], which enforces loop-consistency constraints to mitigate asymmetric delays, and CAT-Sync [4], which improves scalability through topology-aware probing and scheduling. While these methods can achieve high accuracy, their reliance on a single coordinator leads to communication overhead, computational bottlenecks, and limited scalability in large or dynamic environments [9,11,18].

Distributed schemes, in contrast, perform synchronization through peer-to-peer message exchanges without centralized coordination. Classical protocols such as Cristian's algorithm [2] and the Berkeley algorithm [8] estimate pairwise clock offsets through simple message exchanges and periodic averaging. The Classless Time Protocol (CTP) [7] further provides an iterative distributed update rule based on local neighbor interactions. By operating solely through local communication, these methods scale naturally to large systems and avoid the limitations of centralized designs.

However, in wide-area networks, empirical measurements show that one-way delays (OWDs) are often significantly asymmetric and strongly correlated with RTTs [14,17]. Such asymmetry biases pairwise offset estimation and degrades synchronization accuracy, especially when errors accumulate along multi-hop paths. Consequently, methods that rely on local offset averaging or symmetric-delay assumptions may perform less effectively in wide-area network settings.

These observations motivate explicitly incorporating RTT-aware asymmetry modeling into synchronization algorithms; for example, Zhang [21] proposed an Loop-based Estimation with RTT weighting (LERW) model to improve robustness to asymmetric links.

In this paper, we start from the LERW formulation, which incorporates delay asymmetry by assigning RTT-dependent weights to link measurements. We first reformulate this edge-space optimization problem into an equivalent node-space model, referred to as Clock Estimation with RTT Weighting (CERW), where clock offsets become the primary variables while preserving the same loop-consistency constraints.

From the optimality conditions of CERW, we derive a Jacobi-type iterative scheme that naturally admits a fully distributed implementation, allowing each node to update its clock using only local neighbor exchanges. We analyze the convergence of the resulting iteration and characterize its rate through spectral-radius analysis of the iteration matrix. This analysis yields a principled reference-clock selection strategy that accelerates synchronization.

Our main contributions are summarized as follows:

- We establish the equivalence between the edge-space LERW formulation and the node-space CERW formulation, transforming the problem into a representation that is more amenable to scalable distributed synchronization.
- From this formulation, we derive a Jacobi-based distributed clock synchronization algorithm and analyze its convergence.
- We further characterize the spectral radius of the iteration matrix and derive a principled reference-clock selection strategy that accelerates network-wide synchronization.

2 Models in Clock Synchronization

2.1 Four-Timestamps Estimation

We first review the standard pairwise clock offset estimation used in protocols such as NTP [15]. Consider two clocks C_i and C_j with absolute clock times τ_i and τ_j, respectively, and let owd_{ij} and owd_{ji} denote the one-way delays in the two directions. The clock offset of C_j relative to C_i is defined as $\text{offset}_{ij} \triangleq \tau_j - \tau_i$.

During a four-timestamp exchange, node i sends a request at time T_1^{ij}, which is received at node j at time T_2^{ij}, and the reply is sent at T_3^{ij} and received back at T_4^{ij}. From clock propagation, the timestamp relations satisfy

$$T_2^{ij} - T_1^{ij} = owd_{ij} + (\tau_j - \tau_i), \tag{1}$$

$$T_4^{ij} - T_3^{ij} = owd_{ji} + (\tau_i - \tau_j). \tag{2}$$

Hence, the offset estimator is

$$\widetilde{\text{offset}}_{ij} = \frac{(T_2^{ij} - T_1^{ij}) - (T_4^{ij} - T_3^{ij})}{2}. \tag{3}$$

This estimator is exact only under the symmetry assumption $owd_{ij} = owd_{ji}$. In general networks, asymmetric delays introduce bias, and pairwise measurements alone are insufficient. If the one-way delays were known, the offsets could be corrected accordingly; thus delay estimation and offset estimation are fundamentally equivalent problems.

2.2 Node-Parameterized Synchronization Model

We next consider the three-node network in Fig. 1. Besides the pairwise RTT constraints obtained from four-timestamp exchanges, the cycle $1 \to 2 \to 3 \to 1$ introduces an additional loop-consistency constraint:

$$owd_{12} + owd_{23} + owd_{31} = b_{\text{loop}}, \tag{4}$$

where

$$b_{\text{loop}} = (T_2^{12} - T_1^{12}) + (T_2^{23} - T_1^{23}) + (T_2^{31} - T_1^{31}), \tag{5}$$

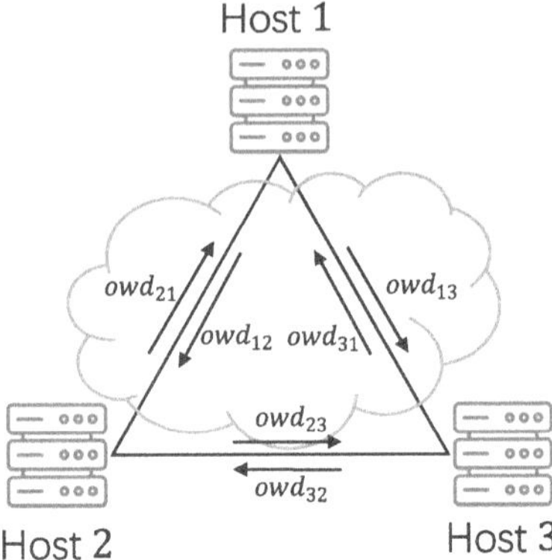

Fig. 1. Three-node network example with asymmetric OWDs. Conventional four-timestamp offset estimation assumes path symmetry and may introduce bias when links are asymmetric. By forming a loop among the nodes, additional consistency constraints can be exploited to jointly refine delay and clock offset estimation.

which is directly computable from the observed timestamps along the cycle.

In the above three-node example, there are six unknown one-way delays but only four independent equations, rendering the system underdetermined. Consequently, the delays cannot be uniquely recovered from pairwise timestamp measurements alone.

More generally, consider a connected network modeled as an undirected graph $G = (V, E)$, where V denotes the set of clocks (nodes) and E the set of communication links (edges). Let owd_{ij} represent the one-way delay on each directed link (i, j) induced by the four-timestamp exchanges. Stacking all directed one-way delays into a vector owd and collecting all measurable delay and loop-consistency relations yields

$$A_{\text{loop}}\,\text{owd} = b, \tag{6}$$

where $A_{\text{loop}} \in \mathbb{R}^{(|E|-|V|+1)\times|E|}$ is the loop-incidence matrix, with one row per independent cycle of the graph, whose number equals $|E| - |V| + 1$ [3], and $b \in \mathbb{R}^{|E|-|V|+1}$ is the associated loop measurement vector.

For the three-node case, stacking the directed delays as

$$\text{owd} = \left[\, owd_{12},\, owd_{21},\, owd_{23},\, owd_{32},\, owd_{31},\, owd_{13} \,\right]^{\top},$$

the constraint matrix becomes

$$A_{\text{loop}} = \begin{bmatrix} 1\,1\,0\,0\,0\,0 \\ 0\,0\,1\,1\,0\,0 \\ 0\,0\,0\,0\,1\,1 \\ 1\,0\,1\,0\,1\,0 \end{bmatrix}, \quad b = \begin{bmatrix} (T_2^{12} - T_1^{12}) + (T_4^{12} - T_3^{12}) \\ (T_2^{23} - T_1^{23}) + (T_4^{23} - T_3^{23}) \\ (T_2^{31} - T_1^{31}) + (T_4^{31} - T_3^{31}) \\ (T_2^{12} - T_1^{12}) + (T_2^{23} - T_1^{23}) + (T_2^{31} - T_1^{31}) \end{bmatrix}. \tag{7}$$

which depends only on timestamp observations.

However, since the number of constraints is smaller than the number of unknowns, the system admits infinitely many feasible solutions. HUYGENS [5] resolves this ambiguity by formulating delay estimation as a global optimization problem, referred to as **Loop-based Estimation (LE)**:

$$\begin{aligned} \min_{\text{owd}} \quad & \sum_{(i,j)\in E} (\text{owd}_{ij} - \text{owd}_{ji})^2, \\ \text{s.t.} \quad & A_{\text{loop}}\,\text{owd} = b. \end{aligned} \tag{8}$$

The same problem can also be reformulated from the perspective of delay asymmetry. Defining the delay asymmetry on each link as $\Delta_{ij} = \text{owd}_{ij} - \frac{\text{RTT}_{ij}}{2}$, we obtain **Asymmetry-based Estimation (AE)** model :

$$\begin{aligned} \min_{\Delta} \quad & \sum_{(i,j)\in E} |\Delta_{ij}|^2, \\ \text{s.t.} \quad & A_{\text{loop}}\,\Delta = c. \end{aligned} \tag{9}$$

Here, c represents the adjusted loop imbalance after removing symmetric delay components from b. For example, in a loop $(1,2,3,1)$, it can be written as $c_{\text{loop}:1,2,3,1} = (T_3^{12} + T_3^{23} + T_3^{31}) - (T_4^{12} + T_4^{23} + T_4^{31})$.

To account for heterogeneous link reliability, Zhang *et al.* [21] further introduced **Loop-based Estimation with RTT Weighting(LERW)**:

$$\begin{aligned} \min_{\text{owd}} \quad & \sum_{(i,j)\in E} \frac{(\text{owd}_{ij} - \text{owd}_{ji})^2}{\text{RTT}_{ij}^{\alpha}}, \\ \text{s.t.} \quad & A_{\text{loop}}\,\text{owd} = b. \end{aligned} \tag{10}$$

These formulations share the same loop-consistency constraints and differ only in variable choice or weighting. However, they are all defined in the edge space, and require collecting all measurements centrally to solve the optimization problem. This motivates a node-space reformulation, where the number of variables is significantly reduced.

2.3 Node-Parameterized Synchronization Model

Both the LE and AE formulations operate in the *edge space*, where the optimization variables are defined on directed links. Alternatively, the synchronization problem can be reformulated directly in the *node space*, following the idea of CTP [7], where the unknowns are the clock offsets of individual nodes. Let τ_i denote the offset of node C_i relative to the reference clock C_1. We define the **Clock Estimate (CE)** model as:

$$\begin{aligned} \min_{\tau} \quad & \sum_{(i,j)\in E} (\tau_j - \tau_i - \widetilde{\text{offset}}_{ij})^2, \\ \text{s.t.} \quad & \tau_1 = 0. \end{aligned} \tag{11}$$

Here, C_1 is fixed as the reference, and the solution $\tau_2, \ldots, \tau_n$ represents the estimated offsets of the remaining clocks.

Claim. The Asymmetry-based Estimation (AE) model and the Clock Estimate (CE) model are equivalent.

Proof. For a general graph $G(V, E)$, the total number of independent loops equals $|E| - |V| + 1$ [3]. In model AE, we divide the variables into those on the spanning tree (ΔM_t) and those off the tree (ΔM_{nt}), leading to:

$$\begin{aligned} \min_{\Delta M_t,\, \Delta M_{nt}} \quad & ||\Delta M_t||^2 + ||\Delta M_{nt}||^2, \\ \text{s.t.} \quad & [A_t,\, A_{nt}] \begin{bmatrix} \Delta M_t \\ \Delta M_{nt} \end{bmatrix} = c. \end{aligned} \tag{12}$$

Each loop equation contains exactly one non-tree edge, so each variable in ΔM_{nt} can be linearly expressed in terms of the tree variables ΔM_t. By eliminating ΔM_{nt}, we obtain an unconstrained optimization problem:

$$\min_{\Delta M_t} ||\Delta M_t||^2 + ||A_{nt}^{-1}(b - A_t \Delta M_t)||^2. \tag{13}$$

Since A_{nt} is invertible by construction, this reduced model contains $|V| - 1$ independent variables, each corresponding to an edge on the spanning tree that covers all nodes.

Finally, by substituting $-\Delta_{ij} = \tau_j - \tau_i + \widetilde{\text{offset}}_{ij}$, we transform the edge-based model into the node-space formulation (11). The Jacobian matrix T is of dimension $(|V| - 1) \times (|V| - 1)$, where each row corresponds to an edge in a spanning tree. Since the spanning tree guarantees that each node j ($j \neq 1$) appears exactly once, each row has diagonal element -1 in column j. If the edge connects j to the reference node 1, all off-diagonal elements are zero. Otherwise, the entry in column i is $+1$ and all other off-diagonal elements are zero. Hence T is diagonally dominant and therefore invertible, guaranteeing that the node-space and edge-space formulations are fully equivalent for arbitrary connected topologies.

Remark 1. Huygens [5] solves the LE model by computing the minimum-norm solution $\Delta = A^\top (AA^\top)^{-1} c$, where $A \in \mathbb{R}^{(|E|-|V|+1)\times|E|}$ is the loop-incidence matrix. This requires forming the pseudo-inverse of A, leading to a computational complexity of $\mathcal{O}(|E|^3)$.

In contrast, the proposed node-based formulations CE reduce the problem to solving a linear system of size $(|V|-1)\times(|V|-1)$, resulting in a lower complexity of $\mathcal{O}(|V|^3)$. Therefore, the node-based models are computationally more efficient and scale better for large networks.

Based on the above derivation, we equivalently reformulate the LERW model in the node space, leading to the following **Clock Estimation with RTT Weighting (CERW)** formulation:

$$\begin{aligned} \min_{\tau} \quad & \sum_{(i,j)\in E} \frac{(\tau_j - \tau_i - \widetilde{\text{offset}}_{ij})^2}{\text{RTT}_{ij}^{\alpha}}, \\ \text{s.t.} \quad & \tau_1 = 0. \end{aligned} \tag{14}$$

Compared with (11), this weighted objective can be viewed as a least-squares problem that accounts for delay asymmetry and heterogeneous link reliability while preserving the compact node-based representation. This form is particularly suitable for scalable distributed iterative updates, which we derive next.

3 Distributed Algorithm

Instead of solving the CERW model centrally, we derive an equivalent Jacobi-type iterative form from the optimization problem. The resulting updates depend only on neighbor information, which naturally enables a fully distributed implementation. Based on this iteration, we present the distributed synchronization algorithm.

3.1 Equivalent Linear System Formulation

For model CERW, if we set the variable τ_1 equal to 0, then the problem becomes an unconstrained problem for variables $\tau_2, ..., \tau_N$. Then the optimal solution of the problem needs to satisfy that the first derivatives of all variables are 0: Consider the CERW least-squares objective

$$\mathcal{L}_{\mathrm{CERW}}(\tau) = \sum_{(i,j)\in E} \frac{\left(\tau_j - \tau_i - \widetilde{\mathrm{offset}_{ij}}\right)^2}{\mathrm{RTT}_{ij}^{\alpha}}. \tag{15}$$

For a fixed node j, only the terms involving τ_j contribute to the derivative. Taking derivative w.r.t. τ_j gives

$$\frac{\partial \mathcal{L}_{\mathrm{CERW}}}{\partial \tau_j} = 2 \sum_{(i,j)\in E} \frac{\tau_j - \tau_i - \widetilde{\mathrm{offset}_{ij}}}{\mathrm{RTT}_{ij}^{\alpha}}. \tag{16}$$

Setting it to zero yields

$$\sum_{(i,j)\in E} \frac{\tau_j - \tau_i - \widetilde{\mathrm{offset}_{ij}}}{\mathrm{RTT}_{ij}^{\alpha}} = 0, \tag{17}$$

which leads to the weighted linear relation

$$\Big(\sum_{(i,j)\in E} \frac{1}{\mathrm{RTT}_{ij}^{\alpha}}\Big)\tau_j - \sum_{(i,j)\in E} \frac{\tau_i}{\mathrm{RTT}_{ij}^{\alpha}} = \sum_{(i,j)\in E} \frac{\widetilde{\mathrm{offset}_{ij}}}{\mathrm{RTT}_{ij}^{\alpha}}. \tag{18}$$

From the connection information of the graph with the timestamps information and set the first column and the first row of matrix to 0, and the diagonal line to 1 to get matrix A. We define vectors $\tau = (\tau_1, \tau_2, \tau_3, ..., \tau_n)$, then Eq. 18 can be expressed as a system of linear equations:

$$\mathbf{A}\tau = \mathbf{b} \tag{19}$$

where matrix A is $N \times N$ which elements satisfy:

$$a_{ij} = \begin{cases} 1, & if \quad i = j = 1 \\ \sum\limits_{(i,j)\in E} \dfrac{1}{\mathrm{RTT}_{ij}^{\alpha}}, & if \quad i = j \neq 1, \\ -\dfrac{1}{\mathrm{RTT}_{ij}^{\alpha}}, & if \quad (i,j) \in E \quad and \quad i,j \neq 1, \\ 0, & else. \end{cases} \tag{20}$$

b is $(N) \times 1$ which elements satisfy:

$$b_j = \begin{cases} 1, & if \quad j = 1 \\ \sum\limits_{(i,j)\in E} \dfrac{\widetilde{\mathrm{offset}}_{ij}}{\mathrm{RTT}_{ij}^{\alpha}} & if \quad j \neq 1 \end{cases} \tag{21}$$

3.2 Jacobi-Based Distributed Algorithms

Based on the above model, we decompose matrix A into the sum of the diagonal matrix D, the strict lower triangular matrix L, and the strict upper triangular matrix U:

$$A = D + L + U \tag{22}$$

Then according to the Jacobi iteration, the update of the vector τ can become:

$$\tau^{(l+1)} = D^{-1}(b - (L + U)\tau^{(l)}) \tag{23}$$

We keep the reference clock $\tau_1 = 0$ unchanged and calculate $\tau_i, i \in V \setminus \{1\}$ iteratively. Specific to each element, it can be expressed as:

$$\tau_j^{(l+1)} = \begin{cases} 1, & if \quad j = 1 \\ \dfrac{\sum\limits_{(i,j)\in E} \frac{\tau_j}{\mathrm{RTT}_{ij}^{\alpha}} + \sum\limits_{(i,j)\in E} \frac{\widetilde{\mathrm{offset}}_{ij}}{\mathrm{RTT}_{ij}^{\alpha}}}{\sum\limits_{(i,j)\in E} \frac{1}{\mathrm{RTT}_{ij}^{\alpha}}} & if \quad j \neq 1 \end{cases} \tag{24}$$

Before the iterations start, each node probes its neighbors using four-timestamp exchanges to obtain pairwise $\widetilde{\mathrm{offset}}_{ij}$ and the corresponding RTTs. The offsets are then shared with the peer, which sets $\widetilde{\mathrm{offset}}_{ji} = -\widetilde{\mathrm{offset}}_{ij}$.

All clocks are initialized with $\tau_1^{(0)} = 0$ for the reference node and $\tau_i^{(0)} = 0$ for all $i \neq 1$. During iteration l, each node maintains its local estimate $\tau_i^{(l)}$ and exchanges it with its neighbors. The clock offsets are updated according to the Jacobi iteration until convergence or a maximum number of rounds is reached. The overall procedure is summarized in Algorithm 1.

Algorithm 1 Jacobi-based Distributed Clock Synchronization Algorithm (CERW)

Require: Network graph $G(V, E)$, reference clock 1, maximum iterations $L_{\max}$, weighting exponent α
Ensure: Estimated clock offsets $\{\tau_i\}$
1: **Initialization:**
2: Initialize $\tau_1^{(0)} = 0$ and $\tau_i^{(0)} = 0, \forall i \neq 1$
3: Each node probes its neighbors and computes $\widetilde{\text{offset}}_{ij}$ and RTT_{ij} from timestamp exchanges
4: Exchange measurements: set $\widetilde{\text{offset}}_{ji} = -\widetilde{\text{offset}}_{ij}$ and $\text{RTT}_{ji} = \text{RTT}_{ij}$.
5: **for** $l = 0, 1, 2, \ldots, L_{\max} - 1$ **do**
6: Each node i sends $\tau_i^{(l)}$ to its neighbors
7: **for all** $i \in V \setminus \{1\}$ **in parallel do**
8: Update clock:

$$\tau_i^{(l+1)} = \frac{\sum_{j:(i,j)\in E} \frac{\tau_j^{(l)}}{\text{RTT}_{ij}^{\alpha}} + \sum_{j:(i,j)\in E} \frac{\widetilde{\text{offset}}_{ij}}{\text{RTT}_{ij}^{\alpha}}}{\sum_{j:(i,j)\in E} \frac{1}{\text{RTT}_{ij}^{\alpha}}}$$

9: **end for**
10: **end for**
11: Apply clock correction using $\{\tau_i\}$

4 The Choice of Reference Clock

In this section, we first establish the convergence of the proposed distributed Jacobi iteration. Based on the resulting iteration matrix, we then analyze its spectral radius to characterize the convergence rate and derive a principled strategy for selecting the reference clock that achieves the fastest convergence. Without loss of generality, for ease of analysis, we relabel the nodes such that the reference clock is indexed as node 1.

4.1 Convergence Analysis

For the linear system $Ax = b$, if A is symmetric with positive diagonal entries, a necessary and sufficient condition for the convergence of the Jacobi method is that both A and $2D - A$ are positive definite [20], where $D = \text{diag}(A)$.

Consider the j-th row of A. We have

$$|a_{jj}| - \sum_{i\neq j} |a_{ji}| = \begin{cases} \frac{1}{\text{RTT}_{1j}^2}, & if \quad (j,1) \in E, \\ 0, & if \quad (j,1) \notin E, \end{cases}$$

Hence A is weakly diagonally dominant. Moreover, when the underlying graph is connected, the associated matrix is irreducible [10]. By classical results on irreducibly diagonally dominant symmetric matrices, A is positive definite.

Similarly, for $2D - A$,

$$|2d_{jj} - a_{jj}| - \sum_{i \neq j} |a_{ji}| = \begin{cases} \frac{1}{\mathrm{RTT}_{1j}^2}, & if \quad (j,1) \in E, \\ 0, & if \quad (j,1) \notin E, \end{cases}$$

which shows that $2D - A$ is also weakly diagonally dominant and irreducible. Therefore, $2D - A$ is positive definite as well.

Since both A and $2D - A$ are positive definite, the Jacobi iteration converges.

4.2 The Choice of Reference Clock

Our goal is to identify the reference clock that yields the fastest convergence in the distributed Jacobi iteration. The overall proof strategy is illustrated in Fig. 2. We provide convergence guarantees for the proposed Jacobi iteration and derive a spectral-radius–based criterion for reference-clock selection for both the CE and CERW models.

Lemma 1. *[19] For the iterative format $x^{(l+1)} = Bx^{(l)} + C$, $-ln\rho(B)$ is said to be its asymptotic convergence velocity, where $\rho(B)$ is the spectral radius of B.*

According to the lemma, a smaller $\rho(B)$ implies faster convergence. Therefore, we aim to select the reference clock that minimizes $\rho(B)$ in the iteration matrix $B = D^{-1}(U + L)$.

To analyze this, we rearrange the system matrix A such that the reference clock is listed first, followed by its k neighboring nodes, and then the remaining $n - k - 1$ nodes. In this structure, the first $k + 1$ rows of $B = D^{-1}(U + L)$ have a row-sum equal to 1, while the others have row-sums strictly less than 1. Applying the Gershgorin circle theorem [6]:

$$|\lambda - a_{ii}| \leq \sum_{j \neq i} |a_{ij}|, i = 1, 2...n. \tag{25}$$

we can only conclude that $\lambda_{\max} \leq 1$, which provides a loose upper bound on $\rho(B)$.

To refine this, we introduce a diagonal scaling transformation $D_1^{-1} B D_1$, where the diagonal elements of D_1 and the eigenvalues of the transformed matrix remain unchanged. When the element ith element of D_1 is α, it means that the first row element of matrix B is divided by α, and the first column is multiplied by α. We hope to achieve the goal of reducing the sum of rows with a value of 1 by making this transformation: some columns will increase in size at the cost of affecting other rows.

We first establish the convergence result for the CE model. The optimality conditions lead to a linear system $A\tau = b$, whose coefficient matrix A has the

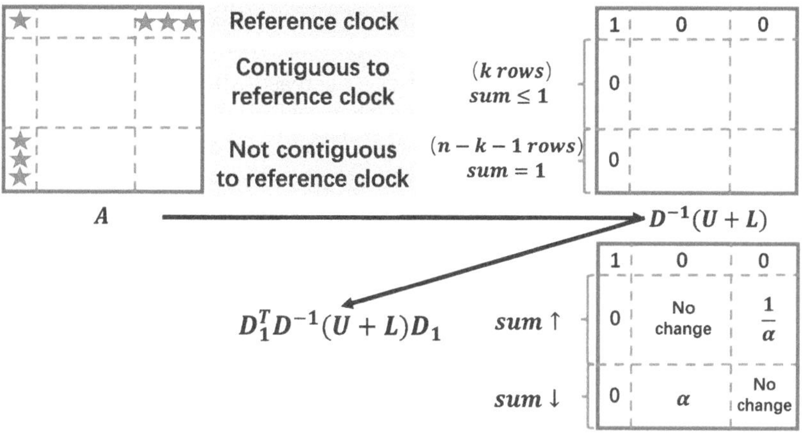

Fig. 2. Deriving the spectral radius through diagonal matrix transformation for convergence analysis.

following structure:

$$a_{ij} = \begin{cases} 1, & \text{if } i = j = 1, \\ k_j, & \text{if } i = j \neq 1, \\ -1, & \text{if } (i,j) \in E \text{ and } i, j \neq 1, \\ 0, & \text{otherwise.} \end{cases}$$

Based on this matrix form, we analyze the Jacobi iteration and derive bounds on its convergence rate. To tighten the bound, we choose the diagonal scaling so that the two types of row sums become approximately equal. Specifically, the rows that originally sum to 1 are reduced to

$$\frac{\alpha}{n-k} + \frac{n-k-1}{n-k},$$

while the other rows are increased to

$$\frac{k}{n} + \frac{n-k-1}{n\alpha}.$$

We then set these two expressions equal and solve for α, which is equivalent to solving the quadratic

$$nx^2 + \big(n(n-k-1) - k(n-k)\big)\,x - (n-k-1)(n-k) = 0, \tag{26}$$

and taking the positive root x^*. The resulting theoretical upper bound of the convergence factor is

$$\rho_{\text{bound}} = \frac{x^*}{n-k} + \frac{n-k-1}{n-k}. \tag{27}$$

This bound characterizes the impact of network connectivity on convergence. As the maximum degree k increases, the theoretical bound ρ_{bound}—corresponding to the spectral radius of B—decreases, indicating faster convergence. Consequently, selecting the node with the largest number of neighbors as the reference clock minimizes the convergence factor and yields the fastest convergence rate. For the CERW model, the analysis becomes more involved due to heterogeneous RTT-based weights. Nevertheless, the same intuition applies: choosing the node with the largest effective weighted degree, i.e.,

$$i = \arg\max_{i} \sum_{(i,j)\in E} \frac{1}{\text{RTT}_{ij}^2},$$

leads to improved convergence. Empirically, this criterion consistently reduces the number of iterations required.

5 Experiments

We conduct three groups of experiments to evaluate the proposed method from both computational and synchronization perspectives: (i) runtime comparison between edge- and node-based formulations, (ii) synchronization accuracy comparison between the proposed distributed Jacobi scheme and the classical Berkeley algorithm, and (iii) convergence analysis under different reference clock selections.

5.1 Simulation Setup

Network Topology. Synthetic network topologies are generated as connected Erdős–Rényi random graphs $G(V, E)$ with varying network sizes. The connectivity probability is chosen to ensure a single connected component, allowing information to propagate through multi-hop paths.

OWD Setting. To model delay asymmetry and reflect its correlation with RTT [17], we introduce RTT-dependent perturbations by drawing $\varepsilon_{ij} \sim \mathcal{N}(0, \sigma^2 RTT_{ij}^2)$. The directed one-way delays are then defined as

$$owd_{ij} = \frac{RTT_{ij}}{2} + \varepsilon_{ij}, \qquad owd_{ji} = \frac{RTT_{ij}}{2} - \varepsilon_{ij}. \tag{28}$$

Consequently, larger-RTT links exhibit stronger delay asymmetry, and the resulting four-timestamp offset measurements become increasingly biased.

Clock Model. Each node maintains a local clock modeled as

$$\tau_i(t) = \alpha_i t + \beta_i, \tag{29}$$

where β_i denotes the initial clock offset and α_i represents the clock drift (frequency skew). The drift parameters are randomly sampled around 1 to simulate oscillator instability and time-varying behavior.

Measurement Noise. To reflect practical timestamp uncertainty, independent Gaussian jitter is added to each timestamp during message exchanges.

This unified setup is used for all experiments, including runtime evaluation of different formulations, synchronization accuracy comparison with classical methods, and convergence analysis of reference clock selection.

5.2 Compared Methods

- **Berkeley.** A reference node periodically collects time differences from all other nodes, computes the average offset, and broadcasts corrections.
- **Huygens.** Huygens adopts a centralized architecture in which a coordinator collects timestamp measurements from all links and solves a global optimization problem to jointly estimate one-way delays and clock offsets.

5.3 Evaluation Metrics

To quantify synchronization accuracy, we measure the error between the estimated clock offsets and the ground-truth relative offsets at each iteration. Let $\tau^{(t)} \in \mathbb{R}^N$ denote the estimated offsets at iteration t, and let $\tau^* \in \mathbb{R}^N$ be the ground-truth solution. We define the per-node error vector as

$$e^{(t)} \triangleq \tau^{(t)} - \tau^*. \tag{30}$$

We report three complementary metrics:

- **Maximum error (worst-case):**

$$\|e^{(t)}\|_\infty = \max_i |e_i^{(t)}|,$$

  which captures the worst synchronized node.
- **Mean error (average performance):**

$$\frac{1}{N}\|e^{(t)}\|_1 = \frac{1}{N}\sum_{i=1}^{N} |e_i^{(t)}|,$$

  which reflects the overall synchronization quality.
- **Convergence factor (ρ):** obtained by fitting the slope of $\log \|e^{(t)}\|_\infty$ after the transient phase, corresponding to the exponential decay rate.

5.4 Results and Discussion

Runtime Comparison of Edge-Based (HUYGENS) vs. Node-Based (CERW) Formulation. To assess computational efficiency, we compare the edge-parameterized formulation used in HUYGENS with the node-parameterized formulation adopted in CERW. Both approaches are implemented

Table 1. Runtime comparison of edge-based (HUYGENS) vs. node-based (CERW) formulations (mean ± std in seconds).

n	Find loops	Huygens	CERW
20	0.0006 ± 0.0001	0.0009 ± 0.0007	**0.0006 ± 0.0017**
50	0.0042 ± 0.0006	0.0013 ± 0.0001	**0.0004 ± 0.0011**
100	0.0242 ± 0.0024	0.0022 ± 0.0002	**0.0004 ± 0.0004**
200	0.2376 ± 0.0353	0.0171 ± 0.0037	**0.0027 ± 0.0028**
500	15.3423 ± 1.0102	0.4164 ± 0.1778	**0.0603 ± 0.0202**

using LSQR [16] and evaluated over 1000 independent runs, reporting the mean and standard deviation of runtime.

Table 1 compares the runtime of the edge-based (HUYGENS) and node-based (CERW) formulations. HUYGENS requires an additional preprocessing step to enumerate independent loops, which already incurs noticeable overhead. Moreover, even considering only the solving time, it remains slower than CERW. By avoiding loop construction and operating directly in the node space, CERW achieves significantly lower runtime and better scalability as the network size increases. In terms of memory footprint, CERW requires $O(|V|^2)$ storage compared to $O(|E|^2)$ for HUYGENS, offering a clear advantage in sparse networks.

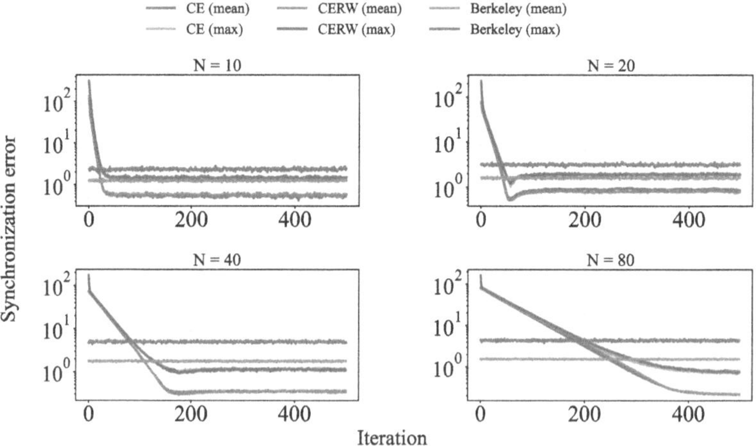

Fig. 3. Synchronization error versus iteration for different network sizes. Across all settings, CE and CERW converge and attain lower errors than the Berkeley algorithm, while CERW consistently provides a slight additional improvement over CE.

Performance Comparison of CERW and Berkeley. Figure 3 compares the synchronization errors of CE, CERW, and the Berkeley algorithm under different network sizes. Both CE and CERW converge significantly faster and achieve lower steady-state errors than Berkeley across all settings. While Berkeley relies on simple pairwise averaging and suffers from persistent bias under asymmetric delays, the proposed loop-consistency– based methods effectively exploit multi-hop information through distributed iterations. Moreover, CERW consistently attains slightly lower errors than CE due to its RTT-aware modeling.

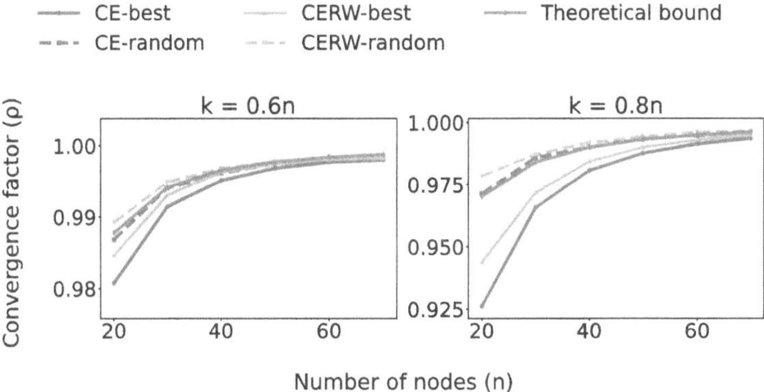

Fig. 4. Convergence factor ρ versus the number of nodes under different reference-clock selection strategies. For both CE and CERW, selecting the reference clock using our spectral-radius criterion consistently achieves faster convergence and performance close to the theoretical bound compared with random selection.

Impact of Reference Clock Selection. We evaluate the effect of reference-clock selection on the distributed Jacobi iteration under four configurations: CE-best, CE-random, CERW-best, and CERW-random. Convergence is measured using the empirical convergence factor ρ and the number of iterations required to reach predefined accuracy thresholds.

As shown in Fig. 4, selecting the optimal reference clock consistently yields smaller ρ for both CE and CERW, indicating faster error decay, whereas random selection leads to noticeably slower convergence. Table 2 further confirms that the optimal-reference schemes require substantially fewer iterations to reach the same accuracy levels, even in large networks. These results validate the spectral-radius analysis and demonstrate that proper reference-clock selection significantly accelerates distributed synchronization.

6 Conclusion

This paper presented an RTT-aware distributed clock synchronization method for wide-area networks with delay asymmetry. Starting from LERW, we established its equivalence to a node-space model CERW, which enables a

Table 2. Average iterations required to reach different accuracy thresholds under varying network sizes. The two proposed methods (CE-best and CERW-best) are highlighted in bold.

Threshold	Method	n					
		20	30	40	50	60	70
10	**CE-best**	**1.9**	**6.1**	**11.5**	**14.3**	**23.2**	**48.7**
	CE-random	6.1	19.6	34.5	44.2	49.5	78.4
	CERW-best	**2.9**	**8.4**	**16.1**	**19.4**	**29.0**	**65.8**
	CERW-random	12.2	24.4	34.5	40.1	63.2	79.3
1	**CE-best**	**27.0**	**63.0**	**110.0**	**163.6**	**243.8**	**354.6**
	CE-random	89.1	195.9	259.1	349.7	410.9	454.9
	CERW-best	**38.8**	**85.3**	**152.9**	**228.1**	**322.9**	**414.8**
	CERW-random	137.7	232.7	313.5	381.2	446.1	472.6
0.1	**CE-best**	**56.1**	**129.2**	**228.7**	**348.8**	**471.1**	**491.4**
	CE-random	187.5	328.1	434.1	487.7	498.7	500.0
	CERW-best	**80.1**	**173.9**	**310.1**	**430.1**	**488.0**	**495.9**
	CERW-random	264.8	374.6	461.7	487.3	498.3	499.4

scalable representation of the synchronization problem. Based on this formulation, we derived a Jacobi-type distributed iteration and provided a convergence analysis. Spectral-radius analysis further led to a principled reference-clock selection strategy that accelerates synchronization. Extensive simulations indicate that the proposed approach generally provides improved convergence speed and reduced synchronization error compared with existing methods, while maintaining scalability across large networks. These results suggest the benefit of combining RTT-aware modeling with distributed iterative synchronization for wide-area environments.

References

1. IEEE standard for a precision clock synchronization protocol for networked measurement and control systems. IEEE Std 1588-2019 (Revision of IEEE Std 1588-2008), pp. 1–499 (2020). https://doi.org/10.1109/IEEESTD.2020.9120376
2. Cristian, F.: Probabilistic clock synchronization. Distrib. Comput. **3**(3), 146–158 (1989)
3. Diestel, R.: Graph Theory. Springer (2025)
4. Fan, Z., Li, X., Xu, Y., Li, Y., Yang, T., Uhlig, S.: Work-in-progress: a novel clock synchronization system for large-scale clusters. In: 2022 IEEE Real-Time Systems Symposium (RTSS), pp. 519–522 (2022). https://doi.org/10.1109/RTSS55097.2022.00056
5. Geng, Y., et al.: Exploiting a natural network effect for scalable, fine-grained clock synchronization. In: Proceedings of the 15th USENIX Conference on Networked Systems Design and Implementation, NSDI 2018, pp. 81–94. USENIX Association, USA (2018)

6. Gershgorin, S.A.: Über die abgrenzung der eigenwerte einer matrix. Izvestiya Akademii Nauk SSSR Seriya Matematika **7**, 749–754 (1931)
7. Gurewitz, O., Cidon, I., Sidi, M.: Network classless time protocol based on clock offset optimization. IEEE/ACM Trans. Network. **14**(4), 876–888 (2006). https://doi.org/10.1109/TNET.2006.880181
8. Gusella, R., Zatti, S.: The accuracy of the clock synchronization achieved by TEMPO in Berkeley UNIX 4.3 BSD. IEEE Trans. Softw. Eng. **15**(7), 847–853 (2002)
9. Heller, B., Sherwood, R., McKeown, N.: The controller placement problem. In: Proceedings of the First Workshop on Hot Topics in Software Defined Networks, HotSDN 2012, pp. 7–12. Association for Computing Machinery, New York, NY, USA (2012). https://doi.org/10.1145/2342441.2342444
10. Horn, R.A., Johnson, C.R.: Matrix Analysis. Cambridge University Press (2012)
11. Karakus, M., Durresi, A.: A survey: control plane scalability issues and approaches in software-defined networking (SDN). Comput. Netw. **112**, 279–293 (2017). https://doi.org/10.1016/j.comnet.2016.11.017. https://www.sciencedirect.com/science/article/pii/S138912861630411X
12. Lamport, L.: Time, clocks, and the ordering of events in a distributed system. Commun. ACM **21**(7), 558–565 (1978). https://doi.org/10.1145/359545.359563
13. Liskov, B.: Practical uses of synchronized clocks in distributed systems. In: Proceedings of the Tenth Annual ACM Symposium on Principles of Distributed Computing, pp. 1–9 (1991)
14. Liu, Y., et al.: What causes delay asymmetry: a large-scale one-way delay measurement and empirical study. In: GLOBECOM 2022 - 2022 IEEE Global Communications Conference, pp. 6127–6132 (2022). https://doi.org/10.1109/GLOBECOM48099.2022.10000938
15. Mills, D.: Internet time synchronization: the network time protocol. IEEE Trans. Commun. **39**(10), 1482–1493 (1991). https://doi.org/10.1109/26.103043
16. Paige, C.C., Saunders, M.A.: LSQR: an algorithm for sparse linear equations and sparse least squares. ACM Trans. Math. Softw. (TOMS) **8**(1), 43–71 (1982)
17. Pathak, A., Pucha, H., Zhang, Y., Hu, Y.C., Mao, Z.M.: A measurement study of internet delay asymmetry. In: Claypool, M., Uhlig, S. (eds.) PAM 2008. LNCS, vol. 4979, pp. 182–191. Springer, Heidelberg (2008). https://doi.org/10.1007/978-3-540-79232-1_19
18. Rekhter, Y., Hares, S., Li, T.: A Border Gateway Protocol 4 (BGP-4). RFC 4271 (2006). https://doi.org/10.17487/RFC4271. https://www.rfc-editor.org/info/rfc4271
19. Varga, R.S.: Matrix Iterative Analysis, 2nd edn. Springer (2009). https://doi.org/10.1007/978-3-642-05156-2
20. Young, D.M.: Iterative Solution of Large Linear Systems. Academic Press, New York (1971)
21. Zhang, W., Zhenyu, M., Zhang, L., Yanwei, X.: A round trip time weighting model for one-way delay estimation. East Asian J. Appl. Math. **14**(1), 179–194 (2024). https://doi.org/10.4208/eajam.2022-330.120623. https://global-sci.com/article/82403/a-round-trip-time-weighting-model-for-oneway-delay-estimation

Harmony in Rocq

Savan Kan and Sergueï Lenglet(✉)

Sorbonne Paris Nord, Villetaneuse, France
lenglet@lipn.univ-paris13.fr

Abstract. The POPLmark challenge has been a source of progress for the representation of binders in proof assistants for sequential calculi. In the same spirit, the Concurrent Calculi Formalization Benchmark proposes a set of challenges covering issues with the representation of concurrent systems models such as process algebra. One of them is about scope extrusion, i.e., the dynamic extension of the scope of a binder during reduction. The benchmark proposes to formalize the harmony lemma, a correspondence result between two semantics of a minimal π-calculus. We present an answer to this challenge in Rocq using de Bruijn indices and the library Autosubst. Our goal is to assess how this library, developed for sequential languages, helps in a concurrent setting.

Keywords: Process calculi · Harmony lemma · De Bruijn indices

1 Introduction

Representing binders in proofs assistant is a source of overhead code in formalized proofs to the point that the POPLmark challenge [2,4] has been proposed to stimulate the research in that area. It resulted in the study or development of techniques, libraries, or proof systems dedicated to simplify the representation of binders. Among them, Autosubst [21] and Autosubst 2 [22] are tools which, given the definition of a language, generate the definitions of its syntax and capture-avoiding substitution using de Bruijn indices [5] for the Rocq (formerly Coq) proof assistant. The tools also generate and prove basic properties of this substitution as well as a tactic `asimpl` to automatically decide terms equalities involving substitution.

The POPLmark challenge focuses on the representation of binders for sequential calculi, using type systems for the λ-calculus as testbeds. Concurrent and distributed systems models such as process algebras [19] raise some specific issues w.r.t. binders, as advocated by the recently proposed Concurrent Calculi Formalization Benchmark [6]. Among them is *scope extrusion*, the dynamic evolution of the scope of a binder. For example, an agent may own a private communication channel, represented as a restricted name; sending that private channel to

Artefacts available in https://archive.softwareheritage.org/swh:1:dir:1ba31f2c30b147ef5918e061f43f1e11fd33b46f.

Published by Springer Nature Switzerland AG 2026
L. Bocchi and B. Kulahcioglu Ozkan (Eds.): FORTE 2026, LNCS 16589, pp. 20–37, 2026.
https://doi.org/10.1007/978-3-032-28187-6_2

another agent to communicate secretly later on requires to extend the scope of that name to include the recipient.

The semantics of process calculi can be defined using two different styles in which the manipulation of scopes is more or less explicit. In a *reduction semantics*, the structures of communicating agents as well as the scopes of their restricted names are considered flexible, and can be reorganized at will using a *structural congruence* to make two agents communicate. In contrast, in a *labelled transition system* (LTS in short), the structure of the agents is preserved as much as possible during communication, which means that scope extrusion is explicit and performed only when needed. The correspondence between the reduction semantics and LTS of a system is expressed by a so-called harmony lemma [19], whose proof can be tedious, depending on the number of constructs in the calculus. To keep things manageable, the benchmark[1] consists in formalizing a harmony lemma for a minimal (finite) π-calculus [19], with just enough constructs to exhibit scope extrusion.

So far, the challenge has been completed [7] using Beluga [16], a prover specialized in the representation of binders. We want to complete the benchmark in Rocq, to see what the difficulties can be in a general purpose prover. A previous comparison [3] of four techniques (de Bruijn indices, nominal [17], Higher-Order Abstract Syntax [15], and locally nameless [8]) for the formalization of a higher-order π-calculus [18] in Rocq concluded in the de Bruijn representation being shorter, but with significant overhead in the manipulation of indices. The first-order π-calculus has been formalized using de Bruijn indices [11,14], but all these works do not use Autosubst or any other automation libraries. The goal of this experience report is to assess how much Autosubst can help with scope extrusion.

The rest of the paper is organized as follows. Section 2 presents the syntax and semantics of the π-calculus of the benchmark, that we recast using de Bruijn indices in Sect. 3. Section 4 discusses the consequences of this representation choice on the proof of the harmony lemma. Section 5 evaluates the pros and cons of de Bruijn indices and Autosubst. Section 6 discusses related work and Sect. 7 concludes the paper. We use the recent OCaml reimplementation of Autosubst 2 [10] to generate the syntax, boilerplate properties, and `asimpl` tactic. Our developments are available online [12], and we use the (🐓) symbol throughout the paper to signal hyperlinks to the code repository.

2 The π-Calculus

We remind the syntax and semantics of the π-calculus fragment of the benchmark.

[1] Henceforth, we simply write "the benchmark" or "the challenge" to refer to the scope extrusion challenge of the concurrent benchmark.

2.1 Syntax

We let x, y, ... range over channel names, and define processes as follows.

$$P, Q, R ::= \oslash \mid P \,|\, Q \mid x!y.P \mid x?(\,).yP \mid (\nu x)P$$

Informally, $\oslash$ is the inactive process that does nothing,[2] and $P \,|\, Q$ are the processes P and Q running in parallel, potentially exchanging messages. The output $x!y.P$ is sending the name y on channel x and then continues as P, while the input $x?(y).P$ is waiting for a name on x to replace y in P. The process $(\nu x)P$ restricts the scope of x to P, making the occurrences of x in P distinct from the ones outside its scope. An input $x?(y).P$ binds y in P, and a restriction $(\nu x)P$ binds x in P. We write $\mathsf{fn}(P)$ for the set of free names of P, and $P\{y/x\}$ for the capture-avoiding substitution of x by y in P, both defined as usual. In this section, we identify processes up to α-conversion of their bound names, and in examples, we assume bound names to be chosen distinct from free names.

A communication may happen when an input is in parallel with an output on the same name. For example, using the semantics of Sect. 2.2, we have:

$$x?(y).P \,|\, x?(z).Q \,|\, x!t.R \longrightarrow x?(y).P \,|\, Q\{t/z\} \,|\, R$$

The calculus is non-deterministic: the communication could have also been with the first input. A name restriction on x may forbid a communication, as in $x?(y).P \,|\, x?(z).Q \,|(\nu x)x!t.R$, because it makes the output name x distinct from the input ones. However, a restriction on t does not prevent it, but the scope of t has to be expanded during the communication to include the receiver.

$$x?(y).P \,|\, x?(z).Q \,|(\nu t)x!t.R \longrightarrow x?(y).P \,|(\nu t)(Q\{t/z\} \,|\, R)$$

This phenomenon is known as *scope extrusion*. Its semantics can be expressed either with a structural congruence relation, which expands the scope of names before a communication, or with a labelled transition system, where scope extrusion happens during communication.

2.2 Reduction Semantics

Reduction semantics describes the semantics of a process calculus using structural congruence, written $P \equiv Q$, a relation which reorganizes processes to end up with the two communicating sub-processes in parallel. We define $\equiv$ as the smallest congruence relation verifying the axioms given in Fig. 1. The first three axioms state that parallel composition is associative, commutative, with $\oslash$ as neutral. Axiom ScResPar is needed to perform scope extrusion: assuming $x \notin \mathsf{fn}(Q)$—a condition that can be always fulfilled using α-conversion—the scope of x is extended to include Q. The last two axioms help in managing name restrictions.

[2] We do not use the usual **0** notation to avoid confusion with the de Bruijn index 0.

Structural congruence axioms:

$$\frac{\textsc{ScParAssoc}}{P \,|\, (Q \,|\, R) \equiv (P \,|\, Q) \,|\, R} \qquad \frac{\textsc{ScParComm}}{P \,|\, Q \equiv Q \,|\, P} \qquad \frac{\textsc{ScParInact}}{P \,|\, \oslash \equiv P}$$

$$\textsc{ScResPar}\ \frac{x \notin \mathsf{fn}(Q)}{((\nu x)P) \,|\, Q \equiv (\nu x)(P \,|\, Q)} \qquad \frac{\textsc{ScResInact}}{(\nu x)\oslash \equiv \oslash} \qquad \textsc{ScRes}\ \frac{x \neq y}{(\nu x)(\nu y)P \equiv (\nu y)(\nu x)P}$$

Reduction rules:

$$\frac{\textsc{RCom}}{x!y.P \,|\, x?(z).Q \longrightarrow P \,|\, Q\{y/z\}} \qquad \textsc{RRes}\ \frac{P \longrightarrow Q}{(\nu x)P \longrightarrow (\nu x)Q} \qquad \textsc{RPar}\ \frac{P \longrightarrow Q}{P \,|\, R \longrightarrow Q \,|\, R}$$

$$\textsc{RStruct}\ \frac{P \equiv P' \qquad P' \longrightarrow Q' \qquad Q' \equiv Q}{P \longrightarrow Q}$$

Fig. 1. Structural congruence and reduction relation

The reduction relation $P \longrightarrow Q$ is also defined in Fig. 1. The communication happens in rule RCom, assuming the output and input processes are in parallel. The rule RRes and RPar are congruence rules, and the rule RStruct allows to use structure congruence on the source and target of a reduction relation. For example, starting from $x?(y).P \,|\, (x?(z).Q \,|\, (\nu t)x!t.R)$, we can use structural congruence to rewrite this process as $(\nu t)(x!t.R \,|\, x?(z).Q) \,|\, x?(y).P$, assuming $t \notin \mathsf{fn}(Q)$. Using RCom, RRes, and RPar, we can then reduce this latter process into $(\nu t)(R \,|\, Q\{t/z\}) \,|\, x?(y).P$, which is itself structurally congruent to $x?(y).P \,|\, (\nu t)(Q\{t/z\} \,|\, R)$.

2.3 Labelled Transition System

A labelled transition system (LTS) uses labels to express the interactions capabilities of a process, like sending a receiving a name on a given channel. For the π-calculus, there are four actions α, defined as follows.

$$\alpha ::= x?y \mid x!y \mid x!(y) \mid \tau$$

The action $x?y$ is an input on x of the name y. The actions $x!y$ and $x!(y)$ are an output and a bound output, respectively, where y is sent on x, as a bound name in the second case. Finally, τ is an internal action, where the process is reducing by itself. We define the free names $\mathsf{fn}(\alpha)$ and the bound names $\mathsf{bn}(\alpha)$ of an action as follows.

$$\begin{array}{llll} \mathsf{fn}(x?y) = \{x, y\} & \mathsf{fn}(x!y) = \{x, y\} & \mathsf{fn}(x!(y)) = \{x\} & \mathsf{fn}(\tau) = \emptyset \\ \mathsf{bn}(x?y) = \emptyset & \mathsf{bn}(x!y) = \emptyset & \mathsf{bn}(x!(y)) = \{y\} & \mathsf{bn}(\tau) = \emptyset \end{array}$$

$$\textsc{Out}\ \frac{}{x!y.P \xrightarrow{x!y} P} \qquad \textsc{In}\ \frac{}{x?(z).P \xrightarrow{x?y} P\{y/z\}} \qquad \textsc{ParL}\ \frac{P \xrightarrow{\alpha} P' \qquad \mathsf{bn}(\alpha) \cap \mathsf{fn}(Q) = \emptyset}{P \mid Q \xrightarrow{\alpha} P' \mid Q}$$

$$\textsc{Res}\ \frac{P \xrightarrow{\alpha} P' \qquad z \notin \mathsf{n}(\alpha)}{(\nu z)P \xrightarrow{\alpha} (\nu z)P'} \qquad \textsc{Open}\ \frac{P \xrightarrow{x!z} P' \qquad z \neq x}{(\nu z)P \xrightarrow{x!(z)} P'}$$

$$\textsc{CommL}\ \frac{P \xrightarrow{x!y} P' \qquad Q \xrightarrow{x?y} Q'}{P \mid Q \xrightarrow{\tau} P' \mid Q'} \qquad \textsc{CloseL}\ \frac{P \xrightarrow{x!(z)} P' \qquad Q \xrightarrow{x?z} Q' \qquad z \notin \mathsf{fn}(Q)}{P \mid Q \xrightarrow{\tau} (\nu z)(P' \mid Q')}$$

Fig. 2. LTS rules

We also define the names of an action as $\mathsf{n}(\alpha) = \mathsf{fn}(\alpha) \cup \mathsf{bn}(\alpha)$.

A transition $P \xrightarrow{\alpha} P'$ means that P becomes P' after doing α. The rules defining the LTS are given in Fig. 2, where we omit the symmetric of the rules involving parallel composition. The Out and In rules express the capabilities of the output and input processes, respectively. In particular, an input process $x?(z).P$ can receive any name y. The actions $x!y$ and $x?(y)$. are unhindered by neither by processes in parallel (rules ParL and omitted ParR), nor by a restriction on a name $z \notin \{x, y\}$ (rule Res). A communication happens between two processes able to send and receive on the same name (rules CommL and CommR).

The rules Open, CloseL, and CloseR are implementing scope extrusion using the action $x!(y)$. If a process P is able to send z on x (with $x \neq z$), then $(\nu z)P$ is sending the bound name z, which means that the scope of z has to be extended. The name restriction does not appear at the right of the arrow in the conclusion of the Open rule, unlike in the Res one. In fact, it is implicit in $x!(z)$: in a transition $P \xrightarrow{x!(z)} P'$, the action $x!(z)$ binds the occurrences of z in P', Consequently, α-renaming z in $x!(z)$ results in renaming z also in P'.

The fact that $x!(z)$ binds z explains the side-condition in rule ParL and ParR: if $P \xrightarrow{x!(z)} P'$, then we have $P \mid Q \xrightarrow{x!(z)} P' \mid Q$ only if $z \notin \mathsf{fn}(Q)$, otherwise any occurrence of z in Q would be captured by the action. Similarly in rules CloseL and CloseR, the implicit restriction on z in the label of the output premise is restored in the conclusion to include the recipient of z, provided again that z in not free in the input process.

We illustrate how scope extrusion happens in the LTS using our running example $x?(y).P \,|\, (x?(z).Q \,|\, (\nu t)x!t.R)$, where we assume $t \notin \mathsf{fn}(Q)$.

$$\dfrac{\dfrac{}{x?(y).Q \xrightarrow{x?t} Q\{t/z\}}\ \textsc{In} \qquad \dfrac{\dfrac{}{x!t.R \xrightarrow{x!t} R}\ \textsc{Out}}{(\nu t)x!t.R \xrightarrow{x!(t)} R}\ \textsc{Open}}{\dfrac{x?(z).Q \,|\, (\nu t)x!t.R \xrightarrow{\tau} (\nu t)(Q\{t/z\} \,|\, R)}{x?(y).P \,|\, (x?(z).Q \,|\, (\nu t)x!t.R) \xrightarrow{\tau} x?(y).P \,|\, (\nu t)(Q\{t/z\} \,|\, R)}\ \textsc{ParR}}\ \textsc{CloseR}$$

3 Representation with de Bruijn Indices

We present how we encode the syntax and semantics of the previous section using de Bruijn indices.

3.1 Syntax

Representing a syntax using de Bruijn indices consists in replacing the entity being bound (here, the names) with natural numbers, which indicate how many enclosing binders (inputs or name restrictions) separate the bound name from its binder. We let n, m range over natural numbers, standing for de Bruijn indices. The syntax of the π-calculus becomes as follows.

$$P, Q, R ::= \oslash \ \mid\ P \,|\, Q \ \mid\ n!m.P \ \mid\ ?.\mathrm{n}P \ \mid\ (\nu)P$$

For example, the process $(\nu x)(\nu y)x!y.\oslash$ is represented as $(\nu)(\nu)1!0.\oslash$: the index 1 skips the first binder to refer to the outermost one, while the index 0 refers to the innermost one. The process $(\nu z)x?(y).y!z.\oslash$ can be represented as $(\nu)1?.0!1.\oslash$. The index 0 refers to the first enclosing binder, in that case the input. The two occurrences of 1 are different names. The second occurrence of 1 ignores its first enclosing binder (the input) to refer to the next one (the name restriction). The first occurrence of 1 ignores its enclosing binder (the name restriction), but there is no other surrounding binder to refer to. The first occurrence of 1 is therefore a free name, and could be replaced by any non-zero index.

Renamings, functions from indices to indices, are needed to keep the correspondence between indices and their binder when defining the semantics. We let σ range over renamings and write $\sigma(n)$ the application of σ to n. The σ-calculus of explicit substitutions [1] distinguishes several primitives on renamings, namely the *identity* id, *shift* $\uparrow$, the *cons* of m on σ written $m \cdot \sigma$[3], and the *composition* $\sigma \circ \sigma'$ of two renamings, defined as follows.

$$\begin{array}{lll} \mathsf{id}(n) = n & (m \cdot \sigma)(0) = m & (\sigma \circ \sigma')(n) = \sigma'(\sigma(n)) \\ \uparrow(n) = n + 1 & (m \cdot \sigma)(n+1) = \sigma(n) & \end{array}$$

[3] In the σ-calculus, the cons is between a term and a substitution, to define explicit substitutions as mappings from indices to terms. In our fragment of the π-calculus, mappings from indices to indices are enough.

$$\frac{\textsc{ScResPar}}{((\nu)P) \mid Q \equiv (\nu)(P \mid Q[\uparrow])} \qquad \frac{\textsc{ScRes}}{(\nu)(\nu)P \equiv (\nu)(\nu)P[\leftrightarrow]} \qquad \frac{\textsc{RCom}}{n!m.P \mid n?.Q \longrightarrow P \mid Q[m \cdot \mathsf{id}]}$$

Fig. 3. Selected congruence and reduction rules with a de Bruijn representation

Applying a renaming σ to a process P, written $P[\sigma]$, is defined as follows.

$$\begin{aligned} \oslash[\sigma] &= \oslash & (n?.P)[\sigma] &= \sigma(n)?.P[\Uparrow \sigma] \\ (P \mid Q)[\sigma] &= P[\sigma] \mid Q[\sigma] & ((\nu)P)[\sigma] &= (\nu)P[\Uparrow \sigma] \\ (n!m.P)[\sigma] &= \sigma(n)!\sigma(m).P[\sigma] \end{aligned}$$

When going through a binder, the renaming σ is *lifted*,[4] written $\Uparrow \sigma$, so that σ does not apply to 0. Lifting leaves 0 unchanged, and $(\Uparrow \sigma)(n+1)$ is computed as $\sigma(n)$, since we ignore 0. The result of the computation is then shifted, to avoid an unwanted capture by the binder. As a result, lift does not need to be a primitive, at it can be defined as $\Uparrow \sigma = 0 \cdot (\sigma \circ \uparrow)$.

In the result of a communication between a sender $n!m.P$ and a receiver $n?.Q$, the substitution applied to Q should map 0 to m, and all the indices $n \geq 1$ should be decreased, since we remove the input binder. Such a substitution can also be defined using the primitives as $m \cdot \mathsf{id}$.

The σ-calculus consists of the renaming primitives listed above with rewrite rules to manipulate them. The calculus is terminating [1], confluent [9], and complete [20]. Autosubst exploits this fact to decide unconditional equalities involving renamings defined using these primitives. The Autosubst tactic `asimpl` applies the rewrite rules until it reaches normal forms on both sides of the equality, and then checks that the two resulting normal forms are equal or not. Given the π-calculus syntax in a specific format (🐓), the Autosubst tool generates Rocq files with the renaming primitives (🐓), the inductive definition of processes (🐓), and the `asimpl` tactic tailored for our language (🐓).

3.2 Reduction Semantics

Most of the rules of Fig. 1 are unchanged or easy to adapt in a de Bruijn representation (🐓) . The three rules with significant changes are RCom, ScResPar, and ScRes; their de Bruijn variants are presented in Fig. 3. What changes in rule RCom is the substitution applied to Q, as explained in Sect. 3.1. In rule ScResPar, the process Q is shifted to avoid capture when extending the scope of the name restriction.

The rule ScRes switches the two topmost name restrictions. With de Bruijn indices, it means that the two indices 0 and 1 should be exchanged, so that the outermost binder becomes the innermost one. To do so, we introduce a *swap* renaming written $\leftrightarrow$, defined so that $\leftrightarrow(0) = 1$, $\leftrightarrow(1) = 0$, and $\leftrightarrow(n) = n$ for $n \geq 2$. It can be defined using the primitives as $\leftrightarrow = 1 \cdot 0 \cdot (\uparrow \circ \uparrow)$ (🐓).

[4] The "lift" operation is sometimes called "up", in particular in Autosubst.

$$\textsc{Out}\ \frac{}{n!m.P \xrightarrow{n!m} P} \qquad \textsc{In}\ \frac{}{n?.P \xrightarrow{n?m} P[m \cdot \mathsf{id}]} \qquad \textsc{ParL}\ \frac{P \xrightarrow{\alpha} P' \quad \mathsf{nb}(\alpha)}{P \mid Q \xrightarrow{\alpha} P' \mid Q} \qquad \textsc{BParL}\ \frac{P \xrightarrow{n!()} P'}{P \mid Q \xrightarrow{n!()} P' \mid Q[\uparrow]}$$

$$\textsc{Res}\ \frac{P \xrightarrow{\alpha[\uparrow]} P' \quad \mathsf{nb}(\alpha)}{(\nu)P \xrightarrow{\alpha} (\nu)P'} \qquad \textsc{BRes}\ \frac{P \xrightarrow{\uparrow(n)!()} P'}{(\nu)P \xrightarrow{n!()} (\nu)P'[\leftrightarrow]} \qquad \textsc{Open}\ \frac{P \xrightarrow{\uparrow(n)!0} P'}{(\nu)P \xrightarrow{n!()} P'}$$

$$\textsc{CommL}\ \frac{P \xrightarrow{n!m} P' \quad Q \xrightarrow{n?m} Q'}{P \mid Q \xrightarrow{\tau} P' \mid Q'} \qquad \textsc{CloseL}\ \frac{P \xrightarrow{n!()} P' \quad Q[\uparrow] \xrightarrow{\uparrow(n)?0} Q'}{P \mid Q \xrightarrow{\tau} (\nu)(P' \mid Q')}$$

Fig. 4. LTS rules in de Bruijn syntax

We can prove by straightforward inductions that structural congruence and reduction are preserved by renamings.

Lemma 1. *For all P, Q, and σ, if $P \equiv Q$ then $P[\sigma] \equiv Q[\sigma]$.*

Lemma 2. *For all P, Q, and σ, if $P \longrightarrow Q$ then $P[\sigma] \longrightarrow Q[\sigma]$.*

Remark 1. Structural congruence is not defined as the symmetric closure of axiomatic rules, as in the benchmark paper [6]. Instead, we duplicate the rules and prove the resulting relation is symmetric. This choice makes the proof of Lemma 3 shorter, with less inductive cases.

3.3 LTS

The main difficulty in adapting the LTS is to handle the bound output action, which contains a hidden binder. We change the LTS actions as follows.

$$\alpha ::= n?m \mid n!m \mid n!() \mid \tau$$

The idea is that $P \xrightarrow{n!()} P'$ is sending the bound name 0 on the channel n, and the action $n!()$ is binding the occurrences of 0 in P'. Since the emitted name is always 0, we no longer write it in the label. Because most of the LTS rules differs for a bound output, we write $\mathsf{nb}(\alpha)$ to state that α is not a bound action. We extend the application of renamings to actions $\alpha[\sigma]$ as follows.

$$(n?m)[\sigma] = \sigma(n)?\sigma(m) \qquad (n!m)[\sigma] = \sigma(n)!\sigma(m)$$
$$\tau[\sigma] = \tau \qquad (n!())[\sigma] = \sigma(n)!()$$

Figure 4 contains the LTS rules adapted to de Bruijn indices, except for the symmetric of the rules involving parallel composition. Renaming application has higher precedence than the syntax operators, so that, e.g., $P \mid Q[\sigma] = P \mid (Q[\sigma])$.

The rules OUT, COMML, and COMMR are the same as in Fig. 2, except that channel names are now indices. The rule IN has been changed with the same renaming as in rule RCOM (Fig. 3). The rules PARL and PARR now distinguish whether the action is a bound output or not. If not, then there is no side-condition, since an unwanted capture cannot happen in that case. Otherwise, we prevent the capture of 0 in the parallel process Q by shifting Q.

A process $(\nu)P$ can send or receive on a channel n only if P can do the same action on $n+1$. It explains why α or n are shifted in the premises of rules RES, BRES or OPEN, but not in the conclusions. As a result, if P is sending or receiving on 0, then $(\nu)P$ cannot do that action, mimicking the conditions on z in rules RES and OPEN of Fig. 2.

The rule OPEN reflects the meaning of a bound output: if P is able to send 0 on $n+1$ to become P', then $(\nu)P$ is sending the bound name 0 on n, and the occurrences of 0 in P' are bound by the action.

In the rule BRES, we need to swap 0 and 1 in P' in the conclusion, as illustrated by the following example.

$$(\nu x) y!x.x!z.\varnothing \xrightarrow{y!(x)} x!z.\varnothing$$

$$(\boldsymbol{\nu}) \mathit{2}!\mathbf{0}.\mathbf{0}!1.\varnothing \xrightarrow{\mathit{1}!()} \mathbf{0}!1.\varnothing$$

The indices and binders for x are in bold, those for y are in italics, and those for z are left normal. Note that 2 in the process and 1 in the label are the same free name because there is one enclosing binder in the process but none in the label. Suppose that we want to bind z, by simply adding a (ν) on both sides.

$$(\nu)(\boldsymbol{\nu}) \mathit{2}!\mathbf{0}.\mathbf{0}!1.\varnothing \xrightarrow{\mathit{0}!()} (\nu)0!\mathbf{1}.\varnothing$$

In the right process, 0 refers to the new name restriction, while 1 refers to the implicit restriction in the label, which is not what we want. The correct structure of binders requires us to swap 0 and 1.

$$(\nu)(\boldsymbol{\nu}) \mathit{2}!\mathbf{0}.\mathbf{0}!1.\varnothing \xrightarrow{\mathit{0}!()} (\nu)\mathbf{1}!0.\varnothing$$

The added restriction traverses the implicit binder in the label, which explains why we need to swap 0 and 1 in the conclusion of the rule BRES.

In the rules CLOSEL and CLOSER, the receiving process Q is shifted to avoid capture by the bound output. Because Q is expected to receive the message on the channel n, $Q[\uparrow]$ is doing the input on $n+1$. Since 0 cannot occurs in $Q[\uparrow]$, we know that any occurrence of 0 in Q' are instances of the bound name received from P. Therefore, the name restriction $(\nu)(P' \mid Q')$ in the conclusion binds only the name sent by P. As an example, consider the following communication.

$$((\nu z)(\nu x) y!x.x!z.\varnothing) \mid y?(t).t!u.\varnothing \xrightarrow{\tau} (\nu x)(((\nu z)x!z.\varnothing) \mid x!u.\varnothing)$$

The process $y?(t).t!u.\oslash$ can be translated as $Q = \mathit{0}?.\underline{0}!\overline{1}.\oslash$ with $Q[\uparrow] = \mathit{1}?.\underline{0}!\overline{2}.\oslash$. The communication is then reflected by the following partial derivation.

$$\textsc{CloseL}\ \frac{(\nu)(\boldsymbol{\nu})\mathit{2}!\mathbf{0}.\mathbf{0}!1.\oslash \xrightarrow{\mathit{0}!()} (\nu)\mathbf{1}!0.\oslash \qquad \mathit{1}?.\underline{0}!\overline{2}.\oslash \xrightarrow{\mathit{1}?\mathbf{0}} \mathbf{0}!\overline{1}.\oslash}{((\nu)(\boldsymbol{\nu})\mathit{2}!\mathbf{0}.\mathbf{0}!1.\oslash) \mid \mathit{0}?.\underline{0}!\overline{1}.\oslash \xrightarrow{\tau} (\boldsymbol{\nu})(((\nu)\mathbf{1}!0.\oslash) \mid \mathbf{0}!\overline{1}.\oslash)}$$

The resulting process corresponds to $(\nu x)(((\nu z)x!z.\oslash) \mid x!u.\oslash)$.

4 Harmony Lemma

We explain how the de Bruijn representation affects the proof of the harmony lemma [19, Lemma 1.4.15]. We follow the general proof strategy suggested by the benchmark.

4.1 Reduction Semantics Implies LTS

To prove that reduction semantics implies τ-transitions, we need a first result showing that a transition can be matched by a congruent process.

Lemma 3 (Lemma 7 in [6] 🐓). *For all P, α, P', and Q, if $P \equiv Q$ and $P \xrightarrow{\alpha} P'$, then there exists Q' such that $Q \xrightarrow{\alpha} Q'$ and $P' \equiv Q'$.*

The proof is necessarily long, as we have to consider all possible transitions from P and all possible cases for $P \equiv Q$; fortunately, many cases can be proved automatically using a basic level of Rocq automation. The proof can be done by induction on the derivation of $P \equiv Q$, and then by case analysis on $P \xrightarrow{\alpha} P'$, or conversely, by induction on the LTS and then case analysis on the structural congruence.

Some preliminary results are necessary in both proof strategies, in particular to handle the ScResPar axiom $((\nu)P) \mid Q \equiv (\nu)(P \mid Q[\uparrow])$. Going left to right, we might have an hypothesis about Q making a transition $Q \xrightarrow{\alpha} Q'$, but we need a transition from $Q[\uparrow]$ to conclude. To this end, we prove a more general result about renaming and the LTS.

Lemma 4 (🐓). *For all P, Q, and σ,*

- *for all α such that $\mathsf{nb}(\alpha)$, if $P \xrightarrow{\alpha} Q$, then $P[\sigma] \xrightarrow{\alpha[\sigma]} Q[\sigma]$;*
- *for all n, if $P \xrightarrow{n!()} Q$, then $P[\sigma] \xrightarrow{\sigma(n)!()} Q[\Uparrow \sigma]$.*

The renaming σ is lifted in the bound output case so that the index 0 still refers to the bound name being sent.

Conversely, going from right to left in ScResPar, we might have an hypothesis about $Q[\uparrow]$ making a transition, but we need a transition from Q to conclude. We therefore need the inversion of Lemma 4.

Lemma 5. *For all P, Q, and σ,*

- 🐓 *for all n and m, if $P[\sigma] \xrightarrow{n!m} Q$, then there exist n', m', and Q' such that $n = \sigma(n')$, $m = \sigma(m')$, $Q = Q'[\sigma]$, and $P \xrightarrow{n'!m'} Q'$;*
- 🐓 *for all n, if $P[\sigma] \xrightarrow{n!()} Q$, then there exist n' and Q' such that $n = \sigma(n')$, $Q = Q'[\Uparrow \sigma]$, and $P \xrightarrow{n'!()} Q'$;*
- 🐓 *for all n and m, if $P[\sigma] \xrightarrow{n?\sigma(m)} Q$, then there exist n' and Q' such that $n = \sigma(n')$, $Q = Q'[\sigma]$, and $P \xrightarrow{n'?m} Q'$;*
- 🐓 *if σ is injective and $P[\sigma] \xrightarrow{\tau} Q$, then there exists Q' such that $Q = Q'[\sigma]$ and $P \xrightarrow{\tau} Q'$.*

The output and bound output cases are as expected, with a lifted renaming in the bound case. In the input case, the received name should be in the image of σ, so that we can invert the transition. Otherwise, a weaker result simply says that $n = \sigma(n')$ (🐓). Finally, we need the extra hypothesis that σ is injective for τ-transitions. Indeed, suppose $P[\sigma] \xrightarrow{\tau} Q$ comes from a communication, with $P = P_1 \,|\, P_2$, $Q = Q_1 \,|\, Q_2$, $P_1[\sigma] \xrightarrow{n!m} Q_1$, and $P_2[\sigma] \xrightarrow{n?m} Q_2$, for some P_1, P_2, Q_1, Q_2, n and m. By the first item, there exist n' and m' such that $n = \sigma(n')$, $m = \sigma(m')$. By the third item, there exists n'' such that $n = \sigma(n'')$. To conclude that $n' = n''$, we need σ to be injective.

The proof strategy for Lemma 3 depends on how to handle a particular subcase, involving congruence w.r.t. parallel composition and the CloseR rule. In that subcase, we have $P \,|\, R \equiv Q \,|\, R$ because $P \equiv Q$, and $P \,|\, R \xrightarrow{\tau} (\nu)(P' \,|\, R')$ because $P[\uparrow] \xrightarrow{\uparrow(n)?0} P'$ and $R \xrightarrow{n!()} R'$ for some P, Q, R, P', R', and n.

Suppose we proceed by induction on the structural congruence derivation, and then by case analysis on the LTS. The induction hypothesis is then that any transition from P is matched by Q. However, we have a transition from $P[\uparrow]$, on which we cannot apply Lemma 5—the index 0 is not in the image of $\uparrow$—so we cannot get a transition from P itself. A way to circumvent the issue is to first prove Lemma 3 for input actions only, and then use that result to prove Lemma 3 for the remaining actions. The input-only proof is simpler since the CloseR subcase does not arise. To handle the CloseR subcase in the non-input proof, from $P \equiv Q$ we get $[\uparrow]\mathrm{P} \equiv Q[\uparrow]$ by Lemma 1, and then we apply the input-only result to get a transition from $Q[\uparrow]$ and conclude from there.

An alternative strategy is to prove Lemma 3 by induction on the derivation of the LTS, and then by case analysis on structural congruence. In the subcase of parallel composition with CloseR, the induction hypothesis then tells us that the transition $P[\uparrow] \xrightarrow{\uparrow(n)?0} P'$ can be matched by any process structurally congruent to $P[\uparrow]$. Since we have $P \equiv Q$, we have $P[\uparrow] \equiv Q[\uparrow]$ by Lemma 1, and we can apply the induction hypothesis and conclude that subcase.

We applied the latter strategy because overall, it results in a simpler proof of Lemma 3. However, transitivity becomes the problematic subcase in that strategy: for example, we could have $P \,|\, R \xrightarrow{\alpha} P'$ and $P \,|\, R \equiv Q$ because $P \,|\, R \equiv S \equiv Q$ for some S. To conclude, we would need an inner induction on the derivation $P \mid R \equiv Q$, and we would have to do the same for every (outer) induction case on the LTS. To avoid this, we define a non-transitive structural congruence $\equiv^{\text{nt}}$ (), prove Lemma 3 on $\equiv^{\text{nt}}$ (), and then extend the result to $\equiv$ ().

After Lemma 3, the remaining results are much simpler to prove. First, we describe the shape of reducing processes up to structural congruence. We define $(\nu^0)P = P$ and $(\nu^{k+1})P = (\nu)(\nu^k)P$ for $k \in \mathbb{N}$ ().

Lemma 6 (Lemma 9 in [6]). *For all P and Q, if $P \longrightarrow Q$, then there exist n, m, k, R_1, R_2, and S such that:*

$$P \equiv (\nu^k)((n!m.R_1 \mid n?.R_2) \mid S)$$
$$Q \equiv (\nu^k)((R_1 \mid R_2[m \cdot \mathsf{id}]) \mid S).$$

The proof is by a straightforward induction on $P \longrightarrow Q$. We can then prove that reduction steps imply τ-steps.

Theorem 1 (Theorem 4 in [6]). *For all P and Q, if $P \longrightarrow Q$, then there exists Q' such that $P \xrightarrow{\tau} Q'$ and $Q \equiv Q'$.*

If $P \longrightarrow Q$, then we have $P \equiv P'$ and $Q \equiv Q'$ with P' and Q' defined in Lemma 6. We can check that $P' \xrightarrow{\tau} Q'$. By Lemma 3, there exists Q'' such that $P \xrightarrow{\tau} Q''$ and $Q' \equiv Q''$. By transitivity we have $Q \equiv Q''$, and the result holds.

4.2 LTS Implies Reduction Semantics

To prove the reverse implication, we need results similar to Lemma 6 but to describe the processes in a transition $P \xrightarrow{\alpha} Q$. We define $\uparrow^0 = \mathsf{id}$ and $\uparrow^{k+1} = \uparrow^k \circ \uparrow$ for $k \in \mathbb{N}$ (). For all σ, we define $\Uparrow^0 \sigma = \sigma$, and $\Uparrow^{k+1} \sigma = \Uparrow (\Uparrow^k \sigma)$ for $k \in \mathbb{N}$ ().

Lemma 7 (). *For all P, Q, n, and m, if $P \xrightarrow{n!m} Q$, then there exist R, S, and k such that*

$$P \equiv (\nu^k)(\uparrow^k (n)! \uparrow^k (m).R \mid S), \text{ and } Q \equiv (\nu^k)(R \mid S).$$

There are similar results for the input () and bound output cases () . Using these results, we can prove that τ-transitions imply reduction steps.

Theorem 2 (Theorem 3 in [6]). *For all P, Q, if $P \xrightarrow{\tau} Q$, then $P \longrightarrow Q$.*

The proof is by induction on the derivation of $P \xrightarrow{\tau} Q$. For example, in the case of CommL, we have $P_1 \mid P_2 \xrightarrow{\tau} Q_1 \mid Q_2$, with $P_1 \xrightarrow{n!m} Q_1$ and $P_2 \xrightarrow{n?m} Q_2$ for some n and m. Then using Lemma 7 and the equivalent result for inputs, we know that there exists k, l, R_1, R_2, S_1, and S_2 such that

$$P_1 \equiv (\nu^k)(\uparrow^k (n)! \uparrow^k (m).R_1 \mid R_2), \text{ and } P_2 \equiv (\nu^l)(\uparrow^l (n)?.S_1 \mid S_2).$$

To reduce $P_1 \mid P_2$, we need to reorganize the parallel compositions and name restrictions using structural congruence.

$$\begin{aligned} P_1 \mid P_2 &\equiv (\nu^k)((\uparrow^k (n)!\, \uparrow^k (m).R_1 \mid R_2) \mid P_2[\uparrow^k]) \\ &\equiv (\nu^k)((\uparrow^k (n)!\, \uparrow^k (m).R_1 \mid R_2) \mid (\nu^l)(\Uparrow^l \uparrow^k (\uparrow^l (n))?.S_1[\Uparrow^{l+1} \uparrow^k] \mid S_2[\Uparrow^l \uparrow^k])) \\ &\equiv (\nu^{k+l})((\uparrow^{l+k} (n)!\, \uparrow^{l+k} (m).R_1[\uparrow^l] \mid \Uparrow^l \uparrow^k (\uparrow^l (n))?.S_1[\Uparrow^{l+1} \uparrow^k]) \mid \\ &\qquad\qquad (R_2[\uparrow^l] \mid S_2[\Uparrow^l \uparrow^k])) \end{aligned}$$

To reduce, we need to prove that $\uparrow^{l+k} (n) = (\Uparrow^l \uparrow^k)(\uparrow^l (n))$ ( ) . We then show that the result of the communication is structurally congruent with $Q_1 \mid Q_2$ to conclude that case. The proofs of the four communication cases are similar and can be factorized (,), so that the above manipulation of indices is done once.

Remark 2. In Sangiorgi and Walker's book [19], the implication is written with an extra structural congruence: if $P \xrightarrow{\tau} P' \equiv Q$ for some P', then $P \longrightarrow Q$. However $P \xrightarrow{\tau} P'$ implies $P \longrightarrow P'$ by Theorem 2, and $P \longrightarrow P' \equiv Q$ implies $P \longrightarrow Q$ by the RStruct rule.

5 Assessment

As pointed out in previous works [11,14], the main benefit of de Bruijn syntax is that the LTS is written without side-conditions involving sets of names. Instead, we avoid capture by applying renamings. It simplifies the proofs, as we do not have to manipulate sets when using the rules. It is specific to the *monadic* π-calculus, where only one name is sent. As soon as we consider a *polyadic* calculus [13]—where several names can be sent at once—or a higher-order calculus [18]—where processes are sent, we would have to compute the set of free names of the message to know whether a name should be extruded or not.

The drawback is as usual the arithmetics on de Bruijn indices. Scope extrusion manifests itself by the swap operation, and the fact that we have to distinguish cases in the LTS for the bound output. In general, writing the rules of Fig. 4 requires some literacy with de Bruijn indices, especially for BRes, CloseL, and CloseR. We also have to be careful to introduce lifts when needed, like in Lemmas 4 and 5. The proof of Theorem 2 also showcases heavy manipulations of shift and lift.

The LTS written as in Fig. 2 is not easy to translate because bindings are left implicit in the case of the bound output. A cleaner way to write the LTS would be to use *abstractions* for inputs $P \xrightarrow{x} (y)Q$ and *concretions* [18] for (bound) outputs $P \xrightarrow{\overline{x}} (\nu y)\langle y\rangle P$. The transition $P \xrightarrow{x} (y)Q$ means that P is waiting for a name z on x to continue as $Q\{z/y\}$, and the transition $P \xrightarrow{\overline{x}} (\nu y)\langle y\rangle P$ means that P is sensing the bound name y. The benefit of abstractions and concretions is that the binder is explicit in the syntax; the problem is that the LTS is no longer uniform, as a process may transition to a process, an abstraction or a concretion.

Autosubst helps when proving results about renamings, as long as they are expressed in terms of the σ-calculus primitives (cf Sect. 3.1), which is the case of the swap operation. The tactic `asimpl` solves unconditional renaming equalities, including the ones involving swap, like the following one.

Lemma 8. *For all P, $P[\uparrow][\leftrightarrow] = P[\Uparrow\uparrow]$.*

Autosubst does not help in proving conditional results, like the ones involving the index 0, which plays a specific role in the formalization.

Lemma 9. *For all σ and n, $(\Uparrow \sigma)(n) \neq 0$ implies $n \neq 0$.*

The proofs of such results require to make de Bruijn indices explicit—Autosubst hides them in a datatype—and are usually solved by simple case analyses. Finally, Autosubst also does not help in proving results involving $\uparrow^k$ and $\Uparrow^k$, because those results usually require an induction on k.

Lemma 10. *For all σ, n, and k, $(\Uparrow^k \sigma)(\uparrow^k (n)) = \uparrow^k (\sigma(n))$.*

In the end, out of the 1100 lines of code we had to write, 460 of them are lemmas and proofs about renamings, including the proofs of Lemmas 4 and 5. It is an improvement over an early de Bruijn implementation [11], where three quarters of the lemmas are devoted to binder management. A way to further reduce that proportion would be for Autosubst to generate the definitions of $\leftrightarrow$, $\Uparrow^k$, and $\uparrow^k$ and some results about them: it would reduce the 460 lines of code about renamings to approximately 200.

6 Related Work

Cecilia and Momigliano's Work. A first formalization of the scope extrusion challenge of the benchmark has been done in Beluga [7], a proof system [16] which relies on a Higher-Order Abstract Syntax (HOAS) encoding [15] of bindings. The principle is to represent binders using the function space of the proof system logic, delegating the definition of capture-avoiding substitution and freshness conditions to the meta-level. The definitions of the syntax and semantics of a language are closer to the pen-and-paper ones and therefore easier to write than with de Bruijn indices.

The authors report the formalization of the harmony lemma to be somewhat straightforward in Beluga, with usual workarounds to bypass the limitations of the prover's logic, like the lack of existential quantification or the lack of lexicographic induction. The management of fresh names and substitutions is mostly absent, except for one result–if $P \xrightarrow{\alpha} P'$, and $x \notin \mathsf{fn}(P)$, then $x \notin \mathsf{fn}(P')$–which requires some non-trivial developments.

An important difference with the benchmark (and our work) is that they use a *late* LTS semantics. The benchmark LTS is *early* because the input transition $\xrightarrow{x?y}$ indicates the received name y, and the instantiation is done already at the level of the axiom (rule IN in Fig. 2). In contrast, the input transition of a late LTS does not know the received message, and instantiation happens during communication. Cecilia and Momigliano prove that the two LTSs produce equivalent τ-transitions and therefore the semantics are the same. However, they do not discuss the choice of a late LTS semantics for the proof of the harmony lemma, which could lead to a simpler proof than with an early one, as we suspect to be the case with de Bruijn indices (see the discussion of Perera and Cheney's work below).

Rocq being a general purpose proof system, it is not surprising that the proof is much shorter in Beluga (700 lines of code) than ours (1100 lines of code, excluding the code automatically generated by Autosubst). It is not clear that a HOAS representation in Rocq would lead to a simpler formalization, because of the lack of support for HOAS in this prover. A previous experimentation in Coq [3] for a richer process calculus resulted in longer developments in HOAS than with de Bruijn indices.

Other Formalizations. The benchmark paper [6] lists previous formalizations of process calculi in proof assistants, none of which are proving the harmony lemma. Some of them use de Bruijn indices [11,14]: our representation relies on the same renamings as in these papers, sometimes under different designations–e.g., $\uparrow$ is called push and $m \cdot \mathsf{id}$ is written pop m in [14]. Hirschkoff's formalization [11] is about congruence proofs for a bisimilarity, while Perera and Cheney's [14] is about concurrence and causality.

The equivalent of the CLOSEL rule is much simpler in Perera and Cheney's work than in Fig. 4 because they use a late LTS. We rewrite some of their rules below using our notations.

$$\textsc{InLate}\ \frac{}{n?.P \xrightarrow{n} P} \qquad \textsc{InParLLate}\ \frac{P \xrightarrow{n} P'}{P \,|\, Q \xrightarrow{n} P' \,|\, Q[\uparrow]} \qquad \textsc{CloseLLate}\ \frac{P \xrightarrow{n!()} P' \qquad Q \xrightarrow{n} Q'}{P \,|\, Q \xrightarrow{\tau} (\nu)(P' \,|\, Q')}$$

In a late transition $P \xrightarrow{n} P'$, the index 0 in P' is meant to be substituted, so when putting a process Q in parallel, it should be shifted to avoid unwanted capture. Besides, in a bound output, the message is also 0, so there is no need to substitute 0 for 0 in the rule CLOSELLATE above. We do not need to shift Q (as in rule CLOSEL in Fig. 4) because the parallel rule INPARLLATE already ensures that the occurrences of 0 in Q' are from the late input, and not from other processes in parallel. We conjecture that a late LTS would lead to simpler developments for the harmony lemma proof.

Ambal et al. [3] compare four formalization techniques in Coq for HOπ, a process calculus where messages are executable processes. A consequence is that several names of the message process may be restricted, resulting in several extruded names in a single communication. The paper formalizes a soundness proof for a bisimilarity; it contains a proof of Lemma 3 for HOπ, but not of the harmony lemma. In that paper, a bound output is written in a de Bruijn syntax using a concretion as $P \xrightarrow{\overline{n}} (\nu^k)\langle Q\rangle R$, meaning that P is sending Q with the indices $l < k$ in Q being bound. The equivalent of the BRES rule uses a more general permutation $\overset{k}{\leftrightarrow}$, which maps indices $l < k$ to $k+1$, k to 0, and $l > k$ to l. It also applies a "down" operation $\downarrow$ to the message Q, reducing its unbound indices by 1.

$$\textsc{OpenHO}\ \frac{P \xrightarrow{\overline{n}} (\nu^k)\langle Q\rangle R \quad n \neq 0 \quad k \in \mathsf{fn}(Q)}{(\nu)P \xrightarrow{\overline{\downarrow(n)}} (\nu^{k+1})\langle Q\rangle R} \qquad \textsc{BResHO}\ \frac{P \xrightarrow{\overline{n}} (\nu^k)\langle Q\rangle R \quad n \neq 0 \quad k \notin \mathsf{fn}(Q)}{(\nu)P \xrightarrow{\overline{\downarrow(n)}} (\nu^k)\langle Q[\Uparrow^k \downarrow]\rangle(\nu)R[\overset{k}{\leftrightarrow}]}$$

We conjecture that the rules could be rewritten with "down" replaced by shift.

$$\textsc{OpenHO}\ \frac{P \xrightarrow{\overline{\uparrow(n)}} (\nu^k)\langle Q\rangle R \qquad k \in \mathsf{fn}(Q)}{(\nu)P \xrightarrow{\overline{n}} (\nu^{k+1})\langle Q\rangle R} \qquad \textsc{BResHO}\ \frac{P \xrightarrow{\overline{\uparrow(n)}} (\nu^k)\langle Q[\Uparrow^k \uparrow]\rangle R}{(\nu)P \xrightarrow{\overline{n}} (\nu^k)\langle Q\rangle(\nu)R[\overset{k}{\leftrightarrow}]}$$

Getting rid of $\downarrow$ is worth it, as most of the properties of $\downarrow$ are conditional (they apply to indices that are not 0), and cannot be directly proved using `asimpl`. However, it is not clear how to easily get rid of the side-condition in rule OPENHO, so that the rule applies only when Q contains k.

7 Conclusion

We complete the scope extrusion challenge in Rocq using de Bruijn indices and Autosubst. The de Bruijn representation of the LTS does not have any side-condition but uses renamings to manage binders. The way the LTS is written has some influence on the proof strategy for Lemma 3, as discussed in Sect. 4.1. One also need to be careful to introduce lifts when proving results about bound outputs (see Lemmas 4 and 5).

Autosubst alleviates the burden of administrative proofs thanks to the `asimpl` tactic, which can solve automatically the unconditional equalities involving renamings. The conditional lemmas or inductively defined renamings still require manual proofs, and some familiarity with de Bruijn syntax is necessary to carry on some proofs, in particular for Theorem 2.

We use *unscoped* de Bruijn indices; in a *scoped* syntax, the type of processes `proc n` specifies the upper bound n of the indices of a process of that type. While having this extra information can be useful in some cases (e.g., to define closing substitutions [3]), we do not see how a scoped syntax would help in simplifying the proofs in the benchmark case.

The π-calculus used for the benchmark is minimal: it lacks usual constructs such as (guarded) sums, replication, recursion, or matching. Extending the proofs to some of these construct may be challenging. For example, recursion is a binder which introduces a new category of variables and a substitution operation replacing these variables with processes. Autosubst 2 [22] in particular handles multi-sorted substitutions and should help in proving the results about the interactions between the two substitutions, such as one distributes over the other.

Acknowledgments. We thank Giovanni Bernardi, Hugo Férée, Matteo Manighetti and Meven Lennon-Bertrand for the discussions around this work. We thank the anonymous reviewers for their comments.

References

1. Abadi, M., Cardelli, L., Curien, P., Lévy, J.: Explicit substitutions. J. Funct. Program. **1**(4), 375–416 (1991)
2. Abel, A., et al.: Poplmark reloaded: mechanizing proofs by logical relations. J. Funct. Program. **29** (2019)
3. Ambal, G., Lenglet, S., Schmitt, A.: Hoπ in coq. J. Autom. Reason. **65**(1), 75–124 (2021)
4. Aydemir, B.E., et al.: Mechanized metatheory for the masses: the poplmark challenge. In: Hurd, J., Melham, T.F. (eds.) Theorem Proving in Higher Order Logics, TPHOLs 2005. LNCS, vol. 3603, pp. 50–65. Springer (2005)
5. de Bruijn, N.G.: Lambda calculus notation with nameless dummies: a tool for automatic formula manipulation, with application to the church-rosser theorem. Indag. Math. **75**(5), 381–392 (1972)
6. Carbone, M., et al.: The concurrent calculi formalisation benchmark. In: Castellani, I., Tiezzi, F. (eds.) Coordination Models and Languages - 26th IFIP WG 6.1 International Conference, COORDINATION 2024, Held as Part of the 19th International Federated Conference on Distributed Computing Techniques, DisCoTec 2024, Groningen, The Netherlands, 17–21 June 2024, Proceedings. Lecture Notes in Computer Science, vol. 14676, pp. 149–158. Springer (2024)
7. Cecilia, G., Momigliano, A.: A beluga formalization of the harmony lemma in the π-calculus. In: Rabe, F., Coen, C.S. (eds.) Proceedings Workshop on Logical Frameworks and Meta-Languages: Theory and Practice, LFMTP@FSCD 2024, Tallinn, Estonia, 8 July 2024. EPTCS, vol. 404, pp. 1–17 (2024)
8. Charguéraud, A.: The locally nameless representation. J. Autom. Reason. **49**(3), 363–408 (2012)
9. Curien, P., Hardin, T., Lévy, J.: Confluence properties of weak and strong calculi of explicit substitutions. J. ACM **43**(2), 362–397 (1996)
10. Dapprich, A.: Generating Infrastructural Code for Terms with Binders using MetaCoq and OCaml. Bachelor's thesis, Saarland University (2021)
11. Hirschkoff, D.: A full formalisation of pi-calculus theory in the calculus of constructions. In: Proceedings of the 10th International Conference on Theorem Proving in Higher Order Logics, vol. 1275, pp. 153–169. Springer (1997)
12. Kan, S., Lenglet, S.: Harmony in Rocq (2026). https://depot.lipn.univ-paris13.fr/lenglet/scorpion/
13. Milner, R.: The polyadic pi-calculus (abstract). In: Cleaveland, R. (ed.) CONCUR 1992, Third International Conference on Concurrency Theory, Stony Brook, NY, USA, 24–27 August 1992, Proceedings. Lecture Notes in Computer Science, vol. 630, p. 1. Springer (1992)
14. Perera, R., Cheney, J.: Proof-relevant π-calculus: a constructive account of concurrency and causality. Math. Struct. Comput. Sci. **28**(9), 1541–1577 (2018)
15. Pfenning, F., Elliott, C.: Higher-order abstract syntax. In: PLDI 1988, pp. 199–208. ACM, Atlanta, Georgia, USA (1988)

16. Pientka, B., Dunfield, J.: Beluga: a framework for programming and reasoning with deductive systems (system description). In: Giesl, J., Hähnle, R. (eds.) IJCAR 2010. LNCS (LNAI), vol. 6173, pp. 15–21. Springer, Heidelberg (2010). https://doi.org/10.1007/978-3-642-14203-1_2
17. Pitts, A.M.: Nominal logic, a first order theory of names and binding. Inf. Comput. **186**(2), 165–193 (2003)
18. Sangiorgi, D.: Bisimulation for higher-order process calculi. Inf. Comput. **131**(2), 141–178 (1996)
19. Sangiorgi, D., Walker, D.: The Pi-Calculus: A Theory of Mobile Processes. Cambridge University Press (2001)
20. Schäfer, S., Smolka, G., Tebbi, T.: Completeness and decidability of de bruijn substitution algebra in coq. In: Leroy, X., Tiu, A. (eds.) Proceedings of the 2015 Conference on Certified Programs and Proofs, CPP 2015, Mumbai, India, 15–17 January 2015, pp. 67–73. ACM (2015)
21. Schäfer, S., Tebbi, T., Smolka, G.: Autosubst: reasoning with de bruijn terms and parallel substitutions. In: Urban, C., Zhang, X. (eds.) ITP 2015. LNCS, vol. 9236, pp. 359–374. Springer, Cham (2015). https://doi.org/10.1007/978-3-319-22102-1_24
22. Stark, K., Schäfer, S., Kaiser, J.: Autosubst 2: reasoning with multi-sorted de bruijn terms and vector substitutions. In: Mahboubi, A., Myreen, M.O. (eds.) CPP 2019, pp. 166–180. ACM (2019)

Control Flow-Based Symmetry Reduction for Parameterised Boolean Equation Systems

Menno Bartels(✉), Maurice Laveaux, Thomas Neele, and Tim A. C. Willemse

Eindhoven University of Technology, Eindhoven, Netherlands
{m.m.g.bartels,m.laveaux,t.s.neele,t.a.c.willemse}@tue.nl

Abstract. Symmetry reduction is a technique that combats the state space explosion problem for model checking. The main idea of symmetry reduction is to merge symmetric states. Two states are symmetric if they can be mapped onto each other such that their semantics is preserved. To carry out symmetry reduction, one first has to identify symmetries for the system at hand. In this work we introduce the concept of symmetries for systems of fixed point equations called parameterised Boolean equation systems. We propose a technique that extracts a symmetry group from the control flow found in such an equation system. We implemented a prototype tool with which we highlight that our technique can effectively find symmetries and in turn achieve substantial reductions.

Keywords: Model checking · Parameterised Boolean equation system · Symmetry reduction · Control flow · Parity games

1 Introduction

Within the area of model checking, symmetry reduction is a technique that aims to combat the well-known state space explosion problem. To reduce the effort spent on answering the model checking problem, symmetry reduction merges symmetric states of a system. Assume that states are represented as vectors of values. Then two states are symmetric, if there exists a mapping that rearranges the state vectors into one another. During solving, a reduced state space is generated that takes into account the symmetries between states. This reduced state space is sufficient to answer the model checking problem fully. In turn, the model checking problem can be more efficiently answered.

Model checking tools like CADP [9] and mCRL2 [2] use *parameterised Boolean equation systems* (PBESs) [10] to encode the μ-calculus model checking problem. PBESs are systems of fixpoint equations ranging over predicate formulas. In mCRL2, a PBES is constructed from a system specification and a

Artefact available at https://doi.org/10.5281/zenodo.19333256.

Published by Springer Nature Switzerland AG 2026
L. Bocchi and B. Kulahcioglu Ozkan (Eds.): FORTE 2026, LNCS 16589, pp. 38–55, 2026.
https://doi.org/10.1007/978-3-032-28187-6_3

μ-calculus formula to be verified. *Solving* a PBES and obtaining the answer to the model checking problem is achieved by converting it to a parity game [14]. This conversion resembles state space exploration. Then, the solving of the generated parity game is done using standard techniques, like the recursive algorithm [30]. Unfortunately, this approach suffers from the state space explosion. The underlying parity game tends to grow exponentially with the number of parallel, possibly identical, components in the system which makes it infeasible to generate it.

When a model contains parallel processes that are instantiated using the same process definition, the associated PBES typically contains a symmetric structure. However, the notion of concurrent processes is lost when translating the model to a PBES. This makes it challenging to identify these symmetries in a PBES. Checking all possible permutations of state vectors is intractable, and the state space itself cannot be used in the process: we need to compute symmetries *a priori* in order to truly avoid the state space explosion. To address this, we develop the theory for symmetry reduction for PBESs. An advantage of this approach is that both the system model and the property to verify are automatically taken into account, since they are together captured in the PBES, possibly yielding better reductions.

We make the following contributions. (1) We define the notion of symmetry in the context of PBESs. This involves applying permutations to predicate formulas. We show that symmetries preserve the solution of a PBES (Theorem 1). Building on [17], this also holds in the context of the reduced parity game (Theorem 2). (2) We present a technique that extracts symmetries from a PBES using control flow. We constructively build up a set of symmetries, such that at every stage in the construction the control flow information is taken into account. The resulting *syntactic symmetries* qualify for reducing the parity game (Theorem 3). (3) We implemented a prototype tool with which we highlight that our technique can effectively find symmetries. Our results showcase the substantial reductions that can be achieved in terms of state space size and solving times.

Related Work. Symmetry reduction for model checking has been studied extensively [25]. Although symmetry reduction does not give guarantees on effectiveness, it has been applied successfully in practice [11,12,16,28,29]. One approach to achieve symmetry reduction is to extend the data structures at hand with functionality to encode symmetry [12,26]. This encoding then enables pruning the generation of the state space, if the property that is being checked allows for this. Alternatively, bottom up approaches have been developed [4,5]. These first consider the semantics of the property and then generate a tailored quotient structure. This structure is then used to answer the model checking problem fully, with respect to the provided formula.

The notion of control flow has been studied in the context of linear processes in [23] and on PBESs in [15]. It provides a way to identify parameters that can be used as program counters of the internal processes of a system. In [15,23] this information is used to perform a liveness analysis. There, a reduction is achieved by discarding parameters that are identified as not alive. Detection of control flow can be done statically by inspecting the syntax of the model. This means that control flow can be identified before the underlying state space is generated.

Previously, several other approaches have been developed for reducing PBESs or parity games. Some of these operate purely on syntax, such as elimination of constant or non-influential parameters [21] or quantifiers [18]. Other approaches, like symbolic bisimulation quotienting [19] and partial-order reduction (POR) [20], operate on semantics (i.e., parity games) and are therefore more akin to our approach. In particular, both POR and symmetry reduction involve first performing static analysis on the input PBES before reducing the generated parity game *on-the-fly*.

Outline. We work out preliminary definitions in Sect. 2. In Sect. 3 we discuss permutations and symmetries. We introduce control flow in Sect. 4.1. Section 4.2 explains our proposed technique to extract symmetries. We give brief implementation details and show the results of our experiments in Sect. 5.

2 Preliminaries

We use abstract data types, denoted $D, E, \dots$, each having a semantic domain, written $\mathbb{D}, \mathbb{E}, \dots$. For Booleans we use B and for natural numbers we use N, with $\mathbb{B} = \{\mathsf{true}, \mathsf{false}\}$ and $\mathbb{N}$ as their semantic counterparts. We fix a set of variables $\mathcal{D}$. To denote that a variable $d \in \mathcal{D}$ is of type D we write $d : D$. If v is a value in $\mathbb{D}$ we write $v \in \mathbb{D}$. We use bold font to denote vectors. With $\boldsymbol{d}$ we denote a vector of variables, with $\boldsymbol{D}$ a vector of types, with $\boldsymbol{v}$ a vector of values and with $\boldsymbol{\mathbb{D}}$ a vector of semantic domains. For a vector $\boldsymbol{x}$, we write x_k for its k'th parameter.

Definition 1. *A* predicate formula *is a first-order formula consisting of* terms *and Boolean connectives, generated by the following grammar.*

$$\varphi := b \mid \varphi \oplus \varphi \mid \mathcal{Q} e : D \,.\, \varphi \mid X(\boldsymbol{t}) \qquad\qquad b, t := x \mid f \mid t(t, \dots, t)$$

Here b is a *term* of type B, X is a predicate variable from a predicate variable set $\mathcal{X}$ and $\boldsymbol{t}$ is a vector of terms t, each of type D. Moreover, x is a parameter of type D and f is a function of type $D^n \to D$ for $n \in \mathbb{N}$. Lastly $\mathcal{Q} \in \{\forall, \exists\}$ and $\oplus \in \{\vee, \wedge\}$. The set of all predicate formulas is denoted with Φ. The set of all terms is written as T, and the set of vectors of terms is $\boldsymbol{T}$. Without loss of generality, we consider any non-Boolean term to have arbitrary type D.

Definition 2. *Let $d, d' \in \mathcal{D}$ be variables.* Syntactic substitution *on a predicate formula φ, written $\varphi[d := d']$, is defined as follows.*

$$\begin{aligned}
x[d := d'] &= \begin{cases} d' & \text{if } x = d \\ x & \text{otherwise} \end{cases} \\
f[d := d'] &= f \\
t(t, \dots, t)[d := d'] &= t[d := d'](t[d := d'], \dots, t[d := d']) \\
(\varphi_1 \oplus \varphi_2)[d := d'] &= \varphi_1[d := d'] \oplus \varphi_2[d := d'] \\
(\mathcal{Q} e : D.\varphi)[d := d'] &= \mathcal{Q} e : D.(\varphi[d := d']) \\
X(\boldsymbol{t})[d := d'] &= X(\boldsymbol{t}[d := d'])
\end{aligned}$$

For a vector of terms we have $(t_1, \ldots, t_n)[d := d'] = (t_1[d := d'], \ldots, t_n[d := d'])$. When φ contains a quantifier that binds e, we require that $d \neq e$ and $d' \neq e$. The semantics of a predicate formula φ is defined in the context of a *data environment* $\delta : \mathcal{D} \to \mathbb{D}$ and a *predicate environment* $\eta : \mathcal{X} \to 2^{\mathbf{D}}$. We write $[\![\varphi]\!]\eta\delta$ where:

$$
\begin{aligned}
[\![b]\!]\eta\delta &= [\![b]\!]\delta \\
[\![\varphi \oplus \psi]\!]\eta\delta &= [\![\varphi]\!]\eta\delta \text{ and/or } [\![\psi]\!]\eta\delta \\
[\![\mathcal{Q}e : D \,.\, \varphi]\!]\eta\delta &= \text{for all/some } v \in \mathbb{D}, [\![\psi]\!]\eta\delta[v/e] \\
[\![X(\boldsymbol{t})]\!]\eta\delta &= [\![\boldsymbol{t}]\!]\delta \in \eta(X)
\end{aligned}
$$

For terms, the semantics is defined in the context of a data environment δ.

$$
[\![x]\!]\delta = \delta(x) \qquad [\![f]\!]\delta = [\![f]\!] \qquad [\![t(t, \ldots, t)]\!]\delta = [\![t]\!]\delta([\![t]\!]\delta, \ldots, [\![t]\!]\delta)
$$

We assume any function symbol f to have a defined semantics that does not depend on any environment. For a vector of terms, we have $[\![\boldsymbol{t}]\!]\delta = ([\![t_1]\!]\delta, \ldots, [\![t_n]\!]\delta)$. To update an environment we write $\delta[v/d]$ where $\delta[v/d](x) = v$ if $x = d$, else $\delta[v/d](x) = \delta(x)$. For multiple updates we write $\delta[v/d][w/e]$ as $\delta[v/d, w/e]$. For vectors of equal length, $\delta[\boldsymbol{v}/\boldsymbol{d}]$ denotes the update of every d_k with v_k.

A *parameterised Boolean equation system* (PBES) [10] is a sequence of fixpoint equations of the form $\sigma X(\boldsymbol{d} : \boldsymbol{D}) = \varphi_X$. Here $X \in \mathcal{X}$ is a predicate variable, φ_X is a predicate formula and σ is either the least fixpoint operator μ or the greatest fixpoint operator ν. To denote an arbitrary PBES we write $\mathcal{E}$. For an equation $(\sigma X(\boldsymbol{d}\colon \boldsymbol{D}) = \varphi_X) \in \mathcal{E}$ we call the predicate formula φ_X the *right-hand side* of bound predicate variable X. We write $\mathsf{bnd}(\mathcal{E})$ for the set of all predicate variables bound by a fixed point operator in $\mathcal{E}$. We consider PBESs that are *closed* and *well-formed*, i.e., no free variables occur and every predicate variable occurring is bound by exactly one equation. Every equation in $\mathcal{E}$ is assigned a *rank*. This is a natural number such that $\mathsf{rank}_{\mathcal{E}}(X) \leq \mathsf{rank}_{\mathcal{E}}(Y)$ if the equation for X occurs before the equation for Y in $\mathcal{E}$. Moreover, $\mathsf{rank}_{\mathcal{E}}(X)$ is an even number if and only if the equation for X has a greatest fixed point. For some bound predicate variable $\hat{X}$, each PBES has an *initial valuation* $\hat{X}(\hat{\boldsymbol{v}})$, where for parameter d_k in $\boldsymbol{d}$ the initial value is denoted with $\mathsf{init}(d_k) = \hat{v}_k$.

We examine PBESs in *standard recursive form* (SRF) [19]. This normal form requires that all right-hand side formulas φ_X occurring in the PBES are either disjunctive or conjunctive, meaning they are in of one of the two following shapes:

$$
\bigvee_{j \in J_X} \exists \boldsymbol{e}_j \colon \boldsymbol{E}_j.\, f_j(\boldsymbol{d}, \boldsymbol{e}_j) \wedge X_j(\boldsymbol{g}_j(\boldsymbol{d}, \boldsymbol{e}_j)) \text{ or } \bigwedge_{j \in J_X} \forall \boldsymbol{e}_j \colon \boldsymbol{E}_j.\, f_j(\boldsymbol{d}, \boldsymbol{e}_j) \vee X_j(\boldsymbol{g}_j(\boldsymbol{d}, \boldsymbol{e}_j))
$$

The disjuncts and conjuncts occurring in the formulas are called *clauses*. In the equation for a predicate variable X the clauses range over a finite index set $J_X \subset \mathbb{N}$. Any $f_j(\boldsymbol{d}, \boldsymbol{e}_j)$ is a term of sort B and any $\boldsymbol{g}_j(\boldsymbol{d}, \boldsymbol{e}_j)$ is a vector of terms, each of sort D. We write $g_{j,k}(\boldsymbol{d}, \boldsymbol{e}_j)$ for the k'th entry of $\boldsymbol{g}_j(\boldsymbol{d}, \boldsymbol{e}_j)$. For any PBES-SRF $\mathcal{E}$ we define the mapping $\mathsf{op}_{\mathcal{E}}(X) \colon \mathsf{bnd}(\mathcal{E}) \to \{\wedge, \vee\}$ which returns whether the right-hand side a predicate variable is disjunctive or conjunctive.

Example 1. Consider the following PBES-SRF $\mathcal{E}$. Here Z denotes integers.

$$\begin{aligned}
\mu X(c_1{:}B, d_1{:}Z, c_2{:}B, d_2{:}Z) &= (\neg c_1 \vee Y(c_1, 1, c_2, d_2)) \wedge (\neg c_2 \vee Y(c_1, d_1, c_2, 1)) \\
\nu Y(c_1{:}B, d_1{:}Z, c_2{:}B, d_2{:}Z) &= (c_1 \wedge Y(\neg c_1, 2, c_2, d_2)) \vee (c_2 \wedge Y(c_1, d_2, \neg c_2, 2)) \\
&\quad \vee (\neg c_1 \wedge \neg c_2 \wedge (d_1 + d_2 \geq 4) \\
&\quad\quad \wedge X(\neg c_1, d_1 - d_2, \neg c_2, d_2 - d_1))
\end{aligned}$$

We assume that every equation has exactly the same vector of data parameters $\boldsymbol{d}$ of type $\boldsymbol{D}$, where the length of $\boldsymbol{d}$ is set to $n \in \mathbb{N}$. Any parameter that does not occur in an equation can be added and copied in all predicate variables occurring throughout the PBES. This means that this assumption does not impact generality. Additionally, because disjunction and conjunction are idempotent, we may also safely assume that within one equation there exists only one copy of each clause. The latter assumption is essential for the existence of bijections between clauses. This will become relevant in Sect. 4.2.

The standard semantics for PBESs is the denotational fixed point semantics [10]. We forego using this and instead consider the *parity game semantics* of PBESs. This game semantics provides an operational view on PBESs and is provably equivalent to the denotational semantics [6]. From the outcome of the parity game one can conclude whether a value is a solution to the corresponding PBES-SRF. A *parity game* is a two player game played on a directed graph. The two players are called *even* ($\Diamond$) and *odd* ($\Box$). The objective of the two players is to *win* as many vertices as possible.

Definition 3. *A* parity game *is a directed graph $M = (V, E, \Omega, \mathcal{P})$, where V is the set of vertices, E the edge relation, $\Omega\colon V \to \mathbb{N}$ the priority function and $\mathcal{P}\colon V \to \{\Diamond, \Box\}$ the ownership function.*

The rules of a parity game are as follows. Each vertex in the game has a priority and an owner, as defined by Ω and $\mathcal{P}$, respectively. Initially a token is placed on some vertex in the graph. The player that owns the vertex on which the token is placed moves the token over an outgoing edge to a next vertex. This process continues indefinitely or until the token is on a vertex without any outgoing edges in which case the token is stuck. During the game, the token moves along a possibly infinite path called a *play*. If a play is finite, it is won by the player that does *not* own the vertex on which the token is stuck. If a play is infinite, then it is won by player $\Diamond$ if the minimal priority that occurs infinitely often along the play is even. Else it is won by player $\Box$.

To denote an arbitrary player, we write p. A *strategy* is partial function $\sigma_p\colon V \to V$ that prescribes how p moves the token to a successive vertex in the game. For vertices owned by p, a strategy σ_p may be undefined, for vertices not owned by p, it is always undefined. If $\sigma_p(v)$ is defined, then it must be the case that $(v, \sigma_p(v)) \in E$. A play $v_1 v_2 \dots$ is consistent with a strategy σ_p if for any v_i that is owned by p and for which $\sigma_p(v_i)$ is defined it holds that $\sigma_p(v_i) = v_{i+1}$. The player p wins a vertex v if and only if there exists a strategy σ_p such that all plays starting in v that are consistent with σ_p are won by p.

We now define the solution to a PBES-SRF using the *associated parity game*.

Definition 4. *The* solution *of $\mathcal{E}$ is the mapping $[\![\mathcal{E}]\!]\colon \mathsf{bnd}(\mathcal{E}) \to 2^{\mathbf{D}}$ where*

$$[\![\mathcal{E}]\!](X) = \{\boldsymbol{v} \in \mathbb{D} \mid X(\boldsymbol{v}) \text{ won by } \Diamond \text{ in } M_{\mathcal{E}}\}$$

Here $M_{\mathcal{E}} = (V, E, \Omega, \mathcal{P})$ is the *associated parity game* for $\mathcal{E}$. We have that $V = \{X(\boldsymbol{v}) \mid X \in \mathsf{bnd}(\mathcal{E}), \boldsymbol{v} \in \mathbf{D}^n\}$ and $(X(\boldsymbol{v}), Y(\boldsymbol{w})) \in E$ if there exists $j \in J_X$ and $\boldsymbol{v}_j \in \mathbf{E}_j$ such that $X_j = Y$, $[\![f_j(\boldsymbol{d}, \boldsymbol{e}_j)]\!]\delta[\boldsymbol{v}/\boldsymbol{d}, \boldsymbol{v}_j/\boldsymbol{e}_j]$ holds and $\boldsymbol{w} = [\![g_j(\boldsymbol{d}, \boldsymbol{e}_j)]\!]\delta[\boldsymbol{v}/\boldsymbol{d}, \boldsymbol{v}_j/\boldsymbol{e}_j]$. Moreover, $\Omega(X(\boldsymbol{v})) = \mathsf{rank}_{\mathcal{E}}(X)$ and $\mathcal{P}(X(\boldsymbol{v})) = \Box$ iff $\mathsf{op}_{\mathcal{E}}(X) = \wedge$ else $\mathcal{P}(X(\boldsymbol{v})) = \Diamond$.

We recall that since the associated parity game is the semantics underlying a PBES-SRF, deciding the winner of a vertex $X(\boldsymbol{v})$ is equivalent to checking whether $\boldsymbol{v}$ is an element of the solution to the equation for X in $\mathcal{E}$ [19]. In turn, this means that the model checking problem that is encoded in the PBES-SRF can be solved by determining the winner of the initial valuation $\hat{X}(\hat{\boldsymbol{v}})$ in the associated parity game.

Example 2. The associated parity game for Example 1 is depicted in Fig. 1. We use t and f as shorthand for the semantic values true and false.

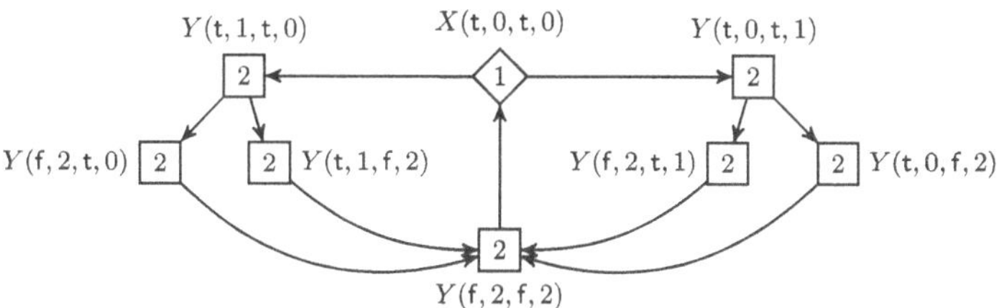

Fig. 1. The associated parity game $M_{\mathcal{E}}$ for for Example 1

3 Symmetries

A symmetry is a mapping of an object onto itself such that the semantics of the object is preserved. The mappings we use are *permutations*. We define how to apply permutations to predicate formulas and show that they form a *group*. A detailed treatment of group theory can be found in [24].

A *permutation* on a set S is a bijection $\pi\colon S \to S$. We define the $\mathsf{per}(S)$ as the set of all permutations on S. Together with function composition, $\mathsf{per}(S)$ is a *group*. This means that for $\alpha, \beta \in \mathsf{per}(S)$, $\alpha \circ \beta$ is again a permutation on S. Also for every permutation π there exists a unique inverse, denoted π^{-1}. We define how to apply group elements to other objects by means of a *group action*.

Definition 5. *Let $(G, \circ)$ be a group and S be a set. A* group action *is a function $\mathsf{act}\colon G \times S \to S$ such that for any $\alpha, \beta \in G$ and $x \in S$ we have:*

$$\mathsf{act}(\mathrm{id}, x) = x \qquad\qquad \mathsf{act}(\alpha, \mathsf{act}(\beta, x)) = \mathsf{act}(\alpha \circ \beta, x)$$

If a group action exists we say that the group G acts on the set S. As shorthand, we write $\alpha(x)$ to refer to the action $\mathsf{act}(\alpha, x)$.

Example 3. We write permutations in disjoint cycle notation. Let $S = \{1, 2, 3\}$. Then $\alpha = (123)$ is defined as $\alpha(1) = 2, \alpha(2) = 3$ and $\alpha(3) = 1$. It maps 1 and 2 to the element on their right, and 3 is mapped back to the first. Likewise for $\beta = (12)(3) = (12)$, $\beta(1) = 2, \beta(2) = 1$ and $\beta(3) = 3$. We omit identity cycles.

Let $\mathsf{var} = \{d_1, \ldots, d_n\}$ be the set of free variables that may occur in predicate formulas and let $[n] := \{1, \ldots, n\}$. Given a term t and a permutation $\pi \in \mathsf{per}([n])$ we define $t[\pi] = t[d_1 := d_{\pi(1)}, d_2 := d_{\pi(2)}, \ldots, d_n := d_{\pi(n)}]$. Here each free variable d_i occurring in t is syntactically substituted by $\pi(d_i)$, simultaneously. Sometimes we write $t[d_i := d_{\pi(i)}]_{i \in [n]}$ to denote $t[\pi]$. Using this we define how permutation act on predicate formulas. We write $\pi(\varphi)$ and define:

$$\begin{aligned} \pi(b) &= b[\pi] \\ \pi(\varphi_1 \oplus \varphi_2) &= \pi(\varphi_1) \oplus \pi(\varphi_2) \\ \pi(\mathcal{Q}e : D.\varphi) &= \mathcal{Q}e : D.\, \pi(\varphi) \\ \pi(X(t_1, \ldots, t_n)) &= X(t_{\pi^{-1}(1)}[\pi], \ldots, t_{\pi^{-1}(n)}[\pi]) \end{aligned}$$

This definition yields a group action on the set of predicate formulas Φ, i.e. the set of predicate formulas itself is closed under inverses and composition of permutations. Note that for a vector of terms, a permutation affects only the *positions* of the entries and not the *indices*. This is important for proving compositionality of the group action. For a vector of values $\boldsymbol{v} = (v_1, \ldots, v_n)$, the application of a permutation is $\pi((v_1, \ldots, v_n)) = (v_{\pi^{-1}(1)}, \ldots, v_{\pi^{-1}(n)})$. For a data environment a permutation remaps the image of every parameter in the domain of the environment, to the image of the permuted parameter. For a predicate environment applying a permutation substitutes for every vector of values, its permuted counterpart. We give the definition of applying a permutation to an environment.

$$\pi(\delta) = \delta[\delta(d_{\pi(i)})/d_i]_{i \in [n]} \qquad \pi(\eta) = \eta[\{\pi^{-1}(\boldsymbol{v}) \mid \boldsymbol{v} \in \eta(X)\}/X]_{X \in \mathcal{X}}$$

We point out that interpreting a permuted predicate formula in some environments coincides with interpreting the original formula in permuted environments.

Lemma 1. *Let $\pi \in \mathsf{per}([n])$ then for any $\varphi \in \Phi$ and environments η and δ:*

$$[\![\pi(\varphi)]\!]\eta\delta = [\![\varphi]\!]\pi(\eta)\pi(\delta)$$

Proof. This can be proven by structural induction on predicate formula φ.

A permutation is a *semantic symmetry* for $\mathcal{E}$ if for every equation the solution of the bound predicate variable is preserved after applying the permutation. Moreover, a permutation is a *syntactic symmetry* if it leaves intact the syntactic structure of the PBES-SRF. This in turn also preserves its semantics. First we give the definition of a semantic symmetry.

Definition 6. *A permutation* $\pi \in \mathsf{per}([n])$ *is a* semantic symmetry *for* $\mathcal{E}$ *if for every* $(\sigma X(\boldsymbol{d}\colon \boldsymbol{D}) = \varphi_X) \in \mathcal{E}$ *we have that* $[\![\pi(\varphi_X)]\!]\eta\delta = [\![\varphi_X]\!]\eta\delta$.

When checking whether a value is in the solution of a PBES-SRF, we can use the result of its symmetric counterparts. For each set of symmetric values, we only inspect whether one of them is in the solution.

Theorem 1. *Let* π *be a symmetry for* $\mathcal{E}$. *Then for* $X \in \mathsf{bnd}(X)$ *and* $\boldsymbol{v} \in \mathbb{D}$ *it holds that* $X(\boldsymbol{v})$ *is won by* $\Diamond$ *in* $M_{\mathcal{E}}$ *if and only if* $X(\pi(\boldsymbol{v}))$*is won by* $\Diamond$ *in* $M_{\mathcal{E}}$.

We fix a group of symmetries G. The *orbit* of a vector of values $\boldsymbol{v} \in \mathbb{D}$ is defined as $\theta(\boldsymbol{v}) = \{\boldsymbol{v}' \in \mathbb{D} \mid \exists \pi \in G \,.\, \pi(\boldsymbol{v}) = \boldsymbol{v}'\}$. Vectors of values that are in the same orbit are called *symmetric*. We use orbits to define *quotient parity games* [17]. To check if $\boldsymbol{v}$ is in the solution of X in $\mathcal{E}$, it suffices to solve the quotient parity game associated with $\mathcal{E}$. The quotient game typically has fewer vertices, as the construction involves merging vertices that contain symmetric vectors of values.

Definition 7. *Consider the associated parity game* $M_{\mathcal{E}}$. *Let* G *be a symmetry group. The* quotient parity game *with respect to* G *is defined as* $M_{\mathcal{E}}^G = (V^G, E^G, \Omega^G, \mathcal{P}^G)$, *where we have vertex set* $V^G = \{X(\theta(\boldsymbol{v})) \mid \boldsymbol{v} \in \mathbb{D}\}$, *edge relation* $E^G = \{(X(\theta(\boldsymbol{v})), Y(\theta(\boldsymbol{w}))) \mid (X(\boldsymbol{v}), Y(\boldsymbol{w})) \in E\}$, *priority function* $\Omega^G(X(\theta(\boldsymbol{v}))) = \Omega(X(\boldsymbol{v}))$ *and ownership function* $\mathcal{P}^G(X(\theta(\boldsymbol{v}))) = \mathcal{P}(X(\boldsymbol{v}))$.

Example 4. Consider the symmetry group $G = \{\mathrm{id}, (13)(24)\}$. The quotient parity game $M_{\mathcal{E}}^G$ for Example 2, is depicted in Fig. 2. For every orbit only a representative vertex is shown. For example, when solving for $Y(f, 2, t, 1)$ we also get the result for the vertex $Y(t, 1, f, 2)$, as these vertices are symmetric in $M_{\mathcal{E}}$.

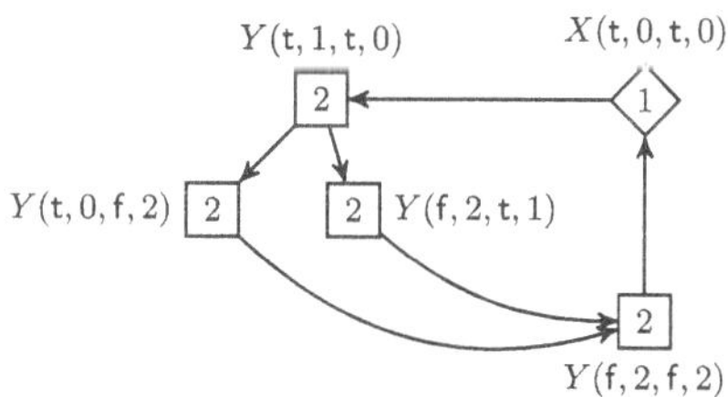

Fig. 2. The quotient parity game $M_{\mathcal{E}}^G$ for Example 4

In our framework, generating the quotient game corresponds to carrying out symmetry reduction. Instead of generating the whole parity game, we take into account the symmetric structure of the PBES-SRF to generate states that represent orbits. This speeds up solving the model checking problem since the reduction often leaves us with fewer states. In fact, the effort of solving is dependent on the size of the parity game underlying the PBES-SRF.

Theorem 2. *Let* G *be a symmetry group. Then for* $X \in \mathsf{bnd}(\mathcal{E})$ *and* $v \in \mathbb{D}$ *it holds that* $X(\boldsymbol{v})$ *is won by* $\Diamond$ *in* $M_{\mathcal{E}}$ *if and only if* $X(\theta(\boldsymbol{v}))$ *is won by* $\Diamond$ *in* $M_{\mathcal{E}}^G$.

4 Extracting Symmetries from Control Flow Graphs

To extract symmetries from a system we consider *syntactic symmetries*. This kind of symmetry does not involve a semantic check. It is based on a purely syntactical equivalence. This choice serves as a practical heuristic – searching for semantics symmetries involves a check for semantic equivalence, which is undecidable in general [3,27]. Nevertheless, the theory presented in Sect. 3 can still be applied, as any syntactic symmetry is a semantic symmetry.

Definition 8. *A permutation* $\pi \in \mathsf{per}([n])$ *is a* syntactic symmetry *for PBES-SRF* $\mathcal{E}$ *if for every* $(\sigma X(\boldsymbol{d}\colon \boldsymbol{D}) = \varphi_X) \in \mathcal{E}$ *and for all* $j \in J_X$ *there exists* $j' \in J_X$ *such that* $X_j = X_{j'}$, $\pi(f_j(\boldsymbol{d}, \boldsymbol{e}_j)) = f_{j'}(\boldsymbol{d}, \boldsymbol{e}_{j'})$ *and* $\pi(\boldsymbol{g}_j(\boldsymbol{d}, \boldsymbol{e}_j)) = \boldsymbol{g}_{j'}(\boldsymbol{d}, \boldsymbol{e}_{j'})$.

Here J_X is the index set for φ_X. Then $f_j(\boldsymbol{d}, \boldsymbol{e}_j)$ is the Boolean term that occurs in clause $j \in J_X$. Likewise $\boldsymbol{g}_j(\boldsymbol{d}, \boldsymbol{e}_j)$ is the vector of terms that occurs in j.

Syntactic symmetries act on predicate formulas and preserve the set of clauses that occur in right-hand side formulas of a PBES-SRF. Hence, any syntactic symmetry is indeed a semantic symmetry. From hereon out we consider only syntactic symmetries and refer to them simply as a *symmetry*.

4.1 Control Flow Graphs

We introduce control flow parameters (CFP) and controls flow graphs (CFG) [15,23] for PBES-SRFs. The search for symmetries exploits control flow to select only permutations that preserve the CFG structure. The control flow of a PBES-SRF is defined using the values of parameters before and after passing through a given clause. To make this explicit we define *source* and *target* functions.

Definition 9. *Consider a partial function* $h\colon \mathsf{bnd}(\mathcal{E}) \times \mathbb{N} \times \mathbb{N} \to \mathbb{D}$. *If for all* $X \in \mathsf{bnd}(\mathcal{E})$, $j \in J_X$, $k \leq n$ *and* δ, *we have that* $h(X, j, k) = v$, *then* h *is a:*

$$\begin{array}{ll} \text{source } \textit{function if:} & [\![f_j(\boldsymbol{d}, \boldsymbol{e}_j)]\!]\delta \implies [\![d_k]\!]\delta = v \\ \text{target } \textit{function if:} & [\![f_j(\boldsymbol{d}, \boldsymbol{e}_j)]\!]\delta \implies [\![g_{j,k}(\boldsymbol{d}, \boldsymbol{e}_j)]\!]\delta = v \end{array}$$

A *source* (resp. *target*) function returns the unique value, if it exists, of parameter d_k right before (resp. after) passing through predicate X_j in φ_X. The definitions allow for under-approximating source and target functions. In practice, we exploit this by performing a purely syntactical analysis on f_j and $\boldsymbol{g}_j$, respectively. From here on, for any given PBES-SRF $\mathcal{E}$ we fix functions src and tgt.

In a PBES-SRF $\mathcal{E}$, a parameter *rules* a clause if both src and tgt are defined for this parameter. The set of all clauses ruled by d_k in φ_X is written $\mathsf{rules}(d_k, X) = \{j \in J_X \mid d_k \text{ rules } j\}$. A clause j may also *copy* a parameter d_k. This means that value of the parameter gets copied over in the recursive call to the predicate variable within the clause, i.e. $[\![g_{j,k}(\boldsymbol{d}, \boldsymbol{e}_j)]\!]\delta = [\![d_k]\!]\delta$ for all δ.

A *control flow parameter* (CFP) is a parameter for which at every point in the system we can deduce its value.

Definition 10. *A parameter d_k is a* control flow parameter *if for all $X \in \mathsf{bnd}(\mathcal{E})$ and $j \in J_X$ we have that either d_k rules j or d_k is copied by j.*

With $\mathsf{cfp}(\mathcal{E})$ we denote the set of CFPs of a PBES-SRF $\mathcal{E}$. A parameter that is not a CFP is called a *data parameter* (DP). For the set of DPs that occur in $\mathcal{E}$ we write $\mathsf{dp}(\mathcal{E})$. The set of semantic values that a CFP c_k can attain is the set $\mathsf{values}(c_k)$ that is defined as

$$\{\mathsf{init}(c_k)\} \cup \bigcup_{\substack{X \in \mathsf{bnd}(\mathcal{E}),\\ j \in \mathsf{rules}(c_k, X)}} \{v \in D \mid v = \mathsf{src}(X, j, k) \vee v = \mathsf{tgt}(X, j, k)\}$$

We define *control flow graphs* (CFG). These make explicit the information that we can statically deduce for the CFPs. In a CFG the vertices consist of predicate variable and the values a CFP attains. The edges depict the clauses in the PBES-SRF that are responsible for a change in value for a CFP.

Definition 11. *Let $\mathcal{E}$ be a PBES-SRF. The control flow graph (CFG) of a control flow parameter $c_k \in \mathsf{cfp}(\mathcal{E})$ is a directed graph $\mathsf{G}_k = (\mathsf{V}_k, \mathsf{E}_k)$ where*

$$\begin{aligned}
\mathsf{V}_k &= \{X(v) \mid X \in \mathsf{bnd}(\mathcal{E}), v \in \mathsf{values}(c_k)\}\\
\mathsf{E}_k &= \{(X(v), j, Y(w)) \mid j \in \mathsf{rules}(c_k, X) \wedge \mathsf{src}(X, j, k) = v \wedge\\
&\qquad\qquad\qquad\qquad \mathsf{tgt}(X, j, k) = w \wedge Y = X_j\}
\end{aligned}$$

Example 5. We reconsider Example 1. First we remark that c_1 and c_2 are the control flow parameters of $\mathcal{E}$. These have G_{c_1} and G_{c_2} as their control flow graphs. The labeling on the edges denotes the index of the clause in the right-hand side formula that is responsible for changing the value of the control flow parameter. For example, in the first clause of φ_X the predicate variable Y and the value of c_1 is copied. Hence the edge $(X(\mathsf{true}), 1, Y(\mathsf{true}))$ is in G_{c_1}.

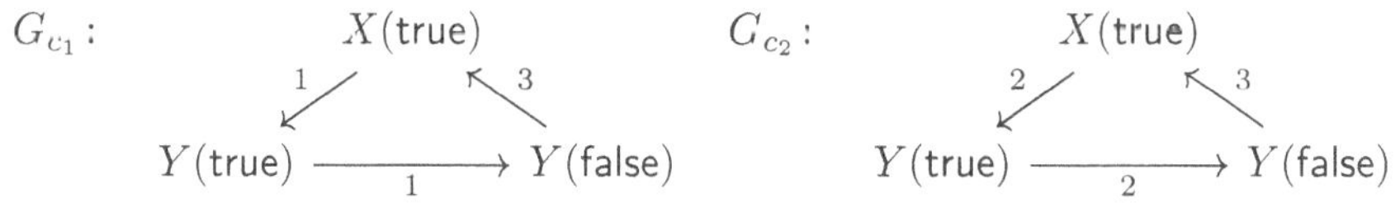

G_{c_1}: $X(\mathsf{true}) \xrightarrow{1} Y(\mathsf{true})$, $Y(\mathsf{true}) \xrightarrow{1} Y(\mathsf{false})$, $Y(\mathsf{false}) \xrightarrow{3} X(\mathsf{true})$

G_{c_2}: $X(\mathsf{true}) \xrightarrow{2} Y(\mathsf{true})$, $Y(\mathsf{true}) \xrightarrow{2} Y(\mathsf{false})$, $Y(\mathsf{false}) \xrightarrow{3} X(\mathsf{true})$

We point out how data parameters are related to clauses in a PBES-SRF. To this end we define when a data parameter is *used for*, *used in* and *changed by* a clause in a PBES-SRF. This allows us to compare CFGs in terms of the data parameters that are interacted with. We introduce $\mathsf{fv}(\varphi) \subseteq \mathcal{D}$ as the set of data parameters freely occurring in formula φ.

Definition 12. *Consider the PBES-SRF $\mathcal{E}$ and an equation $(\sigma X(\boldsymbol{d} \colon \boldsymbol{D}) = \varphi_X)$. Consider a clause j for some index $j \in J_X$. We say that a data parameter d_k is:*

- used for *clause j if $d_k \in \mathsf{fv}(f_j)$;*
- used in *clause j if there exists some $l \leq n$ such that $d_k \in \mathsf{fv}(g_{j,l}(\boldsymbol{d}, \boldsymbol{e}_j))$ where if $X = X_j$ then $k \neq l$;*
- changed by *clause j if $X = X_j$ and $d_k \neq g_{j,k}(\boldsymbol{d}, \boldsymbol{e}_j)$.*

We denote the data parameters that are used for, used in and changed by $j \in J_X$ as $\mathsf{uf}(X,j)$, $\mathsf{ui}(X,j)$ and $\mathsf{cb}(X,j)$, respectively. For an edge $e = (X(\boldsymbol{v}), j, Y(\boldsymbol{w}))$ we write $\mathsf{uf}(e)$ for $\mathsf{uf}(X,j)$, likewise we write $\mathsf{ui}(e)$ and $\mathsf{cb}(e)$.

Example 6. Recall Example 1. Here $\mathsf{cb}(X,1) = \mathsf{cb}(Y,1) = \{d_1\}$, $\mathsf{cb}(X,2) = \mathsf{cb}(Y,2) = \{d_2\}$ and $\mathsf{uf}(Y,3) = \mathsf{ui}(Y,3) = \mathsf{cb}(Y,3) = \{d_1, d_2\}$.

4.2 Extracting Symmetries from CFGs

In this section we present our technique that extracts symmetries for a PBES-SRF. This technique can be summarized as follows. First the CFPs are identified and then partitioned based on the size and shape of their CFGs. Next, we generate a set of permutations that leaves intact this partition. This set is then refined by discarding the permutations that do not induce an isomorphism on the CFGs of the PBES-SRF. For those that are left, we check which are an actual symmetry by comparing against Example 8. What remains is a set of permutations that is a symmetry group for the PBES-SRF at hand.

We define *compatibility* as a means to compare the CFPs. Two CFPs are compatible if their CFGs have equal vertex sets, the sizes of the data sets are equal and the number of edges between vertices is equal.

Definition 13. *Let c and c' be two CFPs. Then* $\mathsf{compatible}$ *is defined as*

$$\begin{aligned}\mathsf{compatible}(c, c') := (\mathsf{V}_c = \mathsf{V}_{c'}) \wedge \forall s, s' \in \mathsf{V}_c \cup \mathsf{V}_{c'}.(&\mathsf{sizes}(c, s, s') = \mathsf{sizes}(c', s, s') \\ &\wedge |\{j \mid (s, j, s') \in \mathsf{E}_c\}| = |\{j \mid (s, j, s') \in \mathsf{E}_{c'}\}|)\end{aligned}$$

where $\mathsf{sizes}(c, s, s') = \{(|\mathsf{uf}(e)|, |\mathsf{ui}(e)|, |\mathsf{cb}(e)|) \mid e = (s, j, s') \in \mathsf{E}_c\}$

In general there can be multiple edges between two vertices in a control flow graph, i.e., multiple clauses change the value of a CFP in the same way. Because of this sizes is defined as set. This way we can identify if there is a discrepancy in the sizes of the sets uf, ui and cb for any of the edges.

Example 7. Recall Example 5. Both CFGs have $\{X(\mathsf{true}), Y(\mathsf{true}), Y(\mathsf{false})\}$ as their vertex set. Between every two vertices there is only one edge in either CFG. This gives $\mathsf{sizes}(c_1, Y(\mathsf{false}), X(\mathsf{true})) = \mathsf{sizes}(c_2, Y(\mathsf{false}), X(\mathsf{true})) = \{(2,2,2)\}$. From Example 6 we see that the set sizes equal for all corresponding edges. Hence, c_1 and c_2 are compatible.

A maximal set of compatible CFPs is called a *clique*. The set of all cliques for a PBES-SRF is denoted $\mathsf{cliques}(\mathcal{E})$. As compatibility is an equivalence relation, this is a partition. Next we define the set of DPs that play a role for any of the CFPs within a clique.

Definition 14. *The set of data parameters for a clique I is defined as follows.*

$$\mathsf{dp}(I) = \bigcup_{c \in I, e \in \mathsf{E}_c} (\mathsf{cb}(e) \cup \mathsf{uf}(e) \cup \mathsf{ui}(e))$$

In the search for symmetries we use *clique permutation.* These permutations interchange CFPs within one clique. Also, they never swap a CFP with a DP.

Definition 15. *The set of clique permutations for a clique I is the following.*

$$\mathsf{cliqper}(I) = \{\alpha\beta \mid \alpha \in \mathsf{per}(I), \beta \in \mathsf{per}(\mathsf{dp}(I))\}$$

Example 8. Recall Example 5. For this example there is only one clique $I = \{c_1, c_2\}$ with $\mathsf{dp}(I) = \{d_1, d_2\}$. From this we get that $\mathsf{per}(I) = \{\mathrm{id}, (c_1c_2)\}$ and $\mathsf{per}(\mathsf{dp}(I)) = \{\mathrm{id}, (d_1d_2)\}$. So $\mathsf{cliqper}(I) = \{\mathrm{id}, (c_1c_2), (d_1d_2), (c_1c_2)(d_1d_2)\}$.

A clique permutation is a *candidate symmetry* if applying the permutation to PBES-SRF leaves intact the structure of the CFGs. To capture when this structure is left intact we first define when a permutation *complies* with a CFP.

Definition 16. *A clique permutation π* complies *with a CFP c if and only if there exists a bijection $\zeta \colon \mathsf{E}_c \to \mathsf{E}_{\pi(c)}$, such that for all $e \in E_c$ it holds that*

$$\pi(\mathsf{uf}(e)) = \mathsf{uf}(\zeta(e)) \wedge \pi(\mathsf{ui}(e)) = \mathsf{ui}(\zeta(e)) \wedge \pi(\mathsf{cb}(e)) = \mathsf{cb}(\zeta(e))$$

We write $\mathsf{complies}(\pi, c)$ when π complies with c and $\mathsf{complies}(\pi, I)$ is the conjunction of $\mathsf{complies}(\pi, c)$ for $c \in I$. Next we define the set of candidate symmetries.

Definition 17. *Let I be a clique. The set of* candidate symmetries *for I is*

$$\mathsf{candidates}(I) = \{\pi \mid \pi \in \mathsf{cliqper}(I) \wedge \mathsf{complies}(\pi, I)\}$$

As the set of clique permutations is a group, we deduce that the complies predicate also preserves inverse and composition. From this we conclude that the set of candidate symmetries also is a group.

We specify how to *combine* the candidates for each individual clique, such that we generate candidate symmetries for $\mathcal{E}$ as a whole. We combine the candidate sets for two cliques in such a way that all the permutations created, again comply with both cliques by construction.

Definition 18. *For two cliques I_1 and I_2 we define:*

$$\mathsf{combine}(I_1, I_2) = \{\alpha_1\alpha_2\beta \mid \alpha_1\beta \in \mathsf{candidates}(I_1) \wedge \alpha_2\beta \in \mathsf{candidates}(I_2)\}$$

The operator $\mathsf{combine}$ is associative and commutative. Because of this, we can also write $\mathsf{combine}(\mathcal{I})$, where $\mathcal{I}$ is a non-empty set of cliques, to denote the iterative application of $\mathsf{combine}$ on the cliques in $\mathcal{I}$. If $\mathcal{I}$ only contains one clique, then $\mathsf{combine}$ just returns the candidates of that clique. If $\mathcal{I} = \emptyset$ then $\mathsf{combine}$ returns no candidates, i.e., the empty set. The set of candidate symmetries for $\mathcal{E}$ is now defined as $\mathsf{candidates}(\mathcal{E}) = \mathsf{combine}(\mathsf{cliques}(\mathcal{E}))$. Like the set of candidates for a clique, the set of candidates for a PBES-SRF is a group.

To construct the candidate symmetries for a PBES-SRF we only consider the structure of the CFGs. Therefore, the set of candidates we computed is an over-approximation of the set of syntactic symmetries. As a final step, we check each candidate against the definition To perform this check we define the predicate $\mathsf{symcheck}$ that resembles Definition 8. We have that $\mathsf{symcheck}(\pi, \mathcal{E}) = \mathsf{true}$ if and only if π is a syntactic symmetry.

Definition 19. *Consider the PBES-SRF $\mathcal{E}$ and a candidate symmetry π. We define the predicate* symcheck *as follows*

$$\mathsf{symcheck}(\pi, \mathcal{E}) := \bigwedge_{X \in \mathsf{bnd}(\mathcal{E})} \bigwedge_{j \in J_X} \bigvee_{j' \in J_X} (\pi(f_j) = f_{j'}) \wedge (X_j = X_{j'}) \wedge (\pi(g_j) = g_{j'})$$

The predicate symcheck performs a purely syntactic check leaving us with syntactical symmetries. We point out that this predicate can be weakened (e.g. by considering logical equivalence) to possibly obtain more symmetries.

Definition 20. *The set of* syntactic symmetries *for $\mathcal{E}$ is defined as follows.*

$$\mathsf{symmetries}(\mathcal{E}) = \{\pi \mid \pi \in \mathsf{candidates}(\mathcal{E}) \wedge \mathsf{symcheck}(\pi, \mathcal{E})\}$$

Example 9. Recall Example 5. We have that $\mathsf{complies}((c_1c_2)(d_1d_2), I)$ holds. Also the identity permutation trivially complies with I. The other clique permutations do not comply with I. Hence, $\mathsf{candidates}(I) = \{\mathrm{id}, (c_1c_2)(d_1d_2)\}$. As there is only one clique $\mathsf{combine}(\mathcal{E}) = \mathsf{candidates}(I)$. The permutation $(c_1c_2)(d_1d_2)$ is a syntactic symmetry for $\mathcal{E}$. This means that $\mathsf{symmetries}(\mathcal{E}) = \{\mathrm{id}, (c_1c_2)(d_1d_2)\}$.

Consider a PBES-SRF with n parameters. Naively, the set of permutations that have to be checked with symcheck is of size $n!$. When selecting the set of candidates, an upper bound for this number is $|\mathcal{I}_1|! \cdot \ldots |\mathcal{I}_m|! \cdot |\mathsf{dp}(\mathcal{E})|!$, for $1 \leq i \leq m$, $\mathcal{I}_i \in \mathsf{cliques}(E)$. This illustrates that selecting the candidates is worthwhile.

The set $\mathsf{symmetries}(\mathcal{E})$ is a subgroup of the set of candidates, meaning it is also a group. Moreover, every permutation in $\mathsf{symmetries}(\mathcal{E})$ is a syntactic symmetry for $\mathcal{E}$. Because of this, we can use $\mathsf{symmetries}(\mathcal{E})$: a PBES-SRF can now be solved by using the extracted set of symmetries to generate the quotient parity game. This is illustrated by the following theorem.

Theorem 3. *Let $G = \mathsf{symmetries}(\mathcal{E})$. Then for $X \in \mathsf{bnd}(\mathcal{E})$ and $v \in \mathbb{D}$ it holds that $\boldsymbol{v}$ is in the solution of X in $\mathcal{E}$ if and only if $X(\theta(\boldsymbol{v}))$ won by $\diamond$ in $M_{\mathcal{E}}^G$.*

5 Experiments

Setup. We implemented our technique for extracting symmetries within the mCRL2 toolset. Our tool converts a given PBES into a PBES-SRF, then carries out a control flow analysis and subsequently generates and checks candidate symmetries. As listing all symmetries is often expensive, the tool outputs the first symmetry it comes across and then terminates. The generation of quotient games is implemented as an extension of the existing mCRL2 tool `pbessolve`. For effectively storing quotient games, we use orbit representatives. To compute these we use GAP [8] – a tool for computational discrete algebra with an emphasis on computational group theory. Using an external tool introduces computational overhead. To make a fair comparison, we call GAP in the original approach using the identity symmetry, i.e. no reduction is applied. The experiments were run five times on a machine with an Intel core i7-12700H processor and 16GB of memory running Ubuntu 22.04. A reproduction artefact is available in the form of a preconfigured VM [1]. The source code of the mCRL2 tools used together with the models, properties and chosen symmetries are also available[1].

We compare three workflows using `pbessolve`. The first one serves as a baseline without symmetry reduction. The next workflow showcases the proposed technique. Our tool automatically identifies a symmetry and then applies symmetry reduction using the first symmetry it finds. As the tool outputs the first symmetry it comes across, it is often the case that there are different symmetries that give more reduction. Using the analysis the tool provides, we manually identify such a symmetry. For the last workflow we apply symmetry reduction with this well-chosen symmetry to showcase the potential reduction symmetry reduction can achieve. We set a timeout (t-o) of 30 min for both solving and detection. When solving timed out, the number of states is not computed and when detection timed out, solving was not done.

Cases. The benchmark set consists of mCRL2 models of Peterson's algorithm [22] (mutex), the dining philosophers (dining) and two models that take inspiration from models found in [7] (alloc and routing). As the numbers in the model names suggest, dining, alloc and routing are variable in the number of philosophers, clients and servers they include, respectively. We check the following properties: always some action can be performed (no_deadlock), any confirm action is preceded by a request action (no_conf_before_req), no infinite sequence of eat actions exists (no_inf_eat), every sequence of lookup actions is finite (fin_lu), there are no consecutive query actions (no_con_query). As shown in Table 1 some of these properties hold (✓) and some do not (×).

Discussion. Our findings are presented in Table 1 The numbers concern the three workflows of `pbessolve`: using no symmetry reduction (Original), symmetry reduction with detected symmetry (First) and symmetry reduction with hand-picked symmetry (Chosen). We show the number of states in the associated parity game ($|V|$), and the mean total runtime for solving over five runs (Time). Additionally, the time for symmetry detection is given (Detection).

The results show that symmetry reduction is always beneficial when applied. In every case where symmetry reduction is applied the size of the parity game ($|V|$) reduces (approximately) linearly with the amount of symmetric parameters in the symmetry used. Consequently, the running time of `pbessolve` (Time) decreases similarly. Adding up the time spent on symmetry detection shows that our tool outperforms the original tool in most cases. In two cases the time spent on symmetry detection exceeds the time saved in solving. In the first case the detected symmetry is of the same size as the hand-picked symmetry (♠). Because of this the tool might have to check a substantial amount of smaller candidates before an actual symmetry is found. In the second case, the candidates to be checked are compatible, but do not comply (■). To deduce compliance a semantic check is performed. This is more costly than the syntactic check needed

[1] https://github.com/mmgbartels/pbes-symmetry-experiments

Table 1. Results for symmetry detection and reduction. Numbers given for three runs of `pbessolve`: no symmetry reduction (Original), using detected symmetry (First), using hand-picked symmetry (Chosen). Depicted are the number of parity game states ($|V|$), mean total time in seconds (Time), and time for detection in seconds (Detection). Timeout (t-o) is 30 min.

			$\lvert V\rvert$			Time			
Model	Property	Result	Original	First	Chosen	Original	First	Detection	Chosen
mutex	no_deadlock	✓	125	64	64	0.11	0.11	+0.03	0.11
alloc4	no_conf_before_req	✓	33223	18919	8503	2.98	1.80	+0.04	0.88
	no_deadlock	✓	46515	26526	11910	5.50	3.21	+0.03	1.54
alloc5	no_conf_before_req	✓	237799	135511	47623	26.408	15.587	+0.039	5.637
	no_deadlock	✓	329601	188058	66009	49.241	28.256	+0.035	10.304
alloc6	no_conf_before_req	✓	1695751	966775	283631	232.27	133.93	+0.05	40.93
	no_deadlock	✓	2330643	1330122	389868	427.05	246.42	+0.04	75.20
alloc7	no_conf_before_req*	✓	-	6876343	1722487	t-o	1176.48	+0.10	307.69
	no_deadlock	✓	-	-	2350749	t-o	t-o	0.06	559.83
dining5	no_deadlock	×	5464	1100	1100	0.778	0.247	+1.521$^\spadesuit$	0.251
	no_inf_eat	✓	3916	788	788	0.454	0.175	+1.126$^\spadesuit$	0.177
dining6	no_deadlock	×	25167	4261	4261	4.10	0.81	+54.44$^\spadesuit$	0.83
	no_inf_eat	✓	17952	3036	3036	2.07	0.48	+39.93$^\spadesuit$	0.45
dining7	no_deadlock	×	115271	-	16475	21.85	-	t-o	3.40
	no_inf_eat	✓	82060	-	11728	11.14	-	t-o	1.81
routing4	fin_lu	✓	95656	51808	24088	12.19	6.85	+4.92	3.45
	no_con_query	✓	105973	57373	26683	11.66	6.48	+0.11	3.20
	no_deadlock	×	141738	76684	35684	20.51	11.62	+0.08	5.44
routing5	fin_lu	✓	1100920	598288	220216	179.17	98.76	+697.60$^\blacksquare$	37.31
	no_con_query	✓	1223773	664873	244789	175.11	96.81	+0.85	36.84
	no_deadlock	×	1625559	882806	325159	315.66	173.42	+0.66	65.67
routing6	fin_lu	✓	-	-	2052928	t-o	-	t-o	448.25
	no_con_query*	✓	-	7468873	2287363	t-o	1399.12	+24.39	445.09
	no_deadlock	×	-	-	3020467	t-o	t-o	23.13	794.21
routing7	fin_lu	-	-	-	-	t-o	-	t-o	t-o
	no_con_query	-	-	-	-	t-o	t-o	1093.68	t-o
	no_deadlock	-	-	-	-	t-o	t-o	1266.98	t-o

for compatibility. The experiments also show that using a hand-pick symmetry may further reduce the effort needed (Chosen). Moreover, our technique is able to solve the model checking problem in cases where the original approach times out ($\bigstar$).

6 Conclusions and Future Work

We have defined the theory of symmetries for PBESs and showed that permutations act on predicate formulas. This enabled us to carry out symmetry based quotienting on the parity game semantics underlying PBESs. We presented a technique to extract syntactic symmetries using the control flow found in a PBES. With a prototype tool we have shown the effectiveness of our technique and the substantial reductions that can be obtained.

One direction for future work is to improve the selection and check of candidate symmetry. Other syntactic (and possibly semantic) notions can be used to rule out candidates at an even earlier stage. This could make the technique more scalable – the number of candidates depends on the number of parameters, which typically grows with the number of components in a model. To improve the selection of candidates it would be interesting to investigate the use of colored graphs like is done in [7]. There GAP is used to obtain a group of candidates using a colored graph containing the structural information of the system at hand. This approach might speed up the selection of the candidates, as our current implementation generates and checks these in a naive manner. Moreover, this technique can generate more interesting symmetries, which in turn leads to more reduction. Another direction for future work could investigate, in addition to permuting only the parameters, also permuting the values that these parameters can attain. With this extension, symmetry reduction can also be applied in the presence of so-called data symmetries [13].

References

1. Bartels, M., Laveaux, M., Neele, T., Willemse, T.: Artefact for paper: "Control Flow-Based Symmetry Reduction for Parameterised Boolean Equation Systems" (2026). https://doi.org/10.5281/zenodo.19333256
2. Bunte, O., et al.: The mCRL2 toolset for analysing concurrent systems. In: Vojnar, T., Zhang, L. (eds.) TACAS 2019. LNCS, vol. 11428, pp. 21–39. Springer, Cham (2019). https://doi.org/10.1007/978-3-030-17465-1_2
3. Church, A.: A note on the Entscheidungsproblem. J. Symb. Log. **1**(1), 40–41 (1936). https://doi.org/10.2307/2269326
4. Clarke, E.M., Emerson, E.A., Jha, S., Sistla, A.P.: Symmetry reductions in model checking. In: CAV. LNCS, pp. 147–158. Springer (1998). https://doi.org/10.1007/BFB0028741
5. Clarke, E.M., Jha, S., Enders, R., Filkorn, T.: Exploiting symmetry in temporal logic model checking. Formal Methods Syst. Des. **9**(1/2), 77–104 (1996). https://doi.org/10.1007/BF00625969
6. Cranen, S., Luttik, B., Willemse, T.A.C.: Evidence for fixpoint logic. In: CSL, pp. 78–93. LIPIcs, Schloss Dagstuhl (2015). https://doi.org/10.4230/LIPICS.CSL.2015.78
7. Donaldson, A.F.: Automatic Techniques for Detecting and Exploiting Symmetry in Model Checking. Ph.D. thesis, University of Glasgow, UK (2007)
8. The GAP Group: GAP – Groups, Algorithms, and Programming, Version 4.15.1 (2025). https://www.gap-system.org
9. Garavel, H., Lang, F., Mateescu, R., Serwe, W.: CADP 2011: a toolbox for the construction and analysis of distributed processes. Int. J. Softw. Tools Technol. Transf. **15**(2), 89–107 (2013). https://doi.org/10.1007/S10009-012-0244-Z
10. Groote, J.F., Willemse, T.A.C.: Parameterised boolean equation systems. Theor. Comput. Sci. **343**(3), 332–369 (2005). https://doi.org/10.1016/J.TCS.2005.06.016
11. Hendriks, M., Behrmann, G., Larsen, K., Niebert, P., Vaandrager, F.: Adding symmetry reduction to UPPAAL. In: Larsen, K.G., Niebert, P. (eds.) FORMATS 2003. LNCS, vol. 2791, pp. 46–59. Springer, Heidelberg (2004). https://doi.org/10.1007/978-3-540-40903-8_5

12. Ip, C.N., Dill, D.L.: Better verification through symmetry. Formal Methods Syst. Des. **9**(1/2), 41–75 (1996). https://doi.org/10.1007/BF00625968
13. Jackson, D., Jha, S., Damon, C.: Isomorph-free model enumeration: a new method for checking relational specifications. ACM Trans. Program. Lang. Syst. **20**(2), 302–343 (1998). https://doi.org/10.1145/276393.276396
14. Kant, G., van de Pol, J.: Efficient instantiation of parameterised boolean equation systems to parity games. In: GRAPHITE, pp. 50–65. EPTCS (2012). https://doi.org/10.4204/EPTCS.99.7
15. Keiren, J.J.A., Wesselink, W., Willemse, T.A.C.: Liveness analysis for parameterised boolean equation systems. In: Cassez, F., Raskin, J.-F. (eds.) ATVA 2014. LNCS, vol. 8837, pp. 219–234. Springer, Cham (2014). https://doi.org/10.1007/978-3-319-11936-6_16
16. Kwiatkowska, M., Norman, G., Parker, D.: Symmetry reduction for probabilistic model checking. In: Ball, T., Jones, R.B. (eds.) CAV 2006. LNCS, vol. 4144, pp. 234–248. Springer, Heidelberg (2006). https://doi.org/10.1007/11817963_23
17. Markey, N., Vester, S.: Symmetry reduction in infinite games with finite branching. In: Cassez, F., Raskin, J.-F. (eds.) ATVA 2014. LNCS, vol. 8837, pp. 281–296. Springer, Cham (2014). https://doi.org/10.1007/978-3-319-11936-6_21
18. Neele, T.: (Re)moving quantifiers to simplify parameterised boolean equation systems. In: ARQNL@IJCAR, pp. 64–80. CEUR Workshop Proceedings, CEUR-WS.org (2022)
19. Neele, T., Willemse, T.A.C., Groote, J.F.: Finding compact proofs for infinite-data parameterised boolean equation systems. Sci. Comput. Program. **188**, 102389 (2020). https://doi.org/10.1016/J.SCICO.2019.102389
20. Neele, T., Willemse, T.A.C., Wesselink, W., Valmari, A.: Partial-order reduction for parity games and parameterised boolean equation systems. Int. J. Softw. Tools Technol. Transf. **24**(5), 735–756 (2022). https://doi.org/10.1007/S10009-022-00672-0
21. Orzan, S., Wesselink, W., Willemse, T.A.C.: Static analysis techniques for parameterised boolean equation systems. In: Kowalewski, S., Philippou, A. (eds.) TACAS 2009. LNCS, vol. 5505, pp. 230–245. Springer, Heidelberg (2009). https://doi.org/10.1007/978-3-642-00768-2_22
22. Peterson, G.L.: Myths about the mutual exclusion problem. Inf. Process. Lett. **12**(3), 115–116 (1981). https://doi.org/10.1016/0020-0190(81)90106-X
23. van de Pol, J., Timmer, M.: State space reduction of linear processes using control flow reconstruction. In: Liu, Z., Ravn, A.P. (eds.) ATVA 2009. LNCS, vol. 5799, pp. 54–68. Springer, Heidelberg (2009). https://doi.org/10.1007/978-3-642-04761-9_5
24. Rotman, J.: An Introduction to the Theory of Groups. Graduate Texts in Mathematics, vol. 148. Springer (2012). https://doi.org/10.1007/978-1-4612-4176-8
25. Sistla, A.P.: Employing symmetry reductions in model checking. Comput. Lang. Syst. Struct. **30**(3–4), 99–137 (2004). https://doi.org/10.1016/J.CL.2004.02.002
26. Sistla, A.P., Godefroid, P.: Symmetry and reduced symmetry in model checking? In: Berry, G., Comon, H., Finkel, A. (eds.) CAV 2001. LNCS, vol. 2102, pp. 91–103. Springer, Heidelberg (2001). https://doi.org/10.1007/3-540-44585-4_9
27. Turing, A.M.: On computable numbers, with an application to the Entscheidungsproblem. Proc. London Math. Soc. **s2-42**(1), 230–265 (1937). https://doi.org/10.1112/PLMS/S2-42.1.230
28. Volk, M., Junges, S., Katoen, J.: Fast dynamic fault tree analysis by model checking techniques. IEEE Trans. Ind. Inform. **14**(1), 370–379 (2018). https://doi.org/10.1109/TII.2017.2710316

29. Wahl, T., Blanc, N., Emerson, E.A.: **SVISS**: symbolic verification of symmetric systems. In: Ramakrishnan, C.R., Rehof, J. (eds.) TACAS 2008. LNCS, vol. 4963, pp. 459–462. Springer, Heidelberg (2008). https://doi.org/10.1007/978-3-540-78800-3_34
30. Zielonka, W.: Infinite games on finitely coloured graphs with applications to automata on infinite trees. Theor. Comput. Sci. **200**(1–2), 135–183 (1998). https://doi.org/10.1016/S0304-3975(98)00009-7

NeuroNL2LTL: A Neurosymbolic Framework for Natural Language Translation of Linear Temporal Logic

Paapa Kwesi Quansah and Ernest Bonnah(✉)

Baylor University, Waco, TX 76706, USA
{paapa_quansah1,ernest_bonnah}@baylor.edu

Abstract. Effectively translating between natural language (NL) and formal logics like Linear Temporal Logic (LTL) requires expertise that limits formal verification's reach in safety-critical development. Template-based approaches sacrifice expressiveness for reliability; neural methods achieve fluency but provide no correctness guarantees. We present NeuroNL2LTL, a neurosymbolic architecture unifying learned translation with formal verification. NeuroNL2LTL routes translation through an intermediate representation whose mapping to LTL is structure-preserving by construction. Generated specifications undergo satisfiability and non-triviality checking; a minimal-edit repair mechanism corrects near-miss outputs before they reach downstream tools. The central innovation is verifier-in-the-loop training: verification outcomes serve as reward signals for reinforcement learning, producing neural components that optimize directly for formal correctness. On 200,000+ requirements spanning aerospace, robotics, autonomous vehicles, and ten additional domains, NeuroNL2LTL achieves 28% semantic equivalence with reference specifications while ensuring 86% of outputs are verified satisfiable. The system also generates contextually grounded explanations from LTL, enabling domain experts to validate specifications without specialized training. This work demonstrates that formal verification can function as both training objective and runtime filter for neural specification systems, allowing us to build neural-based tools whose reliability derives from logical guarantees rather than statistical confidence.

Keywords: Neurosymbolic · Linear Temporal Logic · Natural Language

1 Introduction

Temporal formalisms such as Linear Temporal Logic (LTL) [34] provide a rich semantics to unambiguously specify liveness and safety properties, sequencing constraints, response guarantees in safety-critical hardware, software, and communication systems [37], dynamical systems [3,40], etc. Using model checkers

Published by Springer Nature Switzerland AG 2026
L. Bocchi and B. Kulahcioglu Ozkan (Eds.): FORTE 2026, LNCS 16589, pp. 56–73, 2026.
https://doi.org/10.1007/978-3-032-28187-6_4

like SPIN [17], Spot [11], etc., and theorem provers, we can then verify system designs against these specifications with mathematical guarantee certainty and correctness [8]. Despite the expressive power of LTL, formalizing requirements as LTL specifications requires specialized mathematical expertise and familiarity. However, while domain experts who understand system behavior rarely possess formal methods expertise, formal methods specialists rarely possess domain knowledge of system operation. This mismatch introduces requirement translation and specification errors in succinctly and compactly formalizing behavior-critical systems.

This paper introduces NeuroNL2LTL, a neurosymbolic framework for contextually grounded translation of requirements between NL and LTL. Our proposed tool accepts complex, unrestricted requirements alongside domain context: definitions of atomic propositions, domain labels, and semantic grounding information. The architecture decomposes translation into two stages. First, a neural encoder maps NL requirements to an Intermediate Technical Language (ITL) whose syntax mirrors LTL's logical structure while remaining human-readable. A deterministic converter then produces LTL from ITL through structure-preserving transformation. This decomposition localizes potential errors: the neural component may produce malformed or incorrect ITL, but the ITL-to-LTL mapping is sound by construction. At inference time, the Spot model checker [11] verifies each generated formula for satisfiability and non-triviality, filtering outputs that would fail basic sanity checks. A minimal-edit repair module attempts to correct near-miss generations before rejection. One of the system's central methodological contributions is verifier-in-the-loop training. Rather than optimizing neural parameters against reference translations alone, our tool incorporates verification outcomes as reinforcement learning rewards. The neural encoder learns to produce ITL that survives formal checking, not merely ITL that resembles training examples.

We train our proposed framework on a corpus of over 200,000 requirement-specification pairs spanning thirteen domains including aerospace, autonomous vehicles, robotics, and medical devices. Each training instance includes domain context: definitions mapping atomic propositions to their domain-specific meanings. The system achieves 28% semantic equivalence with reference LTL specifications on held-out data, with 86% of generated formulas verified satisfiable and non-trivial. Ablation experiments isolate the contribution of each architectural component: removing verifier-in-the-loop training reduces semantic equivalence over 30 relative percentage points; disabling repair reduces syntactic correctness by 10 points. NeuroNL2LTL also generates natural language explanations from LTL, grounding explanations in domain-specific proposition definitions so that domain experts can validate specifications without reading temporal logic directly. Human evaluation confirms that generated explanations are fluent, accurate, and contextually appropriate.

The contributions of this work are as follows. We present the first neurosymbolic architecture for contextually grounded translation that uses formal verification outcomes to directly optimize neural translation toward logical correctness. We introduce an intermediate representation that isolates neural uncertainty from deterministic logical transformation, enabling targeted repair when generation fails. We demonstrate that satisfiability and non-triviality checking function as effective runtime filters, catching classes of errors that supervised training alone does not prevent. We provide a methodology for contextual LTL explanation generation, validated through human evaluation across technical domains. Together, these contributions establish that formal verification can serve as supervision signal for learning systems, a principle applicable beyond LTL to any domain where neural outputs admit formal checking.

2 Preliminaries

Let AP be a finite set of *atomic propositions* and $\Sigma = 2^{AP}$ be the powerset of AP. For any alphabet A, we write A^* for the set of finite sequences over A and A^ω for the set of infinite sequences. A *trace*, $t \in \Sigma^\omega$, is an infinite sequence of events $t = e_0, e_1, e_2, \dots$, where $e_i \in \Sigma$ and $i \in \mathbb{N}$. For a trace t, we represent the ith event by $t[i]$.

2.1 Linear Temporal Logic

Linear Temporal Logic (LTL) extends propositional logic with temporal operators that express properties over infinite sequences of states [34]. The syntax of LTL formulas is defined inductively as:

$$\varphi ::= \top \mid p \mid \neg\varphi \mid \varphi_1 \wedge \varphi_2 \mid \mathbf{X}\varphi \mid \mathbf{G}\varphi \mid \mathbf{F}\varphi \mid \varphi_1 \, \mathbf{U} \, \varphi_2$$

where $\top$ stands for true, p is an atomic proposition in AP. The operators $\neg$, and $\wedge$ represent the conjunction and negation Boolean operators respectively. The operators **X**, **G**, **F**, and **U** denote the next, globally, eventually, and until operators respectively. The disjunction operator ($\vee$) can be derived from the negation and conjunction operators. Likewise, the implication operator ($\rightarrow$) can also be derived from the negation and disjunction operators. Similarly, non-primitive operators such as **W** (weak until) and **R** (release) can be derived from the standard operators defined in the grammar.

2.2 Verification Properties

The symbolic backend of the proposed framework verifies two properties of the generated formulas. A formula φ is *satisfiable* if the language defined by $\mathcal{L}(\varphi) = \{t \mid t[0] \models \varphi\}$ is non-empty. A formula is *non-trivial* if it is neither valid nor unsatisfiable; formally, $\mathcal{L}(\varphi) \neq \emptyset$ and $\mathcal{L}(\varphi) \neq (2^{AP})^\omega$. Trivial formulas, comprising tautologies and contradictions, typically signal translation failures because requirements that hold vacuously or preclude all executions cannot capture genuine system constraints.

We then employ the Spot library [12] for verification. Specifically, Spot translates LTL formulas into Büchi automata to evaluate language emptiness. To establish semantic equivalence, our framework verifies that $\mathcal{L}(\varphi_1) = \mathcal{L}(\varphi_2)$ by confirming the emptiness of the symmetric difference: $\mathcal{L}(\varphi_1 \wedge \neg\varphi_2) = \emptyset$ and $\mathcal{L}(\neg\varphi_1 \wedge \varphi_2) = \emptyset$.

2.3 The Contextual Grounding Problem

The translation problem addressed by our proposed framework is not syntax-to-syntax conversion but contextually grounded translation. A NL requirement r is accompanied by a domain context $\mathcal{C}$ that defines the interpretation of atomic propositions. Formally, $\mathcal{C} : AP \rightarrow \text{DESCRIPTIONS}$ maps each proposition to a natural language description of the condition it represents. For example, in an automotive domain: $\mathcal{C}(p)$ = "lane departure detected"; $\mathcal{C}(q)$ = "obstacle detection active"; $\mathcal{C}(r)$ = "driver override requested"

Given requirement r and context $\mathcal{C}$, the translation task is to generate an LTL formula φ over AP such that φ captures the temporal constraints expressed in r with propositions interpreted according to $\mathcal{C}$. The reverse task produces a natural language explanation r' from φ that grounds temporal structure in the domain-specific meanings provided by $\mathcal{C}$. This formulation distinguishes contextually grounded translation from context-free approaches that treat propositions as abstract symbols. A system without access to $\mathcal{C}$ cannot determine whether "the sensor must eventually calibrate after detecting an obstacle" should translate to $\mathbf{G}(q \rightarrow \mathbf{F}s)$ or $\mathbf{G}(p \rightarrow \mathbf{F}r)$; the mapping depends on which proposition denotes sensor calibration in the target domain.

2.4 Intermediate Technical Language

Our framework routes translation through an Intermediate Technical Language (ITL) that mirrors LTL's logical structure in human-readable form. The ITL grammar is defined by a deterministic mapping $\mathcal{T}$: LTL $\rightarrow$ ITL that operates recursively on the abstract syntax tree of an LTL formula:

$$\begin{aligned}
\mathcal{T}(p) &= \text{“}p\text{”} \qquad\qquad \mathcal{T}(\top) = \text{“true”} \quad \mathcal{T}(\bot) = \text{“false”}\\
\mathcal{T}(\neg\varphi) &= \text{“not”} \cdot \mathcal{T}(\varphi)\\
\mathcal{T}(\varphi_1 \wedge \varphi_2) &= \mathcal{T}(\varphi_1) \cdot \text{“and”} \cdot \mathcal{T}(\varphi_2)\\
\mathcal{T}(\varphi_1 \vee \varphi_2) &= \mathcal{T}(\varphi_1) \cdot \text{“or”} \cdot \mathcal{T}(\varphi_2)\\
\mathcal{T}(\varphi_1 \rightarrow \varphi_2) &= \text{“if”} \cdot \mathcal{T}(\varphi_1) \cdot \text{“, then”} \cdot \mathcal{T}(\varphi_2)\\
\mathcal{T}(\varphi_1 \leftrightarrow \varphi_2) &= \mathcal{T}(\varphi_1) \cdot \text{“if and only if”} \cdot \mathcal{T}(\varphi_2)\\
\mathcal{T}(\mathbf{X}\varphi) &= \text{“in the next state,”} \cdot \mathcal{T}(\varphi)\\
\mathcal{T}(\mathbf{G}\varphi) &= \text{“always,”} \cdot \mathcal{T}(\varphi)\\
\mathcal{T}(\mathbf{F}\varphi) &= \text{“eventually,”} \cdot \mathcal{T}(\varphi)\\
\mathcal{T}(\varphi_1 \,\mathbf{U}\, \varphi_2) &= \mathcal{T}(\varphi_1) \cdot \text{“until”} \cdot \mathcal{T}(\varphi_2)\\
\mathcal{T}(\varphi_1 \,\mathbf{R}\, \varphi_2) &= \mathcal{T}(\varphi_1) \cdot \text{“releases”} \cdot \mathcal{T}(\varphi_2)\\
\mathcal{T}(\varphi_1 \,\mathbf{W}\, \varphi_2) &= \mathcal{T}(\varphi_1) \cdot \text{“weakly until”} \cdot \mathcal{T}(\varphi_2)
\end{aligned}$$

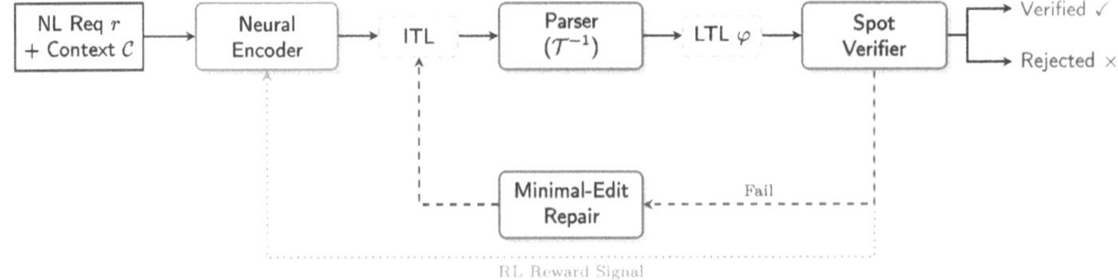

Fig. 1. The architecture of NeuroNL2LTL framework.

where $\cdot$ denotes string concatenation. The mapping $\mathcal{T}$ is total over the LTL fragment and invertible: an ITL string can be parsed back to LTL by reversing the keyword mappings and reconstructing the AST. We denote the inverse $\mathcal{T}^{-1}$: ITL $\rightarrow$ LTL.

Proposition 1 (*Structure Preservation*) For any LTL formula φ: $\mathcal{T}^{-1}(\mathcal{T}(\varphi)) \equiv \varphi$.

Proof Sketch: The proof follows by structural induction on φ. Each LTL operator maps to a unique ITL keyword, and the recursive structure of $\mathcal{T}$ preserves operator scope and precedence. The round-trip property ensures that ITL functions as a lossless intermediate representation. ITL serves two purposes in architecture. First, it provides a more natural target for neural generation than raw LTL syntax: keywords like "until" and "eventually" are closer to natural language than symbols like **U** and **F**, reducing the representational distance the neural encoder must bridge. Second, it localizes the source of translation errors. If the neural component produces malformed output, the error lies in the NL-to-ITL mapping; the ITL-to-LTL conversion is deterministic and correct by construction. This decomposition enables targeted repair: near-miss ITL strings can be corrected without reasoning about LTL syntax directly.

3 The System Architecture

3.1 System Overview

NeuroNL2LTL translates between natural language requirements and Linear Temporal Logic through a neurosymbolic architecture that decomposes the problem into neural and symbolic components with clearly defined interfaces. The neural components handle the ambiguity inherent in natural language while the symbolic components enforce logical correctness. This section presents the architecture, details each component, and explains how formal verification integrates into the training process. As shown in Fig. 1, our proposed neurosymbolic framework comprises four stages, namely, neural encoding, ITL-to-LTL conversion, LTL verification, and minimal-edit repair. The details of the stages are discussed below.

Neural Encoding: The neural encoder implements a sequence-to-sequence model that maps natural language to ITL. The encoder receives a structured input consisting of three elements: the natural language requirement r, a domain label d (e.g., "aerospace", "robotics"), and the context mapping $\mathcal{C}$ rendered as natural language definitions of atomic propositions. We initialize the encoder from a pretrained large language model (Flan-T5-XL) that has undergone continued pretraining on a corpus of approximately five billion tokens drawn from technical documentation across the thirteen target domains. This domain adaptation improves the model's handling of specialized terminology and temporal phrasing patterns common in requirements documents. The adapted model is then fine-tuned on more than $200k+$ paired (NL, ITL) examples using standard supervised learning before the verifier-in-the-loop training stage described in Sect. 3.2. At inference time, we apply grammar-constrained decoding to bias generation toward syntactically valid ITL. The decoder maintains a set of valid next tokens at each generation step according to the ITL grammar, assigning zero probability to tokens that would produce unparseable output. This constraint reduces but does not eliminate syntactic errors; the repair module handles cases where constrained decoding fails. The neural decoder for LTL-to-NL translation shares the same base architecture but is initialized in a different mode. It receives an ITL string (obtained by applying $\mathcal{T}$ to the input LTL) together with domain context $\mathcal{C}$ and generates natural language. Conditioning on both logical structure and domain definitions enables the decoder to produce explanations grounded in application-specific terminology rather than abstract logical paraphrase.

Deterministic ITL-to-LTL Conversion: The parser implements the inverse mapping $\mathcal{T}^{-1}$ from ITL strings to LTL formulas. We implement the parser using Lark, a parsing toolkit that generates parsers from EBNF grammars. The ITL grammar is unambiguous: each valid ITL string corresponds to exactly one parse tree, and the parse tree determines a unique LTL formula. Parsing proceeds in two phases, i.e., lexical analysis and syntactic analysis. The lexical analysis tokenizes the input string, identifying ITL keywords ("always", "eventually", "until", "releases", "weakly until", "if", "then", "and", "or", "not", "in the next state", "if and only if") and atomic proposition identifiers. Syntactic analysis constructs an abstract syntax tree according to the grammar. The AST is then traversed to emit the corresponding LTL formula string in Spot's input format.

Proposition 2 (*Parser Correctness*) For any ITL string s in the language of the ITL grammar, if the parser produces LTL formula φ, then $\mathcal{T}(\varphi) = s$.

Proof Sketch. This property holds by construction: the parser inverts each production rule of $\mathcal{T}$. We verified the property empirically by round-trip testing on the full dataset: for each LTL formula φ, we computed $\mathcal{T}(\varphi)$, parsed the result to obtain φ', and confirmed $\varphi \equiv \varphi'$ using Spot's equivalence checker. All 15,000,000 unique formulas generated at this stage passed this test. If parsing fails, the input string violates the ITL grammar. The parser returns a structured error indicating the failure location and expected tokens, which guides the repair module.

Verification Backend. Successfully parsed LTL formulas undergo verification using the Spot library. Spot converts LTL formulas to equivalent Büchi automata and provides decision procedures for standard properties. NeuroNL2LTL checks two properties:

Satisfiability. A formula φ is satisfiable if $\mathcal{L}(\varphi) \neq \emptyset$. Spot determines satisfiability by constructing the Büchi automaton for φ and checking whether the automaton accepts any infinite word. An unsatisfiable formula represents a contradictory requirement that no system execution can satisfy.

Non-triviality. A formula φ is non-trivial if it is neither unsatisfiable nor valid. We check validity by testing whether $\neg\varphi$ is unsatisfiable. A valid formula (tautology) provides no constraint on system behavior; a translation that produces $\top$ or a logical equivalent has failed to capture the requirement's content.

Formulas that pass both checks are emitted as verified output. Formulas that fail either check are passed to the repair module with an error classification (unsatisfiable, trivial, or syntactically malformed from an earlier parsing failure). The verification backend also supports semantic equivalence checking for evaluation. Given formulas φ_1 and φ_2, Spot tests whether $\mathcal{L}(\varphi_1) = \mathcal{L}(\varphi_2)$ by checking that both $\varphi_1 \wedge \neg\varphi_2$ and $\neg\varphi_1 \wedge \varphi_2$ are unsatisfiable. This equivalence check is the primary metric for translation accuracy: a generated formula is correct if it is semantically equivalent to the reference formula.

Minimal-Edit Repair. When parsing or verification fails, the repair module attempts to correct the error through minimal edits. The module operates in two layers: a fast heuristic layer for common errors and a learned layer for structural errors that heuristics cannot resolve.

Heuristic Repair. The first layer addresses syntactic errors that arise from predictable failure modes: unbalanced parentheses, missing operators between subformulas, and operator precedence ambiguities. The heuristics apply a ranked sequence of edits: parenthesis insertion or deletion at the error location, operator insertion between adjacent propositions, and keyword normalization (e.g., correcting "eventual" to "eventually"). Each edit is validated by re-parsing; the first edit that yields a parseable ITL string is accepted. If no single edit succeeds within a fixed budget of m attempts, control passes to the learned layer.

Learned Repair. The second layer employs a graph neural network trained to correct malformed ITL abstract syntax trees. When an ITL string parses partially (producing a partial AST with error nodes), the GNN receives the partial AST as input and predicts a sequence of edit operations: node relabeling, edge redirection, subtree deletion, or subtree insertion. The GNN was trained on pairs of malformed and corrected ASTs collected during NeuroNL2LTL's development, with successful repairs (those producing verifiable LTL) providing positive training signal.

The repair module returns either a corrected ITL string or a failure indication. Repaired strings re-enter the pipeline at the parsing stage. If repair fails after both layers, the translation is rejected, and no output is returned. Repair cost, defined as the number of edit operations applied, provides a training signal: formulas requiring extensive repair indicate unreliable neural generation, while formulas requiring no repair indicate successful translation. The verifier-in-the-loop training stage (described in Sect. 3.2) penalizes high repair costs to incentivize direct generation of correct formulas.

3.2 Verifier-in-the-Loop Training

Supervised training on paired (NL, ITL) examples teaches the neural encoder to produce outputs that resemble training data. This objective is necessary but insufficient: a model can achieve low loss on reference examples while still generating formulas that fail verification. Verifier-in-the-loop training addresses this gap by incorporating verification outcomes directly into the learning objective.

We formulate the problem as reinforcement learning. The neural encoder acts as a policy π_θ that maps input (requirement, context) pairs to ITL strings. The symbolic backend provides a reward signal R based on the generated ITL and its corresponding LTL. The training objective maximizes expected reward: $\mathcal{J}(\theta) = \mathbb{E}_{(r,\mathcal{C})\sim\mathcal{D}}\left[\mathbb{E}_{s\sim\pi_\theta(\cdot|r,\mathcal{C})}\left[R(s)\right]\right]$, where $\mathcal{D}$ is the training distribution over requirements and contexts.

The reward function combines three components derived from the symbolic backend:

$$\begin{aligned} R(s) = {} & \alpha \cdot \mathbb{1}[\text{parse}(s) \text{ succeeds}] \\ & + \beta \cdot \mathbb{1}[\text{sat}(\mathcal{T}^{-1}(s)) \wedge \text{nontriv}(\mathcal{T}^{-1}(s))] \\ & - \gamma \cdot \text{repair\_cost}(s) \end{aligned}$$

where α, β, γ are weighting coefficients. The first term rewards syntactically valid ITL. The second term rewards LTL formulas that pass satisfiability and non-triviality checks. The third term penalizes formulas that required repair, incentivizing direct generation of correct output. We optimize $\mathcal{J}(\theta)$ using Group Relative Policy Optimization (GRPO), a variant of policy gradient methods that computes advantages relative to a group of samples from the same input. For each training example, we sample multiple ITL candidates from π_θ, compute rewards for each, and update parameters to increase the probability of higher-reward candidates relative to lower-reward ones.

This training procedure directly optimizes for formal properties checked by the symbolic backend. The neural encoder then learns to produce strings that survive parsing, convert to satisfiable non-trivial LTL, and require minimal repair rather than merely to imitate reference ITL strings. Ablation experiments (Sect. 4) demonstrate that verifier-in-the-loop training improves semantic equivalence by over 30 relative percentage points compared to supervised training alone.

3.3 Correctness Considerations

NeuroNL2LTL provides guarantees at different levels of the architecture. The ITL-to-LTL conversion is correct by construction: the parser implements $\mathcal{T}^{-1}$ exactly, and round-trip testing confirms that $\mathcal{T}^{-1}(\mathcal{T}(\varphi)) \equiv \varphi$ for all formulas in the dataset. The verification backend inherits Spot's correctness: satisfiability and non-triviality checks are sound and complete for LTL over infinite traces.

The neural encoder provides no formal guarantees. A generated ITL string that passes verification is guaranteed to be satisfiable and non-trivial, but it is not guaranteed to capture the intended meaning of the input requirement. Semantic equivalence with the intended specification depends on the accuracy of neural translation, which our evaluation measures empirically.

This separation clarifies the role of each component. The symbolic backend acts as a filter: it cannot verify that a translation is correct (in the sense of matching intent), but it can verify that a translation is not obviously wrong (in the sense of being unsatisfiable or trivial). Verifier-in-the-loop training improves the neural encoder's reliability, but the final output remains a proposal that downstream processes, including human review, may validate further.

4 Evaluation

This section presents an empirical evaluation of NeuroNL2LTL across multiple dimensions: translation accuracy, comparison with baseline systems, effectiveness of the verification filter, repair module performance, and ablation studies isolating individual architectural contributions.

4.1 Experimental Setup

Dataset. We evaluate on the VERIFY corpus comprising 218,871 requirement-specification pairs across thirteen domains: aerospace, automotive/autonomous vehicles, robotics, medical devices, industrial automation, home automation, smart grid/energy management, financial/transaction systems, networking/distributed systems, security/authentication, build pipelines/CI-CD, version control, and web services/APIs. Each instance contains a natural language requirement, domain context (natural language definitions for atomic propositions), the canonical ITL representation, and the reference LTL formula verified by Spot. The dataset spans LTL formulas with abstract syntax tree depths from 1 to 22, with a mean depth of 5.0. We partition the data into complexity strata: simple (depth 1–4, 31% of instances), medium (depth 5–8, 42%), high (depth 9–12, 19%), and very high (depth 13+, 8%). We reserve 10% of each stratum for testing, ensuring the test set reflects the full complexity distribution.

Metrics. We evaluate using four metrics:

Semantic Equivalence (SemEq): The primary metric. A generated formula φ_g is semantically equivalent to the reference φ_r if $\mathcal{L}(\varphi_g) = \mathcal{L}(\varphi_r)$, verified using Spot's equivalence checker. We report the percentage of test instances where the generated formula is semantically equivalent to the reference.

Syntactic Correctness (SynCorr): The percentage of outputs that parse successfully as valid ITL and convert to well-formed LTL. This measures whether the neural encoder produces structurally valid output before considering semantic correctness.

Satisfiability (Sat): The percentage of syntactically correct outputs that Spot verifies as satisfiable (non-contradictory).

Non-triviality (NonTriv): The percentage of satisfiable outputs that are also non-trivial (neither tautologies nor contradictions).

Table 1. NeuroNL2LTL syntactic correctness and verification results on the VERIFY test set. Sat conditions on SynCorr; NonTriv conditions on Sat.

Complexity	SynCorr (%)	Sat (%)	NonTriv (%)
Simple (depth 1–4)	96.2	98.1	97.3
Medium (depth 5–8)	94.8	97.4	96.1
High (depth 9–12)	91.3	95.8	94.2
Very High (depth 13+)	87.6	93.1	91.8
Overall	**93.7**	**96.8**	**95.4**

Note that Sat and NonTriv are conditional metrics: Sat conditions on syntactic correctness, and NonTriv conditions on satisfiability. The unconditional rate of outputs passing all three checks (syntactically correct, satisfiable, and non-trivial) is the product SynCorr × Sat × NonTriv.

Baselines. We compare NeuroNL2LTL against two categories of baselines.

Large Language Models (Zero-Shot and Few-Shot): We evaluate GPT-4o, Gemini 1.5 Pro, and Claude 3.5 Sonnet in both zero-shot and 5-shot configurations. For zero-shot, we provide the task description, domain context, and requirement, prompting the model to output LTL directly. For 5-shot, we prepend five (requirement, context, LTL) examples from the training set, selected to cover diverse temporal operators. We use greedy decoding (temperature 0) for reproducibility. We compare NeuroNL2LTL against four systems from the literature: Lang2LTL [33], NL2TL [5], CopyNet-LTL [28], and a Seq2Seq-Attn baseline trained on VERIFY. Note that Lang2LTL, NL2TL, and CopyNet-LTL were designed for simpler, domain-specific commands (primarily robot navigation) without contextual grounding. Our evaluation on complex, multi-domain requirements with explicit proposition definitions represents a distribution shift for these systems.

Implementation. NeuroNL2LTL uses Flan-T5-XL (3B parameters) as the base model, with continued pretraining (CPT) on 5B tokens of technical documentation followed by supervised fine-tuning on 180k training pairs and verifier-in-the-loop training using GRPO for 10k steps. We use the Spot library (version 2.11.6) for all verification. The repair module's GNN uses a 4-layer graph attention network with 256-dimensional hidden states. All experiments run on 4× NVIDIA H200 GPUs.

4.2 Main Results: Translation Accuracy

We present the results on the performance of NeuroNL2LTL on the test set. Table 1 reports syntactic correctness, satisfiability, and non-triviality stratified by formula complexity, and Table 2 reports semantic equivalence alongside baselines. NeuroNL2LTL achieves 27.8% semantic equivalence overall, with 93.7% of outputs syntactically correct. Of syntactically correct outputs, 96.8% are satisfiable and 95.4% of those are non-trivial, yielding an unconditional verification pass rate (syntactically correct, satisfiable, and non-trivial) of 86.2%. Syntactic

Table 2. Comparison with baseline systems on contextually grounded translation.

Category	System	SemEq (%)	SynCorr (%)
LLMs	GPT-4o (zero-shot)	8.3	67.4
	GPT-4o (5-shot)	14.7	78.2
	Gemini 1.5 Pro (zero-shot)	7.1	63.8
	Gemini 1.5 Pro (5-shot)	12.9	74.6
	Claude 3.5 Sonnet (zero-shot)	9.2	71.3
	Claude 3.5 Sonnet (5-shot)	15.4	79.8
Neural NL-to-LTL	Lang2LTL [33]	2.1	41.2
	NL2TL [5]	6.8	58.7
	CopyNet-LTL [28]	1.4	38.9
	Seq2Seq-Attn (our data)	11.2	82.4
	NeuroNL2LTL (ours)	**27.8**	**93.7**

correctness remains high (87.6%+) even at very high complexity, indicating that the grammar-constrained decoding and repair mechanisms successfully produce parseable output regardless of formula depth. The gap between syntactic correctness and semantic equivalence represents formulas that are well-formed but do not capture the intended meaning.

4.3 Comparison with Baselines

We now present the results of the comparisons of NeuroNL2LTL against baseline systems in Table 2.

LLM Baselines. General-purpose LLMs struggle with contextually grounded translation. GPT-4o achieves 8.3% semantic equivalence zero-shot and 14.7% with 5-shot prompting. The primary failure mode is incorrect grounding: LLMs frequently generate syntactically valid LTL using proposition names that do not match the provided context, or they hallucinate propositions not defined in the context. Few-shot examples improve syntactic correctness substantially (67.4% → 78.2% for GPT-4o) but provide limited benefit for semantic equivalence, suggesting that the models learn output format but not the grounding task. Claude 3.5 Sonnet performs best among LLMs (15.4% 5-shot), likely due to stronger instruction following. However, all LLMs remain well below NeuroNL2LTL's 27.8%, a gap of 12–20% points.

Neural NL-to-LTL Baselines. Systems designed for simpler domains perform poorly on our benchmark. Lang2LTL achieves only 2.1% semantic equivalence; inspection reveals that the model produces formulas appropriate for robot navigation commands (simple sequences of goals) but cannot represent the nested temporal structures in our requirements. CopyNet-LTL shows similar limitations (1.4%). NL2TL performs better (6.8%) because it leverages GPT-4's language understanding, but its chain-of-thought prompting strategy does not explicitly handle domain context or proposition grounding. The Seq2Seq-Attn baseline, trained on our data but without NeuroNL2LTL's architectural components, achieves 11.2% semantic equivalence. This baseline isolates the contribution of our architecture: the 16.6% point improvement (11.2% → 27.8%) derives from

Table 3. Classification of errors and filter effectiveness. Of 72.2% total errors, the verification filter catches 28.4%, while 71.6% pass undetected.

Error Type	% of Errors	Caught by Filter
Syntactic (parse failure)	8.7%	Yes (at parsing)
Unsatisfiable	12.3%	Yes (Spot)
Trivial (tautology)	7.4%	Yes (Spot)
Satisfiable, non-trivial, semantically wrong	71.6%	No
Total caught by filter	**28.4%**	—

Table 4. Distribution of semantic error types among formulas that pass verification.

Error Category	Frequency
Incorrect logical scope	41%
Temporal operator mismatch (U/W/R confusion)	28%
Propositional atom error (wrong/missing/hallucinated)	17%
Contextual grounding failure	9%
Other	5%

ITL decomposition, domain adaptation, grammar-constrained decoding, repair, and verifier-in-the-loop training.

4.4 Verification Filter Effectiveness

The symbolic backend serves as a runtime filter, rejecting formulas that fail satisfiability or non-triviality checks. We analyze what errors this filter catches.

Methodology. We examine the 72.2% of test instances where NeuroNL2LTL produces a formula that is *not* semantically equivalent to the reference. For each such instance, we classify whether the generated formula: (a) failed parsing (syntactic error), (b) parsed but was unsatisfiable, (c) was satisfiable but trivial, or (d) was satisfiable, non-trivial, but semantically incorrect.

Table 3 presents the results. The verification filter catches 28.4% of errors: 8.7% at parsing, 12.3% as unsatisfiable, and 7.4% as trivial. The remaining 71.6% of errors produce formulas that are satisfiable and non-trivial but semantically different from the reference.

Interpretation. Satisfiability and non-triviality checking provide necessary but not sufficient conditions for correctness. They catch gross errors (contradictions, tautologies, malformed syntax) but cannot detect semantic mismatches where the generated formula constrains behavior differently than intended. This is expected: determining whether a formula matches an informal requirement's intent requires understanding that intent, which is beyond what syntactic verification can provide.

Table 5. Repair module effectiveness.

Stage	Inputs	Success Rate
Initial parse failures	6.3% of outputs	—
Heuristic repair	6.3%	71.4%
GNN repair (after heuristic failure)	1.8%	68.2%
Initial verification failures	4.2% of parsed outputs	—
Heuristic repair	4.2%	62.3%
GNN repair (after heuristic failure)	1.6%	54.8%
Overall repair success	10.5% of outputs	**87.3%**

The 28.4% error detection rate still provides value. In a pipeline without this filter, contradictory or vacuous specifications would propagate to downstream verification, producing misleading results. The filter ensures that outputs passed to model checkers are at least logically coherent.

Error Type Analysis. Among the 71.6% of undetected semantic errors, we manually analyzed 100 samples and categorized them according to error type (Table 4):

Incorrect logical scope (41%) is the dominant failure mode. The neural encoder misplaces operators in the AST, changing precedence and nesting. For example, generating $(p\,U\,q) \rightarrow r$ instead of $p\,U\,(q \rightarrow r)$ produces a satisfiable, non-trivial formula with different semantics. Temporal operator mismatch (28%) involves confusion between semantically similar operators, most commonly substituting weak-until for until or release for until. These error types suggest directions for improvement: explicit scope prediction, contrastive training on operator distinctions, or interactive disambiguation when natural language is ambiguous.

4.5 Repair Module Effectiveness

The repair module attempts to correct outputs that fail parsing or verification. We evaluate its success rate and contribution to overall performance.

Methodology. We track all test instances where the initial neural encoder output fails parsing or verification. For each, we record whether heuristic repair succeeds, whether GNN repair succeeds (if heuristics fail), and the final outcome.

Table 5 presents the results. Of the 10.5% of outputs requiring repair, 87.3% are successfully recovered. Heuristic repair resolves most cases: 71.4% of parse failures and 62.3% of verification failures. The GNN layer handles more complex structural errors, recovering 68.2% of parse failures and 54.8% of verification failures that heuristics cannot resolve.

Repair and Semantic Correctness. Repair improves syntactic correctness and verification pass rates but does not guarantee semantic correctness. Among repaired outputs, semantic equivalence with reference formulas is 18.4%, lower than the 29.1% for outputs that required no repair. This suggests that outputs needing

Table 6. Ablation study. Each row removes one component from the full NeuroNL2LTL system.

Configuration	SemEq	SynCorr	Sat	NonTriv
NeuroNL2LTL (full)	27.8	93.7	96.8	95.4
– Verifier-in-the-loop	18.2	89.4	91.2	89.8
– Repair module	24.1	83.2	94.7	93.1
– Domain adaptation (CPT)	22.4	90.1	95.3	94.1
– Grammar-constrained decoding	25.3	86.8	95.9	94.6
– ITL (direct NL→LTL)	16.7	78.4	92.1	90.3
– Domain context	19.3	92.8	96.2	94.9

repair are systematically harder cases where the neural encoder's initial attempt was further from correct.

Contribution to Overall Performance. Without the repair module (ablation in Sect. 4.6), syntactic correctness drops from 93.7% to 83.2%, a 10.5% point decrease. Semantic equivalence drops from 27.8% to 24.1%. The repair module thus contributes approximately 3.7% points to semantic equivalence by salvaging outputs that would otherwise be rejected.

4.6 Ablation Studies

We isolate the contribution of each architectural component through ablation experiments. The ablation results are presented in Table 6.

Verifier-in-the-Loop Training. Removing RL fine-tuning with verification rewards reduces semantic equivalence from 27.8% to 18.2%, a decrease of 9.6% points (34.5% relative). This is the largest single-component contribution. The verification reward signal teaches the encoder to produce outputs that survive formal checking, not merely outputs that resemble training examples.

Repair Module. Disabling repair reduces syntactic correctness from 93.7% to 83.2% and semantic equivalence from 27.8% to 24.1%. The repair module rescues approximately 10% of outputs that would otherwise be rejected.

Domain Adaptation. Removing continued pretraining (CPT) on technical corpora reduces semantic equivalence from 27.8% to 22.4%. Domain adaptation improves the model's handling of specialized terminology and temporal phrasing patterns.

Grammar-Constrained Decoding. Without grammar constraints, syntactic correctness drops from 93.7% to 86.8%, but semantic equivalence drops only modestly (27.8% → 25.3%). The repair module partially compensates for syntactic errors introduced by unconstrained decoding.

ITL Decomposition. Replacing the two-stage NL→ITL→LTL pipeline with direct NL→LTL translation reduces semantic equivalence from 27.8% to 16.7%

and syntactic correctness from 93.7% to 78.4%. ITL provides a more learnable intermediate target and enables grammar-constrained decoding, which is not feasible for raw LTL syntax.

Domain Context. Removing proposition definitions from the input reduces semantic equivalence from 27.8% to 19.3%. Without context, the model cannot correctly ground domain-specific terms to atomic propositions, confirming that contextual grounding is essential for this task.

5 Related Work

Pattern-based approaches for translating natural language to temporal logic [13,15,20] guarantee correctness for requirements that fit predefined templates but cannot express specifications outside that finite vocabulary. In addition, structured specification languages such as FRET [14], EARS [30] and Propel [38] impose similar tradeoffs. Though they improve requirements quality through guided authoring, they offer no machine-checkable output. These tools trade expressiveness for reliability: complex nested temporal dependencies, biconditional relationships, and domain-specific conditions fall outside their scope. Neural-based approaches enable a more expressive mode of translating natural language to temporal logic [5,10,28,33,39]. Though successful, all of these systems accept unrestricted natural language, yet none provides correctness guarantees on their output, and none incorporates domain-specific proposition definitions as explicit input. A complementary line of work mines temporal specifications from system traces rather than natural language [4,25,31,36]. Neurosymbolic architectures offer a path toward combining the expressiveness of neural methods with formal guarantees. Semantic loss functions [41], DeepProbLog [29], and Scallop [26] constrain or correct neural outputs using symbolic reasoning at inference time. Neural theorem provers [16,21,35] and AlphaProof [18] invert this relationship, using learned models to guide symbolic proof search. Our work pursues a distinct integration: verification outcomes during *training* rather than at inference alone. This connects to reinforcement learning from verifiable rewards [27] and code generation with execution feedback [22], but targets a domain where satisfiability and non-triviality provide deterministic supervision without annotation infrastructure, unlike RLHF [7,32], Constitutional AI [1], or RLAIF [24], which rely on human or model-generated preference signals.

When neural generation fails, automated repair can recover. Program repair techniques fix source code bugs through search or learning [6,23,42]; syntax repair recovers from malformed parser input via minimal edits [9]; specification repair corrects formulas that fail realizability checks [2,19]. NeuroNL2LTL draws on all three traditions but targets structural errors in the intermediate representation rather than semantic bugs. NeuroNL2LTL differs from prior work in three respects. It decomposes translation through an intermediate representation that isolates neural uncertainty from deterministic symbolic conversion. It incorporates domain context as explicit input, addressing the proposition grounding problem that context-free approaches leave open. It uses formal verification outcomes as reinforcement learning reward, optimizing directly for logical correctness rather than reference similarity.

6 Conclusion

We presented NeuroNL2LTL, a neurosymbolic system for translating natural language requirements to Linear Temporal Logic. The architecture decomposes translation through an Intermediate Technical Language that isolates neural uncertainty from symbolic parsing. A deterministic parser converts ITL to LTL with guaranteed correctness. The Spot verification backend filters contradictory and vacuous formulas. A two-stage repair module recovers from generation failures. Verifier-in-the-loop training using GRPO optimizes directly for verification success. Empirical evaluation establishes that NeuroNL2LTL achieves 27.8% semantic equivalence on complex, multi-domain requirements, outperforming large language model baselines by 12–20% points and prior neural NL-to-LTL systems by 16–26% points. Ablation studies confirm that verifier-in-the-loop training contributes 9.6% points, the largest single-component improvement. The verification filter catches 28.4% of errors, ensuring logical coherence even when semantic correctness is not achieved.

References

1. Bai, Y., et al.: Constitutional AI: harmlessness from ai feedback. arXiv preprint arXiv:2212.08073 (2022)
2. Bloem, R., Könighofer, B., Könighofer, R., Wang, C.: Shield synthesis: runtime enforcement for reactive systems. In: Baier, C., Tinelli, C. (eds.) TACAS 2015. LNCS, vol. 9035, pp. 533–548. Springer, Heidelberg (2015). https://doi.org/10.1007/978-3-662-46681-0_51
3. Cai, M., Hasanbeig, M., Xiao, S., Abate, A., Kan, Z.: Modular deep reinforcement learning for continuous motion planning with temporal logic. arXiv preprint arXiv:2102.12855 (2021)
4. Camacho, A., McIlraith, S.A.: Learning interpretable models expressed in linear temporal logic. In: Proceedings of the International Conference on Automated Planning and Scheduling, vol. 29, pp. 621–630 (2019)
5. Chen, Y., Gandhi, R., Zhang, Y., Fan, C.: NL2TL: transforming natural languages to temporal logics using large language models. arXiv preprint arXiv:2305.07766 (2023)
6. Chen, Z., Kommrusch, S., Tufano, M., Pouchet, L.N., Poshyvanyk, D., Monperrus, M.: Sequencer: sequence-to-sequence learning for end-to-end program repair. IEEE Trans. Software Eng. **47**(9), 1943–1959 (2019)
7. Christiano, P.F., Leike, J., Brown, T., Martic, M., Legg, S., Amodei, D.: Deep reinforcement learning from human preferences. In: Advances in Neural Information Processing Systems, vol. 30 (2017)
8. Clarke, E.M., Henzinger, T.A., Veith, H., Bloem, R., et al.: Handbook of Model Checking, vol. 10. Springer (2018)

9. Corchuelo, R., Pérez, J.A., Ruiz, A., Toro, M.: Repairing syntax errors in LR parsers. ACM Trans. Program. Lang. Syst. (TOPLAS) **24**(6), 698–710 (2002)
10. Cosler, M., Hahn, C., Mendoza, D., Schmitt, F., Trippel, C.: nl2spec: interactively translating unstructured natural language to temporal logics with large language models. In: International Conference on Computer Aided Verification, pp. 383–396. Springer (2023)
11. Duret-Lutz, A., Lewkowicz, A., Fauchille, A., Michaud, T., Renault, É., Xu, L.: Spot 2.0 — a framework for LTL and ω-automata manipulation. In: Artho, C., Legay, A., Peled, D. (eds.) ATVA 2016. LNCS, vol. 9938, pp. 122–129. Springer, Cham (2016). https://doi.org/10.1007/978-3-319-46520-3_8
12. Duret-Lutz, A., Poitrenaud, D.: Spot: an extensible model checking library using transition-based generalized BU/SPL UML/CHI automata. In: The IEEE Computer Society's 12th Annual International Symposium on Modeling, Analysis, and Simulation of Computer and Telecommunications Systems, 2004.(MASCOTS 2004). Proceedings, pp. 76–83. IEEE (2004)
13. Dwyer, M.B., Avrunin, G.S., Corbett, J.C.: Patterns in property specifications for finite-state verification. In: Proceedings of the 21st International Conference on Software Engineering, pp. 411–420 (1999)
14. Giannakopoulou, D., Mavridou, A., Rhein, J., Pressburger, T., Schumann, J., Shi, N.: Formal requirements elicitation with fret. In: International Working Conference on Requirements Engineering: Foundation for Software Quality (REFSQ-2020). No. ARC-E-DAA-TN77785 (2020)
15. Grunske, L.: Specification patterns for probabilistic quality properties. In: Proceedings of the 30th International Conference on Software Engineering, pp. 31–40 (2008)
16. Han, J.M., Rute, J., Wu, Y., Ayers, E.W., Polu, S.: Proof artifact co-training for theorem proving with language models. arXiv preprint arXiv:2102.06203 (2021)
17. Holzmann, G.J.: The SPIN Model Checker: Primer and Reference Manual, vol. 1003. Addison-Wesley, Reading (2004)
18. Hubert, T., et al.: Olympiad-level formal mathematical reasoning with reinforcement learning. Nature 1–3 (2025)
19. Könighofer, B., et al.: Shield synthesis. Formal Methods Syst. Des. **51**(2), 332–361 (2017)
20. Konrad, S., Cheng, B.H.: Real-time specification patterns. In: Proceedings of the 27th International Conference on Software Engineering, pp. 372–381 (2005)
21. Lample, G., et al.: Hypertree proof search for neural theorem proving. Adv. Neural. Inf. Process. Syst. **35**, 26337–26349 (2022)
22. Le, H., Wang, Y., Gotmare, A.D., Savarese, S., Hoi, S.C.H.: Coderl: mastering code generation through pretrained models and deep reinforcement learning. Adv. Neural. Inf. Process. Syst. **35**, 21314–21328 (2022)
23. Le, X.B.D., Chu, D.H., Lo, D., Le Goues, C., Visser, W.: S3: syntax-and semantic-guided repair synthesis via programming by examples. In: Proceedings of the 2017 11th Joint Meeting on Foundations of Software Engineering, pp. 593–604 (2017)
24. Lee, H., et al.: Rlaif: scaling reinforcement learning from human feedback with AI feedback (2023)
25. Lemieux, C., Park, D., Beschastnikh, I.: General LTL specification mining (t). In: 2015 30th IEEE/ACM International Conference on Automated Software Engineering (ASE), pp. 81–92. IEEE (2015)
26. Li, Z., Huang, J., Naik, M.: Scallop: a language for neurosymbolic programming. Proc. ACM Program. Lang. **7**(PLDI), 1463–1487 (2023)

27. Lightman, H., et al.: Let's verify step by step. In: The Twelfth International Conference on Learning Representations (2023)
28. Liu, J.X., et al.: Grounding complex natural language commands for temporal tasks in unseen environments. In: Conference on Robot Learning, pp. 1084–1110. PMLR (2023)
29. Manhaeve, R., Dumancic, S., Kimmig, A., Demeester, T., De Raedt, L.: Deepproblog: neural probabilistic logic programming. Adv. Neural Inf. Process. Syst. **31** (2018)
30. Mavin, A., Wilkinson, P., Harwood, A., Novak, M.: Easy approach to requirements syntax (ears). In: 2009 17th IEEE International Requirements Engineering Conference, pp. 317–322. IEEE (2009)
31. Neider, D., Gavran, I.: Learning linear temporal properties. In: 2018 Formal Methods in Computer Aided Design (FMCAD), pp. 1–10. IEEE (2018)
32. Ouyang, L., et al.: Training language models to follow instructions with human feedback. Adv. Neural. Inf. Process. Syst. **35**, 27730–27744 (2022)
33. Pan, J., Chou, G., Berenson, D.: Data-efficient learning of natural language to linear temporal logic translators for robot task specification. In: 2023 IEEE International Conference on Robotics and Automation (ICRA), pp. 11554–11561. IEEE (2023)
34. Pnueli, A.: The temporal logic of programs. In: 18th Annual Symposium on Foundations of Computer Science (SFCS 1977), pp. 46–57. IEEE (1977)
35. Polu, S., Sutskever, I.: Generative language modeling for automated theorem proving. arXiv preprint arXiv:2009.03393 (2020)
36. Roy, R., Fisman, D., Neider, D.: Learning interpretable models in the property specification language. arXiv preprint arXiv:2002.03668 (2020)
37. Rozier, K.Y.: Linear temporal logic symbolic model checking. Comput. Sci. Rev. **5**(2), 163–203 (2011)
38. Smith, R.L., Avrunin, G.S., Clarke, L.A., Osterweil, L.J.: Propel: an approach supporting property elucidation. In: Proceedings of the 24th International Conference on Software Engineering, pp. 11–21 (2002)
39. Wang, C., Ross, C., Kuo, Y.L., Katz, B., Barbu, A.: Learning a natural-language to LTL executable semantic parser for grounded robotics. In: Conference on Robot Learning, pp. 1706–1718. PMLR (2021)
40. Xie, G., Yin, Z., Li, J.: Temporal logic based motion planning with infeasible LTL specification. In: 2020 Chinese Control And Decision Conference (CCDC), pp. 4899–4904. IEEE (2020)
41. Xu, J., Zhang, Z., Friedman, T., Liang, Y., Broeck, G.: A semantic loss function for deep learning with symbolic knowledge. In: International Conference on Machine Learning, pp. 5502–5511. PMLR (2018)
42. Ye, H., Martinez, M., Monperrus, M.: Neural program repair with execution-based backpropagation. In: Proceedings of the 44th International Conference on Software Engineering, pp. 1506–1518 (2022)

Sound Automatic Lock Placement for Concurrent Programs with Pointers

Nicolas Waldburger, Florian Faissole, Ryo Okabe(✉), and Denis Cousineau

Mitsubishi Electric R&D Centre Europe, Rennes, France
{n.waldburger,f.faissole,r.okabe,d.cousineau}@fr.merce.mee.com

Abstract. We propose a lightweight method for automatic lock placement in concurrent POSIX programs with explicit pointer manipulation, such as C programs. Given a program that lacks sufficient user-placed mutexes or contains none at all, our method introduces new mutexes to prevent data races. The method is formally proven to guarantee the absence of data races and mainly consists of three steps. The first step performs lockset analysis and may-happen-in-parallel analysis. The second step conducts a concurrent points-to analysis derived from a Steensgaard-like procedural analysis, where per-thread points-to graphs are unified using a special completion rule. The final step places locks to prevent any data race while respecting a lock ordering to avoid deadlocks. Since lock placement is a complex and error-prone task, our method aims at helping developers write correct concurrent programs.

Keywords: Concurrent programming · Static analysis · Formal methods · Points-to analysis · Alias analysis

1 Introduction

Concurrent programs are cumbersome to implement and difficult to debug. They are prone to several categories of errors, including data races, deadlocks, starvation and generic race conditions. To prevent such errors, meticulous implementation of concurrency controls, such as mutual exclusion and synchronization, is required. Moreover, conventional testing is insufficient for detecting concurrency errors due to the numerous possibilities of threads interleaving.

A data race occurs when two conflicting accesses to a shared variable are executed without proper synchronization [2,15]. Preventing data races with mutexes is prone to errors such as missing locks and introduction of deadlocks. Pointers increase the difficulty as they obscure which variables a statement accesses.

Some abstract interpretation-based static analyzers [7,12,18,24] specifically target concurrent programs. They offer a sound and highly precise analysis that detects all data races and deadlocks. Thus these static analyzers help reduce verification complexity. However, they do not reduce the implementation effort.

Languages designed with correct-by-construction principles like Cyclone [9,10], Rust [16] and SPARK [3] incorporate type systems that prevent data

Published by Springer Nature Switzerland AG 2026
L. Bocchi and B. Kulahcioglu Ozkan (Eds.): FORTE 2026, LNCS 16589, pp. 74–92, 2026.
https://doi.org/10.1007/978-3-032-28187-6_5

races. Nevertheless, these languages often pose a steep learning curve. SCADE [1] covers more categories of concurrency issues. However, its applicability is limited by its graphical nature and by its reliance on message-passing concurrency.

A promising approach to preventing data races is to automate lock placement. This reduces development effort and makes concurrent programming more accessible to non-experts. Several works proposed algorithms for automatic lock placement in atomic sections [4,8,11,17]. The developer specifies which code sections must be treated as atomic, *i.e.*, must execute without any interference from other threads. These tools insert appropriate mutex acquisitions and releases to enforce atomicity while avoiding deadlocks, using two-phase locking and a predetermined lock ordering. However, avoiding data races is not their goal.

Shared-variable identification and points-to analysis are key to automatic lock placement. Rugina et al. [19,20] proposed a flow-sensitive points-to analysis for structured multithreaded programs, which computes a points-to graph for each program point, using graphs summarizing inter-thread interference. Salcianu et al. [21] presented a flow-sensitive points-to analysis for parallel Java programs. Their approach of merging parent and child graphs to derive thread interference is unsound for C, as global pointers allow more general inter-thread interference. Sui et al. [23] developed a sparse flow-sensitive analysis for unstructured multithreaded C programs, propagating points-to information sparsely along def-use chains for scalability. Abstract interpreters compute shared memory locations and their contents, as well as abstract pointer values. Mthread [12] and AstréeA [18] iteratively re-analyze threads that read shared memory to propagate inter-thread interference until reaching a fixpoint. Their path-sensitive analysis is highly precise, but is expensive due to the combinatorial explosion of program paths and thread interleavings. Goblint [24] avoids this problem through thread-modular analysis, using global invariants summarizing inter-thread interference.

Contributions. We propose an automatic lock placement method for concurrent POSIX programs with explicit pointer manipulation (*e.g.*, C programs). Given a program lacking sufficient user-placed mutexes (or containing none), our method operates on the source code by introducing new mutexes to eliminate data races. We build a concurrent points-to analysis derived from an inexpensive Steensgaard-like per-thread analysis, such as the one implemented in the `alias` plugin of Frama-C [13]. The per-thread points-to graphs are unified using a special completion rule. Overall, our approach is designed to run fast, sacrificing precision for efficiency. It targets use cases where development time is key, and contention in the obtained program is not a primary concern. Moreover, our approach is formalized and proven, which gives weight to the soundness claim and is, in our view, a contribution in itself.

Outline. The paper is organized as follows. Section 2 defines our model for concurrent programs and its semantics. Section 3 describes a preliminary analysis of concurrency between statements and the points-to analysis. Section 4 introduces the automatic lock placement technique, and Sect. 5 concludes the paper.

2 A Model for Concurrent Programs

2.1 Concurrent Programs

A concurrent program is a tuple $\mathcal{P} = \langle \mathcal{T}, \mathcal{V}, \mathcal{M}, \mathcal{C} \rangle$ where:

- $\mathcal{T}$ is a finite set of *threads* with a special thread main;
- $\mathcal{V}$ is a finite set of *variables*;
- $\mathcal{M}$ is a finite set of *mutexes*;
- a function $\mathcal{C}$ that maps each thread to its *control flow graph*.

While the method is intended to work on source-level programs, we present it here on control-flow graphs; in practice, tools such as FramaC [6] allow to operate on such abstract representations of the program. A *control-flow graph* is a tuple $(\mathcal{N}, \mathsf{st}, \mathsf{end}, \Delta)$ where $\mathcal{N}$ is a finite set of *nodes* with *starting node* st and *final node* end, and $\Delta \subseteq \mathcal{N} \times \mathsf{Instr} \times \mathcal{N}$ is a finite set of *transitions* labelled by *instructions* from a set Instr described below. We assume that st has no incoming transition, that end has no outgoing transition and that any node is reachable from st. Given $\delta = (n, \iota, n') \in \Delta$, n is the *source* and n' the *target* of δ. A *path* is a sequence of transitions $\delta_1, \ldots, \delta_k$ such that the target of δ_i is the source of δ_{i+1}. Each thread t is described by its CFG $\mathcal{C}(t) = (\mathcal{N}_t, \mathsf{st}_t, \mathsf{end}_t, \Delta_t)$. Threads have disjoint sets of nodes: for all $t \neq t'$, $\mathcal{N}_t \cap \mathcal{N}_{t'} = \emptyset$. We let $\mathcal{N} := \bigcup_{t \in \mathcal{T}} \mathcal{N}_t$ and $\Delta := \bigcup_{t \in \mathcal{T}} \Delta_t$. Each node $n \in \mathcal{N}$ has a single thread, denoted $\mathsf{th}(n)$, such that $n \in \mathcal{N}_{\mathsf{th}(n)}$. Similarly, each transition δ has a single thread $\mathsf{th}(\delta)$ such that $\delta \in \Delta_{\mathsf{th}(\delta)}$.

Our model includes pointers of arbitrary depth (*e.g.*, in C, `*int`, `**int`...). Each variable has a *depth*; for each $k \geq 0$, $\mathcal{V}_k$ denotes the set of variables of depth k. Variables of depth 0 are integer-valued, variables of depth 1 are pointers to integer variables, variables of depth 2 are pointers to pointers to integer variables, and so on. We define the set e_k of *expressions* of depth k as follows:

$$e_0 ::= c \mid e_0 \ \mathsf{op} \ e_0 \mid x_0 \mid {}^*x_1$$
$$\forall k \geq 1, \quad e_k ::= x_k \mid \&x_{k-1} \mid {}^*x_{k+1}$$

where $x_\ell \in \mathcal{V}_\ell$ is a variable of depth ℓ. In words, an expression e_0 of depth 0 can be a constant $c \in \mathbb{N}$, a (binary) operator (*e.g.*, $+$, $-$ or $\times$) applied to two expressions of depth 0, a variable of depth 0 or the dereference of a variable of depth 1. The exact set of operators allowed is irrelevant to our purposes. An expression e_k of depth $k \geq 1$ is either a variable of depth k, the dereference of a variable of depth $k+1$ or the address of a variable of depth $k-1$.

An instruction of Instr is of one of the following types:

Regular assignment: $\mathsf{x_k} := \mathsf{e_k}$ where $k \in \mathbb{N}$, $x_k \in \mathcal{V}_k$ and e_k is an expression of depth k;

Dereference assignment: $^*\mathsf{x}_{\mathsf{k}+1} := \mathsf{e}_\mathsf{k}$ where $k \in \mathbb{N}$, $x_{k+1} \in \mathcal{V}_{k+1}$ and e_k is an expression of depth k;
Conditional guard: $\mathtt{true}(\mathsf{e}_0), \mathtt{false}(\mathsf{e}_0)$ with e_0 an expression of depth 0;
Locking and unlocking: $\mathtt{lock}(\mathsf{m}), \mathtt{unlock}(\mathsf{m})$ where $m \in \mathcal{M}$;
Thread creation: $\mathtt{create}(\mathsf{t})$ where $t \in \mathcal{T} \setminus \{\mathsf{main}\}$;
Joining: $\mathtt{join}(\mathsf{t})$ where $t \in \mathcal{T} \setminus \{\mathsf{main}\}$.

```
 1 int** dbl_ptr;      9 main() {             17 t1() {               25 t2() {
 2 int* p;            10   dbl_ptr = &p;      18   lock(m);           26   lock(m);
 3 int* q;            11   q = &j;            19   dbl_ptr = &q;      27   *dbl_ptr = p;
 4 int k;             12   k=0, j=0;          20   p = &k;            28   *q = 2;
 5 int j;             13   create(t1);        21   unlock(m);         29   unlock(m);
 6 int out;           14   create(t2);        22   return;            30   return;
 7                    15   out = k;           23 }                    31 }
 8                    16 }                    24
```

Fig. 1. An example of concurrent program, written in C-like syntax. There is a possible data race: if `t1` runs before `t2`, the instruction at line 27 makes `q` in alias with `p` so that `q` points to `k`, making `t2` at line 28 race with `main` at line 15.

We introduce an example of concurrent program in Fig. 1. Here, the set of threads is $\mathcal{T} = \{\mathtt{main}, \mathtt{t1}, \mathtt{t2}\}$, the set of variables is $\mathcal{V} = \{\mathtt{dbl\_ptr}, \mathtt{p}, \mathtt{q}, \mathtt{k}, \mathtt{j}, \mathtt{out}\}$ (`dbl_ptr` has depth 2, `p` and `q` have depth 1, `j`, `k` and `out` have depth 0) and the set of mutexes is $\mathcal{M} = \{\mathtt{m}\}$. The CFG of thread `t1` is represented in Fig. 2.

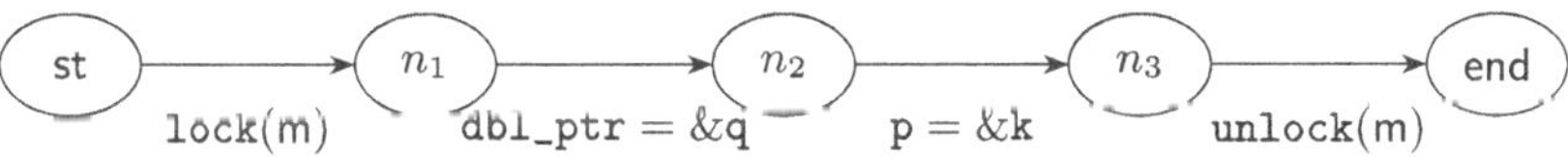

Fig. 2. The CFG of thread `t1`. In the code, nodes are program locations in between transitions; for example n_1 is between lines 18 and 19.

2.2 Semantics

We define the set of configurations of our system. The *state* of a thread is an element of $\mathsf{States} := \mathcal{N} \uplus \{\mathsf{Uncreated}, \mathsf{Joined}\}$. State Uncreated is self-explanatory. A thread t whose state is a node $n \in \mathcal{N}$ is *active*. A thread t is in Joined once $\mathtt{join}(\mathsf{t})$ has been performed. A configuration is a tuple $\gamma = \langle \mathsf{St}, \nu, \mathsf{h} \rangle$ where:

- $\mathsf{St} : \mathcal{T} \to \mathsf{States}$ maps each thread to its state,
- $\nu : \mathcal{V} \to \mathbb{N} \cup \mathcal{V} \cup \{\#\}$ maps each variable to its value, which is either an integer (for variables in $\mathcal{V}_0$), the variable that it points to (for variables in $\mathcal{V}_k$, $k \geq 1$) or a special value # when the variable has not been initialized.
- $\mathsf{h} : \mathcal{M} \to \mathcal{T} \cup \{\bot\}$ maps each mutex to the thread holding it, and $\bot$ if none.

The valuation ν must be *well-formed*: $\nu(x_0) \in \mathbb{N} \cup \{\#\}$ for all $x_0 \in \mathcal{V}_0$ and $\nu(x_{k+1}) \in \mathcal{V}_k \cup \{\#\}$ for all $k \geq 0$ and $x_{k+1} \in \mathcal{V}_{k+1}$. The initial configuration is $\gamma_0 = \langle \mathsf{St}_0, \nu_0, \mathsf{h}_0 \rangle$ where $\mathsf{St}_0(\mathsf{main}) = \mathsf{st}_{\mathsf{main}}$ and $\mathsf{St}_0(t) = \mathsf{Uncreated}$ for all $t \neq \mathsf{main}$ (only main is created), $\nu_0(x) = \#$ for all $x \in \mathcal{V}$ (variables are uninitialized) and $\mathsf{h}_0(m) = \bot$ for all $m \in \mathcal{M}$ (no mutex is held).

We explain how expressions of depth 0 (integer-valued expressions) are evaluated. Let ν be a valuation, let e be an expression of depth 0. The evaluation $\mathsf{ev}_\nu(e) \in \mathbb{N}$ is defined recursively by:

- if $e = c \in \mathbb{N}$ then $\mathsf{ev}_\nu(e) = c$;
- if $e = x_0$ with $x_0 \in \mathcal{V}_0$ then $\mathsf{ev}_\nu(e) = \nu(x_0)$;
- if $e = {}^*x_1$ with $x_1 \in \mathcal{V}_1$ then $\mathsf{ev}_\nu(e) = \nu(\nu(x_1))$;
- if $e = e_a \;\mathsf{op}\; e_b$ then $\mathsf{ev}_\nu(e) = (\mathsf{ev}_\nu(e_a)) \;\mathsf{op}\; (\mathsf{ev}_\nu(e_b))$.

We use convention that $\nu(\#) = \#$, so that $\nu(\nu(x_1)) = \#$ if $\nu(x_1) = \#$.

Let $\gamma = \langle \mathsf{St}, \nu, \mathsf{h} \rangle$, $\gamma' = \langle \mathsf{St}', \nu', \mathsf{h}' \rangle$ and $\delta = (n, \iota, n') \in \Delta$. There is a *step* $\gamma \xrightarrow{\delta} \gamma'$ when, by letting $t = \mathsf{th}(\delta)$, we have $\mathsf{St}(t) = n$ and the following are true.

Assignments. If ι is an assignment, then we must have $\mathsf{St}'(t) = n'$, $\mathsf{St}(\tilde{t}) = \mathsf{St}'(\tilde{t})$ for all $\tilde{t} \neq t$ and $\mathsf{h}' = \mathsf{h}$. Moreover, the left-hand side of the assignment is either of the form $\mathsf{x_k}$ or $^*\mathsf{x_{k+1}}$; in the latter case, we require that $\nu(x_{k+1}) \neq \#$ (otherwise the step is not possible). Let $x \in \mathcal{V}_k$ be the variable equal to x_k in the first case and to $\nu(x_{k+1})$ in the second case ($\nu(x_{k+1}) \in \mathcal{V}_k$ as ν is well-formed). We require that $\nu(z) = \nu'(z)$ for all $z \in \mathcal{V} \setminus \{x\}$. The value accessed at the right-side must be correctly initialized, otherwise the step is not possible. We make a case disjunction on the right-hand side:
  - if it is an expression e of depth 0 ($k = 0$) then $\nu'(x) = \mathsf{ev}_\nu(e) \neq \#$ (if the expression evaluates to $\#$ then the step is not possible);
  - if it is a variable $y \in \mathcal{V}_k$ then $\nu'(x) = \nu(y) \neq \#$;
  - if it is a $^*y$ (which implies $y \in \mathcal{V}_{k+1}$) then $\nu'(x) = \nu(\nu(y)) \neq \#$ (we have $\nu(y) \in \mathcal{V}_k$ by well-formedness);
  - if it is a $\&y$ (which implies $k \geq 1$ and $y \in \mathcal{V}_{k-1}$) then $\nu'(x) = y$.

Conditional guards. If ι is $\texttt{true}(\mathsf{e_0})$ then $\mathsf{ev}_\nu(e_0) \notin \{0, \#\}$ and if ι is $\texttt{false}(\mathsf{e_0})$ then $\mathsf{ev}_\nu(e_0) = 0$; in both cases, $\nu' = \nu$, $\mathsf{St}'(t) = n'$, $\mathsf{St}(\tilde{t}) = \mathsf{St}'(\tilde{t})$ for all $\tilde{t} \neq t$ and $\mathsf{h}' = \mathsf{h}$.

Mutex operations. If ι is $\texttt{lock}(\mathsf{m})$ then $\mathsf{h}(m) = \bot$ and $\mathsf{h}'(m) = t$, and if ι is $\texttt{unlock}(\mathsf{m})$ then $\mathsf{h}(m) = t$ and $\mathsf{h}'(m) = \bot$; in both cases $\nu' = \nu$, $\mathsf{St}'(t) = n'$ and $\mathsf{St}(\tilde{t}) = \mathsf{St}'(\tilde{t})$ for all $\tilde{t} \neq t$.

Create. If ι is $\texttt{create}(\mathsf{t_c})$ then $\mathsf{St}(t_c) = \mathsf{Uncreated}$, $\mathsf{St}'(t_c) = \mathsf{st}_{t_c}$, $\mathsf{St}'(t) = n'$, $\mathsf{St}(\tilde{t}) = \mathsf{St}'(\tilde{t})$ for all $\tilde{t} \in \mathcal{T} \setminus \{t, t_c\}$, $\nu' = \nu$ and $\mathsf{h}' = \mathsf{h}$.

Join. If ι is $\texttt{join}(\mathsf{t_j})$ then $\mathsf{St}(t_j) = \mathsf{end}_{t_j}$, $\mathsf{St}'(t_j) = \mathsf{Joined}$, $\mathsf{St}'(t) = n'$, $\mathsf{St}(\tilde{t}) = \mathsf{St}'(\tilde{t})$ for all $\tilde{t} \in \mathcal{T} \setminus \{t, t_j\}$, $\nu' = \nu$ and $\mathsf{h}' = \mathsf{h}$.

The valuation ν' is well-formed by construction. From now on, we implicitly assume that all considered valuations are well-formed. Given a sequence $s = \delta_1, \ldots, \delta_k \in \Delta^*$, we let $\gamma_0 \xrightarrow{s} \gamma_k$ when there are $\gamma_1, \ldots, \gamma_{k-1}$ such that $\gamma_i \xrightarrow{\delta_i} \gamma_{i+1}$ for all $i \leq k-1$. We denote $\gamma_1 \xrightarrow{*} \gamma_k$ the existence of such a sequence. A configuration γ' is *reachable* when $\gamma_0 \xrightarrow{*} \gamma'$. An *execution* is an alternating sequence $\rho = \gamma_0, \delta_1, \gamma_1, \ldots, \delta_k, \gamma_k$ such that $\gamma_i \xrightarrow{\delta_{i+1}} \gamma_{i+1}$ for all $i \leq k-1$.

Example 1. On the example of Fig. 1, by letting `t1` return before `t2` starts and with `main` stopping after line 14 and `t2` stopping after line 27, we obtain a reachable configuration $\gamma = \langle \mathsf{St}, \nu, \mathsf{h} \rangle$ where:

- $\mathsf{St}(\texttt{main}) = n_{14\to 15}$, $\mathsf{St}(\texttt{t1}) = \mathsf{Returned}$ and $\mathsf{St}(\texttt{t2}) = n_{27\to 28}$ where $n_{\ell_1 \to \ell_2}$ denotes the node between lines ℓ_1 and ℓ_2;
- $\nu(\texttt{dbl\_ptr}) = \texttt{q}$, $\nu(\texttt{p}) = \nu(\texttt{q}) = \texttt{k}$, $\nu(\texttt{k}) = \nu(\texttt{j}) = 0$ and $\nu(\texttt{out}) = \#$;
- $\mathsf{h}(\texttt{m}) = \texttt{t2}$.

From γ, `main` and `t2` may perform concurrent accesses to `k`, *i.e.*, a data race.

3 Analysis of the Program

We start with an analysis of the program composed of two parts. The first part, called *preliminary analysis*, analyzes when two statements may run in parallel as well as when locks are held. The second part analyzes the points-to relation. Neither part performs any sort of value analysis: we aim for a fast analysis at the cost of lessened precision.

3.1 Preliminary Analysis

We compute, for every node n, three sets: $U(n), J(n) \subseteq \mathcal{T}$ and $L(n) \subseteq \mathcal{M}$. When $\mathsf{th}(n)$ is in n, threads in $U(n)$ cannot be created yet, threads in $J(n)$ must already be joined, and mutexes in $L(n)$ are held by $\mathsf{th}(n)$.

Lockset Analysis. We start with the analysis of mutexes held. Trivially, $L(\mathsf{st}_t) = \emptyset$. For a node n, a mutex m is in $L(n)$ when it is guaranteed to be locked when $\mathsf{th}(n)$ is in n, *i.e.*, when, for every n' with a transition $(n', \iota, n) \in \Delta$: ι is not $\texttt{unlock}(\mathsf{m})$ and, if ι is $\texttt{lock}(\mathsf{m})$, then $m \in L(n')$. Overall, $(L(n))_{n \in \mathcal{N}}$ is the greatest $|\mathcal{N}|$-uple of subsets of $\mathcal{M}$ (for pointwise subset ordering) that satisfies:

$$\forall t \in \mathcal{T},\ L(\mathsf{st}_t) := \emptyset$$

$$\forall n \in \mathcal{N} \setminus \{\mathsf{st}_t \mid t \in \mathcal{T}\}, L(n) :=$$

$$\bigcap_{\substack{n' \in \mathcal{N}, \iota \in \mathsf{Instr} \\ \iota \neq \texttt{lock}(\_) \\ \iota \neq \texttt{unlock}(\_) \\ (n', \iota, n) \in \Delta}} \boldsymbol{\ell}[n'] \cap \bigcap_{\substack{n' \in \mathcal{N}, m \in \mathcal{T} \\ (n', \texttt{lock}(\mathsf{m}), n) \in \Delta}} (\boldsymbol{\ell}[n'] \cup \{m\}) \cap \bigcap_{\substack{n' \in \mathcal{N}, m \in \mathcal{T} \\ (n', \texttt{unlock}(\mathsf{m}), n) \in \Delta}} (\boldsymbol{\ell}[n'] \setminus \{m\})$$

We use convention $\bigcap_{x \in \emptyset} \_ = \mathcal{M}$. The existence of such a $\mathcal{N}$-uple $(L(n))_{n \in \mathcal{N}}$ can be proved using the Knaster-Tarski theorem. In practice, this fixpoint analysis is easy to implement by exploring the control flow of each thread; performing an actual fixpoint computation is needed only when the CFG has a cycle. This analysis is sound:

Proposition 2. *For every $n \in \mathcal{N}_t$, for every $\gamma = \langle \mathsf{St}, \nu, \mathsf{h} \rangle$ such that $\gamma_0 \xrightarrow{*} \gamma$ and $\mathsf{St}(\mathsf{th}(n)) = n$, for every $m \in L(n)$, we have $\mathsf{h}(m) = \mathsf{th}(n)$.*

Analysis of Joined Threads. We continue with the analysis of joined threads. Trivially, $J(\mathsf{st}_{\mathsf{main}}) = \emptyset$. When a thread $t \neq \mathsf{main}$ has been created by a transition $(n_1, \mathtt{create}(\mathsf{t}), n_2)$, threads in $J(n_2)$ can be considered joined at the start of t. If there are several transitions creating t, we must conservatively intersect over all such transitions, giving constraint $J(\mathsf{st}_t) \subseteq \bigcap_{(n_1,\mathtt{create}(\mathsf{t}),n_2)\in\Delta} J(n_2)$. For $n \neq \mathsf{st}_{\mathsf{th}(n)}$, a thread t is considered joined if the following holds for every $(n', \iota, n) \in \Delta$. If ι is not a join, then we need $t \in J(n')$. If ι is a $\mathtt{join}(\mathsf{t})$, there is no condition. Finally, if ι is a $\mathtt{join}(\mathsf{t_j})$ with $t_j \neq t$, then t must be in $J(\mathsf{end}_{t_j})$: if t must be joined at the end of t_j, then once t_j is joined, t must also be joined. Overall, $(J(n))_{n\in\mathcal{N}}$ is the greatest $|\mathcal{N}|$-uple of subsets of thread such that:

$$
\begin{aligned}
&J(\mathsf{st}_{\mathsf{main}}) := \emptyset \\
&\forall t \in \mathcal{T} \setminus \{\mathsf{main}\},\ J(\mathsf{st}_t) := \bigcap_{\substack{n_1,n_2\in\mathcal{N} \\ (n_1,\mathtt{create}(\mathsf{t}),n_2)\in\Delta}} J(n_1) \\
&\forall n \in \mathcal{N} \setminus \{\mathsf{st}_t \mid t \in \mathcal{T}\}, \\
&J(n) := \bigcap_{n_p\in\mathsf{P}_o(n)} J(n_p) \cap \bigcap_{(n_p,t_j)\in\mathsf{P}_j(n)} (J(n_p) \cup \{t_j\} \cup J(\mathsf{end}_{t_j}))
\end{aligned}
$$

where we use the convention $\bigcap_{x\in\emptyset} \_ = \mathcal{T}$ and where

$$
\begin{aligned}
&\mathsf{P}_j(n) := \{(n_p, t_j) \in \mathcal{N} \times \mathcal{T} \mid (n_p, \mathtt{join}(\mathsf{t_j}), n) \in \Delta\} \\
&\mathsf{P}_o(n) := \{n_p \in \mathcal{N} \mid \exists \iota \text{ s.t. } (n_p, \iota, n) \in \Delta \text{ and } \iota \notin \{\mathtt{join}(\mathsf{t}) \mid t \in \mathcal{T}\}\}.
\end{aligned}
$$

This analysis is sound:

Proposition 3. *For every $n \in \mathcal{N}$, for every $\gamma = \langle \mathsf{St}, \nu, \mathsf{h} \rangle$ such that $\gamma_0 \xrightarrow{*} \gamma$ and $\mathsf{St}(\mathsf{th}(n)) = n$, for every $t_j \in J(n)$, we have $\mathsf{St}(t_j) = \mathsf{Joined}$.*

Analysis of Uncreated Threads. Finally, we present the analysis of uncreated threads. It relies on the same principles but is more complex. There are two main challenges: how a creation transition $(n', \mathtt{create}(\mathsf{t_c}), n)$ impacts $U(n)$, and what lies in the set $U(\mathsf{st}_t)$ of the starting node of a thread.

To explain our solution, we illustrate it on the following running example. Consider a program where executions behave as follows. A thread $t_1 = \mathsf{main}$ creates a thread t_2, then joins t_2, then creates another thread t_3; t_2 itself creates a thread t_4. See opposite for a depiction of the creation graph.

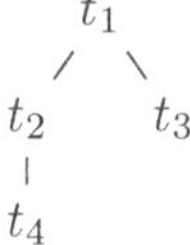

Consider the transition $(n', \mathtt{create}(\mathtt{t}_2), n) \in \Delta_{t_1}$ creating t_2. We must have $t_2 \notin U(n)$. Moreover, t_2 may in turn create thread t_4, so that, at n, t_4 is potentially created. We express this with constraint

$$U(n) \subseteq (\mathcal{T} \setminus \{t_2\}) \cap \bigcap_{n_2 \in \mathcal{N}_{t_2}} U(n_2).$$

We now explain which threads are considered uncreated at a starting node st_t. First, consider the situation at the start node st_{t_2} of t_2. Obviously, we must have $U(\mathsf{st}_{t_2}) \subseteq \mathcal{T} \setminus \{t_2\}$. Since $(n', \mathtt{create}(\mathtt{t}_2), n) \in \Delta_{t_1}$ is the transition creating t_2, at the start of t_2, threads in $\mathcal{T} \setminus U(n)$ are possibly created. Moreover, t_1 keeps running in parallel with t_2: subsequent nodes of t_1 are also taken into account, but only until t_2 is joined. In particular, t_3 is never created before t_2 is joined, so it is uncreated at every node in t_2. This leads us to the constraint

$$U(\mathsf{st}_{t_2}) \subseteq \bigcap_{n \in \mathcal{N}_{t_1}, t_2 \notin U(n), t_2 \notin J(n)} U(n).$$

Consider now the case of the starting node of t_4. While t_2 cannot run in parallel with t_3, its child t_4 can: t_4 remains active after t_2 is joined. If t_4 obtained information from its parent's nodes only, it would wrongly deduce that t_3 is uncreated. For this reason, there is a transfer of information from the *grandparents* to the *grandchildren*, here from t_1 to t_4. This here gives $U(\mathsf{st}_{t_4}) \subseteq \bigcap_{n \in \mathcal{N}_{t_1}} U(n)$.

We define $(U(n))_{n \in \mathcal{N}}$ as the greatest $|\mathcal{N}|$-uple of subsets of $\mathcal{T}$ such that:

$$U(\mathsf{st}_{\mathsf{main}}) := \mathcal{T} \setminus \{\mathsf{main}\}$$

$$\forall t \in \mathcal{T} \setminus \{\mathsf{main}\}, U(\mathsf{st}_t) := (\mathcal{T} \setminus \{t\}) \cap \bigcap_{\substack{n \in \mathcal{N}_{\mathsf{par}}(t) \\ t \notin J(n), t \notin U(n)}} U(n) \cap \bigcap_{n \in \mathcal{N}_{\mathsf{gpar}}(t)} U(n)$$

$$\forall n \in \mathcal{N} \setminus \{\mathsf{st}_t \mid t \in \mathcal{T}\},$$

$$U(n) := \bigcap_{n_p \in \mathsf{P}_{\mathsf{o}}(n)} U(n_p) \cap \bigcap_{(n_p, t_c) \in \mathsf{P}_{\mathsf{cr}}(n)} \left((U(n_p) \setminus \{t_c\}) \cap \bigcap_{n_c \in \mathcal{N}_{t_c}} U(n_c) \right)$$

where we use convention $\bigcap_{x \in \emptyset} \_ = \mathcal{T}$ and where:

$$\mathsf{P}_{\mathsf{cr}}(n) := \{(n_p, t_{\mathsf{child}}) \in \mathcal{N} \times \mathcal{T} \mid (n_p, \mathtt{create}(\mathtt{t}_{\mathsf{child}}), n) \in \Delta\}$$

$$\mathsf{P}_{\mathsf{o}}(n) := \{n_p \in \mathcal{N} \mid \exists \iota \text{ s.t. } (n_p, \iota, n) \in \Delta \text{ and } \iota \notin \{\mathtt{create}(\mathtt{t}) \mid t \in \mathcal{T}\}\}$$

$$\mathcal{N}_{\mathsf{par}}(t) := \{n \in \mathcal{N} \mid \exists t_{\mathsf{par}} \in \mathcal{T} : n \in \mathcal{N}_{t_{\mathsf{par}}} \wedge (\exists n_1, n_2 : (n_1, \mathtt{create}(\mathtt{t}), n_2) \in \Delta_{t_{\mathsf{par}}})\}$$

$$\mathcal{N}_{\mathsf{gpar}}(t) := \{n \in \mathcal{N} \mid \exists t_{\mathsf{par}}, t_{\mathsf{gpar}} \in \mathcal{T} : n \in \mathcal{N}_{t_{\mathsf{gpar}}} \wedge (\exists n_1, n_2 : (n_1, \mathtt{create}(\mathtt{t}_{\mathsf{par}}), n_2) \in \Delta_{t_{\mathsf{gpar}}}) \wedge (\exists n_1, n_2 : (n_1, \mathtt{create}(\mathtt{t}_{\mathsf{gpar}}), n_2) \in \Delta_{t_{\mathsf{par}}})\}$$

This analysis is sound:

Proposition 4. *For every $n \in \mathcal{N}$, for every $\gamma = \langle \mathsf{St}, \nu, \mathsf{h} \rangle$ such that $\gamma_0 \xrightarrow{*} \gamma$ and $\mathsf{St}(\mathsf{th}(n)) = n$, we have $\mathsf{St}(t) = \mathsf{Uncreated}$ for each $t \in U(n)$.*

3.2 Points-to Analysis

In this section, we introduce a points-to analysis of the concurrent program. Such an analysis is needed to understand which variables are really accessed, in particular for data race detection. For example, if $\nu(x) = y$ then an access to $^*x$ is an access to y, which may race with a concurrent access to y. We compute an overapproximation of the points-to graph at each node n, *i.e.*, a relation $\rightarrow_{\mathsf{pto}(n)}$ on $\mathcal{V}$ such that, for every reachable γ where $\mathsf{th}(n)$ is in n, if x points to y in γ then $x \rightarrow_{\mathsf{pto}(n)} y$ (this claim will be made more formal later).

Points-to Graphs. A *points-to graph* (PTG) is a labelled (directed) graph $\mathsf{PTG} = (V, E, \lambda)$ with $\lambda : V \rightarrow 2^{\mathcal{V}}$ (vertices are labelled by sets of variables) such that, for every $x \in \mathcal{V}$, there is a unique vertex $\mathsf{ver}(x) \in V$ for which $x \in \lambda(\mathsf{ver}(x))$. Moreover, each vertex $v \in V$ has a depth $k \in \mathbb{N}$ and $\lambda(v)$ may only contain variables of depth k; children of v must have depth $k - 1$ (as a consequence, points-to graphs are acyclic). Given a valuation ν, we let $\mathsf{PTG}(\nu)$ be the PTG $(\mathcal{V}, E_\nu, \lambda_{\mathsf{id}})$ with set of vertices $\mathcal{V}$, with an edge $(x, y) \in E_\nu$ if and only if $\nu(x) = y$ and with $\lambda_{\mathsf{id}}(x) = \{x\}$. Given $x, y \in \mathcal{V}$ and a PTG $\mathsf{PTG} = (V, E, \lambda)$, x *points to* y in PTG, denoted $x \rightarrow_{\mathsf{PTG}} y$ (or simply $x \rightarrow y$ when PTG is clear from context), when there is an edge from $\mathsf{ver}(x)$ to $\mathsf{ver}(y)$ in PTG.

Definition 5. *Given* $\mathsf{PTG} = (V, E, \lambda)$ *and* $v_1, v_2 \in V$ *of same depth, the points-to graph obtained from* PTG *by* merging v_1 *and* v_2 *is the PTG* (V', E', λ') *s.t.:*

- $V' := (V \setminus \{v_1, v_2\}) \cup \{v\}$ *with* $v \notin V$ *a fresh vertex;*
- *the set of parents (resp. children) of* v *is the union of the set of parents (resp. children) of* v_1 *and* v_2*; formally* $E' := \{(u, w) \in E \mid u, w \notin \{v_1, v_2\}\} \cup \{(u, v) \mid (u, v_1) \in E \vee (u, v_2) \in E\} \cup \{(v, w) \mid (v_1, w) \in E \vee (v_2, w) \in E\}$;
- $\lambda'(v) = \lambda(v_1) \cup \lambda(v_2)$ *and* $\lambda'(v') = \lambda(v')$ *for all* $v' \in V' \setminus \{v\}$.

Note that if $v_1 = v_2$ then merging v_1 and v_2 has no effect.

Given two points-to graphs PTG and PTG', we let $\mathsf{PTG} \preccurlyeq \mathsf{PTG}'$ when PTG' can be obtained from PTG by merging vertices and adding edges. It is easy to see that $\mathsf{PTG} \preccurlyeq \mathsf{PTG}'$ implies that, for every $x, y \in \mathcal{V}$, if $x \rightarrow_{\mathsf{PTG}} y$ then $x \rightarrow_{\mathsf{PTG}'} y$.

Definition 6. *Given* $\mathsf{PTG} = (V, E, \lambda)$ *and* $\mathsf{PTG}' = (V', E', \lambda')$, *the* union points-to graph $\mathsf{PTG} \sqcup \mathsf{PTG}'$ *is the points-to graph* $(V_\sqcup, E_\sqcup, \lambda_\sqcup)$ *such that:*

- $V_\sqcup \subseteq 2^{V \cup V'}$ *is the set of equivalence classes of the transitive closure of the relation* $\sim$ *on* $V \uplus V'$ *defined by letting, for each* $v \in V$ *and* $v' \in V'$, $v \sim v'$ *whenever* $\lambda(v) \cap \lambda'(v') \neq \emptyset$;
- *given* $W_1, W_2 \in V_\sqcup$, *there is an edge* $(W_1, W_2) \in E_\sqcup$ *if and only if there are* $v_1 \in W_1$, $v_2 \in W_2$ *such that* $(v_1, v_2) \in E \cup E'$;
- *for each* $W \in V_\sqcup$, $\lambda_\sqcup(W) := \bigcup_{v \in W \cap V} \lambda(v) \cup \bigcup_{v \in W \cap V'} \lambda'(v)$.

Informally, $\mathsf{PTG} \sqcup \mathsf{PTG}'$ groups vertices of PTG and PTG' so that two variables in the same vertex in PTG or PTG' are in the same vertex in $\mathsf{PTG} \sqcup \mathsf{PTG}'$. By transitivity, if x is in the same vertex as z in PTG and y is in the same vertex as z in PTG', then x and y are in the same vertex in $\mathsf{PTG} \sqcup \mathsf{PTG}'$. The operator $\sqcup$ is associative, commutative and idempotent; it is non-decreasing for $\preccurlyeq$ and, for every PTG and PTG', $\mathsf{PTG} \preccurlyeq \mathsf{PTG} \sqcup \mathsf{PTG}'$. Also, if $\mathsf{PTG} \preccurlyeq \mathsf{PTG}'$ then $\mathsf{PTG}' = \mathsf{PTG} \sqcup \mathsf{PTG}'$.

Procedural Points-to Analysis. Our concurrent points-to analysis is built from a *procedural* points-to analysis, *i.e.*, a points-to analysis that analyzes each thread in isolation. This procedural points-to analysis corresponds to the `alias` plugin of Frama-C [13]. It corresponds to a lightweight, Steensgaard-style [22] points-to analysis, with some limited form of flow-sensitivity as an instruction only affects the analysis at future nodes.

Let $t \in \mathcal{T}$ and consider a path π from st_t to a node $n \in \mathcal{N}_t$. We define the points-to graph $\mathsf{PTG}(\pi)$ generated by π by induction as follows. If π is the empty path, then $\mathsf{PTG}(\pi) = \mathsf{PTG}(\nu_0)$ (the graph with one vertex per variable and no edge). Let $\pi = \pi_p \cdot \delta$. If the instruction ι of δ is an assignment at depth 0 (*i.e.*, integer assignment) or not an assignment, then $\mathsf{PTG}(\pi) = \mathsf{PTG}(\pi_p)$. If the assignment is at depth $k \geq 1$ (*i.e.*, pointer assignment), then $\mathsf{PTG}(\pi)$ is obtained from $\mathsf{PTG} := \mathsf{PTG}(\pi_p)$ with the following transformation (see Fig. 3).

- If ι is $\mathsf{x} := \mathsf{y}$, then we merge $\mathsf{ver}(x)$ and $\mathsf{ver}(y)$.
- If ι is $\mathsf{x} := {}^*\mathsf{y}$ then we add an edge from $\mathsf{ver}(y)$ to $\mathsf{ver}(x)$ (if it not yet exists).
- If ι is ${}^*\mathsf{x} := \mathsf{y}$ then we add an edge from $\mathsf{ver}(x)$ to $\mathsf{ver}(y)$.
- If ι is $\mathsf{x} := \&\mathsf{y}$ then we add an edge from $\mathsf{ver}(x)$ to $\mathsf{ver}(y)$.
- If ι is ${}^*\mathsf{x} := \&\mathsf{y}$, we add a vertex v with $\lambda(v) = \emptyset$ and edges from $\mathsf{ver}(x)$ to v and from v to $\mathsf{ver}(y)$, so that $\mathsf{ver}(y)$ is the grandchild of $\mathsf{ver}(x)$.
- If ι is ${}^*\mathsf{x} := {}^*\mathsf{y}$ then we add a vertex v with $\lambda(v) = \emptyset$ and edges from $\mathsf{ver}(x)$ to v and from $\mathsf{ver}(y)$ to v, so that $\mathsf{ver}(x)$ and $\mathsf{ver}(y)$ have a common child.

Recall that an expression of depth $k \geq 1$ may take three forms: y, ${}^*y$ and $\&y$, so all cases are treated. To obtain $\mathsf{PTG}(\pi)$, after the transformation above, we iteratively merge vertices with a common parent. For example, for instruction $\mathsf{x} := \&\mathsf{y}$, $\mathsf{ver}(y)$ is merged with the child of $\mathsf{ver}(x)$, if there is such a child.

The procedural points-to overapproximation $\alpha(n)$ at node n of thread $t = \mathsf{th}(n)$ is computed as the union of all $\mathsf{PTG}(\pi)$ for all paths π from st_t to n[1]. This analysis is *path-insensitive*, since all paths are taken into account and conditional guards are not considered. This is needed towards concurrent points-to analysis; for example, a $\mathtt{true}(\mathsf{x})$ guard that is impassable in isolation can be crossed when another thread sets x to 1. Moreover, the analysis only accumulates points-to pairs along a path, never losing any: this is called *cumulativity*, and is also needed for concurrent points-to analysis. For example, when analyzing a sequence of

[1] In presence of cycles, this set of paths may be infinite. However, $\mathsf{PTG}(\pi{\cdot}\delta) = PTG(\pi)$ when δ already appears in π, so the set of $\mathsf{PTG}(\pi)$ to consider is finite.

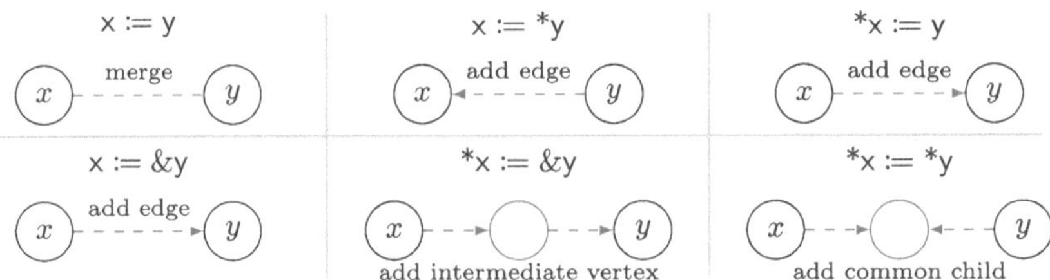

Fig. 3. A depiction of how the procedural points-to analysis takes assignments of depth ≥ 1 into account. Here, vertex with label x is the vertex $\mathsf{ver}(x)$; it may also be labelled by other variables that are not represented. If x and y are in the same vertex, there is nothing to do. In the second step of the transformation (not represented), for every vertex with several children, all children are merged.

instructions $x := \&y; {}^*x := z;$, one should not remove previous points-to edges from y, since in a concurrent setting the value of x may be changed in between the two instructions. Implementation-wise, the `alias` plugin [13] does not explicitly build the points-to graph at each node, but stores it using a persistent union-find datastructure [5] which records changes along a path.

We illustrate the procedural points-to analysis on thread `t1` from Sect. 2.1, using notations from Fig. 2. At `st` and after the `lock(m)` instruction, the points-to graph has no edge. After instruction `dbl_ptr = &p`, there is an edge from `dbl_ptr` to `q`. After `p = &k`, there is an edge from `p` to `k`. The algorithm ends with edges (`dbl_ptr`, `q`) and (`p`, `k`). Each vertex still has a single variable, because there is no assignment of the form $\mathsf{x} := \mathsf{y}$ with x and y pointers.

Concurrent Points-to Analysis. We now introduce how the procedural points-to analysis from above is turned into a concurrent points-to analysis.

Let α be the result of the procedural points-to analysis. Recall that α maps each node n to a points-to graph $\alpha(n)$. In words, the (concurrent) points-to overapproximation at node n makes the union of its procedural points-to analysis $\alpha(n)$ with all procedural points-to analysis $\alpha(n')$ of nodes n' that may have been visited before n in the execution. Therefore, we need, for every node n, an overapproximation of the set of nodes that may have been visited before. Nodes of the same thread $\mathsf{th}(n)$ need not be considered because α is cumulative. We let

$$\mathsf{MHB}(n) := \{n' \mid \mathsf{th}(n') \neq \mathsf{th}(n) \wedge \mathsf{th}(n) \notin J(n') \wedge \mathsf{th}(n') \notin U(n)\}.$$

Thanks to Proposition 3 and Proposition 4, $\mathsf{MHB}(n)$ overapproximates the set of nodes that other threads may have visited before $\mathsf{th}(n)$ is in n.

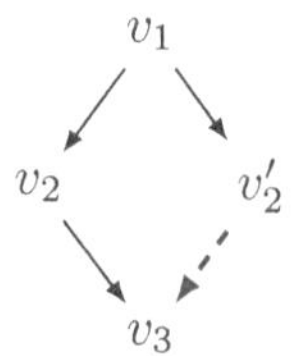

Another ingredient is needed to combine procedural points-to analysis of different threads, which we dub diamond completion rule. It is a weakened notion of merging where two vertices are forced to have the same children, but not the same parents. Given a PTG PTG, we let $\mathsf{DCR}(\mathsf{PTG})$ denote the points-to graph obtained from PTG by applying, until saturation, the *diamond completion*

rule (DCR). The DCR can be applied to $(v_1, v_2, v_2', v_3) \in V^4$ when there are edges (v_1, v_2), (v_1, v_2'), $(v_2, v_3) \in E$; it adds an edge from v_2' to v_3. In $\mathsf{DCR}(\mathsf{PTG})$, all nodes sharing a parent have the same set of children. See the figure opposite for an illustration. We define the concurrent points-to analysis as follows.

Definition 7. *For every* $n \in \mathcal{N}$, $\mathsf{pto}(n) := \mathsf{DCR}\left(\alpha(n) \sqcup \bigsqcup_{n' \in \mathsf{MHB}(n)} \alpha(n')\right)$.

Example 8. In Fig. 4, we illustrate this analysis on the example of Fig. 1. We present how $\mathsf{pto}(n_m)$ is computed, where n_m is the node before the access to `out` in `main`. Since no vertex has been merged in any of the analyses α of the tasks, we only have one variable per vertex. The DCR rule is needed for soundness, because there is indeed an execution where `q` points to `k`, as highlighted in Example 1. Without DCR, the analysis would miss the potential data race on k.

In practice, computing $\mathsf{pto}(n)$ does not require to iterate over *all* nodes in $\mathsf{MHB}(n)$. Since the procedural analysis α is cumulative, it suffices to consider all $n' \in \mathsf{MHB}(n)$ that have no successor in $\mathsf{MHB}(n)$, *i.e.*, who have no successor at all or whose successors n'' are all such that $\mathsf{th}(n) \in J(n'')$.

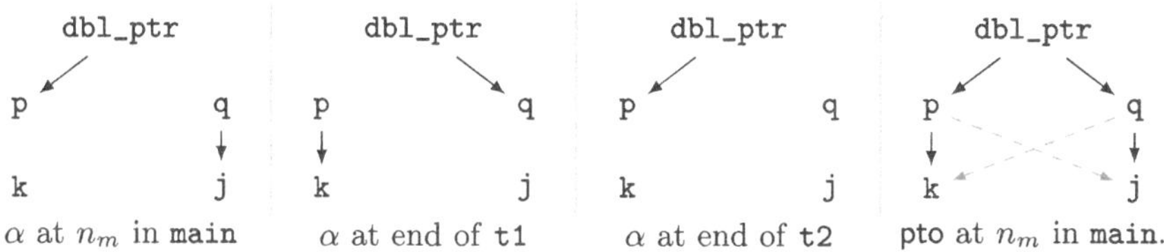

Fig. 4. The computation of the concurrent points-to analysis on the program of Fig. 1 at the node n_m between lines 14 and 15 in `main`. Variable `out` is omitted from the picture. Dashed red edges are those added by DCR.

Soundness of the concurrent points-to analysis pto is stated as follows:

Theorem 9. *For every* $t \in \mathcal{T}$, *for every* $n \in \mathcal{N}_t$, *for every reachable* $\gamma = \langle \mathsf{St}, \nu, \mathsf{h} \rangle$ *such that* $\mathsf{St}(t) = n$, *for every* $x, y \in \mathcal{V}$, *if* $\nu(x) = y$ *then* $x \rightarrow_{\mathsf{pto}(n)} y$.

Proof sketch. We present here the core ideas, some technicalities are omitted and can be found in the long version. We proceed by induction on the length of the execution from γ_0 to γ. The interesting part is when the last step of the execution is $\gamma_1 = \langle \mathsf{St}_1, \nu_1, \mathsf{h}_1 \rangle \xrightarrow{\delta} \gamma_2 = \langle \mathsf{St}_2, \nu_2, \mathsf{h}_2 \rangle$ where $\delta = (n_1, \iota, n_2)$ with ι an assignment of depth $k \geq 1$ (*i.e.*, a pointer assignment). By induction hypothesis, $\mathsf{pto}(n_2)$ has all points-to pairs from ν_1; we prove that it has the (potentially) new points-to pair corresponding to the effect of the assignment. We proceed by case disjunction on the shape of ι.

$\mathsf{x} := \mathsf{y}$. Thanks to $\alpha(n_2)$, x and y are in the same vertex, and thanks to $\mathsf{pto}(n_1)$, $y \rightarrow \nu_1(y)$; therefore $x \rightarrow \nu_1(y)$ in $\mathsf{pto}(n_2)$.

- $\mathsf{x := *y}$. Thanks to $\mathsf{pto}(n_1)$, $y \to \nu_1(y)$ and $\nu_1(y) \to \nu_1(\nu_1(y))$; thanks to $\alpha(n_2)$, $y \to x$. By DCR on $(\mathsf{ver}(y), \mathsf{ver}(\nu_1(y)), \mathsf{ver}(x), \mathsf{ver}(\nu_1(\nu_1(y))))$, $x \to \nu_1(\nu_1(y))$.
- $\mathsf{*x := y}$. Let $p_x := \nu_1(x)$ and $p_y := \nu_1(y)$. We have $\nu_2(p_x) = p_y$. Thanks to $\alpha(n_2)$, $x \to y$. Thanks to $\mathsf{pto}(n_1)$, $x \to p_x$ and $y \to p_y$. By DCR applied to $(\mathsf{ver}(x), \mathsf{ver}(y), \mathsf{ver}(p_x), \mathsf{ver}(p_y))$, $p_x \to p_y$.
- $\mathsf{x := \&y}$. We have $\nu_2(x) = y$. Thanks to $\alpha(n_2)$, $x \to y$.
- $\mathsf{*x := *y}$ Let $p_x := \nu_1(x)$ and $p_y := \nu_1(y)$; we have $\nu_2(p_x) = \nu_1(p_y)$. Thanks to $\mathsf{pto}(n_1)$, $x \to p_x$, $y \to p_y$ and $p_y \to \nu_1(p_y)$. Thanks to $\alpha(n_2)$, $\mathsf{ver}(x)$ and $\mathsf{ver}(y)$ share a child v in $\mathsf{pto}(n_2)$. By DCR applied to $(\mathsf{ver}(y), \mathsf{ver}(p_y), v, \mathsf{ver}(\nu_1(p_y)))$, v has an edge to $\mathsf{ver}(\nu_1(p_y))$. By DCR applied to $(\mathsf{ver}(x), v, \mathsf{ver}(p_x), \mathsf{ver}(\nu_1(p_y)))$, $\mathsf{ver}(p_x)$ has an edge to $\mathsf{ver}(\nu_1(p_y))$. This proves that $p_x \to \nu_1(p_y)$.
- $\mathsf{*x := \&y}$. Let $p_x := \nu_1(x)$; we have $\nu_2(p_x) = y$. Thanks to $\mathsf{pto}(n_2)$, $x \to p_x$. Thanks to $\alpha(n_2)$, there is a vertex v with an edge from $\mathsf{ver}(x)$ to v and an edge from v to $\mathsf{ver}(y)$. By DCR applied to $(\mathsf{ver}(x), v, \mathsf{ver}(p_x), \mathsf{ver}(y))$, $p_x \to y$.

□

Remark 10. The procedural points-to analysis α systematically merges children v_2 and v_2' of a vertex v_1. The concurrent points-to analysis pto does not: it uses DCR instead so that v_2 and v_2' must have the same children, but not the same parents. In fact, α could also rely on DCR instead of merging children, which would give better precision but worse performance (merging allows to keep the number of vertices low). We have not defined α this way because we want it to reflect the implementation from the `alias` plugin of Frama-C.

4 Automatic Mutex Placement

We finally introduce a technique that, from a program $\mathcal{P}$, adds mutexes to obtain a new program $\tilde{\mathcal{P}}$ with no data race. *Data races* are common concurrency bugs which occur when two threads simultaneously access the same memory location.

The transformation must not create deadlocks. A deadlock corresponds to a set of threads each waiting upon a mutex held by another thread in the set. For our purposes, the only blocking operation is locking. Therefore, deadlocks may only occur in the presence of a *cyclic dependency*, *i.e.*, a sequence of mutexes $m_1, \ldots, m_n, m_{n+1} = m_1$ (with $n \geq 2$) such that, for each $i \leq n$, a thread tries to lock m_{i+1} while holding m_i (see, *e.g.*, [14]). A classic strategy for deadlock avoidance is to impose a *lock ordering*, *i.e.*, a total order $\trianglelefteq$ on the set of mutexes such that a mutex smaller for $\trianglelefteq$ must be acquired earlier, *i.e.*, for every $m \trianglelefteq m'$ with $m \neq m'$, a thread can never try to perform a `lock(m)` instruction while holding m'. In order to remain as general as possible, we do not assume any lock ordering for $\mathcal{P}$. Instead, we impose a lock ordering on newly-introduced mutexes; we will prove in Proposition 14 that no deadlock is introduced this way.

The transformations introduces, for each variable x, a new mutex μ_x in charge of protecting x. We let $\mathcal{M}_{\mathsf{new}} := \{\mu_x \mid x \in \mathcal{V}\}$; the full set of mutexes becomes $\mathcal{M} \uplus \mathcal{M}_{\mathsf{new}}$. To prevent deadlocks, we consider an arbitrary ordering $\trianglelefteq$ on $\mathcal{M}_{\mathsf{new}}$.

In our model, the only instructions that access variables are assignments and conditional guards. We call *access instructions* such instructions, and *access transitions* the transitions whose instructions are access instructions. Given an access transition $\delta = (n, \iota, n')$ and a valuation $\nu : \mathcal{V} \to \mathbb{N} \cup \mathcal{V} \cup \{\#\}$, we let $\mathsf{W}_\nu(\delta) \subseteq \mathcal{V}$ (resp. $\mathsf{R}_\nu(\delta) \subseteq \mathcal{V}$) denote the set of variables that are written to (resp. read) in ι, assuming that the current valuation is ν. Formally:

- if ι is a conditional guard `true(e)`, `false(e)`, then $\mathsf{W}_\nu(\delta)$ is empty and $\mathsf{R}_\nu(\delta)$ contains all variables accessed to evaluate e, *i.e.*, any x syntactically appearing in e as well as $\nu(x)$ for any $^*x$ appearing in e (address-of terms $\&x$ are not considered, they cannot be involved in data races);
- if ι is an assignment $x := e$, then $\mathsf{W}_\nu(\delta) = \{x\}$ and $\mathsf{R}_\nu(\delta)$ contains all variables accessed to evaluate e, as defined above, as well as x;
- if ι is an assignment $^*x := e$, then $\mathsf{W}_\nu(\delta) = \{\nu(x)\}$ and $\mathsf{R}_\nu(\delta)$ is as above except that it contains both x and $\nu(x)$.

Note that $\mathsf{W}_\delta(\nu) \subseteq \mathsf{R}_\delta(\nu)$. Given $\delta = (n, \iota, n')$, we overapproximate the set of variables read (resp. written to) by δ thanks to the points-to analysis $\mathsf{pto}(n)$ from Sect. 3.2. We define its may-read set $\mathsf{MR}(\delta)$ (resp. may-write set $\mathsf{MW}(\delta)$) similarly to $\mathsf{R}_\nu(\delta)$ (resp. $\mathsf{W}_\nu(\delta)$) except that for $^*x$, we add all y such that $x \to_{\mathsf{pto}(n)} y$ instead of $\nu(x)$. By Theorem 9, in every execution where δ is applied from $\gamma = \langle \mathsf{St}, \nu, \mathsf{h} \rangle$, $\mathsf{R}_\nu(\delta) \subseteq \mathsf{MR}(\delta)$ and $\mathsf{W}_\nu(\delta) \subseteq \mathsf{MW}(\delta)$.

In our model, an execution ρ has a data race when two consecutive[2] access transitions performed by different threads, among which at least one write, access the same variable. Formally, given two access transitions δ_1 and δ_2 and a variable x, ρ *has a data race between* δ_1 *and* δ_2 *on* x when ρ contains a sequence $\gamma_1 \xrightarrow{\delta_1} \gamma_2 \xrightarrow{\delta_2} \gamma_3$ such that, by letting $\delta_1 = (n_1, \iota_1, n_1')$, $\delta_2 = (n_2, \iota_2, n_2')$, $\gamma_1 = \langle \mathsf{St}_1, \nu_1, \mathsf{h}_1 \rangle$ and $\gamma_2 = \langle \mathsf{St}_2, \nu_2, \mathsf{h}_2 \rangle$, we have $\mathsf{th}(n_1) \neq \mathsf{th}(n_2)$ and $x \in (\mathsf{W}_{\nu_1}(\delta_1) \cap \mathsf{R}_{\nu_2}(\delta_2)) \cup (\mathsf{R}_{\nu_1}(\delta_1) \cap \mathsf{W}_{\nu_2}(\delta_2))$. Recall that $\mathsf{W}_\nu(\delta) \subseteq \mathsf{R}_\nu(\delta)$, so that there can be a data race where both accesses write to x. We say that there is a data in $\mathcal{P}$ when there is a data race in some execution of $\mathcal{P}$.

For every variable x, we compute a *may-race relation* $\mathsf{MayRace}_x$ such that, for all access transitions δ_1, δ_2, if there is an execution ρ with a data race between δ_1 and δ_2 on x then $\delta_1\ \mathsf{MayRace}_x\ \delta_2$. To do so, we define a relation MHP that overapproximates when two access transitions may happen in parallel. Let $\delta_1 = (n_1, \iota_1, n_1')$, $\delta_2 = (n_2, \iota_2, n_2')$, $t_1 := \mathsf{th}(\delta_1)$ and $t_2 := \mathsf{th}(\delta_2)$. We let:

$$\delta_1\ \mathsf{MHP}\ \delta_2 \iff t_1 \neq t_2 \ \wedge\ t_1 \notin U(n_2) \cup J(n_2) \ \wedge\ t_2 \notin U(n_1) \cup J(n_1) \ \wedge\ L(n_1) \cap L(n_2) = \emptyset.$$

[2] Our model is sequential, with no true notion of concurrency. We use the fact that, when two access transitions of different threads are performed consecutively in the model, they may happen concurrently in reality.

$$\forall x \in \mathcal{V}, \quad \delta_1 \ \mathsf{MayRace}_x \ \delta_2 \iff \delta_1 \ \mathsf{MHP} \ \delta_2 \wedge x \in (\mathsf{MW}(\delta_1) \cap \mathsf{MR}(\delta_2)) \cup (\mathsf{MR}(\delta_1) \cap \mathsf{MW}(\delta_2)).$$

Lemma 11. *If there is an execution with a data race between two access transitions δ_1 and δ_2 on a variable x, then δ_1 $\mathsf{MayRace}_x$ δ_2.*

Proof. Let ρ be an execution with a data race between access transitions $\delta_1 = (n_1, \iota_1, n_1')$ and $\delta_2 = (n_2, \iota_2, n_2')$, with witness $\gamma_1 \xrightarrow{\delta_1} \gamma_2 \xrightarrow{\delta_2} \gamma_3$. Let $\gamma_1 = \langle \mathsf{St}_1, \nu_1, \mathsf{h}_1 \rangle$ and $\gamma_2 = \langle \mathsf{St}_2, \nu_2, \mathsf{h}_2 \rangle$. Because δ_1 and δ_2 are access transitions, they do not create or join threads. Also, t_1 and t_2 are created and not joined in γ_1. By Proposition 3 and Proposition 4, $t_1 \notin U(n_2) \cup J(n_2)$ and $t_2 \notin U(n_1) \cup J(n_1)$. Finally, there cannot be $m \in L(n_1) \cap L(n_2)$ thanks to Proposition 2. This proves that δ_1 MHP δ_2. Also, by Theorem 9 and by definition of $\mathsf{MW}(.)$ and $\mathsf{MR}(.)$, for all $i \in \{1, 2\}$, $\mathsf{W}_{\nu_i}(\delta_i) \subseteq \mathsf{MW}(\delta_i)$ and $\mathsf{R}_{\nu_i}(\delta_i) \subseteq \mathsf{MR}(\delta_i)$. Therefore, $x \in (\mathsf{MW}(\delta_1) \cap \mathsf{MR}(\delta_2)) \cup (\mathsf{MR}(\delta_1) \cap \mathsf{MW}(\delta_2))$, so that δ_1 $\mathsf{MayRace}_x$ δ_2. □

We transform program $\mathcal{P}$ into $\tilde{\mathcal{P}}$ by doing the following for every access transition δ. Let $M_\delta := \{\mu_x \mid x \in \mathcal{V}, \exists \delta' : \delta \ \mathsf{MayRace}_x \ \delta'\}$; M_δ contains all mutexes of variables on which δ may be involved in a data race. The transformation adds a $\mathtt{lock}(\mu_\mathsf{x})$ transition before δ and a $\mathtt{unlock}(\mu_\mathsf{x})$ transition after δ for each $\mu_x \in M_\delta$. The locking instructions are inserted in the order given by $\trianglelefteq$: we let $M_\delta = \{m_1, m_2, \ldots, m_k\}$ sorted in increasing order for $\trianglelefteq$, and we add a sequence of transitions with instructions $\mathtt{lock}(\mathsf{m}_1), \ldots, \mathtt{lock}(\mathsf{m}_\mathsf{k})$ right before δ.

Example 12. Consider again the example from Fig. 1. As highlighted in Example 1, there is an execution with a data race on k between transition δ_{15} at line 15 and transition δ_{28} at line 28. Since the points-to analysis is sound, $k \in \mathsf{MW}(\delta_{28})$, and trivially $k \in \mathsf{MR}(\delta_{15})$. Moreover, δ_{28} MHP δ_{15}; indeed, by letting n_{28} and n_{15} the source nodes, $U(n_{28}) = J(n_{28}) = U(n_{15}) = J(n_{15}) = \emptyset$. Also, $L(n_{28}) = \{\mathtt{m}\}$, $L(n_{15}) = \emptyset$ so that $L(n_{28}) \cap L(n_{15}) = \emptyset$. This implies that δ_{28} $\mathsf{MayRace}_k$ δ_{15}. In fact, this is the only may-race relation in this program. Therefore, the program $\tilde{\mathcal{P}}$ has a single new mutex, μ_k. The transformation inserts two $\mathtt{lock}(\mu_\mathsf{k})$ instructions, one between lines 14 and 15 in `main` and one between lines 27 and 28 in `t2`; and two $\mathtt{unlock}(\mu_\mathsf{k})$ instructions, one between lines 15 and 16 in `main` and one between lines 28 and 29 in `t2`. In the obtained $\tilde{\mathcal{P}}$, whenever a thread accesses k, mutex μ_k is held, preventing the data race. Had there been a need for a mutex $\mu_\mathtt{out}$ at line 15, the transformation would have introduced an arbitrary ordering $\trianglelefteq$ on $\{\mu_k, \mu_\mathtt{out}\}$, and inserted instructions $\mathtt{lock}(\mu_\mathsf{k})$ and $\mathtt{lock}(\mu_\mathtt{out})$ between lines 14 and 15 in the order given by $\trianglelefteq$.

The transformation introduces a mutex for every variable, therefore we expect this method to yield lower contention that simpler approaches such as coarse-grained locking. The obtained program is free of data races:

Theorem 13. *There is no data race in $\tilde{\mathcal{P}}$.*

Proof. Suppose by contradiction that there is a data race in $\tilde{\mathcal{P}}$. There are access transitions $\tilde{\delta_1}$ and $\tilde{\delta_2}$ and an execution $\tilde{\rho}$ of $\tilde{\mathcal{P}}$ with a sequence $\gamma_1 \xrightarrow{\tilde{\delta_1}} \gamma_2 \xrightarrow{\tilde{\delta_2}} \gamma_3$ such that, by letting $\gamma_1 = \langle \mathsf{St}_1, \nu_1, \mathsf{h}_1 \rangle$ and $\gamma_2 = \langle \mathsf{St}_2, \nu_2, \mathsf{h}_2 \rangle$, we have $\mathsf{th}(\tilde{\delta_1}) \neq \mathsf{th}(\tilde{\delta_2})$ and $x \in (\mathsf{W}_{\nu_1}(\tilde{\delta_1}) \cap \mathsf{R}_{\nu_2}(\tilde{\delta_2})) \cup (\mathsf{R}_{\nu_1}(\tilde{\delta_1}) \cap \mathsf{W}_{\nu_2}(\tilde{\delta_2}))$. By removing transitions manipulating mutexes in $\mathcal{M}_{\mathsf{new}}$, we convert $\tilde{\rho}$ into an execution ρ of $\mathcal{P}$; $\tilde{\delta_1}$ and $\tilde{\delta_2}$ are access transitions, so there are corresponding transitions δ_1 and δ_2 in $\mathcal{P}$. In ρ, δ_1 and δ_2 occur consecutively; moreover, the values of variables in ρ corresponding to the values in $\tilde{\rho}$ and $x \in (\mathsf{W}_{\nu_1}(\delta_1) \cap \mathsf{R}_{\nu_2}(\delta_2)) \cup (\mathsf{R}_{\nu_1}(\delta_1) \cap \mathsf{W}_{\nu_2}(\delta_2))$. This proves that ρ has a data race between δ_1 and δ_2, so δ_1 $\mathsf{MayRace}_x$ δ_2 by Lemma 11. Hence, $\mu_x \in M_{\delta_1} \cap M_{\delta_2}$, *i.e.*, μ_x is a protecting mutex for both δ_1 and δ_2. Hence, in $\tilde{\rho}$, $\tilde{\delta_1}$ and $\tilde{\delta_2}$ are both surrounded by a $\mathtt{lock}(\mu_\mathsf{x}) - \mathtt{unlock}(\mu_\mathsf{x})$ pair. In γ_2, $\mathsf{th}(\tilde{\delta_1})$ and $\mathsf{th}(\tilde{\delta_2})$ are inside their respective $\mathtt{lock}(\mu_\mathsf{x}) - \mathtt{unlock}(\mu_\mathsf{x})$ pair. They both hold μ_x in γ_2, a contradiction. □

Moreover, executions of $\mathcal{P}$ and of $\tilde{\mathcal{P}}$ correspond, *i.e.*, they coincide on transitions of $\mathcal{P}$. First, any execution of $\tilde{\mathcal{P}}$ can be turned to an execution of $\mathcal{P}$ by removing all $\mathtt{lock}(\mathsf{m})$ and $\mathtt{unlock}(\mathsf{m})$ for all $m \in \mathcal{M}_{\mathsf{new}}$. Conversely, any execution ρ of $\mathcal{P}$ can be turned to an execution $\tilde{\rho}$ of $\tilde{\mathcal{P}}$ as follows. When, in ρ, a thread performs an access transition δ, we make this thread perform in $\tilde{\rho}$ the sequence composed of: all lock transitions protecting δ, δ, all unlock transitions protecting δ. With this construction, mutexes in $\mathcal{M}_{\mathsf{new}}$ are never held outside these sequences, so lock instructions are never blocking.

However, in $\tilde{\mathcal{P}}$, the protection blocks of several access transitions might interleave, so that semantic equivalence between the two programs requires an additional argument that no deadlock is introduced.

Proposition 14. *The transformation does not introduce new deadlocks.*

Proof. We prove that no cyclic lock dependency $m_1, \ldots, m_n, m_{n+1} = m_1$ in $\tilde{\mathcal{P}}$ ($n \geq 2$) involves a mutex in $\mathcal{M}_{\mathsf{new}}$. By contradiction and w.l.o.g., suppose $m_1 = \mu_{x_1} \in \mathcal{M}_{\mathsf{new}}$. There is an execution where some $\mathtt{lock}(\mathsf{m}_2)$ is performed while m_1 is held by the thread. By construction, each $\mathtt{lock}(\mu_{\mathsf{x}_1}) - \mathtt{unlock}(\mu_{\mathsf{x}_1})$ block only contains: an access transition to x_1 (not a locking instruction), instructions of the form $\mathtt{lock}(\mu_\mathsf{y})$ with y s.t. $\mu_{x_1} \trianglelefteq \mu_y$, and unlock instructions. Thus, $m_2 = \mu_{x_2}$ for some $x_2 \neq x_1$ such that $\mu_{x_1} \trianglelefteq \mu_{x_2}$. By direct induction, $m_j = \mu_{x_j}$ with $x_j \neq x_{j+1}$ and $\mu_{x_j} \trianglelefteq \mu_{x_{j+1}}$ for all j, which contradicts $\trianglelefteq$ being an ordering. □

An extra final step consists in removing redundant mutexes. A mutex μ_x is removed if there is $m \neq \mu_x$ known to be held at every access transition protected by μ_x. This cannot happen when $m \in \mathcal{M}$ is a mutex of the original program: it would mean $m \in L(n)$ for every $\delta = (n, \iota, n')$ such that $\mu_x \in M_\delta$, but in that case there is no data race on x and μ_x would not be used in the first place. It can however happen that a new mutexes μ_x is redundant with another new mutex μ_y ($x \neq y$), because any racy access to x in $\mathcal{P}$ is also a racy access to y. This is easy to detect, and in that case we can simply remove μ_x and all its transitions.

It is possible to use a similar technique to protect any user-annotated atomic section AS of the program, so as to guarantee that other threads cannot interfere with AS. This would be done using the classic approach of (weak) two-phase locking. The analysis from Sect. 3 has enough information to identify which variables in AS are vulnerable to interference. For each such variable x, AS would have a single `lock`(μ_x) – `unlock`(μ_x) pair, where the locking (resp. unlocking) is done before (resp. after) any access to x in AS. This also requires to hold μ_x at any transition δ of another thread when δ may interfere with AS on x.

5 Conclusion

We have presented a method to automatically place locks in a concurrent program so as to prevent any data race. Our approach is self-contained and formally proven. It includes a formal model for C-like POSIX concurrent programs, a preliminary analysis of concurrency and a must-lockset analysis. One of the key contribution is a concurrent points-to analysis derived from a procedural, Steensgaard-like points-to analysis such as the one implemented in the `alias` plugin of Frama-C [13]. This is done using a unification technique called diamond completion rule. Our method uses the result of the analysis to automatically place locks and respects a lock ordering to prevent deadlocks.

References

1. Berry, G.: SCADE: synchronous design and validation of embedded control software. In: Next Generation Design and Verification Methodologies for Distributed Embedded Control Systems, pp. 19–33 (2007). https://doi.org/10.1007/978-1-4020-6254-4_2
2. Boehm, H.J.: How to miscompile programs with "benign" data races. In: 3rd USENIX Workshop on Hot Topics in Parallelism (HotPar 2011) (2011). https://www.usenix.org/conference/hotpar-11/how-miscompile-programs-benign-data-races
3. Carré, B., Garnsworthy, J.: SPARK—an annotated Ada subset for safety-critical programming. In: Proceedings of the conference on TRI-ADA 1990, pp. 392–402. TRI-Ada 1990 (1990). https://doi.org/10.1145/255471.255563. https://dl.acm.org/doi/10.1145/255471.255563
4. Cherem, S., Chilimbi, T., Gulwani, S.: Inferring locks for atomic sections. In: Proceedings of the 29th ACM SIGPLAN Conference on Programming Language Design and Implementation, PLDI 2008, pp. 304–315 (2008). https://doi.org/10.1145/1375581.1375619
5. Conchon, S., Filliâtre, J.: A persistent union-find data structure. In: Proceedings of the ACM Workshop on ML, 2007, Freiburg, Germany, 5 October 2007, pp. 37–46 (2007). https://doi.org/10.1145/1292535.1292541

6. Cuoq, P., Kirchner, F., Kosmatov, N., Prevosto, V., Signoles, J., Yakobowski, B.: Frama-C - a software analysis perspective. In: Eleftherakis, G., Hinchey, M., Holcombe, M. (eds.) SEFM 2012. LNCS, vol. 7504, pp. 233–247. Springer, Heidelberg (2012). https://doi.org/10.1007/978-3-642-33826-7_16
7. Dacík, T., Vojnar, T.: RacerF: Lightweight Static Data Race Detection for C Code (2025). https://doi.org/10.48550/arXiv.2502.04905. http://arxiv.org/abs/2502.04905
8. Emmi, M., Fischer, J.S., Jhala, R., Majumdar, R.: Lock allocation. ACM SIGPLAN Not. **42**(1), 291–296 (2007). https://doi.org/10.1145/1190215.1190260. https://dl.acm.org/doi/10.1145/1190215.1190260
9. Gerakios, P., Papaspyrou, N., Sagonas, K.: Race-free and memory-safe multithreading: design and implementation in cyclone. In: Proceedings of the 5th ACM SIGPLAN Workshop on Types in Language Design and Implementation, TLDI 2010, pp. 15–26 (2010). https://doi.org/10.1145/1708016.1708020
10. Grossman, D.: Type-safe multithreading in cyclone. In: Proceedings of the 2003 ACM SIGPLAN International Workshop on Types in Languages Design and Implementation, TLDI 2003, pp. 13–25 (2003). https://doi.org/10.1145/604174.604177
11. Hicks, M., Foster, J.S., Pratikakis, P.: Lock inference for atomic sections. In: Proceedings of the First ACM SIGPLAN Workshop on Languages, Compilers, and Hardware Support for Transactional Computing, p. 13 (2006)
12. Kirchner, F., Kosmatov, N., Prévosto, V., Signoles, J., Yakobowski, B.: Frama-C: a software analysis perspective. Formal Aspects Comput. **27**(3), 573 (2015). https://doi.org/10.1007/s00165-014-0326-7. https://cea.hal.science/cea-01808981
13. Le Gall, T., Rochel, J., Faissole, F., Signoles, J., Cousineau, D.: Alias: pointeurs espionnés en série. In: 35es Journées Francophones des Langages Applicatifs (JFLA 2024), pp. 85–104 (2024). https://hal.science/hal-04407140
14. Lin, Y., Kulkarni, S.S.: Automatic repair for multi-threaded programs with deadlock/livelock using maximum satisfiability. In: International Symposium on Software Testing and Analysis, ISSTA 2014, San Jose, CA, USA - 21–26 July 2014, pp. 237–247 (2014). https://doi.org/10.1145/2610384.2610398
15. Lu, S., Park, S., Seo, E., Zhou, Y.: Learning from mistakes: a comprehensive study on real world concurrency bug characteristics. In: Proceedings of the 13th International Conference on Architectural Support for Programming Languages and Operating Systems, pp. 329–339. ASPLOS XIII (2008). https://doi.org/10.1145/1346281.1346323
16. Matsakis, N.D., Klock, F.S.: The rust language. Ada Lett. **34**(3), 103–104 (2014). https://doi.org/10.1145/2692956.2663188
17. McCloskey, B., Zhou, F., Gay, D., Brewer, E.: Autolocker: synchronization inference for atomic sections. In: Conference Record of the 33rd ACM SIGPLAN-SIGACT Symposium on Principles of Programming Languages, POPL 2006, pp. 346–358 (2006). https://doi.org/10.1145/1111037.1111068
18. Miné, A., et al.: Taking static analysis to the next level: proving the absence of run-time errors and data races with Astrée. In: 8th European Congress on Embedded Real Time Software and Systems (ERTS 2016) (2016). https://hal.science/hal-01271552
19. Rugina, R., Rinard, M.: Pointer analysis for multithreaded programs. In: Proceedings of the ACM SIGPLAN 1999 Conference on Programming Language Design and Implementation, PLDI 1999, pp. 77–90 (1999). https://doi.org/10.1145/301618.301645. https://dl.acm.org/doi/10.1145/301618.301645

20. Rugina, R., Rinard, M.C.: Pointer analysis for structured parallel programs. ACM Trans. Program. Lang. Syst. **25**(1), 70–116 (2003). https://doi.org/10.1145/596980.596982. https://dl.acm.org/doi/10.1145/596980.596982
21. Salcianu, A., Rinard, M.: Pointer and escape analysis for multithreaded programs. In: Proceedings of the Eighth ACM SIGPLAN Symposium on Principles and Practices of Parallel Programming, PPoPP 2001, pp. 12–23 (2001). https://doi.org/10.1145/379539.379553. https://dl.acm.org/doi/10.1145/379539.379553
22. Steensgaard, B.: Points-to analysis in almost linear time. In: Conference Record of POPL'96: The 23rd ACM SIGPLAN-SIGACT Symposium on Principles of Programming Languages, Papers Presented at the Symposium, St. Petersburg Beach, Florida, USA, 21–24 January 1996, pp. 32–41 (1996). https://doi.org/10.1145/237721.237727
23. Sui, Y., Di, P., Xue, J.: Sparse flow-sensitive pointer analysis for multithreaded programs. In: Proceedings of the 2016 International Symposium on Code Generation and Optimization, CGO 2016, pp. 160–170. (2016). https://doi.org/10.1145/2854038.2854043. https://dl.acm.org/doi/10.1145/2854038.2854043
24. Vojdani, V., Vene, V.: Goblint: path-sensitive data race analysis. In: Annales Univ. Sci. Budapest., Sect. Comp. vol. 30, pp. 141–155 (2009)

Formal Modeling of Beefy, a Protocol for Supporting Light Clients

Daniel O. Dirdal[1(✉)], Leander Jehl[1], Bhargav Nagaraj Bhatt[2], Hein Meling[1], and Nejm Saadallah[1]

[1] University of Stavanger, Stavanger, Norway
daniel.o.dirdal@uis.no
[2] Morpho Association, Paris, France

Abstract. Blockchain systems involve participants with diverse roles and resource constraints. Resource-constrained participants, called light clients, cannot download the full blockchain but still need to verify the state to participate. To support this, a justification layer above the finality layer can provide succinct proofs of block finalization. In this work, we motivate the need for such a justification layer, describe how it can support light clients, and outline the properties it should satisfy. We study Beefy, a justification layer protocol deployed in the Polkadot ecosystem, and present a formal specification of the protocol in TLA$^+$. We use the explicit-state model checker TLC to verify safety and liveness properties and the symbolic model checker Apalache to validate an inductive invariant. In particular, we show that mandatory blocks containing validator set changes can achieve justification even under asynchronous conditions. We also compare our specification with Polkadot's informal specification and implementation, demonstrating that the informal specification admits a deadlock, a flaw not present in the deployed implementation.

Keywords: Blockchain · Light Clients · Justification Layer · Model Checking · TLA$^+$

1 Introduction

Blockchain systems provide a decentralized platform for maintaining a shared ledger in an adversarial environment, relying on participants with different roles and resource capabilities. The participants typically include *validators*, who run a Byzantine Fault Tolerant (BFT) consensus protocol to agree on the canonical chain and, by necessity, act as *full nodes* storing and relaying chain data and state. Other full nodes may store and relay data without participating in consensus. Another type of participant, *clients*, submit transactions or query the chain's state. Clients must verify that the blockchain state they observe is valid; naively, this requires downloading and validating every block. To mitigate this cost, a class of clients known as *light clients* [12] instead verify only block headers and rely on the validator set to guarantee the correctness of the blockchain state.

Published by Springer Nature Switzerland AG 2026
L. Bocchi and B. Kulahcioglu Ozkan (Eds.): FORTE 2026, LNCS 16589, pp. 93–111, 2026.
https://doi.org/10.1007/978-3-032-28187-6_6

To enable light clients to securely follow the canonical chain, blockchain systems employ a *justification layer*, a lightweight protocol that runs on top of a *finality layer* providing *provable finality*. The finality layer finalizes blocks through a BFT consensus protocol, while the justification layer generates *succinct proofs* of finalized blocks via an additional round of validator voting. These proofs, secured by the collective agreement of the validator set, allow light clients to track the chain and enable cross-chain interoperability, supporting secure asset transfers between independent blockchains.

The proof-of-stake blockchain Polkadot [8] deploys BEEFY (Bridge Efficiency Enabling Finality Yielder) [3] as a justification layer protocol on top of its finality layer protocol GRANDPA [33]. GRANDPA provides fast provable finality for the blockchain, while BEEFY enables light clients to track finalized blocks and supports cross-chain bridging. For example, the Snowbridge protocol uses BEEFY to bridge Polkadot to Ethereum, currently securing over $70 million [34].

Ensuring the correctness of BEEFY is critical, as it underpins cross-chain bridging from Polkadot to external blockchains. Cross-chain bridges have historically been among the most targeted and exploited components in blockchain systems, with losses exceeding $2.8 billion [13].

We present a formal specification of BEEFY in the TLA$^+$ specification language [23], which is well suited for modeling concurrent, reactive, and asynchronous systems. We validate the specification on finite models using two complementary model checkers: the explicit-state model checker TLC [40] and the bounded symbolic model checker Apalache [20]. Although BEEFY is deployed within the broader Polkadot architecture, our model deliberately abstracts away the underlying finality layer and unnecessary details. This enables us to focus on BEEFY as a message-driven voting protocol operating over finalized blocks.

Although we verify standard consensus safety properties such as agreement, these follow directly from the construction of BEEFY and are therefore not the primary focus of our work. Instead, we investigate more subtle aspects of the protocol, in particular the correct handling of *mandatory* blocks, which contain validator set changes. For mandatory blocks, we verify both safety and liveness assuming only eventual block delivery, and validate a candidate inductive invariant that implies the safety properties. We further show that liveness properties for non-mandatory blocks require stronger assumptions. We compare our formal specification with Polkadot's informal specification and highlight that the informal specification permits a deadlock.

2 Background

This section outlines the system model and underlying assumptions, followed by an overview of the block lifecycle and motivation for the justification layer.

2.1 System Model and Assumptions

The system consists of a set of n validators $\Pi = \{p_1, \ldots, p_n\}$, of which up to $f < n/3$ can be Byzantine faulty; the remaining validators are *honest* and follow the protocol [24]. We assume $n = 3f + 1$ and denote the set of honest validators by Π_h. A *quorum certificate* for a message m consists of $2f + 1$ votes from distinct validators, certifying supermajority agreement on m.

We assume a *partially synchronous* network [15], in which messages sent by honest validators are delivered to all other honest validators within a bounded delay Δ, but only after some unknown *global stabilization time* (GST). Formally, if an honest validator sends a message at time t, all other honest validators will receive it no later than $\max(t, \text{GST}) + \Delta$.

The system advances through a sequence of *epochs*, each composed of a fixed number of *slots*. In each slot, a single proposer is elected to produce a *block* containing a list of transactions and metadata describing a proposed state transition. A slot may contain zero, one, or more block proposals. We assume variable slot durations, so the rate of block production depends on network conditions.

We model the blockchain as a rooted tree of blocks, where each block has an associated *height* equal to its distance from the genesis block (with genesis at height 0). The canonical chain is the unique chain consisting of finalized blocks. Because at most one block at any given height can be finalized, the canonical chain contains a unique finalized block at each height.

2.2 Block Lifecycle

We adopt Polkadot's block lifecycle model [8], which divides the blockchain architecture into three distinct layers: (1) The *block production layer*, which is responsible for proposing and propagating new blocks. (2) The *finality layer*, which finalizes blocks to ensure consensus on a single canonical chain. (3) The *justification layer*, which produces succinct proofs of finality.

The layers operate largely independently but are coupled through a few dependencies. Block production builds on the highest finalized block, the finality layer finalizes proposed blocks, and the justification layer justifies finalized blocks. These dependencies are illustrated in Fig. 1.

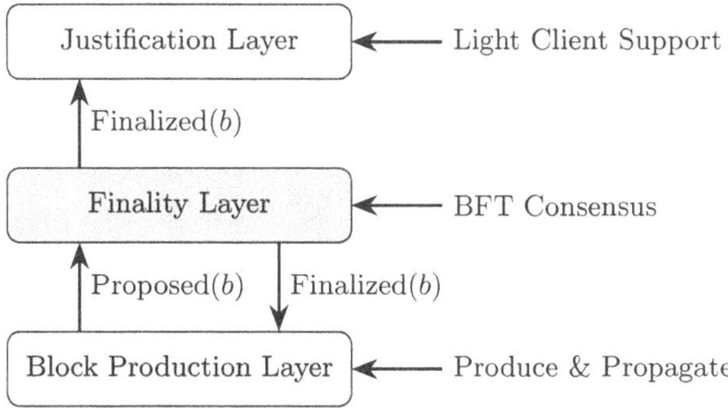

Fig. 1. Blocks are proposed by the block production layer, finalized by the finality layer, and then made available to both the block production and justification layers.

An alternative way to visualize the interaction between the layers—one that more closely reflects how the protocols operate in practice—is shown in Fig. 2. The figure illustrates the perspective of a single validator, highlighting its view of the highest justified, the highest finalized, and the current head of the chain. Different validators may hold different views of the chain due to network delays. The figure also highlights that the justification layer lags behind the finality layer, which in turn lags behind block production, as each layer operates on different parts of the chain and progresses at its own pace.

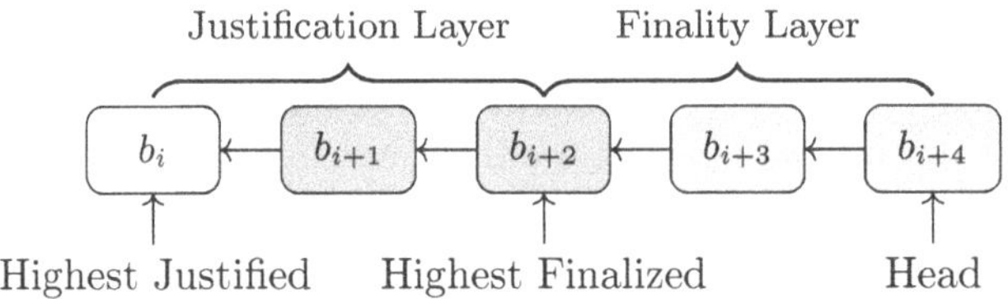

Fig. 2. Validator view of justified, finalized, and head.

For example, consider a validator v with the view illustrated in Fig. 2. Validator v would be working to justify b_{i+1} or b_{i+2}, and to finalize b_{i+3} or b_{i+4}. Only block proposals extending v's highest finalized block, b_{i+2}, would be accepted. If selected as a block proposer, v would extend block b_{i+4}.

Depending on the system, the validator set Π may be shared across protocol layers or differ between them. For example, Polkadot uses a unified staked validator set [8,17], meaning the justification layer inherits the security and trust assumptions of the underlying layers. For the remainder of this paper, we focus solely on the validator set of the justification layer and assume the block production and finality layers operate correctly.

The Ethereum [9] blockchain also supports a light client protocol via its Altair fork [16]. Unlike Polkadot's justification layer (Fig. 1), Ethereum's protocol operates directly on the block production layer rather than on finalized blocks. It uses a periodically rotating subset of the validators, called a *sync committee*, which collectively votes on the head of the chain; in Fig. 2, this corresponds to voting for the head block b_{i+4} instead of a finalized block.

2.3 The Need for a Justification Layer

Although light clients can follow the finality layer directly, consensus protocols are designed for well-provisioned validators that participate in consensus and re-execute transactions, prioritizing fast finality, large validator sets, and low message complexity. Light clients, by contrast, have limited compute and bandwidth and download only block headers, creating a fundamental mismatch.

Even when downloading only block headers, light clients must verify proofs of finality, and the cost of this verification depends on the structure of the consensus protocol. In such protocols, finality is established through quorum certificates produced during voting phases. Broadly, consensus protocols fall into two categories: (i) Protocols with distinct vote types across phases [6,33]. Here, finality is determined by a dedicated final-phase certificate, so a light client needs to verify only that certificate. (ii) Protocols with a single, pipelined vote type [10,39]. In these systems, finality emerges from a sequence of consecutive certificates, typically two or three, requiring a light client to verify certificates for the target block and up to two of its successors.

Finality protocols also differ in granularity: some finalize multiple blocks at once [10,33], while others finalize blocks individually [6]. This affects how much data a light client must process to remain synchronized. In all cases, the client must either download every finalized header and verify its quorum certificate or rely on validators to supply succinct ancestry proofs.

One might think a justification layer is simply a checkpointing mechanism, but the two serve different purposes and operate differently. Checkpointing is mainly used for *garbage collection* and *node synchronization*, allowing nodes to prune history or bootstrap from a snapshot. It typically occurs at fixed intervals and only needs to complete eventually. In contrast, the justification layer runs continuously on top of the finality layer and is time-sensitive. Its goal is not merely to agree on state snapshots, but to allow light clients to verify and follow the finalized chain. To avoid stale views, the justification layer must remain closely synchronized with finality, unlike checkpointing.

In essence, the justification layer aims to: (1) Let light clients track the finalized blocks while staying closely aligned with the finality layer. (2) Impose minimal overhead on validators. (3) Provide succinct justification proofs, typically quorum certificates, using aggregatable or threshold signatures such as BLS [4]. (4) Allow light clients to verify ancestry between justified blocks using commitment structures such as Merkle Mountain Ranges, which support efficient inclusion proofs and incremental updates [7,37].

3 BEEFY Overview

BEEFY is a justification layer protocol that supports light clients and cross-chain bridging by providing succinct proofs of finalized blocks, enabling secure and efficient tracking of the finalized chain. Built on top of the finality layer, it operates exclusively on the canonical chain of finalized blocks and therefore assumes a fork-free view of the blockchain, avoiding consensus complexities such as fork resolution and equivocation. The only faulty behavior BEEFY must address is validators voting for blocks outside the finalized chain.

Operating solely on finalized blocks allows BEEFY to rely on a single type of quorum certificate, called a *justification proof.* A justification proof is considered *valid* for a block b if it satisfies (1), i.e., it contains signatures from at least $2f+1$ distinct validators attesting to b's justification:

$$\mathrm{Justified}(b) \triangleq \left|\{v \in \Pi \mid \mathrm{Voted}(v, b)\}\right| \geq 2f + 1. \tag{1}$$

Here, $\mathrm{Voted}(v, b)$ is true if validator v has voted for block b. A valid justification proof enables light clients and cross-chain bridges to track the finalized chain.

Since honest validators vote only for finalized blocks, $f+1$ signatures would, in principle, suffice to ensure that a justification proof for a block b includes at least one honest vote. However, BEEFY requires $2f+1$ signatures because these proofs are used in a probabilistic sampling protocol for cross-chain bridging. As part of sampling, only $m < f$ signatures are randomly checked to reduce costs; requiring $2f+1$ signatures guarantees that a majority are honest, making it highly likely that the sampled subset includes at least one honest signature [3].

Each attempt by validators to generate a justification proof for a finalized block is called a *round*. Since the canonical chain contains at most one finalized block per height, rounds are in one-to-one correspondence with finalized block heights. A round number r and a height h refer to the same block iff $r = h$. We use the terms round and height interchangeably and denote the finalized block at height/round i by b_i.

At a high level, BEEFY works as follows. Whenever a validator receives either (i) a finalized block or (ii) a justification proof that advances its view of the finalized or justified chain, it updates its state and executes the *round selection algorithm* (Algorithm 1). The algorithm then outputs a round r, and the validator votes for block b_r.

Since BEEFY operates only on finalized blocks, validator set changes are handled by the underlying layers. At the start of each epoch, the validator set Π may be replaced by a new set Π'. To ensure safety during this transition, the first finalized block of each epoch must include Π' and a cryptographic commitment to it, denoted $C(\Pi')$. Such blocks are called *mandatory blocks.*

If a proposer omits Π' or $C(\Pi')$, honest validators in the underlying layers reject the block and the duty to produce a valid block passes to the next proposer. This process repeats until a valid block b is produced and finalized. By construction, b is the first finalized block of the new epoch and is therefore a mandatory block that must be justified. Once b is justified, validators can safely update from Π to Π' and thus verify later justification proofs against Π'.

To allow light clients to verify justification proofs safely, mandatory blocks must be justified in strict sequential order. A justification proof that depends on Π' is valid only if the light client has already accepted $C(\Pi')$. To enforce sequential ordering, validators ignore justification proofs for blocks whose height exceeds that of their highest mandatory block M while M remains unjustified, ensuring that mandatory blocks are justified strictly sequentially. Non-mandatory blocks only need to be justified at increasing heights. Honest validators are required to store justification proofs for mandatory blocks in the set $\mathcal{M}$, allowing validators to easily provide these proofs to light clients and other validators. Proofs for non-mandatory blocks, however, need not be stored beyond an epoch, and can therefore be pruned.

3.1 Round Selection

The round selection algorithm ensures that mandatory blocks are justified in order and keeps the justification layer up-to-date with the finality layer. If a mandatory block has not yet been justified, the algorithm forces validators to vote for the earliest such block, guaranteeing sequential justification. Once all mandatory blocks are justified, voting can proceed for non-mandatory blocks.

At a high level, validators compute rounds using a *bounded jump* based on the gap between their highest justified and finalized heights. The jump progresses in powers of two, so when the gap is small, rounds advance roughly one by one, and validators vote on consecutive finalized blocks. As the gap grows, several consecutive finalized blocks may fall within the same power of two interval, creating a many-to-one mapping from block heights to rounds. Validators therefore skip intermediate finalized blocks within the same interval, reducing communication overhead while still allowing honest validators to converge. Intuitively, the next round is either the lowest unjustified mandatory block or the highest finalized block whose height differs from the last justified block by a power of two.

Validators compute rounds deterministically using Algorithm 1, which takes three input parameters: J, F, and E [17]. J represents the height of the highest justified block and F the height of the highest finalized block observed by the validator (see Fig. 2). E is the height of a mandatory block, defined as either (i) the first finalized block of the earliest epoch whose block b_E has not yet been justified, or (ii) the first finalized block of the current epoch. Since justification only applies to finalized blocks, it follows that $F \geq J$.

Algorithm 1. Round Selection

```
function SelectRound(J, F, E)          ▷ J = highest justified, F = highest finalized
    if J = F then
        return no vote
    if Justified(b_E) then
        E' ← nextMandatory(J, F, E)     ▷ height of next mandatory block or ∞
        jump ← p(⌊(F − J + 1)/2⌋)       ▷ p(x) smallest power of two ≥ x
        r ← min(E', J + jump)
    else
        r ← E                           ▷ force current mandatory block
    return r
```

Example 1 demonstrates the behavior of the round selection algorithm.

Example 1. Suppose J is fixed at 0 (genesis block), E is ignored, and finalized blocks arrive sequentially as b_1, b_2, b_3 and so on. These finalized blocks are highlighted in blue in Fig. 3, which also shows how Algorithm 1 maps rounds to these blocks. The number above each group indicates the round to which those blocks are mapped. For example, blocks b_1 and b_2 both map to round 1, illustrating how consecutive blocks can share the same round. The figure also demonstrates the jumping mechanism, where the round and number of blocks per round double at each step, except between the first and second step. This exception arises from the flooring operation in the jump calculation.

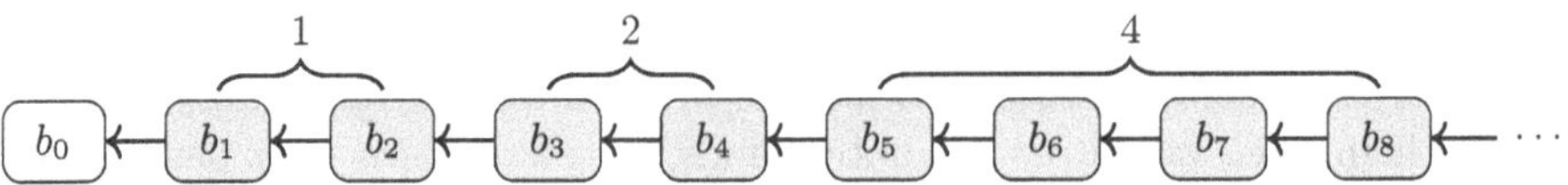

Fig. 3. Round selection behavior with fixed J and sequential arrival of finalized blocks.

3.2 Handling Divergent Validator Views

From this point on, our description of BEEFY differs from Polkadot's informal specification [17], following its implementation instead [36]. Polkadot's specification restricts a validator to at most one active round, whereas we allow validators to participate in multiple rounds simultaneously. Limiting validators to a single round can lead to a deadlock when validators have divergent views of J and F (see Sect. 7 for an example).

To support participation in multiple rounds, each validator maintains a local set $\mathcal{A}$ that records the rounds it is currently trying to justify. Each round r is classified according to the validator's local state as follows: (1) *active* if $r \in (J, F]$ and $r \in \mathcal{A}$, meaning the validator is trying to justify r; (2) *stale* if $r \leq J$; (3) *inactive* if it is neither active nor stale. Because validators may have inconsistent views of J, F, and $\mathcal{A}$, they can classify rounds differently. Whenever J is updated, the validator prunes $\mathcal{A}$ by removing all rounds $\leq J$, thus discarding stale rounds.

The goal of the round selection algorithm is to ensure that at least $2f + 1$ validators eventually converge on the same round. Convergence is therefore defined with respect to such a quorum and can occur in the following cases: (i) Values of J and F are aligned. (ii) A new mandatory block is identified. (iii) Validators share the same J but have differing F values that fall within the same power of two interval relative to J, causing the round selection algorithm to return the same round (Example 1). (iv) Validators hold different J but update F sequentially such that their active rounds intersect (Example 2).

Example 2. Let $\Pi = \{v_0, v_1, v_2, v_3\} = \Pi_h$, and suppose each validator $v_i \in \Pi$ has a distinct height for its highest justified block, i.e., $J[v_i] = i$, where i is the height of block b_i. We assume finalized blocks are received strictly in sequence: if a validator v has $F[v] = k$, it receives block b_{k+1} next, then b_{k+2}, and so on. After executing the round selection algorithm for each newly received block, the validators' active rounds are shown in Table 1. Although the sets of active rounds differ, they intersect. Notably, round 4 appears in the sets of v_0, v_2, and v_3, showing that a justification proof can be formed even when validators have different values of J.

4 Specification

When specifying the BEEFY protocol, we base it on the description in Sect. 3. Our goal is to isolate BEEFY as a message-driven voting protocol operating atop a

Table 1. Each row i lists the set of active rounds computed by validator v_i.

Validator	Value of J	Active Rounds
v_0	0	$\{1, 2, 4, 8, 16, \dots\}$
v_1	1	$\{2, 3, 5, 9, 17, \dots\}$
v_2	2	$\{3, 4, 6, 10, 18, \dots\}$
v_3	3	$\{4, 5, 7, 11, 19, \dots\}$

stream of finalized blocks, rather than replicating the full architecture depicted in Fig. 1, with the corresponding TLA$^+$ specification available at [14]. To achieve this isolation, we introduce a set of modeling abstractions that preserve the core behavior. We describe five such abstractions below.

(i) We assume a fixed validator set that does not change over time, even across epoch boundaries. Although we model mandatory blocks, they do not include validator set updates as they would in a concrete program. Supporting dynamic validator sets would require specifying exactly when an update should occur, for example, whether it takes effect once the mandatory block of epoch n is justified or after k additional epochs.
(ii) We model block production and the finality layer as a single black-box component that outputs a canonical chain of finalized blocks. This lets us ignore forks, non-finalized blocks, and intermediate steps between block proposal and finalization. Since honest validators vote only on finalized blocks, omitting non-finalized blocks merely excludes faulty validators voting on them. Within our model, the finality layer finalizes one block at a time at consecutive heights.
(iii) We model updates to F such that whenever a validator updates from F to F', it also receives all intermediate blocks between F and F'. However, the round selection algorithm is invoked only for block F', even if intermediate blocks exist. We do not impose the same modeling choice for updates to J, since there is no guarantee that blocks between J and J' have justification proofs.
(iv) We model votes by mapping each block to the set of validators that have voted for it, rather than tracking the votes received by each validator individually. This eliminates per-validator bookkeeping and message passing. The blockchain is modeled as a shared structure in which validators can receive blocks whenever possible and update their value of F accordingly. A validator can update its value of J once a justification proof for a later block exists.
(v) In a concrete program, an epoch typically consists of a fixed number of slots, and each block is assigned to a specific slot, such that the epoch can be derived from the slot number. In our specification, we take the opposite approach: blocks carry only an epoch number, with the requirement that a block's epoch is greater than or equal to its parent. This abstraction offers two advantages: (i) it naturally accommodates epochs without any blocks,

and (ii) it removes the need to define a bound on the number of slots per epoch. As a result, each block is identified solely by its ID, height, parent, and epoch number.

Our TLA$^+$ specification follows the standard TLA$^+$ structure, in which the system is described by a single formula defining a state machine [23]:

$$Spec \triangleq Init \land \square[Next]_{vars} \land L \tag{2}$$

The specification *Spec* asserts that any behavior[1] must start in a state satisfying the initial predicate *Init*, and that all system transitions must either correspond to an *action* described in *Next* or leave the variables *vars* unchanged (a *stuttering step*). In addition, all behaviors must satisfy the fairness constraints specified by L. The use of fairness constraints will be explored in Sect. 5.2.

In TLA$^+$, it is common to classify each action in *Next* as either a *system* action or an *environment* action [23]. System actions capture the protocol's internal behavior, such as processing justification proofs and casting votes. Environment actions represent everything outside the protocol's internal scope, such as producing and finalizing blocks. For the justification layer, the only relevant interaction with the environment is receiving finalized blocks; how those blocks are produced is outside its concern. This separation clearly distinguishes the behavior managed by the protocol from what is provided by the environment.

We model the behavior of honest validators using a two-step procedure controlled by a program counter *pc*. For each honest validator $v \in \Pi_h : pc[v] \in$ {"Receive","Vote"} indicates whether the validator is ready to receive a finalized block or a justification proof ("Receive"), or running the round selection algorithm and casting a vote ("Vote"). Whenever J or F is updated, *pc* is set to "Vote", and after voting it is reset to "Receive".

The behavior of faulty validators is left unconstrained: they may vote for any finalized block at any time. Unlike honest validators, they maintain no local state and are assumed to possess a global view of the system, enabling them to act arbitrarily based on that information.

Validator behavior is simple under normal operation; however, updating E requires handling an edge case. Although epochs typically contain at least one finalized block, it is theoretically possible for an epoch to contain none. In that case, transitioning from E to E' requires skipping one or more empty epochs. While rare in systems such as Polkadot, where epochs span 2400 slots, this scenario is captured in our specification.

Whenever J or F is updated, the validator checks whether E should be updated to the height of a later mandatory block. If the block b_E is justified and $\text{epoch}[b_F] > \text{epoch}[b_E]$, then the validator considers the set of block heights

$$\mathcal{E} = \{\text{height}[b] \mid b \in \mathcal{B}_F \land \text{epoch}[b] > \text{epoch}[b_E]\},$$

[1] A *behavior* is an infinite sequence of states, where a *state* is any assignment of values to variables. A step of a behavior is any pair of consecutive states in the behavior.

where $\mathcal{B}_F$ denotes the set of finalized blocks with height at most F. The new value of E is set to the minimum of $\mathcal{E}$, i.e., the height of the first finalized block in the earliest epoch following the current E. For finalized blocks, this check is an optimization, since the round selection algorithm already ensures validators vote for the next mandatory block whenever the computed round exceeds it.

5 Properties

In this section, we formally define *safety* and *liveness* properties of BEEFY and verify them through model checking [22].

Several safety properties follow directly from BEEFY's construction. Two examples are as follows: (i) All justified blocks lie on a single chain: a justification proof requires at least $2f + 1$ votes, while at most f validators may be faulty, so two conflicting blocks cannot both obtain justification proofs. (ii) Every justified block is also finalized: the finality layer maintains a canonical chain of finalized blocks, and honest validators vote only for finalized blocks, thus all justified blocks must be finalized. These properties are immediate consequences of how justification proofs are constructed and of the canonical chain structure, and are therefore not the primary focus of our verification. Nevertheless, we verified (i) and (ii) via model checking of a specification different from the one described in Sect. 4, where block production and the finality layer are modeled as distinct actions.

Properties related to mandatory blocks are more subtle. Recall from Sect. 3.1 that while a mandatory block remains unjustified, honest validators do not vote for any non-mandatory block. This rule ensures that mandatory blocks cannot be skipped and, consequently, that every mandatory block is eventually justified. In Sect. 5.3, we verify safety and liveness properties for mandatory blocks in an asynchronous model using TLC, and use Apalache to validate a candidate inductive invariant that implies the safety properties.

Properties concerning non-mandatory blocks—such as how far the justification layer lags behind the finality layer, or how many rounds an honest validator has active simultaneously—are dependent on having a concrete notion of when blocks become justified. Verifying these properties would require a synchronous network model, and we leave this for future work.

5.1 Safety

Before formalizing safety properties for mandatory blocks, we start with some definitions. Let $\mathcal{B}$ denote the set of all blocks in the system, and let $\mathcal{B}_{Fin} \subseteq \mathcal{B}$ denote the set of finalized blocks.

To identify mandatory blocks, we introduce the auxiliary operator IsMan(b), which determines whether a finalized block $b \in \mathcal{B}_{Fin}$ is mandatory:

$$\text{IsMan}(b) \triangleq \forall c \in \mathcal{B}_{Fin} : \text{epoch}[b] = \text{epoch}[c] \Rightarrow \text{height}[b] \leq \text{height}[c] \quad (3)$$

A block is mandatory if it is the first finalized block within its epoch.

We define two safety properties for mandatory blocks. These ensure that justification proceeds sequentially and that honest validators do not skip mandatory blocks when executing the round selection algorithm.

If a block is justified, then all mandatory blocks with height less than or equal to b are also justified:

$$\forall b, c \in \mathcal{B} : \text{Justified}(b) \land \text{IsMan}(c) \land \text{height}[c] \leq \text{height}[b] \Rightarrow \text{Justified}(c) \quad (4)$$

This ensures that the justification of any block implies the justification of all earlier mandatory blocks.

For every honest validator $v \in \Pi_h$ and each round $r \in \mathcal{A}[v]$, all mandatory blocks with height strictly less than r are stored in $\mathcal{M}[v]$, the set of mandatory blocks maintained by v:

$$\forall v \in \Pi_h : \forall r \in \mathcal{A}[v] : \forall b \in \mathcal{B} : \text{IsMan}(b) \land \text{height}[b] < r \Rightarrow b \in \mathcal{M}[v] \quad (5)$$

This ensures that an honest validator only includes a round in $\mathcal{A}[v]$ if all lower mandatory blocks have already been justified and stored in $\mathcal{M}[v]$. The block at height r is excluded, as it may still be in the process of being justified.

5.2 Liveness

We define two liveness properties to ensure mandatory blocks are eventually justified and received by all honest validators.

Every mandatory block will eventually be justified:

$$\forall b \in \mathcal{B} : \text{IsMan}(b) \leadsto \text{Justified}(b) \quad (6)$$

The temporal operator $\leadsto$ ("leads to") expresses that whenever the left-hand condition becomes true, the right-hand condition must hold either immediately or at some future point. Thus, for every mandatory block b, once $\text{IsMan}(b)$ holds, $\text{Justified}(b)$ must hold now or in the future.

Mandatory blocks are eventually received by all honest validators:

$$\forall b \in \mathcal{B} : \text{IsMan}(b) \leadsto \big(\forall v \in \Pi_h : J[v] \geq \text{height}[b]\big) \quad (7)$$

In other words, if b is a mandatory block, every honest validator v will eventually have $J[v] \geq \text{height}[b]$. Combined with safety property (5), this entails that all honest validators eventually receive and store every mandatory block in $\mathcal{M}[v]$.

To verify the liveness properties, we impose fairness constraints on protocol actions to prevent honest validators from indefinitely postponing enabled actions. TLA$^+$ provides two fairness conditions for actions: *weak fairness*, which requires continuously enabled actions to eventually occur, and *strong fairness*, which requires infinitely often enabled actions to eventually occur. In our specification, once an action becomes enabled, it remains enabled until it is taken or disabled by a higher-priority action. We therefore assume weak fairness for all actions in *Next* corresponding to honest validators, and no fairness for faulty validators.

The liveness properties hold even under full asynchrony due to our assumption of weak fairness on the following actions: finalized blocks are continually produced, blocks are eventually received, validators cast a vote whenever enabled, and justification proofs are eventually received. Whenever a mandatory block remains unjustified, honest validators will keep voting on it each time the round selection algorithm is invoked. Although network delays may prevent agreement on non-mandatory blocks, validators eventually converge on mandatory blocks, which therefore become justified.

5.3 Model Checking

Although the specification allows an arbitrary number of blocks, epochs, and validators, we construct a finite-state model to verify mandatory blocks in the asynchronous setting by leveraging two properties. First, honest validators never vote for a non-mandatory block if any mandatory block remains unjustified. Second, the first finalized block of each epoch is always mandatory.

For the finite model, we consider $|\Pi| = 4$, with three honest validators and one faulty, the minimal configuration tolerating a single faulty validator ($f = 1$). We also bound the number of epochs to at most three, including the initial epoch (epoch 0), allowing behaviors to span up to two additional epochs, which may themselves be empty. Thus, at most three mandatory blocks can occur.

Despite having only one faulty validator, the model exhibits a large number of possible next-state actions, due to the faulty validator's ability to vote for any finalized block at any time. This creates numerous interleavings, primarily driven by the faulty validator's actions, for each honest step, all of which must be considered by the model checker. This structure gives rise to many possible long traces before honest progress accumulates, which is challenging for bounded model checkers such as Apalache, which reason about executions up to a fixed step bound and often require reductions that shorten traces. In contrast, explicit-state model checkers such as TLC are driven primarily by the reachable state space rather than by an a priori bound on trace length.

With this setup, we verify behaviors containing 4, 5, and 6 blocks. The model checking results are summarized in Table 2, which were computed on an AMD Ryzen 5900X with 64 GB of memory running Ubuntu 24.04. The second column reports runtimes for safety-only checking, while the third column reports runtimes for liveness-only checking; for liveness checking, no safety properties are evaluated. The fourth column gives the number of distinct states explored, while the fifth column reports how many of these states arise from a faulty validator.

The table highlights the state-explosion problem: both the number of states and runtime grow exponentially. A major contributor is the faulty validator, which accounts for roughly 52%–63% of the states. Note that these faulty state counts are approximate: when running with multiple cores, TLC updates per-action counters non-deterministically, so they may vary across runs, unlike the deterministic total state count.

Liveness checking increases runtime substantially, as shown in Table 2. Safety properties are evaluated at each state and can be checked in parallel, whereas

Table 2. Runtime and state-space data for different numbers of blocks.

$\|\mathcal{B}\|$	Safety	Liveness	Distinct States	Distinct Faulty
4	27 s	7 m 08 s	669 k	350 k
5	09 m 09 s	10 h 38 m 13 s	12 M	7 M
6	2 h 29 m 09 s	–	187 M	118 M

liveness checking relies on a sequential algorithm for finding strongly connected components, forcing TLC to pause state exploration. To reduce overhead, liveness is checked only periodically (after $\approx 10\%$ increase in distinct states). Moreover, liveness in TLA$^+$ is evaluated under fairness assumptions, which must be incorporated into the cycle detection, further increasing computational and memory costs. For $|\mathcal{B}| = 6$, liveness checking exhausted available memory.

To gain additional confidence beyond finite-state checking with TLC, we formulated a candidate inductive invariant, Inv, and used Apalache to validate and iteratively strengthen it through a counterexample-driven process. An *inductive invariant* is a predicate over system states that satisfies two conditions: (i) every initial state satisfies Inv, and (ii) for any state that satisfies Inv, every valid next-state transition also produces a state that satisfies Inv. By induction, this ensures that Inv holds in all reachable states. If Inv implies the safety properties of interest, then those properties hold in all behaviors of the specification.

We used Apalache to check inductiveness over finite instances—executions with up to 6 blocks, 4 validators, and 3 epochs. For all such instances, the invariant is inductive, providing strong evidence that it may generalize to parameterized system sizes. Establishing this formally would require a formal proof, for example using TLAPS, which we leave for future work. The inductive invariant identified here provides a natural starting point for such a proof.

6 Related Work

While substantial work exists on formal verification of BFT-based consensus protocols, including Tendermint, HotStuff, Jolteon, and DAG-based [2,5,19,31,32,35], these efforts focus on verifying safety or liveness at the consensus layer. In contrast, we assume a correct finality layer and study a justification-layer protocol built atop it, allowing us to abstract from the underlying consensus mechanism and focus specifically on properties unique to the justification layer.

There is also work on the design of light client protocols [7,12], but these works do not formally specify their protocols or verify their properties.

The line of work closest to ours is the formal verification of cross-chain and interoperability protocols [11,25–27,30,38], using tools such as TLA$^+$, Isabelle/HOL [28], Event-B [1], and Quint [18]. Wei et al. [38] use TLA$^+$ and TLC to analyze the IBC protocol on finite models; like our work, they rely on abstractions and explicit bounds to keep model checking tractable. Nehaï et al. [27] provide a TLA$^+$ formal proof of a cross-chain swap, trading exhaustive exploration for a more manual process. Marić et al. [26] verify safety properties of a fail-safe cross-chain bridge in Isabelle/HOL, but do not verify liveness properties. Llambías et al. [25] formalize a gateway-based blockchain interoperability solution in Event-B, while Pillai et al. [30] verify a burn-to-claim interoperability protocol with the PAT model checker. Recent work by Chaidos et al. [11] uses Quint, an executable specification language closely related to TLA$^+$, to model-check blockchain bridges and identify bounded counterexamples and potential attack vectors. Taken together, these works study different cross-chain interoperability designs and make varying trade-offs between automation, abstraction level, and verification guarantees. In contrast, we provide a formal specification and verification of a justification-layer protocol, rather than of a cross-chain interoperability design.

7 Lessons Learned

In this section, we present one key finding from our formal specification of BEEFY and four lessons learned from the specification and verification process.

Our finding is that model checking revealed a deadlock in Polkadot's informal specification, which we denote as *ISpec*. In Sect. 3.2, we explained that our specification, denoted *Spec*, differs from *ISpec*, and that *ISpec* admits behaviors that can deadlock. Specifically, *ISpec* restricts each validator to at most one round at a time, whereas *Spec* permits multiple concurrent rounds. Restricting validators to a single round does not by itself imply deadlock. However, *ISpec* further requires that a round concludes for a validator only after it collects $2f+1$ votes for that round or receives a justification proof for a later round. Because *ISpec* does not guarantee that all validators participate in the same round, validators may wait indefinitely in different rounds. As a result, no round gathers sufficient votes to conclude, and no further justification proofs are generated. We illustrate such a deadlocking behavior of *ISpec* in Example 3.

Example 3. Let $\Pi = \{v_1, v_2, v_3, v_4\}$ be the set of validators, where v_1, v_2, and v_3 are honest, and v_4 is faulty and remains silent. Each honest validator starts with $J = F = 0$, corresponding to the genesis block b_0. Subsequently, blocks b_1, b_2, and b_3 are proposed and finalized, forming the chain $b_0 \leftarrow b_1 \leftarrow b_2 \leftarrow b_3$, where the subscript indicates the block height. Eventually, each validator updates its view of the highest finalized block, resulting in $F[v_1] = 1$, $F[v_2] = 2$, and $F[v_3] = 3$. When the round selection algorithm is invoked, the resulting votes are $\{(v_1, b_1), (v_2, b_1), (v_3, b_2)\}$. In this state, no block has collected enough votes to form a justification proof. Later, v_1 and v_2 update their views to $F = 3$. However, because they have already participated in an active round (round 1), they do not invoke the round selection algorithm again, thus resulting in a deadlock.

We discovered the deadlocking behavior of Example 3 while model checking an earlier version of our specification that more closely followed *ISpec*; this specification is also publicly available at [14]. In the earlier version, a validator could vote only if no vote existed for any blocks in the interval $(b_J, b_F]$, preventing it from reconsidering its vote, thereby enabling the deadlock described above.

After discussing this behavior with the Web3 Foundation (the third author of this paper[2]), we confirmed that the deadlock was a bug in *ISpec*, and that it cannot occur in the implementation, which allows validators to participate in multiple rounds simultaneously [29].

The first lesson concerns the choice of atomicity granularity. When formalizing an informal specification, determining which operations to model as atomic steps is a central design decision. Rather than starting from a highly abstract model and refining it stepwise, we found it more effective to formalize each procedure directly and then merge fine-grained steps into coarser ones, balancing readability against state-space size. For example, we represent updates to J, F, and E as a single step, while casting a vote remains a separate step. Representing the protocol using two steps, rather than one or three, proved to be a good compromise between understandability and state-space size.

The second lesson concerns the modeling abstractions we employed in Sect. 4. We found that carefully chosen abstractions can drastically reduce the state space while preserving the properties under verification. For example, abstraction ii models block production and the finality layer as a single black-box component by combining them into a single atomic step. This eliminates intermediate states and actions, such as faulty validators voting on non-finalized blocks, that are irrelevant when focusing on mandatory blocks. Another example, abstraction v, replaces slot numbers with epoch numbers, observing that the justification layer depends only on the sequence of finalized blocks and epoch boundaries. Rather than fixing each epoch to contain a predetermined number of slots, the model reasons directly over epochs and blocks, thus abstracting away unnecessary slot-level details. Overall, our experience reinforces that every modeling detail should be motivated by the properties under verification and balanced against its impact on state-space size and the readability of the specification. This challenge is not unique to our work: Wei et al. [38] similarly report the need to apply abstractions to keep the verification through model checking feasible.

The third lesson concerns the cost of liveness verification in TLC, which is inherently more expensive than safety checking as described in Sect. 5.3. The runtime measurements in Table 2 illustrate the asymmetry: for $|\mathcal{B}| = 4$, safety checking completes in 36 s, whereas liveness checking takes over seven minutes; for $|\mathcal{B}| = 6$, liveness checking exhausts available memory. We found it useful to first verify safety properties on the largest feasible model, including invariants expected to be violated, before attempting liveness checking.

The final lesson concerns verification workflow. After checking the basic safety and liveness properties on the largest feasible model with TLC, we found it effective to use Apalache to check whether candidate invariants are inductive. If a candidate invariant is not inductive, Apalache produces a counterexample from a satisfying pre-state to a violating post-state, which supports iterative refinement. This follows the recommended TLA$^+$ workflow [21]: use TLC first, Apalache second to check inductiveness, and TLAPS last for formal proofs, with

[2] Previously affiliated with Web3 Foundation Research.

each step requiring more effort but yielding stronger guarantees. The same trade-off appears in related work: Nehaï et al. [27] and Marić et al. [26] likewise use proof-oriented verification rather than model checking alone, gaining stronger guarantees for the properties they verify at the cost of less automation.

8 Conclusion

We have presented a formal specification of BEEFY and shown that model checking safety and liveness properties for mandatory blocks, together with using Apalache to help discover and validate a candidate inductive invariant through counterexamples, is a viable verification approach. Building on this, we showed that, although the underlying layers are complex, modeling only the guarantees they provide allowed us to abstract away most details, making verification of the justification layer feasible. We also showed that Polkadot's informal specification admitted a deadlock that could be resolved by allowing multiple active rounds, highlighting how formal specification and model checking can reveal subtle flaws in informal designs.

References

1. Abrial, J.R.: Modeling in Event-B: System and Software Engineering. Cambridge University Press (2010). https://doi.org/10.1017/CBO9781139195881
2. Bertrand, N., Ghorpade, P., Rubin, S., Scholz, B., Subotić, P.: Reusable formal verification of DAG-based consensus protocols. In: Dutle, A., Humphrey, L., Titolo, L. (eds.) NFM 2025. LNCS, vol. 15682, pp. 138–158. Springer, Cham (2025). https://doi.org/10.1007/978-3-031-93706-4_9
3. Bhatt, B.N., Shirazi, F., Stewart, A.: Trustless bridges via random sampling light clients. In: Avarikioti, Z., Christin, N. (eds.) 7th Conference on Advances in Financial Technologies (AFT 2025). Leibniz International Proceedings in Informatics (LIPIcs), vol. 354, pp. 31:1–31:24. Schloss Dagstuhl – Leibniz-Zentrum für Informatik, Dagstuhl, Germany (2025). https://doi.org/10.4230/LIPIcs.AFT.2025.31
4. Boneh, D., Drijvers, M., Neven, G.: Compact multi-signatures for smaller blockchains. Cryptology ePrint Archive, Paper 2018/483 (2018). https://eprint.iacr.org/2018/483
5. Braithwaite, S., et al.: A tendermint light client (2020). https://arxiv.org/abs/2010.07031
6. Buchman, E., Kwon, J., Milosevic, Z.: The latest gossip on BFT consensus (2019). https://arxiv.org/abs/1807.04938
7. Bunz, B., Kiffer, L., Luu, L., Zamani, M.: FlyClient: super-light clients for cryptocurrencies. In: 2020 IEEE Symposium on Security and Privacy, SP 2020, San Francisco, CA, USA, 18–21 May 2020. pp. 928–946. IEEE (2020). https://doi.org/10.1109/SP40000.2020.00049
8. Burdges, J., et al.: Overview of polkadot and its design considerations (2020). https://arxiv.org/abs/2005.13456
9. Buterin, V.: A next-generation smart contract and decentralized application platform. Whitepaper (2014). https://github.com/ethereum/wiki/wiki/White-Paper

10. Buterin, V., Griffith, V.: Casper the friendly finality gadget (2019). https://arxiv.org/abs/1710.09437
11. Chaidos, P., et al.: Crossing with confidence: Formal analysis and model checking of blockchain bridges. Cryptology ePrint Archive, Paper 2026/292 (2026). https://eprint.iacr.org/2026/292
12. Chatzigiannis, P., Baldimtsi, F., Chalkias, K.: SoK: blockchain light clients. In: Eyal, I., Garay, J. (eds.) FC 2022. LNCS, vol. 13411. pp. 615–641. Springer, Heidelberg (2022). https://doi.org/10.1007/978-3-031-18283-9_31
13. DefiLlama: Hacks (2025). https://defillama.com/hacks. Accessed 18 Nov 2025
14. Dirdal, D.O.: Formal specification of BEEFY (2025). https://github.com/relab/formal-modeling-beefy-artifacts
15. Dwork, C., Lynch, N., Stockmeyer, L.: Consensus in the presence of partial synchrony. J. ACM **35**(2), 288–323 (1988). https://doi.org/10.1145/42282.42283
16. Foundation, E., Contributors, C.S.: Ethereum consensus specification: altair light client sync protocol (2024). https://ethereum.github.io/consensus-specs/specs/altair/light-client/sync-protocol/
17. Foundation, W.: Finality. https://spec.polkadot.network/sect-finality
18. Informal Systems: Quint: The quint specification language (2026). https://quint-lang.org/
19. Jehl, L.: Formal verification of HotStuff. In: Peters, K., Willemse, T.A.C. (eds.) FORTE 2021. LNCS, vol. 12719, pp. 197–204. Springer, Cham (2021). https://doi.org/10.1007/978-3-030-78089-0_13
20. Konnov, I., Kukovec, J., Tran, T.H.: TLA+ model checking made symbolic. Proc. ACM Program. Lang. **3**(OOPSLA) (2019). https://doi.org/10.1145/3360549
21. Konnov, I., Kuppe, M., Merz, S.: Specification and Verification with the TLA+ Trifecta: TLC, Apalache, and TLAPS. In: Margaria, T., Steffen, B. (eds.) ISoLA 2022. LNCS, vol. 13701, pp. 88–105. Springer, Cham (2022). https://doi.org/10.1007/978-3-031-19849-6_6
22. Lamport, L.: Proving the correctness of multiprocess programs. IEEE Trans. Softw. Eng. SE **3**(2), 125–143 (1977). https://doi.org/10.1109/TSE.1977.229904
23. Lamport, L.: Specifying Systems: The TLA+ Language and Tools for Hardware and Software Engineers. Addison-Wesley Longman Publishing Co., Inc., USA (2002)
24. Lamport, L., Shostak, R., Pease, M.: The byzantine generals problem. ACM Trans. Program. Lang. Syst. **4**, 382–401 (1982)
25. Llambías, G., González, L., Ruggia, R.: Formalising a gateway-based blockchain interoperability solution with event-B. In: 2024 IEEE International Conference on Blockchain and Cryptocurrency (ICBC), pp. 1–9. (2024). https://doi.org/10.1109/ICBC59979.2024.10634427
26. Marić, F., Scholz, B., Subotić, P.: Formal verification of a fail-safe cross-chain bridge. In: Marmsoler, D., Xu, M. (eds.) 6th International Workshop on Formal Methods for Blockchains (FMBC 2025). Open Access Series in Informatics (OASIcs), vol. 129, pp. 8:1–8:18. Schloss Dagstuhl – Leibniz-Zentrum für Informatik, Dagstuhl (2025). https://doi.org/10.4230/OASIcs.FMBC.2025.8
27. Nehaï, Z., Bobot, F., Tucci-Piergiovanni, S., Delporte-Gallet, C., Fauconnier, H.: A TLA+ formal proof of a cross-chain swap. In: Proceedings of the 23rd International Conference on Distributed Computing and Networking., ICDCN 2022, pp. 148–159. Association for Computing Machinery, New York (2022). https://doi.org/10.1145/3491003.3491006

28. Nipkow, T., Paulson, L.C., Wenzel, M.: Isabelle/HOL: A Proof Assistant for Higher-Order Logic. Lecture Notes in Computer Science, vol. 2283. Springer, Cham (2002). https://doi.org/10.1007/3-540-45949-9
29. ParityTech: Polkadot SDK. https://github.com/paritytech/polkadot-sdk
30. Pillai, B., Hóu, Z., Biswas, K., Muthukkumarasamy, V.: Formal verification of the burn-to-claim blockchain interoperable protocol. In: Li, Y., Tahar, S. (eds.) ICFEM 2023. LNCS, vol. 14308, pp. 249–254. Springer Nature Singapore, Singapore (2023). https://doi.org/10.1007/978-981-99-7584-6_15
31. Qiu, L., Kim, Y., Shin, J.Y., Kim, J., Honoré, W., Shao, Z.: Lido: linearizable byzantine distributed objects with refinement-based liveness proofs. Proc. ACM Program. Lang. **8**(PLDI) (2024). https://doi.org/10.1145/3656423
32. Qiu, L., Xiao, J., Shin, J.Y., Shao, Z.: Lido-DAG: a framework for verifying safety and liveness of DAG-based consensus protocols. Proc. ACM Program. Lang. **9**(PLDI) (2025). https://doi.org/10.1145/3729306
33. Stewart, A., Kokoris-Kogia, E.: Grandpa: a byzantine finality gadget (2020). https://arxiv.org/abs/2007.01560
34. Team, S.: Snowbridge (2025). https://docs.snowbridge.network/. Accessed 18 Nov 2025
35. Team, T.: Tendermint specifications (2020). https://github.com/tendermint/tendermint/tree/master/spec
36. Technologies, P.: Beefy (2025). https://github.com/paritytech/polkadot-sdk/tree/master/substrate/client/consensus/beefy
37. Todd, P.: Making UTXO set growth irrelevant with low-latency delayed TXO commitments (2016). https://lists.linuxfoundation.org/pipermail/bitcoin-dev/2016-May/012715.html
38. Wei, Q., Zhao, X., Zhu, X.Y., Zhang, W.: Formal analysis of IBC protocol. In: 2023 IEEE 31st International Conference on Network Protocols (ICNP) (2023). https://doi.org/10.1109/ICNP59649.2023.10355573
39. Yin, M., Malkhi, D., Reiter, M.K., Gueta, G.G., Abraham, I.: HotStuff: BFT consensus with linearity and responsiveness. In: Proceedings of the 2019 ACM Symposium on Principles of Distributed Computing, PODC 2019, pp. 347–356. Association for Computing Machinery, New York (2019). https://doi.org/10.1145/3293611.3331591
40. Yu, Y., Manolios, P., Lamport, L.: Model checking TLA$^+$ specifications. In: Pierre, L., Kropf, T. (eds.) CHARME 1999. LNCS, vol. 1703, pp. 54–66. Springer, Heidelberg (1999). https://doi.org/10.1007/3-540-48153-2_6

Soundness of Typed Transitions in the Linear π-Calculus

Adrian Francalanza[1], Marco Giunti[2](✉), and Antonio Ravara[3]

[1] Faculty of ICT, University of Malta, Msida, Malta
[2] Faculty of Science and Technology, University of Algarve, Faro, Portugal
mgiunti@ualg.pt
[3] NOVA LINCS and NOVA FCT, Caparica, Portugal

Abstract. We present a Coq mechanisation for a Labelled Transition System (*LTS*) with global information about resource visibility and capability. The LTS states are linear π-calculus processes, *i.e.*, concurrent programs that can dynamically create and share linear and unrestricted channels on other channels, paired with the type environment that typechecks them. The type environment is augmented with auxiliary information relating to the usage status and visibility (from an interacting process perspective). This global information determines what transitions are allowed. In turn, the transitions themselves update the global information as computation progresses. The mechanisation shows that the LTS (i) observes subject reduction for well-typed linear π-calculus processes, (ii) preserves Barendregt's convention for binders, and (iii) is deployed as a certified OCaml interpreter extracted from Coq. To the best of our knowledge, this is the first mechanisation of a typed LTS for the linear π-calculus.

1 Introduction

The linear π-calculus [24], by Kobayashi *et al.*, is an influential extension of the π-calculus [27] where channels are partitioned into either linear or unrestricted. The authors develop a type system to ensure that linear channels are used exactly once, and prove a subject reduction (*SR*) property that guarantees that such usage is invariant over reductions. The calculus has been studied for its computational properties [41,42] and has acted as a foundation for more expressive formalisms such as session types [8].

Despite its merits, the linear π-calculus lacks a mechanised *typed Labelled Transition System (LTS)* that permits compositional reasoning on typed computation. Such a typed LTS judgement would take the form below to encode the following information:

$$\Gamma \triangleright P \xrightarrow{\alpha} \Gamma' \triangleright P' \qquad (1)$$

(*i*) environment Γ typechecks process P, *i.e.*, $\Gamma \vdash P$, (*ii*) process P interacts with some implicit observer process Q, denoted by the action α, (*iii*) the observer Q is itself *typed*, with respect to some implicit type environment Δ, *i.e.*, $\Delta \vdash Q$, where (*iv*) the two type environments are in agreement, *i.e.*, there exists some environment Λ that constitutes the composition of the two environment, $\Gamma + \Delta = \Lambda$, (*v*) after interacting with Q, process P transitions to a new state, P', that typechecks *wrt.* the (possibly different) environment

Published by Springer Nature Switzerland AG 2026
L. Bocchi and B. Kulahcioglu Ozkan (Eds.): FORTE 2026, LNCS 16589, pp. 112–129, 2026.
https://doi.org/10.1007/978-3-032-28187-6_7

Γ', *i.e.*, $\Gamma' \vdash P'$, and (*vi*) on its part, $\Delta \triangleright Q$ transitions on the dual of action α, *i.e.*, $\overline{\alpha}$, to a new state $\Delta' \triangleright Q'$ that also preserves typing.

Challenges. Several obstacles hinder the mechanisation of these behavioral frameworks in state-of-the-art proof assistants. For instance, binding constructs require proper handling of bound identifiers in order to model alpha conversion [3]; name scope extrusion further complicates this handling in the case of the π-calculus since the scope becomes dynamic. Another obstacle is the reliance on environment splitting assertions of the form $\exists \Gamma_1, \Gamma_2. \Gamma = \Gamma_1 + \Gamma_2$ when defining transition rules for parallel processes [36,43]: the inherent underspecification of how these splitting are described (note the existential quantifications) complicates the mechanisation of proof searches. The idiomatic name scoping construct, $(\nu n)P$, though central to delineate locality, poses complications other than the handling of scope extrusion. For instance, a typed LTS based on the typing of [24], cannot be used to detect and locate deadlocks by *reporting offending scoped channels via their name*, since these are subject to *change* through alpha-conversion; in a reduction semantics, this mechanism is used to distinguish between the different instances of scoped names generated by replicated/recursive processes. Name scoping also makes it hard to model and reason about resource constrained computation where accounting for the number of (scoped and free) channels in use is required. For instance, the standard structural equivalence rule $(\nu n)P \equiv P$, valid whenever n is not a free name in P, can be used both to garbage collect redundant names but also to *introduce them arbitrarily*, since the rule is symmetric.

Proposed Solution. To this end, this paper proposes a linear π-calculus reformulation, for how free and scoped channel names are represented in the LTS states $\Gamma \triangleright P$ of Eq. (1): *all* channel names are recorded in the environment, Γ, to permit *global resource reasoning* on channels, and a *uniform mechanism to reference* them. In order to still differentiate between global (*i.e.*, free) and local channels, *flags* are introduced in the environment mappings of Γ. Concretely, *visible* (v) and *hidden* (h) flags are used to correspond to free and local channels, respectively. Accordingly, the process P delimits locality via a hiding construct, $(\kappa n)P$, instead of the customary construct $(\nu n)P$, that has *no binding* functionality. To preserve locality and compositionality, the reformulation employs a third flag, *illegal* (i), which acts as the dual of the hidden flag for environment splitting, *i.e.*, $\mathtt{h} + \mathtt{i} = \mathtt{h}$. Typechecking across parallel processes can thus still be expressed in the Kobayashi *et al.* style of [24] using a (lifted) environment split. The flag annotations also permit the computation steps described in Eq. (1) to globally refer to hidden channels directly by their name, while also representing the hidden channels of the implicit observer Q (discussed earlier) via the (dual) illegal flag, i. The downside of our proposed mechanism is that the behaviour previously modelled via alpha-conversion needs to be explicitly managed by the LTS of Eq. (1).

Main Contributions. 1. The definition of a compositional typed LTS for the linear π-calculus that manages names globally and book-keeps type information after transitions. The LTS does not employ (underspecified) environment splitting nor does it rely on structural equivalence, supporting a mechanisation leading to a certified interpreter. 2. The validation of the proposed typed LTS via a mechanised SR stating that if $\Gamma \vdash P$ then $\Gamma' \vdash P'$ as well. This is the first such result for a π-calculus relying on typed labelled semantics. 3. The mechanisation of the preservation of Barendregt's convention – bound variables are distinct from free ones and all binders bind variables not already in scope, a result [7,38] that here is a corollary of SR.

Outline. Section 2 introduces the language, the type algebra, and the type system, and illustrates their mechanisation in Coq. Section 3 presents the typed labelled semantics and its mechanisation. Section 4 contains the SR theorem; details of its mechanised proof are outlined in the technical report . We conclude the section by showing how to extract a certified interpreter. Section 5 discusses related and future work, and the reusability of the techniques introduced herein. The paper contains links as *rooster images* that point to a public repository containing the *Coq development*; for instance points to the proof of SR.[1]

2 A Linear π-calculus

We employ a minimal version of the synchronous π-calculus, where replicated input is the only source of infinite behaviour. Instead of the usual name binding construct $(\nu n)P$, our calculus uses a Church-style hiding construct, $(\kappa\, n)P$, which does *not* assume alpha-conversion. The syntax given in Definition 1 assumes distinct enumerable sets for (channel) *names* $n, a, b, c, d \in \text{NAMES}$, and *variables* $x, y, z \in \text{VARS}$, and collectively refers to the set $\text{NAMES} \cup \text{VARS}$ as *identifiers*, ranged over by u, v. $N, L \subset \text{NAMES}$ denote *finite* sets of names and $M \Subset \text{NAMES}$ denote finite *multisets* of names, where $|M|$ converts M into a set by removing duplicates.

Definition 1 (Process syntax).

$$P, Q, R \in \text{PROC} ::= \mathsf{nil} \quad (\textit{inert}) \quad \mid *u?x.P \quad (\textit{replication}) \quad \mid P \| Q \quad (\textit{composition})$$
$$\mid u?x.P \quad (\textit{input}) \quad \mid u!v.P \quad (\textit{output}) \quad \mid (\kappa\, n)P \quad (\textit{hiding})$$

We often omit trailing nil and write $u!v$ in lieu of $u!v.\mathsf{nil}$. Our syntax only contains binders for variables, namely $u?x.P$ and $*u?x.P$ which have a static scope. The language does *not* employ name binders (whose scope is dynamic). We mimic the Barendregt's convention for names by only considering well-formed processes, Definition 2, where all hidden (restricted) names are disjoint from one another and also from visible (free) names. Formally, we let $\mathsf{hid}(P)$ be the multi-set of the hidden names of P where $\mathsf{hid}((\kappa\, n)P) = \mathsf{hid}(P) \uplus n$ ($\uplus$ being multi-set union); the remaining cases are homomorphic. In similar fashion, we let $\mathsf{vis}(P)$ be the multi-set of the names of P that are not hidden; the names of P are defined as $\mathbf{nm}(P) = \mathsf{hid}(P) \uplus \mathsf{vis}(P)$, and assume the predicate $\mathsf{noDup}(M) = \nexists n\,.\,\{n, n\} \Subset M$. The substitution of a *free* variable x of P with an identifier v, is noted as $P\{v/x\}$. Dynamic generation of "fresh" names at runtime (cf. Sect. 3) is mimicked by the *relabelling of a hidden* name n with another name n' not occurring "elsewhere", noted $P\{\!|n'/n|\!\}$. The following paragraph clarifies this point.

Definition 2. *A process P is* well-formed *iff* $\mathsf{noDup}(\mathsf{hid}(P))$ *and* $\mathsf{hid}(P) \Cap \mathsf{vis}(P) = \emptyset$.

[1] We find it appropriate to use the old name of the Rocq Prover since we work with an older version (Coq 8.8.2).

Mechanisation of Processes. We implement name and variables with type `name` (an alias for `nat`), thus avoiding any syntactic distinction among the two: this simplifies the treatment of type environments (*cf.* Sect. 2.2). A semantic distinction is introduced by the mechanised type system (*cf.* Sect. 2.3). Channels are implemented as *pairs of naturals* to allow us to track the replicated process body from where they are generated. See Remark 1.

```
Notation name := nat.
Inductive dproc : Set := | dZero : dproc | dBang : name → name → name → name → dproc → dproc
  | dPar : dproc → dproc → dproc | dNu : name → name → dproc → dproc
  | dInp : name → name → name → name → dproc → dproc | dOut : name → name → name → name →
  dproc → dproc.
Lemma nat_pair_eq_dec : ∀ n m : name * name, {n = m} + {n ≠ m}.
```

We import `Coq.Lists.List` with `secLabs` providing *hidden channels* of processes (*cf.* hid).

```
Fixpoint secLabs (p : dproc) := match p with | dZero ⇒ nil | dPar p q ⇒ secLabs q ++ secLabs p
  | dBang p | dInp p | dOut p ⇒ secLabs p | dNu h i p ⇒ secLabs p ++ (h, i) :: nil end.
```

The substitution $P\{v/x\}$ is implemented as `pmap v1 v2 x1 x2`. Relabelling is only defined for processes that do not reuse a hidden channel twice (*cf.* Definition 2 and `List.NoDup`). Function `dep_relabel` receives a process, a multiset of channels, and *a proof* that the hidden channels of the process are unique, and returns a process where all hidden channels are relabelled by *shifting* the second entry of each channel with the maximal value among the second entries of the input multiset (*cf.* Remark 1).

```
Fixpoint max (l : list (nat*nat)) : nat := match l with | nil ⇒ 0
  | (_, x) :: t ⇒ let m := max t in if x <? m then m else x end.
Fixpoint dep_relabel (p : dproc) (s : list (name*name)) : NoDup s → dproc :=
  match p with | dZero ⇒ fun _ ⇒ p
  | dBang x1 x2 y1 y2 p ⇒ fun pf : NoDup s ⇒ dBang x1 x2 y1 y2 (dep_relabel p s pf)
  | dInp x1 x2 y1 y2 p ⇒ fun pf : NoDup s ⇒ dInp x1 x2 y1 y2 (dep_relabel p s pf)
  | dOut x1 x2 y1 y2 p ⇒ fun pf : NoDup s ⇒ dOut x1 x2 y1 y2 (dep_relabel p s pf )
  | dPar p q ⇒ fun pf : NoDup s ⇒ dPar (dep_relabel p s pf) (dep_relabel q s pf)
  | dNu h i p ⇒ fun pf : NoDup s ⇒ dNu h (i + max s) (pmap (dep_relabel p s pf) h i h (i + max s))
  end.
```

We use function `dep_relabel` in the definition of the *typed labelled transition system* of processes defined in Sect. 3.

Remark 1. Representing channels as pairs of `nat` is a design choice that yields two advantages. First, it allows us to generate fresh names (*i.e.*, globally unique) via `dep_relabel` in a *local manner* by simply incrementing the second element: starting with a set of unique pairs of the form `n 0`, any k increments to the second element will yield a unique pair `n k`. Second, by maintaining the first element `n` constant, we are able to retain the provenance of a dynamically generated channel; during bug reporting, this allows us to relate errors detected on dynamic code back to the channels specified in the static code.

2.1 Types and Type Environments

Types T in the universe TYP include channel types of the form $p[T]^m$, where $p \in$ POL describes the channel *input* and *output* polarities, and $m \in$ MUL describes *linear* or *unrestricted* multiplicities. We abstract over base types considering a single one, bt.

Definition 3 (Type syntax).

$$T, S ::= \mathsf{bt} \quad (base) \quad | \ p[T]^m \quad (channel) \qquad m ::= \omega \quad (unrestricted) \quad | \ \iota \quad (linear)$$
$$p, q ::= \updownarrow \quad (I/O) \quad | \ \emptyset \quad (empty) \qquad | \downarrow \quad (input) \quad | \uparrow \quad (output)$$

Type environments, ranged over by Γ and Δ, map identifiers to pairs $(\mathtt{f}, T)$, where $\mathtt{f} \in \{\mathtt{v}, \mathtt{h}, \mathtt{i}\}$ is a *flag*. The notation $\Gamma\backslash_a$ refers to Γ_1 whenever $\Gamma = \Gamma_1, a\colon (\mathtt{f}, T)$. Without name scoping, every Γ typing a process P (*cf.* Sect. 2.3) includes *all* the names of P, $\mathbf{nm}(P)$ in its domain. To compensate, flags capture the visibility of an identifier in the process being typed: *visible* ($\mathtt{v}$), *hidden* ($\mathtt{h}$), or *illegal* ($\mathtt{i}$). We refer to channels typed using linear (*resp.* unrestricted) channel types as linear (*resp.* unrestricted) channels, irrespective of their visibility status.

Mechanisation of Type Environments The representation of types in Coq follows Definition 3. Channel types are produced with constructor `chan`; type bt is renamed `Top`. The flags `vis`, `hid`, and `ill` deploy $\mathtt{v}$, $\mathtt{h}$, and $\mathtt{i}$, respectively. Type environments are represented as lists of type `typeEnv` (*cf.* Remark 2). In order to preserve their semantics, we use the predicate `isMap` asserting that a type environment implements a partial function.

```
Inductive pol : Set := empty | inp | out | io.
Inductive mode : Set := lin | un.
Inductive piType : Set := | Chan : mode → pol → piType → piType | Top : piType.
Inductive flag : Set := hid | ill | vis.
Definition typeEnv := list ((name * name) * flag * piType).
Definition isMap (g : typeENv) := ∀ x f1 t1 f2 t2, In (x, f1, t1) g ∧ In (x, f2, t2) g →
  f1 = f2 ∧ t1 = t2.
```

The *maximum* of a type environment Γ, is the maximal second entry in the domain of Γ. This is the threshold that is used by function `dep_relabel` 🐓 to perform the shifting.

```
Fixpoint domain (g: typeEnv) : list (nat * nat) :=
  match g with | (x, _, _) :: t ⇒ x :: domain t | nil ⇒ nil end.
Definition maximum (g : typeEnv) := max(domain(g)).
```

Remark 2. Type environments are represented as lists, rather than partial functions,*e.g.*, [4], because of the definition of the splitting relation $\Gamma_1 + \Gamma_2 = \Gamma$ of Fig. 1. The syntactic manipulation of flags and types in type environments with equal domain (*cf.* Sect. 2.2) is the core mechanism deployed by environment splitting. This kind of transformation is better served by data structures rather than functions. Still, we pay the price of carrying dependent proofs establishing that the list representations do indeed abstract maps.

2.2 Type Algebra

Figure 1 introduces an algebra on types based on the splitting (partial) operation $T_1 + T_2$. The operation is defined in terms of the polarity splitting of linear and unrestricted channels, which are treated differently, using, respectively, the symmetric operators $\uplus$ and $\sqcup$ (symmetric rules are elided): $\uplus$ is akin to set disjoint union (*i.e.*, a *partial* operation), whereas $\sqcup$ is akin to set union (*i.e.*, a *total* operation). Figure 1 also defines a type subtraction operation; we abuse terminology and say that T is a *super-type* of S (*resp.* S is a subtype of T) when $T - S$ is defined. Environment splitting, $\Gamma_1 + \Gamma_2$, derived from

Type Operations

$$\emptyset \uplus p = p \qquad \downarrow \uplus \uparrow = \updownarrow \qquad \updownarrow \sqcup p = \updownarrow \qquad \emptyset \sqcup p = p \qquad \downarrow \sqcup \downarrow = \downarrow \qquad \uparrow \sqcup \uparrow = \uparrow \qquad \downarrow \sqcup \uparrow = \updownarrow$$

$$\mathsf{bt}+\mathsf{bt} = \mathsf{bt} \qquad p[T]^\iota + q[T]^\iota = p \uplus q[T]^\iota \qquad p[T]^\omega + q[T]^\omega = p \sqcup q[T]^\omega$$

$$\mathsf{bt} - \mathsf{bt} = \mathsf{bt} \qquad p[T]^m - \emptyset[T]^m = p[T]^m$$

$$p[T]^\iota - p[T]^\iota = \emptyset[T]^\iota \qquad \updownarrow [T]^\iota - \downarrow [T]^\iota = \uparrow [T]^\iota \qquad \updownarrow [T]^\iota - \uparrow [T]^\iota = \downarrow [T]^\iota$$

$$p[T]^\omega - p[T]^\omega = p[T]^\omega \qquad \updownarrow [T]^\omega - \downarrow [T]^\omega = \updownarrow [T]^\omega \qquad \updownarrow [T]^\omega - \uparrow [T]^\omega = \updownarrow [T]^\omega$$

Flag Combination

$$\mathtt{h} + \mathtt{i} = \mathtt{h} = \mathtt{i} + \mathtt{h} \qquad \mathtt{v} + \mathtt{v} = \mathtt{v} \qquad \mathtt{i} + \mathtt{i} = \mathtt{i}$$

Environment Splitting Relation

$$\emptyset + \emptyset = \emptyset \qquad \frac{\Gamma_1 + \Gamma_2 = \Gamma_3 \qquad (T = \mathsf{bt} \ \vee \ T = p[S]^\omega)}{(\Gamma_1, u{:}(\mathtt{f}, T)) + (\Gamma_2, u{:}(\mathtt{g}, T)) = \Gamma_3, u{:}(\mathtt{f} + \mathtt{g}, T)}$$

$$\frac{\Gamma_1 + \Gamma_2 = \Gamma_3}{(\Gamma_1, u{:}(\mathtt{f}, p[T]^\iota)) + (\Gamma_2, u{:}(\mathtt{g}, q[T]^\iota)) = \Gamma_3, u{:}(\mathtt{f} + \mathtt{g}, p \uplus q[T]^\iota)}$$

Fig. 1. Operations on Types and Type Environments

Kobayashi *et al.* [24] is overloaded to handle visibility flags. Visible and illegal flags are idempotent, but hidden flags act as the commutative identity for the illegal flag. We follow [15] and require that split environments have the same domain.

Mechanisation of Environment Splitting. Each total operation on polarities, types, and flags of Fig. 1 is implemented as a `Fixpoint`, while partial operations in the same figure are deployed as relations defined with the command `Inductive`. We let `pol_cup` and `pol_plus` implement the polarity operators $\sqcup$ and $\uplus$, respectively, and `typ_plus` and `typ_remove` implement the type operators $+$ and $-$, respectively, and `flag_plus` implement the flag operator $+$. Predicate `flagOf g a f` (`typeOf g a t`) asserts that the flag (type) of channel a in the environment Γ is $\mathtt{f}$ (T). We use function `rm` to remove a channel n from a type environment Γ. The splitting $\Gamma_1 + \Gamma_2 = \Gamma_3$ of Fig. 1 is defined through the inductive predicate `tEnv_split`, written `tEnv_split g1 g2 g3 pf1 pf2 pf3`: each parameter `pf` $_i$, $1 \leq i \leq 3$, is a proof that Γ_i is a map.

```
Inductive tEnv_split (g1 : typeEnv) (g2 : typeEnv) (g3 : typeEnv) (pf1 : isMap g1) (pf2 : isMap g2)
  (pf3 : isMap g3) : Prop :=
  | SpNil : g1 = nil → g2 = nil → g3 = nil → tEnv_split g1 g2 g3 pf1 pf2 pf3
  | SpLin : ∀ n f f' g p q p' t g''' pf' pf'' pf''', flag_plus f g f' → pol_plus p q p' →
     In (n, f, Chan lin p t) g1 → In (n, g, Chan lin q t) g2 → rm n g3 = g''' → flagOf g3 n f' →
     typeOf g3 n (Chan lin p' t) → tEnv_split (rm n g1) (rm n g2) g''' pf' pf'' pf''' →
     tEnv_split g1 g2 g3 pf1 pf2 pf3
  | SpUn : ∀ n f f' g p t g''' pf' pf'' pf''', flag_plus f g f' → In (n, f, Chan un p t) g1 →
     In (n, g, Chan un p t) g2 → tEnv_split (rm n g1) (rm n g2) g''' pf' pf'' pf''' → rm n g3 = g''' →
     flagOf g3 n f' → typeOf g3 n (Chan un p t) → tEnv_split g1 g2 g3 pf1 pf2 pf3
  | SpTop : ∀ n f f' g g''' pf' pf'' pf''', flag_plus f g f' → In (n, f, Top) g1 →
     In (n, g, Top) g2 → rm n g3 = g''' → flagOf g3 n f' →
     tEnv_split (rm n g1) (rm n g2) g''' pf' pf'' pf''' → typeOf g3 n Top →
     tEnv_split g1 g2 g3 pf1 pf2 pf3.
```

Consumed predicate

$$\frac{}{\mathtt{cons}(\emptyset)} \qquad \frac{\mathtt{cons}(\Gamma)}{\mathtt{cons}(\Gamma, u\colon (\mathtt{f}, \mathsf{bt}))} \qquad \frac{\mathtt{cons}(\Gamma)}{\mathtt{cons}(\Gamma, u\colon (\mathtt{f}, \emptyset[T]^{\iota}))} \qquad \frac{\mathtt{cons}(\Gamma)}{\mathtt{cons}(\Gamma, u\colon (\mathtt{f}, p[T]^{\omega}))}$$

Typing Rules

$$\textsc{tNil}\ \frac{\mathtt{cons}(\Gamma)}{\Gamma \vdash \mathsf{nil}} \qquad \textsc{tInU}\ \frac{\Gamma, u{:}(\mathtt{v}, p[T]^{\omega}), x{:}(\mathtt{v}, T) \vdash P \qquad \downarrow \in p \qquad \mathtt{cons}(\mathtt{proj}_{\mathtt{v,i}}(\Gamma))}{\Gamma, u{:}(\mathtt{v}, p[T]^{\omega}) \vdash *u?x.P}$$

$$\textsc{tIn}\ \frac{\Gamma, u{:}(\mathtt{v}, p[T]^{m} - \downarrow [T]^{m}), x{:}(\mathtt{v}, T) \vdash P \qquad \downarrow \in p}{\Gamma, u{:}(\mathtt{v}, p[T]^{m}) \vdash u?x.P} \qquad \textsc{tNew}\ \frac{\Gamma, n{:}(\mathtt{v}, T) \vdash P}{\Gamma, n{:}(\mathtt{h}, T) \vdash (\kappa\, n)\,(P)}$$

$$\textsc{tPar}\ \frac{\Gamma_1 \vdash P_1 \qquad \Gamma_2 \vdash P_2}{\Gamma_1 + \Gamma_2 \vdash P_1 \,||\, P_2} \qquad \textsc{tOut}\ \frac{\Gamma, u{:}(\mathtt{v}, p[T]^{m} - \uparrow [T]^{m}), v{:}(\mathtt{v}, T' - T) \vdash P \qquad \uparrow \in p}{\Gamma, u{:}(\mathtt{v}, p[T]^{m}), v{:}(\mathtt{v}, T') \vdash u!v.P}$$

Fig. 2. Linear Type System

2.3 Type System

The type system is defined via the standard substructural typing rules in Fig. 2 using the type algebra of Fig. 1. It is a cosmetic variant of [24], and enforces the invariant that linear I/O capabilities are used exactly once through the predicate $\mathtt{cons}(\Gamma)$, to ensure that all linear permissions in a type environment are consumed. We let $\mathtt{proj}_{\mathtt{v,i}}(\emptyset) = \emptyset$, $\mathtt{proj}_{\mathtt{v,i}}(\Gamma, u\colon (\mathtt{f}, T)) = \mathtt{proj}_{\mathtt{v,i}}(\Gamma), u\colon (\mathtt{f}, T)$ when $\mathtt{f} \in \{\mathtt{v}, \mathtt{i}\}$, and $\mathtt{proj}_{\mathtt{v,i}}(\Gamma, u\colon (\mathsf{h}, T)) = \mathtt{proj}_{\mathtt{v,i}}(\Gamma)$. Note that whereas statically scoped variables add to the premise typing environment in rules tIn and tInU, hidden names are expected to be part of the conclusion type environment carrying the hidden $\mathtt{h}$ flag in rule tNew. All typing rules are syntax directed. Rule tPar poses the only source of under-specification when typechecking (bottom-up) for how to split the linear permissions across the environments Γ_1 and Γ_2.

Mechanisation of the typing rules The predicate $\mathtt{cons}$ is implemented by the inductive type `cons`. The mechanisation of the rules follows. The predicate `typeCheck` receives an environment Γ and a proof that Γ satisfies `isMap`. To ease the explanation of the rules, we use the notation $\Gamma\backslash_n$ to indicate `rm g n`.

```
Inductive typeCheck (g : typeEnv) (pf : isMap g) : dproc → Prop :=
  | TNil :  cons g pf → typeCheck g pf dZero
  | TNew : ∀ p n t pf1, In (n, hid, t) g → typeCheck ((n, vis, t) :: (rm n g)) pf1 p →
     typeCheck g  pf (dNu (fst n) (snd n) p)
  | TPar : ∀ g1 g2 p1 p2 pf1 pf2, tEnv_split g1 g2 g pf1 pf2 pf → typeCheck g1 pf1 p1 →
     typeCheck g2 pf2 p2 → typeCheck g pf (dPar p1 p2)
  | TOutL : ∀ u p t v t' q t1 t2 pf1, type_remove (Chan lin p t) (Chan lin out t) t1 →
     type_remove t' t t2 → typeCheck ((u, vis, t1) :: (v, vis, t2) :: (rm v (rm u g))) pf1 q →
     In (u, vis, Chan lin p t) g → In (v, vis, t') g →
     typeCheck g pf (dOut (fst u) (snd u) (fst v) (snd v) q)
  | TOutUn : ∀ u p t v t' q t2 pf1, (p = io ∨ p = out) → type_remove t' t t2 →
     In (u, vis, Chan un p t) g → In (v, vis, t') g → typeCheck ((v, vis, t2) :: (rm v g)) pf1 q →
     typeCheck g pf (dOut (fst u) (snd u) (fst v) (snd v) q)
  | TInL : ∀ u p t x q t1 pf1, type_remove (Chan lin p t) (Chan lin inp t) t1 →
     In (u, vis, Chan lin p t) g → ¬ In x (domain g) → snd x < maximum g →
     typeCheck ((u, vis, t1) :: (x, vis, t) :: rm u g) pf1 q →
     typeCheck g pf (dInp (fst u) (snd u) (fst x) (snd x) q)
  | TInUn : ∀ u p t x q pf1, (p = io ∨ p = inp) → In (u, vis, Chan un p t) g → ¬ In x (domain g) →
```

```
    snd x < maximum g → typeCheck ((x, vis, t) :: g) pf1 q →
    typeCheck g pf (dInp (fst u) (snd u) (fst x) (snd x) q)
  | TInU : ∀ u p t x q pf1 pf2, (p = io ∨ p = inp) → In (u, vis, Chan un p t) g →
    ¬ In x (domain g) → snd x < maximum g → cons (vis_proj g ++ ill_proj g) pf2 →
    typeCheck ( (x, vis, t) :: g) pf1 q → typeCheck g pf (dBang (fst u) (snd u) (fst x) (snd x) q).
```

Case `TNil` accepts the inert process iff the predicate `cons` ❦ holds. Case `TNew` applies when the process is $(\kappa\, n)\,(P)$, and channel n has flag h and type T in Γ, and $\Gamma\backslash_n, n\colon (\mathsf{v}, T)$ type checks P. Case `TPar` applies when we have a parallel process $P_1 \parallel P_2$ and environments Γ_1 and Γ_2 such that $\Gamma_1 + \Gamma_2 = \Gamma$ and $\Gamma_1 \vdash P_1$ and $\Gamma_2 \vdash P_2$. For each output (cf.TOUT) and input (cf.TIN) rule of Fig. 2 we have two versions corresponding to a linear or unrestricted channel subject. Case `TOutL` applies when we have an output process $u!v.Q$, and u is a linear channel of Γ. We require that: (1) both u and v are visible; (2) the subtraction T_1 of the output capability of u from the type of u is defined; (3) the subtraction T_2 of the payload type of u from the type of v is defined; (4) the environment $\Gamma\backslash_u\backslash_v, u\colon (\mathsf{v}, T_1), v\colon (\mathsf{v}, T_2)$ type checks Q. Case `TOutUn` applies when we have an output process $u!v.Q$, and u is an unrestricted channel of Γ. We weaken the conditions (2) and (4) of `TOutL`: (2) u possesses the output capability; (4) the environment $\Gamma\backslash_v, v\colon (\mathsf{v}, T_2)$ type checks Q. The rules of the input $u?x.P$ and of the replicated input $*u?x.P$ follow (*cf.* `TInL`, `TInUn`, and `TInU`, respectively). In these rules, the variable x occurring as subject of the input is treated differently from a name, although it belongs to the same syntactic category (*cf.* `name`). In particular, in all these rules we require that: (1) u is visible; (2) the input capability of u with payload T is available; (3) x *is not used* in Γ and its second component is smaller than the maximum. The first part of (3) implements a "freshness' check that avoids clashing of variables: the assumption does not pose any limitation because we can always rename all clashing variables when typing processes at compile time. The second part of (3) is a *sanity check* that is needed to preserve the soundness of relabelling; the technical report further discusses this point. Case `TInL` applies when we have an input process $u?x.Q$, and u is a linear channel of Γ: in addition to (1)–(3) above, we require that $\Gamma\backslash_u, u\colon T_1, x\colon (\mathsf{v}, T)$ types the continuation Q, where the subtraction T_1 of the input capability of u from the type of u must be defined. Case `TInUn` applies when we have an input process $u?x.Q$, and u is an unrestricted channel of Γ. We require that (4) $\Gamma, x\colon (\mathsf{v}, T)$ types Q. The last case, `TInU`, applies when we have a replicated input process $*u?x.P$ and u is an unrestricted channel of Γ. We require that (4) the projection ❦ of the visible and illegal names of Γ is consumed, and (5) $\Gamma, x\colon (\mathsf{v}, T)$ types Q.

3 Typed Labelled Transitions

Figure 3 presents the operational semantics of our process language as a LTS over *configurations*: these are pairs of environments Γ, and processes, P, written as $\Gamma \triangleright P$, and constitute the states of our LTS. Similarly to previous work, e.g. [17, 18], when writing $\Gamma \triangleright P$ we assume that *there exists* an environment that *type checks P*. However, in our setting the environment Γ_1 s.t. $\Gamma_1 \vdash P$ has *less or equal information* on the channels of P, i.e., $\exists \Gamma_2.\ \Gamma = \Gamma_1 + \Gamma_2$; in contrast, Γ_1 has more or equal information in [17, 18], i.e., $\Gamma_1 <: \Gamma$. Note that, in our configurations $\Gamma \triangleright P$ channels are hidden (respectively visible) in Γ, only if they are hidden (respectively visible) in P.

Typed Transitions

$$\text{LOUT}\ \frac{T'' = T' - T}{\Gamma, a{:}(\mathtt{v}, \uparrow [T]^{\iota}), n{:}(\mathtt{v}, T') \triangleright a!n.P \xrightarrow{a!n} \Gamma, a{:}(\mathtt{v}, \emptyset[T]^{\iota}), n{:}(\mathtt{v}, T'') \triangleright P}$$

$$\text{uRIN}\ \frac{\downarrow \in p \qquad T'' = T' + T \qquad \mathtt{f} \neq \mathtt{h} \qquad (\Gamma', P') = \mathsf{rlb}((\Gamma, c{:}(\mathtt{v}, p[T]^{\omega}), n{:}(\mathtt{f}, T')), P)}{\Gamma, c{:}(\mathtt{v}, p[T]^{\omega}), n{:}(\mathtt{f}, T') \triangleright *c?x.P \xrightarrow{c?n} \Gamma, c{:}(\mathtt{v}, p[T]^{\omega}), n{:}(\mathtt{v}, T''), \Gamma' \triangleright P[^{n}/_{x}] \parallel *c?x.P'}$$

$$\text{PARL}\ \frac{\Gamma \triangleright P_1 \xrightarrow{\alpha} \Gamma' \triangleright P_1'}{\Gamma \triangleright P_1 \parallel P_2 \xrightarrow{\alpha} \Gamma' \triangleright P_1' \parallel P_2} \qquad \text{OPEN}\ \frac{\Gamma, n{:}(\mathtt{v}, T) \triangleright P \xrightarrow{n'!n} \Gamma' \triangleright P'}{\Gamma, n{:}(\mathtt{h}, T) \triangleright (\kappa n)(P) \xrightarrow{n'!n} \Gamma' \triangleright P'}$$

$$\text{HIDE}\ \frac{\Gamma, n{:}(\mathtt{v}, T) \triangleright P \xrightarrow{\alpha} \Gamma', n{:}\ (\mathtt{v}, S) \triangleright P' \quad n \notin \mathbf{nm}(\alpha)}{\Gamma, n{:}(\mathtt{h}, T) \triangleright (\kappa n)(P) \xrightarrow{\alpha} \Gamma', n{:}\ (\mathtt{h}, S) \triangleright (\kappa n)(P')}$$

$$\text{uCOML}\ \frac{\begin{array}{c} S' = S - T \quad \Gamma, c{:}(\mathtt{v}, \updownarrow [T]^{\omega}), n{:}(\mathtt{v}, S) \triangleright P_1 \xrightarrow{c!n} \Gamma_1 \triangleright P_1' \\ \Gamma, c{:}(\mathtt{v}, \updownarrow [T]^{\omega}), n{:}(\mathtt{v}, S') \triangleright P_2 \xrightarrow{c?n} \Gamma_2, c{:}(\mathtt{v}, \updownarrow [T]^{\omega}), n{:}(\mathtt{v}, S) \triangleright P_2' \end{array}}{\Gamma, c{:}(\mathtt{v}, \updownarrow [T]^{\omega}), n{:}(\mathtt{v}, S) \triangleright P_1 \parallel P_2 \xrightarrow{\tau} \Gamma_2, c{:}(\mathtt{v}, \updownarrow [T]^{\omega}), n{:}(\mathtt{v}, S) \triangleright P_1' \parallel P_2'}$$

$$\text{LCLSL}\ \frac{\begin{array}{c} S' = S - T \quad \Gamma, a{:}(\mathtt{v}, \uparrow [T]^{\iota}), n{:}(\mathtt{h}, S) \triangleright P_1 \xrightarrow{a!n} \Gamma_1 \triangleright P_1' \\ \Gamma, a{:}(\mathtt{v}, \downarrow [T]^{\iota}), n{:}(\mathtt{i}, S') \triangleright P_2 \xrightarrow{a?n} \Gamma, a{:}(\mathtt{v}, \emptyset[T]^{\iota}), n{:}(\mathtt{v}, S) \triangleright P_2' \end{array}}{\Gamma, a{:}(\mathtt{v}, \updownarrow [T]^{\iota}), n{:}(\mathtt{h}, S) \triangleright P_1 \parallel P_2 \xrightarrow{\tau} \Gamma, a{:}(\mathtt{v}, \emptyset[T]^{\iota}), n{:}(\mathtt{h}, S) \triangleright (\kappa n)(P_1' \parallel P_2')}$$

Fig. 3. Labelled Transition System (Selected Rules)

The LTS is a ternary relation, where the first and third elements are a configuration and the second element is a label, ranged over by α. It is written as $\Gamma \triangleright P \xrightarrow{\alpha} \Gamma' \triangleright P'$ where α is either an internal (or idle) action τ, an input action $n?n'$, or an output action $n!n'$. The set of names of an action, $\mathbf{nm}(\alpha)$, are the empty if the action is idle and $\{n, n'\}$ otherwise. In the case of the input action, the judgement $\Gamma \triangleright P \xrightarrow{n?n'} \Gamma' \triangleright P'$ denotes that the configuration $\Gamma \triangleright P$ interacts with a (context) process, Q, that typechecks *wrt.* an environment Δ that can be composed with Γ, *i.e.*, $\Gamma + \Delta$ is defined. The transition therefore models the communication where $\Gamma \triangleright P$ inputs on channel n the name n' sent to it by the context $\Delta \triangleright Q$, to then evolve to P'. The interpretation of the output transition, $\Gamma \triangleright P \xrightarrow{n!n'} \Gamma' \triangleright P'$, is analogous. *Scope extruding* outputs, a characteristic feature of π-calculus LTSs, is described as an outputted name n' has visibility $\mathtt{h}$ in Γ; this also implies that the context interacted with must typecheck *wrt.* some environment Δ where the visibility of n' is $\mathtt{i}$, due to the requirement $\mathtt{h}+\mathtt{i}=\mathtt{h}$ from Fig. 1.

The LTS rules were designed along their mechanisation following a feedback-loop methodology where the high level definitions were tuned by considering the Coq implementation, and vice-versa (*e.g.,* to see how actions can do away with binding when expressing scope extrusion). The transition rules are *split-free*, *i.e.*, they do not employ the environment splits, $\Gamma_1 + \Gamma_2$. There are two reasons for this. First, this eliminates under-specification for derivations involving parallel processes, making the system more algorithmic: in Sect. 4, we defend this thesis by presenting a certified OCaml interpreter extracted from the Coq code. Second, rule premises use the same environment for the most part (*e.g.*, PARL in Fig. 3), meaning that the implicit context with whom the process interacts is preserved for sub-derivations, in keeping with the intended interpretation of the transition. It is worth noting that, although transition derivations may start with a configuration $\Gamma \triangleright P$ at the root that is *typeable*, *i.e.*, $\Gamma \vdash P$, this need *not* be the case for configurations in the premises. Note also that processes in a transition are always *closed* (as opposed to the judgements of Fig. 2, where processes may contain free variables).

We have five rules for prefixes; here we cover two of them. Rule LOUT allows an output process $a!n.P$ to transition with an output on a *linear* channel a and payload n (both *visible*) whenever the environment maps a to a linear channel type with *only* the output capability, $\uparrow$, to allow the observer to hold the dual input capability, $\downarrow$; the environment should also map n to a supertype of T, the declared payload type of a, captured by the condition $T''=T'-T$. The configuration transitions with action $a!n$ to reach a configuration where the environment has no capabilities left for a, and n has the remainder capability obtained by removing T from the prior type of n.

Rule URIN describes the semantics of a replicated input $*c?x.P$ receiving a name n. Unlike the output case, the flag f of n is constrained, namely f $\neq$ h, since hidden flags are reserved for hidden channels in P; whenever f $=$ h, the observer can only be typed with flag i for n, and thus can never send the name n. The configuration reached always carries flag v for n. “Intrusion” of fresh names from the observer is expressed when the flag of n is i in the source configuration, meaning that the observer is typed with visibility h for n. The rule requires that (*i*) the environment possesses *at least* the input capability for c; (*ii*) the type of c does not change in the reached configuration. Replication comports that a transition labelled by $c?n$ spawns a *relabelled* copy P' of the input body P, to preserve the (encoding of) Barendregt's convention. The definition of the operator rlb is axiomatic, and is mechanised by passing the domain of the environment to function `dep_relabel` introduced in Section 2; we avoid all details of the axiomatisation and refer to the paragraph on the mechanisation. Note, however, the addition of a *fresh environment* Γ' to the configuration transitioned to, containing the *new entries* needed to type check the hidden names of the relabelled continuation P'.

Rule OPEN models scope extrusion, removing a hiding construct $(\kappa\, n)P$ enveloping P by sending the name n as the payload of an output on some channel n'. We mimic the mechanism from the typing rule TNEW of Fig. 2 and change the visibility of n from h to v in the premise, once the restriction is peeled off. Our framework does *not* rely on alpha-conversion, since it requires n to be in the type environment domain carrying the flag h. From the premise we (implicitly) know that the process transitioned to, namely P', does not restrict the name n and, accordingly, the configuration transitioned to in the conclusion must map n to a visible flag (v). Our formalism does not employ a dedicated syntax for the open output action (as found in [17,35]), since this information can be obtained from the flag of the payload in the environment. The other rule handling name restriction is HIDE. It is analogous to rule OPEN in many respects, but (*i*) the action does not concern the name being restricted in the conclusion; (*ii*) the restriction construct (and hidden flag) is preserved in the configuration transitioned to.

We have five rules for parallel processes (apart from the symmetric ones); we only discuss three of them. Independent transitions across processes is described by rule PARL. Its conclusion permits parallel processes $P_1 \parallel P_2$ to transition whenever the (left) sub-process P_1 can transition with the *same* environment of the parallel composition, Γ. The environment of the configuration reached is that reached by the sub-process in the premise. This formulation avoids the need to split the environment while preserving the implicit observer with which the interaction occurs, namely some $\Delta \triangleright Q$ that is in agreement with $\Gamma \triangleright P_1 \parallel P_2$, *i.e.*, $\Gamma + \Delta$ is defined.

Rule uCOML allows a communication of a visible channel on a unrestricted channel c, given that: (i) the environment of the premises retains the full capability on c; (ii) the reached environment differs from the starting environment by possibly extending the environment with new entries (*e.g.*, whenever the input action has been fired by using uRIN) The premises require that n is visible and that the output and input actions, $c!n$ and $c?n$, can be performed in the respective sub-processes with designated environments; these are obtained by providing the necessary conditions for the action by splitting the type of n accordingly using the object type of channel c (the type of channel c need *not* be split since it is unrestricted). The environment reached after the communication is the one reached by the input action premise, which takes into account the case where the input $c?n$ is the result of a replicated input that may extend the domain of the environment. Rule lCLSL allows for sending a hidden channel n over a linear channel a, whenever the environment in the premises has the full capability of a. It requires that: (*i*) the premises split the capabilities for output and input; (*ii*) the premises split the flag of n, which is hidden, as the visibility $\mathbf{h}$ for the premise executing the output, and $\mathtt{i}$ for the premise executing the input; (*iii*) the environment reached after the transition is equal to the starting environment but for the type of a, where both (linear) capabilities are now consumed *i.e.*, channel a now has empty capabilities.

Mechanisation of LTS rules The LTS in Fig. 3 is implemented by type `lts 🙵` which is defined using a proof that the domain 🙵 of the initial environment Γ does not contain duplicates (*cf.* `List.NoDup`); this is stronger than `isMap(Gamma)` and is used with `List.In` to implement conditions of the form $\Gamma(u) = (\mathtt{f}, T)$, from now on written as `In (u, f, t) g`.

```
Inductive lts (g : typeEnv) : dproc → action → typeEnv → dproc → NoDup (domain g) → Prop :=
| parL : ∀ p1 a g1 q p2 pf, lts g p1 a g1 p2 pf → lts g (dPar p1 q) a g1 (dPar p2 q) pf
| lOut : ∀ p a1 a2 b1 b2 pf t t1 t2 g1, type_remove t1 t t2 → In ((a1, a2), vis, Chan lin out t) g→
  g1=(((a1, a2), vis, Chan lin empty t):: ((b1, b2), vis, t2):: (rm (a1,a2) (rm (b1,b2) g))) →
  In ((b1, b2), vis, t1) g → lts g (dOut a1 a2 b1 b2 p) (aOut a1 a2 b1 b2) g1 p pf
| uRin : ∀ pol p a1 a2 x1 x2 b1 b2 pf f t t1 t2 g1, pol = inp ∨ pol = io → type_plus t1 t t2 →
  f ≠ hid → In ((a1, a2), vis, Chan un pol t) g → In ((b1, b2), f, t1) g →
  let q := dep_relabel p (domain g) pf in
  g1 = (newEntries g (secLabs q) (maximum g)) ++ (((b1, b2), vis, t2) :: rm (b1, b2) g) →
  lts g (dBang a1 a2 x1 x2 p) (aIn a1 a2 b1 b2) g1 (dPar (pmap p x1 x2 b1 b2) (dBang a1 a2 x1 x2 q)) pf
| lclsL : ∀ p1 p2 q1 q2 a1 a2 b1 b2 s s1 t pf pf1 pf2 g1, let g0 := rm (a1, a2) (rm (b1, b2) g) in
  type_remove s t s1 → In ((a1, a2), vis, Chan lin io t) g → In ((b1, b2), hid, s) g →
  g1 = (((a1, a2), vis, Chan lin empty t) :: ((b1, b2), hid, s) :: g0) →
  lts (((a1, a2), vis, Chan lin out t) :: ((b1, b2), hid, s) :: g0) p1 (aOut a1 a2 b1 b2)
      (((a1, a2), vis, Chan lin empty t) :: ((b1, b2), vis, s1) :: g0) p2 pf1 →
  lts (((a1, a2), vis, Chan lin inp t) :: ((b1, b2), ill, s1) :: g0) q1 (aIn a1 a2 b1 b2)
      (((a1, a2), vis, Chan lin empty t) :: ((b1, b2), vis, s) :: g0) q2 pf2 →
  lts g (dPar p1 q1) (aTau a1 a2) g1 (dNu b1 b2 (dPar p2 q2)) pf
| ucomL : ∀ g1 p1 p2 q1 q2 a1 a2 b1 b2 s s1 t pf pf1 pf2, let g0 := rm (b1, b2) g in
  let g' := ((b1, b2), vis, s1):: g0 in type_remove s t s1 → In ((a1, a2), vis, Chan un io t) g →
  In ((b1, b2), vis, s) g → In ((a1, a2), vis, Chan un io t) g1 → In ((b1, b2), vis, s) g1 →
```

```
  lts g p1 (aOut a1 a2 b1 b2) (((b1, b2), vis, s1) :: g0) p2 pf1 →
  lts g' q1 (aIn a1 a2 b1 b2) g1 q2 pf2 → lts g (dPar p1 q1) (aTau a1 a2) g1 (dPar p2 q2) pf
| open : ∀ p a1 a2 b1 b2 g1 p' t pf pf1, In ((b1, b2), hid, t) g →
  lts (((b1, b2), vis, t) :: rm (b1, b2) g) p (aOut a1 a2 b1 b2) g1 p' pf1 →
  lts g (dNu b1 b2 p) (aOut a1 a2 b1 b2) g1 p' pf
| hide : ∀ b1 b2 t p a  h1 h2 h' h'' t' p' pf pf1 g1, notHidden b1 b2 a →
g = h1 ++ (b1, b2, hid, t) :: h2 →
  lts (h1 ++ (b1, b2, vis, t) :: h2) p a (h' ++ (b1, b2, vis, t') :: h'') p' pf1 →
  g1 = (h' ++ (b1, b2, hid, t') :: h'') → lts g (dNu b1 b2 p) a g1 (dNu b1 b2 p') pf.
(* | uOut ···| lIn ···| uIn ···| lcomL ···| uclsL ···*)
```

The input cases rely on function pmap (*cf.* Sect. 2) to substitute a variable with a name in the continuation process. The replication case uRin uses function newEntries to build an environment containing only the *hidden* entries that have been *shifted* by function dep_relabel. Function InB checks if a channel a is mapped by an environment Γ while also returning the entry associated to a, when $a \in \mathsf{dom}(\Gamma)$.

```
Fixpoint newEntries (g : typeEnv) (l : list (name * name)) (max : nat) : typeEnv :=
  match l with | nil ⇒ nil
  | (a1, a2) :: tail ⇒ let (_, notNew) := InB (a1, a2) g in if notNew then newEntries g tail max
  else let (pair, _) := InB (a1, a2 - max) g in
  ((a1, a2), fst pair, snd pair) :: newEntries g tail max end.
```

In the communication cases, *cf.* lcomL, lclsL, ucomL, and uclsL, we record the channel that is the subject of the τ-communication. This simplifies the proof of subject reduction, and has no semantic impact (*cf.* [24]). In the inductive cases—the communication cases, open, and hide—we build the hypotheses environment by manipulating the input environment. For instance, in rule open we receive an environment Γ and a process $(\kappa\, b)P$ to obtain hypothesis In (b, hid, t) g. We then take as hypothesis an output transition from ((b, vis, t):: rm b g) and P: since we check typings by using the predicate In, the position of the entry in the list is irrelevant. Rule hide makes uses of the predicate notHidden to verify that the name b hidden in $(\kappa\, b)P$ does not occur in the action, ∀ b c. notHidden b (aTau c). Differently to the other rules, hide makes uses of Datatypes.app to define the structure of the input environment; this is similar to the use of the predicate In (*cf.* List.in_split). This format specifies the shape of the environment of the hypothesis, which is key to determine the environment reached by applying the rule.

4 Subject Reduction, and Other Results

We discuss aspects of the mechanisation of subject reduction, outlining also auxiliary results: Barendregt's convention preservation and the extraction of a certified OCaml interpreter. The technical report contains a few details of the proof of subject reduction.

We start by setting axiomatic conditions to rule out divergent defining equations of the form $T = p[T]^m$ and $P = u!v.P$.

```
Parameter nonRecTypes: (∀ m p t, t = Chan m p t → False) ∧
   (∀ m m1 m2 p p1 p2 t, Chan m1 p1 t = Chan m p (Chan m2 p2 t) → False).
Parameter nonDivergentProcesses : ∀ g p a g' nd_pf, ¬ lts g p a g' p nd_pf.
```

The first result says that the hidden channels of a process P relabelled w.r.t. a non-duplicated superset of the hidden channels of P does not contain duplicates. Function List.count_occ counts the occurrences of pairs of names in a list (*cf.* Sect. 2).

```
Definition incl_ (l m: list (name*name)) := ∀ a:name*name, In a l →
  In a m ∧ count_occ nat_pair_eq_dec l a = count_occ nat_pair_eq_dec m a.
Proposition prop27 : ∀ (p :dproc) (s : list (name*name)) (pf : NoDup s),
  incl_ (secLabs p) s → NoDup (secLabs (dep_relabel p s pf)).
```

The next result relies on a *sanity check* of the hidden channels of process P w.r.t. environment Γ in $\Gamma \triangleright P$. We require that the second entry of a hidden channel of P (1) is positive (*cf.* `sl_pos`), and (2) is less than or equal than the maximum of Γ. Both requirements are essential to preserve the soundness of the relabelling mechanism. We establish that the domain of Δ—the environment returned by function `newEntries` applied to Γ and the hidden channels of the relabelling of P and the maximum of Γ—and the domain of Γ are disjoint, provided that the sanity check on P and Γ holds.

```
Lemma new_entries_disjoint: ∀ g p pf, sl_pos p → max (secLabs p) <= maximum g →
  disjoint (domain g) (domain (newEntries g (secLabs (dep_relabel p (domain g) pf)) (maximum g))).
```

First Milestone. The first result clarifies the semantics of our split-free system: if $\Gamma_1 + \Gamma_2 = \Gamma$ and $\Gamma_1 \vdash P$ and $\Gamma \triangleright P \xrightarrow{\alpha} \Gamma' \triangleright P'$ then there is $\mathcal{K}_1$ s.t. $\Gamma_1 \triangleright P \xrightarrow{\alpha} \mathcal{K}_1 \triangleright P'$. That is, a process that (i) is *typed by a subenvironment* Γ_1 of Γ, and (ii) does a transition w.r.t. Γ, can do *the same transition* w.r.t. Γ_1. The proof of `split_lts_exist_lts` is closed by applying `dependent induction` [25] to $\Gamma \triangleright P \xrightarrow{\alpha} \Gamma' \triangleright P'$ while relying on `split_not_exist_lts`.

```
Lemma split_lts_exist_lts: ∀ g1 g2 g p a g' p' pf1 pf2 pf nd_pf nd_pf1,
  tEnv_split g1 g2 g pf1 pf2 pf → typeCheck g1 pf1 p → lts g p a g' p' nd_pf → sl_pos p →
  ∃ k1, lts g1 p a k1 p' nd_pf1.
```

Second Milestone. The second milestone consists of a collection of results on typing. The *substitution lemma* states that if $\Gamma, b\colon (\mathtt{f}, S_1), x\colon (\mathsf{v}, S) \vdash P$ and $\mathtt{f} \neq \mathsf{h}$ and $S_1 + S = S_2$ then $\Gamma, b\colon (\mathsf{v}, S_2) \vdash P\{b/x\}$. The requirement `x2 < maximum g ∨ x2 < b2` is needed to maintain the invariant on the maximum of the environment (*cf.* Sect. 2.1).

```
Lemma typeCheck_substitution: ∀ b1 b2 x1 x2 f s1 s s2 g pf pf1 p (nd_pf:NoDup (domain g)),
  In (b1, b2, f, s1) g → In (x1, x2, vis, s) g → (x1,x2)≠ (b1, b2) → (x2 < maximum g ∨ x2 < b2)→
  f ≠ hid → type_plus s1 s s2 → typeCheck g pf p →
  typeCheck ((b1, b2, vis, s2) :: rm (b1, b2) (rm (x1, x2) g)) pf1 (pmap p x1 x2 b1 b2).
```

Another result is that *typing is preserved by relabelling* (*cf.* uRIN of Fig. 3): if $\Gamma \vdash P$ and $\mathsf{rlb}(\Gamma, P) = \mathcal{K}, Q$ then $\mathcal{K}, \Gamma{\downarrow_{\mathrm{i}}} \vdash Q$. The operator $\Gamma{\downarrow_{\mathrm{i}}}$, mechanised as `illECast`, casts the polarity of linear hidden and illegal channels (only) to empty.

```
Lemma typeCheck_dep_relabel2: ∀ p g pf nd_pf pf1 k, sl_pos p →
  typeCheck g pf p → k = newEntries g (secLabs (dep_relabel p (domain g) nd_pf)) (maximum g) →
  typeCheck (k ++ illECast g) pf1 (dep_relabel p (domain g) nd_pf).
```

4.1 Subject Reduction Theorem

The design of the typed LTS of Fig. 3 which omits the use of environment splitting (*cf.* Fig. 1), requires a stronger (and harder) result to close subject reduction.

Lemma 1 (Strong subject reduction). *If* $\Gamma_1 \vdash P$ *and* $\Gamma_1 + \Gamma_2 = \Gamma$ *and* $\Gamma \triangleright P \xrightarrow{\alpha} \mathcal{H} \triangleright P'$ *and* $\Gamma_1 \triangleright P \xrightarrow{\alpha} \mathcal{K}' \triangleright P'$ *then* $\mathcal{K}' \vdash P'$.

The need for Lemma 1 comes from the combination of the typing (*cf.* tPAR, Fig. 2) and LTS (*cf.* PARL, Fig. 3) rules for parallel composition. Consider the parallel case, $P = P_1 \parallel Q_1$, for Theorem 1. When apply induction, the goal is $\Gamma' \vdash P_2 \parallel Q_1$, where $\Gamma \triangleright P_1 \xrightarrow{\alpha} \Gamma' \triangleright P_2$ with the following IH: if $\Gamma \vdash P_1$ then $\Gamma' \vdash P_2$. The main complication is that, in general, $\Gamma \nvdash P_1$. By inversion of $\Gamma \vdash P_1 \parallel Q_1$, we indeed obtain $\Gamma_1 \vdash P_1$ and $\Gamma_2 \vdash P_2$ and $\Gamma_1 + \Gamma_2 = \Gamma$ which is insufficient to complete the proof. Instead, the fine-grained formulation of Lemma 1 allows us to prove the desired result and obtain Theorem 1 as a byproduct. The outline of the mechanisation of Lemma 1 is in report; its proof takes 16k loc.

Theorem 1 (Subject reduction). *If* $\Gamma \vdash P$ *and* $\Gamma \triangleright P \xrightarrow{\alpha} \Gamma' \triangleright P'$ *then* $\Gamma' \vdash P'$.

4.2 Other Results

Barendregt's convention (*BC*) preservation The convention is implemented by `wf`. Typed processes satisfy BC: this result and subject reduction enforce preservation.

```
Definition wf (p : dproc) : Prop := NoDup (secLabs p) ∧ disjoint (fn p) (secLabs p).
Corollary wf_preserve g1 p1 a g2 p2 pf nd_pf: sl_pos p1 → typeCheck g1 pf p1 →
   lts g1 p1 a g2 p2 nd_pf → wf p2.
```

LTS typing avoids cases such as $\Gamma \triangleright P \xrightarrow{a?b} \Gamma' \triangleright P'$ where $\mathsf{fn}(P') \cap \mathsf{hid}(P') = \emptyset$ does not hold. *E.g.*, Rule uRIN of Fig. 3 would rule this out when $P = *a?x.x!v.\mathsf{nil} \parallel (\kappa\, b)Q$ and $b \in \mathsf{fn}(P') \wedge b \in \mathsf{hid}(P')$ since it requires the flag of channel b *not* to be hid.

Extraction of a certified interpreter The LTS of Sect. 3 can be deployed soundly in mainstream programming languages. Function `elts` receives a type environment Γ, a process P, an action α, and other optional arguments, and returns (i) a pair (Γ', P'), or (ii) none: in case (i), we show that $\Gamma \triangleright P \xrightarrow{\alpha} \Gamma' \triangleright P'$: that is, the interpreter is sound. The code is extracted to OCaml and contains less than fifty types/values.

5 Conclusions

We present an LTS semantics for the linear π-calculus that lends itself well to mechanically-checked software. We defend that the semantics can be used as a basis for building automated static analyses of linear π-calculus system models that is equipped with mechanisms to report channel names that are determined to be the source of a defect. The certified runnable code extracted from the mechanisation permits the study of elaborate examples (that go beyond small pen-and-paper inspections) via simulations, implementing Klein *et al.*'s "run your research" challenge [23].

Approaches to Mechanising the π-Calculus. There are various different ways of dealing with name binding and scope extrusion in mobile process calculi. They may take an axiomatic approach, building on theories to deal with (capture avoiding) α-conversion (inspired by seminal work on mechanising the λ-calculus [9]), or they may be based on logical techniques.

The axiomatic approach can be either first-order, *e.g.*, [11,16,26], or higher-order, *e.g.*, [1,22,33,34,44], via the Higher-Order Abstract Syntax or/and the "Theory of Contexts". The main limitations of these approaches are the cumbersome and heavy representation of bound names, not being preserved by the semantics of the calculus, and the existence of "exotic" terms and the extra work needed to exclude them.

The logical approaches are based on either Nominal Logics [2,31] or on the Concurrent Logical Framework (CLF) [5,37,39]. Proponents of the former argue that formal proofs become similar to those in books by simplifying the reasoning about bound names and allowing processes to be equated up-to α-conversion. However, Nominal Logics require equivariance lemmata, stating that name permutations are preserved by the operations of the static and dynamic semantics: static analyses based on such a framework would find it hard to refer to a specific bound name working up-to α-conversion. CFL uses a special quantifier (∇) for encoding both judgements and fixed points. It provides a formal treatment of bound names and highlights the differences between the various classical definitions of bisimulation via the interplay of quantifiers. Although its focus is on proof systems, proof search, and modal characterisations of equivalences, it has been used to show type safety of a behavioural type system for the π-calculus [40]. It is however not clear if algorithmic type checking/inference or code extraction are possible.

There are several works [1,2,20–22,28–30,32–34] that mechanise semantic theories of the π-calculus to prove type preservation and safety results [6,10,11,19,45]. These works however use reduction semantics, not LTSs. The type systems presented are declarative and, by admission of the authors, "turning" them into type checking and/or type inference algorithms is an added challenge. In our case, the type checking algorithm can be derived from the rules by adding a return environment containing the capabilities not consumed by parallel processes, following [12,13]. Type inference can be obtained by indicating which channels are meant to be linear (*cf.* [14]). None of these works feature the extraction of an interpreter from the semantic mechanisation. This is relatively straightforward in our case, because we designed the LTS with this intent.

Concurrent Benchmark **Challenges** [3]. We address all challenges (one partially):

Linearity and Behavioural Type Systems: we define a π-calculus with linear types and prove type preservation (*i.e.*, subject-reduction). Instead of using the more straightforward approach with reduction semantics, we used an LTS-based semantics which is more compositional. Our approach is original—it uses neither α nor structural congruence—and features an important novelty, a split-free typed LTS.

Name Passing and Scope Extrusion: type environments have information on name visibility and usage permission, dynamically managing linearity via capabilities updates due to scope intrusion/extrusion, while also dealing soundly with binding.

Coinduction and Infinite Processes: the minimal calculus we use has infinite processes via replicated inputs. Using the relabelling mechanism, the LTS takes care of incremental name generation (as showing in Sect. 4). Work on a behavioural equivalence is in progress; the mechanisation of that is left for future work.

Reusable Mechanisms. We develop an innovative, simple yet general treatment of bound names, capabilities, and type environment operations for substructural type systems and labelled transition systems. We contend that the constructions that are reusable in other contexts (program calculi) are the following. 1. The treatment of binders leading to an α-congruence free calculus that preserve Barendregt's convention for typed processes. 2. Type environments with visible and hidden (scoped) entries, internalising identifier observability and usage permission. 3. Substructural manipulation of resource policies with an algebra on types and an associated split-free semantics for the language. 4. A general soundness theorem leading to the extraction of a certified interpreter.

Acknowledgements. This work was partly supported by the DReason project (2024.15569.PEX, https://doi.org/10.54499/2024.15569.PEX), NOVA LINCS (UID/04516/2025) with the financial support of FCT.IP (https://doi.org/10.54499/UID/04516/2025) and the UOM Research Seed Fund CPSRP01-26 (Runtime Verification and Adaptation for Industry 5.0).

References

1. Affeldt, R., Kobayashi, N.: A Coq library for verification of concurrent programs. In: Schürmann, C. (ed.) Proceedings of the Fourth International Workshop on Logical Frameworks and Meta-Languages, LFM@IJCAR 2004. Electronic Notes in Theoretical Computer Science, vol. 199, pp. 17–32. Elsevier (2004). https://doi.org/10.1016/J.ENTCS.2007.11.010
2. Bengtson, J., Parrow, J.: Formalising the pi-calculus using nominal logic. Log. Methods Comput. Sci. **5**(2) (2009). http://arxiv.org/abs/0809.3960
3. Carbone, M., et al.: The concurrent calculi formalisation benchmark. In: Castellani, I., Tiezzi, F. (eds.) COORDINATION 2024. LNCS, vol. 14676, pp. 149–158. Springer, Cham (2024). https://doi.org/10.1007/978-3-031-62697-5_9
4. Castegren, E., Wrigstad, T.: OOlong: a concurrent object calculus for extensibility and reuse. SIGAPP Appl. Comput. Rev. **18**(4), 47–60 (2019). https://doi.org/10.1145/3307624.3307629
5. Cervesato, I., Pfenning, F., Walker, D., Watkins, K.: A concurrent logical framework II: examples and applications. Technical report, Carnegie Mellon University (2007). https://doi.org/10.1184/R1/6587294.v1
6. Ciccone, L., Padovani, L.: A dependently typed linear π-calculus in Agda. In: 22nd International Symposium on Principles and Practice of Declarative Programming, PPDP 2020, pp. 8:1–8:14. ACM (2020). https://doi.org/10.1145/3414080.3414109
7. Copello, E., Szasz, N., Tasistro, Á.: Formalisation in constructive type theory of Barendregt's variable convention for generic structures with binders. In: Blanqui, F., Reis, G. (eds.) 13th International Workshop on Logical Frameworks and Meta-Languages: Theory and Practice, LFMTP@FSCD 2018. EPTCS, vol. 274, pp. 11–26 (2018). https://doi.org/10.4204/EPTCS.274.2
8. Dardha, O., Giachino, E., Sangiorgi, D.: Session types revisited. Inf. Comput. **256**, 253–286 (2017). https://doi.org/10.1016/j.ic.2017.06.002
9. de Bruijn, N.J.: Lambda calculus notation with nameless dummies. Indag. Math. **75**(5), 381–392 (1972)
10. Sudan, M.: List decoding: algorithms and applications. In: van Leeuwen, J., Watanabe, O., Hagiya, M., Mosses, P.D., Ito, T. (eds.) TCS 2000. LNCS, vol. 1872, pp. 25–41. Springer, Heidelberg (2000). https://doi.org/10.1007/3-540-44929-9_3

11. Gay, S.J.: A framework for the formalisation of pi calculus type systems in Isabelle/HOL. In: Boulton, R.J., Jackson, P.B. (eds.) TPHOLs 2001. LNCS, vol. 2152, pp. 217–232. Springer, Heidelberg (2001). https://doi.org/10.1007/3-540-44755-5_16
12. Gay, S.J., Hole, M.: Subtyping for session types in the pi calculus. Acta Inform. **42**(2–3), 191–225 (2005). https://doi.org/10.1007/S00236-005-0177-Z
13. Giunti, M.: Algorithmic type checking for a pi-calculus with name matching and session types. J. Log. Algebraic Methods Program. **82**(8), 263–281 (2013). https://doi.org/10.1016/J.JLAP.2013.05.003
14. Giunti, M.: GoPi: compiling linear and static channels in Go. In: Bliudze, S., Bocchi, L. (eds.) COORDINATION 2020. LNCS, vol. 12134, pp. 137–152. Springer, Cham (2020). https://doi.org/10.1007/978-3-030-50029-0_9
15. Giunti, M., Vasconcelos, V.T.: Linearity, session types and the pi calculus. Math. Struct. Comput. Sci. **26**(2), 206–237 (2016). https://doi.org/10.1017/S0960129514000176
16. Gordon, A.D., Melham, T.: Five axioms of alpha-conversion. In: Goos, G., Hartmanis, J., van Leeuwen, J., von Wright, J., Grundy, J., Harrison, J. (eds.) TPHOLs 1996. LNCS, vol. 1125, pp. 173–190. Springer, Heidelberg (1996). https://doi.org/10.1007/BFb0105404
17. Hennessy, M.: A Distributed Pi-Calculus. Cambridge University Press (2007)
18. Hennessy, M., Rathke, J.: Typed behavioural equivalences for processes in the presence of subtyping. Math. Struct. Comput. Sci. **14**(5), 651–684 (2004). https://doi.org/10.1017/S0960129504004281
19. Henry-Gréard, L.: Proof of the subject reduction property for a π-calculus in Coq. Technical report RR-3698, INRIA (1999). https://inria.hal.science/inria-00072970
20. Hirschkoff, D.: A full formalisation of π-calculus theory in the calculus of constructions. In: Gunter, E.L., Felty, A. (eds.) TPHOLs 1997. LNCS, vol. 1275, pp. 153–169. Springer, Heidelberg (1997). https://doi.org/10.1007/BFb0028392
21. Hirschkoff, D.: Mise en Oevre de Preuves de Bisimulation. Ph.D. thesis, Ecole Nationale des Pont et Chausseees (1999)
22. Honsell, F., Miculan, M., Scagnetto, I.: Pi-calculus in (co)inductive-type theory. Theor. Comput. Sci. **253**(2), 239–285 (2001). https://doi.org/10.1016/S0304-3975(00)00095-5
23. Klein, C., et al.: Run your research: on the effectiveness of lightweight mechanization. In: Field, J., Hicks, M. (eds.) 39th ACM SIGPLAN-SIGACT Symposium on Principles of Programming Languages, POPL 2012, pp. 285–296. ACM (2012). https://doi.org/10.1145/2103656.2103691
24. Kobayashi, N., Pierce, B.C., Turner, D.N.: Linearity and the pi-calculus. ACM Trans. Program. Lang. Syst. **21**(5), 914–947 (1999). https://doi.org/10.1145/330249.330251
25. McBride, C.: Elimination with a motive. In: Callaghan, P., Luo, Z., McKinna, J., Pollack, R., Pollack, R. (eds.) TYPES 2000. LNCS, vol. 2277, pp. 197–216. Springer, Heidelberg (2002). https://doi.org/10.1007/3-540-45842-5_13
26. Melham, T.F.: A mechanized theory of the pi-calculus in HOL. Nordic J. Comput. **1**(1), 50–76 (1994)
27. Milner, R.: Communicating and Mobile Systems - the Pi-Calculus. Cambridge University Press (1999)
28. Aït Mohamed, O.: Mechanizing a π-calculus equivalence in HOL. In: Thomas Schubert, E., Windley, P.J., Alves-Foss, J. (eds.) TPHOLs 1995. LNCS, vol. 971, pp. 1–16. Springer, Heidelberg (1995). https://doi.org/10.1007/3-540-60275-5_53
29. Orchard, D.A., Yoshida, N.: Using session types as an effect system. In: 8th International Workshop on Programming Language Approaches to Concurrency- and Communication-cEntric Software, PLACES 2015. EPTCS, vol. 203, pp. 1–13 (2015). https://doi.org/10.4204/EPTCS.203.1

30. Perera, R., Cheney, J.: Proof-relevant pi-calculus: a constructive account of concurrency and causality. Math. Struct. Comput. Sci. **28**(9), 1541–1577 (2018). https://doi.org/10.1017/S096012951700010X
31. Pitts, A.M.: Nominal logic, a first order theory of names and binding. Inf. Comput. **186**(2), 165–193 (2003). https://doi.org/10.1016/S0890-5401(03)00138-X
32. Röckl, C.: A first-order syntax for the pi-calculus in Isabelle/HOL using permutations. Electron. Notes Theor. Comput. Sci. **58**(1), 1–17 (2001). https://doi.org/10.1016/S1571-0661(04)00276-2
33. Röckl, C., Hirschkoff, D.: A fully adequate shallow embedding of the [pi]-calculus in Isabelle/HOL with mechanized syntax analysis. J. Funct. Program. **13**(2), 415–451 (2003). https://doi.org/10.1017/S0956796802004653
34. Röckl, C., Hirschkoff, D., Berghofer, S.: Higher-order abstract syntax with induction in Isabelle/HOL: formalizing the π-calculus and mechanizing the theory of contexts. In: Honsell, F., Miculan, M. (eds.) FoSSaCS 2001. LNCS, vol. 2030, pp. 364–378. Springer, Heidelberg (2001). https://doi.org/10.1007/3-540-45315-6_24
35. Sangiorgi, D., Walker, D.: The Pi-Calculus - A Theory of Mobile Processes. Cambridge University Press (2001)
36. Sano, C., Kavanagh, R., Pientka, B.: Mechanizing session-types using a structural view: enforcing linearity without linearity. Proc. ACM Program. Lang. **7**(OOPSLA2), 374–399 (2023). https://doi.org/10.1145/3622810
37. Tiu, A., Miller, D.: Proof search specifications of bisimulation and modal logics for the π-calculus. ACM Trans. Comput. Logic **11**(2) (2010). https://doi.org/10.1145/1656242.1656248
38. Urban, C., Norrish, M.:. A formal treatment of the Barendregt variable convention in rule inductions. In: Pollack, R. (ed.) ACM SIGPLAN International Conference on Functional Programming, Workshop on Mechanized Reasoning About Languages with Variable Binding, MERLIN 2005, pp. 25–32. ACM (2005). https://doi.org/10.1145/1088454.1088458
39. Watkins, K., Cervesato, I., Pfenning, F., Walker, D.: A concurrent logical framework: the propositional fragment. In: Berardi, S., Coppo, M., Damiani, F. (eds.) TYPES 2003. LNCS, vol. 3085, pp. 355–377. Springer, Heidelberg (2004). https://doi.org/10.1007/978-3-540-24849-1_23
40. Watkins, K., Cervesato, I., Pfenning, F., Walker, D.: Specifying properties of concurrent computations in CLF. Electron. Notes Theor. Comput. Sci. **199**, 67–87 (2008). Proceedings of the Fourth International Workshop on Logical Frameworks and Meta-Languages (LFM 2004). https://doi.org/10.1016/j.entcs.2007.11.013
41. Yoshida, N., Berger, M., Honda, K.: Strong normalisation in the pi-calculus. In: 16th Annual IEEE Symposium on Logic in Computer Science, LICS 2001, pp. 311–322. IEEE Computer Society (2001). https://doi.org/10.1109/LICS.2001.932507
42. Yoshida, N., Honda, K., Berger, M.: Linearity and bisimulation. J. Log. Algebraic Methods Program. **72**(2), 207–238 (2007)
43. Zackon, D., Sano, C., Momigliano, A., Pientka, B.: Split decisions: explicit contexts for substructural languages. In: Stark, K., Timany, A., Blazy, S., Tabareau, N. (eds.) 14th ACM SIGPLAN International Conference on Certified Programs and Proofs, CPP 2025, pp. 257–271. ACM (2025). https://doi.org/10.1145/3703595.3705888
44. Zalakain, U.: Type-checking session-typed π-calculus with Coq. Master's thesis, University of Glasgow (2019). https://umazalakain.info/static/Z19/msc-thesis.pdf
45. Zalakain, U., Dardha, O.: π with leftovers: a mechanisation in Agda. In: Peters, K., Willemse, T.A.C. (eds.) FORTE 2021. LNCS, vol. 12719, pp. 157–174. Springer, Cham (2021). https://doi.org/10.1007/978-3-030-78089-0_9

Automata Learning with an Incomplete but Inductive Teacher

Daniel Stan[1,2(✉)], Adrien Pommellet[1], and Juliette Jacquot[1]

[1] Laboratoire de Recherche de l'EPITA, 14-16 Rue Voltaire, Le Kremlin-Bicêtre, France
{daniel.stan,adrien.pommellet,juliette.jacquot}@epita.fr
[2] ICube, UMR 7357, Université de Strasbourg, Strasbourg, France
http://www.lre.epita.fr/

Abstract. *Active automata learning* (AAL) under a *Minimally Adequate Teacher* (MAT) has been successfully used to infer a regular language through membership and equivalence queries. This language might not be fully characterized: we are thus interested in finding *any* solution in a *target class* of possibly many regular languages. Some problems such as *regular language separation* or *inductive invariant synthesis* in the context of *regular model checking* (RMC) may indeed admit more than one answer. We therefore introduce IdMAT: a new teacher formalism answering queries with respect to any language in the target class, all at once. Such a teacher—tailored towards invariant synthesis—might provide *incomplete* "don't know" answers, but also *inductive* facts of the form "if w_1 is accepted, so is w_2". We pair IdMAT with a novel AAL algorithm L^{IndA} that 1. encodes all uncertainties as a unique SAT instance and does not fork, 2. leverages incremental SAT solving and UNSAT core analysis, and 3. handles counterexamples—of the simple or inductive type—in a frugal manner inspired by the Rivest-Schapire refinement technique. We finally evaluate a prototype implementation in the context of regular language separation and RMC.

Keywords: Active Learning · Incremental SAT Solving · UNSAT core · Regular Model Checking

1 Introduction

A central challenge in the formal verification of distributed systems is that the number of participating processes is often not known *a priori*. In particular, *parameterized* model checking [11] addresses the correctness of a system where the number of copies of a process is a *parameter*. A successful approach in this context—known as *regular model checking* [1] (RMC)—consists in encoding individual configurations as finite words, sets of configurations as regular languages, and transitions as transducers. For example, safety RMC consists in determining whether, from a regular set of *initial* configurations S_0, one can

Published by Springer Nature Switzerland AG 2026
L. Bocchi and B. Kulahcioglu Ozkan (Eds.): FORTE 2026, LNCS 16589, pp. 130–148, 2026.
https://doi.org/10.1007/978-3-032-28187-6_8

guarantee that the system is *safe* and never reaches a regular set of *bad* configurations S_b. By writing the successor (resp. predecessor) function Post (resp. Pre) and its transitive closure Post* (resp. Pre*), this amounts to checking whether $\text{Post}^*(S_0) \cap \text{Pre}^*(S_b) = \emptyset$. RMC is, in general, undecidable; nevertheless, if one can find a language L and effectively verify that it contains only reachable states and no bad states, then the system is safe.

Example 1. Two tokens are initially located at both extremities of a track of even length $2 \times n$; $n \in \mathbb{N} \setminus \{0\}$ is a *parameter* of the system. Both tokens can only move synchronously in opposite directions. We want to prove that a collision can't happen, i.e. that the two tokens can't end up in the same position.

A configuration is a word on the alphabet $\Sigma = \{\bullet, \circ\}$ with exactly two $\bullet$ letters, where $\bullet$ represents a position occupied by a token. The system's starting configuration is $\bullet(\circ\circ)^{n-1}\bullet$. Thus, the set of initial configurations for every possible value of n is $S_0 = \mathcal{L}(\bullet(\circ\circ)^*\bullet)$. The set of forbidden configurations is $S_b = \mathcal{L}(\circ^*\bullet\circ\bullet\circ^*)$ (the two tokens can overlap next step).

The transition relation $\hookrightarrow$ of the system is such that the tokens can only move toward or away from each other. As an example, $\circ\bullet\circ\circ\bullet\circ \hookrightarrow \circ\circ\bullet\bullet\circ\circ$ and $\circ\bullet\circ\circ\bullet\circ \hookrightarrow \bullet\circ\circ\circ\circ\bullet$. Thus, if we consider the set Post* of successors induced by $\hookrightarrow$, $\{\circ\circ\bullet\bullet\circ\circ, \bullet\circ\circ\circ\circ\bullet\} \subseteq \text{Post}^*(\{\circ\bullet\circ\circ\bullet\circ\})$.

To synthesize such a language, one may resort to *active automata learning* [3] under a *Minimally Adequate Teacher* (MAT): a *learner* infers a formal model (here, a regular language L over a finite alphabet Σ) by asking membership—does $w \in \Sigma$ belong to L?—and equivalence—given a language H, does $H = L$, and if it does not, what is a counterexample?—queries to a *teacher*. However, in some cases, it may happen that the learner is actually interested in learning *any* language in a *target* class of languages.

Consider the *regular language separation* problem: finding a regular language L—known as a *separator*—such that $L_1 \subseteq L$ and $L \subseteq \overline{L_2}$ for some disjoint languages L_1 and L_2. Multiple solutions may exist: words in L_1 (resp. L_2) should (resp. should not) belong to L, but words that belong to neither are under no such constraint. Yet, dedicated AAL techniques can yield a separator under the *inexperienced* [17] or *incomplete* [19] teacher framework iMAT that allows "don't know" answers to membership queries if a word's membership is unspecified; it also replaces equivalence queries with *validity* queries testing separation.

RMC is a variation of this problem; however, one may not be able to directly decide whether L separates $\text{Post}^*(S_0)$ and $\text{Pre}^*(S_b)$, e.g. if we cannot compute these two sets in the first place. But another similar, sound approach known as *regular inductive invariant synthesis* can also guarantee safety: finding a regular language I called an *inductive invariant* such that $S_0 \subseteq I$, $I \subseteq \overline{S_b}$, and $\text{Post}(I) \subseteq I$. The language I then obviously separates $\text{Post}^*(S_0)$ and $\text{Pre}^*(S_b)$. This approach remains *incomplete*: a safe system may not admit an invariant.

Example 2. Consider Example 1. The language $I = \mathcal{L}(\circ^*\bullet(\Sigma^2)^*\bullet\circ^*)$ is a regular inductive invariant. The system is therefore safe for any value of n.

Were we to learn regular inductive invariants, we can easily check whether a hypothesis H submitted to the teacher is inductive, i.e. $\text{Post}(H) \subseteq H$; if it is not, an *inductive counterexample* such that $(c_1 \in H) \wedge (c_2 \notin H)$ yet $c_2 \in \text{Post}^*(\{c_1\})$ can be found. Similarly, if $w_2 \in \text{Post}^*(\{w_1\})$ for some words w_1 and w_2, then any regular inductive invariant I verifies $w_1 \in I \rightarrow w_2 \in I$; the learner can make use of the *inductive pair* (w_1, w_2).

Our Contributions. We introduce a new AAL framework IdMAT for non-uniquely specified targets that allows both inductive pairs and counterexamples (Sect. 3). We pair this framework with L^{IndA}, a SAT-based AAL algorithm that extends Angluin's L^* algorithm [3], making use of incremental SAT solving and UNSAT core analysis (Sect. 4). Inspired by Rivest and Schapire [24], we design a frugal analysis method for simple and inductive counterexamples (Sect. 4.4 and 4.5). Finally, we discuss our Python implementation [26] of this framework, then its application to regular language separation and RMC (Sect. 3.2 and 5). When omitted or sketched, the full definitions and proofs can be found in the technical report [25] and its appendix.

1.1 Related Work

Chen et al. [6]'s algorithm L^{Sep} aims to learn a separator to two *regular* languages by treating "don't know" answers as if they were the third letter $\square$ of an alphabet already containing 1 and 0, then relying on Angluin's L^* algorithm [3] to infer an incompletely specified finite state machine—also known as a 3DFA. The latter's minimal *specification* yields the minimal regular separator. Yaacov et al. [31] use a similar approach to learn concise bug descriptions.

Moeller et al. [19] focus on the generic regular language separation problem. Their $L^*_{\square}$ AAL algorithm maintains a queue of *incomplete observation tables* (IOT, as defined in Section 4), of which they fill in the blanks with a SAT solver to generate hypotheses. Whenever the current IOT results in an UNSAT instance, its UNSAT core [18] is used to insert one or more IOTs, one new prefix at a time.

Grinchtein et al. [12] synthesize minimal network invariants. They allow inductive counterexamples of the form "$w \in \text{Post}(I)$ but $w \notin I$" that they handle by maintaining an IOT queue and forking the current learner instance—one fork accepts the counterexample, the other rejects it.

As RMC amounts to determining whether the reachable fragment $\text{Post}^*(S_0)$ contains a bad configuration, many techniques have been developed in order to compute this language, be it abstraction [2], widening [28], acceleration [16] or AAL [21,22,30]. Other recent techniques combine abstraction with learning, and look for an invariant of a given specific shape [8,9].

Chen et al. [7] use L^* with a *generous* teacher accepting *any* regular inductive invariant. Instead of "don't know", this teacher is *strict* (resp. *non-strict*) as it returns 0 (resp. 1), thus targeting the smallest (resp. biggest) invariant. It may be that neither are regular, despite a regular invariant existing.

Neider et al. [21,22] compute regular inductive invariants with an L^*-like AAL algorithm that allows "don't know" answers. They maintain a single IOT instead of a queue but rely on an iterative SAT-based synthesis algorithm to generate a hypothesis by treating the IOT as a passive learning sample.

The IdMAT framework formalizes these various use cases by framing incomplete learning as looking for an unspecified language in a *target class.* A lack of consensus within the target class—a word is accepted by some targets but rejected by others—results in "don't know" answers to membership queries, although IdMAT may—subsuming iMAT [19] when it does not—nevertheless return inductive constraints verified by every language in the target class.

Moreover, among the L^* variants tailored for incomplete teachers, our AAL algorithm L^{IndA} is the only one that doesn't maintain a learner queue or synthesize hypotheses with the help of a passive learning algorithm: instead, it takes a single call to a SAT solver to generate a hypothesis from L^{IndA}'s only IOT. However, L^{IndA} does not necessarily return the smallest automaton in the target class: this property is of limited use for RMC, as any inductive invariant proves safety. Finally, rather than indiscriminately adding the entire set of prefixes [12,21,22] or suffixes [19] of a counterexample to the table, we extend Rivest-Schapire's algorithm [24] to incomplete teachers, for simple and inductive counterexamples alike.

2 Preliminaries

2.1 Regular Languages

An *alphabet* is a finite set Σ. A *word* w over Σ is any finite sequence over Σ. Its *length* is written $|w|$. A *language* L is a subset of the set Σ^* of words. Given $w_1, w_2 \in \Sigma^*$ and $L_1, L_2 \subseteq \Sigma^*$, $w_1 \cdot w_2$ denotes their *concatenation*—symbol $\cdot$ may be omitted—and $L_1 \cdot L_2 = \{w_1 \cdot w_2 \mid w_1 \in L_1, w_2 \in L_2\}$. For any $i \in \mathbb{N}$, $w[i]$ stands for the i-th letter of w if $0 \leq i < |w|$, and $w[i] = \varepsilon$ otherwise. For $0 < i \leq |w|$, w^i is the *prefix* $w[0] \cdots w[i-1]$. For $0 \leq i < |w|$, ${}^i w$ is the *suffix* $w[i] \cdots w[|w|-1]$. Both w^i and ${}^i w$ are equal to ε for other values of i.

Definition 1. *A* Deterministic Finite Automaton *(DFA)* $\mathcal{A} = (Q, \Sigma, \delta, q_i, F)$ *is a tuple s.t.* Q *is a finite* set of states, Σ *a finite alphabet,* $\delta : Q \times \Sigma \to Q$ *a* transition function, $q_i \in Q$ *the* initial *state,* $F \subseteq Q$ *the set of* final *states.*

The inductive closure $\delta^* : Q \times \Sigma^* \to Q$ of δ is s.t. for $w \in \Sigma \setminus \{\varepsilon\}$ and $q \in Q$, $\delta^*(q, \varepsilon) = q$ and $\delta^*(q, w) = \delta(q', {}^1 w)$ where $q' = \delta^*(q, w[0])$. If $\delta^*(q_i, w) = q$, w is an *access sequence* for state q. $\mathcal{A}$ *accepts* w if $\delta^*(q_i, w) \in F$; we denote this predicate $\mathcal{A}(w)$. The language $\mathcal{L}(\mathcal{A})$ *accepted* by $\mathcal{A}$ is the set of all words accepted by $\mathcal{A}$. A language is *regular* or *rational* if it is accepted by some DFA. $\mathrm{Reg}(\Sigma)$ denotes the set of regular languages over Σ, characterized as follows:

Definition 2 (Congruence relation). *Given* $L \subseteq \Sigma^*$, $\equiv_{\mathrm{L}}$ *is the equivalence relation on* Σ^* *such that* $w_1 \equiv_{\mathrm{L}} w_2$ *if and only if* $\forall s \in \Sigma^*, w_1 \cdot s \in L \leftrightarrow w_2 \cdot s \in L$.

Theorem 1 (Myhill-Nerode). *L is regular if and only if $\equiv_{\mathrm{L}}$ has finite index.*

From $\equiv_{\mathrm{L}}$'s finite quotient space $\Sigma^*/\equiv_{\mathrm{L}}$, one can infer the unique minimal (in terms of states) DFA $\mathcal{A}_L = (\Sigma^*/\equiv_{\mathrm{L}}, \Sigma, \delta_L, [\varepsilon]_{\equiv_{\mathrm{L}}}, F_L)$ accepting L, where $\delta_L([p]_{\equiv_{\mathrm{L}}}, a) = [pa]_{\equiv_{\mathrm{L}}}$ and $F_L = \{[w]_{\equiv_{\mathrm{L}}} \mid w \in L\}$. It is called L's *canonical* DFA.

If $w_1 \cdot s \in L \not\leftrightarrow w_2 \cdot s \in L$ for some $s \in \Sigma^*$, we say that s *distinguishes* w_1 and w_2; it is witness to $w_1 \not\equiv_{\mathrm{L}} w_2$. A *state cover* of L is a set P such that for any congruence class $[w]_{\equiv_{\mathrm{L}}} \in \Sigma^*/\equiv_{\mathrm{L}}$, there exists a unique $p \in P$, $p \in [w]_{\equiv_{\mathrm{L}}}$. A set S is a *characterization set* of L if for any $w_1, w_2 \in \Sigma^*$ such that $w_1 \not\equiv_{\mathrm{L}} w_2$, there exists $s \in S$ distinguishing w_1 and w_2.

2.2 Active Automata Learning

We recommend Steffen et al.'s chapter [27] for a more thorough introduction to active automata learning.

The MAT Framework. Let $L \in \mathrm{Reg}(\Sigma)$ be a target language. The *Minimally Adequate Teacher* (MAT) for L consists of two functions: a *membership* oracle $\texttt{MEM} : w \in \Sigma^* \mapsto$ "$w \in L$?" $\in \{0, 1\}$ and an *equivalence* oracle $\texttt{EQ} : \mathrm{Reg}(\Sigma) \to \Sigma^* \cup \{1\}$ such that $\texttt{EQ}(H) = 1$ if $H = L$ and $\texttt{EQ}(H) = w$ s.t. $w \in H \not\leftrightarrow w \in L$ otherwise—w is said to be a *counterexample. Active Automata Learning* (AAL) is a two player game consisting in a *learner* using the MAT to compute L, trying to perform as few calls to the oracles MEM and EQ—respectively called membership queries (MQs) and equivalence queries (EQs)—as possible.

Data Structures. Angluin's L^* algorithm [3] maintains two sets $P, S \subseteq \Sigma^*$, informally called the sets of *prefixes* and *suffixes*. They determine the MQs to be submitted to the MAT, the answers to which being stored in a table:

Definition 3. *An* Observation Table *(OT) is a function* $\mathfrak{T} : (P \cup (P \cdot \Sigma)) \times S \to \{0, 1\}$ *such that* $\mathfrak{T}(p, s) = \texttt{MEM}(p \cdot s)$ *(also written* $\mathfrak{T}(p \cdot s) = \texttt{MEM}(p \cdot s)$*).*

The set $P \cdot \Sigma$ is called the *frontier*, and $\mathfrak{C} = (P \cup (P \cdot \Sigma)) \cdot S$, the set of *cells* of $\mathfrak{T}$. The latter is the set of words one needs to query to fill in the table.

An OT $\mathfrak{T}$ induces a congruence relation $\equiv_{\mathfrak{T}}$ over $P \cup (P \cdot \Sigma)$ such that $w_1 \equiv_{\mathfrak{T}} w_2$ if and only if $\forall s \in S$, $\texttt{MEM}(w_1 \cdot s) = \texttt{MEM}(w_2 \cdot s)$, i.e. lines w_1 and w_2 of $\mathfrak{T}$ are identical. Note that $\equiv_{\mathfrak{T}}$ under-approximates $\equiv_{\mathrm{L}}$, as $w_1 \not\equiv_{\mathfrak{T}} w_2 \to w_1 \not\equiv_{\mathrm{L}} w_2$.

An OT is *sharp* if $\forall p_1, p_2 \in P$ such that $p_1 \neq p_2$, $p_1 \not\equiv_{\mathfrak{T}} p_2$: its prefixes are demonstrably pairwise distinguished. It is *closed* if $\forall w \in P \cdot \Sigma$, $\exists p \in P$, $p \equiv_{\mathfrak{T}} w$: any line labeled by a word $w \in P \cdot \Sigma$ in the frontier is identical to a line labeled by a prefix p. If $\mathfrak{T}$ is sharp and closed, this prefix p is unique, called the *representative* of w, and written $\sigma_{\mathfrak{T}}(w)$. A sharp and closed OT induces a *hypothesis* $\mathcal{H}_{\mathfrak{T}} = (P, \Sigma, \delta_{\mathfrak{T}}, \varepsilon, F_{\mathfrak{T}})$ such that $F_{\mathfrak{T}} = \{p \in P \mid \texttt{MEM}(p) = 1\}$ and $\forall p \in P$, $\forall a \in \Sigma$, $\delta_{\mathfrak{T}}(p, a) = \sigma_{\mathfrak{T}}(p \cdot a)$.

For any $w \in \Sigma^*$, we define $\sigma_{\mathfrak{T}}(w) = \delta^*_{\mathfrak{T}}(p, w)$. This does not contradict the previous definition of $\sigma_{\mathfrak{T}}(w)$ on $P \cdot \Sigma$ by design of $\delta_{\mathfrak{T}}$. Moreover, $\mathcal{H}_{\mathfrak{T}}(\sigma_{\mathfrak{T}}(w)) =$

$\mathcal{H}_{\mathfrak{T}}(w)$ for any $w \in \Sigma^*$ and $\sigma_{\mathfrak{T}}(p) = p$ for any $p \in P$. Intuitively, $\sigma_{\mathfrak{T}}(w)$ is the prefix in P identifying the state w leads to in $\mathcal{H}_{\mathfrak{T}}$.

The Learning Algorithm L^*. Initially, $P = S = \{\varepsilon\}$. Algorithm L^* queries the MAT as it computes $\mathfrak{T}$, then seeks closure defects, i.e. whether $\exists p \cdot a \in P \cdot \Sigma$ such that $\forall p' \in P$, $p \cdot a \not\equiv_{\mathfrak{T}} p'$. If one such $p \cdot a$ exists, it is added to P. The OT is therefore always kept sharp by design. Once it is closed, the learner computes $\mathcal{H}_{\mathfrak{T}}$. If $\mathtt{EQ}(\mathcal{H}_{\mathfrak{T}})$ returns a counterexample w, then it can be proven that there exists a *refining* suffix of w s.t. its addition to S causes a closure defect.

The sharpness of $\mathfrak{T}$ guarantees termination due to the elements of P demonstrably belonging to different classes of the quotient space $\Sigma^*/\equiv_{\mathrm{L}}$. L^*'s correction is a consequence of $\equiv_{\mathfrak{T}}$ being an under-approximation of $\equiv_{\mathrm{L}}$. As L^* ends, P is a state cover of L and S a characterization set.

Counterexample Analysis. A method designed by Rivest and Schapire [24] (RS) infers a refining suffix s of a counterexample w in $\mathcal{O}(\log|w|)$ MQs. Intuitively, it consists in replacing a prefix of w with its representative and observing at which point doing so alters MEM's output. Formally, for $i \in [0 \,..\, |w|]$, we consider the i-th *partial computation* $c^{\mathfrak{T}}_{w,i} = \sigma_{\mathfrak{T}}(w^i) \cdot {}^i w$—we may omit $\mathfrak{T}$ whenever contextually relevant—and its matching *evaluation predicate* $\alpha_w(i) = \mathtt{MEM}(c_{w,i})$.

Definition 4. *A* breaking point *(BP) w.r.t. counterexample $w \in \Sigma^*$ to $\mathcal{H}_{\mathfrak{T}}$ is $i \in [0 \,..\, |w|-1]$ s.t. $\alpha_w(i) \neq \alpha_w(i+1)$.*

If i is a BP, ${}^i w$ separates $\sigma(w^i) \cdot w[i]$ and $\sigma(w^{i+1})$, yet $\sigma(w^i) \cdot w[i] \equiv_{\mathfrak{T}} \sigma(w^{i+1})$. Thus, adding ${}^i w$ to S causes a closure defect and induces a refinement of $\mathcal{H}$. A BP always exists due to $\alpha_w(0) \neq \alpha_w(|w|)$. If we explore table $[\alpha_i(w)]_{i \in [0..|w|]}$ dichotomically, finding a BP only requires a logarithmic number of MQs.

2.3 SAT Solving

Given a set of *variables* $\mathcal{V}$, we consider the set $\varphi := 0 \mid 1 \mid x \in \mathcal{V} \mid \neg\varphi \mid \varphi \wedge \varphi \mid \varphi \vee \varphi \mid \varphi \rightarrow \varphi \mid \varphi \leftrightarrow \varphi$ of *propositional formulas* (PFs) $\mathcal{F}_0$. A *valuation* v is a partial function $v : \mathcal{V} \rightarrow \{0,1\}$. A valuation v' *subsumes* v if v is a subset of v' in terms of binary relations over $\mathcal{V} \times \{0,1\}$. The PF $v[\varphi]$ is obtained by replacing any variable $x \in \mathcal{V}$ occuring in φ by $v(x)$ whenever the latter is defined.

A *model* m for a formula φ—written $m \vDash \varphi$—is a valuation s.t. $m[\varphi] = 1$ according to Boolean semantics and every variable of φ belongs to m's domain. The *satisfiability* (SAT) problem for a PF φ consists in determining whether a model for φ exists; φ is said to be SAT if it does, and UNSAT otherwise.

A *set of clauses* is a finite set $\mathcal{C}$ of PFs in conjunctive normal form (CNF), interpreted as the PF $\bigwedge_{c \in \mathcal{C}} c$. If $\mathcal{C}$ is UNSAT, an *UNSAT core* of $\mathcal{C}$ is a minimal (according to $\subseteq$) subset $\mathcal{C}'$ of $\mathcal{C}$ such that $\mathcal{C}'$ is UNSAT as well. A *SAT solver* is a program that decides for any set of clauses $\mathcal{C}$ whether $\mathcal{C}$ is SAT or not and returns a model m of $\mathcal{C}$ if it is. A solver is *incremental* if we can add new clauses to $\mathcal{C}$ and try to solve the updated problem without resetting the solver.

3 The IdMAT Framework

3.1 Inductive Oracles

We introduce an extension to the MAT framework where the target language is not unique: given a *target class* $\mathcal{T} \subseteq 2^{\Sigma^*}$, the goal of the learner in this setting is to identify *one* unspecified language $T \in \mathcal{T}$. To this end, we introduce an inductive teacher IdMAT consisting of two oracles:

Definition 5. *An* inductive membership oracle *is a function* $\texttt{MEM} : \Sigma^* \times 2^{\Sigma^*} \rightarrow \{0,1\} \cup 2^{\Sigma^* \times \Sigma^*}$ *such that for any finite set* $A \subseteq \Sigma^*$ *and* $w \in \Sigma^*$, *exactly one of the following holds:*

- $\texttt{MEM}(w, A) = 1$ *and* $\forall T \in \mathcal{T}, w \in T$; *every target language accepts* w.
- $\texttt{MEM}(w, A) = 0$ *and* $\forall T \in \mathcal{T}, w \notin T$; *every target language rejects* w.
- $\texttt{MEM}(w, A) \subseteq \{(w_1, w_2) \in (A \times \{w\}) \cup (\{w\} \times A) \mid \forall T \in \mathcal{T}, w_1 \in T \rightarrow w_2 \in T\}$.

Intuitively, the third case of Definition 5 is an *incomplete* answer that states that w's membership status is not constant over the target class. Nevertheless, the learner can provide "hint words" in a set A, and the teacher can then provide *inductive pairs* (w_1, w_2) relating $w \in \{w_1, w_2\}$ to these words, in the form "For any target T, if w_1 belongs to T, then so must w_2.". As a shorthand, we write $\texttt{MEM}(w) = \texttt{MEM}(w, \emptyset)$ reducing the possible answers to 0, 1 or $\emptyset$, that is, respectively "Yes", "No" or "Don't know" answers.

Similarly, the following Definition 6 generalizes equivalence queries to account for inductive pairs being counterexamples. Moreover, notice that while the oracles are not-uniquely defined, the provided counterexamples must be consistent with the answers returned by the membership oracle:

Definition 6. *An* inductive validity oracle *is a function* $\texttt{VAL} : \text{Reg}(\Sigma) \rightarrow \{1\} \cup \Sigma^* \cup (\Sigma^* \times \Sigma^*)$ *such that for any hypothesis* $H \in \text{Reg}(\Sigma)$:

- $\texttt{VAL}(H) = 1$ *if and only if* $H \in \mathcal{T}$; *the hypothesis belongs to the target class.*
- *If* $\texttt{VAL}(H) = w \in \Sigma^*$, *then* $\texttt{MEM}(w) \in \{0, 1\}$ *and* $w \in H \leftrightarrow \texttt{MEM}(w) = 0$; *word* w *is a* simple *counterexample.*
- *If* $\texttt{VAL}(H) = (w_1, w_2) \in \Sigma^* \times \Sigma^*$, *then* $(w_1, w_2) \in \texttt{MEM}(w_1, \{w_2\})$, $w_1 \in H$ *but* $w_2 \notin H$; *pair* (w_1, w_2) *is an* inductive *counterexample.*

3.2 Instantiating IdMAT

Regular Language Separation. Consider two languages $L_1, L_2 \subseteq \Sigma^*$. Let $\mathcal{T}_{\text{sep}} = \{L \in \text{Reg}(\Sigma) \mid L_1 \subseteq L \subseteq \overline{L_2}\}$ be the target class of regular separators. For any $w \in \Sigma^*$, finite $A \subseteq \Sigma^*$, and $H \in \text{Reg}(\Sigma)$, IdMAT oracles complying with Definitions 5 and 6 are defined as follows:

- $\texttt{MEM}(w, A) = 1$ if $w \in L_1$, 0 if $w \in L_2$, and $\emptyset$ otherwise.
- $\texttt{VAL}(H)$ is any word in $(H \setminus L_2) \cup (L_1 \setminus H)$ if $H \notin \mathcal{T}_{\text{sep}}$, and 1 otherwise.

They are effective if $w \in L_1$, $w \in L_2$, $L_1 \subseteq L$ and $L \subseteq \overline{L_2}$ are decidable for every $w \in \Sigma^*$ and $L \in \mathrm{Reg}(\Sigma)$. The inductive capabilities (hint words, inductive counterexamples) of the IdMAT are ignored, restricting MEM's output to 0, 1 and the "don't know" answer $\emptyset$, thus subsuming Moeller et al.'s iMAT framework [19].

Regular Model Checking. Let $\mathcal{R} = (\Sigma, \hookrightarrow, S_0, S_b)$ be a *regular transition system* (RTS) with $S_0, S_b \in \mathrm{Reg}(\Sigma)$ and $\hookrightarrow \in \mathrm{Reg}(\Sigma \times \Sigma)$ a length-preserving finite transducer inducing an effectively computable *successor* relation Post : $\mathrm{Reg}(\Sigma) \to \mathrm{Reg}(\Sigma)$ such that $\mathrm{Post}(L) = \{w_2 \mid w_1 \in L, (w_1, w_2) \in \hookrightarrow\}$. Similarly, Pre : $\mathrm{Reg}(\Sigma) \to \mathrm{Reg}(\Sigma)$ must be an effectively computable *predecessor* relation such that $\mathrm{Pre}(L) = \{w_1 \mid w_2 \in L, (w_1, w_2) \in \hookrightarrow\}$. However, note that $\mathrm{Post}^*(L) = \bigcup_{k \geq 0} \mathrm{Post}^k(L)$ and $\mathrm{Pre}^*(L) = \bigcup_{k \geq 0} \mathrm{Pre}^k(L)$ may not be computable.

Consider the class $\mathcal{T}_{\mathrm{ind}} = \{I \subseteq \Sigma^* \mid (S_0 \subseteq I) \wedge (I \subseteq \overline{S_b}) \wedge (\mathrm{Post}(I) \subseteq I)\}$ of inductive invariants. For every $w \in \Sigma^*$, finite $A \subseteq \Sigma^*$, and $H \in \mathrm{Reg}(\Sigma)$, consider the IdMAT oracles complying with Definitions 5 and 6:

- $\mathtt{MEM}(w, A) = 1$ if $w \in \mathrm{Post}^*(S_0 \cap \Sigma^{|w|})$, 0 if $w \in \mathrm{Pre}^*(S_b \cap \Sigma^{|w|})$, and $\{w\} \times (\mathrm{Post}^*(\{w\}) \cap A) \cup (\mathrm{Pre}^*(\{w\}) \cap A) \times \{w\}$ otherwise.
- $\mathtt{VAL}(H) = w$ for some $w \in (S_0 \setminus H) \cup (S_b \cap H)$ if such a word exists, else (w_1, w_2) for some $w_1 \in H$ and $w_2 \notin H$ such that $(w_1, w_2) \in \mathtt{MEM}(w_1, \{w_2\})$ if such a pair exists, else 1.

These oracles are effectively computable: $\hookrightarrow$ is length-preserving and $S_0 \cap \Sigma^{|w|}$ is finite, thus $\mathrm{Post}^*(S_0 \cap \Sigma^{|w|})$ is finite and can be found using an iterative fixpoint algorithm. The same is true of $\mathrm{Pre}^*(S_b \cap \Sigma^{|w|})$, $\mathrm{Post}^*(\{w\}) \cap A$, and $\mathrm{Pre}^*(\{w\}) \cap A$. Moreover, $\mathrm{Post}(H)$ is regular and we can look for inductive counterexamples by seeking $w_2 \in \mathrm{Post}(H) \setminus H$ then computing $w_1 \in \mathrm{Pre}^*(\{w_2\}) \cap H$.

Example 3. Consider Example 1. Words $w_1 = $ ●○○●○ and $w_2 = $ ○●●○○ belong neither to $\mathrm{Post}^*(S_0)$ nor $\mathrm{Pre}^*(S_b)$, being configurations of odd length with an even number of ○ empty positions in-between their two ● tokens. Yet $w_2 \in \mathrm{Post}^*(\{w_1\})$, thus (w_1, w_2) is an inductive pair and $(w_1, w_2) \in \mathtt{MEM}(w_1, \{w_2\})$.

4 The L^{IndA} Active Learning Algorithm

We assume that the oracles defined in Sect. 3.1 are effectively computable for a non-empty target class $\mathcal{T}$. We aim to find one $T \in \mathcal{T} \cap \mathrm{Reg}(\Sigma)$ if it exists and to this end introduce L^{IndA}, a new AAL algorithm under the IdMAT framework.

4.1 Data Structures

Algorithm L^{IndA} is based on L^*. Similarly, it maintains two sets P and S and an OT variant $\mathfrak{T}$ that also accounts for incomplete answers:

Definition 7. *An* Incomplete Observation Table *(IOT) is* $\mathfrak{T} : (P \cup (P \cdot \Sigma)) \times S \to \{0, 1, \square\}$ *s.t.* $\mathfrak{T}(p, s) = \square$ *if* $\mathtt{MEM}(p \cdot s) \notin \{0, 1\}$ *and* $\mathtt{MEM}(p \cdot s)$ *otherwise.*

Symbol $\square$ stands for incomplete answers to MQs, in a similar fashion to $L^*_\square$ [19]. An IOT is shown in Example 4. A sub-table $\mathfrak{T}_B$ of $\mathfrak{T}$ for some $B \subseteq P$ is $\mathfrak{T}$'s restriction to $(B \cup (B \cdot \Sigma)) \times S$. Unlike L^* under the MAT framework or $L^*_\square$ under iMAT, we must also account for inductive answers to MQs that constrain $\mathfrak{T}$'s $\square$ cells, since $\mathfrak{T}$ does not fully record these:

Definition 8. *Let* $U = \{w \in \mathfrak{C} \mid \mathfrak{T}(w) = \square\}$ *be the set of* incomplete *cells. The set of* inductive pairs *is* $\mathrm{IP} = \bigcup_{w \in U} \mathtt{MEM}(w, U)$.

4.2 Outlining the Learning Loop

Unlike other AAL algorithms for incomplete teachers, L^{IndA} does not maintain several IOTs nor use passive learning algorithms to infer a hypothesis from the table. Instead, our intuition is to maintain a single IOT $\mathfrak{T}$, but design P and S in such a fashion they will at some point respectively *contain* a state cover B—known as a *basis*—and a characterization set of some $T \in \mathcal{T} \cap \mathrm{Reg}(\Sigma)$.

To infer a hypothesis H that we can submit to the IdMAT, a prefix-closed subset $B \subseteq P$ called the *basis* is chosen, inducing a sub-table $\mathfrak{T}_B$. The "blanks" of $\mathfrak{T}_B$ are then "filled"—i.e. $\square$ cells are arbitrarily assigned values—in a manner that makes the resulting table sharp, closed, and compliant with the inductive constraints recorded in IP. We encode the existence of such a basis and sub-table as a SAT instance $\mathcal{C}_{P,S}$; given a model m to this instance, $\mathfrak{T}_m$ denotes the OT that results from using m to choose a basis B and fill IOT $\mathfrak{T}_B$'s $\square$ cells.

Algorithm 1 summarizes L^{IndA}'s main loop. Similarly to L^*, $P, S = \{\varepsilon\}$ initially. In a broad sense, closure defects result in P being updated while counterexamples yield new suffixes to add to S, although the finer details of these steps significantly differ from L^* under the MAT framework. Note that if the target class is a singleton $\mathcal{T} \cap \mathrm{Reg}(\Sigma) = \{L\}$, `MEM` never returns incomplete answers, and a run of L^{IndA} is essentially identical to a run of L^* with RS under the MAT framework: it maintains the same OT and performs the same queries.

Algorithm 1. The learning algorithm L^{IndA}.

```
P, S ← {ε}
loop
    Update the IOT 𝔗 and the clauses C_{P,S}.                ▷ See Sect. 4.3 and [25, A].
    while C_{P,S} is satisfied by some model m do
        From m, build a hypothesis H_m.                       ▷ See Sect. 4.3 and [25, A].
        c ← VAL(H_m)
        if c = 1 then return H_m                              ▷ An invariant has been found.
        else if c = w ∈ Σ* then
            Analyze w and update S, 𝔗 and C_{P,S}.             ▷ See Sect. 4.4.
        else if c = (w1, w2) then
            Analyze (w1, w2) and update S, 𝔗 and C_{P,S}.      ▷ See Sect. 4.5.
    P ← P ∪ {p · a | (clos_{p,a}) ∈ UnsatCore(C_{P,S})}       ▷ See Sect. 4.3.
```

4.3 Generating the Hypothesis

We encode as a SAT instance the existence of both a basis B and a membership assignment function that would make the resulting sub-table sharp and closed. A set of clauses $\mathcal{C}_{P,S}$ [25, A] guarantees that, if m is a model of $\mathcal{C}_{P,S}$, then it yields a sub-table $\mathfrak{T}_m$ of $\mathfrak{T}$ that is sharp and closed. For each $w \in \mathfrak{C}$ such that $\mathfrak{T}(w) = \square$, we introduce a variable x_w representing w's membership status. For every $p \in P$, a variable b_p determines whether p belongs to B. Finally, variable $e_{p,a,q}$ states that $p \cdot a \in P \cdot \Sigma$ must be equivalent to $q \in P$ w.r.t. the OT generated. Of particular interest are the clauses $(\texttt{clos}_{p,a})$ for $p \in P$ and $a \in \Sigma$ that guarantee $p \cdot a \equiv_{\mathfrak{T}_m} p'$ for some $p' \in P$, hence, $\mathfrak{T}_m$'s closure:

$$b_p \rightarrow \bigvee_{p' \in P} e_{p,a,p'} \qquad (\texttt{clos}_{p,a})$$

Moreover, for any pair $(w_1, w_2) \in \text{IP}$, there exists a clause $x_{w_1} \rightarrow x_{w_2}$ in $\mathcal{C}_{P,S}$.

Using the UNSAT Core to Extend the Set of Prefixes. Should the instance $\mathcal{C}_{P,S}$ end up being UNSAT, then it can be proven (see [25, A] for a detailed proof) that its core always contains at least one clause $(\texttt{clos}_{p,a})$. Then for each $(p, a) \in P \times \Sigma$ such that $(\texttt{clos}_{p,a})$ is in the core, we add $p \cdot a$ to P. Intuitively, an UNSAT instance means that, no matter the basis chosen and the values assigned to $\square$ cells, the resulting sub-table will contain a closure defect. Theorem 4 later states that these core-based refinements guarantee termination.

Example 4. Consider the following IOT $\mathfrak{T}$ induced by Example 1 after counterexample ●○● to hypothesis $H = \Sigma^*$ results in a first refinement of $\mathfrak{T}$.

Due to $|P| = 1$, the only possible basis is $B = \{\varepsilon\}$ and $\mathfrak{T}_B = \mathfrak{T}$. The closure condition results in $\varepsilon \equiv_{\mathfrak{T}_m}$ ○ $\equiv_{\mathfrak{T}_m}$ ● for any possible model m. Thus, $\mathfrak{T}_m(\varepsilon,$ ○●$) = 0$ and $\mathfrak{T}_m($○, ●$) = 1$. But both cells describe the membership status of word ○●. There is a contradiction, the instance is UNSAT, and ○, ● are added to P.

		S		
		ε	●	○●
P	ε	□	□	□
P · Σ	○	□	□	□
	●	□	1	0

Building the Hypothesis. If the instance is SAT, we denote m the model returned by the SAT solver and $\mathfrak{T}_m$ the resulting □-free sub-table. From $\mathfrak{T}_m$, a hypothesis $\mathcal{H}_m$ can be built, as described in Sect. 2.1.

Example 5. Consider the updated IOT resulting from Example 4's refinement. Were the SAT solver to pick $B = \{\varepsilon, ●\}$ as a basis, grayed lines ○○ and ○● are dropped from $\mathfrak{T}_B$. Filling the remaining lines and □ cells as depicted results in a sharp, closed table $\mathfrak{T}_m$ from which we can infer the following two state DFA $\mathcal{H}_m$:

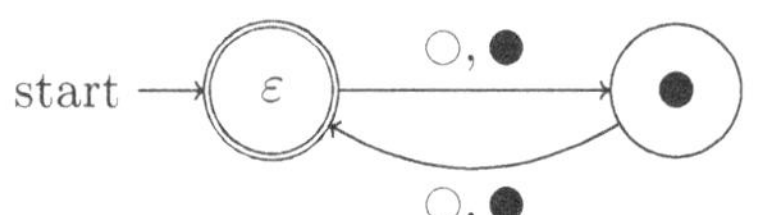

		S		
		ε	●	○●
P	ε	1	0	1
	○	0	1	0
	●	0	1	0
P · Σ	○○	□	□	□
	○●	□	□	0
	●○	1	0	1
	●●	1	0	1

4.4 Analyzing Simple Counterexamples

Under incomplete teachers, the evaluation predicate introduced in Sect. 2.2 may return incomplete answers. Thus, the existence of a breaking point is no longer guaranteed—as shown in Example 6—and incomplete learning algorithms revert to adding the entire set of prefixes [12,21,22] (resp. suffixes [19]) of a counterexample w to P (resp. S) in order to induce a refinement.

We introduce a counterexample analysis algorithm that can reduce the number of suffixes added to S, in a fashion similar to RS under the MAT framework. To this end, the evaluation predicate must account for incomplete answers and membership assumptions made by model m while assigning values to □ cells:

Definition 9. *Given a counterexample $w \in \Sigma^*$ to $\mathcal{H}_m$ and $i \in [0 .. |w|]$, the* incomplete evaluation predicate *is 1.* $\alpha_w(i) = \mathtt{MEM}(c_{w,i}^{\mathfrak{T}_m})$ *if* $\mathtt{MEM}(c_{w,i}^{\mathfrak{T}_m}) \in \{0,1\}$, *else 2.* $\alpha_w(i) = m[x_{c_{w,i}^{\mathfrak{T}_m}}]$ *if* $m[x_{c_{w,i}^{\mathfrak{T}_m}}]$ *is defined, else 3.* $\alpha_w(i) = \square$.

While a BP may not exist, some intervals can nevertheless provide L^{IndA} with a set of new suffixes whose addition to S induces a refinement of the hypothesis:

Definition 10. *A* Breaking Interval *(BI) is an interval* $[i .. j]$, $i, j \in [0 .. |w|]$, $i < j$, *such that* $\{\alpha_w(i), \alpha_w(j)\} \subseteq \{0,1\}$ *and* $\alpha_w(i) \neq \alpha_w(j)$.

Property 1. $\{\alpha_w(0), \alpha_w(|w|)\} \subseteq \{0,1\}$, $\alpha_w(0) \neq \alpha_w(|w|)$, and $[0 .. |w|]$ is a BI.

Example 6. Consider counterexample $w =$ ○●○○○● $\in \mathrm{Pre}^*(S_b)$ to hypothesis $\mathcal{H}_m$ of Example 5. Let us perform a RS analysis of w: we split w into a prefix w^i and a suffix ${}^i w$, compute the representative $\sigma_{\mathcal{H}_m}(w^i)$ of w^i, explicit the partial computation $c_{w,i}^{\mathfrak{T}_m} = \sigma_{\mathcal{H}_m}(w^i) \cdot {}^i w$, and finally perfom a query $\mathtt{MEM}(c_{w,i}^{\mathfrak{T}_m})$ to compute $\alpha_w(i)$. It results in the following RS table that lacks a BP:

i	0	1	2	3	4	5	6
w^i	ε	○	○●	○●○	○●○○	○●○○○	○●○○○●
$\sigma_{\mathcal{H}_m}(w^i)$	ε	●	ε	●	ε	●	ε
${}^i w$	○●○○○●	●○○○●	○○○●	○○●	○●	●	ε
$c_{w,i}^{\mathfrak{T}_m}$	○●○○○●	●●○○○●	○○○●	●○○●	○●	●●	ε
$\alpha_w(i)$	0	□	□	1	□	1	1

Yet [0 .. 3] is a BI. We add suffixes ●○○○●, ○○○●, and ○○● to S.

Theorem 2. *Let m be a model for the set of clauses $\mathcal{C}_{P,S}$, w a counterexample to $\mathcal{H}_m$, $[i \mathrel{..} j]$ a breaking interval of w, and $S' = S \cup \{^{i+1}w, \ldots, {}^{j}w\}$. Then any model m' subsuming m does not satisfy the updated set of clauses $\mathcal{C}_{P,S'}$.*

Intuitively, assume that there exists an OT $\mathfrak{T}_{m'}$ synthesized from a model m' of $\mathcal{C}_{P,S'}$ that shares $\mathfrak{T}_m$'s basis and membership assumptions—resulting in the same hypothesis being generated and w still being a counterexample. By definition of S', partial computations $c_{w,k}^{\mathfrak{T}_{m'}} = \sigma_{\mathfrak{T}_{m'}}(w^k) \cdot {}^k w$ belong to $\mathfrak{T}_{m'}$'s cells for any $k \in [i+1 \mathrel{..} j]$. Therefore, m' must assign a value to predicate $\alpha_w(k)$. But, due to $\alpha_w(i) \neq \alpha_w(j)$, $[i \mathrel{..} j]$ must contain a BP that causes a closure defect invalidating $m' \models \mathcal{C}_{P,S'}$. By contradiction, no such m' exists.

Property 1 guarantees a BI always exists. Its proof and that of Theorem 2 are detailed in [25, B.1 and B.2]. Finding a BI requires at most $\mathcal{O}(|w|)$ MQs, a weaker result than the $\mathcal{O}(\log |w|)$ MQs needed under the MAT framework: binary search is no longer an efficient option due to □ answers.

Use of Simple Counterexamples in L^{IndA}. Given a simple counterexample w to hypothesis $\mathcal{H}_m$, we find a BI $[i \mathrel{..} j]$ and add $\{^{i+1}w, \ldots, {}^{j}w\}$ to S, resulting in new columns being inserted in the IOT $\mathfrak{T}$. The set of clauses $\mathcal{C}_{P,S}$ is then updated *incrementally*: new clauses are added to further constrain the current instance of the SAT solver without resetting it. Depending on how MQs are carried out, we may be looking for the shortest BI or for one that maximizes i (hence, minimizes the length of the longest suffix added). We experimentally evaluate these two options in Sect. 5, in particular in the context of RMC.

4.5 Analysing Inductive Counterexamples

We briefly show how to handle inductive counterexamples to hypothesis $\mathcal{H}_m$ of the form $w = (w_1, w_2)$ in a similar fashion to simple counterexamples, inducing a refinement of $\mathcal{H}_m$ by *frugally* expanding S. Intuitively, we introduce a *two-dimensional* incomplete evaluation predicate $\alpha_w(i,j)$, querying the teacher and the model to determine whether $(c_{w_1,i}, c_{w_2,j})$ is an inductive pair for $(i,j) \in [0 \mathrel{..} |w_1|] \times [0 \mathrel{..} |w_2|]$. We look for a *breaking rectangle* (BR) $[i \mathrel{..} i'] \times [j \mathrel{..} j']$ s.t. $\{\alpha_w(i,j), \alpha_w(i',j')\} \subseteq \{0,1\}$, and $\alpha_w(i,j) \neq \alpha_w(i',j')$, from which we deduce which suffixes of w_1 and w_2 to add to S.

Theorem 3. *Let m be a model for the set of clauses $\mathcal{C}_{P,S}$, $w = (w_1, w_2)$ an inductive counterexample to $\mathcal{H}_m$, $[i \mathrel{..} i'] \times [j \mathrel{..} j']$ a breaking rectangle, and $S' = S \cup \{^{i}w_1, \ldots, {}^{i'}w_1\} \cup \{^{j}w_2, \ldots, {}^{j'}w_2\}$. Then any model m' subsuming m does not satisfy the updated set of clauses $\mathcal{C}_{P,S'}$.*

We refer the reader to [25, C] for formal definitions and proofs. Finding a suitable BR requires at most $\mathcal{O}(|w_1| \times |w_2|)$ MQs.

Example 7. Example 5 featured an inductive hypothesis s.t. $\text{Post}(H) \subseteq H$.

However, its IOT can also yield another hypothesis with three states $B = \{\varepsilon, \bigcirc, \bullet\}$ if we choose to "fill in the blanks" differently:

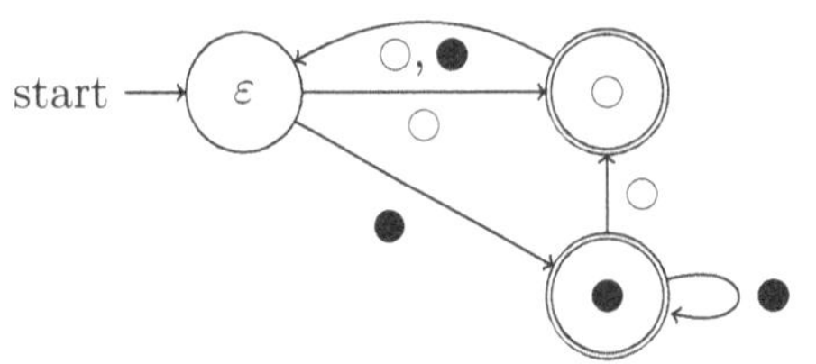

		S		
		ε	●	○●
P	ε	$\boxed{0}$	$\boxed{1}$	$\boxed{0}$
	○	$\boxed{1}$	$\boxed{0}$	$\boxed{1}$
	●	$\boxed{1}$	1	0
P · Σ	○○	$\boxed{0}$	$\boxed{1}$	$\boxed{0}$
	○●	$\boxed{0}$	$\boxed{1}$	0
	●○	$\boxed{1}$	0	1
	●●	$\boxed{1}$	$\boxed{1}$	$\boxed{0}$

$\alpha_w(k,l)$		k					
		0	1	2	3	4	5
l	0	1	1	□	1	1	1
	1	1	1	□	1	1	1
	2	□	□	□	□	□	□
	3	□	□	□	□	□	□
	4	0	0	□	0	0	0
	5	0	0	□	0	0	0

This hypothesis is not inductive: $(w_1, w_2) = (\bullet\bigcirc\bigcirc\bullet\bigcirc, \bigcirc\bullet\bullet\bigcirc\bigcirc)$ is an inductive pair by Example 3, yet $w_1 \in H$ and $w_2 \notin H$. It yields the 2D RS table to the left. Rectangle $[5] \times [1 .. 4]$ is breaking; thus, we add suffixes $\{{}^5w_1, {}^1w_2, {}^2w_2, {}^3w_2, {}^4w_2\} = \{\varepsilon, \bullet\bullet\bigcirc\bigcirc, \bullet\bigcirc\bigcirc, \bigcirc\bigcirc, \bigcirc\}$ to S.

Use of Inductive Counterexamples in L^{IndA}. Given an inductive counterexample (w_1, w_2) to hypothesis $\mathcal{H}_m$, we find a breaking rectangle $[i .. i'] \times [j .. j']$ then update S (hence the IOT $\mathfrak{T}$ as well) with $\{{}^iw_1, \ldots, {}^{i'}w_1\} \cup \{{}^jw_2, \ldots, {}^{j'}w_2\}$. Again, the resulting new clauses are added to the solver incrementally. We may be looking for the smallest rectangle (in terms of area) or one that maximizes (i, j).

4.6 Termination and Correctness

Under the MAT framework for a unique target $L \in \text{Reg}(\Sigma)$, L^* maintains a set P of words that are pairwise distinguished under $\equiv_L$. This invariant guarantees termination and correctness: to fix a closure defect, one adds a new element to P; the algorithm ends when P is a state cover of L.

However, L^{IndA}'s target class may contain more than one regular language. Nevertheless, we can prove that for any $T \in \mathcal{T}$, there exists a subset $B \subseteq P$ of words pairwise distinguished under $\equiv_T$ that grows with core-induced refinements, guaranteeing that targets of index $n+1$ can be learnt after at most n refinements. For any variable v appearing in the algorithm, let $v^{(n)}$ denote its value after the n-th UNSAT core analysis.

Lemma 1 ([25, **D.1**]). *Let $T \in \mathcal{T}$. Assume that L^{IndA} has not ended after $n \in \mathbb{N}$ UNSAT core refinements. Then there exists a prefix-closed set $B_n \subseteq P^{(n)}$ of size $n+1$ such that $\forall p, q \in B_n$, if $p \neq q$ then $p \not\equiv_T q$.*

Theorem 4 ([25, **D.2**]). *Assume $\mathcal{T}$ contains a language $T \in \mathcal{T}$ s.t. $\equiv_T$ has index $n \in \mathbb{N} \setminus \{0\}$. Then L^{IndA} terminates after at most $n-1$ UNSAT core refinements.*

Core-based refinements may add more than one prefix: hence, a target with $n+1$ states might require less than n refinements to be learnt. In the worst case scenario, the algorithm may add up to $|P| \times |\Sigma|$ prefixes each refinement, leading to an exponential number of prefixes. This is less likely to happen if some structure of $\mathcal{T}$ can be inferred from MQs—that is, if the teacher does not always return incomplete answers.

5 Experiments

We implemented[1] L^{IndA} in Python using the PySAT `1.8.dev16` [14,15] library, as it allows us to tap into the incremental SAT solver CaDiCaL `1.95` [5], a choice motivated by the results of the SAT competition [4]. Our library also features basic automata manipulation, including language separation and RMC-related operations for the IdMAT implementation.

Each run is performed on an Ubuntu 24.04 LTS virtual machine with 8 vCPU and 16GB of RAM. A run is considered failed when it timeouts after 10 minutes, or when it uses more than 200 MB of RAM. Since SAT solving and UNSAT core extraction are non-deterministic processes, we resort to running every experiment 3 times then consider the best-of-three (Bo3) runtime and query complexity.

These experiments aim at addressing the following research questions:

(Rq1) What is the impact of using a single SAT solver without forking or maintaining a learner queue—that is, using L^{IndA} instead of $L^*_\square$?

(Rq2) Does the introduction of inductive queries results in more instances being solved within the allotted time-frame?

(Rq3) What is the most efficient way to introduce new suffixes during counterexample analysis?

5.1 Language Separation Benchmark

To address *(Rq1)*, we consider the Nerode tool from [19] that implements the $L^*_\square$ algorithm mentioned in Sect. 1.1. Nerode is compiled from its repository[2] and ran with CLI options `-s -pq` on the same hardware, with the same time and memory constraints. The benchmark set does not consider inductive queries as they are not supported by Nerode and focus instead here on the language separation problem of Oliveira and al. [23] as formatted by [20].

[1] https://gitlab.lre.epita.fr/aa/string-chc-lib [26].

[2] https://github.com/cornell-pl/nerode-public/commit/9d32ef8.

Individual instances running times are reported comparatively in Fig. 1a: Nerode and L^{IndA} solved 96% and 98% of presented instances with an average runtime of 24 s and 6 s, respectively. We therefore conclude that the use of L^{IndA} is beneficial to the overall learning time. We can also remark that the improvement could be even greater as L^{IndA} is programmed in an interpreted language while Nerode is written and compiled in OCaml.

5.2 Inductive Queries: an Ablation Study

To answer *(Rq2)*, we now consider 28 RMC models from two different sources: parameterized protocols from the RMCbenchmark from [7], in a custom automata/transducer text file; and handcrafted token passing protocols, in Python format, inspired by Example 1.

As a baseline, we consider a `strict` (resp. `non-strict`) teacher—as defined in Sect. 1.1—that targets $\mathrm{Post}^*(S_0)$ (resp. $\mathrm{Pre}^*(S_b)$). This setting did not allow us to achieve comparable[3] performances to [7]; thus, we perform an ablation study on L^{IndA} instead. Table 1 displays the number of the instances solved and the Bo3 runtime/query complexity of the various AAL algorithms for the models they can solve within the allotted time-frame. It shows that L^{IndA} instantiated with an inductive teacher is able to solve more models—with the RS optimization, all solvable models save one—than `strict` and `non-strict` teachers thanks to the expressivity of the IdMAT framework, although it comes at the expense of runtime and query complexity compared to `non-strict`.

5.3 Rivest-Schapire-Like (RS) Counterexample Analysis *(Rq3)*

We perform another ablation study on the dataset previously introduced in Sect. 5.2; we compare the refinement method that consists in adding every suffix of a counterexample to S—in a similar fashion to $L^*_\square$ [19]—to our adaptation of the RS analysis technique under the IdMAT framework detailed in Sects. 4.4 and 4.5. Based on the type of BIs and BRs selected, two variants are considered: do we seek to minimize the number of new suffixes added to S (option `small`), or the length of the longest suffix added (option `short`)?

Figure 1b compares the runtime of both RS variants with a RS-free execution of L^{IndA} and shows an overall improvement. Table 1 also highlights a slight increase in the number of models solved when either variant of RS is enabled. Variant `small` is shown to be faster than `short`: in particular, it performs a significantly smaller amount of MQs.

---

[3] We conjecture that this is due to our Python implementation that exhaustively computes $\mathrm{Post}^*(S_0 \cap \Sigma^n)$ and $\mathrm{Pre}^*(S_b \cap \Sigma^n)$.

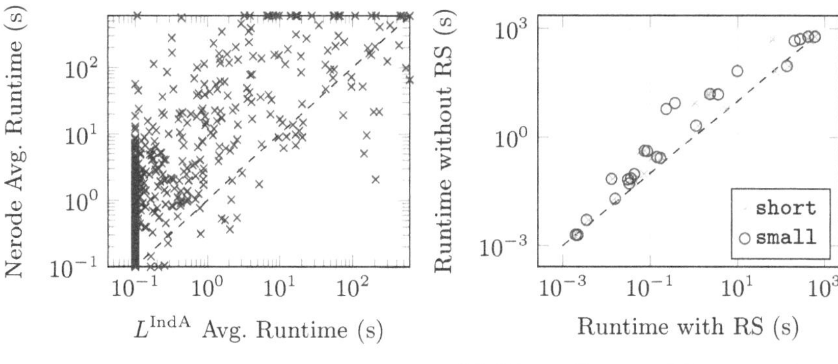

(a) Language separation benchmark (b) Rivest-Shapire ablation study.

Fig. 1. Runtime analysis and average values.

Table 1. Number of RMC models solved at least once. We average Bo3 query complexity and runtime on the set of common models every algorithm can solve.

	L^{IndA} `small`	L^{IndA} w.o. RS	L^{IndA} `short`	`strict`	`non-strict`	Common	V. Best
#Models	23	22	23	17	18	13	24
Solved freq.	0.79	0.75	0.80	0.61	0.64	-	-
Avg. Time	1.4	29.0	6.2	34.5	1.1	-	-
Avg. #`MEM`	203.4	733.6	644.2	591.4	146.1	-	-
Avg. #`VAL`	3.6	4.5	7.2	4.2	2.7	-	-

6 Conclusion and Further Developments

We devised an inductive learning framework IdMAT that targets classes of languages and subsumes the incomplete learning framework iMAT [19]. Under IdMAT, we designed a new AAL algorithm L^{IndA} that leverages incremental SAT solving and UNSAT core analysis, as well as a new frugal refinement method inspired by the well-known RS technique [24] that we also extended to inductive counterexamples. We implemented L^{IndA} and benchmarked it in the context of regular language separation and invariant synthesis.

In the footsteps of [17,19,22], we based L^{IndA} on Angluin's L^* [3]. However, it remains to be seen whether state-of-the-art active learning algorithms such as $L^{\#}$ [29] or L^{λ} [13] can be extended to the IdMAT framework. The latter algorithm is of great interest to us as it tends to reduce the overall *symbol complexity*—the sum of the length of all words that have been queried—of the learning process: indeed, given a MQ on a word w of length n, the oracle must exhaustively compute $\text{Post}^*(S_0 \cap \Sigma^n)$ and $\text{Pre}^*(S_b \cap \Sigma^n)$ (see Sect. 3.2); the smaller the n, the faster the computation. Another promising lead to explore these sets consists in relying on GPUs and a matrix-based representation of the finite transducer that encodes the system's transitions.

Finally, we should also investigate the use of *symbolic* alphabets, as RTS are often partially or fully encoded symbolically [10].

References

1. Abdulla, P.A.: Regular model checking. Int. J. Softw. Tools Technol. Transf. **14**(2), 109–118 (2012). https://doi.org/10.1007/S10009-011-0216-8
2. Abdulla, P.A., Haziza, F., Holík, L.: Parameterized verification through view abstraction. Int. J. Softw. Tools Technol. Transf. **18**(5), 495–516 (2016). https://doi.org/10.1007/S10009-015-0406-X
3. Angluin, D.: Learning regular sets from queries and counterexamples. Inf. Comput. **75**(2), 87–106 (1987). https://doi.org/10.1016/0890-5401(87)90052-6
4. Balyo, T., Heule, M., Iser, M., Järvisalo, M., Suda, M. (eds.): Proceedings of SAT Competition 2023: Solver, Benchmark and Proof Checker Descriptions. Department of Computer Science Series of Publications B, Department of Computer Science, University of Helsinki, Finland (2023)
5. Biere, A., Faller, T., Fazekas, K., Fleury, M., Froleyks, N., Pollitt, F.: Cadical 2.0. In: Gurfinkel, A., Ganesh, V. (eds.) Computer Aided Verification, pp. 133–152. Springer, Cham (2024)
6. Chen, Y.-F., Farzan, A., Clarke, E.M., Tsay, Y.-K., Wang, B.-Y.: Learning minimal separating DFA's for compositional verification. In: Kowalewski, S., Philippou, A. (eds.) TACAS 2009. LNCS, vol. 5505, pp. 31–45. Springer, Heidelberg (2009). https://doi.org/10.1007/978-3-642-00768-2_3
7. Chen, Y., Hong, C., Lin, A.W., Rümmer, P.: Learning to prove safety over parameterised concurrent systems. In: Stewart, D., Weissenbacher, G. (eds.) 2017 Formal Methods in Computer Aided Design, FMCAD 2017, Vienna, Austria, 2–6 October 2017, pp. 76–83. IEEE (2017). https://doi.org/10.23919/FMCAD.2017.8102244
8. Czerner, P., Esparza, J., Krasotin, V., Welzel-Mohr, C.: Computing inductive invariants of regular abstraction frameworks. In: Majumdar, R., Silva, A. (eds.) 35th International Conference on Concurrency Theory (CONCUR 2024). Leibniz International Proceedings in Informatics (LIPIcs), vol. 311, pp. 19:1–19:18. Schloss Dagstuhl – Leibniz-Zentrum für Informatik, Dagstuhl, Germany (2024). https://doi.org/10.4230/LIPIcs.CONCUR.2024.19. https://drops.dagstuhl.de/entities/document/10.4230/LIPIcs.CONCUR.2024.19
9. Esparza, J., Raskin, M., Welzel-Mohr, C.: Regular model checking upside-down: an invariant-based approach. Log. Methods Comput. Sci. **21**(1), 4 (2025). https://doi.org/10.46298/LMCS-21(1:4)2025
10. Esparza, J., Raskin, M.A., Welzel, C.: Regular model checking upside-down: an invariant-based approach. In: Klin, B., Lasota, S., Muscholl, A. (eds.) 33rd International Conference on Concurrency Theory, CONCUR 2022, 12–16 September 2022, Warsaw, Poland. LIPIcs, vol. 243, pp. 23:1–23:19. Schloss Dagstuhl - Leibniz-Zentrum für Informatik (2022). https://doi.org/10.4230/LIPICS.CONCUR.2022.23
11. German, S.M., Sistla, A.P.: Reasoning about systems with many processes. J. ACM **39**(3), 675–735 (1992)
12. Grinchtein, O., Leucker, M., Piterman, N.: Inferring network invariants automatically. In: Furbach, U., Shankar, N. (eds.) Automated Reasoning, pp. 483–497. Springer, Heidelberg (2006)

13. Howar, F., Steffen, B.: Active automata learning as black-box search and lazy partition refinement. In: Jansen, N., Stoelinga, M., van den Bos, P. (eds.) A Journey from Process Algebra via Timed Automata to Model Learning - Essays Dedicated to Frits Vaandrager on the Occasion of His 60th Birthday. Lecture Notes in Computer Science, vol. 13560, pp. 321–338. Springer (2022). https://doi.org/10.1007/978-3-031-15629-8_17
14. Ignatiev, A., Morgado, A., Marques-Silva, J.: PySAT: a python toolkit for prototyping with SAT oracles. In: SAT, pp. 428–437 (2018). https://doi.org/10.1007/978-3-319-94144-8_26
15. Ignatiev, A., Tan, Z.L., Karamanos, C.: Towards universally accessible SAT technology. In: SAT, pp. 4:1–4:11 (2024). https://doi.org/10.4230/LIPICS.SAT.2024.16
16. Jonsson, B., Nilsson, M.: Transitive closures of regular relations for verifying infinite-state systems. In: Graf, S., Schwartzbach, M. (eds.) TACAS 2000. LNCS, vol. 1785, pp. 220–235. Springer, Heidelberg (2000). https://doi.org/10.1007/3-540-46419-0_16
17. Leucker, M., Neider, D.: Learning minimal deterministic automata from inexperienced teachers. In: Margaria, T., Steffen, B. (eds.) ISoLA 2012. LNCS, vol. 7609, pp. 524–538. Springer, Heidelberg (2012). https://doi.org/10.1007/978-3-642-34026-0_39
18. Liffiton, M.H., Sakallah, K.A.: Algorithms for computing minimal unsatisfiable subsets of constraints. J. Autom. Reason. **40**(1), 1–33 (2008). https://doi.org/10.1007/S10817-007-9084-Z
19. Moeller, M., Wiener, T., Solko-Breslin, A., Koch, C., Foster, N., Silva, A.: Automata learning with an incomplete teacher. In: Ali, K., Salvaneschi, G. (eds.) 37th European Conference on Object-Oriented Programming, ECOOP 2023, 17–21 July 2023, Seattle, Washington, United States. LIPIcs, vol. 263, pp. 21:1–21:30. Schloss Dagstuhl - Leibniz-Zentrum für Informatik (2023). https://doi.org/10.4230/LIPICS.ECOOP.2023.21
20. Moeller, M., Wiener, T., Solko-Breslin, A., Koch, C., Foster, N., Silva, A.: Automata learning with an incomplete teacher (artifact). Dagstuhl Artifacts Ser. **9**(2), 21:1–21:3 (2023). https://doi.org/10.4230/DARTS.9.2.21. https://drops.dagstuhl.de/entities/document/10.4230/DARTS.9.2.21
21. Neider, D.: Applications of automata learning in verification and synthesis. Ph.D. thesis, RWTH Aachen University (2014). http://darwin.bth.rwth-aachen.de/opus3/volltexte/2014/5169
22. Neider, D., Jansen, N.: Regular model checking using solver technologies and automata learning. In: Brat, G., Rungta, N., Venet, A. (eds.) NFM 2013. LNCS, vol. 7871, pp. 16–31. Springer, Heidelberg (2013). https://doi.org/10.1007/978-3-642-38088-4_2
23. Oliveira, A.L., Silva, J.P.M.: Efficient algorithms for the inference of minimum size DFAs. Mach. Learn. **44**(1/2), 93–119 (2001). https://doi.org/10.1023/A:1010828029885
24. Rivest, R.L., Schapire, R.E.: Inference of finite automata using homing sequences. Inf. Comput. **103**(2), 299–347 (1993). https://doi.org/10.1006/INCO.1993.1021
25. Stan, D., Pommellet, A., Jacquot, J.: Automata Learning with an Incomplete but Inductive Teacher (Technical Report). CoRR abs/2602.21073 (2026). https://doi.org/10.48550/ARXIV.2602.21073
26. STAN, D., Pommellet, A., Jacquot, J.: LIndA: Automata Learning with an Incomplete but Inductive Teacher (Artifact) (2026). https://doi.org/10.5281/zenodo.18770274

27. Steffen, B., Howar, F., Merten, M.: Introduction to active automata learning from a practical perspective. In: Bernardo, M., Issarny, V. (eds.) SFM 2011. LNCS, vol. 6659, pp. 256–296. Springer, Heidelberg (2011). https://doi.org/10.1007/978-3-642-21455-4_8
28. Touili, T.: Regular model checking using widening techniques. In: Mayr, R. (ed.) Verification of Parameterized Systems, VEPAS 2001, Satellite Workshop of ICALP 2001, Crete, Greece, 13 July 2001. Electronic Notes in Theoretical Computer Science, vol. 50, pp. 342–356. Elsevier (2001). https://doi.org/10.1016/S1571-0661(04)00187-2
29. Vaandrager, F., Garhewal, B., Rot, J., Wißmann, T.: A new approach for active automata learning based on apartness. In: TACAS 2022. LNCS, vol. 13243, pp. 223–243. Springer, Cham (2022). https://doi.org/10.1007/978-3-030-99524-9_12
30. Vardhan, A., Sen, K., Viswanathan, M., Agha, G.: Learning to verify safety properties. In: Davies, J., Schulte, W., Barnett, M. (eds.) ICFEM 2004. LNCS, vol. 3308, pp. 274–289. Springer, Heidelberg (2004). https://doi.org/10.1007/978-3-540-30482-1_26
31. Yaacov, T., Weiss, G., Amram, G., Hayoun, A.: Automata models for effective bug pattern description. In: 28th ACM/IEEE International Conference on Model Driven Engineering Languages and Systems, MODELS 2025, Grand Rapids, MI, USA, 5–10 October 2025, pp. 119–129. IEEE (2025). https://doi.org/10.1109/MODELS67397.2025.00017

Binary and Two-Party Asynchronous Subtypings are Equivalent

Maurizio Murgia[✉]

Gran Sasso Science Institute, L'Aquila, Italy
maurizio.murgia@gssi.it

Abstract. Asynchronous session subtyping is a refinement relation that allows safe reordering of messages. It was introduced in the context of binary sessions, and subsequently extended to the multiparty setting (over local types). However, the definitions of binary and multiparty subtypings are fairly different: the former is based on a notion of accumulation of inputs, whereas the latter on a decomposition into single input single output types and a refinement relation over them. Since binary sessions can be encoded as two-party sessions, it is natural to wonder whether binary session subtyping and two-party subtyping are equivalent. We show that the two notions coincide.

1 Introduction

Session types [17,20,37] specify communication protocols, capturing the types of messages that can be sent or received over a network and in which order. A key feature of session types is that they allow for typechecking implementations against protocols. This is typically performed through static [24,25,28,33,34] or dynamic [2,3] typechecking, as well as API generation [23,32]. The original theory of binary session types, where every session is composed by two participants communicating over the two endpoints of a channel, has been subsequently extended to multiparty asynchronous interactions [21,22], where sessions consists of $n \geq 2$ roles, which communicate over FIFO channels. Another important extension of binary session types is the introduction of session subtyping [15], which allows for the safe replacement of one program for another in every execution context, provided that the new one is typed by a subtype (in accordance with the Liskov substitution principle [29]). For instance, consider a protocol for a client-server interaction where the server offers to its clients to either login or to register a new account (we ignore message payload for simplicity). From the server's perspective, such a protocol can be expressed as the (binary) session type $\mathbb{B} = ?login \,\&\, ?register$, where ? denotes input, & an external choice, *login* and *register* are communication labels. In turn, a client would follow the dual protocol $\overline{\mathbb{B}} = !login \oplus !register$, where ! is for output and $\oplus$ for internal choice. The server may then be extended with new functionalities, such as a reset password operation. The new type of the server would be $\mathbb{B}' = ?login \,\&\, ?register \,\&\, ?reset$.

Published by Springer Nature Switzerland AG 2026
L. Bocchi and B. Kulahcioglu Ozkan (Eds.): FORTE 2026, LNCS 16589, pp. 149–160, 2026.
https://doi.org/10.1007/978-3-032-28187-6_9

Intuitively, such a change would be transparent to old clients that either register or login, as both options remain available.

When asynchronous communication comes into play, it turns out that output actions may be safely executed before input actions [9]. For instance, let $\mathbb{B} = ?a.!b$ and $\overline{\mathbb{B}} = !a.?b$. Session type $\mathbb{B}$ waits for message a and then sends message b, while $\overline{\mathbb{B}}$ exhibits dual behaviour. Let $\mathbb{B}' = !b.?a$: it sends b and then waits for a (that is, it anticipates the output action). We observe that $\mathbb{B}'$ can be safely composed with $\overline{\mathbb{B}}$: $\mathbb{B}'$ and $\overline{\mathbb{B}}$ will send a message for the other party, then receive a message from their own queue, without getting stuck and without communication mismatches. For this reason, $\mathbb{B}'$ is a binary asynchronous subtype of $\mathbb{B}$. In the context of multiparty session types, we can also reorder actions of the same polarity but referring to different roles [19]. Consider the following local[1] multiparty session types $\mathbb{S}_r = p!a.q!a, \mathbb{S}_p = r?a = \mathbb{S}_q$, where p, q, r are roles. Note that actions now also contain the role of the communication partner: $p!a$ means send message a to p. We have that $\mathbb{S}_r$, impersonated by role r, sends a to p and then to q, while p and q will just wait for such messages. We have that $\mathbb{S}'_r = q!a.p!a$ is a subtype of $\mathbb{S}_r$, as the reordering of sends does not introduce deadlocks and it is transparent from the point of view of p and q.

From the above discussion, multiparty subtyping is larger than binary subtyping, as the former allows for more kind of reorderings. But what happens if we consider the two party fragment of multiparty session types? Intuitively two party and binary subtypings should coincide. However, definitions of binary and multiparty subtypings are quite different: the former is based on a notion of accumulation of inputs, the latter on a decomposition into single input single output types and a refinement relation over them. This makes the equivalence of the two notions not entirely obvious, so that, in a private communication, a researcher told me to suspect that binary subtyping may not imply the two party one. Here we show that, instead, they coincide.

2 Preliminaries

In this section we describe binary and multiparty session types, and the corresponding subtypings. We remark that here we consider only local multiparty types, and not global ones.

2.1 Binary Session Types

Binary session types are a formalism to describe communication protocols over binary channels. A binary channel consists of two endpoints. All messages sent to an endpoint can be received from the other one. When the communication is asynchronous, each endpoint has a queue: output is non-blocking and appends the message to the tail of the receiver's queue. Input from a non-empty queue

[1] The kind of multiparty session types considered in this paper are always local. We will therefore omit the adjective local from now on.

consumes the message at its head. So messages are stored in FIFO order. A binary session type is associated to an endpoint, not to the whole channel.

We assume a finite set of *communication labels* ranged over by $a, b, \ldots$.

Definition 1. Binary session types $\mathbb{B}$ *are defined co-inductively as follows:*

$$\mathbb{B} \stackrel{coind}{::=} \oplus_{i\in I} !a_i.\mathbb{B}_i \mid \&_{i\in I} ?a_i.\mathbb{B}_i \mid \mathsf{end}$$

where index sets I are finite and labels in selections ($\oplus$) and branchings ($\&$) are pairwise distinct.

Selection $\oplus_{i\in I} !a_i.\mathbb{B}_i$ models a protocol where the participant sends a message a_k $(k \in I)$ of her choice, and then continues as $\mathbb{B}_k$. Dually, $\&_{i\in I} ?a_i.\mathbb{B}_i$ models a protocol where the participant waits to receive one among the messages a_i, and then behaves as the corresponding continuation. With end we model a terminated protocol. We consider a coinductive syntax without recursion, which generalises standard regular session types and can encode context-free ones.

Towards binary asynchronous subtyping, we introduce the auxiliary notions of asynchronous context and the predicate $\& \in \mathbb{B}$.

Definition 2. *Asynchronous contexts $\mathcal{A}$ are defined inductively as follows:*

$$\mathcal{A} ::= []^n \mid \&_{i\in I} ?a_i.\mathcal{A}_i$$

We write $\mathcal{A}[]^{n\in N}$ to denote a context with holes indexed by elements of N and $\mathcal{A}[\mathbb{B}_n]^{n\in N}$ to denote the same context when the hole $[]^n$ has been filled with $\mathbb{B}_n$.

So, an asynchronous context is just a session type with only branchings (no selections nor end) and with some holes $[]^n$. When all such holes are filled, we obtain a binary session type.

Definition 3. *We define the* must input *predicate $\& \in \mathbb{B}$ inductively as follows:*

$$\frac{}{\& \in \&_{i\in I} ?a_i.\mathbb{B}_i} \qquad \frac{\forall i \in I : \& \in \mathbb{B}_i}{\& \in \oplus_{i\in I} !a_i.\mathbb{B}_i}$$

The predicate $\& \in \mathbb{B}$ intuitively holds when every maximal path of $\mathbb{B}$ (seen as a tree) contains at least an input action.

Definition 4 (Binary asynchronous subtyping [9]). *Binary asynchronous subtyping is defined coinductively by the following rules:*

$$\frac{\forall i \in I:\ \mathbb{B}_i \leq_B \mathbb{B}'_i}{\oplus_{i\in I} !a_i.\mathbb{B}_i \leq_B \oplus_{i\in I\cup J} !a_i.\mathbb{B}'_i}\ \textsf{RefBSel1} \qquad \frac{\forall i \in I:\ \mathbb{B}_i \leq_B \mathbb{B}'_i}{\&_{i\in I\cup J} ?a_i.\mathbb{B}_i \leq_B \&_{i\in I} ?a_i.\mathbb{B}'_i}\ \textsf{RefBBra}$$

$$\frac{}{\mathsf{end} \leq_B \mathsf{end}}\ \textsf{RefBEnd} \qquad \frac{\forall i \in I : \mathbb{B}_i \leq_B \mathcal{A}[\mathbb{B}^n_i]^{n\in N} \quad \& \in \mathcal{A} \quad \& \in \mathbb{B}_i}{\oplus_{i\in I} !a_i.\mathbb{B}_i \leq_B \mathcal{A}[\oplus_{i\in I\cup J_n} !a_i.\mathbb{B}^n_i]^{n\in N}}\ \textsf{RefBSel2}$$

Rule RefBSel1 allows to derive that a selection type is a subtype of another selection type as soon as the subtype can output a subset of labels (output co-variance), and the corresponding continuations are also related by subtyping. Rule RefBBra is dual, as it applies to branching and requires that the subtype offers more labels than the supertype (input contra-variance). Rule RefBEnd is the only rule for the end type, and stipulates that a terminated protocol can only be a subtype of a terminated protocol. Rule RefBSel2 enables message reorderings: outputs of the subtype are not immediately matched by the supertype, but they must be available after some inputs. Condition $\& \in \mathbb{B}_i$ imposes that the subtype must eventually perform some inputs: this makes the subtyping eventual reception preserving. Condition $\& \in \mathcal{A}$ does not affect the notion of subtyping, but just rules out situation when both rule RefBSel1 and RefBSel2 are applicable.

Example 1. Let $\mathbb{B} = !a.(?b\&?c)$ and $\mathbb{B}' = ?b.!a\&?c.(!a\oplus!b)$. Observe that $\mathbb{B}'$ can be rewritten as $\mathcal{A}[!a]^1[!a\oplus!b]^2$ where $\mathcal{A} = ?b[]^1\&?c.[]^2$. We can then derive $\mathbb{B} \leq_B \mathbb{B}'$ as follows:

$$\dfrac{\dfrac{\dfrac{}{\mathsf{end} \leq_B \mathsf{end}} \quad \dfrac{}{\mathsf{end} \leq_B \mathsf{end}}}{?b\&?c \leq_B \mathcal{A}[\mathsf{end}]^1[\mathsf{end}]^2 = ?b\&?c} \quad \dfrac{}{\& \in \mathcal{A}} \quad \dfrac{}{\& \in ?b\&?c}}{\mathbb{B} \leq_B \mathbb{B}'}$$

2.2 Multyparty Session Types

Multiparty session types extend binary ones in that every session is composed of many participants. Concretely, every selection specifies to which participant (more precisely, to which role) messages are sent, and similarly branchings specify from which role messages are received.

We assume a finite set of roles ranged over by $p, q, \ldots$.

Definition 5. *Multiparty session types $\mathbb{S}$ are defined coinductively as follows:*

$$\mathbb{S} \overset{coind}{::=} \oplus_{i\in I}\, p!a_i.\mathbb{S}_i \mid \&_{i\in I}\, p?a_i.\mathbb{S}_i \mid \mathsf{end}$$

where index sets I are finite and labels in selections and branchings are pairwise distinct.

We now define the notions of Single Output, Single Input and Single Input Single Output types. Such types have a crucial role in the definition of Multiparty asynchronous subtyping.

Definition 6. *We define Single Output (SO) types $\mathbb{U}$, Single Input (SI) types $\mathbb{V}$ and Single Input Single Output type (SISO) $\mathbb{W}$ coinductively as follows:*

$$\mathbb{U} \overset{coind}{::=} p!a.\mathbb{U} \mid \&_{i\in I}\, p?a_i.\mathbb{U}_i \mid \mathsf{end} \qquad \mathbb{V} \overset{coind}{::=} \oplus_{i\in I}\, p!a_i.\mathbb{V}_i \mid p?a.\mathbb{V} \mid \mathsf{end}$$

$$\mathbb{W} \overset{coind}{::=} p!a.\mathbb{W} \mid p?a.\mathbb{W} \mid \mathsf{end}$$

If a sequence $\mathbb{W}$ contains the action $p \diamond a$ where $\diamond \in \{!, ?\}$, we write $p \diamond a \in \mathbb{W}$. We define $act(p \diamond a) = (p \diamond)$ and $act(\mathbb{W}) = \{ \text{act}(p \diamond a) \mid p \diamond a \in \mathbb{W}\}$.

We now define two notions of sequences of actions, A^p and B^p, which are parameterised by a role p. Sequences A^p can only contain input actions from roles different from p. In contrast, B^p can contain output actions to roles different from p, and arbitrary input actions.

Definition 7 (Finite sequences). *Sequences A^p and B^p are inductively defined as follows: $A^p ::= q?a \mid q?a.\, A^p$ and $B^p ::= r?a \mid q!a \mid r?a.\, B^p \mid q!a.\, B^p$ with $q \neq p$.*

We now define SISO refinement, which crucially captures the kind of swapability allowed by multiparty subtyping.

Definition 8 (SISO refinement [19]). *The refinement relation $\precsim$ over SISO-trees is co-inductively defined as below:*

$$\dfrac{}{\mathsf{end} \precsim \mathsf{end}}\ \mathsf{RefEnd} \qquad \dfrac{\mathbb{W} \precsim \mathbb{W}'}{p?a.\mathbb{W} \precsim p?a.\mathbb{W}'}\ \mathsf{RefIn} \qquad \dfrac{\mathbb{W} \precsim \mathbb{W}'}{p!a.\mathbb{W} \precsim p!a.\mathbb{W}'}\ \mathsf{RefOut}$$

$$\dfrac{\mathbb{W} \precsim A^p.\mathbb{W}' \quad act(\mathbb{W}) = act(A^p.\mathbb{W}')}{p?a.\mathbb{W} \precsim A^p.p?a.\mathbb{W}'}\ \mathsf{RefA} \qquad \dfrac{\mathbb{W} \precsim B^p.\mathbb{W}' \quad act(\mathbb{W}) = act(B^p.\mathbb{W}')}{p!a.\mathbb{W} \precsim B^p.p!a.\mathbb{W}'}\ \mathsf{RefB}$$

We briefly comment on rules RefA and RefB (the other three are straightforward). The former allows the subtype to reorder receive actions, as long as this reordering does not swap inputs from the same participant. The condition $act(\mathbb{W}) = act(A^p.\mathbb{W}')$ crucially disallows starvation, which is the situation where an action is perpetually postponed. Rule RefB handles the reordering of outputs: outputs to different roles can be swapped freely, and outputs can precede inputs.

SISO refinement expresses swapability over two sequences of actions. Session types, rather than sequences, can be seen as trees with selection and branching points. Multiparty subtyping exploits a decomposition of types in sets of SO and SI types, defined below.

Definition 9 (SO and SI decomposition for multiparty session types [19]). *The tree decomposition maps $[\![.]\!]_{\mathsf{SO}}$ from MST $\mathbb{S}$ to SO-trees $\mathbb{U}$ and $[\![.]\!]_{\mathsf{SI}}$ from MST $\mathbb{S}$ to SI-trees $\mathbb{V}$ are coinductively defined as follows:*

$$\begin{aligned}
[\![\mathsf{end}]\!]_{\mathsf{SO}} &= \{\mathsf{end}\}\\
[\![\oplus_{i\in I}\, p!a_i.\mathbb{S}_i]\!]_{\mathsf{SO}} &= \{p!a_i.U_i \mid i \in I, \mathbb{U}_i \in [\![\mathbb{S}_i]\!]_{\mathsf{SO}}\}\\
[\![\&_{i\in I}\, p?a_i.\mathbb{S}_i]\!]_{\mathsf{SO}} &= \{\&_{i\in I}\, p?a_i.\mathbb{U}_i \mid i \in I, \mathbb{U}_i \in [\![\mathbb{S}_i]\!]_{\mathsf{SO}}\}
\end{aligned}$$

$$\begin{aligned}
[\![\mathsf{end}]\!]_{\mathsf{SI}} &= \{\mathsf{end}\}\\
[\![\oplus_{i\in I}\, p!a_i.\mathbb{S}_i]\!]_{\mathsf{SI}} &= \{\oplus_{i\in I}\, p!a_i.\mathbb{V}_i \mid i \in I, \mathbb{V}_i \in [\![\mathbb{S}_i]\!]_{\mathsf{SI}}\}\\
[\![\&_{i\in I}\, p?a_i.\mathbb{S}_i]\!]_{\mathsf{SI}} &= \{p?a_i.\mathbb{V}_i \mid i \in I, \mathbb{V}_i \in [\![\mathbb{S}_i]\!]_{\mathsf{SI}}\}
\end{aligned}$$

Multiparty asynchronous subtyping (MAS) is defined in a forall-exists manner over SO and SI decompositions, capturing output covariance and input contravariance, and then resorting to SISO-refinement.

Definition 10 (Multiparty asynchronous subtyping). *The binary relation* $\leq_M$ *on* $\mathbb{T} \times \mathbb{T}$ *is defined by* $T \leq_M T'$ *holds iff* $\forall U \in [\![T]\!]_{\mathsf{SO}} : \forall V' \in [\![T']\!]_{\mathsf{SI}} : \exists W \in [\![U]\!]_{\mathsf{SI}} : \exists W' \in [\![V']\!]_{\mathsf{SO}} : W \precsim W'$.

Example 2. To illustrate MAS, consider showing $T \leq T'$ where:

$$T = p?c.q!d.\mathsf{end} \,\&\, p?e.q!d.\mathsf{end} \qquad T' = q!d.(p?c.\mathsf{end} \,\&\, p?e.\mathsf{end})$$

Since T is an SO-tree, $[\![T]\!]_{\mathsf{SO}} = \{T\}$. T' is not an SI-tree hence $[\![T']\!]_{\mathsf{SI}} = \{q!d.p?c.\mathsf{end}, q!d.p?e.\mathsf{end}\}$. Universal quantification over $[\![T']\!]_{\mathsf{SI}}$ requires that T is checked against *both* $q!d.p?c.\mathsf{end}$ and $q!d.p?e.\mathsf{end}$. To do so, note $p?c.q!d.\mathsf{end} \in [\![T]\!]_{\mathsf{SI}}$ and $p?c.q!d.\mathsf{end} \precsim q!d.p?c.\mathsf{end}$ likewise $p?e.q!d.\mathsf{end} \in [\![T]\!]_{\mathsf{SI}}$ and $p?e.q!d.\mathsf{end} \precsim q!d.p?e.\mathsf{end}$ since

$$\dfrac{\dfrac{\overline{\overline{\mathsf{end} \precsim \mathsf{end}}}\ \mathsf{RefEnd}}{q!d.\mathsf{end} \precsim q!d.\mathsf{end}}\ \mathsf{RefOut}}{p?c.q!d.\mathsf{end} \precsim q!d.p?c.\mathsf{end}}\ \mathsf{RefA} \qquad \dfrac{\dfrac{\overline{\overline{\mathsf{end} \precsim \mathsf{end}}}\ \mathsf{RefEnd}}{q!d.\mathsf{end} \precsim q!d.\mathsf{end}}\ \mathsf{RefOut}}{p?e.q!d.\mathsf{end} \precsim q!d.p?e.\mathsf{end}}\ \mathsf{RefA}$$

3 Comparing Binary and Two Party Async Subtypings

In this section we compare binary subtyping with multiparty subtyping. Due to the possibility of reordering inputs w.r.t. inputs (resp. outputs w.r.t. outputs) from (resp. to) different roles, multiparty subtyping is more permissive in general. It remains to investigate what happens in the two party fragment of multiparty session types, where two party session types are multiparty types that interact with at most one role p. This corresponds to two party interactions, as the first participant is the agent implementing the current (local) type, while the second is an agent impersonating the role p (or just an agent if the current type is end). Note that requiring exactly one role would have made end not two party).

Definition 11. *We define* $R(\mathbb{S}) = \{p \mid p\diamond \in act(\mathbb{S})$ *for some* $\diamond \in \{!, ?\}\}$. *We say that* $\mathbb{S}$ *is two party if* $|\ R(\mathbb{S})\ | \leq 1$.

Since binary and two party types are formally different mathematical objects, we introduce the mapping $\mathbb{B}(\_)$ from multiparty types to binary ones. Such a mapping simply cleans up role information, leaving action labels and type structure unchanged.

Definition 12.

$$\mathbb{B}(\mathsf{end}) = \mathsf{end} \quad \mathbb{B}(\oplus_{i\in I}\, p!a_i.\mathbb{S}_i) = \oplus_{i\in I}\, !a_i.\mathbb{B}(\mathbb{S}_i) \quad \mathbb{B}(\&_{i\in I}\, p?a_i.\mathbb{S}_i) = \&_{i\in I}\, ?a_i.\mathbb{B}(\mathbb{S}_i)$$

3.1 SISO Types

We first compare the two subtypings for SISO types. We start with an example.

Example 3. Let $\mathbb{W}_1 = (p!a.p!a.p?b)^\omega$ and $\mathbb{W}_2 = (p?b.p!a)^\omega$, where notation $\mathbb{W}^\omega$ stands for the infinite repetition of $\mathbb{W}$. The derivation of $\mathbb{W}_1 \precsim \mathbb{W}_2$ is infinite, but can be depicted as follows:

$$\dfrac{\vdots}{\mathbb{W}_1 \precsim (p?b)^{i+1}.\mathbb{W}_2}\;\textsf{RefB}$$

$$\vdots$$

$$\dfrac{\vdots}{\mathbb{W}_1 \precsim (p?b)^{i}.\mathbb{W}_2}\;\textsf{RefB}$$

$$\vdots$$

$$\dfrac{\dfrac{\dfrac{\dfrac{\vdots}{\mathbb{W}_1 \precsim p?b.\mathbb{W}_2}\;\textsf{RefB}}{p?b.\mathbb{W}_1 \precsim p?b.p?b.\mathbb{W}_2}\;\textsf{RefIn} \quad act(p?b.\mathbb{W}_1) = \{p!, p?\} = act(p?b.p?b.\mathbb{W}_2)}{p!a.p?b.\mathbb{W}_1 \precsim p?b.p!a.p?b.\mathbb{W}_2 = p?b.\mathbb{W}_2}\;\textsf{RefB} \quad act(p!a.p?b.\mathbb{W}_1) = \{p!, p?\} = act(p?b.\mathbb{W}_2)}{\mathbb{W}_1 = p!a.p!a.p?b.\mathbb{W}_1 \precsim p?b.p!a.\mathbb{W}_2 = \mathbb{W}_2}\;\textsf{RefB}$$

Let $\mathbb{B}_i = \mathbb{B}(\mathbb{W}_i)$ $(i \in \{1,2\})$. A derivation for $\mathbb{B}(\mathbb{W}_1) \leq_B \mathbb{B}(\mathbb{W}_2)$ has a similar shape (we omit the derivation for $\& \in \mathbb{B}$ predicates):

$$\dfrac{\vdots}{\mathbb{B}_1 \leq_B (?b)^{i+1}.\mathbb{B}_2}\;\textsf{RefBSel2}$$

$$\vdots$$

$$\dfrac{\vdots}{\mathbb{B}_1 \leq_B (?b)^{i}.\mathbb{B}_2}\;\textsf{RefBSel2}$$

$$\vdots$$

$$\dfrac{\dfrac{\dfrac{\dfrac{\vdots}{\mathbb{B}_1 \leq_B ?b.\mathbb{B}_2}\;\textsf{RefBSel2}}{?b.\mathbb{B}_1 \leq_B ?b.?b.\mathbb{B}_2}\;\textsf{RefBBra} \quad \dfrac{}{\& \in ?b[]} \quad \dfrac{}{\& \in ?b.\mathbb{B}_1}}{!a.?b.\mathbb{B}_1 \leq_B ?b.!a.?b.\mathbb{B}_2 = ?b.\mathbb{B}_2}\;\textsf{RefBSel2} \quad \dfrac{}{\& \in ?b[]} \quad \dfrac{}{\& \in !a.?b.\mathbb{B}_1}}{\mathbb{B}_1 = !a.!a.?b.\mathbb{B}_1 \leq_B ?b.!a.\mathbb{B}_2 = \mathbb{B}_2}\;\textsf{RefBSel2}$$

□

Observe that, in the two party setting, rule RefA of definition 8 never applies: if a SISO type $\mathbb{W}$ has the form $A^p.p?a.\mathbb{W}'$ then A^p contains at least one input action from some role $q \neq p$. Hence $R(\mathbb{W}) \supseteq \{p, q\}$, and so $\mathbb{W}$ is not two party. For SISO types, rules RefEnd, RefIn and RefOut match precisely respectively rules RefBEnd, RefBBra and RefBSel1 of definition 4. Rules RefB and RefBSel2, albeit similar, differ in that the former requires $act(\mathbb{W}) = act(B^p.\mathbb{W}')$, the latter $\& \in \mathbb{B}(\mathbb{W})$. Observe that for two party types, B^p must contain at least one input action. Hence $p? \in act(B^p.\mathbb{W}')$. So, $act(\mathbb{W}) = act(B^p.\mathbb{W}')$ implies $p? \in act(\mathbb{W})$, that is $\mathbb{W}$ eventually performs an input. Then also $\mathbb{B}(\mathbb{W})$ must input eventually, hence $\& \in \mathbb{B}(\mathbb{W})$. With a dual argument we can conclude that $\& \in \mathbb{B}(\mathbb{W})$ implies $p? \in act(\mathbb{W})$. Since the asynchronous context $\mathcal{A}$ (which corresponds to $\mathbb{B}(B^p)[]$) of rule RefBSel2 must contain at least one input action, we intuitivety have that $p? \in act(B^p.\mathbb{W}')$ must hold. The remaining fact that $p! \in act(\mathbb{W}) \iff p! \in act(B^p.\mathbb{W}')$ intuitively holds because, from the rules of definition 4, we can observe that every output in the subtype must be matched in the supertype, and that outputs in the supertype cannot be skipped. The formal argument is a bit more complex. We therefore have the following propositions, which together establish the equivalence of binary and two party subtypings in the SISO fragment. Note that the direction binary subtyping implies two party subtyping requires that the two party types interact with the same role: obviously, $p!a \not\leq_M q!a$ but $\mathbb{B}(p!a) = !a \leq_B !a = \mathbb{B}(q!a)$.

Proposition 1. *For all two party SISO-trees $\mathbb{W}_1, \mathbb{W}_2$: If $\mathbb{W}_1 \leq_M \mathbb{W}_2$ then $\mathbb{B}(\mathbb{W}_1) \leq_B \mathbb{B}(\mathbb{W}_2)$.*

Proposition 2. *For all two party SISO-trees $\mathbb{W}_1, \mathbb{W}_2$ with $R(\mathbb{W}_1) = R(\mathbb{W}_2)$: If $\mathbb{B}(\mathbb{W}_1) \leq_B \mathbb{B}(\mathbb{W}_2)$ then $\mathbb{W}_1 \leq_M \mathbb{W}_2$.*

3.2 Types with Branching and Selection

In the general setting, the two subtyping definitions look fairly different:

- Binary subtyping handles reorderings, co- and contra-variance simultaneously with a kind of simulation, where every immediate output in the subtype must be matched by the supertype possibly skipping some inputs. If the subtype is a branching, then the supertype must be a branching offering a subset of the subtype inputs.
- Multiparty subtyping checks reorderings by means of the SISO refinement relation, while co- and contra-variance are dealt with the SO and SI decompositions.

Example 4. Consider the following two party types:

$$\mathbb{S}_1 = p!a.(p?c \& p?d) \;\oplus\; p!b.(p?c \& p?d \& p?e)$$
$$\mathbb{S}_2 = p?c.(p!a \oplus p!b) \;\&\; p?d.(p!a \oplus p!b \oplus p!c)$$

We first show that $\mathbb{B}(\mathbb{S}_1) \leq_B \mathbb{B}(\mathbb{S}_2)$ (we omit the simple derivations of the $\& \in \mathbb{B}$):

$$\dfrac{\dfrac{\mathsf{end} \leq_B \mathsf{end} \quad \mathsf{end} \leq_B \mathsf{end}}{?c\&?d \leq_B ?c\&?d} \quad \dfrac{\mathsf{end} \leq_B \mathsf{end} \quad \mathsf{end} \leq_B \mathsf{end}}{?c\&?d\&?e \leq_B ?c\&?d} \quad \dfrac{}{\& \in ?c\&?d[]} \quad \dfrac{}{\& \in ?c\&?d} \quad \dfrac{}{\& \in ?c\&?d\&?e}}{\mathbb{B}(\mathbb{S}_1) = !a.(?c\&?d) \oplus !b.(?c\&?d\&?e) \leq_B ?c.(!a \oplus !b) \;\&\; ?d.(!a \oplus !b \oplus !c) = \mathbb{B}(\mathbb{S}_2)}$$

Also $\mathbb{S}_1 \leq_M \mathbb{S}_2$ holds, as depicted in the table below. The top row contains the two elements of $\llbracket \mathbb{S}_1 \rrbracket_{\mathsf{SO}}$, the left column the two elements of $\llbracket \mathbb{S}_2 \rrbracket_{\mathsf{SI}}$. The other cells show the pair of corresponding SISO types in the SISO refinement relation.

	$p!a.(p?c \;\&\; p?d)$	$p!b.(p?c \;\&\; p?d)$
$p?c.(p!a \oplus p!b)$	$p!a.p?c \precsim p?c.p!a$	$p!b.p?c \precsim p?c.p!b$
$p?d.(p!a \oplus p!b \oplus p!c)$	$p!a.p?d \precsim p?d.p!a$	$p!b.p?d \precsim p?d.p!b$

At a first glance, the way the two subtypings are established look very different. However, after a deeper inspection, we can observe that the derivation tree of

$\mathbb{B}(\mathbb{S}_1) \leq_B \mathbb{B}(\mathbb{S}_2)$ has four branches - excluding the $\& \in \mathbb{B}$ predicates. When checking $\mathbb{S}_1 \leq_M \mathbb{S}_2$, we derived four SISO refinements. Moreover, consider the left most branch of the derivation tree for $\mathbb{B}(\mathbb{S}_1) \leq_B \mathbb{B}(\mathbb{S}_2)$: it corresponds to the choice of the $!a$ label from the subtype selection, and to the choice of label $?c$ from the supertype branching. These choices intuitively correspond to the SO type $p!a.(p?c\&p?d) \in [\![\mathbb{S}_1]\!]_{\mathsf{SO}}$ and the SI type $p?c.(p!a \oplus p!b) \in [\![\mathbb{S}_2]\!]_{\mathsf{SI}}$, which lead to the $p!a.p?c \precsim p?c.p!a$ cell in the two party subtyping table. □

Our main result is the equivalence of binary and two party subtypings, as stated by the following theorems.

Theorem 1. *For all two-party session types* $\mathbb{S}_1, \mathbb{S}_2$*, if* $\mathbb{B}(\mathbb{S}_1) \leq_B \mathbb{B}(\mathbb{S}_2)$ *and* $R(\mathbb{S}_1) = R(\mathbb{S}_2)$ *then* $\mathbb{S}_1 \leq_M \mathbb{S}_2$*.*

Theorem 2. *For all two-party session types* $\mathbb{S}_1, \mathbb{S}_2$*, if* $\mathbb{S}_1 \leq_M \mathbb{S}_2$ *then* $\mathbb{B}(\mathbb{S}_1) \leq_B \mathbb{B}(\mathbb{S}_2)$*.*

4 Related Work and Conclusions

Session subtyping was introduced by Gay and Hole in the late 90 s [15,16], as a refinement relation between synchronous binary types. The first work on session subtyping in the asynchronous setting is due to Mostrous et al. [31] for multiparty session types. A related asynchronous subtyping relation is [30], which targets binary sessions in the involved setting of higher order process calculi. Both [30,31] allow message reorderings in the same way as the subtypings studied in this paper, but they do not preserve eventual reception: there, $(!a)^\omega$ is a subtype of $?a.(!a)^\omega$. The definition of subtyping used in this paper comes from [9,10] for the binary case and [18,19] for multiparty types. We remark that here we do not consider the carrier types in communications for simplicity. Asynchronous session subtyping received several attention in recent years. For instance, due to undecidability of asynchronous subtyping [6,26], there have been quite a few proposals of sound subtyping checkers, both for binary [1,5] and multiparty [4,13] types, as well as proof assistant mechanisations [14]. Some authors introduced other notions of asynchronous subtypings, in particular fair subtyping [7,8,11,12,35,36] preserves the possibility of termination (in contrast with the subtypings studied here, which preserve a specific notion of progress [19]). The decidable subtyping in [27] takes into account more general types with directed and mixed choices than the aforementioned works, but it disallows message reorderings.

Acknowledgement. Work partially supported by the MUR "dipartimento di eccellenza".

References

1. Bacchiani, L., Bravetti, M., Lange, J., Zavattaro, G.: A session subtyping tool. In: Damiani, F., Dardha, O. (eds.) COORDINATION 2021. LNCS, vol. 12717, pp. 90–105. Springer, Cham (2021). https://doi.org/10.1007/978-3-030-78142-2_6
2. Bartoletti, M., Murgia, M., Scalas, A., Zunino, R.: Verifiable abstractions for contract-oriented systems. J. Log. Algebraic Methods Program. **86**(1), 159–207 (2017)
3. Bocchi, L., Chen, T.-C., Demangeon, R., Honda, K., Yoshida, N.: Monitoring networks through multiparty session types. Theoret. Comput. Sci. **669**, 33–58 (2017)
4. Bocchi, L., King, A., Murgia, M., Thompson, S.: Abstract subtyping for asynchronous multiparty sessions. In: Bouyer, P., van de Pol, J. (eds.) 36th International Conference on Concurrency Theory, CONCUR 2025, Aarhus, Denmark, 26–29 August 2025. LIPIcs, vol. 348, pp. 10:1–10:19. Schloss Dagstuhl - Leibniz-Zentrum für Informatik (2025)
5. Bravetti, M., Carbone, M., Lange, J., Yoshida, N., Zavattaro, G.: A sound algorithm for asychronous session subtyping and its implementation. Logical Methods Comput. Sci. **17**(1), 1–35 (2021)
6. Bravetti, M., Carbone, M., Zavattaro, G.: Undecidability of asynchronous session subtyping. Inf. Comput. **256**, 300–320 (2017)
7. Bravetti, M., Lange, J., Zavattaro, G.: Fair refinement for asynchronous session types. In: FOSSACS 2021. LNCS, vol. 12650, pp. 144–163. Springer, Cham (2021). https://doi.org/10.1007/978-3-030-71995-1_8
8. Bravetti, M., Padovani, L., Zavattaro, G.: A sound and complete characterization of fair asynchronous session subtyping. In: Bouyer, P., van de Pol, J. (eds.) 36th International Conference on Concurrency Theory, CONCUR 2025, Aarhus, Denmark, 26–29 August 2025. LIPIcs, vol. 348, pp. 11:1–11:17. Schloss Dagstuhl - Leibniz-Zentrum für Informatik (2025)
9. Chen, T.-C., Dezani-Ciancaglini, M., Scalas, A., Yoshida, N.: On the preciseness of subtyping in session types. Logical Methods Comput. Sci. **13**(2), 1–61 (2017)
10. Chen, T.-C., Dezani-Ciancaglini, M., Yoshida, N.: On the preciseness of subtyping in session types. In: Principles and Practice of Declarative Programming, pp. 135–146. ACM Press, New York (2014)
11. Ciccone, L., Dagnino, F., Padovani, L.: Fair termination of multiparty sessions. In: Ali, K., Vitek, J. (eds.) 36th European Conference on Object-Oriented Programming, ECOOP 2022, Berlin, Germany, 6–10 June 2022. LIPIcs, vol. 222, pp. 26:1–26:26. Schloss Dagstuhl - Leibniz-Zentrum für Informatik (2022)
12. Ciccone, L., Padovani, L.: Fair termination of binary sessions. Proc. ACM Program. Lang. **6**(POPL), 1–30 (2022)
13. Cutner, Z., Yoshida, N., Vassor, M.: Deadlock-free asynchronous message reordering in rust with multiparty session types. In: Symposium on Principles and Practice of Parallel Programming, pp. 246–261. ACM Press, New York (2022)
14. Ekici, B., Yoshida, N.: Completeness of asynchronous session tree subtyping in coq. In: Bertot, Y., Kutsia, T., Norrish, M. (eds.) International Conference on Interactive Theorem Proving. LIPIcs, vol. 309, pp. 13:1–13:20. Schloss Dagstuhl - Leibniz-Zentrum für Informatik (2024)
15. Gay, S., Hole, M.: Types and subtypes for client-server interactions. In: Swierstra, S.D. (ed.) ESOP 1999. LNCS, vol. 1576, pp. 74–90. Springer, Heidelberg (1999). https://doi.org/10.1007/3-540-49099-X_6

16. Gay, S., Hole, M.: Subtyping for session types in the pi calculus. Acta Inform. **42**, 191–225 (2005)
17. Gay, S., Vasconcelos, V.T.: Session Types. Cambridge University Press (2025)
18. Ghilezan, S., Pantovic, J., Prokic, I., Scalas, A., Yoshida, N.: Precise subtyping for asynchronous multiparty sessions. Proc. ACM Program. Lang. **5**(POPL), 1–28 (2021)
19. Ghilezan, S, Pantovic, J., Prokic, I., Scalas, A., Yoshida, N.: Precise subtyping for asynchronous multiparty sessions. ACM Trans. Comput. Log. **24**(2), 14:1–14:73 (2023)
20. Honda, K., Vasconcelos, V.T., Kubo, M.: Language primitives and type discipline for structured communication-based programming. In: Hankin, C. (ed.) ESOP 1998. LNCS, vol 1381, pp. 22–138. Springer, Heidelberg (1998). https://doi.org/10.1007/bfb0053567
21. Honda, K., Yoshida, N., Carbone, M.: Multiparty asynchronous session types. In: Principles of Programming Languages, pp. 273–284. ACM (2008)
22. Honda, K., Yoshida, N., Carbone, M.: Multiparty asynchronous session types. J. ACM **63**(1), 9:1–9:67 (2016)
23. Hu, R., Yoshida, N.: Hybrid session verification through endpoint API generation. In: Stevens, P., Wąsowski, A. (eds.) FASE 2016. LNCS, vol. 9633, pp. 401–418. Springer, Heidelberg (2016). https://doi.org/10.1007/978-3-662-49665-7_24
24. Hu, R., Yoshida, N., Honda, K.: Session-based distributed programming in java. In: Vitek, J. (ed.) ECOOP 2008. LNCS, vol. 5142, pp. 516–541. Springer, Heidelberg (2008). https://doi.org/10.1007/978-3-540-70592-5_22
25. Lagaillardie, N., Neykova, R., Yoshida, N.: Stay safe under panic: affine rust programming with multiparty session types. In: European Conference on Object-Oriented Programming, vol. 222, pp. 4:1–4:29. Schloss Dagstuhl, Leibniz-Zentrum für Informatik, Dagstuhl (2022)
26. Lange, J., Yoshida, N.: On the undecidability of asynchronous session subtyping. In: Esparza, J., Murawski, A.S. (eds.) FoSSaCS 2017. LNCS, vol. 10203, pp. 441–457. Springer, Heidelberg (2017). https://doi.org/10.1007/978-3-662-54458-7_26
27. Li, E., Stutz, F., Wies, T.: Deciding subtyping for asynchronous multiparty sessions. In: Weirich, S. (eds.) ESOP 2024. LNCS, vol. 14576, pp. 176–205. Springer, Berlin (2024). https://doi.org/10.1007/978-3-031-57262-3_8
28. Lindley, S., Garrett Morris, J.: Embedding session types in Haskell. In: International Symposium on Haskell, pp. 133–145. ACM Press, New York (2016)
29. Liskov, B., Wing, J.: A behavioral notion of subtyping. ACM Trans. Program. Lang. Syst. **16**(6), 1811–41 (1994)
30. Mostrous, D., Yoshida, N.: Session-based communication optimisation for higher-order mobile processes. In: Curien, P.-L. (ed.) TLCA 2009. LNCS, vol. 5608, pp. 203–218. Springer, Heidelberg (2009). https://doi.org/10.1007/978-3-642-02273-9_16
31. Mostrous, D., Yoshida, N., Honda, K.: Global principal typing in partially commutative asynchronous sessions. In: Castagna, G. (ed.) ESOP 2009. LNCS, vol. 5502, pp. 316–332. Springer, Heidelberg (2009). https://doi.org/10.1007/978-3-642-00590-9_23
32. Neykova, R., Hu, R., Yoshida, N., Abdeljallal, F.: A session type provider: compile-time API generation of distributed protocols with interaction refinements in F#. In: Compiler Construction, pp. 128–138. ACM Press, New York (2018)
33. Ng, N., Yoshida, N., Honda, K.: Multiparty session C: safe parallel programming with message optimisation. In: Furia, C.A., Nanz, S. (eds.) TOOLS 2012. LNCS,

vol. 7304, pp. 202–218. Springer, Heidelberg (2012). https://doi.org/10.1007/978-3-642-30561-0_15
34. Orchard, D., Yoshida, N.: Session types with linearity in haskell. In: Behavioural Types: from Theory to Tools, pp. 219–241. River Publishers, Gistrup (2017)
35. Padovani, L.: Fair subtyping for multi-party session types. In: De Meuter, W., Roman, G.-C. (eds.) COORDINATION 2011. LNCS, vol. 6721, pp. 127–141. Springer, Heidelberg (2011). https://doi.org/10.1007/978-3-642-21464-6_9
36. Padovani, L., Zavattaro, G.: Fair termination of asynchronous binary sessions. In: Aldrich, J., Silva, A. (eds.) 39th European Conference on Object-Oriented Programming, ECOOP 2025, Bergen, Norway, 30 June–2 July 2025. LIPIcs, pp. 24:1–24:29. Schloss Dagstuhl - Leibniz-Zentrum für Informatik (2025)
37. Takeuchi, K., Honda, K., Kubo, M.: An interaction-based language and its typing system. In: Halatsis, C., Maritsas, D., Philokyprou, G., Theodoridis, S. (eds.) PARLE 1994. LNCS, vol. 817, pp. 398–413. Springer, Heidelberg (1994). https://doi.org/10.1007/3-540-58184-7_118

TARZAN: A Region-Based Library for Forward and Backward Reachability of Timed Automata

Andrea Manini(✉), Matteo Rossi, and Pierluigi San Pietro

Politecnico di Milano, Milan, Italy
{andrea.manini,matteo.rossi,pierluigi.sanpietro}@polimi.it

Abstract. The zone abstraction, widely adopted for its notable practical efficiency, is the de facto standard in the verification of Timed Automata (TA). Nonetheless, region-based abstractions have been shown to outperform zones in specific subclasses of TA. To complement and support mature zone-based tools, we introduce TARZAN, a C++ region-based verification library for TA. The algorithms implemented in TARZAN use a novel region abstraction that tracks the order in which clocks become unbounded. This additional ordering induces a finer partitioning of the state space, enabling backward algorithms to avoid the combinatorial explosion associated with enumerating all ordered partitions of unbounded clocks, when computing immediate delay predecessor regions.

We validate TARZAN by comparing forward reachability results against the state-of-the-art tools Uppaal and TChecker. The experiments confirm that zones excel when TA have large constants and strict guards. In contrast, TARZAN exhibits superior performance on closed TA and TA with punctual guards. Finally, we demonstrate the efficacy of our backward algorithms, establishing a foundation for region-based analysis in domains like Timed Games, where backward exploration is essential.

1 Introduction

Formally verifying the behavioral correctness of real-time systems (also including distributed systems) is essential for ensuring that critical properties hold. Since their introduction, Timed Automata (TA) have become one of the most widely adopted formalisms for modeling and analyzing such systems [15,28].

A key challenge in the verification of TA is their infinite state space, addressed by the *region* [2] abstraction, which provides a finite representation enabling algorithmic verification. Alternatives include *Binary Decision Diagrams* [32] and *zones* [17], the latter requiring *normalization* for state space finiteness [10]. Zones, typically implemented using *Difference Bound Matrices (DBMs)* [16], are used in tools such as Uppaal [7], TChecker [18], Kronos [14], and Synthia [25].

Supported by Politecnico di Milano. Artefacts available in https://doi.org/10.5281/zenodo.18656202.

Published by Springer Nature Switzerland AG 2026
L. Bocchi and B. Kulahcioglu Ozkan (Eds.): FORTE 2026, LNCS 16589, pp. 161–178, 2026.
https://doi.org/10.1007/978-3-032-28187-6_10

Zones have been shown to be highly efficient in practice and, over the last decades, have become the de facto standard for the formal verification of TA, although they have well-known limitations [12,21,33]. Yet, prior work has demonstrated that for the class of *closed* TA, *i.e.*, TA containing only non-strict guards, region-based abstractions may outperform state-of-the-art zone-based tools [19].

The promising performance of region-based abstractions on appropriate subclasses of TA motivated the development of TARZAN (Timed Automata Region and Zone library for real-time systems ANalysis) [23], a C++20 library designed to support and complement state-of-the-art zone-based tools for the formal verification of TA. Currently, TARZAN supports only region-based reachability of TA; optimizations leveraging zones are deferred to future work. The implementation of backward reachability algorithms enables the extension of TARZAN to domains in which backward analysis is essential, such as Timed Games [22].

When compared against zone-based state-of-the-art tools including Uppaal and TChecker, TARZAN exhibits superior performance on TA and networks of TA featuring *punctual* guards, *i.e.*, guards with equality constraints, and on closed TA, even with large constants or many clocks. However, the size of constants remains a significant bottleneck in other classes of TA (*e.g.*, zones excel in TA with strict guards). Moreover, since TARZAN only supports reachability analysis, using forward reachability to verify safety properties for unreachable regions requires exploring the entire reachable state space. We show in this paper that backward reachability can enhance the verification of safety properties.

Related Works. Abstractions related to regions have already been proposed to better capture the semantics of TA. In [34], regions are encoded as Boolean formulae via discrete interpretations. The *slot-based* abstraction [3] groups regions by time using integer-bounded intervals over a global clock. A data structure, known as *time-dart* [19], compactly encodes configurations of TA and their time successors without explicit enumeration. In [11], regions of bounded TA are represented as tuples combining integer clock values and a partition of clocks that reflects the ordering of their fractional parts. The region abstraction is extended in [13] to *durational-action* TA and in [1] to real-time recursive systems.

To the best of our knowledge, no region-based library for TA verification, nor any libraries or tools based on the aforementioned abstractions, currently exist. Consequently, we compare TARZAN against the state-of-the-art tools Uppaal and TChecker. Existing libraries that explicitly support the analysis of TA using DBM-based zone representations include [27,30]. Other libraries offer more general polyhedral abstractions beyond zones, such as those provided by [4,26].

Contributions. The main contribution of this work is two-fold: (i) we first introduce a refined region representation that tracks the order in which clocks become unbounded. While this representation may increase the total number of regions by inducing a finer partitioning of the state space, a major advantage is that it guarantees at most three immediate delay predecessors for any region; (ii) building on this new representation, we develop and implement algorithms in

TARZAN for computing delay and discrete successors and predecessors of regions. Existing tools may integrate TARZAN to enhance their verification capabilities.

This paper is organized as follows: Sect. 2 introduces the necessary theoretical background. Section 3 presents the proposed new region representation, from which a classification of regions is derived. Section 4 details the algorithms (and their pseudocode) to compute discrete successors and immediate delay predecessors of regions using this representation. Section 5 presents an overview of TARZAN and provides an empirical evaluation of forward and backward reachability. Section 6 concludes and outlines future developments. An extended version [24] provides additional algorithms, proofs, and full experimental results.

2 Theoretical Background

The timing behavior of real-time systems is naturally modeled by the formalism of TA, which is obtained by extending classical finite-state automata with real-valued clocks. In the following, we use the term *action* to refer to the events that a real-time system can exhibit.TA are defined as follows [2]:

Definition 1. *A* Timed Automaton $\mathcal{A}$ *is a tuple* $\mathcal{A} = (Act, Q, Q_0, X_\mathcal{A}, T, Inv)$, *where* Act *is a finite set of actions,* Q *is a finite set of locations,* $Q_0 \subseteq Q$ *is a set of initial locations,* $X_\mathcal{A}$ *is a finite set of clocks,* $T \subseteq Q \times Act \times \Gamma(X_\mathcal{A}) \times 2^{X_\mathcal{A}} \times Q$ *is a transition relation, and* $Inv : Q \to \Gamma(X_\mathcal{A})$ *is an invariant-assignment function.*

Let $\mathcal{A}$ be a TA. Clocks are special variables that can only be reset or compared against non-negative integer constants. The value of all clocks is initialized to zero and grows with derivative 1 until a reset occurs. When a clock is reset, its value becomes zero; after a reset, it starts increasing again. $\Gamma(X_\mathcal{A})$ is the set of *clock guards*, *i.e.*, conditions over clocks that must be satisfied for a transition to fire. Clock guards are defined by the following grammar: $\gamma := \xi \mid \gamma \wedge \gamma$, where $\xi := x \sim c$ is a *clock constraint*, $x \in X_\mathcal{A}$, $c \in \mathbb{N}$, and $\sim \in \{\leq, <, =, >, \geq\}$. We write $\xi \in \gamma$ to indicate that the clock constraint ξ occurs within the guard γ. For instance, if $\gamma := x_1 < c \wedge x_2 \geq c$, then $\xi_1 := x_1 < c$ and $\xi_2 := x_2 \geq c$, where $\xi_1, \xi_2 \in \gamma$. The powerset $2^{X_\mathcal{A}}$ indicates that a transition may reset a subset of the clocks. We denote by $c_m \in \mathbb{N}$ the maximum constant appearing in $\mathcal{A}$ and assume, without loss of generality, that it is the same for all clocks of $\mathcal{A}$.

A pair (q, v) is a *configuration* of a TA $\mathcal{A}$, where $q \in Q$ and $v : X_\mathcal{A} \to \mathbb{R}_{\geq 0}$ is a *clock valuation* function. We denote by $Eval_\mathcal{A}$ the set of all clock valuations of $\mathcal{A}$. Given a subset $Y \subseteq X_\mathcal{A}$ of clocks, we denote by $v[Y \leftarrow 0]$ the clock valuation defined as $v[Y \leftarrow 0](x) = 0$ if $x \in Y$ and $v[Y \leftarrow 0](x) = v(x)$ otherwise. Given a constant $\delta \in \mathbb{R}_{\geq 0}$ and a clock $x \in X_\mathcal{A}$, the value $(v + \delta)(x)$ is defined as $v(x) + \delta$.

The *transition system* $TS(\mathcal{A}) = (S, Act \cup \mathbb{R}_{\geq 0}, I, \hookrightarrow)$ captures the semantics of a TA $\mathcal{A}$, where $S = Q \times Eval_\mathcal{A}$, $I = \{(q, v) \mid q \in Q_0 \wedge \forall x \in X_\mathcal{A} : v(x) = 0\}$, and $\hookrightarrow$ is the transition relation containing: (i) *discrete* transitions $((q, v), a, (q', v'))$ if there exists a transition $(q, a, \gamma, Y, q') \in T$ in $\mathcal{A}$ such that v satisfies both γ and $Inv(q)$, and $v'(x) = v[Y \leftarrow 0](x)$ satisfies $Inv(q')$, where $a \in Act$, for all $x \in X_\mathcal{A}$, and (ii) *delay* transitions $((q, v), \delta, (q, v'))$ if there exists a constant

$\delta \in \mathbb{R}_{\geq 0}$ such that $v'(x) = (v + \delta)(x)$ satisfies $Inv(q)$, for all $x \in X_{\mathcal{A}}$. A full description of the standard transition system semantics of TA is covered in [5, Chapter 9].

The infinite state space of TA can be conveniently analyzed by resorting to a finite abstraction, known as the *region* abstraction [2]. For any real number $m \in \mathbb{R}$, we denote its integral and fractional parts by $\lfloor m \rfloor$ and $fr(m)$, respectively.

Definition 2 (Clock equivalence relation). *Let* $\mathcal{A} = (Act, Q, Q_0, X_{\mathcal{A}}, T, Inv)$ *be a TA. Two clock valuations* $v, v' \in Eval_{\mathcal{A}}$ *are called* clock-equivalent, *denoted by* $v \cong v'$, *if, and only if, it either holds that:* (i) $v(x) > c_m$ *and* $v'(x) > c_m$, *for all* $x \in X_{\mathcal{A}}$, *or* (ii) *for any* $x, y \in X_{\mathcal{A}}$, *with* $v(x), v'(x) \leq c_m$ *and* $v(y), v'(y) \leq c_m$, *it holds that:* (ii$_a$) $\lfloor v(x) \rfloor = \lfloor v'(x) \rfloor$ *and* $fr(v(x)) = 0 \Leftrightarrow fr(v'(x)) = 0$, *and* (ii$_b$) $fr(v(x)) \sim fr(v(y)) \Leftrightarrow fr(v'(x)) \sim fr(v'(y))$, *where* $\sim \in \{<, =\}$.

Definition 3 (Region). *Let* $\mathcal{A}$ *be a TA and* $s = (q, v)$ *be a configuration of* $\mathcal{A}$. *The* clock region $[v]$ *of* $v \in Eval_{\mathcal{A}}$ *is the set of all clock valuations equivalent to* v *under the relation of Definition 2. The* state region $[s]$ *of* s *is:* $[s] = (q, [v]) = \{(q, v') \mid v' \in [v]\}$; $[s]$ *is* initial *iff* $q \in Q_0$ *and* $\forall v' \in [v], \forall x \in X_{\mathcal{A}} : v'(x) = 0$.

In the remainder of this work, we focus on state regions, referred to simply as *regions*. Let $\mathcal{A}$ be a TA and $[s] = (q, [v])$ a region of $\mathcal{A}$. A region $[s'] = (q', [v'])$ is an *immediate delay successor* of $[s]$ if either: (i) $q = q' \wedge [v] = [v']$ and, for all $\bar{v} \in [v]$ and $x \in X_{\mathcal{A}}$, $\bar{v}(x) > c_m$, or (ii) $q = q' \wedge [v] \neq [v']$ and for all $\bar{v} \in [v]$ there exists $\delta \in \mathbb{R}_{>0}$ such that $\bar{v} + \delta \in [v'] \wedge \forall\, 0 \leq \delta' \leq \delta : \bar{v} + \delta' \in ([v] \cup [v'])$. A region $[s']$ is a *delay successor* of $[s]$ if there exists a finite sequence of regions $[s_0], [s_1], \ldots, [s_n]$ such that $[s_0] = [s]$, $[s_n] = [s']$, and each $[s_{i+1}]$ is an immediate delay successor of $[s_i]$, for $0 \leq i < n$. A region $[s']$ is a *discrete successor* of $[s]$ if $[v'] = [v[Y \leftarrow 0]]$, where $Y \subseteq X_{\mathcal{A}}$ is the subset of clocks reset over the discrete transition from $[s]$ to $[s']$. Symmetric definitions can be given for *immediate delay predecessors*, *delay predecessors*, and *discrete predecessors*.

3 Representing Regions with Ordered Clock Partitions

We introduce a new region representation that captures the order in which clocks become unbounded (exceeding c_m). For bounded clocks (with value up to c_m), only the ordering of their fractional part is preserved. Our representation builds on [11], which focuses on TA with bounded clocks. By also handling unbounded clocks, we significantly extend the applicability of region-based state space exploration to a broader class of TA. While forward exploration remains unaffected, our representation influences backward exploration (Theorem 1 and Theorem 2).

Let $\mathcal{A} = (Act, Q, Q_0, X_{\mathcal{A}}, T, Inv)$ be a TA, $q \in Q$. Furthermore, let $\boldsymbol{\ell}, \mathfrak{r} \in \mathbb{N}$ be two integers such that $\boldsymbol{\ell} + \mathfrak{r} \leq |X_{\mathcal{A}}|$. We denote by $X_i \subseteq X_{\mathcal{A}}$ a subset of clocks of $\mathcal{A}$, for $-\boldsymbol{\ell} \leq i \leq \mathfrak{r}$. We require that these subsets induce a partition of $X_{\mathcal{A}}$, *i.e.*, $X_{\mathcal{A}} = \bigcup_i X_i$ and, for all indices $-\boldsymbol{\ell} \leq i, j \leq \mathfrak{r}$ such that $i \neq j$, $X_i \cap X_j = \varnothing$.

Finally, we introduce a function $h : X_{\mathcal{A}} \rightarrow \{0, \ldots, c_m\}$ that assigns an integer value to each clock in $X_{\mathcal{A}}$. A region of $\mathcal{A}$ can be represented as follows:

$$\mathcal{R} := \{q, h, X_{-\ell}, X_{-(\ell-1)}, \ldots, X_{-1}, X_0, X_1, \ldots, X_{(\mathfrak{r}-1)}, X_{\mathfrak{r}}\}. \tag{1}$$

Set X_0 is always present even if empty; the other sets are omitted when empty. The sets $X_{-\ell}, \ldots, X_{-1}$ represent unbounded clocks, capturing the ordering in which these clocks become unbounded (*e.g.*, all clocks in X_{-1} become unbounded simultaneously and prior to all clocks in X_{-2}). Conversely, the sets $X_1, \ldots, X_{\mathfrak{r}}$ represent bounded clocks, capturing the ordering of their fractional parts (*e.g.*, the fractional parts of all clocks in X_1 are equal and less than the fractional parts of all clocks in X_2). X_0 contains bounded clocks that have no fractional part (we also say these clocks *are in the unit*). The integers ℓ and $\mathfrak{r}$ denote the number of sets containing unbounded and bounded clocks, respectively ($\mathfrak{r}$ does not consider X_0). Their values are automatically updated whenever a set is inserted into or removed from $\mathcal{R}$. We use a subscript to disambiguate between different regions: for instance, $q_{\mathcal{R}}$ refers to the location q of $\mathcal{R}$, $X_{\mathcal{R},0}$ to the set X_0 of $\mathcal{R}$, and $\ell_{\mathcal{R}}$ indicates the number of sets containing unbounded clocks in $\mathcal{R}$.

For conciseness, we also refer to the elements of a region $\mathcal{R}$ as its *structure*. Two regions $\mathcal{R}, \mathcal{R}'$ are *structurally equivalent* if the following holds: $q_{\mathcal{R}} = q_{\mathcal{R}'} \wedge \ell_{\mathcal{R}} = \ell_{\mathcal{R}'} \wedge \mathfrak{r}_{\mathcal{R}} = \mathfrak{r}_{\mathcal{R}'}$ and, for all $-\ell_{\mathcal{R}} \leq i \leq \mathfrak{r}_{\mathcal{R}}$, $X_{\mathcal{R},i} = X_{\mathcal{R}',i}$.

Example 1. Let $\mathcal{A}$ be a TA with clocks $X_{\mathcal{A}} = \{x, y, z, w\}$ and $c_m = 5$. Consider the region defined as: $\{(x, y, z, w) \mid 2 < x < 3, 2 < y < 3, z > 5, w > 5, x = y\}$, *i.e.*, a region (assumed to be in $q \in Q$) in which x and y are bounded and equal (they have the same fractional part), while clocks z and w are unbounded (we assume that z became unbounded before w). The region is represented using Eq. 1 as: $\mathcal{R} = \{q, h(x) = 2, h(y) = 2, h(z) = 5, h(w) = 5, X_{-2}, X_{-1}, X_0, X_1\}$, where $X_{-2} = \{w\}, X_{-1} = \{z\}, X_0 = \varnothing, X_1 = \{x, y\}, \ell = 2$, and $\mathfrak{r} = 1$.

Definition 4 (Region class). *If the order in which clocks become unbounded is tracked, regions can be classified in four distinct* classes—*Z (Zero), P (Positive), M (Mixed), and U (Unbounded)—defined as:* (i) *Class Z:* $\ell \geq 0 \wedge \mathfrak{r} = 0 \wedge X_0 \neq \varnothing$; (ii) *Class P:* $\ell \geq 0 \wedge \mathfrak{r} > 0 \wedge X_0 = \varnothing$; (iii) *Class M:* $\ell \geq 0 \wedge \mathfrak{r} > 0 \wedge X_0 \neq \varnothing$; *and* (iv) *Class U:* $\ell > 0 \wedge \mathfrak{r} = 0 \wedge X_0 = \varnothing$.

Class Z denotes regions in which some clocks may be unbounded, while all bounded clocks have no fractional part and at least one clock must be bounded. Class P denotes regions where some clocks may be unbounded, and all bounded clocks have a fractional part greater than zero (again, at least one clock must be bounded). Class M denotes regions where some clocks may be unbounded and the bounded clocks are partitioned into those with no fractional part and those with a fractional part greater than zero (at least two clocks must be bounded, one with no fractional part and one with a fractional part greater than zero). Finally, class U denotes regions in which all clocks are unbounded. Notice that the region presented in Example 1 belongs to class P. This classification into different classes lies at the core of the algorithms that compute the immediate delay successor and immediate delay predecessors of a given region.

Transitioning Between Classes. Let $\mathcal{R}_Z$, $\mathcal{R}_P$, $\mathcal{R}_M$, and $\mathcal{R}_U$ be regions of classes Z, P, M, and U, respectively. Transitions from a region to its immediate delay successor induce the following deterministic transitions between classes:

- *From* $\mathcal{R}_Z$ *to* $\mathcal{R}_P$: at least one clock $x \in X_{\mathcal{R}_Z,0}$ must increase such that its fractional part becomes greater than zero, while remaining bounded. Other clocks in $X_{\mathcal{R}_Z,0}$ can either become unbounded or remain bounded and grow at the same rate of x, *i.e.*, all bounded clocks have the same fractional part.
- *From* $\mathcal{R}_Z$ *to* $\mathcal{R}_U$: all clocks in $X_{\mathcal{R}_Z,0}$ become unbounded simultaneously.
- *From* $\mathcal{R}_P$ *to* $\mathcal{R}_Z$: it must hold that $\mathfrak{r}_{\mathcal{R}_P} = 1$. All clocks in $X_{\mathcal{R}_P,1}$ must reach the next unit (they will be inserted into $X_{\mathcal{R}_Z,0}$) and their integer value is incremented by 1, as they have a fractional part greater than zero.
- *From* $\mathcal{R}_P$ *to* $\mathcal{R}_M$: it must hold that $\mathfrak{r}_{\mathcal{R}_P} > 1$. All clocks in $X_{\mathcal{R}_P,\mathfrak{r}_{\mathcal{R}_P}}$ must reach the next unit (they will be inserted into $X_{\mathcal{R}_M,0}$) and their integer value is incremented by 1, as they have the biggest fractional part.
- *From* $\mathcal{R}_M$ *to* $\mathcal{R}_P$: clocks in $X_{\mathcal{R}_M,0}$ can become unbounded or their fractional part can become greater than zero while remaining bounded.

The missing transitions between classes are explained as follows. By Definition 4, transitioning to $\mathcal{R}_U$ is only possible from $\mathcal{R}_Z$, since $\mathfrak{r}_{\mathcal{R}_U} = 0 \wedge X_{\mathcal{R}_U,0} = \varnothing$ must hold. It is not possible to transition from $\mathcal{R}_Z$ to $\mathcal{R}_M$, since all clocks will exit from $X_{\mathcal{R}_Z,0}$. An immediate delay successor of $\mathcal{R}_M$ has at least one clock with a nonzero fractional part, making it impossible to transition from $\mathcal{R}_M$ to $\mathcal{R}_Z$.

Transitions between classes contain no self-loops; the immediate delay successor of a region is always a distinct region. $\mathcal{R}_U$ has no delay successors other than itself: unbounded clocks can grow indefinitely. The structure of regions influences transitioning between classes; *e.g.*, from $\mathcal{R}_M$ with $\mathfrak{r}_{\mathcal{R}_M} = 3$, several cycles between $\mathcal{R}_P$ and $\mathcal{R}_M$ are required before reaching $\mathcal{R}_Z$ via delay transitions; this becomes possible once $\mathfrak{r}_{\mathcal{R}_M}$ decreases to 1 as some clocks become unbounded.

4 Discrete Successors and Immediate Delay Predecessors

We present algorithms computing discrete successor and immediate delay predecessor regions. For brevity, immediate delay successor and discrete predecessor algorithms are deferred to the extended version [24].

Discrete Successors. Algorithm 1, whose time complexity is $O(|T| \cdot |X_\mathcal{A}|)$, computes the discrete successors of a given region $\mathcal{R}$. In particular, a set storing the resulting discrete successors is initialized in Line 2 and returned in Line 13. The loop in Line 3 iterates over all transitions t of the original TA that exit from the current location $q_\mathcal{R}$ of $\mathcal{R}$, identifying all possible discrete successors of $\mathcal{R}$. If the guard γ of t is satisfied by combining the integer values of the clocks of $\mathcal{R}$, as returned by $h_\mathcal{R}$, with their fractional parts (Line 4), a copy $\boldsymbol{R}$ of $\mathcal{R}$ is created to represent the successor region (Line 5). The location of $\boldsymbol{R}$ is updated to the target location q of t (Line 6). The loop in Line 7 iterates over all integers $-\ell_{\boldsymbol{R}} \leq i \leq \mathfrak{r}_{\boldsymbol{R}}$, enabling the inner loop in Line 8 to examine each clock set of $\boldsymbol{R}$. If a clock x is reset in t, its integer value is set to zero (Line 9). Moreover, if x is either unbounded or has a nonzero fractional part (Line 10), it is inserted into $X_{\boldsymbol{R},0}$ and removed from its previous clock set (Line 11). Finally, the resulting region $\boldsymbol{R}$ is added to the result set in Line 12.

Algorithm 1: `find-discrete-successors`($\mathcal{R}$)

Data: $\mathcal{R}$: a region.
Result: The discrete successors of $\mathcal{R}$.

```
1  begin
2    res ← ∅;
3    foreach t = (q_R, a, γ, Y, q) ∈ T do
4      if γ is satisfied by R then
5        R ← copy of R;
6        q_R ← q;
7        for i = −ℓ_R to r_R do
8          foreach x ∈ X_{R,i} such that x ∈ Y do
9            h_R(x) ← 0;
10           if i ≠ 0 then
11             X_{R,0} ← X_{R,0} ∪ {x}; X_{R,i} ← X_{R,i} \ {x};
12       res ← res ∪ {R};
13   return res;
```

Immediate Delay Predecessors. The following theorem (whose proof is shown in the extended version [24]) establishes that, when tracking the order in which clocks become unbounded, the number of immediate delay predecessors of a given region does not exhibit exponential blow-up.

Theorem 1. *If the order in which clocks become unbounded is tracked, the number of immediate delay predecessors of a given region is at most three.*

Indeed, if the order in which clocks become unbounded is not tracked, computing the immediate delay predecessors of regions with unbounded clocks would require enumerating all ordered partitions of the unbounded clocks, as every order in which the clocks become unbounded would then be admissible (regions without unbounded clocks would have a unique immediate delay predecessor).

The immediate delay predecessors of a given region $\mathcal{R}$ are computed by Algorithm 2, whose time complexity is $O(|X_{\mathcal{A}}|)$ (we refer to *predecessors* in its description). In particular, Line 2 initializes a set, returned in Line 20, storing the computed predecessors. The algorithm proceeds by analyzing the class of $\mathcal{R}$ to compute its predecessors by modifying a copy $\boldsymbol{R}$ of $\mathcal{R}$, created in Line 3.

If $\mathcal{R}$ is of class U (Line 4), the predecessor is obtained by inserting set $X_{\boldsymbol{R},-\ell_{\boldsymbol{R}}}$, which contains the clocks that became unbounded while exiting from the unit, into $X_{\boldsymbol{R},0}$. Then, $X_{\boldsymbol{R},-\ell_{\boldsymbol{R}}}$ is removed from $\boldsymbol{R}$ (Line 5).

Algorithm 2: `find-immediate-delay-predecessors`($\mathcal{R}$)

Data: $\mathcal{R}$: a region where no clock x is such that: $h_{\mathcal{R}}(x) = 0 \wedge x \in X_{\mathcal{R},0}$.
Result: The immediate delay predecessors of $\mathcal{R}$.

```
1  begin
2      res ← ∅;
3      R ← copy of 𝓡;
4      if X_{𝓡,0} = ∅ ∧ 𝔯_𝓡 = 0 then
5          insert clocks of X_{R,−ℓ_R} in X_{R,0} and remove X_{R,−ℓ_R} from R;
6      else if X_{𝓡,0} ≠ ∅ then
7          X_tmp ← ∅;
8          foreach x ∈ X_{R,0} do
9              h_R(x) ← h_R(x) − 1;
10             X_tmp ← X_tmp ∪ {x}; X_{R,0} ← X_{R,0} \ {x};
11         insert X_tmp to the right of X_{R,𝔯_R};
12     else
13         insert clocks of X_{R,1} in X_{R,0} and remove X_{R,1} from R;
14         if ℓ_𝓡 ≥ 1 then
15             R_1 ← copy of 𝓡;
16             insert clocks of X_{R_1,−ℓ_{R_1}} in X_{R_1,0} and remove X_{R_1,−ℓ_{R_1}} from R_1;
17             R_2 ← copy of R_1;
18             insert clocks of X_{R_2,1} into X_{R_2,0} and remove X_{R_2,1} from R_2;
19             res ← res ∪ {R_1, R_2};
20     return (res ∪ {R});
```

For regions of class Z or class M (Line 6), an auxiliary set X_{tmp} is initialized (Line 7). The integer part of each clock $x \in X_{\boldsymbol{R},0}$ (Line 8) is decremented by 1 (Line 9), and x is moved from $X_{\boldsymbol{R},0}$ to X_{tmp} (Line 10). Since these clocks must have the highest fractional part, X_{tmp} is inserted to the right of $X_{\boldsymbol{R},\mathfrak{r}_R}$ (Line 11).

If $\mathcal{R}$ is of class P (Line 12), the algorithm considers both the cases where the predecessor is of class Z or class M. First, clocks in $X_{\boldsymbol{R},1}$ (those that left the unit) are moved into $X_{\boldsymbol{R},0}$ (Line 13). Then, Line 14 checks whether unbounded clocks must also be handled. If so, two additional regions are created. The first, $\boldsymbol{R}_1$, is created on Line 15 as a copy of $\mathcal{R}$ and updated on Line 16 to represent the case in which all clocks with zero fractional part in the predecessor became unbounded. After $\boldsymbol{R}_1$ is updated, it is copied in $\boldsymbol{R}_2$ (Line 17), which is modified on Line 18 to capture the case in which only a subset of those clocks became unbounded. Both $\boldsymbol{R}_1$ and $\boldsymbol{R}_2$ are collected on Line 19 in the result set.

Example 2. Let $\mathcal{A}$ be a TA having clocks $X_{\mathcal{A}} = \{x, y\}$ and maximum constant $c_m = 2$. Consider the region $\mathcal{R}_0$ as depicted in Fig. 1a. Here, triangles are used to symbolically represent entire regions rather than individual points (*e.g.*, the triangle corresponding to $\mathcal{R}_2$ represents the region $\{(x, y) \mid 1 < x < 2 \wedge y > 2\}$). For this reason, they are not drawn on the diagonals, as would be implied by

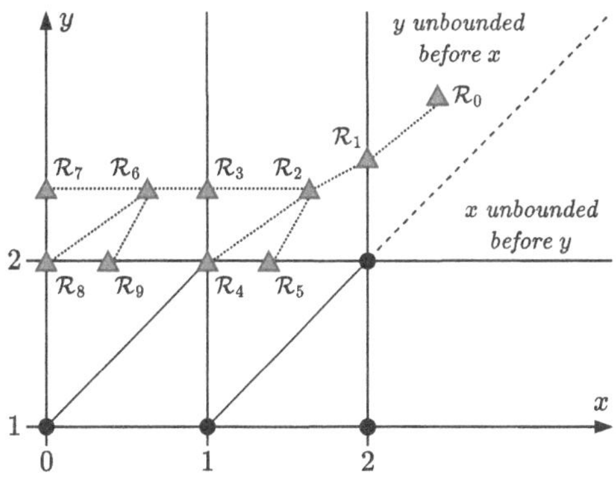

(a) Partial computation of delay predecessors of $\mathcal{R}_0$.

Region	Class	Unbounded
$\mathcal{R}_0$	U	yes, $\{x, y\}$
$\mathcal{R}_1$	Z	yes, $\{y\}$
$\mathcal{R}_2$	P	yes, $\{y\}$
$\mathcal{R}_3$	Z	yes, $\{y\}$
$\mathcal{R}_4$	Z	no, $\varnothing$
$\mathcal{R}_5$	M	no, $\varnothing$
$\mathcal{R}_6$	P	yes, $\{y\}$
$\mathcal{R}_7$	Z	yes, $\{y\}$
$\mathcal{R}_8$	Z	no, $\varnothing$
$\mathcal{R}_9$	M	no, $\varnothing$

(b) Table listing regions $\mathcal{R}_i$, $0 \leq i \leq 9$, their class, and their unbounded clocks (if any).

Fig. 1. Example of delay predecessors computation from $\mathcal{R}_0$ (left), stopped upon reaching bounded regions, and a table with additional information about the regions (right). Triangles symbolically represent entire regions rather than specific points within them.

Definition 2. For visual clarity, the figure does not represent the portion of the state space where $y < 1$. Since $\mathcal{R}_0$ lies above the diagonal originating from $(2, 2)$, it corresponds to the case in which y became unbounded before x. $\mathcal{R}_0$ can be represented as: $\mathcal{R}_0 = \{q,\ h(x) = 2,\ h(y) = 2,\ X_{-2} = \{x\},\ X_{-1} = \{y\},\ X_0 = \varnothing\}$.

We compute the delay predecessors of $\mathcal{R}_0$ using Algorithm 2. For conciseness, we stop the computation when reaching a bounded region or because no further delay predecessors exist. The algorithm yields a single immediate delay predecessor of class Z (Fig. 1b): $\mathcal{R}_1 = \{q,\ h(x) = 2,\ h(y) = 2,\ X_{-1} = \{y\},\ X_0 = \{x\}\}$. Applying the same algorithm to $\mathcal{R}_1$ yields a single immediate delay predecessor: $\mathcal{R}_2 = \{q,\ h(x) = 1,\ h(y) = 2,\ X_{-1} = \{y\},\ X_0 = \varnothing,\ X_1 = \{x\}\}$. Then, from $\mathcal{R}_2$, three immediate delay predecessors can be computed. Two of them ($\mathcal{R}_4$ and $\mathcal{R}_5$) are not further analyzed in this example, as they are already bounded. Consider the region: $\mathcal{R}_3 = \{q,\ h(x) = 1,\ h(y) = 2,\ X_{-1} = \{y\},\ X_0 = \{x\}\}$. This region is structurally equivalent to $\mathcal{R}_1$, except that the integer value of x has been decremented by 1. The computation from $\mathcal{R}_1$ applies similarly from $\mathcal{R}_3$.

The computation of delay predecessors can be optimized. Assume that, for a region $\mathcal{R}$, Algorithm 2 can be applied n times. Furthermore, assume that all clocks in $\mathcal{R}$ are bounded and that $\mathfrak{r}_{\mathcal{R}} > 0$ holds. We define the *period* of $\mathcal{R}$ as $\theta = 2 \cdot (\mathfrak{r}_{\mathcal{R}} + 1)$ if $X_{\mathcal{R},0} \neq \varnothing$; $\theta = 2 \cdot \mathfrak{r}_{\mathcal{R}}$ otherwise. Then, decrement the integer value of every clock of $\mathcal{R}$ by $\lfloor n/\theta \rfloor$ (ensuring their integer value does not go below zero), obtaining a new region $\mathcal{R}'$. After this step, if none of the clocks of $\mathcal{R}'$ are equal to zero (with no fractional part), it suffices to apply Algorithm 2 only $n \bmod \theta$ times to $\mathcal{R}'$ to obtain the final result, possibly stopping earlier if one or more clocks become equal to zero during this process. Similar optimizations can also be applied when some clocks are unbounded.

Discrete Predecessors (Intuition). When computing a discrete successor, a subset of clocks may be reset, and therefore appear with value zero in the successor region. Discrete predecessors computation aims to reverse this operation. However, starting from a region in which the value of some clocks is zero (with no fractional part), a challenge arises, since the original values of these clocks prior to being reset are unknown. As a result, all possible combinations of values for the reset clocks must be considered (including cases where they may have been unbounded) to ensure all discrete predecessors are computed. This process can be simplified using the guard of the transition over which discrete predecessors are computed, as it may constrain the possible values of clocks prior to reset.

The following theorem (whose proof is shown in the extended version [24]) establishes that, when tracking the order in which clocks become unbounded, the number of discrete predecessors of a given region suffers from an inherent exponential blow-up that cannot be avoided in general.

Theorem 2. *Let $\mathcal{A}$ be a TA such that $n = |X_{\mathcal{A}}|$ and let $\mathcal{R}$ be a region of $\mathcal{A}$. If the order in which clocks become unbounded must be tracked, then the number of discrete predecessors of $\mathcal{R}$ over a single transition is $O\left((\frac{c_m+1}{\ln 2})^n \cdot (n+1)!\right)$.*

5 Implementation and Experimental Evaluation

This section introduces Tarzan along with a detailed empirical evaluation of its forward and backward reachability algorithms. To express reachability queries, we use the standard Computation Tree Logic formula $\exists\Diamond(\varphi)$, meaning that there exists a path in the state space in which φ eventually holds true.

5.1 The Tarzan library

Tarzan is a C++20 library for performing forward and backward reachability analysis of TA and networks of TA, using either breadth-first (BFS) or depth-first (DFS) state space exploration. Tarzan supports shared integer variables (specified through general arithmetic expressions), urgent locations, and invariants. The semantics of both invariants and networks in Tarzan follows that of Uppaal [8]. Support for networks of TA and integer variables in backward reachability is currently under development. Successor and predecessor algorithms were revised to allow each clock to have its own maximum constant.

Tarzan accepts .txt input files, parsed using the Boost Spirit X3 library, containing a TA representation written in a domain-specific language called *Liana*. Each file represents a single TA; a network of TA is defined using multiple files.

Networks of TA. A *network* of size n is the parallel composition of n individual TA [5, Chapter 9]. Given regions $\mathcal{R}_1, \dots, \mathcal{R}_n$, each corresponding to a TA $\mathcal{A}_1, \dots, \mathcal{A}_n$ in the network, a *network region* $\overline{\mathcal{R}}$ is defined as $\overline{\mathcal{R}} := \{\mathcal{R}_1, \dots, \mathcal{R}_n\}$. To compute both immediate delay and discrete successors of $\overline{\mathcal{R}}$, Tarzan relies on specialized data structures that generalize the applicability of the algorithms originally developed for individual regions to network regions. These data structures ensure the correctness of on-the-fly immediate delay and discrete successor computation across the Cartesian product of $\mathcal{A}_1, \dots, \mathcal{A}_n$. In particular, a C++

double-ended queue maintains the relative ordering of the fractional parts of all clocks within $\overline{\mathcal{R}}$, partitioning these clocks into ordered equivalence classes. This ordering captures the evolution over time of all clocks within $\overline{\mathcal{R}}$, including which clocks will exit the unit (possibly becoming unbounded), reach the next unit, or be reset. Furthermore, a C++ set identifies the regions in $\overline{\mathcal{R}}$ that are of class Z or M. Since the generalized algorithms for network regions operate by applying the successor algorithms to a subset of individual regions in $\overline{\mathcal{R}}$, this classification is essential for computing immediate delay successors; indeed, regions of class Z or M contain clocks that will exit the unit; hence, their immediate delay successors must be computed prior to those of regions of class P.

Implementation Considerations. Since the focus of this paper is the implementation of algorithms using the new representation of Eq. (1), most optimizations are deferred to future work. Currently, TARZAN does not implement any optimizations for state space exploration, except for symmetry reduction [9]. Memory compression optimizations are also not implemented. The algorithms also suffer when computing delay successors (predecessors), as these computations require generating a sequence of immediate delay successors (predecessors). This limitation could be mitigated through the optimization described in Sect. 4 for delay predecessors (which can be adapted for delay successors as well). Furthermore, since TARZAN only performs reachability analysis, proving that a region is unreachable going forward requires exploring the entire reachable state space. Due to the aforementioned limitations, a BFS exploration must visit all delay successors (predecessors) before visiting discrete successors (predecessors), which is typically unnecessary and increases the verification time. For this reason, unless stated otherwise, all experiments follow a DFS strategy.

5.2 Forward Reachability Benchmarks

We compared TARZAN against Uppaal 5.0 and TChecker (commit d711ace) in forward reachability[1]. The benchmarks (adjusted to ensure compatibility across all tools) come from publicly available repositories, published literature, or manually crafted when required. If possible, the reachability queries match those of the original benchmarks; otherwise, they have been adapted to fit the capabilities of the tools. Uppaal was run with standard DBM without memory optimizations; TChecker was configured with the `covreach` flag to match the algorithm used in Uppaal. Experiments were conducted on a MacBook Pro equipped with an M3 chip and 24 GB of RAM.

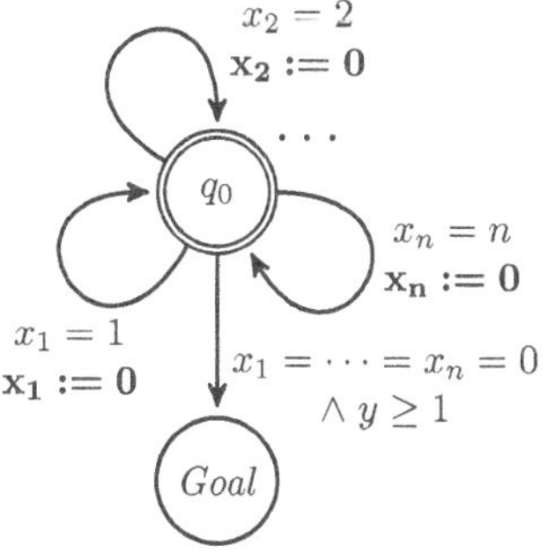

Fig. 2. `flower`. q_0 is initial.

[1] To ensure a fair comparison, symmetry reduction was disabled in both TARZAN and Uppaal; notably, this optimization cannot be manually controlled in TChecker.

In the following, tables report Verification Time (VT), Execution Time (ET), memory (Mem, representing the Maximum Resident Set Size), and the number of stored regions and states. ET measures the time elapsed between issuing the verification command and receiving the result from the tool. Timings are in seconds, memory in MB. The size of a network is denoted by K (for `flower`, K indicates the number of clocks). All values are averages over five runs, with a timeout of 600 s set on ET. Timeouts are reported as TO, ε denotes times below 0.001 s, and out-of-memory events are denoted by OOM. Bold cells indicate the fastest VT (on ties, the fastest ET). KO indicates that an error occurred during verification. The complete benchmark suite is in the extended version [24].

TA with Punctual Guards. Region-based abstractions can outperform zone-based approaches when TA are *closed*, *i.e.*, contain only non-strict guards. This is particularly evident when guards are *punctual*, *i.e.*, restricted to equality constraints. The `flower` TA [19] depicted in Fig. 2, which is also used in our evaluation of backward reachability, satisfies these requirements. It consists of two locations: q_0 (which is initial) and *Goal*, and it features $n+1$ clocks, denoted by $x_1, \ldots, x_n, y$. The guards over clocks x_i are punctual; the guard on y is non-strict. Since y is never reset, the behavior of `flower` is equivalent to a model featuring only punctual guards. To reach *Goal*, all clocks x_i must simultaneously be exactly zero, while y must satisfy $y \geq 1$. Specifically, when transitioning to *Goal*, y must be equal to the least common multiple of $1, 2, \ldots, n$. Similar behavior is shown in the additional examples reported in Table 1: these are networks of TA with only punctual guards. In all these experiments, punctual guards force zones to be repeatedly and finely split, as reflected by the large number of states shown in Table 1. The results indicate that Uppaal and TChecker experience a substantial decrease in performance when $K \geq 8$.

Table 1. When all transitions have punctual guards, regions may outperform zones. Here, `flower` is a single TA, while the others are networks of TA.

K	TARZAN				TChecker				UPPAAL			
	VT	ET	Mem	Regions	VT	ET	Mem	States	VT	ET	Mem	States
▶ `boolean` [23] :: [Query: $\exists\Diamond(ctr_1 = 1 \wedge ctr_2 = 1 \wedge \cdots \wedge ctr_K = 1)$] ◀												
4	ε	0.013	7.78	24	ε	**0.007**	**6.47**	**185**	0.001	0.052	18.85	185
6	**0.003**	**0.016**	**13.42**	**425**	0.088	0.096	13.80	8502	0.075	0.128	19.91	8502
8	**0.013**	**0.027**	**29.10**	**1009**	75.461	75.980	220.82	566763	77.204	77.523	81.79	566763
▶ `flower` [19] :: [Query: $\exists\Diamond(Flower.Goal)$] ◀												
5	ε	**0.013**	**7.92**	**95**	0.001	0.007	6.35	150	0.001	0.056	18.82	150
7	ε	**0.022**	**10.65**	**573**	0.322	0.330	13.12	3508	0.399	0.455	19.76	3508
9	**0.007**	**0.022**	**58.62**	**9161**	—	TO	—	—	—	TO	—	—
▶ `gates` [23] :: [Query: $\exists\Diamond(Unlocker.Goal)$] ◀												
5	ε	**0.013**	**8.84**	**76**	0.001	0.008	7.19	549	0.001	0.055	19.01	549
7	ε	**0.014**	**11.23**	**151**	0.110	0.122	21.08	32979	0.035	0.092	22.79	32979
9	**0.001**	**0.015**	**15.43**	**251**	47.895	48.771	806.72	3071646	5.228	6.509	451.71	3071646
▶ `ring` [23] :: [Query: $\exists\Diamond(P_0.Goal \wedge P_1.Goal \wedge \ldots \wedge P_K.Goal)$] ◀												
4	**0.001**	**0.015**	**12.40**	**542**	0.020	0.029	11.56	7738	0.010	0.065	19.52	7738
6	**0.011**	**0.025**	**48.96**	**3397**	12.137	12.561	268.93	1180575	3.406	3.715	128.87	1180575
8	**0.204**	**0.225**	**687.77**	**47063**	—	TO	—	—	—	TO	—	—

Closed TA. Two networks of closed TA were adapted from the benchmarks available from [29]: `medicalWorkflow` models medical checks for patients, while `mpeg2` models the homonymous compression standard, where compression leverages a given number of bidirectional frames (BFrames). Since TARZAN does not currently support broadcast channels, these models were rewritten into equivalent versions that use only point-to-point channels. The results in Table 2 reveal a high number of stored states. This indicates that these models restrict the evolution of clocks in a way that forces zones to be repeatedly and finely split, thus pushing these models into a category where zone-based abstractions exhibit poor performance, a phenomenon already demonstrated in the above experiments (see Table 1). Furthermore, both Uppaal and TChecker exhibit an unexpectedly high verification time in `medicalWorkflow`. This indicates that the dominant cost in this benchmark originates from zone manipulation, whose operations may have quadratic or cubic complexity in the number of clocks [19]. Region-based analysis avoids this overhead, as its fundamental operations have linear complexity in the number of clocks. Interestingly, TChecker aborted execution on the largest instances of `medicalWorkflow` raising the error: *"ERROR: value out of bounds"*.

Table 2. The results are derived from networks of closed TA, where guards may either be punctual or contain non-strict inequalities. In this setting, TARZAN can handle both large networks (`medicalWorkflow`) and large constants (`mpeg2`).

K	TARZAN				TChecker				UPPAAL			
	VT	ET	Mem	Regions	VT	ET	Mem	States	VT	ET	Mem	States
▶ `medicalWorkflow` [29] :: [Query: $\exists\Diamond(Patient_1.Done \wedge Patient_2.Done \wedge \cdots \wedge Patient_{K-2}.Done)$] ◀												
12	0.007	0.021	33.39	660	0.011	0.030	22.63	639	**0.002**	**0.059**	**20.83**	**582**
22	0.056	0.072	204.97	2715	0.316	0.560	173.75	3774	**0.032**	**0.093**	**31.76**	**2862**
42	**0.609**	**0.647**	**2271.65**	**15025**	13.571	16.096	2517.18	25544	1.275	1.379	230.07	16522
72	**5.781**	**5.959**	**12891.17**	**68990**	355.827	389.223	16109.45	126949	54.200	54.838	2799.57	74762
102	**27.918**	**28.466**	**13780.57**	**189555**	KO	KO	KO	KO	593.317	597.306	12364.67	202302
▶ `mpeg2` [29] :: [Query: $\exists\Diamond(BFrame_1.Bout \wedge BFrame_2.Bout \wedge \cdots \wedge BFrame_{K-4}.Bout)$] ◀												
8	0.365	0.385	451.46	26916	0.003	0.014	8.96	531	**0.001**	**0.058**	**19.46**	**537**
12	**0.796**	**0.819**	**718.63**	**27238**	8.405	8.663	252.70	383103	1.621	1.766	112.33	383109
16	**1.364**	**1.392**	**1032.46**	**27704**	—	TO	—	—	—	TO	—	—

Large Constants. When constants are large, zones are still preferable. Table 3 reports results from two real-world case studies: the Carrier Sense Multiple Access/Collision Detection protocol (`CSMA/CD`) [20] and `pagerank` [6], a mechanism used to prioritize Web keyword search results. The latter is presented in two variants: in the first, the last two digits of the original constants were truncated, while the second uses the full constants. The largest constant in `CSMA/CD` is 808, whereas in `pagerank` they are 101 (truncated) and 10162 (full).

Safety Properties. When safety properties must be verified using forward reachability, TARZAN requires to explore the entire reachable state space. Table 4 reports the results for the Fischer mutual exclusion protocol [31]. The verified property specifies that two given processes must never be in the critical section simultaneously. In the remainder of this section, we demonstrate that backward reachability may enhance the verification of safety properties by exploring only a restricted subset of the state space, potentially avoiding out-of-memory events.

Table 3. Large constants negatively impact the VT of regions, unlike zones. Here, the first row of `pagerank` corresponds to the variant with truncated constants.

K	TARZAN				TChecker				UPPAAL			
	VT	ET	Mem	Regions	VT	ET	Mem	States	VT	ET	Mem	States
▶ CSMA/CD [20] :: [Query: $\exists\Diamond \begin{pmatrix} P_1.senderRetry \wedge P_2.senderRetry \wedge P_3.senderTransm \\ \wedge P_4.senderRetry \wedge \cdots \wedge P_7.senderRetry \end{pmatrix}$] ◀												
21	0.198	0.215	364.96	20936	0.004	0.038	30.32	232	**0.001**	**0.061**	**20.24**	**269**
31	0.674	0.701	1194.45	47526	0.018	0.218	117.03	371	**0.002**	**0.064**	**21.11**	**554**
51	3.364	3.431	5351.35	131906	0.293	1.386	837.12	1381	**0.010**	**0.077**	**23.89**	**1424**
▶ `pagerank` [6] :: [Query: $\exists\Diamond(Stage_7.Completed)$] ◀												
9	0.068	0.085	179.33	4193	0.002	0.086	58.54	1129	**0.002**	**0.076**	**22.89**	**1129**
9	4.227	4.361	10950.36	257311	0.002	0.085	58.53	1129	**0.002**	**0.076**	**23.01**	**1129**

Table 4. Safety properties require TARZAN to visit the entire reachable state space.

K	TARZAN				TChecker				UPPAAL			
	VT	ET	Mem	Regions	VT	ET	Mem	States	VT	ET	Mem	States
▶ `fischer` [31] :: [Query: $\exists\Diamond(Fischer_1.cs \wedge Fischer_2.cs)$] ◀												
4	0.644	0.669	1098.36	180032	ε	**0.007**	**6.75**	**220**	0.001	0.055	18.96	220
5	19.627	19.849	12948.99	3920652	0.004	0.011	9.30	727	**0.002**	**0.057**	**19.07**	**727**
6	—	—	OOM	—	0.024	0.032	12.25	2378	**0.008**	**0.064**	**19.43**	**2378**

5.3 Backward Reachability Analysis with TARZAN

We begin with a backward unreachability example on `flower`, and then compare its forward and backward reachability results. The entire `flower` reachable state space, when considering five clocks and computed going forward starting from the initial region $\mathcal{R}_0 = \{q_0, h(x_1) = h(x_2) = h(x_3) = h(x_4) = h(y) = 0, X_0\}$, where $X_{\mathcal{R}_0,0} = \{x_1, x_2, x_3, x_4, y\}$, resulted in 1517 regions, computed in 1.18 ms.

Backward reachability can offer a practical advantage for proving unreachability, since it may avoid a complete state space exploration. Consider the region $\mathcal{R}_1 = \{q_0, h(x_1) = 1, h(x_2) = 2, h(x_3) = h(x_4) = 0, h(y) = 1, X_{-1}, X_0\}$, where $X_{\mathcal{R}_1,-1} = \{x_2, y\}$ and $X_{\mathcal{R}_1,0} = \{x_1, x_3, x_4\}$. $\mathcal{R}_1$ is unreachable: it requires both x_2 and y to become unbounded simultaneously, but the constraint $y \geq 1$ forces y to become unbounded before x_2. TARZAN classifies $\mathcal{R}_1$ as unreachable by verifying that $\mathcal{R}_0$ is unreachable from $\mathcal{R}_1$, requiring 272 regions in 0.245 ms. By adjusting $\mathcal{R}_1$ with the correct ordering in which clocks become unbounded, we obtain $\mathcal{R}_2 = \{q_0, h(x_1) = 1, h(x_2) = 2, h(x_3) = h(x_4) = 0, h(y) = 1, X_{-2}, X_{-1}, X_0\}$, where $X_{\mathcal{R}_2,-2} = \{x_2\}$, $X_{\mathcal{R}_2,-1} = \{y\}$, and $X_{\mathcal{R}_2,0} = \{x_1, x_3, x_4\}$. Region $\mathcal{R}_2$ is reachable. Reaching $\mathcal{R}_0$ from $\mathcal{R}_2$ required 263 regions in 0.378 ms.

Now, consider the version of `flower` with $K = n + 1$ clocks. Let $\mathcal{R}_K$ denote the region in location *Goal* in which all clocks x_i are exactly equal to zero (no fractional part) and $y \geq 1$ holds. Table 5 reports the VT and number of regions stored by TARZAN when checking the forward and backward reachability of $\mathcal{R}_K$. The results show that forward reachability is generally faster and requires fewer regions, while backward reachability remains comparable in this setting.

Backward reachability was employed to verify that in `fischer` two processes cannot occupy the critical section simultaneously. As backward reachability does

Table 5. Backward reachability results. `fischer` goes out of memory at $K = 6$. Tests use DFS except `trainAHV93`, for which BFS is faster. `flower` checks reachability, `fischer` unreachability, and `trainAHV93` reachability (rows 1,2) and unreachability (rows 3,4).

▶ `flower` [19] :: DFS ◀				▶ `fischer` [23] :: DFS ◀				▶ `trainAHV93` [23] :: BFS ◀			
Forward $K = 11, 13, 15, 17$		*Backward* $K = 11, 13, 15, 17$		*Forward* $K = 3, 4, 5, 6$		*Backward* $K = 3, 4, 5, 6$		*Forward* $K = 4, 5, 4, 5$		*Backward* $K = 4, 5, 4, 5$	
VT	**Regions**	**VT**	**Regions**	**VT**	**Regions**	**VT**	**Regions**	**VT**	**Regions**	**VT**	**Regions**
0.028	30761	0.060	38669	0.007	9083	ε	264	ε	1241	0.171	118868
0.412	370331	0.615	388911	0.141	183459	0.001	1316	0.026	31516	66.877	31051667
7.188	5142671	9.414	4921043	4.061	4182681	0.008	8724	0.013	17124	0.030	26914
16.212	11023829	21.497	11077295	—	—	0.100	77084	1.000	912597	0.635	614220

not currently support networks of TA nor integer variables, we developed a script to construct a single TA version of `fischer` [23], in which the *pid* variable is directly encoded within its locations. The safety property to be verified with K processes is described as follows: processes 1 through $K-2$ are requesting access to the critical section, with their clocks strictly between 1 and 2; processes $K-1$ and K are both in the critical section, with their clocks greater than 2; *pid* is equal to K. A preliminary phase was necessary to compute the initial subset of regions from which backward reachability was started. This required considering all ordered partitions of the fractional parts of bounded clocks as well as all ordered partitions of unbounded clocks. Clock constraints in the property were introduced to enable the manual computation of this subset. Backward reachability results, reported in Table 5, demonstrate superior performance compared to forward reachability, to the extent that an out-of-memory event becomes feasible. Indeed, the unreachable portion of the state space limited the backward exploration to a relatively small number of regions. We evaluated the same property with Uppaal (which uses forward reachability) on the same `fischer` model and obtained: for $K = 3$, 88 states in 0.001 s; for $K = 4$, 460 states in 0.004 s; for $K = 5$, 2765 states in 0.025 s; and for $K = 6$, 19042 states in 0.214 s. In this comparison, TARZAN outperformed Uppaal when using backward reachability.

Backward reachability was also applied to `trainAHV93` [23] (we developed a script to convert it into a single TA version). Exploration was conducted in BFS, as it achieved better performance on this model. `trainAHV93` allows two or more trains to be in the crossing while the gate is down. Rows 1,2 of Table 5 report the results for (i) reaching the first region detected by the BFS exploration in which at least two trains occupy the crossing while the gate is down, and (ii) computing the backward predecessors from this region to an initial one. In this case, backward reachability requires substantially more regions than forward reachability. We also verified the safety property stating that whenever a train is in the crossing, the number of trains in the crossing cannot be zero (*i.e.*, no counter malfunction). Such property with $K-2$ trains, a gate, and a controller, is described as follows: trains 1 to $K-3$ are not in the crossing and their clocks are strictly between 2 and 3; train $K-2$ is in the crossing and its clock is exactly 4; the gate's clock is strictly between 1 and 2, and the controller's clock is greater than 1. As in `fischer`, we first explicitly identified the initial subset of regions from which backward reachability was started. Rows 3, 4 of Table 5 show that, in this case, forward and backward reachability perform comparably.

6 Conclusion and Future Works

We introduced TARZAN, a region-based verification library supporting forward and backward reachability for TA. Our experiments demonstrated that TARZAN exhibits superior performance on closed TA and TA with punctual guards, while zone-based approaches remain better suited to other classes of TA. We showed that backward reachability with TARZAN is often feasible in practice and effective for verifying safety properties. For this reason, the integration of TARZAN into existing tools has the potential to enhance their verification capabilities.

Future work will proceed in several directions. We plan to integrate additional optimizations into TARZAN, with a particular focus on improving the computation of delay successors and predecessors, while leveraging symbolic techniques to reduce memory usage. In addition, we will extend backward reachability algorithms to networks of TA, thereby laying the foundation for applying TARZAN to the synthesis of winning strategies in Timed Games. Finally, we intend to explore hybrid approaches that complement TARZAN with zone-based techniques, thereby combining the strengths of both abstractions.

References

1. Abdulla, P.A., Atig, M.F., Stenman, J.: Dense-timed pushdown automata. In: Proceedings of the 2012 27th Annual IEEE/ACM Symposium on Logic in Computer Science, LICS 2012, pp. 35–44. IEEE Computer Society, USA (2012). https://doi.org/10.1109/LICS.2012.15
2. Alur, R., Dill, D.L.: A theory of timed automata. Theoret. Comput. Sci. **126**(2), 183–235 (1994)
3. André, E., Jacobs, S., Karra, S.L., Sankur, O.: Parameterized verification of timed networks with clock invariants (2024)
4. Apron developers: Apron. https://github.com/antoinemine/apron. Accessed 24 Nov 2025
5. Baier, C., Katoen, J.P.: Principles of Model Checking (Representation and Mind-Series). The MIT Press (2008)
6. Baresi, L., Bersani, M.M., Marconi, F., Quattrocchi, G., Rossi, M.: Using formal verification to evaluate the execution time of spark applications. Formal Aspects Comput. **32**(1), 33–70 (2020)
7. Behrmann, G., David, A., Larsen, K.G.: A tutorial on UPPAAL. In: Bernardo, M., Corradini, F. (eds.) SFM-RT 2004. LNCS, vol. 3185, pp. 200–236. Springer, Heidelberg (2004). https://doi.org/10.1007/978-3-540-30080-9_7
8. Bengtsson, J., Yi, W.: Timed automata: semantics, algorithms and tools. In: Desel, J., Reisig, W., Rozenberg, G. (eds.) ACPN 2003. LNCS, vol. 3098, pp. 87–124. Springer, Heidelberg (2004). https://doi.org/10.1007/978-3-540-27755-2_3

9. Bošnački, D., Dams, D., Holenderski, L.: Symmetric spin. In: Havelund, K., Penix, J., Visser, W. (eds.) SPIN 2000. LNCS, vol. 1885, pp. 1–19. Springer, Heidelberg (2000). https://doi.org/10.1007/10722468_1
10. Bouyer, P.: Forward analysis of updatable timed automata. Formal Methods Syst. Design **24**(3), 281–320 (2004)
11. Bouyer, P., Brinksma, E., Larsen, K.G.: Optimal infinite scheduling for multi-priced timed automata. Formal Methods Syst. Design **32**(1), 3–23 (2008)
12. Bouyer, P., Fahrenberg, U., Larsen, K.G., Markey, N.: Quantitative analysis of real-time systems using priced timed automata. Commun. ACM **54**(9), 78–87 (2011)
13. Bouzenada, A., Saidouni, D.E., Díaz, G.: A finite representation of durational action timed automata semantics. Mathematics **12**(24) (2024)
14. Bozga, M., Daws, C., Maler, O., Olivero, A., Tripakis, S., Yovine, S.: Kronos: a model-checking tool for real-time systems. In: Hu, A.J., Vardi, M.Y. (eds.) CAV 1998. LNCS, vol. 1427, pp. 546–550. Springer, Heidelberg (1998). https://doi.org/10.1007/BFb0028779
15. Daszczuk, W.B.: Modeling and verification of asynchronous systems using timed integrated model of distributed systems. Sensors **22**(3) (2022). https://doi.org/10.3390/s22031157, https://www.mdpi.com/1424-8220/22/3/1157
16. Dill, D.L.: Timing assumptions and verification of finite-state concurrent systems. In: Sifakis, J. (ed.) CAV 1989. LNCS, vol. 407, pp. 197–212. Springer, Heidelberg (1990). https://doi.org/10.1007/3-540-52148-8_17
17. Henzinger, T., Nicollin, X., Sifakis, J., Yovine, S.: Symbolic model checking for real-time systems. Inf. Comput. **111**(2), 193–244 (1994)
18. Herbreteau, F., Srivathsan, B., Tran, T.T., Walukiewicz, I.: Why liveness for timed automata is hard, and what we can do about it. ACM Trans. Comput. Logic **21**(3)(2020)
19. Jørgensen, K.Y., Larsen, K.G., Srba, J.: Time-darts: a data structure for verification of closed timed automata. Electron. Proc. Theor. Comput. Sci. **102**, 141–155 (2012)
20. Kiviriga, A., Larsen, K.G., Nyman, U.: Randomized reachability analysis in Uppaal: fast error detection in timed systems. In: Lluch Lafuente, A., Mavridou, A. (eds.) FMICS 2021. LNCS, vol. 12863, pp. 149–166. Springer, Cham (2021). https://doi.org/10.1007/978-3-030-85248-1_9
21. Lehmann, S., Schupp, S.: Bounded DBM-based clock state construction for timed automata in Uppaal. Int. J. Softw. Tools Technol. Transfer **25**(1), 19–47 (2023)
22. Maler, O., Pnueli, A., Sifakis, J.: On the synthesis of discrete controllers for timed systems. In: Mayr, E.W., Puech, C. (eds.) STACS 1995. LNCS, vol. 900, pp. 229–242. Springer, Heidelberg (1995). https://doi.org/10.1007/3-540-59042-0_76
23. Manini, A.: Tarzan: timed automata region and zone library for real-time systems analysis (2025). https://github.com/andreamanini98/TARZAN
24. Manini, A., Rossi, M., San Pietro, P.: Tarzan: a region-based library for forward and backward reachability of timed automata (extended version) (2026). https://arxiv.org/abs/2602.15435
25. Peter, H.-J., Ehlers, R., Mattmüller, R.: Synthia: verification and synthesis for timed automata. In: Gopalakrishnan, G., Qadeer, S. (eds.) CAV 2011. LNCS, vol. 6806, pp. 649–655. Springer, Heidelberg (2011). https://doi.org/10.1007/978-3-642-22110-1_52
26. PPL developers: Ppl: Parma polyhedra library. https://github.com/BUGSENG/PPL. Accessed 24 Nov 2025
27. PyDBM developers: PyDBM. https://launchpad.net/pydbm. Accessed 24 Nov 2025

28. Rodriguez-Navas, G., Proenza, J.: Using timed automata for modeling distributed systems with clocks: challenges and solutions. IEEE Trans. Softw. Eng. **39**(6), 857–868 (2012). https://doi.org/10.1109/TSE.2012.73
29. TAPAAL Developers: TAPAAL: timed-arc petri net analyzer. https://www.tapaal.net/download/. Accessed 15 Nov 2025
30. UDBM developers: UDBM: UPPAAL DBM library. https://github.com/UPPAALModelChecker/UDBM. Accessed 24 Nov 2025
31. UPPAAL Developers: UPPAAL. https://uppaal.org/. Accessed 15 Nov 2025
32. Wang, F.: Efficient verification of timed automata with BDD-like data structures. Int. J. Softw. Tools Technol. Transf. **6**(1), 77–97 (2004)
33. Yovine, S.: Model checking timed automata. In: Rozenberg, G., Vaandrager, F.W. (eds.) EEF School 1996. LNCS, vol. 1494, pp. 114–152. Springer, Heidelberg (1998). https://doi.org/10.1007/3-540-65193-4_20
34. Yu, F., Wang, B.-Y.: Toward unbounded model checking for region automata. In: Wang, F. (ed.) ATVA 2004. LNCS, vol. 3299, pp. 20–33. Springer, Heidelberg (2004). https://doi.org/10.1007/978-3-540-30476-0_7

Deadlock-Free Context-Free Session Types

Andreia Mordido[1] and Jorge A. Pérez[2(✉)]

[1] LASIGE, Faculdade de Ciências, Universidade de Lisboa, Lisbon, Portugal
[2] University of Groningen, Groningen, The Netherlands
j.a.perez@rug.nl

Abstract. We tackle the problem of statically ensuring that message-passing programs never run into *deadlocks*. We focus on concurrent functional programs governed by *context-free session types*, which can express rich tree-like structures not expressible in regular session types. We propose a new type system based on context-free session types: it enforces both protocol conformance and deadlock freedom, also for programs implementing cyclic communication topologies with recursion and polymorphism. We show how the *priority-based* approach to deadlock freedom can be extended to this expressive setting. We prove that well-typed concurrent programs respect their protocols and never deadlock.

1 Introduction

A long-standing issue in concurrent programming is ensuring the absence of *deadlocks*: states in which processes are forever blocked awaiting a message. Motivated by this challenge, this paper develops new compositional verification techniques that ensure deadlock freedom for processes that exchange messages by following some *protocols*. We focus on *session types*, which specify reciprocal protocols on heterogeneously typed channels [13,14]. As key novelty, we consider *context-free* session types (CFSTs) [27], in which sequential composition, non-regular recursion, and polymorphism can jointly specify tree-like structures not expressible in regular session types. By targeting CFSTs, our work broadens the range of concurrent processes that can be verified to be deadlock-free.

The expressiveness of CFSTs leads to challenges in the study of notions such as type equivalence [3] and subtyping [26]. Addressing deadlock freedom is not an exception, for two reasons. *First*, enforcing deadlock freedom entails performing *non-local analyses* on the behavior of processes. The goal is to identify circular dependencies between processes that cannot be detected by analyzing each process in isolation. Existing disciplines based on CFSTs prioritize programming flexibility; as they rely on purely local analyses, they accept deadlocked processes as typable. *Second*, there is no "obviously small" formulation of CFSTs for studying deadlock freedom. For regular session types, useful deadlock analyses can be done in a setting without recursion, whereas in the case of CFSTs one must include recursion *and* polymorphism—indeed, they are "entangled" [27]: limiting recursion would make our system degenerate into regular session types;

Published by Springer Nature Switzerland AG 2026
L. Bocchi and B. Kulahcioglu Ozkan (Eds.): FORTE 2026, LNCS 16589, pp. 179–196, 2026.
https://doi.org/10.1007/978-3-032-28187-6_11

removing polymorphism would prevent us from having recursion. Defined on top of a concurrent functional language, our CFSTs thus combine three distinctive features: sequential composition, non-regular recursion, and polymorphism.

We handle this formulation of CFSTs by extending the original proposal by Thiemann and Vasconcelos [27]. To carry out the non-local analyses required, we follow the *priority-based* approach pioneered by Kobayashi [15,17], later streamlined by Padovani [22]. The key idea is to endow each communication action with a *priority*, an integer that denotes its urgency: immediately enabled actions have a higher priority than those that appear later on in the process. This idea allows to detect processes that are stuck due to insidious circular dependencies between threads, as their associated actions cannot be given a valid priority. The approach supports processes organized in *cyclic network topologies*, which abound in practical distributed scenarios; it also extends to processes with recursion and polymorphism, in which priority management requires care.

Originally developed for variants of the π-calculus with *linear types* [19], here we build upon the type systems by Padovani and Novara [24,25], who adopted the priority-based approach in [22] to higher-order concurrent programs. Following their approach, but casting it in the more expressive setting of CFSTs, we develop a type system and associated meta-theoretical results of *type preservation* (protocol conformance, Theorem 1) and *deadlock freedom* (Theorem 3).

Contributions and Outline. This paper's contributions are two-fold. First, in the context of a call-by-value concurrent language, we endow CFSTs with a priority-based mechanism to guarantee deadlock freedom. Second, we devise novel mechanisms for supporting polymorphic types with priorities, namely constructs for channel creation and polymorphic recursion at the level of priorities.

Section 2 motivates our work via examples written in FreeST [2], a functional programming language with CFSTs. Section 3 introduces the type language and notions of type duality and priorities. Section 4 introduces expressions, configurations, and the typing rules. Section 5 presents the operational semantics and proves type preservation and deadlock freedom. Section 6 discusses related work and concludes the paper. *The online appendix* [21] *contains additional material.*

2 Deadlock Freedom in Programs with CFSTs

A Classic Deadlock Scenario. Consider a communicating program involving two processes that share two channels. They aim to send in one channel the value received in the other, but do so in an order that prevents synchronization. Each process holds two linear *endpoints*: one obeys the type $\mathsf{T} = ?\mathbf{Int}; \mathbf{Wait}$, meaning that it first *receives* an integer and then *waits* to be closed; the other follows the type *dual* to T (denoted $!\mathbf{Int}; \mathbf{Close}$), which *sends* an integer and then *closes* the channel. In FreeST, each process can be implemented as follows:

```
1  f : T → dualof T 1→ ()
2  f x y = let (n,x) = receive x in
```

```
3        let y = send n y in
4        wait x; close y
```

where '1→ ' in the type of f represents a *linear* function, to be used *once*. When a FreeST program launches two parallel processes, each running an instance of function f, the program type-checks, but deadlocks: both processes block indefinitely, each waiting to receive a value that the other never sends.

To avoid deadlocks, one solution is to prescribe the intended order of operations in the program body. We annotate the types with priorities associated to the corresponding operation, following Padovani and Novara [24,25]. Priorities are integers that indicate an action's *urgency* in the protocol. Throughout the paper we use colour teal to highlight priorities in our type system.

Revisiting the classic deadlock scenario, the types that govern the two channels should now be typed differently, priority-wise:

```
1  type R = ?p Int; Wait (p+2)
2  type S = ?q Int; Wait (q+2)
```

Type R extends T with priorities: it receives an **Int** at priority p and then waits at priority p+2 ; type S extends T similarly, under priority q . To showcase the use of priorities, we could consider two variants of function f (the meaning of priority bounds on arrows, shown within [] after the arrow, is formalized in Sect. 3):

```
3  f : R →[top, bot] dualof S 1→[p, q+2] ()
4  f x y =
5    let (n,x) = receive x in    -- priority: p
6    let y = send n y in         -- priority: q
7    ...
8  g : S →[top, bot] dualof R 1→[q, p+2] ()
9  g y x = ...
```

By following the priorities of the arguments' types, we detect a mismatch: function f requires p < q (Lines 5 and 6) whereas function g requires q < p . The type checker flags the mismatch when f and g run in parallel: no priorities p and q satisfy both constraints, so this deadlocked state is rejected statically. The fix is to swap the operations receive/send and wait/close in one of the functions.

Recursion and Polymorphism over Priorities. To express repetitive protocols, session types leverage recursion and are usually equi-recursive. Recursion introduces challenges [24] that are familiar to issues found in the theory of CFSTs [27].

Consider a protocol that sends a stream of unit values, defined by the type Stream as $\mu\beta.!\mathsf{Unit};\beta$. We could write a recursive program for two interacting Streams. However, with equi-recursive types, iterating the protocol forces reusing the same priorities for later actions, which makes repeated sends/receives inconsistent; this motivates us to define *polymorphic recursion* at the level of priorities.

We propose *priority abstractions* to allow the type to evolve while avoiding inconsistent states. We use a quantifier $\forall\iota^{\varphi}$ to abstract over priorities and bind a *priority variable* ι to a *priority interval* φ, as proposed in [24]. The type Stream can be defined by: $\mu\beta.(\forall\iota^{(\bot,\top)}.!^{\iota}\mathsf{Unit};\beta)$. A channel of this type first instantiates the priority variable ι with an integer in interval $(\bot,\top)$ that materializes the order/urgency of the send operation, sends a unit value and finally recurs.

The instantiation of priorities *on channels* cannot be arbitrary. When creating a channel (using **new**), we assign a *priority sequence* predefined for the channel's endpoints. Such a sequence intuitively acts as a 'stack' of priorities, common to both endpoints. With this mechanism for channel creation, we could define a client function as follows (noting that () represents Unit in FreeST):

```
1  type Stream = ∀ i ∈ (bot, top) ⇒ !i() ; Stream
2
3  client: ∀ p ∈ (bot, top)⇒ Stream →[top, bot] dualof Stream
4                                    1→[p, top] ()
5  client c1 c2 =
6    let c1 = send () (inst c1) in          -- c1 : Stream
7    let (_,c2) = receive (inst c2) in      -- c2 : Stream
8    client{next c1} c1 c2
```

Listing 1.1. Example of polymorphism over priorities on session and functional types.

We overload ∀ for priority-quantified sessions (Line 1) and functions (Line 3); the two are instantiated differently (**inst** *vs.* {...}). In Line 6, **inst** c1 uses the next priority for c1, sends () at priority ρ, and pops ρ from c1's stack (returning c1 with type Stream); in Line 8, the recursive call to client explicitly instantiates p with the **next** priority assigned to c1.

The consistency of program operations is verified at compile time, according to the priorities fixed upon channel creation. The function main below creates two channels of type Stream that are used by two threads, one executing client and another executing newclient (similar to client with **send** and **receive** swapped):

```
9  main : ()
10 main =
11   let (w1, r1) = new Stream 1 2 () in
12   let (w2, r2) = new Stream 2 2 () in
13   fork (\_:() 1→ client{next w1} w1 r2);
14   newclient{next w2} w2 r1
```

Listing 1.2. Creation of polymorphic channels with priority sequences.

For priority-polymorphic sessions, **new** allocates dual endpoints and fixes their priority sequence, ensuring that both endpoints are always governed by the same priorities. This sequence is determined by two user-provided numbers, an *initial value* and an *increment*. In Lines 11–12, endpoints for reading and writing are created: r1 and w1 get the priority sequence [1, 3, 5, ...] from 2 (initial value) and 2 2 (increment), while r2 and w2 get [2, 4, 6, ...] from 2 2 ; recursive calls instantiate their priority variables with the channels' **next** priorities.

Non-regular Recursion. The classic example that capitalises on all the features of CFSTs is exchanging binary trees [3,27]. Consider the type TreeChannel, defined as $\mu\beta.(\forall^{S}\iota^{(\bot,\top)}.\&^{\iota}\{\mathsf{LeafC} : \mathsf{Skip}, \mathsf{NodeC} : ?^{\iota+1}\mathsf{Int};\beta;\beta\})$: it first instantiates the priority variable ι and then offers two branches: one with label LeafC, which does nothing; and another with label NodeC, which receives an integer under priority $\iota + 1$ and then receives the left and right subtrees. Consider a function receiveTree in our approach (assuming **data** Tree = Leaf | Node **Int** Tree Tree):

```
1  receiveTree : ∀ p ∈ (bot, top) ⇒ ∀ a :: p ⇒
2                TreeChannel; a →[top,top] (Tree, a)
3  receiveTree c =
4    match (inst c) with {
5      LeafC c →
6        (Leaf, c),
7      NodeC c →
8        let (x, c) = receive c in
9        let (left, c) = receiveTree{next c} @(TreeChannel;a)
             c in
10       let (right, c) = receiveTree{next c} @a c in
11       (Node x left right, c) }
```

This function inputs a channel of type 'TreeChannel; a ', where a is a *type variable* that represents a type with priority p ∈ (bot, top) . This variable is instantiated in a function call through the @ operator (Lines 9–10). Since channel c is polymorphic, receiveTree first instantiates its priority variable (**inst** c in Line 4). The **match** expression handles the choices on channel c. The recursive calls apply polymorphic recursion on priorities *and* types: they instantiate the priority variable p with the **next** priority assigned to the operations in channel c; note that **next** c has different values in Lines 9 and 10. The function returns a pair with a reconstruction of the node and the continuation of the channel.

3 Context-Free Session Types, with Priorities

We define types in two syntactic categories: functional types and session types. We rely on some base sets: $\ell \in L$ stands for labels, α stands for functional type variables, β stands for session type variables, and m stands for multiplicities (relevant for arrow types). We use γ as a meta-variable for type variables (functional or session). As we have seen, ρ, ι, and φ stand for priorities, priority variables, and priority intervals, respectively. We use $\bot$ and $\top$ to stand for the lowest and highest priority, respectively. Also, we write $\overline{\pi}$ to denote a priority sequence, as motivated in Sect. 2. The full grammar of types is in Fig. 1.

Having two syntactic categories avoids the need for a kinding system [1, 27], but entails some duplication: polymorphic types can either have a functional body, in which case the quantifier binds a *functional* type variable, or the body can be a session, in which case the quantifier binds a *session* type variable; the same for recursive types. This means that in addition to $\alpha \neq \beta$, we also have two different (but overloaded) $\forall$ and μ operators. Recursive types keep their body's original "nature", whereas polymorphic types are always functional. (We leave the details of this choice to previous work on context-free session types [3].)

T, U ::=	(Functional types)	S ::=	(Session types)
Unit	unit type	$\mid \mathsf{Skip}$	type skip
$\mid T \rightarrow_m^{\rho_1,\rho_2} U$	function type	$\mid !^\rho T$	send value of type T
$\mid T \times U$	product type	$\mid ?^\rho T$	receive value of type T
$\mid \alpha$	(functional) type variable	$\mid \oplus^\rho \{\ell \colon S_\ell\}_{\ell \in L}$	internal choice
$\mid \mu\alpha.T$	rec. functional type	$\mid \&^\rho \{\ell \colon S_\ell\}_{\ell \in L}$	external choice
$\mid \forall \alpha^\rho.T$	poly. functional type	$\mid S_1; S_2$	sequential composition
$\mid \forall \beta^\rho.S$	poly. session type	$\mid \mathsf{Close}^\rho$	ready to be closed
$\mid \forall^{\mathsf{F}} \iota^\varphi.T$	priority abstraction	$\mid \mathsf{Wait}^\rho$	wait to be closed
$\mid S$	session type	$\mid \beta$	(session) type variable
		$\mid \mu\beta.S$	recursive session type
		$\mid \forall^{\mathsf{S}} \iota^\varphi.S$	priority abstraction

$$m ::= \mathsf{lin} \mid \mathsf{un} \qquad \text{(Multiplicities)}$$
$$\rho ::= \bot \mid n \mid \top \mid \iota \mid \rho + n \qquad \text{(Priorities)}$$
$$\varphi ::= [\rho_1, \rho_2] \mid (\rho_1, \rho_2] \mid [\rho_1, \rho_2) \mid (\rho_1, \rho_2) \qquad \text{(Intervals)}$$
$$\Delta ::= \epsilon \mid \Delta, \alpha :: \rho \mid \Delta, \beta :: \rho \qquad \text{(Polymorphic variables)}$$
$$\Theta ::= \epsilon \mid \Theta, \iota \in \varphi \qquad \text{(Priority variables)}$$

Fig. 1. Types, priorities and priority variables, polymorphic and priority contexts.

As discussed in Sect. 2, the distinguishing feature of our work is the extension of CFSTs with priority annotations to enforce deadlock freedom [20,24,25]. The function type $T \rightarrow_m^{\rho_1,\rho_2} U$ features a *lower priority bound* ρ_1 which indicates that the closure of the function contains channels with priority ρ_1 or greater, and an *upper priority bound* ρ_2, which stands for the maximum priority that is pending in the function and will be triggered once the function is applied (see the explanation by Padovani and Novara [24] for further details). The m denotes the function's multiplicity: $m = \mathsf{lin}$ means that the function can be used once, whereas $m = \mathsf{un}$ means that it can be used zero or more times.

In polymorphic types ($\forall \alpha^\rho.T$, $\forall \beta^\rho.S$), the type variable is given a priority ρ. Priorities are defined via priority variables ι, that are abstracted through a $\forall$ binder that assigns a priority interval φ to ι. Since priority applications are handled differently, we distinguish between binders for functional types $\forall^{\mathsf{F}}$ and for session types $\forall^{\mathsf{S}}$; the superscript is omitted when clear from context. To define channel creation, we write $\mathcal{S}^\forall$ to denote session types that contain a priority abstraction $\forall^{\mathsf{S}}$; session types without priority binders are denoted by $\mathcal{S}$.

Following [20,23,24], our synchronizations (send/receive, internal/external choice, close/wait) operate under a priority ρ. Type Skip and sequential composition do not explicitly represent an operation, so do not have priorities.

Figure 1 defines priorities ρ and priority intervals φ. Priorities can be $\top$ (which are given to *unrestricted types*, cf. [28]), integers n, priority variables

$$\frac{\Delta, \gamma :: \rho \mid \Theta \vdash T \quad \mathsf{fpv}(\rho) \in \mathsf{dom}(\Theta)}{\Delta \mid \Theta \vdash \forall \gamma^{\rho}.T}\ \text{F-TAbs} \qquad \frac{\Delta \mid \Theta, \iota \in \varphi \vdash T \quad \mathsf{fpv}(\varphi) \in \mathsf{dom}(\Theta)}{\Delta \mid \Theta \vdash \forall^{\mathrm{F}} \iota^{\varphi}.T}\ \text{F-PAbsF}$$

$$\frac{\Delta \mid \iota \in \varphi \vdash S \quad \mathsf{fpv}(\varphi) \in \mathsf{dom}(\Theta)}{\Delta \mid \epsilon \vdash \forall^{\mathrm{S}} \iota^{\varphi}.S}\ \text{F-PAbsS}$$

Fig. 2. Type formation.

ι, and a *displacement* $\rho + n$, which represents the addition of integers extended with the rules $\bot + n = \bot$ and $\top + n = \top$. Priority intervals can be closed or open to account for the inclusion of the limits.

We denote the set of *free type variables* in a type T as $\mathsf{ftv}(T)$ and the set of *free priority variables* in a priority ρ (resp., interval φ) as $\mathsf{fpv}(\rho)$ (resp., $\mathsf{fpv}(\varphi)$). We adopt the usual notions of substitution for both type and priority substitutions: we denote by $T[^{U}/_{\gamma}]$ the substitution of a type U for a type variable γ in T and by $T[^{\rho}/_{\iota}]$ the substitution of a priority ρ for a priority variable ι in T.

Not all types are well formed. For example, we do not wish to define the type '$\forall\alpha^{\iota}.?^{\rho}\alpha$' if ι and ρ are free variables. To define type formation we use typing contexts for polymorphic and priority variables, denoted Δ and Θ, respectively, are presented in Fig. 1. We record polymorphic variables with the corresponding priority assignment in Δ and priority variables with their respective range in Θ.

The judgement $\Delta \mid \Theta \vdash T$ denotes that type T is well-formed under the polymorphic context Δ and the priority context Θ. The standard CFST type-formation rules are as in [27]; the complete set of rules appears in [21]. Figure 2 shows only the new or modified type formation rules introduced in this work.

Rule F-TAbs states that a polymorphic type $\forall\gamma^{\rho}.T$ can only assign a type variable γ to a priority ρ if all the free priority variables in ρ are defined in Θ; furthermore, T should be well-formed under the extended environment $\Delta, \gamma :: \rho$. Similarly, rule F-PAbsF states that a priority variable ι can only be assigned to φ through the $\forall^{\mathrm{F}}$ binder if all the free variables occurring in φ are defined in Θ; furthermore, the body of the type should be well-formed under the priority environment $\Theta, \iota \in \varphi$. Rule F-PAbsS imposes the same conditions but requires the priority environment to be empty, thus enforcing that the $\forall^{\mathrm{S}}$ binder occurs at most once in a well-formed type; this restriction is meant to simplify the representation of priority sequences (cf. the definition of priority maps in Fig. 3).

Priorities govern the order of operations. This is apparent in polymorphic types, which can be instantiated with different priority values. For this reason, priorities are closely related to typing environments and a natural *priority ordering* will be imposed in the typing rules (cf. Sect. 4), rather than in type formation rules. The typing rules will allow to ensure that there are no viable programs for types such as $!^{2}(!^{1}\mathsf{Int})$, where the operation that follows in the payload is *more urgent*, i.e., has lower priority, than sending the message itself.

Duality is paramount to establish compatible communication between two endpoints of a channel. This notion is defined only over session types; the def-

$$
\begin{array}{rll}
n & ::= & 1 \mid 2 \mid \ldots \qquad \text{(Natural numbers)}\\
\sigma & ::= & \rho \mid \mathsf{next}^k x \qquad \text{(Priority values)}\\
c & ::= & \mathsf{fork} \mid \mathsf{send} \mid \mathsf{receive} \mid \mathsf{close} \mid \mathsf{wait} \mid () \mid \mathsf{select}\, k \mid \mathsf{fix} \qquad \text{(Constants)}\\
v & ::= & x \mid c \mid \lambda_m x : T.e \mid (v,v) \mid \Lambda\alpha.v \mid \mathbb{A}\iota.v \mid \mathsf{close}\{\sigma\} \mid \mathsf{wait}\{\sigma\} \mid \mathsf{fork}\{\sigma_1\}\\
& & \mid \mathsf{fork}\{\sigma_1\}\{\sigma_2\} \mid \mathsf{send}\{\sigma_1\} \mid \mathsf{send}\{\sigma_1\}[T] \mid \mathsf{send}\{\sigma_1\}[T]\{\sigma_2\}\\
& & \mid \mathsf{send}\{\sigma_1\}[T]\{\sigma_2\}\{\sigma_3\} \mid \mathsf{send}\{\sigma_1\}[T]\{\sigma_2\}\{\sigma_3\}[S] \mid \mathsf{send}\{\sigma_1\}[T]\{\sigma_2\}\{\sigma_3\}[S]v\\
& & \mid \mathsf{receive}\{\sigma_1\} \mid \mathsf{receive}\{\sigma_1\}[T] \mid \mathsf{receive}\{\sigma_1\}[T]\{\sigma_2\} \mid \mathsf{receive}\{\sigma_1\}[T]\{\sigma_2\}\{\sigma_3\}\\
& & \mid \mathsf{receive}\{\sigma_1\}[T]\{\sigma_2\}\{\sigma_3\}[S] \mid \boxed{x\{\sigma\}} \qquad \text{(Values)}\\
e & ::= & v \mid ee \mid (e,e) \mid \mathsf{let}\, x = e\, \mathsf{in}\, e \mid \mathsf{let}\,(x_1,x_2) = e\, \mathsf{in}\, e \mid e;e \mid e[T] \mid e\{\sigma\}\\
& & \mid \mathsf{match}\, e\, \mathsf{with}\, \{\ell \to e_\ell\}_{\ell\in L} \mid \mathsf{new}\, \mathcal{S} \mid \mathsf{new}\, \mathcal{S}^{\forall}\, n_1\, n_2 \mid \mathsf{inst}^{\Psi}\, x \qquad \text{(Expressions)}\\
\mathcal{C} & ::= & \phi\langle e\rangle \mid \mathcal{C} \parallel \mathcal{C} \mid (\nu xy^{\bar{\pi}})\,\mathcal{C} \qquad \text{(Configurations)}\\
\phi & ::= & \circ \mid \bullet \qquad \text{(Thread flags)}\\
\Gamma & ::= & \epsilon \mid \Gamma, x : T \qquad \text{(Typing contexts)}\\
\Psi & ::= & \epsilon \mid \Psi, x : T \mapsto \bar{\pi} \qquad \text{(Priority maps)}
\end{array}
$$

Fig. 3. The syntax of values, expressions, configurations, priorities and typing contexts.

inition is standard [3,27] and is presented in [21]. Crucially, duality preserves priorities (e.g., $\overline{!^\rho T} = ?^\rho T$). The dual of a priority abstraction ($\overline{\forall \beta^\varphi.S}$) is the priority abstraction of the dual session type, $\forall \beta^\varphi.\overline{S}$.

4 Statics: Configurations and Typing Rules

Here we present our concurrent functional language with sessions, which extends earlier works [3,27] with applications and abstractions over priority variables. Our language adopts a *call-by-value* strategy; as usual in functional sessions (cf. [10]), session communication arises at the level of *configurations*, which is where deadlocks could occur. A configuration is either an expression, a parallel composition of configurations, or a configuration in the scope of a channel restriction $(\nu xy^{\bar{\pi}})$ that binds together the (dual) endpoints x and y. It is convenient to consider configurations with a *flag* ϕ, useful to indicate whether the configuration is the main thread ($\phi = \bullet$) or is a child thread ($\phi = \circ$). The syntax of constants, (runtime) values, expressions and configurations is given in Fig. 3.

Further novelties concern priorities and their associated constructs. Priority values σ can be a priority ρ (cf. Fig. 1) or an element from the priority sequence associated with a channel x, denoted $\mathsf{next}^k x$ (for the k-th element in the sequence). Priority abstractions are of the form $\mathbb{A}\iota.e$, where $\mathbb{A}$ binds a priority variable ι that might occur free in e. Like type abstractions, priority abstractions of the form $\mathbb{A}\iota.v$ are values. Priority applications over an expression e are denoted by $e\{\sigma\}$ and $\mathsf{inst}^{\Psi}\, e$ (we often omit Ψ as it is easily inferred from the context). In Fig. 3, the box enclosing priority applications over channel names $x\{\sigma\}$ means that they are *runtime values*, not present in source programs.

There are several forms of partial applications for constants, which are considered values; they will be justified by the types presented in Fig. 5. We denote by $\mathsf{fv}(e)$ the set of free (term) variables occurring in e. We have two different ways of declaring sessions ('new –'), depending on whether the session type involved contains a priority abstraction or not; if that is the case, session declaration requires the initial value and increment for the associated priority sequence. We use $e_1; e_2$ as an abbreviation for $\mathsf{let}\, x = e_1 \,\mathsf{in}\, e_2$ when e_1 has type Unit.

Typing Contexts and Priority Split. Figure 3 also defines the syntax of *typing contexts* (for term variables) and of *priority maps*. The priority map Ψ relates type assignments $x : T$ with priority sequences $\bar{\pi}$. This map is essential to determine the **next** priority assigned to a channel. We write $\Psi(x)$ instead of $\Psi(x : T)$ when the type T is unimportant or clear from the context. A type T may appear more than once in Ψ, associated with different variables. We write $\Psi(T)$ to denote the (possibly empty) set of variables associated with T in Ψ. Given Ψ, we write $\lceil\Psi(x)\rangle\!\rangle$ to denote the first element in the priority sequence for x and $\rangle\!\rangle\Psi(x)\rfloor$ to denote the rest of the sequence. That is, $\Psi(x) = \lceil\Psi(x)\rangle\!\rangle \cdot \rangle\!\rangle\Psi(x)\rfloor$.

Given a priority map $\Psi = \{(x_i : T_i) \mapsto \bar{\pi}_i\}_{i\in I}$, the *priority split* $\Psi = \Psi_1 \circ \Psi_2$ is defined if $\Psi_1 = \{(x_i : T_i) \mapsto \bar{\pi}_i^1\}_{i\in I}$ and $\Psi_2 = \{(x_i : T_i) \mapsto \bar{\pi}_i^2\}_{i\in I}$ and $\bar{\pi}_i = \bar{\pi}_i^1 \cdot \bar{\pi}_i^2$ for each $i \in I$. Hence, $\bar{\pi}_i$ is the sequence that results from appending $\bar{\pi}_i^2$ to $\bar{\pi}_i^1$. We denote by $\Psi|_\Gamma$ the restriction of priority map Ψ to the typing context Γ.

We work modulo α-conversion of bound names (λ-binders and restricted channel endpoints), applying the same renaming to Ψ whenever applicable.

Priority of a Type. To statically check the order of operations, we must determine a type's priority. Remarkably, priorities of polymorphic types heavily depend on the particular *instances* under consideration: for example, the session type Stream in Listing 1.1 is instantiated with two different priority sequences in Listing 1.2. Whereas $\mathsf{r1}$ in Listing 1.2 has *upcoming priority* 1, $\mathsf{r2}$'s next priority is 2, according to the priorities predefined in Lines 11 and 12. For this reason, we must compute the priorities of types according to the typing contexts.

The priority of a type T, defined in Fig. 4, depends on its leading operation. To expose it, we use the *unravel function* [6], which unfolds a type appropriately, adapting the behavior of type abstractions to priority abstractions. The unravel of T, denoted $\mathsf{unr}(T)$, is such that $\mathsf{unr}(\mathsf{Skip}; !^{\rho} S) = !^{\rho} S$, $\mathsf{unr}(\forall^{\mathsf{P}} \iota^{\varphi}.U) = \forall^{\mathsf{P}} \iota^{\varphi}.U$ and $\mathsf{unr}((\forall^{\mathsf{S}} \iota^{\varphi}.S_1); S_2) = \forall^{\mathsf{S}} \iota^{\varphi}.(S_1; S_2)$, assuming that ι does not occur in S_2. Since recursive types are required to be contractive (cf. [21]), the function unr terminates and never returns a recursive type.

Remarkably, the priority of a type is a set of integers. Typically, the set $|T|$ is a singleton, unless T is polymorphic. When T is a polymorphic session type, $|T|$ contains the elements of the priority sequence associated with T. On the other hand, when T represents a priority abstraction, $|T|$ consists of a set of integers that can be instantiated to provide a concrete priority. Formally, $|T|$ relies on contexts Ψ, Δ, Θ, and Γ. However, to lighten up notation, we shall write $|T|_{cond}$ to denote the priority of T, where *cond* specifies the least condition required from Ψ, Δ, Θ, and Γ (which are inferred from the typing rule where the definition is used). We write $|T|$ when no specific condition is used to compute the priority of T. Also, we write $|\Gamma|$ for the expected extension to typing contexts Γ, enabled by $\cdot \sqcap \cdot$. With a little abuse of notation, we write for instance '$\rho < |T|$' and '$|T| < \top$' to mean that for every $\rho_i \in |T|$, $\rho < \rho_i$ and $\rho_i < \top$, respectively. Similarly, we may write '$|T_1| \sqcap |T_2|$' instead of '$\min |T_1| \sqcap \min |T_2|$'. Finally, we write ρ instead of the singleton $\{\rho\}$ when clear from the context.

When the leading operation is a message exchange or a choice, the type inherits the priority of that operation; if it is a function, the priority of the type is the lower priority bound in the arrow. In either case, the priority is a singleton. The priority of a product type $T_1 \times T_2$ is the minimum between the least elements of the sets $|T_1|$ and $|T_2|$.

The priority of a polymorphic type of the form $\forall^{S} \iota^{\varphi}.U$ is a set containing the values in an associated priority sequence; the definition depends on the particular instances in the context. Because different instances of the same session type can result in different priority sequences, it is clear that the leading operation can occur with different priorities in distinct instances. When an instance of the type governs channel x, the priority of the type results from replacing the priority variable with the priority sequence for x. For functional types, we keep track of priority restrictions, updating the environment Θ. For type abstractions, we update the environment for polymorphic variables Δ with the respective restriction. To compute the priority of a type variable γ, we check whether its associated ρ (obtained via Δ) contains free priority variables: if $\mathsf{fpv}(\rho) = \emptyset$ then the priority of γ is $\{\rho\}$; otherwise, we obtain the values of the variables in $\mathsf{fpv}(\rho)$ using Θ. In the figure, $\Theta(\rho)$ represents $\Theta(\iota)$ if $\rho = \iota$ and the displacement of $\Theta(\rho_0)$ by n when $\rho = \rho_0 + n$. In the remaining cases, the priority of a type is $\top$.

$$
|T| = \begin{cases}
n & \text{if } \mathsf{unr}(T) = !^n U, ?^n U, \&^n\{\ell\colon S_\ell\}_{\ell \in L}, \oplus^n\{\ell\colon S_\ell\}_{\ell \in L}, \\
 & \quad \mathsf{Close}^n, \mathsf{Wait}^n, T_1 \rightarrow^{n;\sigma}_{m} T_2, !^n U; S \text{ or } ?^n U; S \\
|T_1| \sqcap |T_2| & \text{if } \mathsf{unr}(T) = T_1 \times T_2 \\
\bigcup_{x \in \Psi(T)} \bigcup_{\rho \in \Psi(x:T)} \{|U[\rho/\iota]|\} & \text{if } \mathsf{unr}(T) = \forall^{S} \iota^{\varphi}.U \\
|U|_{\iota \in \varphi} & \text{if } \mathsf{unr}(T) = \forall^{F} \iota^{\varphi}.U \\
|T|_{\gamma :: \rho} & \text{if } \mathsf{unr}(T) = \forall \gamma^{\rho}.T \\
\rho & \text{if } \mathsf{unr}(T) = \gamma \text{ and } (\gamma :: \rho) \in \Delta \text{ and } \mathsf{fpv}(\rho) = \emptyset \\
\Theta(\rho) & \text{if } \mathsf{unr}(T) = \gamma \text{ and } (\gamma :: \rho) \in \Delta \\
\top & \text{otherwise}
\end{cases}
$$

Fig. 4. Priority of types.

Context Formation and Split. Context formation and context split are standard; see [21] for their definition. Context split handles the distribution of bindings depending on their priority, recalling that types with priority $\top$ are unrestricted. The typing environments needed to determine the priority of T are prescribed by the typing rules, where context split is invoked (see cf. Fig. 6).

$$\text{send} : \forall \iota_1^{(\bot,\top)}.\forall \alpha^{\iota_1}.\forall \iota_2^{(\bot,\iota_1)}.\forall \iota_3^{(\iota_2,\top)}.\forall \beta^{\iota_3}.\alpha \rightarrow_{\text{un}}^{\top,\bot} !^{\iota_2}\alpha;\beta \rightarrow_{\text{lin}}^{\top,\iota_2} \beta$$

$$\text{receive} : \forall \iota_1^{(\bot,\top)}.\forall \alpha^{\iota_1}.\forall \iota_2^{(\bot,\iota_1)}.\forall \iota_3^{(\iota_2,\top)}.\forall \beta^{\iota_3}.?^{\iota_2}\alpha;\beta \rightarrow_{\text{un}}^{\top,\iota_2} \alpha \times \beta$$

$$\text{fork} : \forall \iota_1^{(\bot,\top)}.\forall \iota_2^{[\bot,\top]}.(\text{Unit} \rightarrow_{\text{un}}^{\iota_1,\iota_2} \text{Unit}) \rightarrow_{\text{un}}^{\top,\bot} \text{Unit}$$

$$\text{fix} : \forall \iota^{[\bot,\top]}.\forall \alpha^{\iota}.((\alpha \rightarrow_{\text{un}}^{\top,\bot} \alpha) \rightarrow_{\text{un}}^{\top,\bot} (\alpha \rightarrow_{\text{un}}^{\top,\bot} \alpha)) \rightarrow_{\text{un}}^{\top,\bot} (\alpha \rightarrow_{\text{un}}^{\top,\bot} \alpha)$$

$$\text{close} : \forall \iota^{(\bot,\top)}.\text{Close}^{\iota} \rightarrow_{\text{un}}^{\top,\iota} \text{Unit} \qquad \text{wait} : \forall \iota^{(\bot,\top)}.\text{Wait}^{\iota} \rightarrow_{\text{un}}^{\top,\iota} \text{Unit} \qquad () : \text{Unit}$$

Fig. 5. Types for constants.

Types for constants are defined in Fig. 5. By upgrading priorities to the level of types, we can give proper (functional) types to all constants, instead of relying on type schemes [20,24]. Following Padovani and Novara [24], our priority binders control the order of operations in a type. A representative case is send. This type first binds the priority ι_1 of the payload, then requires the priority of the send operation to be lower (i.e., more urgent) than that of the payload and, finally, the lowest priority of the continuation channel should be higher than that of the send operation. Once every type and priority variables are instantiated, function send expects an input value to be sent, followed by a channel of type $!^{\iota_2}\alpha;\beta$, and returns the continuation channel β. It has latent effect ι_2, meaning that as soon as function send is fully applied, it triggers operations with priority at most ι_2.

The types for constants should clarify the different forms of values in Fig. 3. Consider the type of send: we can apply it to a priority and get a partial application $\text{send}\{\sigma_1\}$, or further make a type application and get $\text{send}\{\sigma_1\}[T]$. Then, we can do one or two priority applications again, reaching $\text{send}\{\sigma_1\}[T]\{\sigma_2\}$ and $\text{send}\{\sigma_1\}[T]\{\sigma_2\}\{\sigma_3\}$. At this point, we are left with another type application yielding $\text{send}\{\sigma_1\}[T]\{\sigma_2\}\{\sigma_3\}[S]$, which has type $T \rightarrow_{\text{un}}^{\top,\bot} !^{\sigma_2}T;S \rightarrow_{\text{lin}}^{\top,\sigma_2} S$. Before we get send fully applied, we can do a term-level application of the previous expression to a value v and get the expression $\text{send}\{\sigma_1\}[T]\{\sigma_2\}\{\sigma_3\}[S]v$, which is still a value. For the other constants, the reasoning is similar.

Typing Rules. The typing judgement $\Delta \mid \Gamma \mid \Theta \mid \Psi \vdash e : T \diamond \bar{\pi} \diamond \rho$ means that an expression e has type T and latent effect ρ under the typing environments Δ, Γ, Θ, and Ψ. The evaluation of expression e might yield a sequence of priorities $\bar{\pi}$ which predetermines the possible instantiations of polymorphic channels—this annotation is useful for creating new channels. The predefined priorities are mapped to the corresponding channel names and stored in Ψ.

Figure 6 presents selected typing rules for expressions and Fig. 7 presents the typing rules for configurations, which result from incorporating the priority-based approach to deadlock freedom [20,24,25] in the type system of context-free session types [3,27]. Now we discuss the typing rules of Fig. 6; the complete set of typing rules (together with additional discussion) is given in [21].

Constants are typed through T-Const according to the types in Fig. 5; they have no priority effect ($\bot$), do not yield any priority sequence ($\bar{\pi} = \epsilon$), and assume

T-Const
$$\frac{\Delta \mid \Theta \vdash \Gamma \qquad |\Gamma| = \top}{\Delta \mid \Gamma \mid \Theta \mid \Psi \vdash c : \mathsf{typeof}(c) \diamond \epsilon \diamond \bot}$$

T-Var
$$\frac{\Delta \mid \Theta \vdash \Gamma \qquad |\Gamma| = \top}{\Delta \mid \Gamma, \gamma : T \mid \Theta \mid \Psi \vdash \gamma : T \diamond \epsilon \diamond \bot}$$

T-TAbs
$$\frac{\Delta, \gamma :: \rho \mid \Gamma \mid \Theta \mid \Psi \vdash e : T \diamond \epsilon \diamond \sigma \qquad |\Gamma| = \top \quad \mathsf{fpv}(\rho) \in \mathsf{dom}(\Theta)}{\Delta \mid \Gamma \mid \Theta \mid \Psi \vdash \Lambda\gamma.e : \forall \gamma^{\rho}.T \diamond \epsilon \diamond \bot}$$

T-PAbs
$$\frac{\Delta \mid \Gamma \mid \Theta, \iota \in \varphi \mid \Psi \vdash e : T \diamond \epsilon \diamond \sigma \qquad |\Gamma| = \top \quad \mathsf{fpv}(\varphi) \in \mathsf{dom}(\Theta)}{\Delta \mid \Gamma \mid \Theta \mid \Psi \vdash \mathbb{\Lambda}\iota.e : \mathbb{\forall}\iota^{\varphi}.T \diamond \epsilon \diamond \bot}$$

T-TApp
$$\frac{\Delta \mid \Gamma \mid \Theta \mid \Psi \vdash e : \forall \alpha^{\rho}.U \diamond \epsilon \diamond \rho_1 \qquad \Delta \mid \Theta \vdash T \quad \rho \in |T|}{\Delta \mid \Gamma \mid \Theta \mid \Psi \vdash e[T] : U[{}^{T}/_{\alpha}] \diamond \epsilon \diamond \rho_1}$$

T-PApp
$$\frac{\Delta \mid \Gamma \mid \Theta \mid \Psi \vdash e : \mathbb{\forall}\iota^{\varphi}.U \diamond \epsilon \diamond \rho_1 \quad \rho \in \varphi}{\Delta \mid \Gamma \mid \Theta \mid \Psi \vdash e\{\rho\} : U[{}^{\rho}/_{\iota}] \diamond \epsilon \diamond \rho_1}$$

T-Inst
$$\frac{\Delta \mid \Gamma \mid \Theta \mid \Psi \vdash x : \mathbb{\forall}^{\mathsf{S}}\iota^{\varphi}.S \diamond \epsilon \diamond \rho_1 \quad \rho = \lceil \Psi(x) \rangle\!\rangle \quad \rho \in \varphi}{\Delta \mid \Gamma \mid \Theta \mid \Psi \vdash \mathsf{inst}^{\Psi}\, x : S[{}^{\rho}/_{\iota}] \diamond \epsilon \diamond \rho_1}$$

T-App
$$\frac{\Delta \mid \Gamma_1 \mid \Theta \mid \Psi \vdash e_1 : T_1 \to_m^{\rho,\sigma} T_2 \diamond \epsilon \diamond \rho_1 \quad \Delta \mid \Gamma_2 \mid \Theta \mid \Psi \vdash e_2 : T_1 \diamond \epsilon \diamond \rho_2 \qquad \rho_1 < |\Gamma_2| \quad \rho_2 < \rho}{\Delta \mid \Gamma_1 \circ \Gamma_2 \mid \Theta \mid \Psi \vdash e_1 e_2 : T_2 \diamond \epsilon \diamond \rho_1 \sqcup \rho_2 \sqcup \sigma}$$

T-Let
$$\frac{\Delta \mid \Gamma_1 \mid \Theta \mid \Psi \vdash e_1 : T \diamond \epsilon \diamond \rho_1 \quad \exists \Psi_1 . \Psi = \Psi_1 \circ \Psi_2 \text{ and } \Psi|_{\Gamma_2} = \Psi_2|_{\Gamma_2} \qquad \Delta \mid \Gamma_2, x : T \mid \Theta \mid \Psi_2 \vdash e_2 : S \diamond \epsilon \diamond \rho_2 \quad \rho_1 < |\Gamma_2|}{\Delta \mid \Gamma_1 \circ \Gamma_2 \mid \Theta \mid \Psi \vdash \mathsf{let}\, x = e_1 \,\mathsf{in}\, e_2 : S \diamond \epsilon \diamond \rho_1 \sqcup \rho_2}$$

T-LetPair
$$\frac{\begin{array}{c}\Delta \mid \Gamma_1 \mid \Theta \mid \Psi \vdash e_1 : T_1 \times T_2 \diamond \bar{\pi} \diamond \rho_1 \quad \exists \Psi_1 . \Psi = \Psi_1 \circ \Psi_2 \text{ and } \Psi|_{\Gamma_2} = \Psi_2|_{\Gamma_2} \\ \text{if } \bar{\pi} \neq \epsilon \text{ then } \Psi_2' = \Psi_2, x_1 : T_1 \mapsto \bar{\pi}, x_2 : T_2 \mapsto \bar{\pi} \text{ else } \Psi_2' = \Psi_2 \\ \Delta \mid \Gamma_2, x_1 : T_1, x_2 : T_2 \mid \Theta \mid \Psi_2' \vdash e_2 : S \diamond \epsilon \diamond \rho_2 \quad \rho_1 < |\Gamma_2|\end{array}}{\Delta \mid \Gamma_1 \circ \Gamma_2 \mid \Theta \mid \Psi \vdash \mathsf{let}\,(x_1, x_2) = e_1 \,\mathsf{in}\, e_2 : S \diamond \epsilon \diamond \rho_1 \sqcup \rho_2}$$

T-Sel
$$\frac{\Delta \mid \Theta \vdash \Gamma \quad \Delta \mid \Theta \vdash S_\ell \quad \rho < |S_\ell| \;\; (\forall \ell \in L) \quad k \in L \quad |\Gamma| = \top}{\Delta \mid \Gamma \mid \Theta \mid \Psi \vdash \mathsf{select}\, k : \oplus^{\rho}\{\ell \colon S_\ell\}_{\ell \in L} \to_m^{\top, \sqcup_{\ell \in L}|S_\ell|} S_k \diamond \epsilon \diamond \bot}$$

T-Match
$$\frac{\Delta \mid \Gamma_1 \mid \Theta \mid \Psi_1 \vdash e : \&^{\rho}\{\ell \colon S_\ell\}_{\ell \in L} \diamond \epsilon \diamond \rho_1 \quad \rho_1 < |\Gamma_2| \qquad \Delta \mid \Gamma_2 \mid \Theta \mid \Psi_2 \vdash e_\ell : S_\ell \to_{\mathsf{lin}}^{|\Gamma_2|, \rho_2} T \diamond \epsilon \diamond \bot}{\Delta \mid \Gamma_1 \circ \Gamma_2 \mid \Theta \mid \Psi_1 \circ \Psi_2 \vdash \mathsf{match}\, e \,\mathsf{with}\, \{\ell \to e_\ell\}_{\ell \in L} : T \diamond \epsilon \diamond \rho_1 \sqcup \rho_2 \sqcup \rho}$$

T-NewPoly
$$\frac{\Delta \mid \Theta \vdash \Gamma \qquad \Delta \mid \Theta \vdash \mathcal{S}^{\mathbb{\forall}} \qquad |\Gamma| = \top \qquad \bar{\pi} = [n_1 + k \cdot n_2 \mid k \in \mathbb{N}]}{\Delta \mid \Gamma \mid \Theta \mid \Psi \vdash \mathsf{new}\, \mathcal{S}^{\mathbb{\forall}}\, n_1\, n_2 : \mathcal{S}^{\mathbb{\forall}} \times \overline{\mathcal{S}^{\mathbb{\forall}}} \diamond \bar{\pi} \diamond \bot}$$

T-New
$$\frac{\Delta \mid \Theta \vdash \Gamma \qquad \Delta \mid \Theta \vdash \mathcal{S} \qquad |\Gamma| = \top \qquad \mathsf{unr}(\mathcal{S}) \neq \mathsf{Skip}}{\Delta \mid \Gamma \mid \Theta \mid \Psi \vdash \mathsf{new}\, \mathcal{S} : \mathcal{S} \times \overline{\mathcal{S}} \diamond \epsilon \diamond \bot}$$

Fig. 6. Typing rules for expressions, part 1.

that the context Γ has priority $\top$, i.e., it is *unrestricted.* Rule T-Var checks that variables are typed under an unrestricted environment, with no effects.

We have abstractions on types, priorities, and terms. Rule T-TAbs states that a type abstraction $\Lambda\gamma.e$ has type $\forall\gamma^{\rho}.T$ with no effect if e has type T under the extended polymorphic environment $\Delta, \gamma :: \rho$, assuming that the free priority variables occurring in ρ are defined in Θ and that Γ is unrestricted, because we do not want to abstract over linear values. Rule T-PAbs is similar with the expected adaptation to priority abstractions. Rules T-AbsLin and T-AbsUn consider linear and unrestricted functions, which are presented in [21].

Rule T-TApp types the application $e[T]$ requiring that the type variable α is associated to a priority $\rho \in |T|$, interpreted under environment Θ. Rule T-PApp, distinctive of our work, is applicable to functional and session types (recalling that the instantiation of priorities in sessions is only a runtime value), and states that a priority ρ can instantiate ι if ρ belongs to the priority interval assigned to ι; all the occurrences of ι in U are updated with the new value ρ. Rule T-Inst governs channel instantiation: it takes the first priority ρ in the sequence for x ($\rho = \lceil\Psi(x)\rangle\rangle$) and instantiates the continuation type (similarly to rule T-PApp).

Rule T-App is standard for *call-by-value* evaluation [24]: it requires e_1 to have a *more urgent* priority than the typing context for e_2 and the effect of e_2 to be *more urgent* than the priority of the type of e_1 (which has reduced to a value by then). The typing environment is split to properly distribute channels, but the priority map is passed to both premises to ensure that the priority sequence is available for instantiation. Unlike Γ, the priority map Ψ is not a linear resource: it is only consulted by inst^{Ψ} (and updated by 'popping' in sequencing rules).

Rule T-Let uses the full map Ψ in the first premise to enable priority instantiation (e.g., reasoning about next^k), whereas the second premise is checked under an updated map Ψ_2 that reflects the priority information remaining after evaluating e_1 (as captured by Ψ_1 in $\Psi = \Psi_1 \circ \Psi_2$). This rule also checks that the channels used for evaluating e_1 have lower priority than those occurring in e_2. This constraint enforces an increasing order of priorities between successive operations, thus complementing the type formation rules, as observed in Sect. 3.

Rule T-LetPair checks that the effect of e_1 is lower than the lowest priority of the typing environment for e_2. This rule is also responsible for updating the map of priorities when the priority sequence emerging from the evaluation of e_1 is not empty (that is, when the rule preceding T-LetPair is T-NewPoly, see below). More specifically, when the priority sequence $\bar{\pi}$ is not empty, e_2 is typed under the context with a priority extended with a mapping of the new channel endpoints (x_1 and x_2) to the corresponding priority sequence.

Rule T-Sel assigns no effect ($\bot$) to the evaluation of $\mathsf{select}\, k$, requires the priority of the choice operation to be lower than that of the continuation types and also that the typing environment has no channel left, i.e., has priority $\top$. Rule T-Match treats e_ℓ as if it were a function (see T-AbsLin in [21]) and, according to the call-by-value evaluation strategy, requires the evaluation of e to be more urgent than that of e_ℓ; the distribution of channel names by the priority maps follows the usual rules for splitting linear contexts.

$$\frac{\epsilon \mid \Gamma \mid \epsilon \mid \Psi \vdash e : \mathsf{Unit} \diamond \bar{\pi} \diamond \rho}{\Gamma \vdash^{\circ}_{\Psi} \circ\langle e \rangle}\ \textsc{C-Child} \qquad \frac{\epsilon \mid \Gamma \mid \epsilon \mid \Psi \vdash e : T \diamond \bar{\pi} \diamond \rho \quad |T| = \top}{\Gamma \vdash^{\bullet}_{\Psi} \bullet\langle e \rangle}\ \textsc{C-Main}$$

$$\frac{\Gamma_1 \vdash^{\phi_1}_{\Psi_1} \mathcal{C}_1 \quad \Gamma_2 \vdash^{\phi_2}_{\Psi_2} \mathcal{C}_2}{\Gamma_1 \circ \Gamma_2 \vdash^{\phi_1+\phi_2}_{\Psi_1 \circ \Psi_2} \mathcal{C}_1 \parallel \mathcal{C}_2}\ \textsc{C-Par} \qquad \frac{\Gamma, x : S, y : \overline{S} \vdash^{\phi}_{\Psi_2} \mathcal{C} \quad \epsilon \mid \epsilon \vdash S \quad \Psi_2 = \Psi_1, x : S \mapsto \bar{\pi}, y : \overline{S} \mapsto \bar{\pi}}{\Gamma \vdash^{\phi}_{\Psi_1} (\nu x y^{\bar{\pi}})\, \mathcal{C}}\ \textsc{C-New}$$

Fig. 7. Typing rules for configurations.

Typing rules for channel creation distinguish session types with a priority binder (denoted by $\mathcal{S}^{\forall}$) from session types without (denoted by $\mathcal{S}$). Channels of the first kind must be assigned a priority sequence. In rule T-NewPoly, the primitive new receives a session type with a priority abstraction $\mathcal{S}^{\forall}$ that indicates the type of the channel being created and two natural numbers (n_1 and n_2) representing the start and increment of its priority sequence. The rule defines a sequence starting at n_1 and with increment n_2, which is passed as a side effect through the first annotation $\bar{\pi}$ (that should be eventually mapped to the corresponding endpoints and stored in Ψ, cf. rule T-LetPair). Rule T-New requires the typing environment to be unrestricted and type $\mathcal{S}$ to be well-formed and such that $\mathsf{unr}(\mathcal{S}) \neq \mathsf{Skip}$, to ensure that there are some pending operations.

The judgement for configurations $\Gamma \vdash^{\phi}_{\Psi} \mathcal{C}$ means that $\mathcal{C}$ is well-typed under Γ with priority map Ψ. The typing rules are in Fig. 7. Rules C-Child and C-Main distinguish between child and main threads: while any expression (closed for priority and polymorphic variables) with unrestricted type can run in the main thread, only expressions with type Unit can run in a child thread; the expression is evaluated under Γ and Ψ. Rules C-Par splits the context and the priority map, and considers a flag obtained as follows: $\circ + \circ = \circ$, $\circ + \bullet = \bullet$, and $\bullet + \circ = \bullet$ (no rule for $\bullet + \bullet$). Rule C-New types $(\nu x y^{\bar{\pi}})\, \mathcal{C}$: it introduces two dual endpoints of a channel in Γ and extends the map Ψ for x and y with the sequence $\bar{\pi}$.

5 Dynamics: Type Preservation and Deadlock Freedom

We define reduction for expressions and configurations considering a call-by-value evaluation strategy. Reduction rules for expressions are standard for a call-by-value setting; see [21]. Novelties are presented in Fig. 8. A new reduction rule for channel instantiations (E-PInst) and a β-reduction rule for priority-level abstractions (E-PApp). Evaluation contexts also reflect the left-to-right evaluation strategy and are defined by the grammar in the top-left of Fig. 8.

Reduction includes rules to lift reductions from expressions to configurations (Rule R-LiftE) and from configurations to configuration contexts (Rule R-LiftC). Rule R-Fork creates a new *child* thread, while rules R-New and R-NewPoly create a new channel and bind its endpoints and the priority sequence in a restric-

Evaluation contexts

$E ::= [] \mid Ee \mid vE \mid E[T] \mid E\{\rho\} \mid \mathsf{let}\, x = E \,\mathsf{in}\, e$
$\mid \mathsf{let}\,(x_1, x_2) = E \,\mathsf{in}\, e \mid E; e \mid (E, e) \mid (v, E) \mid \mathsf{inst}^{\Psi}\, E$
$\mid \mathsf{match}\, E \,\mathsf{with}\, \{\ell \to e_\ell\}_{\ell \in L}$ (Evaluation contexts)
$\mathcal{F} ::= \phi\langle E \rangle$ (Thread evaluation contexts)
$\mathcal{G} ::= [] \mid \mathcal{G} \,\|\, \mathcal{C} \mid (\nu x y^{\bar{\pi}})\, \mathcal{G}$ (Configuration contexts)

Expression reduction

E-PInst
$\mathsf{inst}^{\Psi}\, x \to x\{\lceil \Psi(x) \rangle\!\rangle\}$

E-PApp
$(\Lambda\iota.v)\{\rho\} \to v[\rho/\iota]$

Configuration reduction

R-LiftE
$$\frac{e_1 \to e_2}{\mathcal{F}[e_1] \to \mathcal{F}[e_2]}$$

R-LiftC
$$\frac{\mathcal{C}_1 \to \mathcal{C}_2}{\mathcal{G}[\mathcal{C}_1] \to \mathcal{G}[\mathcal{C}_2]}$$

R-Fork
$\mathcal{F}[\mathsf{fork}\{\_\}\{\_\}e] \to \mathcal{F}[\,()\,] \,\|\, \circ\langle e\,()\,\rangle$

R-New
$\mathcal{F}[\mathsf{new}\, \mathcal{S}] \to (\nu x y^{\epsilon})\, \mathcal{F}[(x, y)]$ $x, y \notin \mathsf{fv}(\mathcal{F})$ and $\mathsf{unr}(\mathcal{S}) \neq \mathsf{Skip}$

R-NewPoly
$\mathcal{F}[\mathsf{new}\, \mathcal{S}^{\forall}\, n_1\, n_2] \to (\nu x y^{\bar{\pi}})\, \mathcal{F}[(x, y)]$ where $x, y \notin \mathsf{fv}(\mathcal{F})$ and $\bar{\pi} = [n_1 + k \cdot n_2 \mid k \in \mathbb{N}]$

Fig. 8. Evaluation contexts and expression reduction (excerpt).

tion. Rules for send/receive, select/match, and close/wait and for configuration reduction are standard, and rely on a notion of structural congruence ([21]).

We now state our type preservation results; their proofs are presented in [21].

Lemma 1. *If $\Delta \mid \Gamma \mid \Theta \mid \Psi \vdash e_1 : T \diamond \bar{\pi} \diamond \rho$ and $e_1 \to e_2$ then $\Delta \mid \Gamma \mid \Theta \mid \Psi \vdash e_2 : T \diamond \bar{\pi} \diamond \rho$.*

Theorem 1. *If $\Gamma \vdash^{\phi}_{\Psi} \mathcal{C}_1$ and $\mathcal{C}_1 \to \mathcal{C}_2$ then $\Gamma \vdash^{\phi}_{\Psi} \mathcal{C}_2$.*

We now focus on our goal of proving that well-typed (closed) configurations are deadlock-free. Following Kokke and Dardha [20], we rely on some useful notions on expressions. An expression *acts on a channel* x if it is of one of the following forms: $\mathsf{send}\{\rho\}[T]\{\sigma\}[S]vx$, or $\mathsf{receive}\{\rho\}[T]\{\sigma\}[S]x$, or $\mathsf{close}\{\rho\}x$, or $\mathsf{wait}\{\rho\}x$. In this case, the expression is said to be an *action*. Actions need to be extended to a notion that considers the other forms of *readiness* to communicate. We thus define an expression e_1 as *ready* if it is of the form $E[e_2]$, where e_2 is of the form $\mathsf{new}\, \mathcal{S}$, $\mathsf{new}\, \mathcal{S}^{\forall}\, n_1\, n_2$ or $\mathsf{fork}\{\rho\}\{\sigma\}e_3$ or e_2 acts on channel x. In the latter case, e_1 is said to be *ready to act on* x.

We now state progress for the term language; see [21] for its proof.

Theorem 2. *If $\Delta \mid \Gamma \mid \Theta \mid \Psi \vdash e : T \diamond \bar{\pi} \diamond \rho$ and for all $x : T \in \Gamma$, T is a session type, then: (i) e is a value, or (ii) $e \to e'$ for some e', or (iii) e is ready.*

Following [20], we say that a configuration $\mathcal{C}$ is in *canonical form* if it is of the form $(\nu x_1 y_1{}^{\bar{\pi}_1}) \dots (\nu x_n y_n{}^{\bar{\pi}_n})\, \bullet\langle e \rangle$ or, when it has child threads, it is of the form $(\nu x_1 y_1{}^{\bar{\pi}_1}) \dots (\nu x_n y_n{}^{\bar{\pi}_n})\, (\circ\langle e_1 \rangle \,\|\, \dots \,\|\, \circ\langle e_m \rangle \,\|\, \bullet\langle e \rangle)$, where no expression e_i is a value. Intuitively, a configuration is *deadlock-free* if either it reduces forever or, if it terminates, then all child threads are able to reduce to unit and the main thread reduces to an unrestricted value. More precisely:

Definition 1. $\mathcal{C}$ *is* deadlock-free *if* $\mathcal{C} \rightarrow^* \mathcal{C}' \not\rightarrow$ *then* $\mathcal{C}' \equiv \bullet\langle v \rangle$*, where* v *is such that* $\Delta \mid \Gamma \mid \Theta \mid \Psi \vdash v : T \diamond \bar{\pi} \diamond \rho$ *with* $|T| = \top$*.*

We can now establish deadlock freedom (see [21] for details):

Theorem 3. *Suppose* $\epsilon \vdash^{\bullet}_{\epsilon} \mathcal{C}$*. (1) If* $\mathcal{C}$ *is in canonical form, then* $\mathcal{C} \rightarrow \mathcal{D}$ *for some* $\mathcal{D}$ *or* $\mathcal{C} \equiv \bullet\langle v \rangle$*, where* v *is an unrestricted value. (2)* $\mathcal{C}$ *is deadlock-free.*

6 Closing Remarks

We have extended CFSTs for higher-order concurrent programs [3,27] with mechanisms to enforce deadlock freedom [20,24,25]. Our work shows that the high expressiveness of CFSTs (which includes polymorphism and non-regular recursion) does not conflict with strong correctness guarantees, as CFSTs can be effectively extended with deadlock-freedom guarantees while still supporting programs not expressible in regular session types, including those featuring cyclic process networks (see [21] for examples). Our framework's design is aligned with FreeST, a programming language with CFSTs [2]. Future work includes developing ways of relieving programmers from defining correct priority sequences. We believe that inference techniques in prior works [5,16,18] may provide a good starting point.

Related Work. The priority-based approach to deadlock freedom can be traced back to seminal work by Kobayashi [15,17]. The resulting classes of typed, deadlock-free processes can express cyclic process networks and encode typed λ-calculi and the sequencing behavior distinctive of (standard) session types [8,15]. Curry-Howard correspondences between session types and linear logic induce type systems that elegantly ensure deadlock freedom [4,29]. A limitation is their support for tree-like topologies only, which leaves out realistic scenarios with cyclic topologies [9]. To address this shortcoming, logic-based type systems have been extended with priorities in [7] (for synchronous processes without recursive types) and in [11,12] (for asynchronous processes with recursive types).

All previously mentioned works concern processes, not programs. The difference is relevant, as the non-local analyses enabled by priorities can be more directly performed for processes than for programs, where communication arises via functional constructs (cf. Fig. 5). To our knowledge, Padovani and Novara [24,25] were the first to adapt the type system for processes in [22] to the case of higher-order concurrent programs. A source of inspiration for our work, they use polymorphism and a form of *regular* recursion that appears limited to specify some examples. Our proof of deadlock freedom has been also influenced by Kokke and Dardha's work [20], who adapted the approach in [24,25] to the case of regular session types without recursion, which is subsumed by our work.

Acknowledgments. We are grateful to the anonymous reviewers of the current and previous versions of this paper for their constructive feedback. The first author was funded by FCT – Fundação para a Ciência e a Tecnologia, I.P., under the project REACT, ref. 2023.13752.PEX, DOI https://doi.org/10.54499/2023.13752.PEX, and under the LASIGE Research Unit, ref. UID/00408/2025, DOI https://doi.org/10.54499/UID/00408/2025. The second author gratefully acknowledges the support of the Dutch Research Council (NWO) under project "Cyclic Structures in Programs and Proofs" (OCENW.XL.23.089).

References

1. Almeida, B., Mordido, A., Thiemann, P., Vasconcelos, V.T.: Polymorphic lambda calculus with context-free session types. Inf. Comput. **289**(Part), 104948 (2022). https://doi.org/10.1016/J.IC.2022.104948
2. Almeida, B., Mordido, A., Vasconcelos, V.T.: Freest, a concurrent programming language with context-free session types (2019). https://freest-lang.github.io
3. Almeida, B., Mordido, A., Vasconcelos, V.T.: Deciding the bisimilarity of context-free session types. In: TACAS 2020. LNCS, vol. 12079, pp. 39–56. Springer, Cham (2020). https://doi.org/10.1007/978-3-030-45237-7_3
4. Caires, L., Pfenning, F.: Session types as intuitionistic linear propositions. In: Gastin, P., Laroussinie, F. (eds.) CONCUR 2010. LNCS, vol. 6269, pp. 222–236. Springer, Heidelberg (2010). https://doi.org/10.1007/978-3-642-15375-4_16
5. Coppo, M., Dezani-Ciancaglini, M., Yoshida, N., Padovani, L.: Global progress for dynamically interleaved multiparty sessions. Math. Struct. Comput. Sci. **26**(2), 238–302 (2016). https://doi.org/10.1017/S0960129514000188
6. Costa, D., Mordido, A., Poças, D., Vasconcelos, V.T.: Polymorphic higher-order context-free session types. Theor. Comput. Sci. **1001**, 114582 (2024). https://doi.org/10.1016/J.TCS.2024.114582
7. Dardha, O., Gay, S.J.: A new linear logic for deadlock-free session-typed processes. In: Baier, C., Dal Lago, U. (eds.) FoSSaCS 2018. LNCS, vol. 10803, pp. 91–109. Springer, Cham (2018). https://doi.org/10.1007/978-3-319-89366-2_5
8. Dardha, O., Giachino, E., Sangiorgi, D.: Session types revisited. Inf. Comput. **256**, 253–286 (2017). https://doi.org/10.1016/j.ic.2017.06.002
9. Dardha, O., Pérez, J.A.: Comparing type systems for deadlock freedom. J. Log. Algebraic Methods Program. **124**, 100717 (2022). https://doi.org/10.1016/J.JLAMP.2021.100717
10. Gay, S.J., Vasconcelos, V.T.: Linear type theory for asynchronous session types. J. Funct. Program. **20**(1), 19–50 (2010). https://doi.org/10.1017/S0956796809990268
11. van den Heuvel, B., Pérez, J.A.: Deadlock freedom for asynchronous and cyclic process networks. In: Lange, J., Mavridou, A., Safina, L., Scalas, A. (eds.) Proceedings 14th Interaction and Concurrency Experience, ICE 2021, Online, 18th June 2021. EPTCS, vol. 347, pp. 38–56 (2021). https://doi.org/10.4204/EPTCS.347.3
12. van den Heuvel, B., Pérez, J.A.: Asynchronous session-based concurrency: deadlock-freedom in cyclic process networks. Log. Methods Comput. Sci. **20**(4) (2024). https://doi.org/10.46298/LMCS-20(4:6)2024
13. Honda, K.: Types for dyadic interaction. In: Best, E. (ed.) CONCUR 1993. LNCS, vol. 715, pp. 509–523. Springer, Heidelberg (1993). https://doi.org/10.1007/3-540-57208-2_35

14. Honda, K., Vasconcelos, V.T., Kubo, M.: Language primitives and type discipline for structured communication-based programming. In: Hankin, C. (ed.) ESOP 1998. LNCS, vol. 1381, pp. 122–138. Springer, Heidelberg (1998). https://doi.org/10.1007/BFb0053567
15. Kobayashi, N.: Type systems for concurrent programs. In: Aichernig, B.K., Maibaum, T. (eds.) Formal Methods at the Crossroads. From Panacea to Foundational Support. LNCS, vol. 2757, pp. 439–453. Springer, Heidelberg (2003). https://doi.org/10.1007/978-3-540-40007-3_26
16. Kobayashi, N.: Type-based information flow analysis for the pi-calculus. Acta Informatica **42**(4–5), 291–347 (2005)
17. Kobayashi, N.: A new type system for deadlock-free processes. In: Baier, C., Hermanns, H. (eds.) CONCUR 2006. LNCS, vol. 4137, pp. 233–247. Springer, Heidelberg (2006). https://doi.org/10.1007/11817949_16
18. Kobayashi, N., Laneve, C.: Deadlock analysis of unbounded process networks. Inf. Comput. **252**, 48–70 (2017). https://doi.org/10.1016/J.IC.2016.03.004
19. Kobayashi, N., Pierce, B.C., Turner, D.N.: Linearity and the pi-calculus. ACM Trans. Program. Lang. Syst. **21**(5), 914–947 (1999). https://doi.org/10.1145/330249.330251
20. Kokke, W., Dardha, O.: Prioritise the best variation. Log. Methods Comput. Sci. **19**(4) (2023). https://doi.org/10.46298/LMCS-19(4:28)2023
21. Mordido, A., Pérez, J.A.: Deadlock-free context-free session types. CoRR abs/2506.20356 (2025). https://doi.org/10.48550/ARXIV.2506.20356
22. Padovani, L.: Deadlock and lock freedom in the linear π-calculus. In: Proceedings of the Joint Meeting of the Twenty-Third EACSL Annual Conference on Computer Science Logic (CSL) and the Twenty-Ninth Annual ACM/IEEE Symposium on Logic in Computer Science (LICS). CSL-LICS 2014. Association for Computing Machinery, New York, NY, USA (2014)
23. Padovani, L.: Type reconstruction for the linear π-calculus with composite and equi-recursive types. In: Muscholl, A. (ed.) FoSSaCS 2014. LNCS, vol. 8412, pp. 88–102. Springer, Heidelberg (2014). https://doi.org/10.1007/978-3-642-54830-7_6
24. Padovani, L., Novara, L.: Types for Deadlock-Free Higher-Order Concurrent Programs (2014). https://inria.hal.science/hal-00954364, working paper or preprint
25. Padovani, L., Novara, L.: Types for deadlock-free higher-order programs. In: Graf, S., Viswanathan, M. (eds.) FORTE 2015. LNCS, vol. 9039, pp. 3–18. Springer, Cham (2015). https://doi.org/10.1007/978-3-319-19195-9_1
26. Silva, G., Mordido, A., Vasconcelos, V.T.: Subtyping context-free session types. In: Pérez, G.A., Raskin, J. (eds.) 34th International Conference on Concurrency Theory, CONCUR 2023, 18–23 September 2023, Antwerp, Belgium. LIPIcs, vol. 279, pp. 11:1–11:19. Schloss Dagstuhl - Leibniz-Zentrum für Informatik (2023). https://doi.org/10.4230/LIPICS.CONCUR.2023.11
27. Thiemann, P., Vasconcelos, V.T.: Context-free session types. In: Garrigue, J., Keller, G., Sumii, E. (eds.) Proceedings of the 21st ACM SIGPLAN International Conference on Functional Programming, ICFP 2016, Nara, Japan, 18–22 September 2016, pp. 462–475. ACM (2016). https://doi.org/10.1145/2951913.2951926
28. Vasconcelos, V.T.: Fundamentals of session types. Inf. Comput. **217**, 52–70 (2012)
29. Wadler, P.: Propositions as sessions. In: Thiemann, P., Findler, R.B. (eds.) ACM SIGPLAN International Conference on Functional Programming, ICFP 2012, Copenhagen, Denmark, 9–15 September 2012, pp. 273–286. ACM (2012). https://doi.org/10.1145/2364527.2364568

TPTL-DIST: A Calculus for Verifying Real-Time Distributed Systems

Javier Enríquez Mendoza(✉), Sam Speight(✉), and Vincent Rahli(✉)

University of Birmingham, Birmingham, UK
jxe275@student.bham.ac.uk, {s.l.speight,V.Rahli}@bham.ac.uk

Abstract. We introduce TPTL-DIST, a temporal logic and labelled sequent calculus for specifying and verifying real-time distributed systems, formalised in Agda to provide machine-checked correctness and tool support. The logic extends Timed Propositional Temporal Logic (TPTL) with past operators, freeze quantification, comparisons between time expressions, domain-specific atoms, and an induction principle on time. We provide a world-based semantics, develop an interval-annotated calculus, and establish its soundness w.r.t. the semantics. To demonstrate its expressiveness, we encode standard distributed system patterns, and we carry out a mechanized proof of a key real-time property of the Pistis Byzantine broadcast protocol. Our results show that TPTL-DIST provides a uniform, mechanized framework for reasoning about temporal properties of distributed systems.

Keywords: Temporal Logic · Real-Time · Distributed Systems · Byzantine Reliable Broadcast · Agda

1 Introduction

Modern systems, such as smart factories, power grids, high-speed payment processing (e.g., Visa, PayPal), ultra-low-latency 5G networks, and mission-critical air traffic control, rely on distributed systems. In these settings, correctness depends not only on what actions occur, but when they occur as delays can lead to failures. While temporal logics such as LTL and CTL provide well established foundations for reasoning about system behaviour over time, they lack support for real-time properties. Extensions such as TPTL [1] and Timed CTL [2] incorporate clocks and timing constraints, and tools like PRISM [3] and TLA++ [4–6] support modelling and model checking of real-time and distributed systems [7–15]. However, existing formalisms differ from our approach in important ways and face key limitations. (1) Our work leverages a full Agda formalisation, enabling machine-checked reasoning and providing a foundation for verified tool support. (2) Logics like TPTL and Timed CTL cannot express common distributed system events such as message send/receive or agent correctness, and it lacks inductive reasoning over time. (3) Tools like PRISM and TLA+ require exhaustively

Published by Springer Nature Switzerland AG 2026
L. Bocchi and B. Kulahcioglu Ozkan (Eds.): FORTE 2026, LNCS 16589, pp. 197–223, 2026.
https://doi.org/10.1007/978-3-032-28187-6_12

exploring all possible states of the system, which is not always feasible. (4) Existing approaches separate clock reasoning from the communication structure of distributed systems.

To complement the current landscape of approaches, we introduce TPTL-DIST, a fully formalised temporal logic and labelled sequent calculus designed specifically for reasoning about real-time fault-tolerant distributed protocols. The logic extends TPTL with past operators, freeze quantification, a general comparison operator on time expressions, and atomic predicates encoding message transmission, internal events, and agent correctness.

TPTL-DIST's rules are annotated with time intervals and the semantics is given over an abstract world structure equipped with an induction principle for temporal reasoning. A central goal of TPTL-DIST is to provide a uniform framework to state and reason about both temporal and distributed aspects of a protocol. All definitions, rules, and meta-theoretical results are formalized in Agda: https://github.com/jaeem006/TPTL-DIST/blob/main/Index2025.lagda. We use the symbol ⚙ to link to the formalization.

Contributions. Our contributions are as follows, demonstrating that TPTL-DIST provides a principled and mechanized foundation for reasoning about real-time distributed systems:

- TPTL-DIST a new logic for real-time distributed systems, extending TPTL with past operators, quantifiers, comparisons on time expressions, and fault-tolerant distributed system operators.
- A sequent calculus for TPTL-DIST that supports reasoning with intervals, which is sound for the intended semantics.
- A general semantic framework based on ordered worlds, enabling a principled induction rule for unbounded temporal reasoning.
- A mechanization in Agda, covering the logic, calculus and meta-theory.
- A modular design of the Pistis real-time reliable broadcast protocol [16].
- A mechanized proof of Pistis' timeliness property, showcasing TPTL-DIST's support for real-time constraints, message-passing patterns, and induction.

2 Related Work

Several proof systems have been proposed for LTL-like logics. However, the until operator is known to pose difficulties due to its dual character of being both universal and existential. A labeled natural deduction system was proposed in [17] to treat those difficulties. Simplifying and generalizing that system (see Sect. 3), we propose a labeled sequent calculus that allows reasoning about TPTL's temporal operators, in particular until and freeze, in a uniform way.

TPTL. The syntax of TPTL is as follows, where $\mathbf{U}$ and $\bigcirc$ are the usual "until" and "next" LTL operators; p is an atomic proposition; x is a clock variable; c is a clock expression; $\sim \; \in \{\leq, <, =, >, \geq\}$ allows comparing a clock variable with a clock expression; and the *freeze* formula $x \cdot \varphi$ binds the current time to x in φ:

$$\varphi ::= p \mid \varphi \wedge \varphi \mid \neg\varphi \mid \varphi \,\mathbf{U}\, \varphi \mid \bigcirc\varphi \mid x \sim c \mid x \cdot \varphi$$

The *eventually* and *always* operators are defined as usual: $\Diamond\varphi \equiv \top \,\mathbf{U}\, \varphi$ and $\Box\varphi \equiv \neg\Diamond\neg\varphi$, while the freeze operator allows capturing that φ eventually holds by time c: $x \cdot \Diamond(x \leq c \wedge \varphi)$. To understand this, consider TPTL's semantics over the discrete notion of time given by $\mathbb{N}$. A formula's semantics is given in terms of a mapping ρ from $\mathbb{N}$ to states, a point in time $i \in \mathbb{N}$, and a variable valuation v, where a state ρ_n is a pair of a valuation on atoms σ_n and a timestamp τ_n:

$$\begin{array}{llll}
\rho, i, v \models p & \iff p \in \sigma_i & \rho, i, v \models \varphi \wedge \psi & \iff \rho, i, v \models \varphi \text{ and } \rho, i, v \models \psi \\
\rho, i, v \models \neg\varphi & \iff \rho, i, v \not\models \varphi & \rho, i, v \models \bigcirc\varphi & \iff \rho, i+1, v \models \varphi \\
\rho, i, v \models x \sim c & \iff \tau_i - v(x) \sim c & \rho, i, v \models x \cdot \varphi & \iff \rho, i, v[x \mapsto \tau_i] \models \varphi
\end{array}$$
$$\rho, i, v \models \varphi \,\mathbf{U}\, \psi \iff \exists j > i.(\rho, j, v \models \psi) \wedge \forall k \in [i, j).(\rho, k, v \models \varphi)$$

The semantics of "φ eventually holds by time c", i.e., $x \cdot \Diamond(x \leq c \wedge \varphi)$ w.r.t. ρ, i, v states that there exists a time $\tau_j \leq \tau_i + c$ at which φ is true, for some $j > i$. This is achieved by "freezing" the current time τ_i, by mapping x to τ_i in the variable valuation v; by jumping to a later time τ_j thanks to the $\Diamond$ operator; and finally the constraint $x \leq c$ guarantees that $\tau_j \leq \tau_i + c$.

Despite its expressive power, TPTL does not allow formalizing properties of distributed systems such as those relevant to the Pistis real-time Byzantine-resilient reliable broadcast protocol [16], lacking the support for reasoning about agents, messages, communication, etc. TPTL-DIST is designed to address these points, as well as TPTL's lack of support for important time-related reasoning mechanisms, such as reasoning about past properties in addition to future properties, and reasoning inductively over time.

Note that TPTL-DIST aims to support the specification and verification of systems that are required to perform critical actions in a timely fashion. As such, it allows modeling a *real* or *physical*, quantitative notion of time, in addition to a *logical*, qualitative notion of time [18,19].

Other approaches with similar motivation, i.e., formally verifying timing properties of systems, but using different techniques have been proposed in the literature. We illustrate below how our approach relates and differs.

TLA+: Temporal Logic of Actions. The primary distinction with TLA+ lies in its treatment of time. Our system integrates temporal constructs directly into the language's syntax through its freeze and comparison operators. This representation of time allows for simple and intuitive modeling of temporal conditions. By contrast, TLA+ relies on temporal operators such as always and eventually to express time-dependent properties. Although it is feasible to capture a quantitative notion of time in TLA+ using variables that represent time, these variables are treated as ordinary state variables and are not inherently connected to the temporal operators. As a result, while providing great flexibility, the burden of correctly managing time relies on the user explicitly updating those variables, as opposed to the automated management of time in TPTL-DIST.

PRISM: Probabilistic Model Checking. PRISM is primarily designed for the verification of probabilistic properties. It is based on probabilistic temporal logics such as PCTL (Probabilistic Computation Tree Logic) [20,21] and CSL (Continuous Stochastic Logic) [22,23]. In addition to including temporal mechanisms that enable reasoning about time-related properties, PRISM's core strength lies in its ability to handle systems characterized by randomness, uncertainty, and nondeterminism. TPTL-DIST complements PRISM's approach, whose model checking engine imposes some restrictions on the real-time systems and properties that can be verified, providing flexibility to the users thanks to its calculus.

Summary. TLA+ lets users manage time flexibly through variables, requiring careful handling, while PRISM takes a more restricted approach to enable effective model checking. TPTL-DIST provides primitives that do not require careful management of variables, while still providing some flexibility when stating time-related properties, along with a calculus to prove those properties.

3 TPTL-DIST

We now present TPTL-DIST, an extension of TPTL + Past [24], with quantifiers, a more general comparison operator, a "discrete" semantics, and a sequent calculus.

3.1 Syntax

To reason about distributed systems, which are composed of nodes, or agents, communicating by exchanging messages, we fix some types (T) to allow quantifying over agents (**Agent**), sets of agents (**Agents**), and data (**Data**), where **Data** is used to capture the information exchanged between agents ⚙:

$$T \in \mathsf{Type} ::= \textbf{Agent} \mid \textbf{Agents} \mid \textbf{Data}$$

Let v_a range over a set $\mathcal{V}_a$ of variables of type **Agent** and c_a range over a set $\mathcal{C}_a$ of constants of type **Agent**; let v_A range over a set $\mathcal{V}_A$ of variables of type **Agents**; and let v_d range over a set $\mathcal{V}_d$ of variables of type **Data** and c_d range over a set $\mathcal{C}_d$ of constants of type **Data**. Expressions of types **Agent** ⚙, **Agents** ⚙, and **Data** ⚙ are defined as follows:

$$i, j \in \mathsf{Agent} ::= v_a \mid c_a \qquad A \in \mathsf{Agents} ::= v_A \mid [i_1, \ldots, i_n] \qquad d \in \mathsf{Data} ::= v_d \mid c_d$$

TPTL-DIST also includes expressions to capture time constraints, where v_t ranges over a set $\mathcal{V}_t$ of time variables, $\mathbf{0}$ is a constant, capturing an empty amount of time, and $\bullet$ is a binary operation, intuitively adding two time expressions ⚙:

$$t \in \mathsf{TimeExp} ::= v_t \mid \mathbf{0} \mid t \bullet t$$

To compare time expressions, we further introduce the following operators ⚙:

$$\sim \ \in \mathsf{Comparison} ::= \ \sqsubset \ \mid \ \equiv \ \mid \lhd$$

Intuitively, $t_1 \sqsubset t_2$ states that t_1 is strictly lower than t_2, $t_1 \equiv t_2$ states that t_1 and t_2 are equal, and $t_1 \lhd t_2$ states that t_1 is t_2's immediate predecessor.

To reason about distributed systems, one must reason about the knowledge acquired by agents over time. The two main approaches are the *implicit* or *external* representation of knowledge, which is externally assigned to agents; and the *explicit* representation, where knowledge is explicitly "stored" in states, allowing agents to compute and act on their knowledge [25]. We take an explicit approach, introducing a number of atomic expressions that capture knowledge through the exchange of messages between agents. A *distributed* atom a is either a *send* atom $\mathtt{send}(i, d, A)$, stating that agent i sent the data d to the set of agents A; or a *receive* atom $\mathtt{recv}(i, d, j)$, stating that agent i received the data d from agent j; or an *internal event* atom $\mathtt{internal}(i, d)$, stating that d happened at agent i; or a *correct* atom $\mathtt{correct}(i)$, stating that agent i is correct ⚙:

$$a_d \in \mathsf{DistAtom} ::= \mathtt{send}(i, d, A) \mid \mathtt{recv}(i, d, j) \mid \mathtt{internal}(i, d) \mid \mathtt{correct}(i)$$

Furthermore, TPTL-DIST includes atoms to reason about sets of agents as follows, where $n \in \mathbb{N}$, $\mathtt{size}(A, n)$ states that the collection of agents A is of size n, and $i \in A$ states that agent i is in the collection of agents A ⚙:

$$a_s \in \mathsf{SetAtom} ::= \mathtt{size}(A, n) \mid i \in A$$

An atom is then either a *distributed* or a *set* atom: $a \in \mathsf{Atom} ::= a_d \mid a_s$.

TPTL-DIST's syntax includes: (1) propositional connectives; (2) past and future LTL operators; (3) a freeze operator along with a comparison operator on time expressions; (4) quantifiers; (5) atoms to reason about distributed systems. It is defined as follows, where $\mathbf{S}$ and $\mathbf{Y}$ are the "since" and "yesterday" past counterparts of $\mathbf{U}$ and $\bigcirc$, and v is a variable of type T in $\forall v : T.\varphi$ and $\exists v : T.\varphi$ ⚙:

$$\begin{aligned}\varphi \in \mathsf{Formula} ::= {} & a \mid \top \mid \bot \mid \varphi \wedge \varphi \mid \varphi \vee \varphi \mid \varphi \rightarrow \varphi \mid \varphi \,\mathbf{U}\, \varphi \mid \bigcirc \varphi \\ & \mid \varphi \,\mathbf{S}\, \varphi \mid \mathbf{Y}\, \varphi \mid t \sim t \mid v_t \cdot \varphi \mid \forall v : T.\varphi \mid \exists v : T.\varphi\end{aligned}$$

We write $\forall v_1, \ldots, v_n : T.\varphi$ for $\forall v_1 : T. \ldots \forall v_n : T.\varphi$, and similarly for $\exists$. Negation is defined as usual: $\neg\varphi :\equiv \varphi \rightarrow \bot$. We recall the definitions of *eventually* and *always* (in white) as well as their past counterparts (in black) ⚙:

$$\Diamond \varphi :\equiv \top \,\mathbf{U}\, \varphi \qquad \Box \varphi :\equiv \neg \Diamond \neg \varphi \qquad \blacklozenge \varphi :\equiv \top \,\mathbf{S}\, \varphi \qquad \blacksquare \varphi :\equiv \neg \blacklozenge \neg \varphi$$

Thanks to TPTL-DIST's general comparison operator $t_1 \sim t_2$, a time-bounded version of $\Diamond$ can be defined more straightforwardly than in TPTL: $\Diamond_t \varphi :\equiv v_t \cdot \Diamond(v'_t \cdot v'_t \sqsubseteq (v_t \bullet t) \wedge \varphi)$, stating that φ happens sometime in the future by time t, where $t_1 \sqsubseteq t_2$ stands for $t_1 \sqsubset t_2 \vee t_1 \equiv t_2$. Similarly, we define a time-bounded

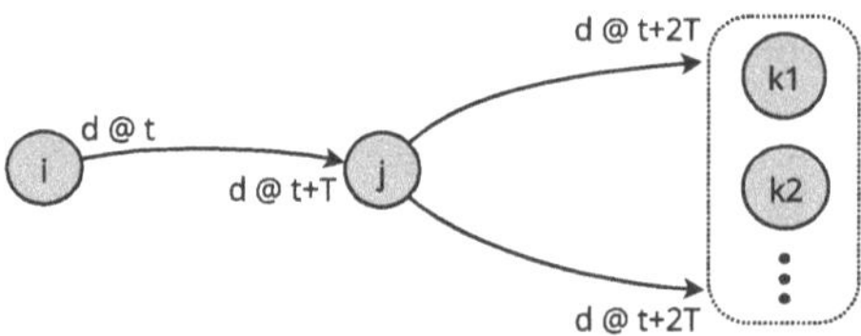

Fig. 1. Forwarding example

version of the $\Box$ operator: $\Box_t\varphi \coloneqq v_t \cdot \Box(v'_t \cdot v'_t \sqsubseteq (v_t \bullet t) \to \varphi)$ stating that φ always holds between now and t. Furthermore, we define the following *strict* version of the *sometimes before* operator $\blacklozenge$ as follows: $\blacktriangleleft\varphi \coloneqq \mathbf{Y}(\blacklozenge\varphi)$, stating that φ happened sometimes in the past, but not now.

3.2 Forwarding Example

We now illustrate aspects of the language using a simple forwarding example, demonstrating how to capture message passing patterns in distributed systems, where agents exchange information by sending/receiving messages (see Appendix A for further examples). In this example, messages are relayed between agents of a synchronous system. Section 3.6 then proves a property of this system in detail, illustrating the use of TPTL-DIST's rules presented in Sect. 3.5.

As illustrated in Fig. 1, in this example, an agent i sends a message d at time t to another agent j, which then forwards d to all other agents. We are then guaranteed that any agent would have received that message by time $t+2T$ assuming that the maximum transmission delay between agents is T.

All agents are assumed to be correct and communication is assumed to be synchronous, ensuring that all sent messages are received within a time interval T, captured by the following formula stating that if an agent sends a message d at time t to a collection of agents, those agents will receive d by time $t+T$:

$$\forall i, j : \textsc{Agent}.\forall d : \textsc{Data}.\forall A : \textsc{Agents}. \quad \Box(\texttt{send}(i, d, A) \to \Diamond_T(j \in A \to \texttt{recv}(j, d, i))) \tag{1}$$

Additionally, we assume that agents immediately forward the information they receive to all other agents, captured by the following formula stating that whenever j receives a message it immediately sends it to k, and this for any k:

$$\forall i, j, k : \textsc{Agent}.\forall d : \textsc{Data}.\Box(\texttt{recv}(j, d, i) \to \texttt{send}(j, d, [k])) \tag{2}$$

As shown in Sect. 3.6, using TPTL-DIST's calculus presented below, one can then derive the following formula from the above assumptions, stating that if an agent i sends a message d to some agent j, then any agent k will also receive d before $2T$ (where $2T$ is simply $T \bullet T$):

$$\forall i, j, k : \textsc{Agent}.\forall d : \textsc{Data}.\Box(\texttt{send}(i, d, [j]) \to \Diamond_{2T}\texttt{recv}(k, d, j)) \tag{3}$$

$\cdot$-*sym*	$\forall w_1, w_2 : \mathcal{W}.w_1 \cdot w_2 = w_2 \cdot w_1$
$\cdot$-*assoc*	$\forall w_1, w_2, w_3 : \mathcal{W}.w_1 \cdot (w_2 \cdot w_3) = (w_1 \cdot w_2) \cdot w_3$
$\preceq$-*trans*	$\forall w_1, w_2, w_3 : \mathcal{W}.w_1 \preceq w_2 \rightarrow w_2 \preceq w_3 \rightarrow w_1 \preceq w_3$
$\cdot$-*unit*	$\forall w : \mathcal{W}.\mathsf{0} \cdot w = w$
$\preceq$-*refl*	$\forall w : \mathcal{W}.w \preceq w$
$\mathsf{0}$-*initial*	$\forall w : \mathcal{W}.\mathsf{0} \preceq w$
monotonicity	$\forall w_1, w_2, w_3, w_4 : \mathcal{W}.w_1 \preceq w_2 \rightarrow w_3 \preceq w_4 \rightarrow w_1 \cdot w_3 \preceq w_2 \cdot w_4$
sub	$\forall w_1, w_2 : \mathcal{W}.w_1 \lhd w_2 \rightarrow w_1 \preceq w_2$
right-density	$\forall w_1, w_2 : \mathcal{W}.w_1 \preceq w_2 \rightarrow w_1 = w_2 \vee \exists w : \mathcal{W}.w_1 \preceq w \wedge w \lhd w_2$
left-density	$\forall w_1, w_2 : \mathcal{W}.w_1 \preceq w_2 \rightarrow w_1 = w_2 \vee \exists w : \mathcal{W}.w_1 \lhd w \wedge w \preceq w_2$
conditional-totality	$\forall w_1, w_2, w : \mathcal{W}.w_1 \preceq w \rightarrow w_2 \preceq w \rightarrow w_1 \preceq w_2 \vee w_2 \preceq w_1$
induction	$\forall P : \mathcal{W} \rightarrow \mathsf{Set}.$ $(\forall w : \mathcal{W}.(\forall u, v : \mathcal{W}.u \preceq v \rightarrow v \lhd w \rightarrow P(u)) \rightarrow P(w)) \rightarrow$ $\forall w : \mathcal{W}.P(w)$

Fig. 2. World axioms

3.3 Semantics

We now adapt and extend TPTL's semantics to our calculus, in particular to account for domain-specific atoms and a more general comparison operator between time expressions. Formulas are interpreted w.r.t. a collection of worlds, which provides meaning to time expressions. The set of worlds $\mathcal{W}$ includes a constant $\mathsf{0}$ and a binary operation $\cdot$ (the semantic counterparts of the time expressions in TimeExp) and is equipped with two relations $\preceq$ and $\lhd$ (the semantic counterparts of the relations in Comparison) satisfying the axioms in Fig. 2 ⚙.

The axioms $\cdot$-*sym*, $\cdot$-*assoc*, $\cdot$-*unit*, $\preceq$-*refl*, $\preceq$-*trans*, *monotonicity* and $\mathsf{0}$-*initial* make $\mathcal{W}$ into a positively ordered (commutative) monoid [26] (though note that we do not require antisymmetry). Ordered commutative monoids have been exhibited as the mathematical structures of resource combination and convertibility [27]. Later, we will interpret time expressions as worlds, and, as such, may think of time as a resource.

We think of $\lhd$ as capturing immediate predecessor in the $\preceq$ relation; hence the *sub* axiom simply expresses that the former is a subrelation of the latter. Axiom *right-density* is used, in particular, along with the induction axiom, to derive the induction rule presented in Sect. 3.5, which is key to proving our main application in Lemma 2. Axiom *conditional-totality*, in the presence of $\preceq$-*refl* and *monotonicity*, is equivalent to totality, by setting $w = w_1 \cdot w_2$.

The *right-density* and *left-density* axioms are in particular used to prove the left-to-right and right-to-left implications of $(\blacklozenge(\mathbf{Y}\,\varphi)) \leftrightarrow (\mathbf{Y}\,(\blacklozenge\varphi))$, respectively. Interestingly, only the former was necessary in Section 4.2.

Following [25,28–30], formulas are interpreted w.r.t. a model, which is a tuple of the form $\langle r, \pi, w, \mathcal{V}\rangle$ consisting of (1) a run r, (2) an interpretation function π, which assigns meaning to atomic formulas, (3) a world $w \in \mathcal{W}$, and (4) a variable valuation $\mathcal{V}$ assigning meaning to free variables. A run r is a function in $\mathcal{W} \rightarrow$ Global, where Global is a global state, i.e., an element of List(ClosedAtom), where ClosedAtom is the type of closed atoms (closed elements

$$
\begin{array}{l}
\boxed{[\![\_]\!] : \mathsf{Type} \rightarrow \mathsf{Set}} \\
[\![\textsc{Agent}]\!] \coloneqq \mathcal{C}_a \\
[\![\textsc{Agents}]\!] \coloneqq \mathsf{List}(\mathcal{C}_a) \\
[\![\textsc{Data}]\!] \coloneqq \mathcal{C}_d
\end{array}
\quad
\begin{array}{l}
\boxed{[\![\_]\!]_\mathcal{V} : \mathsf{TimeExp} \rightarrow \mathcal{W}} \\
[\![v_t]\!]_\mathcal{V} \coloneqq \mathcal{V}(v_t) \\
[\![\mathbf{0}]\!]_\mathcal{V} \coloneqq 0 \\
[\![t_1 \bullet t_2]\!]_\mathcal{V} \coloneqq [\![t_1]\!]_\mathcal{V} \cdot [\![t_2]\!]_\mathcal{V}
\end{array}
\quad
\begin{array}{l}
\boxed{[\![\_]\!] : \mathsf{Comparison} \rightarrow \mathcal{W} \rightarrow \mathcal{W} \rightarrow \mathsf{Set}} \\
[\![\sqsubset]\!] \coloneqq \prec \\
[\![\equiv]\!] \coloneqq = \\
[\![\lhd]\!] \coloneqq \lhd
\end{array}
$$

$$
\begin{array}{l}
\boxed{[\![\_]\!]_\mathcal{V} : \mathsf{Agents} \rightarrow \mathsf{List}(\mathcal{C}_a)} \\
[\![v_A]\!]_\mathcal{V} \coloneqq \mathcal{V}(v_A) \\
[\![[i_1, \ldots, i_n]]\!]_\mathcal{V} \coloneqq [[\![i_1]\!]_\mathcal{V}, \ldots, [\![i_n]\!]_\mathcal{V}]
\end{array}
\quad
\begin{array}{l}
\boxed{[\![\_]\!]_\mathcal{V} : \mathsf{Agent} \rightarrow \mathcal{C}_a} \\
[\![v_a]\!]_\mathcal{V} \coloneqq \mathcal{V}(v_a) \\
[\![c_a]\!]_\mathcal{V} \coloneqq c_a
\end{array}
\quad
\begin{array}{l}
\boxed{[\![\_]\!]_\mathcal{V} : \mathsf{Data} \rightarrow \mathcal{C}_d} \\
[\![v_d]\!]_\mathcal{V} \coloneqq \mathcal{V}(v_d) \\
[\![c_d]\!]_\mathcal{V} \coloneqq c_d
\end{array}
$$

$$
\begin{array}{l}
\boxed{[\![\_]\!]_\mathcal{V} : \mathsf{DistAtom} \rightarrow \mathsf{ClosedAtom}} \\
[\![\mathtt{send}(i, d, A)]\!]_\mathcal{V} \coloneqq \mathtt{send}([\![i]\!]_\mathcal{V}, [\![d]\!]_\mathcal{V}, [\![A]\!]_\mathcal{V}) \\
[\![\mathtt{recv}(i, d, j)]\!]_\mathcal{V} \coloneqq \mathtt{recv}([\![i]\!]_\mathcal{V}, [\![d]\!]_\mathcal{V}, [\![j]\!]_\mathcal{V}) \\
[\![\mathtt{internal}(i, d)]\!]_\mathcal{V} \coloneqq \mathtt{internal}([\![i]\!]_\mathcal{V}, [\![d]\!]_\mathcal{V}) \\
[\![\mathtt{correct}(i)]\!]_\mathcal{V} \coloneqq \mathtt{correct}([\![i]\!]_\mathcal{V})
\end{array}
$$

Fig. 3. Semantics of types, time expressions, comparison operators, agents, collections of agents, data, and distributed atoms

of Atom). An interpretation is a function in Global $\rightarrow$ ClosedAtom $\rightarrow$ Set, which checks whether a given atom is true in a given global state. A variable valuation is a function in $(\mathcal{V}_a \rightarrow \mathcal{C}_a) \cup (\mathcal{V}_A \rightarrow \mathsf{List}(\mathcal{C}_a)) \cup (\mathcal{V}_d \rightarrow \mathcal{C}_d) \cup (\mathcal{V}_t \rightarrow \mathcal{W})$. We write $\mathcal{V}(X_1, \ldots, X_n)$ to indicate that $\mathcal{V}$ is a variable valuation with domain including the free variables of the syntactic expressions X_1 to X_n. We also write $w_1 \prec w_2$ for $\exists w : \mathcal{W}. w_1 \lhd w \wedge w \preceq w_2$.

Figure 3 ✿ introduces the semantics of time expressions $[\![t]\!]_\mathcal{V} \in \mathcal{W}$, types $[\![T]\!] \in \mathsf{Set}$, atoms $[\![a]\!]_\mathcal{V} \in \mathsf{ClosedAtom}$, agents $[\![i]\!]_\mathcal{V} \in \mathcal{C}_a$, collections of agents $[\![A]\!]_\mathcal{V} \in \mathsf{List}(\mathcal{C}_a)$, data $[\![d]\!]_\mathcal{V} \in \mathcal{C}_d$, and comparison operators $[\![\sim]\!] \in \mathcal{W} \rightarrow \mathcal{W} \rightarrow \mathsf{Set}$, while Fig. 4 ✿ defines the semantics of formulas. In particular, the semantics of an atom a_d, checks that the interpretation $[\![a_d]\!]_\mathcal{V}$ is in the global state returned by r at world w.

3.4 Sequents and Rules

Some proof systems have been proposed for LTL-like logics [31,32]. However, the until operator is known to pose difficulties [33]. A labeled natural deduction system was proposed in [17] to circumvent those difficulties, following a long line of work on labeled deduction systems [34–37]. Simplifying and generalizing that system, we propose a labeled sequent calculus that allows reasoning about until and timing properties using the same machinery.

A sequent is of the form $\Gamma \vdash \varphi^{\mathsf{a}}$, where Γ is a list of hypotheses, φ is a formula, and a is a time annotation. Time annotations are as follows, where $\centerdot$ indicates no annotation, meaning the formula is time-irrelevant ✿:

$$\mathsf{a} ::= \centerdot \mid t \mid [t_1, t_2] \mid [t_1, t_2) \mid (t_1, t_2] \mid (t_1, t_2)$$

Such a sequent states that φ holds at time a in the context Γ. An hypothesis is of the form φ^{a}. We write φ for the annotated formula $\varphi^{\centerdot}$. Similar to [17], TPTL-DIST relies on intervals to capture the meaning of $\mathbf{U}$. The formula $\varphi \,\mathbf{U}\, \psi$ is true

$$\begin{array}{lll}
r, \pi, w, \mathcal{V} \models a_d & \Longleftrightarrow & \pi(r(w))(\llbracket a_d \rrbracket_{\mathcal{V}}) \\
r, \pi, w, \mathcal{V} \models i \in A & \Longleftrightarrow & \llbracket i \rrbracket_{\mathcal{V}} \in \llbracket A \rrbracket_{\mathcal{V}} \\
r, \pi, w, \mathcal{V} \models \mathtt{size}(A, n) & \Longleftrightarrow & |\llbracket A \rrbracket_{\mathcal{V}}| = n \\
r, \pi, w, \mathcal{V} \models \top & \Longleftrightarrow & \text{True} \\
r, \pi, w, \mathcal{V} \models \bot & \Longleftrightarrow & \text{False} \\
r, \pi, w, \mathcal{V} \models \neg\varphi & \Longleftrightarrow & \neg(r, \pi, w, \mathcal{V} \models \varphi) \\
r, \pi, w, \mathcal{V} \models \varphi \wedge \psi & \Longleftrightarrow & r, \pi, w, \mathcal{V} \models \varphi \text{ and } r, \pi, w, \mathcal{V} \models \psi \\
r, \pi, w, \mathcal{V} \models \varphi \vee \psi & \Longleftrightarrow & r, \pi, w, \mathcal{V} \models \varphi \text{ or } r, \pi, w, \mathcal{V} \models \psi \\
r, \pi, w, \mathcal{V} \models \varphi \rightarrow \psi & \Longleftrightarrow & r, \pi, w, \mathcal{V} \models \varphi \text{ implies } r, \pi, w, \mathcal{V} \models \psi \\
r, \pi, w, \mathcal{V} \models \forall v : T.\varphi & \Longleftrightarrow & r, \pi, w, \mathcal{V}[v \mapsto z] \models \varphi \text{ for all } z \in \llbracket T \rrbracket \\
r, \pi, w, \mathcal{V} \models \exists v : T.\varphi & \Longleftrightarrow & r, \pi, w, \mathcal{V}[v \mapsto z] \models \varphi \text{ for some } z \in \llbracket T \rrbracket \\
r, \pi, w, \mathcal{V} \models t_1 \sim t_2 & \Longleftrightarrow & \llbracket t_1 \rrbracket_{\mathcal{V}} \llbracket \sim \rrbracket \llbracket t_2 \rrbracket_{\mathcal{V}} \\
r, \pi, w, \mathcal{V} \models v_t \cdot \varphi & \Longleftrightarrow & r, \pi, w, \mathcal{V}[v_t \mapsto w] \models \varphi \\
r, \pi, w, \mathcal{V} \models \varphi \,\mathbf{U}\, \psi & \Longleftrightarrow & \exists w' \succ w.(r, \pi, w', \mathcal{V} \models \psi) \wedge \\
& & \quad \forall w''.w \preceq w'' \prec w' \rightarrow (r, \pi, w'', \mathcal{V} \models \varphi) \\
r, \pi, w, \mathcal{V} \models \bigcirc \varphi & \Longleftrightarrow & \exists w' \rhd w.r, \pi, w', \mathcal{V} \models \varphi \\
r, \pi, w, \mathcal{V} \models \varphi \,\mathbf{S}\, \psi & \Longleftrightarrow & \exists w' \prec w.(r, \pi, w', \mathcal{V} \models \psi) \wedge \\
& & \quad \forall w''.w' \prec w'' \preceq w \rightarrow (r, \pi, w'', \mathcal{V} \models \varphi) \\
r, \pi, w, \mathcal{V} \models \mathbf{Y}\, \varphi & \Longleftrightarrow & \exists w' \lhd w.r, \pi, w', \mathcal{V} \models \varphi
\end{array}$$

Fig. 4. Semantics of formulas

at some time t whenever there exists a later time t' such that φ is true in the interval $[t, t')$ and ψ is true at t'.

As explained below, some rules are only valid when formulas are annotated with *non-empty annotations*. A non-empty annotation is either of the form $\bullet$, or t, or an interval as long as it is non-empty, e.g., of the form $[t_1, t_2]$ if $t_1 \preceq t_2$. Therefore, to state such rules, TPTL-DIST also features sequents of the form $\Gamma \vdash \mathsf{a}$, stating that a is a non-empty annotation in the context Γ.

The semantics of annotated formulas is defined as follows ⚙:

$$r, \pi, \mathcal{V} \models \varphi^{\bullet} \Longleftrightarrow r, \pi, 0, \mathcal{V} \models \varphi \qquad r, \pi, \mathcal{V} \models \varphi^{t} \Longleftrightarrow r, \pi, \llbracket t \rrbracket_{\mathcal{V}}, \mathcal{V} \models \varphi$$
$$r, \pi, \mathcal{V} \models \varphi^{[t_1, t_2]} \Longleftrightarrow \forall w. \llbracket t_1 \rrbracket_{\mathcal{V}} \preceq w \preceq \llbracket t_2 \rrbracket_{\mathcal{V}} \rightarrow r, \pi, w, \mathcal{V} \models \varphi$$
and similarly for the other intervals

The semantics of (1) a list of hypotheses Γ of the form $h_1, \ldots, h_n$, (2) a sequent S of the form $\Gamma \vdash \varphi^{\mathsf{a}}$, and (3) a rule R with premises $S_1, \ldots, S_n$ and conclusion S, are defined as follows ⚙:

$$\begin{array}{lll}
r, \pi, \mathcal{V} \models \Gamma & \Longleftrightarrow & \forall i \in [1, n].r, \pi, \mathcal{V} \models h_i \\
r, \pi \models S & \Longleftrightarrow & \forall \mathcal{V}(\Gamma, \mathsf{a}, \varphi).\ r, \pi, \mathcal{V} \models \Gamma \rightarrow r, \pi, \mathcal{V} \models \varphi^{\mathsf{a}} \\
r, \pi \models R & \Longleftrightarrow & r, \pi \models S_1 \rightarrow \cdots \rightarrow r, \pi \models S_n \rightarrow r, \pi \models S
\end{array}$$

A rule r is valid iff $r, \pi \models r$ for all runs r and interpretations π. as further discussed in Sect. 5, the above semantics is formalized in agda, and we have proved that TPTL-DIST's rules presented below are valid.

3.5 Sequent Calculus

We now present an exert of TPTL-DIST's rules. See Appendix B for the full list.

Propositional Logic Rules. The propositional logic rules are all standard ⚙:

$$\frac{\Gamma, \Delta \vdash \mathsf{a}_1}{\Gamma, \bot^{\mathsf{a}_1}, \Delta \vdash \varphi^{\mathsf{a}}} \bot\mathrm{L} \qquad \frac{\Gamma \vdash \varphi^{\mathsf{a}} \quad \Gamma \vdash \psi^{\mathsf{a}}}{\Gamma \vdash \varphi \wedge \psi^{\mathsf{a}}} \wedge\mathrm{R} \qquad \frac{\Gamma, \varphi^{\mathsf{a}}, \psi^{\mathsf{a}}, \Delta \vdash \delta^{\mathsf{a}_1}}{\Gamma, \varphi \wedge \psi^{\mathsf{a}}, \Delta \vdash \delta^{\mathsf{a}_1}} \wedge\mathrm{L}$$

$$\frac{\Gamma \vdash \varphi^{\mathsf{a}}}{\Gamma \vdash \varphi \vee \psi^{\mathsf{a}}} \vee\mathrm{R}_1 \qquad \frac{\Gamma \vdash \psi^{\mathsf{a}}}{\Gamma \vdash \varphi \vee \psi^{\mathsf{a}}} \vee\mathrm{R}_2 \qquad \frac{\Gamma, \varphi^{t}, \Delta \vdash \delta^{\mathsf{a}} \quad \Gamma, \psi^{t}, \Delta \vdash \delta^{\mathsf{a}}}{\Gamma, \varphi \vee \psi^{t}, \Delta \vdash \delta^{\mathsf{a}}} \vee\mathrm{L}$$

$$\frac{\Gamma, \varphi^{t} \vdash \psi^{t}}{\Gamma \vdash \varphi \to \psi^{t}} \to\mathrm{R} \qquad \frac{\Gamma, \Delta \vdash \varphi^{t} \quad \Gamma, \psi^{t}, \Delta \vdash \delta^{\mathsf{a}}}{\Gamma, \varphi \to \psi^{t}, \Delta \vdash \delta^{\mathsf{a}}} \to\mathrm{L} \qquad \frac{}{\Gamma, \varphi^{\mathsf{a}} \vdash \varphi^{\mathsf{a}}} \mathit{var}$$

Note that the disjunction in the $\vee$L rule cannot be annotated with an interval, since the semantics of intervals is a $\forall$, and $\forall$ does not distribute over $\vee$. Similarly, $\to$R cannot be annotated with intervals either.

Non Empty Annotations. Another issue arises with $\bot$L, which would not hold without the premise $\Gamma, \Delta \vdash \mathsf{a}_1$. For example, the instance $\bot^{\mathsf{a}_1} \vdash \bot^{\boldsymbol{\cdot}}$ is semantically false when a_1 is an empty interval because $\bot^{\mathsf{a}_1}$ is vacuously true. TPTL-DIST features the following rules to prove that annotations are non-empty ⚙:

$$\frac{\Gamma \vdash t_1 \sqsubseteq t_2}{\Gamma \vdash [t_1, t_2]} \qquad \frac{\Gamma \vdash t_1 \sqsubset t_2}{\Gamma \vdash [t_1, t_2)} \qquad \frac{\Gamma \vdash t_1 \sqsubset t_2}{\Gamma \vdash (t_1, t_2]} \qquad \frac{\Gamma \vdash t_1 \sqsubset t \quad \Gamma \vdash t \sqsubset t_2}{\Gamma \vdash (t_1, t_2)}$$

$$\frac{}{\Gamma \vdash t} \qquad \frac{}{\Gamma \vdash \boldsymbol{\cdot}}$$

Temporal Logic Rules. We now present the temporal rules, which illustrate key aspects of our calculus, where v_t is a "fresh" variable ⚙:

$$\frac{\Gamma \vdash t \lessdot t_1 \quad \Gamma \vdash \varphi^{t_1}}{\Gamma \vdash \bigcirc \varphi^{t}} \bigcirc\mathrm{R} \qquad \frac{\Gamma \vdash t \sqsubseteq t_1 \quad \Gamma \vdash \psi^{t_1} \quad \Gamma \vdash \varphi^{[t, t_1)}}{\Gamma \vdash \varphi \,\mathbf{U}\, \psi^{t}} \mathbf{U}\mathrm{R}$$

$$\frac{\Gamma, t \lessdot v_t, \varphi^{v_t}, \Delta \vdash \delta^{\mathsf{a}}}{\Gamma, \bigcirc \varphi^{t}, \Delta \vdash \delta^{\mathsf{a}}} \bigcirc\mathrm{L} \qquad \frac{\Gamma, t \sqsubseteq v_t, \psi^{v_t}, \varphi^{[t, v_t)}, \Delta \vdash \delta^{\mathsf{a}}}{\Gamma, \varphi \,\mathbf{U}\, \psi^{t}, \Delta \vdash \delta^{\mathsf{a}}} \mathbf{U}\mathrm{L}$$

The **U**R rule states that for $\varphi \,\mathbf{U}\, \psi$ to be true at time t, there must exist a time t_1 greater than t at which ψ holds, and φ holds between t and t_1. The **U**L rule states that if $\varphi \,\mathbf{U}\, \psi$ is true at time t then there must be a time v_t (a variable) greater than t at which ψ holds, and φ must be true between t and v_t.

Timed Rules. The rules for the comparison and freeze operators are as follows (we only show some of the comparison rules, as they reflect the axioms in Fig. 2) ⚙:

$$\frac{\Gamma, \varphi[v_t\backslash t]^t, \Delta \vdash \psi^{\mathsf{a}}}{\Gamma, v_t \cdot \varphi^t, \Delta \vdash \psi^{\mathsf{a}}}\ \cdot\mathrm{L} \qquad \frac{\Gamma \vdash \varphi[v_t\backslash t]^t}{\Gamma \vdash v_t \cdot \varphi^t}\ \cdot\mathrm{R}$$

$$\frac{}{\Gamma \vdash t_1 \bullet t_2 \equiv t_2 \bullet t_1^{\mathsf{a}}}\ \bullet sym \qquad \frac{}{\Gamma, t_1 \sqsubseteq t_2, \Delta \vdash t_1 \sqsubseteq t_2^{\mathsf{a}}}\ var_{\sqsubseteq}$$

Note that the annotation on the hypothesis $t_1 \sqsubseteq t_2$ of the $var_{\sqsubseteq}$ rule could be any annotation except an empty interval, unless a is also an empty interval.

Furthermore, TPTL-DIST's ()L, [)L, (]L, []L, ()R, [)R, (]R, and []R rules allow instantiating intervals, such as the following ones, where v_t is a fresh variable ⚙:

$$\frac{\Gamma, \varphi^t, \Delta \vdash \psi^{\mathsf{a}} \quad \Gamma, \Delta \vdash t_1 \sqsubseteq t \quad \Gamma, \Delta \vdash t \sqsubseteq t_2}{\Gamma, \varphi^{[t_1,t_2]}, \Delta \vdash \psi^{\mathsf{a}}}\ []\mathrm{L} \qquad \frac{\Gamma, t_1 \sqsubseteq v_t, v_t \sqsubseteq t_2 \vdash \phi^{v_t}}{\Gamma \vdash \phi^{[t_1,t_2]}}\ []\mathrm{R}$$

$$\frac{\Gamma, \varphi^t, \Delta \vdash \psi^{\mathsf{a}} \quad \Gamma, \Delta \vdash t_1 \sqsubseteq t \quad \Gamma, \Delta \vdash t \sqsubset t_2}{\Gamma, \varphi^{[t_1,t_2)}, \Delta \vdash \psi^{\mathsf{a}}}\ [)\mathrm{L} \qquad \frac{\Gamma, t_1 \sqsubseteq v_t, v_t \sqsubset t_2 \vdash \phi^{v_t}}{\Gamma \vdash \phi^{[t_1,t_2)}}\ [)\mathrm{R}$$

Induction. Furthermore, assuming that worlds satisfy the induction axiom in Fig. 2, the following rule holds, assuming that v_t does not occur free in Γ ⚙:

$$\frac{\Gamma, v_t \cdot \varphi^{[\mathbf{0},v_t)} \vdash \varphi^{v_t}}{\Gamma \vdash \varphi^{v_t}}\ ind$$

Note the use of the freeze operator in the induction hypothesis (IH) $v_t \cdot \varphi^{[\mathbf{0},v_t)}$. It is necessary because not only is v_t the time at which φ is stated to hold, but v_t can also occur free in φ. If the IH were $\varphi^{[\mathbf{0},v_t)}$ (without the freeze operator), then we would be assuming that for any time t in $[\mathbf{0}, v_t)$, the formula φ holds at t, but where the variable v_t in φ is still v_t. However, we want the variable v_t to be t too, which the freeze opeator achieves by binding v_t's occurences in φ.

Another naive attempt at stating this induction hypothesis is $\mathbf{Y}\,(\blacksquare v_t \cdot \varphi)^{v_t}$. However, this fails in capturing the induction hypothesis because $\mathbf{Y}$ requires the existence of a world preceding v_t, which might not exist. To state the induction hypothesis in that fashion, TPTL-DIST would need to include an alternative $\mathbf{Y}$ operator, say $\mathbf{Y}_?$, with semantics $\forall w' \lhd w.(r, \pi, w', \mathcal{V} \models \varphi)$. We instead rely on TPTL-DIST's intervals as shown above. Finally, the hypothesis would have to be $\mathbf{Y}_?\,(\blacksquare v_t \cdot \varphi)^{v_t}$ and not $v_t \cdot \mathbf{Y}\,(\blacksquare \varphi)^{v_t}$, which has a different semantics.

Classical Rules. TPTL-DIST features a *lem* rule to make classical reasoning explicit without multiple conclusions ⚙:

$$\frac{}{\Gamma \vdash \varphi \vee \neg\varphi^{\mathsf{a}}}\ lem$$

Derived Rules. Using the above rules, in particular **UR** and **UL**, right and left rules can be derived for $\Box$ and $\Diamond$, and their past, bounded, and strict versions. These rules will in particular be critical in proving properties of real-time systems as illustrated with a simple example in Sect. 3.6. In all the rules below, v_t stands for a "fresh" variable. For example, the following rules hold for $\Box$, the bounded version of $\Diamond$, and $\blacktriangleleft$ ⚙:

$$\frac{\Gamma, t \sqsubseteq v_t \vdash \varphi^{v_t}}{\Gamma \vdash \Box\varphi^t}\ \Box\mathrm{R} \qquad \frac{\Gamma, \varphi^{t_2}, \Delta \vdash \psi^t \quad \Gamma, \Delta \vdash t_1 \sqsubseteq t_2}{\Gamma, \Box\varphi^{t_1}, \Delta \vdash \psi^t}\ \Box\mathrm{L}$$

$$\frac{\Gamma \vdash \varphi^{t_1} \quad \Gamma \vdash t_1 \sqsubset t}{\Gamma \vdash \blacktriangleleft\varphi^t}\ \blacktriangleleft\mathrm{R} \qquad \frac{\Gamma \vdash \varphi^{t_1} \quad \Gamma \vdash t \sqsubseteq t_1 \quad \Gamma \vdash t_1 \sqsubseteq t_0 \bullet t}{\Gamma \vdash \Diamond_{t_0}\varphi^t}\ \Diamond\_\mathrm{R}$$

$$\frac{\Gamma, \varphi^{v_t}, v_t \sqsubset t_1, \Delta \vdash \psi^t}{\Gamma, \blacktriangleleft\varphi^{t_1}, \Delta \vdash \psi^t}\ \blacktriangleleft\mathrm{L} \qquad \frac{\Gamma, \varphi^{v_t}, t_1 \sqsubseteq v_t, v_t \sqsubseteq t_0 \bullet t_1, \Delta \vdash \psi^t}{\Gamma, \Diamond_{t_0}\varphi^{t_1}, \Delta \vdash \psi^t}\ \Diamond\_\mathrm{L}$$

Soundness

Theorem 1. TPTL-DIST *is sound w.r.t. the semantics presented in Sect. 3.3 and Sect. 3.4, i.e., all the rules presented above are valid.*

3.6 Example

Section 3.2 introduced a simple forwarding example, where agents forward the messages they receive in a synchronous network, guaranteeing that any message sent to a single agent is received by all agents by some time bound. As sketched below, TPTL-DIST allows proving the following property (see Sect. C for full details):

Lemma 1. *This following holds in all models* ⚙: $(Eq.\ 1)^t, (Eq.\ 2)^t \vdash Eq.\ 3^t$.

Proof. Assume $(Eq.\ 1)^t$ and $(Eq.\ 2)^t$, agents a, b, and c, and data d, and prove that $\Box(\mathtt{send}(a, d, [b]) \rightarrow \Diamond_{2T}\mathtt{recv}(c, d, b))$ holds at t. By $\Box$R, it is enough to prove that $\Diamond_{2T}\mathtt{recv}(c, d, b)$ holds at some time v_t, assuming $t \sqsubseteq v_t$ and $\mathtt{send}(a, d, [b])^{v_t}$. In particular, from $\mathtt{send}(a, d, [b])^{v_t}$ and $(Eq.\ 1)^t$, using $\Box$L, we get to further assume that $\Diamond_T(b \in [b] \rightarrow \mathtt{recv}(b, d, a))^{v_t}$. Now by $\Diamond_$L, we can refine this assumption to $\mathtt{recv}(b, d, a)^{v_t'}$ for some v_t' such that $v_t \sqsubseteq v_t'$ and $v_t' \sqsubseteq T \bullet v_t$. From $\mathtt{recv}(b, d, a)^{v_t'}$ and $(Eq.\ 2)^t$, using $\Box$L, we get to further assume $\mathtt{send}(b, d, [c])^{v_t'}$. Once again, using $(Eq.\ 1)^t$ and $\Box$L on that hypothesis. we get to assume $\Diamond_T(c \in [c] \rightarrow \mathtt{recv}(c, d, b))^{v_t'}$, and using $\Diamond_$L, we can refine this assumption to $\mathtt{recv}(c, d, b)^{v_t''}$ for some v_t'' such that $v_t' \sqsubseteq v_t''$ and $v_t'' \sqsubseteq T \bullet v_t'$. Finally, we conclude using $\Diamond_$R, from the fact that $v_t \sqsubseteq v_t''$ and $v_t'' \sqsubseteq 2T \bullet v_t$. $\Box$

4 Real-Time Distributed Systems

4.1 The Pistis Real-Time Reliable Broadcast Protocol

Our main use case is the Pistis real-time Byzantine-resilient reliable broadcast protocol [16]. A broadcast protocol allows messages sent by (correct) nodes in a distributed system to be eventually received (or delivered) by the other (correct) nodes when the network conditions are "good enough". We are in particular interested here in scenarios where nodes can be faulty, where faults can range from benign crashes to more critical adversarial attacks. This fault model is called the *Byzantine* fault model [38, Sec.2.2.6], in which faulty nodes behave arbitrarily. We further assume that nodes can be authenticated, usually achieved through digital signatures. All messages are signed by their senders, meaning that correct nodes cannot be impersonated. Many Byzantine-resilient broadcast protocols exist, providing different properties. In particular, Byzantine consistent broadcast [38, Sec.3.10], guarantees that if a correct node broadcasts a message then that message will be delivered by all other correct nodes. This however does not cover the scenario where the broadcasting node is faulty, in which case only some of the other correct nodes might deliver the message. Byzantine reliable broadcast [38, Sec.3.11] further guarantees that a correct node delivers a message iff all correct nodes deliver that message. More precisely, the guarantees provided by a Byzantine reliable broadcast protocol are: *Validity*, i.e., if a correct node broadcasts a message, then every correct node eventually delivers that message; *No duplication*, i.e., every correct node delivers at most one message; *Integrity*, i.e., if a correct node delivers a message with correct sender i, then that message was broadcast by i; *Consistency*, i.e., if two correct nodes i and j deliver a message, then those messages are the same; and *Totality*, i.e., if a correct node delivers a message then every correct node eventually delivers a message.

Many Byzantine reliable broadcast algorithms have been developed, such as Bracha's algorithm [39], which requires $3f+1$ nodes to tolerate up to f Byzantine faults, and makes use of two message transmission phases (often called *echo* and *ready*) to guarantee the above properties. More recently, algorithms have been designed that further guarantee a timeliness property [16,40]. For example, Pistis [16] builds on top of Bracha's algorithm, and further satisfies *Timeliness*, i.e., there exists a known bound Δ such that if a correct node broadcasts a message m at real-time t, then no correct nodes delivers m after $t + \Delta$.

Pistis achieves timeliness thanks to a *proof-of-connectivity* (PoC) mechanism that requires nodes to become passive when not receiving messages in a timely manner and are therefore likely to deliver messages late. Timeliness would be easily achievable in a *synchronous* network where message transmission is bounded, and the bound, here called d, is known to the nodes. Instead, [16] assumes a more realistic *probabilistic synchronous* network, where messages can arrive after the bound d with low probability. Pistis would still satisfy the above properties in a completely *asynchronous* network where message transmission is unbounded. However, frequent delays beyond d would result in the PoC mechanism making too many nodes become passive, resulting in a system shutdown. Probabilistic synchrony, on the other hand, guarantees that system shutdowns are unlikely.

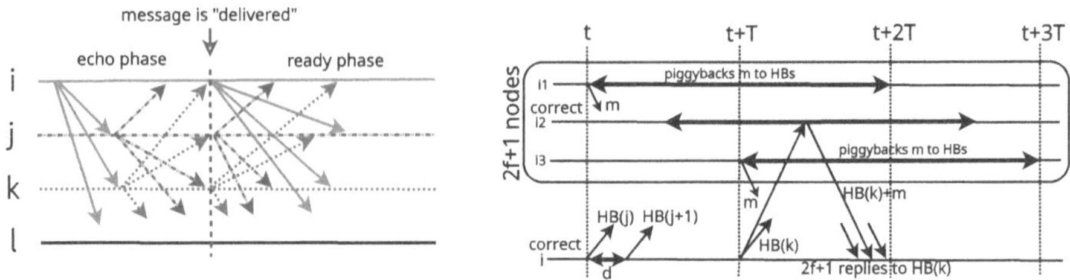

Fig. 5. Pistis: high-level overview (left) & pulling mechanism (right)

Figure 5 illustrates the Pistis protocol with 4 nodes, i.e., at most 1 faulty node. Node i broadcasts a message by sending an echo message to all other nodes, which reply by sending their own echo messages to all other nodes. Nodes that receive $2f+1$ echo messages,[1] including their own, (or a ready message) proceed by sending a ready message to all other nodes. Any node that has not received $2f+1$ echo messages (or one ready message) T units of time after it has sent its echo message becomes passive. Similarly, any node that has not received $2f+1$ ready messages $2T$ units of time after it has sent its ready message becomes passive. We expand on those T and $2T$ bounds below.

We now introduce Pistis in more detail, describing its main functionalities in terms of pushing and pulling messages, leading to a discussion on how it achieves timeliness, while Sect. 4.2 illustrates how to verify real-time properties of distributed systems using TPTL-DIST by proving a property crucial for timeliness.

Pushing. A node that sends a message at time t without receiving $2f+1$ replies by $t+T$, becomes passive. Here, T is a multiple of d, the maximum transmission delay, picked by the system administrator depending on the quality of the network. Assuming synchrony, it would be guaranteed that all messages sent at t are received by correct nodes by $t+d$. However, assuming probabilistic synchrony, we can only derive the weaker *"quorum" synchrony assumption* guaranteeing that if a correct node sends a message at time t, then a "quorum" of $2f+1$ nodes are known to have received it by time $t+T$. This property can be stated as follows, where a "Quorum" is a set of $2f+1$ nodes, $f+1$ of which are therefore correct ⚙:

$$\begin{aligned}&\forall p : \text{Node. correct}(p) \rightarrow \forall m : \text{Msg.}\forall t : \text{Time. } p \text{ sends } m \text{ at } t \rightarrow \\ &\exists Q : \text{Quorum.}\forall q \in Q. \\ &\quad p \text{ receives the acknowledgment within } [t, t+T] \text{ that } q \text{ received } m\end{aligned} \tag{4}$$

Pulling. To guarantee timeliness despite messages arriving late, nodes implement the above PoC mechanism, which sends *heartbeat* messages every d units of time to probe the rest of the system and fetch (or *pull*) broadcast messages. A node that does not receive enough replies to its heartbeats becomes passive, as it risks delivering late. Heartbeats are tagged with unique identifiers, and given

[1] Since there are $3f+1$ nodes, f of which might be faulty, nodes can only expect to receive messages from $2f+1$ nodes.

bounded delivery: $\Box\forall i : \textbf{AGENT}.\forall d : \textbf{DATA}.\texttt{correct}(i) \rightarrow \texttt{internal}(i,d) \rightarrow$
$\exists B : \textbf{AGENTS}.\,\texttt{size}(B, 2f{+}1) \wedge$
$\Diamond_T \blacklozenge \forall j : \textbf{AGENT}.j \in B \rightarrow \texttt{correct}(j) \rightarrow \Diamond_T \texttt{internal}(j,d)$

unbounded delivery: $\Box\forall i : \textbf{AGENT}.\forall d : \textbf{DATA}.\texttt{correct}(i) \rightarrow \texttt{internal}(i,d) \rightarrow$
$\exists B : \textbf{AGENTS}.\,\texttt{size}(B, 2f{+}1) \wedge$
$\forall j : \textbf{AGENT}.j \in B \rightarrow \texttt{correct}(j) \rightarrow \Diamond_T \blacklozenge \texttt{internal}(j,d)$

stay faulty: $\forall i : \textbf{AGENT}.\Box(\texttt{correct}(i) \rightarrow \blacksquare \texttt{correct}(i))$

Fig. 6. Bounded and unbounded delivery in TPTL-DIST

a heartbeat sent by node i, tagged with identifier k, denoted HB(k) in Fig. 5, and sent at time t, $2f{+}1$ replies to HB(k) are expected by $t{+}T$ for i to stay active and therefore correct. PoC guarantees that if a quorum of nodes sends a message within $[t, t{+}T]$, then all correct nodes will receive that message within $[t{+}T, t{+}2T]$, thereby preventing nodes from staying active while not delivering:

$$\begin{array}{l}\forall m : \text{Msg}.\forall t : \text{Time}.\forall Q : \text{Quorum}.(\forall q \in Q.\ q \text{ sends } m \text{ within } [t, t{+}T]) \rightarrow \\ \forall p : \text{Node}.\ \text{correct}(p) \rightarrow p \text{ receives } m \text{ within } [t{+}T, t{+}2T]\end{array} \qquad (5)$$

A simple way to guarantee Eq. 5 is for nodes to reply to heartbeats with the messages they have sent during the last $2T$ time interval. A $2T$ interval is necessary because a node (i_1 in Fig. 5) in Q sending m at t (one end of the $[t, t{+}T]$ interval) piggybacks m to its replies to heartbeats during the interval $[t, t{+}2T]$, while a node (i_3 in Fig. 5) sending m at $t{+}T$ (the other end of the $[t, t{+}T]$ interval) piggybacks m during the interval $[t{+}T, t{+}3T]$, thereby intersecting on the interval $[t{+}T, t{+}2T]$. As Fig. 5 illustrates, these two mechanisms (sending and replying to heartbeats) guarantee that, during the $[t{+}T, t{+}2T]$ interval, correct (non-passive) nodes (i in Fig. 5) obtain messages sent by quorums of nodes. This holds because one correct node (i_2 in Fig. 5) is necessarily at the intersection of the $2f{+}1$ nodes sending replies to HB(k) and the $2f{+}1$ nodes piggybacking m.

Properties. The above components guarantee timeliness, since by prop. 4, if p is correct and broadcasts a message m at time t, then by time $t_d \leq t{+}T$, it receives the acknowledgments that m was received by $2f{+}1$ nodes. It can then start delivering and sending corresponding ready messages. Again by prop. 4, by time $t_d{+}T$, p receives the acknowledgment that this ready message was received by $2f{+}1$ nodes. We then prove by induction on time t_d, that there is a collection B of $2f{+}1$ nodes such that all correct nodes in B started delivering m (and sending corresponding ready messages) during some interval $[t_{d'}, t_{d'}{+}T]$ some time prior to $t_d{+}T$. Therefore, their PoC components will piggyback those ready messages to heartbeats (i.e., to pull requests) during the interval $[t_{d'}{+}T, t_{d'}{+}2T]$. By prop. 5, all correct nodes receive m during that interval.

Therefore, a key point in this proof is that, as captured by *bounded delivery* in Fig. 6 ✿, if a correct node delivers at time t, then there exists a collection B of $2f{+}1$ nodes such that some time t' prior to $t{+}T$, all correct nodes in B have delivered by $t'{+}T$. This follows from the fact that, as captured by the *unbounded delivery* TPTL-DIST formula in Fig. 6, if a correct node delivers at time t, then there exists a collection of $2f+1$ nodes that have delivered some time prior to $t+T$, a consequence of prop. 4. Section 4.2 shows that *unbounded delivery* implies *bounded delivery*, assuming that faulty nodes cannot become correct.

4.2 Proof of Bounded Delivery

We now show how to prove that *bounded delivery* follows from *unbounded delivery* (see Fig. 6), which is key in proving Pistis' timeliness property.

Lemma 2. *The following sequent holds in all models* ⚙:

$$\textit{unbounded delivery}^{\mathbf{0}}, \textit{stay faulty}^{\mathbf{0}} \vdash \textit{bounded delivery}^{\mathbf{0}}$$

Proof. Using $\Box$R, we have to prove *unbounded delivery* $\vdash C^{v_t}$, where v_t is a fresh variable, and C is the formula under the $\Box$ in *bounded delivery*. Using the induction rule from Sect. 3.5, we obtain the additional assumption $v_t \cdot C^{[\mathbf{0},v_t)}$.

We then assume some correct agent i and piece of data d that "happened" at i at time v_t, and have to exhibit a quorum of agents B, such that at some time t before $T \bullet v_t$, d "happened" at all correct agents in B by time $T \bullet t$ (as stated by *bounded delivery*). Instantiating *unbounded delivery* to v_t using $\Box$L, we know that there exists a quorum of agents B, such that d "happened" at all correct agents in B prior to $T \bullet v_t$. Using the classical *lem* rule, we go by cases on whether $\Diamond_T \blacklozenge \forall j : \textbf{AGENT}.j \in B \to \texttt{correct}(j) \to \Diamond_T \texttt{internal}(j, d)$ holds at time v_t, concluding directly if it does.

Let us now assume that the above formula does not hold. Using classical reasoning, we derive that $\Box_T \blacksquare \exists j : \textbf{AGENT}.j \in B \wedge \texttt{correct}(j) \wedge \Box_T \neg \texttt{internal}(j, d)$ holds at v_t. Instantiating both $\Box\_$ and $\blacksquare$ with the current time v_t, we get a correct agent j in B such that $\Box_T \neg \texttt{internal}(j, d)$ holds at v_t (note that the assumption that j is correct is at v_t). From *unbounded delivery*, we also get that $\Diamond_T \blacklozenge \texttt{internal}(j, d)$ holds at v_t. It then follows that $\blacktriangleleft \texttt{internal}(j, d)$ holds at v_t too. Using $\blacktriangleleft$L, it follows that $\texttt{internal}(j, d)$ holds at $v_t' \sqsubset v_t$.

Using [)L, we instantiate the induction hypothesis with v_t', j, and d, and obtain a quorum of agents B' such that $\Diamond_T \blacklozenge \forall j : \textbf{AGENT}.j \in B' \to \texttt{correct}(j) \to \Diamond_T \texttt{internal}(j, d)$ holds at v_t' (we then have to prove that j is correct at $v_t' \sqsubset v_t$, which holds thanks to *stay faulty*). We conclude by instantiating the conclusion with B', and by showing that if $\Diamond_t \blacklozenge A$ holds at $t_1 \sqsubseteq t_2$ then it also holds at t_2. □

5 Conclusion

We have introduced TPTL-DIST, a calculus for verifying time-related properties of fault-tolerant distributed systems, extending TPTL + Past with quantifiers and a general comparison operator, featuring a sequent calculus that relies on intervals to precisely capture timing constraints. TPTL-DIST allows formalizing and verifying non-trivial properties of fault-tolerant algorithms, including one of Pistis' key properties. We now plan on exploring a few directions.

Based on TPTL-DIST, we plan on designing a type system tailored to the unique demands of distributed systems, that would not only allow modeling their properties, but also allow reasoning about running code.

Another direction is to build on the architecture of PRISM to adapt existing model checkers and automated verification techniques to TPTL-DIST. While subsets of TPTL-DIST could be model checked by PRISM, those techniques will need to be adapted to handle TPTL-DIST's freeze and distributed operators.

Finally, all the results discussed above have been formalized in Agda. In particular, we have proved that the rules in Sect. 3.5 are valid according to TPTL-DIST's semantics. Using those proofs, we have started building a verified proof checker for TPTL-DIST in Agda, which opens the door to further automation. In addition, we proved that a large subset of TPTL-DIST has a decidable semantics, which we will integrate in a formally verified automated proof engine.

A Further Examples

In addition to the forwarding (FW) example provided in Sect. 3.2, we further illustrate here aspects of TPTL-DIST through two other simple examples: leader election in a ring (LER) in Sect. A.1, and Byzantine consistent broadcast (BCB) in Sect. A.2. All three examples illustrate how to capture message passing patterns in distributed systems, where agents exchange information by sending/receiving messages. Furthermore, while the LER and BCB examples involve a logical, qualitative notion of time, the FW example involves a physical, quantitative notion of time thanks to formulas of the form $\Diamond_t \varphi$. Finally, the LER example involves a typical inductively proven property, while BCB involves some typical pattern, where agents can only make progress when they have received enough messages from the other agents in the system.

A.1 Leader Election in a Ring

The leader election in a ring problem involves selecting a single leader from a group of agents organized in a ring. Each agent has a unique identifier (id), and the goal is to elect the agent with the highest id. Agents do not have knowledge of the entire ring, and messages can only be passed to the adjacent node according to a fixed (e.g., clockwise) direction. Leader election is crucial for coordination in distributed systems, such as for database replication or time synchronization.

A key property that the algorithm must fulfill is *liveness*, which guarantees that all agents eventually receive the outcome of the election, i.e., the identity of the leader:

$$\forall a : \textsc{Agent}.\exists b, c : \textsc{Agent}.@_0 \Diamond \mathtt{recv}(a, \mathtt{Elected}(c), b) \qquad (6)$$

The @ operator is used to state that a formula is true at a specific point in time: $@_t\varphi :\equiv x \cdot \varphi \wedge x \equiv t$. Both $\mathtt{Propose}(a)$ and $\mathtt{Elected}(a)$ are pieces of data

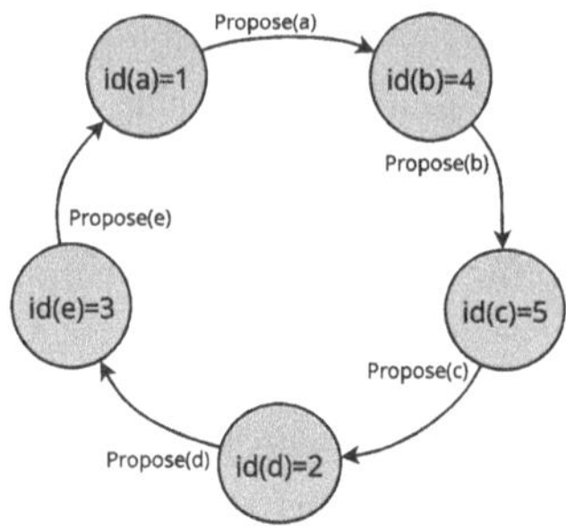

Fig. 7. Leader Election in a Ring

capturing the fact that a was proposed to be the leader, and elected to be the leader, respectively.

We now present a formalization of the classical ring election algorithm [41, 42] in TPTL-DIST. We assume no failures, a synchronous system, a binary predicate $>$ on agents, where $a > b$ captures the fact that a has a higher identifier than b, and a function $\texttt{nhbr} : \textbf{Agent} \to \textbf{Agent}$ returning the neighbour of each agent in the ring.

Initialization: Each agent a suggests itself as the leader, sending its id in a proposal to its neighbour (See Fig. 7):

$$\forall a : \textbf{Agent}.@_0\texttt{send}(a, \texttt{Propose}(a), \{\texttt{nhbr}(a)\}) \tag{7}$$

Proposal Propagation: When an agent a receives an $\texttt{Propose}(c)$ message, it compares c's id to its own id. If c's id is greater than a's, a simply forwards the message to its neighbour, and if c's id is smaller than a's, a forwards its own id to its neighbour:

$$\begin{aligned}\forall a, b, c : \textbf{Agent}.\Box(&\texttt{recv}(a, \texttt{Propose}(c), b) \to \\ &(c > a \to \texttt{send}(a, \texttt{Propose}(c), \{\texttt{nhbr}(a)\}))\wedge \\ &(a > c \to \texttt{send}(a, \texttt{Propose}(a), \{\texttt{nhbr}(a)\})))\end{aligned} \tag{8}$$

Leader Determination: If a receives a proposal containing its own id, it means that a has the highest id. It then sends an $\texttt{Elected}(a)$ message around the ring to announce its election as leader.

$$\forall a, b : \textbf{Agent}.\Box(\texttt{recv}(a, \texttt{Propose}(a), b) \to \texttt{send}(a, \texttt{Elected}(a), \{\texttt{nhbr}(a)\})) \tag{9}$$

Leader Propagation: When an agent a receives an $\texttt{Elected}(b)$ message, it knows that b is the leader, and forwards the message to its neighbour (unless a is b):

$$\begin{aligned}&\forall a, b, c : \textbf{Agent}. \\ &\quad\Box(\texttt{recv}(a, \texttt{Elected}(b), c) \to b > a \to \texttt{send}(a, \texttt{Elected}(b), \{\texttt{nhbr}(a)\}))\end{aligned} \tag{10}$$

The algorithm ends when the leader received an `Elected` message with its own id.

Liveness (election terminates) is proved by induction on time using the following invariant, which states that at time x, if a has not yet received a message informing it that it is the leader (the `leader` operator), then it must be receiving the highest id among its x predecessors in the ring (the `rcvMaxId` operator), where $\texttt{max}(a, x)$ is the agent with the highest id among the x predecessors of a in the ring (it returns a when x is 0):

$$\forall a : \textbf{AGENT}. \bigcirc \square(x \cdot \neg\texttt{leader}(a) \rightarrow \texttt{rcvMaxId}(a, \texttt{max}(a, x))) \tag{11}$$

where

$$\begin{aligned} \texttt{leader}(a) &:\equiv \exists c : \textbf{AGENT}.\blacklozenge\texttt{recv}(a, \texttt{Propose}(a), c) \\ \texttt{rcvMaxId}(a, b) &:\equiv \exists c : \textbf{AGENT}.\texttt{recv}(a, \texttt{Propose}(b), c) \end{aligned}$$

This invariant allows concluding that the election phase terminates after N steps, where N is the number of agents in the ring, with all agents having received the highest agent/leader, including the leader itself. Equation 9 can then be used for the leader to start the final phase and Eq. 10 guarantees that the `Elected` message will go around the ring back to the leader marking the end of the execution of the algorithm.

We further consider that the agents advance in lockstep, meaning that each message takes exactly one unit of time to reach its destination:

$$\forall a, b : \textbf{AGENT}.\forall d : \textbf{DATA}.\square(\texttt{send}(a, d, \{b\}) \rightarrow \bigcirc\texttt{recv}(b, d, a)) \tag{12}$$

Let us now sketch the proof of the above invariant. In the base case where the time $x = 0$, $\texttt{max}(a, x) = a$, which satisfies the invariant, because each agent is assumed to have received a vote for itself at initialization as captured by Eq. 7.

For the induction step, assume the property holds for time x. Then, at time $x+1$, the predecessor of agent a, say b, if not yet the leader, has received $\texttt{max}(b, x)$, which is the agent with the largest id among the x predecessors of b. When b receives this information, it compares its own id with $\texttt{max}(b, x)$. If $b > \texttt{max}(b, x)$ or $b < \texttt{max}(b, x)$, we apply Eq. 8, sending $\texttt{Propose}(b)$ or $\texttt{Propose}(\texttt{max}(b, x))$ to a, respectively. In both cases a receives $\texttt{max}(a, x + 1)$ at time $x + 1$ using Eq. 12.

A.2 The Byzantine Consistent Broadcast

The Byzantine Consistent Broadcast [38, Sec. 3.10] (BCB) is a fundamental broadcast primitive designed for the Byzantine fault model, where faulty agents arbitrarily deviate from their specification, even deliberately trying to prevent an algorithm from achieving its goals. It requires $3f + 1$ agents to tolerate up to f faulty agents.

Every BCB instance has a unique designated sender initiating the broadcast of a message. BCB guarantees the *validity* property, even if the sender is faulty, stating that if a correct agent a broadcasts a message m, then every correct process eventually delivers m. This property is stated as follows in TPTL-DIST, where

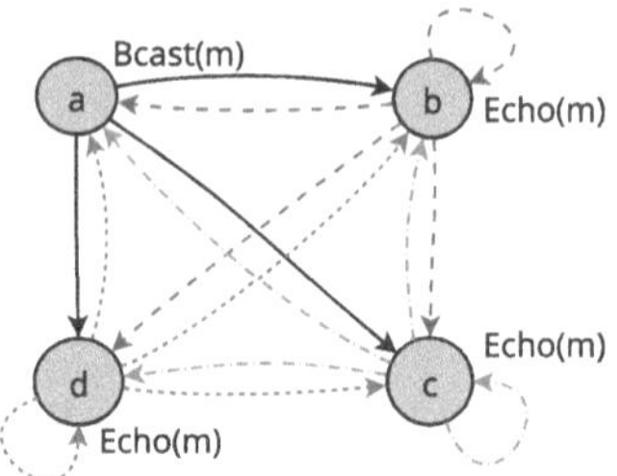

Fig. 8. Byzantine Consistent Broadcast

$\texttt{Bcast}(m), \texttt{Echo}(m), \texttt{Deliver}(m) \in \textbf{Data}$ capture the broadcast, echoing, and delivery of a message m (also a piece of data), respectively:

$$\begin{aligned} &\forall a, b : \textbf{Agent}.\forall m : \textbf{Data}.\texttt{correct}(a) \rightarrow \texttt{correct}(b) \rightarrow \\ &\quad \Box(\texttt{internal}(a, \texttt{Bcast}(m)) \rightarrow \Diamond\texttt{internal}(b, \texttt{Deliver}(m))) \end{aligned} \tag{13}$$

Broadcast: An agent initiates a broadcast through an internal broadcast event of the form $\texttt{internal}(a, \texttt{Bcast}(m))$. When initiating a broadcast, the agent sends a broadcast message to all other agents, where N is the collection of agents in the system:

$$\begin{aligned} &\forall a : \textbf{Agent}.\forall m : \textbf{Data}.\,\texttt{correct}(a) \rightarrow \\ &\quad \Box(\texttt{internal}(a, \texttt{Bcast}(m)) \rightarrow \texttt{send}(a, \texttt{Bcast}(m), N)) \end{aligned} \tag{14}$$

Echo: When an agent receives a broadcast message, it then sends an echo message to all other agents:

$$\begin{aligned} &\forall a, b : \textbf{Agent}.\forall m : \textbf{Data}.\,\texttt{correct}(a) \rightarrow \\ &\quad \Box(\texttt{recv}(a, \texttt{Bcast}(m), b) \rightarrow \texttt{send}(a, \texttt{Echo}(m), b)) \end{aligned} \tag{15}$$

Deliver: Agents deliver on receipt of $2f{+}1$ echoes:

$$\begin{aligned} &\forall a : \textbf{Agent}.\Box(\,\texttt{correct}(a) \rightarrow \\ &\quad \left(\begin{array}{l} \exists B : \textbf{Agents}. \\ \texttt{size}(B, 2f+1)\wedge \\ \forall b : \textbf{Agent}.\,b \in B \rightarrow \\ \qquad \Diamond\texttt{recv}(a, \texttt{Echo}(m), b) \\ \end{array} \right) \rightarrow \\ &\quad \Diamond\texttt{internal}(a, \texttt{Deliver}(m))) \end{aligned} \tag{16}$$

Reliable Communication: We assume reliable communication, i.e., any message sent by a correct agent will eventually be received by all other correct agents:

$$\begin{aligned} &\forall a : \textbf{Agent}.\forall d : \textbf{Data}.\,\forall B : \textbf{Agents}. \\ &\quad \Box(\texttt{correct}(a) \rightarrow \texttt{send}(a, d, B) \rightarrow \\ &\qquad \forall b : \textbf{Agent}.\,b \in B \rightarrow \\ &\qquad\quad \texttt{correct}(b) \rightarrow \Diamond\texttt{recv}(b, d, a)) \end{aligned} \tag{17}$$

Fault Threshold: Finally, we assume that there are at least $2f + 1$ correct agents out of $3f + 1$, where P below is a predicate on agents:

$$\begin{aligned}&\Box(\forall b : \textbf{AGENT}.\texttt{correct}(b) \rightarrow P(b)) \rightarrow \\ &\quad \exists B : \textbf{AGENTS}.\,\texttt{size}(B, 2f+1) \wedge \\ &\qquad \forall b : \textbf{AGENT}.b \in B \rightarrow \texttt{correct}(b) \wedge P(b))\end{aligned} \tag{18}$$

Figure 8 shows a BCB execution, in a system with $3f + 1 = 4$ agents, with at most $f = 1$ Byzantine agent. Agent a broadcasts message m, which is then echoed by all agents (dashed blue lines for b, dashed and dotted green lines for c, and dotted orange lines for d). After received $2f + 1 = 3$ echoes from b, c, d, agent b, for example, delivers.

Let us now sketch a proof of the validity property. Assume correct agents a and b such that a initiates a broadcast of m, i.e., $\texttt{internal}(a, \texttt{Bcast}(m))$ holds. We need to prove that b eventually delivers m, i.e., $\Diamond\texttt{internal}(b, \texttt{Deliver}(m))$. By Eq. 14, a also sends $\texttt{Bcast}(m)$ to all agents in N. By Eq. 17, all correct agents in N receive $\texttt{Bcast}(m)$ and by Eq. 15 they send $\texttt{Echo}(m)$ messages to all other agents in N, including b. Therefore, by Eq. 17, b will receive $\texttt{Echo}(m)$ from all correct agents. Finally, by Eq. 16 and Eq. 18, agent b delivers m.

B Full Set of Rules

Propositional Logic. TPTL-DIST's propositional logic rules are as follows:

$$\frac{\Gamma, \Delta \vdash \mathsf{a}_1}{\Gamma, \bot^{\mathsf{a}_1}, \Delta \vdash \varphi^{\mathsf{a}}}\ \bot\text{L} \qquad \frac{\Gamma \vdash \varphi^{\mathsf{a}} \quad \Gamma \vdash \psi^{\mathsf{a}}}{\Gamma \vdash \varphi \wedge \psi^{\mathsf{a}}}\ \wedge\text{R} \qquad \frac{\Gamma, \varphi^{\mathsf{a}}, \psi^{\mathsf{a}}, \Delta \vdash \delta^{\mathsf{a}_1}}{\Gamma, \varphi \wedge \psi^{\mathsf{a}}, \Delta \vdash \delta^{\mathsf{a}_1}}\ \wedge\text{L}$$

$$\frac{\Gamma \vdash \varphi^{\mathsf{a}}}{\Gamma \vdash \varphi \vee \psi^{\mathsf{a}}}\ \vee\text{R}_1 \qquad \frac{\Gamma \vdash \psi^{\mathsf{a}}}{\Gamma \vdash \varphi \vee \psi^{\mathsf{a}}}\ \vee\text{R}_2 \qquad \frac{\Gamma, \varphi^{t}, \Delta \vdash \delta^{\mathsf{a}} \quad \Gamma, \psi^{t}, \Delta \vdash \delta^{\mathsf{a}}}{\Gamma, \varphi \vee \psi^{t}, \Delta \vdash \delta^{\mathsf{a}}}\ \vee\text{L}$$

$$\frac{}{\Gamma \vdash \top^{\mathsf{a}}}\ \top\text{R} \qquad \frac{\Gamma, \varphi^{t} \vdash \psi^{t}}{\Gamma \vdash \varphi \rightarrow \psi^{t}}\ \rightarrow\text{R} \qquad \frac{\Gamma, \Delta \vdash \varphi^{t} \quad \Gamma, \psi^{t}, \Delta \vdash \delta^{\mathsf{a}}}{\Gamma, \varphi \rightarrow \psi^{t}, \Delta \vdash \delta^{\mathsf{a}}}\ \rightarrow\text{L}$$

TPTL-DIST also includes the following rules. We often make silent use of the *cut* rule to duplicate an hypothesis whenever using a "left" (or elimination) rule on that hypothesis if we wish to retain it because TPTL-DIST's "left" rules discard the formulas being eliminated.

$$\frac{\Gamma, \Delta \vdash \varphi^{\mathsf{a}}}{\Gamma, \psi^{\mathsf{a}_1}, \Delta \vdash \varphi^{\mathsf{a}}}\ \textit{thin} \qquad \frac{\Gamma \vdash \psi^{\mathsf{a}_1} \quad \Gamma, \psi^{\mathsf{a}_1} \vdash \varphi^{\mathsf{a}}}{\Gamma \vdash \varphi^{\mathsf{a}}}\ \textit{cut}$$

$$\frac{}{\Gamma, \varphi^{\mathsf{a}} \vdash \varphi^{\mathsf{a}}}\ \textit{var} \qquad \frac{}{\Gamma \vdash i \in [\ldots, i, \ldots]^{\mathsf{a}}}\ \in\text{R}$$

Non-Empty Annotations

$$\frac{}{\Gamma \vdash \centerdot} \qquad \frac{\Gamma \vdash t_1 \sqsubseteq t_2}{\Gamma \vdash [t_1, t_2]} \qquad \frac{\Gamma \vdash t_1 \sqsubset t_2}{\Gamma \vdash [t_1, t_2)}$$

$$\frac{}{\Gamma \vdash t} \qquad \frac{\Gamma \vdash t_1 \sqsubset t_2}{\Gamma \vdash (t_1, t_2]} \qquad \frac{\Gamma \vdash t_1 \sqsubset t \quad \Gamma \vdash t \sqsubset t_2}{\Gamma \vdash (t_1, t_2)}$$

Temporal Logic Rules. In the following rules v_t is a "fresh" variable:

$$\frac{\Gamma \vdash t \lhd t_1 \quad \Gamma \vdash \varphi^{t_1}}{\Gamma \vdash \bigcirc \varphi^t} \bigcirc\text{R} \qquad \frac{\Gamma \vdash t \sqsubseteq t_1 \quad \Gamma \vdash \psi^{t_1} \quad \Gamma \vdash \varphi^{[t,t_1)}}{\Gamma \vdash \varphi \,\mathbf{U}\, \psi^t} \mathbf{UR}$$

$$\frac{\Gamma, t \lhd v_t, \varphi^{v_t}, \Delta \vdash \delta^{\mathsf{a}}}{\Gamma, \bigcirc \varphi^t, \Delta \vdash \delta^{\mathsf{a}}} \bigcirc\text{L} \qquad \frac{\Gamma, t \sqsubseteq v_t, \psi^{v_t}, \varphi^{[t,v_t)}, \Delta \vdash \delta^{\mathsf{a}}}{\Gamma, \varphi \,\mathbf{U}\, \psi^t, \Delta \vdash \delta^{\mathsf{a}}} \text{UL}$$

$$\frac{\Gamma \vdash t_1 \lhd t \quad \Gamma \vdash \varphi^{t_1}}{\Gamma \vdash \mathbf{Y}\, \varphi^t} \mathbf{YR} \qquad \frac{\Gamma \vdash t_1 \sqsubseteq t \quad \Gamma \vdash \psi^{t_1} \quad \Gamma \vdash \varphi^{[t_1,t)}}{\Gamma \vdash \varphi \,\mathbf{S}\, \psi^t} \text{SR}$$

$$\frac{\Gamma, v_t \lhd t, \varphi^{v_t}, \Delta \vdash \delta^{\mathsf{a}}}{\Gamma, \mathbf{Y}\, \varphi^t, \Delta \vdash \delta^{\mathsf{a}}} \mathbf{YL} \qquad \frac{\Gamma, v_t \sqsubseteq t, \psi^{v_t}, \varphi^{(v_t,t]}, \Delta \vdash \delta^{\mathsf{a}}}{\Gamma, \varphi \,\mathbf{S}\, \psi^t, \Delta \vdash \delta^{\mathsf{a}}} \text{SL}$$

Timed Rules. The rules for the comparison and freeze operators are shown below. We only show some of the comparison rules, as they reflect the axioms in Fig. 2. Furthermore, TPTL-DIST's ()L, [)L, (]L, []L, ()R, [)R, (]R, and []R rules allow instantiating intervals, some of which are shown below (the others are of the same form).

$$\frac{}{\Gamma, t_1 \sqsubseteq t_2, \Delta \vdash t_1 \sqsubseteq t_2^{\mathsf{a}}} var_{\sqsubseteq} \qquad \frac{\Gamma \vdash \varphi[v_t \backslash t]^t}{\Gamma \vdash v_t \cdot \varphi^t} \cdot\text{R}$$

$$\frac{}{\Gamma \vdash t_1 \bullet t_2 \equiv t_2 \bullet t_1^{\mathsf{a}}} \bullet sym \qquad \frac{\Gamma, \varphi[v_t \backslash t]^t, \Delta \vdash \psi^{\mathsf{a}}}{\Gamma, v_t \cdot \varphi^t, \Delta \vdash \psi^{\mathsf{a}}} \cdot\text{L}$$

$$\frac{\Gamma, \varphi^t, \Delta \vdash \psi^{\mathsf{a}} \quad \Gamma, \Delta \vdash t_1 \sqsubseteq t \quad \Gamma, \Delta \vdash t \sqsubseteq t_2}{\Gamma, \varphi^{[t_1,t_2]}, \Delta \vdash \psi^{\mathsf{a}}} []\text{L}$$

$$\frac{\Gamma, t_1 \sqsubseteq v_t, v_t \sqsubseteq t_2 \vdash \phi^{v_t}}{\Gamma \vdash \phi^{[t_1,t_2]}} []\text{R}$$

Predicate Logic Rules. The predicate rules are as follows, where v' is a "fresh" variable and X is a term of type T:

$$\frac{\Gamma \vdash \varphi[v \backslash v']^{\mathsf{a}}}{\Gamma \vdash \forall v : T.\varphi^{\mathsf{a}}} \forall\text{R} \qquad \frac{\Gamma, \varphi[v \backslash X]^{\mathsf{a}_1}, \Delta \vdash \psi^{\mathsf{a}}}{\Gamma, \forall v : T.\varphi^{\mathsf{a}_1}, \Delta \vdash \psi^{\mathsf{a}}} \forall\text{L}$$

$$\frac{\Gamma \vdash \varphi[v \backslash X]^{\mathsf{a}}}{\Gamma \vdash \exists v : T.\varphi^{\mathsf{a}}} \exists\text{R} \qquad \frac{\Gamma, \varphi[v \backslash v']^t, \Delta \vdash \psi^{\mathsf{a}}}{\Gamma, \exists v : T.\varphi^t, \Delta \vdash \psi^{\mathsf{a}}} \exists\text{L}$$

Induction. The induction rule is as follows, where v_t does not occur free in Γ:

$$\frac{\Gamma, v_t \cdot \varphi^{[\mathbf{0},v_t)} \vdash \varphi^{v_t}}{\Gamma \vdash \varphi^{v_t}} ind$$

Classical Rules

$$\frac{}{\Gamma \vdash \varphi \vee \neg\varphi^{\mathsf{a}}} lem$$

Derived Rules. In all the rules below, v_t stands for a "fresh" variable.

$$\frac{\Gamma \vdash \varphi^{t_1} \quad \Gamma \vdash t \sqsubseteq t_1}{\Gamma \vdash \Diamond\varphi^t} \Diamond\mathrm{R} \qquad \frac{\Gamma, \varphi^{v_t}, t_1 \sqsubseteq v_t, \Delta \vdash \psi^t}{\Gamma, \Diamond\varphi^{t_1}, \Delta \vdash \psi^t} \Diamond\mathrm{L}$$

$$\frac{\Gamma, t \sqsubseteq v_t \vdash \varphi^{v_t}}{\Gamma \vdash \Box\varphi^t} \Box\mathrm{R} \qquad \frac{\Gamma, \varphi^{t_2}, \Delta \vdash \psi^t \quad \Gamma, \Delta \vdash t_1 \sqsubseteq t_2}{\Gamma, \Box\varphi^{t_1}, \Delta \vdash \psi^t} \Box\mathrm{L}$$

$$\frac{\Gamma \vdash \varphi^{t_1} \quad \Gamma \vdash t \sqsubseteq t_1 \quad \Gamma \vdash t_1 \sqsubseteq t_0 \bullet t}{\Gamma \vdash \Diamond_{t_0}\varphi^t} \Diamond\_\mathrm{R}$$

$$\frac{\Gamma, \varphi^{v_t}, t_1 \sqsubseteq v_t, v_t \sqsubseteq t_0 \bullet t_1, \Delta \vdash \psi^t}{\Gamma, \Diamond_{t_0}\varphi^{t_1}, \Delta \vdash \psi^t} \Diamond\_\mathrm{L}$$

$$\frac{\Gamma, t \sqsubseteq v_t, v_t \sqsubseteq t_0 \bullet t \vdash \varphi^t}{\Gamma \vdash \Box_{t_0}\varphi^t} \Box\_\mathrm{R}$$

$$\frac{\Gamma, \varphi^{t_2}, \Delta \vdash \psi^t \quad \Gamma, \Delta \vdash t_1 \sqsubseteq t_2 \quad \Gamma, \Delta \vdash t_2 \sqsubseteq t_0 \bullet t_1}{\Gamma, \Box_{t_0}\varphi^{t_1}, \Delta \vdash \psi^t} \Box\_\mathrm{L}$$

$$\frac{\Gamma \vdash \varphi^{t_1} \quad \Gamma \vdash t_1 \sqsubseteq t}{\Gamma \vdash \blacklozenge\varphi^t} \blacklozenge\mathrm{R} \qquad \frac{\Gamma, \varphi^{v_t}, v_t \sqsubseteq t_1, \Delta \vdash \psi^t}{\Gamma, \blacklozenge\varphi^{t_1}, \Delta \vdash \psi^t} \blacklozenge\mathrm{L}$$

$$\frac{\Gamma, v_t \sqsubseteq t \vdash \varphi^{v_t}}{\Gamma \vdash \blacksquare\varphi^t} \blacksquare\mathrm{R} \qquad \frac{\Gamma, \varphi^{t_2}, \Delta \vdash \psi^t \quad \Gamma, \Delta \vdash t_2 \sqsubseteq t_1}{\Gamma, \blacksquare\varphi^{t_1}, \Delta \vdash \psi^t} \blacksquare\mathrm{L}$$

$$\frac{\Gamma \vdash \varphi^{t_1} \quad \Gamma \vdash t_1 \sqsubset t}{\Gamma \vdash \blacktriangleleft\varphi^t} \blacktriangleleft\mathrm{R} \qquad \frac{\Gamma, \varphi^{v_t}, v_t \sqsubset t_1, \Delta \vdash \psi^t}{\Gamma, \blacktriangleleft\varphi^{t_1}, \Delta \vdash \psi^t} \blacktriangleleft\mathrm{L}$$

C Proof of Eq. 3

This section presents a fully worked out proof of eq. 3, a sketch of which was presented in Sect. 3.6.

Let

$$\begin{aligned}
\Gamma_0 &:\equiv (Eq.\ 1)^t, (Eq.\ 2)^t \\
\Gamma_1 &:\equiv \Gamma_0, t \sqsubseteq v_t, \mathtt{send}(a, d, [b])^{v_t}, \mathtt{recv}(b, d, a)^{v'_t}, v_t \sqsubseteq v'_t, v'_t \sqsubseteq T \bullet v_t \\
\Gamma_2 &:\equiv \Gamma_1, \mathtt{send}(b, d, [c])^{v'_t} \\
\Gamma_3 &:\equiv \Gamma_2, \mathtt{recv}(c, d, b)^{v''_t}, v'_t \sqsubseteq v''_t, v''_t \sqsubseteq T \bullet v'_t
\end{aligned}$$

To prove $\Gamma_0 \vdash Eq.\ 3^t$, we start with a few introductions to in particular get the assumption that $\mathtt{send}(a, d, [b])^{v_t}$:

$$\cfrac{\cfrac{\cfrac{\Gamma_0, t \sqsubseteq v_t, \mathtt{send}(a, d, [b])^{v_t} \vdash \Diamond_{2T}\mathtt{recv}(c, d, b)^{v_t}}{\Gamma_0, t \sqsubseteq v_t \vdash \mathtt{send}(a, d, [b]) \to \Diamond_{2T}\mathtt{recv}(c, d, b)^{v_t}} \to\mathrm{R}}{\Gamma_0 \vdash \Box(\mathtt{send}(a, d, [b]) \to \Diamond_{2T}\mathtt{recv}(c, d, b))^t} \Box\mathrm{R}}{\Gamma_0 \vdash Eq.\ 3^t} \forall\mathrm{R}(\times 4)$$

We now instantiate Eq. 1 to, in particular, get the assumption $\mathtt{recv}(b, d, a)^{v'_t}$:

$$\dfrac{\dfrac{\dfrac{\dfrac{\Gamma_1 \vdash \Diamond_{2T}\mathtt{recv}(c,d,b)^{v_t}}{\Gamma_0, t \sqsubseteq v_t, \mathtt{send}(a,d,[b])^{v_t}, \phi_3^{v_t'}, v_t \sqsubseteq v_t', v_t' \sqsubseteq T \bullet v_t \vdash \Diamond_{2T}\mathtt{recv}(c,d,b)^{v_t}}\;{\to}\mathrm{L}\ \&\ {\in}\mathrm{R}}{\Gamma_0, t \sqsubseteq v_t, \mathtt{send}(a,d,[b])^{v_t}, \phi_2^{v_t} \vdash \Diamond_{2T}\mathtt{recv}(c,d,b)^{v_t}}\;\Diamond\_\mathrm{L}}{\Gamma_0, t \sqsubseteq v_t, \mathtt{send}(a,d,[b])^{v_t}, \phi_1^{v_t} \vdash \Diamond_{2T}\mathtt{recv}(c,d,b)^{v_t}}\;{\to}\mathrm{L}\ \&\ var}{\Gamma_0, t \sqsubseteq v_t, \mathtt{send}(a,d,[b])^{v_t} \vdash \Diamond_{2T}\mathtt{recv}(c,d,b)^{v_t}}\;\forall\mathrm{L}(\times 4)\ \&\ \Box\mathrm{L}\ \&\ var_{\sqsubseteq}$$

where

$$\phi_1 \coloneqq \mathtt{send}(a,d,[b]) \to \phi_2$$
$$\phi_2 \coloneqq \Diamond_T(\phi_3)$$
$$\phi_3 \coloneqq b \in [b] \to \mathtt{recv}(b,d,a)$$

We instantiate Eq. 2 to, in particular, get the assumption $\mathtt{send}(b,d,[c])^{v_t'}$:

$$\dfrac{\dfrac{\Gamma_2 \vdash \Diamond_{2T}\mathtt{recv}(c,d,b)^{v_t}}{\Gamma_1, \phi_4^{v_t'} \vdash \Diamond_{2T}\mathtt{recv}(c,d,b)^{v_t}}\;{\to}\mathrm{L}\ \&\ var \qquad \dfrac{}{\Gamma_1 \vdash t \sqsubseteq v_t'^{v_t}}\;{\sqsubseteq}trans\ \&\ var_{\sqsubseteq}}{\Gamma_1 \vdash \Diamond_{2T}\mathtt{recv}(c,d,b)^{v_t}}\;\forall\mathrm{L}(\times 4)\ \&\ \Box\mathrm{L}$$

where

$$\phi_4 \coloneqq \mathtt{recv}(b,d,a) \to \mathtt{send}(b,d,[c])$$

We instantiate Eq. 1 once more, to in particular get the assumption $\mathtt{recv}(c,d,b)^{v_t''}$:

$$\dfrac{\dfrac{\dfrac{\dfrac{\Gamma_3 \vdash \Diamond_{2T}\mathtt{recv}(c,d,b)^{v_t}}{\Gamma_2, \phi_7^{v_t''}, v_t' \sqsubseteq v_t'', v_t'' \sqsubseteq T \bullet v_t' \vdash \Diamond_{2T}\mathtt{recv}(c,d,b)^{v_t}}\;{\to}\mathrm{L}\ \&\ {\in}\mathrm{R}}{\Gamma_2, \phi_6^{v_t'} \vdash \Diamond_{2T}\mathtt{recv}(c,d,b)^{v_t}}\;\Diamond\_\mathrm{L}}{\Gamma_2, \phi_5^{v_t'} \vdash \Diamond_{2T}\mathtt{recv}(c,d,b)^{v_t}}\;{\to}\mathrm{L}\ \&\ var \qquad \dfrac{}{\Gamma_1 \vdash t \sqsubseteq v_t'^{v_t}}\;{\sqsubseteq}trans\ \&\ var_{\sqsubseteq}}{\Gamma_2 \vdash \Diamond_{2T}\mathtt{recv}(c,d,b)^{v_t}}\;\forall\mathrm{L}(\times 4)\ \&\ \Box\mathrm{L}$$

where

$$\phi_5 \coloneqq \mathtt{send}(b,d,[c]) \to \phi_6$$
$$\phi_6 \coloneqq \Diamond_T(\phi_7)$$
$$\phi_7 \coloneqq c \in [c] \to \mathtt{recv}(c,d,b)$$

We finally conclude using in particular the derived rule $\Diamond\_\mathrm{R}$, where $\Gamma_3 \vdash v_t'' \sqsubseteq 2T \bullet v_t^{v_t}$ is trivial but tedious to prove using among other rules, $\sqsubseteq trans$, $\bullet$assoc, and $var_{\sqsubseteq}$:

$$\dfrac{\dfrac{}{\Gamma_3 \vdash v_t \sqsubseteq v_t''^{v_t}}\;{\sqsubseteq}trans\ \&\ var_{\sqsubseteq} \qquad \dfrac{}{\Gamma_3 \vdash v_t'' \sqsubseteq 2T \bullet v_t^{v_t}}}{\Gamma_3 \vdash \Diamond_{2T}\mathtt{recv}(c,d,b)^{v_t}}\;\Diamond\_\mathrm{R}$$

References

1. Alur, R., Henzinger, T.A.: A really temporal logic. J. ACM **41**(1), 181–203 (1994)
2. Baier, C., Katoen, J.: Principles of Model Checking. MIT Press, Cambridge (2008)
3. Kwiatkowska, M., Norman, G., Parker, D.: PRISM 4.0: verification of probabilistic real-time systems. In: Gopalakrishnan, G., Qadeer, S. (eds.) CAV 2011. LNCS, vol. 6806, pp. 585–591. Springer, Heidelberg (2011). https://doi.org/10.1007/978-3-642-22110-1_47
4. Lamport, L.: Specifying Systems: The TLA+ Language and Tools for Hardware and Software Engineers. Addison-Wesley, Boston (2003)
5. Lamport, L.: Real time is really simple. Technical report, MSR-TR-2005-30, p. 72 (2005)
6. Cousineau, D., Doligez, D., Lamport, L., Merz, S., Ricketts, D., Vanzetto, H.: TLA+ Proofs. arXiv: 1208.5933 [cs.SE] (2012)
7. Norman, G., Parker, D., Zou, X.: Verification and control of partially observable probabilistic real-time systems. In: Sankaranarayanan, S., Vicario, E. (eds.) FORMATS 2015. LNCS, vol. 9268, pp. 240–255. Springer, Cham (2015). https://doi.org/10.1007/978-3-319-22975-1_16
8. Oxford, M., Parker, D., Ryan, M.: Quantitative verification of certificate transparency gossip protocols. In: 8th IEEE Conference on Communications and Network Security, CNS 2020, Avignon, France, 29 June–1 July 2020, pp. 1–9. IEEE (2020)
9. Lu, T., Merz, S., Weidenbach, C.: Towards verification of the pastry protocol using TLA^+, pp. 244–258 (2011)
10. Joshi, R., Lamport, L., Matthews, J., Tasiran, S., Tuttle, M.R., Yu, Y.: Checking cache-coherence protocols with TLA^+. Formal Methods Syst. Design **22**(2), 125–131 (2003)
11. Bolosky, W.J., Douceur, J.R., Howell, J.: The Farsite project: a retrospective. Oper. Syst. Rev. **41**(2), 17–26 (2007)
12. Newcombe, C.: Why Amazon chose TLA +, pp. 25–39 (2014)
13. Newcombe, C., Rath, T., Zhang, F., Munteanu, B., Brooker, M., Deardeuff, M.: How Amazon web services uses formal methods. Commun. ACM **58**(4), 66–73 (2015)
14. Chand, S., Liu, Y.A., Stoller, S.D.: Formal verification of multi-paxos for distributed consensus. In: FM 2016: Formal Methods - 21st International Symposium, vol. 9995, pp. 119–136 (2016)
15. Gao, S., et al.: Formal verification of consensus in the taurus distributed database. In: Formal Methods, pp. 741–751 (2021)
16. Kozhaya, D., Decouchant, J., Rahli, V., Veríssimo, P.E.: PISTIS: an event-triggered real-time byzantine-resilient protocol suite. IEEE Trans. Parallel Distrib. Syst. **32**(9), 2277–2290 (2021)
17. Volpe, M.: Labeled natural deduction for temporal logics. Ph.D. thesis. University of Verona, Italy (2010)
18. Kopetz, H.: Real-Time Systems: Design Principles for Distributed Embedded Applications, 1st edn. Kluwer Academic Publishers, USA (1997)
19. Kopetz, H.: Why a global time is needed in a dependable SoS. In: CoRR abs/1404.6772 (2014). arXiv: 1404.6772
20. Hansson, H., Jonsson, B.: A logic for reasoning about time and reliability. Formal Aspects Comput. **6**(5), 512–535 (1994)

21. Bianco, A., de Alfaro, L.: Model checking of probabilistic and nondeterministic systems. In: Thiagarajan, P.S. (ed.) FSTTCS 1995. LNCS, vol. 1026, pp. 499–513. Springer, Heidelberg (1995). https://doi.org/10.1007/3-540-60692-0_70
22. Aziz, A., Sanwal, K., Singhal, V., Brayton, R.: Verifying continuous time Markov chains. In: Alur, R., Henzinger, T.A. (eds.) CAV 1996. LNCS, vol. 1102, pp. 269–276. Springer, Heidelberg (1996). https://doi.org/10.1007/3-540-61474-5_75
23. Baier, C., Katoen, J.-P., Hermanns, H.: Approximative symbolic model checking of continuous-time Markov chains. In: Baeten, J.C.M., Mauw, S. (eds.) CONCUR 1999. LNCS, vol. 1664, pp. 146–161. Springer, Heidelberg (1999). https://doi.org/10.1007/3-540-48320-9_12
24. Bozzelli, L., Murano, A., Sorrentino, L.: Alternating-time temporal logics with linear past. Theoret. Comput. Sci. **813**, 199–217 (2020)
25. Fagin, R., Halpern, J.Y., Moses, Y., Vardi, M.E.: Reasoning About Knowledge. MIT Press, Cambridge (1995)
26. Wehrung, F.: Injective positively ordered monoids I. J. Pure Appl. Algebra **83**(1), 43–82 (1992)
27. Fritz, T.: Resource convertibility and ordered commutative monoids. Math. Struct. Comput. Sci. **27**(6), 850–938 (2017)
28. Kuznets, R., Prosperi, L., Schmid, U., Fruzsa, K.: Epistemic reasoning with byzantine-faulty agents. In: Herzig, A., Popescu, A. (eds.) FroCoS 2019. LNCS (LNAI), vol. 11715, pp. 259–276. Springer, Cham (2019). https://doi.org/10.1007/978-3-030-29007-8_15
29. Baltag, A., Renne, B., Smets, S.: The logic of justified belief, explicit knowledge, and conclusive evidence. Ann. Pure Appl. Logic **165**(1), 49–81 (2014)
30. Baltag, A., Moss, L.S., Solecki, S.: The logic of public announcements, common knowledge, and private suspicions (extended abstract) (2016)
31. Bolotov, A., Basukoski, A., Grigoriev, O., Shangin, V.: Natural deduction calculus for linear-time temporal logic. In: Fisher, M., van der Hoek, W., Konev, B., Lisitsa, A. (eds.) JELIA 2006. LNCS (LNAI), vol. 4160, pp. 56–68. Springer, Heidelberg (2006). https://doi.org/10.1007/11853886_7
32. Bolotov, A., Grigoriev, O., Shangin, V.: Automated natural deduction for propositional linear-time temporal logic. In: 14th International Symposium on Temporal Representation and Reasoning (TIME 2007), pp. 47–58 (2007)
33. Masini, A., Viganò, L., Volpe, M.: A history of until. Electron. Notes Theor. Comput. Sci. **262**, 189–204 (2010)
34. Gabbay, D.M.: Labelled Deductive Systems. Clarendon Press (1996)
35. Simpson, A.K.: The proof theory and semantics of intuitionistic modal logic. Ph.D. thesis, University of Edinburgh, UK (1994)
36. Basin, D., Caleiro, C., Ramos, J., Viganò, L.: Labelled tableaux for distributed temporal logic. J. Log. Comput. **19**(6), 1245–1279 (2009). eprint: https://academic.oup.com/logcom/article-pdf/19/6/1245/2805892/exp022.pdf
37. Viganò, L., Volpe, M.: Labeled natural deduction systems for a family of tense logics. arXiv: 0803.3187 [cs.LO] (2008)
38. Cachin, C., Guerraoui, R., Rodrigues, L.: Introduction to Reliable and Secure Distributed Programming. Springer, Heidelberg (2011)
39. Bracha, G.: Asynchronous Byzantine Agreement Protocols. Inf. Comput. **75**(2), 130–143 (1987)
40. Kozhaya, D., Decouchant, J., Esteves-Verissimo, P.: RT-ByzCast: byzantine-resilient real-time reliable broadcast. IEEE Trans. Comput. **68**(3), 440–454 (2019)

41. Lann, G.L.: Distributed systems - towards a formal approach. In: Information Processing, Proceedings of the 7th IFIP Congress 1977, Toronto, Canada, 8–12 August 1977, pp. 155–160. North-Holland (1977)
42. Chang, E.J.H., Roberts, R.: An improved algorithm for decentralized extrema-finding in circular configurations of processes. Commun. ACM **22**(5), 281–283 (1979)

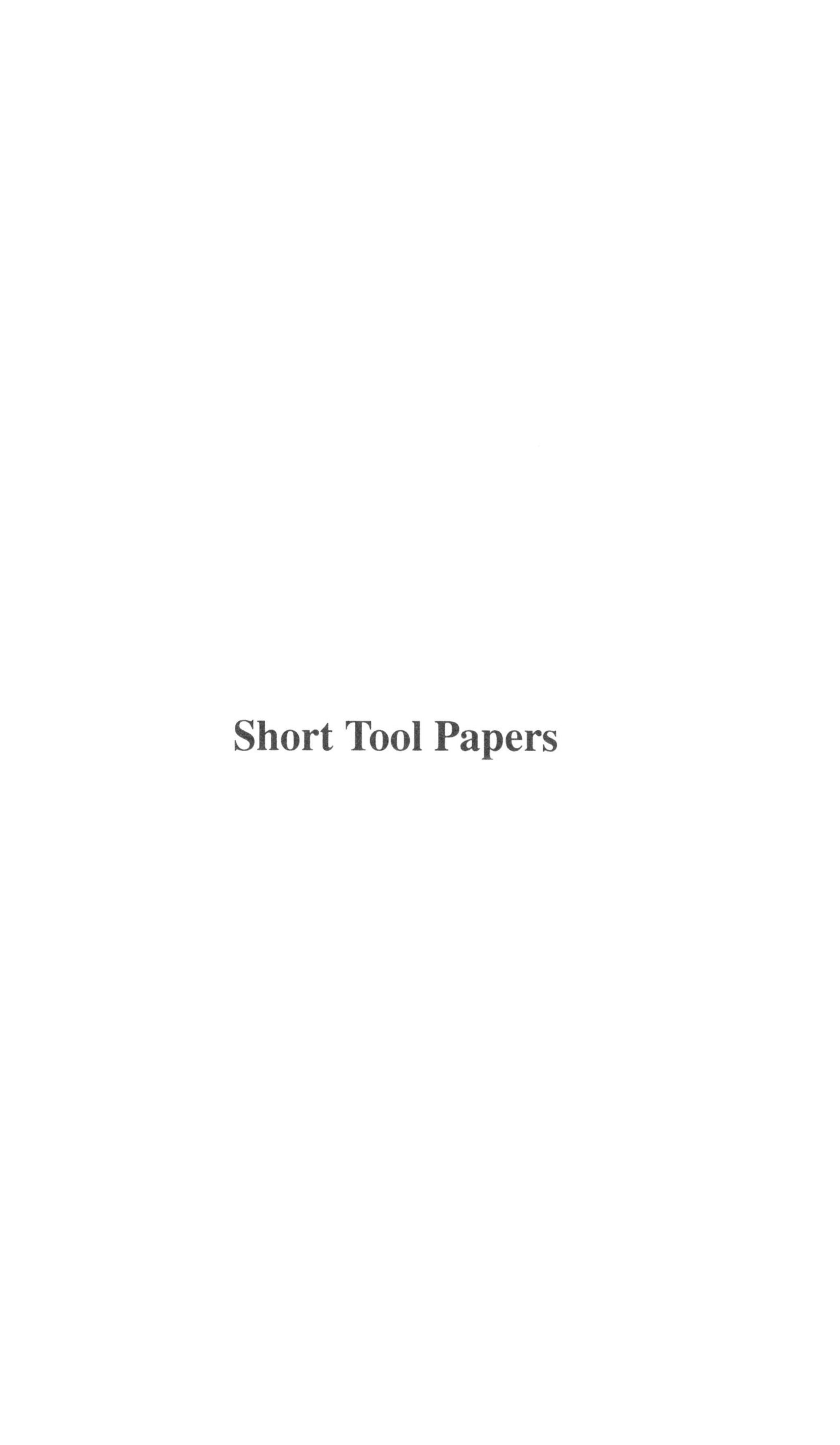

Short Tool Papers

Robustness Against Time Distortions in STARK

Julian de Jong[1], Valentina Castiglioni[1(✉)], and Simone Tini[2]

[1] Eindhoven University of Technology, Eindhoven, The Netherlands
v.castiglioni@tue.nl

[2] University of Insubria, Como, Italy

Abstract. STARK is a tool for the analysis of the robustness of dynamical systems operating under uncertainty. Robustness is expressed as a distance between the nominal and perturbed versions of the behaviour. However, the current version of the tool does not allow for analysing the robustness with respect to time distortions induced by perturbations. To fill this gap, we discuss the integration of a Skorokhod-like technique to the evaluation of distances in STARK. Moreover, we claim that this approach will allow us to extend the expressiveness of STARK with resilience analysis. We make use of a case study from System Biology to showcase the potential of the proposed technique: we analyse the robustness and resilience of the oscillatory behaviour of a gene regulatory network.

Keywords: Robustness · Resilience · Time distortions · Skorokhod · Systems Biology

1 Introduction

The STARK tool has been introduced to model and analyse the behaviour of dynamical systems operating under uncertainty [6], like cyber-physical, autonomous, and biological systems. In STARK, the behaviour of a system is modelled in terms of the modifications that the interaction of a set of *agents* (the logical component of the system) with an *environment* (the physical component) induces on a *data state* (a set of variables and parameters with their current values). To reflect the unpredictability of the environment and approximations in the agents, those modifications are modelled as a sequence of distributions on the data states that are attainable at each step, which we call an *evolution sequence* [3]. To ensure safety and correctness of agents that are sensitive to quantitative input and subject to uncertainty, we require them to be *robust* against *perturbations*. Robustness is a measure of the impact of an unpredictable event (a perturbation) on the behaviour of the system. In STARK, robustness properties are specified as requirements on the evaluations of *distances* between the nominal and perturbed behaviour of a system [5]. The tool offers a language to specify perturbations, one to specify distances, and a sample-based simulation to generate evolution sequences.

Distances over evolution sequences take into account their spatial differences, i.e., the differences in the distributions over data states. The evaluation of such distances is strongly entangled to the discrete-time approach in the simulation: robustness is measured starting from the Wasserstein distance [16] between distributions over data states

Published by Springer Nature Switzerland AG 2026
L. Bocchi and B. Kulahcioglu Ozkan (Eds.): FORTE 2026, LNCS 16589, pp. 227–234, 2026.
https://doi.org/10.1007/978-3-032-28187-6_13

that are reached *at the same time step* in the nominal and perturbed evolution sequences. Hence, the evaluation of robustness cannot take into account potential time distortions or delays in the behaviour of the system that are induced by perturbations. Such a feature becomes particularly limiting when analysing systems that are characterised by an oscillatory behaviour, like power grids and biological systems. Moreover, overcoming such limitation would allow us not only to refine the evaluation of the robustness of a system, but also to evaluate its *resilience*. This is a measure of the ability of a system to recover after a perturbation occurred. Indeed, being able to compare current (perturbed) behaviour with future or past (intended) behaviour is crucial to evaluate recovery.

In this short paper we discuss a possible approach for measuring spatial and temporal distances in evolution sequences, thus paving the way to refine the robustness analysis in STARK and enhance the tool's expressiveness with resilience analysis.

A Skorokhod-Based Approach. The *Skorokhod distance* [2,15] allows us to optimise between spatial and temporal discrepancies under a timing distortion. Hence, to obtain a well defined distance **Sk** over evolution sequences, we will use the Wasserstein distance to quantify the spatial discrepancies between distributions and we will combine it with a non-decreasing retiming function allowing us to determine the optimal pairing of distributions. Briefly, given two evolution sequences $\mathcal{S}_1, \mathcal{S}_2$, $\mathbf{Sk}_{I \to I'}(\mathcal{S}_1, \mathcal{S}_2)$ considers the distributions reached by $\mathcal{S}_1$ in the interval I and uses the retiming to match each of them to a distribution reached by $\mathcal{S}_2$ in the interval I'. We claim that given the nominal behaviour $\mathcal{S}$ of the system and its perturbed one $\mathcal{S}_p$, $\mathbf{Sk}_{I \to I'}(\mathcal{S}, \mathcal{S}_p)$ measures *resilience*, and $\mathbf{Sk}_{I \to I'}(\mathcal{S}_p, \mathcal{S})$ measures *robustness* against the perturbation. We remark that the development of this theory is at a very early stage, and thus we can only share our ideas on the use of the proposed approach in this direction.

We implement a binary search algorithm (available at https://github.com/the-stark-tool/STARK/blob/main/lib/src/main/java/stark/distance/SkorokhodDistanceExpression.java) for the computation of this Skorokhod-like distance in STARK and we showcase the potential of our approach by applying it to the analysis of robustness and resilience of the repressilator gene regulatory network [10].

Related Work. The Skorokhod distance has seen several successful application to the analysis of cyber-physical systems, like conformance analysis [1,8,9], robustness analysis [7,11,14], and monitoring [12]. Our contribution is the enhancement of the expressiveness of STARK that derives from the addition of the Skorokhod approach to it. To the best of our knowledge, ours is the first proposal of the use a Skorokhod-like distance to quantify both the robustness and resilience of a system operating under uncertainty. The binary search approach was inspired by [8], in which, however, time is continuous and retimings are characterised as non-decreasing, surjective functions. Since time is discrete in STARK, we drop the requirement on surjectivity, as it would be too limiting in our setting. This simplification resulted in a novel algorithm for the optimisation of the retimings (Algorithm 2) that scales better than the corresponding one in [8].

2 The Skorokhod Distance in STARK

In STARK the behaviour of a system is modelled as an evolution sequence, i.e., a sequence of probability distributions over data states. Given an evolution sequence $\mathcal{S}$ and a time step $t \in \mathbb{N}$, we denote by $\mathcal{S}^t$ the distribution that is obtained at step t in the sequence. Moreover, we let $\mathbf{d}, \mathbf{d}_i, \ldots$ range over data states. To specify and evaluate robustness properties, the tool offers *Robustness Temporal Logic* (RobTL) [5]. RobTL allows us to specify requirements on the evolution in time of distance between nominal and perturbed behaviours of a system. Distances and perturbations are specified by means of sublanguages in the logic. Examples of expressions defining distances are

$$\texttt{exp} ::= \, <^{\rho} \mid \texttt{F}^{I}\ \texttt{exp} \mid \texttt{G}^{I}\ \texttt{exp} \mid \texttt{exp}\ \texttt{U}^{I}\ \texttt{exp} \mid \min(\texttt{exp}, \texttt{exp}) \mid \max(\texttt{exp}, \texttt{exp}) \mid \ldots$$

where the atomic distance expression $<^{\rho}$, is an atomic distance expression used to evaluate the distance between two distributions, and the temporal expression operators $\texttt{F}^{I}\,\texttt{exp}$ and $\texttt{G}^{I}\texttt{exp}$ allow for evaluating, respectively, the minimal and the maximal value of a given distance $\texttt{exp}$ over the bounded time interval I. Given two evolution sequences $\mathcal{S}_0, \mathcal{S}_1$ and a time step t, the evaluation of expressions in the triple $\mathcal{S}_0, \mathcal{S}_1, t$ is given by function $[\![\cdot]\!]^{t}_{\mathcal{S}_0,\mathcal{S}_1}$ taking values in $\rightarrow [0,1]$ which is defined inductively over expressions. For instance:

$$\begin{aligned} [\![<^{\rho}]\!]^{t}_{\mathcal{S}_0,\mathcal{S}_1} &= \mathbf{W}(m^{\rho})(\mathcal{S}_1^{\tau}, \mathcal{S}_2^{t}) \\ [\![\texttt{F}^{I}\ \texttt{exp}]\!]^{t}_{\mathcal{S}_0,\mathcal{S}_1} &= \min_{t' \in I+t} [\![\texttt{exp}]\!]^{t'}_{\mathcal{S}_0,\mathcal{S}_1} \\ [\![\texttt{G}^{I}\texttt{exp}]\!]^{t}_{\mathcal{S}_0,\mathcal{S}_1} &= \max_{t' \in I+t} [\![\texttt{exp}]\!]^{t'}_{\mathcal{S}_0,\mathcal{S}_1} \end{aligned}$$

where:

- ρ is a (user defined) *rank* function that assigns to each data state $\mathbf{d}$ a rank in $[0,1]$ that is used to capture a specific task of the system;
- $\mathfrak{m}^{\rho}$ is a (user defined) ground distance over the ranks assigned to data states by ρ: for all data states $\mathbf{d}_1, \mathbf{d}_2$ we have $\mathfrak{m}^{\rho}(\mathbf{d}_1, \mathbf{d}_2) \in [0,1]$;
- $\mathbf{W}(\mathfrak{m}^{\rho})$ is the Wasserstein lifting [16] of $\mathfrak{m}^{\rho}$ to distributions over data states, defined for any two distributions μ, ν by

$$\mathbf{W}(m_{\rho})(\mu, \nu) = \inf_{\mathfrak{w} \in \mathfrak{W}(\mu,\nu)} \int_{\mathcal{D}\times\mathcal{D}} m_{\rho}(\mathbf{d}, \mathbf{d}')\, d\mathfrak{w}(\mathbf{d}, \mathbf{d}')$$

where $\mathfrak{W}(\mu, \nu)$ is the set of the *couplings* of μ and ν.

We refer the interested reader to [5] for in depth presentation.

The Skorokhod Distance. While the expressiveness of RobTL allows for specifying arbitrary requirements on the evolution in time of distances between evolution sequences, in most use-cases we encountered so far a combination of the distance expressions above suffices to test system's robustness. We can test the formula $\square^{J} \Delta(\texttt{G}^{I} <^{\rho}, \texttt{p}) \leq \eta$ that specifies that no matter at which step $j \in J$ a given perturbation $\texttt{p}$ is applied, it is always the case that $[\![\texttt{G}^{I} <^{\rho}]\!]^{j}_{\mathcal{S},\mathcal{S}_{\texttt{p}}} \leq \eta$ for a given threshold

$\eta \in [0,1]$, where $\mathcal{S}_{\mathsf{p}}$ is the perturbation of $\mathcal{S}$ via p. Intuitively, if the maximal point-wise distance with respect to ρ is smaller than η, then the system was able to fulfil the task identified by ρ despite being affected by p. However, the step-wise evaluation of $<^{\rho}$ does not account for possible temporal distortions, like delays, induced by p. This usually results in a over pessimistic evaluation of system's robustness.

To overcome this limitation we add a new distance expression to the specification language, based on the Skorokhod metric [2,15]. Let λ be a strictly increasing continuous function from $[0,1]$ to $[0,1]$, and let f, g be real-valued functions from $[0,1]$ to $[0,1]$ that are right-continuous and have left-hand limits. The Skorokhod distance between f, g is then defined as:

$$d(f,g) = \inf_{\lambda} \max \left\{ \sup_{0 \le t \le 1} |\lambda(t)) - t|, \sup_{0 \le t \le 1} |f(t) - g(\lambda(t))| \right\}.$$

Assume that we are interested in evaluating the difference between the behaviour $\mathcal{S}_1$ in the time interval $I = [\mathsf{l}, \mathsf{r}]$ and the behaviour $\mathcal{S}_2$. To account for the effects of perturbations, we allow to inspect the latter behaviour in the interval $I' = [\mathsf{l}', \mathsf{r}']$, where the relations between the left-bounds l, l', and between the right-bounds r, r' vary according to the application context. Then we define *retimings* as non-decreasing functions $\lambda \colon I \to I'$ that match, for every $t \in I$, the distribution $\mathcal{S}_1^t$ with the distribution $\mathcal{S}_2^{\lambda(t)}$. The goal is to find the retiming that minimises the maximum between the maximal offset $|\lambda(t) - t| \cdot \rho_{I \to I'}$, quantifying the time distortion, and the maximal spatial distance $\mathbf{W}(\mathrm{m}^{\rho})(\mathcal{S}_1^t, \mathcal{S}_2^{\lambda(t)})$ over the interval I. Here, $\rho_{I \to I'}$ is a normalisation factor used to guarantee that the offset is in $[0,1]$.

Definition 1 (Skorokhod distance in STARK). *We define the Skorkhod-like distance* $\mathbf{Sk}_{I \to I'}$ *by*

$$\mathbf{Sk}_{I \to I'}(\mathcal{S}_1, \mathcal{S}_2) = \inf_{\lambda \colon I \to I'} \max \left\{ \max_{t \in I} |\lambda(t) - t| \cdot \rho_{I \to I'}, \max_{t \in I} \mathbf{W}(\mathrm{m}^{\rho})(\mathcal{S}_1^t, \mathcal{S}_2^{\lambda(t)}) \right\}$$

for all time intervals I, I' *and evolution sequences* $\mathcal{S}_1, \mathcal{S}_2$.

Robustness and Resilience. While we cannot offer yet a fully developed theory on the specification of robustness and resilience properties using the proposed Skorokhod-like distance, we can share intuition towards why we find this approach promising. Assume that $\mathcal{S}$ represents the nominal behaviour of a system, and let $\mathcal{S}_{\mathsf{p}}$ be the perturbed behaviour. Our claim is that $s_{\mathsf{res}} = \mathbf{Sk}_{I \to I'}(\mathcal{S}, \mathcal{S}_{\mathsf{p}})$ quantifies system's resilience, and $s_{\mathsf{rob}} = \mathbf{Sk}_{J \to J'}(\mathcal{S}_{\mathsf{p}}, \mathcal{S})$ quantifies its robustness, modulo an adequate choice of I, I', J, J'. When we evaluate s_{res} we fix the distributions reached by $\mathcal{S}$ in I and we look for the retiming that minimises the pointwise maximal distances to the matched distributions of $\mathcal{S}_{\mathsf{p}}$ in I'. A small value of s_{res} means that the behaviour $\mathcal{S}_p$ in I' is close enough to $\mathcal{S}$ in I, i.e., that the system recovered its behaviour after the perturbation. However, the minimisation over the retiming might hide some unwanted behaviour in $\mathcal{S}_{\mathsf{p}}$ by simply ignoring some distributions in I'. The evaluation of the max between the spatial distances and the maximal retiming offset and an adequate choice of I' given I should limit the effects of such skips on the evaluation of resilience. We leave as

Algorithm 1. Skorokhod distance

Input Evolution sequences $\mathcal{S}_1, \mathcal{S}_2$, step t, intervals $I = [\mathsf{l}, \mathsf{r}], I' = [\mathsf{l}', \mathsf{r}']$, resolution σ, rank function ρ, ground distance m^{ρ}, time normalisation $\rho_{I \to I'}$.

Output $\mathbf{Sk}_{I+t \to I'+t}(\mathcal{S}_1, \mathcal{S}_2)$, with max deviation σ, and the related offsets.

1: $\mathsf{lb} \leftarrow 0$; $\mathsf{ub} \leftarrow 1$; $\mathsf{ret\_off} \leftarrow [0, \ldots, 0]$; $\mathsf{below\_thr} \leftarrow$ `False`
2: **while** $(!(\mathsf{below\_thr}) \vee \mathsf{ub} - \mathsf{lb} \geq \sigma)$ **do**
3: $\quad\mathsf{thr} \leftarrow (\mathsf{ub} + \mathsf{lb})/2$
4: $\quad(\mathsf{below\_thr}, \mathsf{ret\_off}) \leftarrow$ `Refining_Skorokhod`$(\mathcal{S}_1, \mathcal{S}_2, \mathsf{thr}, t, I, I', \rho, \mathrm{m}^{\rho}, \rho_{I \to I'})$
5: $\quad$**if** $\mathsf{below\_thr}$ **then** $\mathsf{ub} \leftarrow \mathsf{thr}$
6: $\quad$**else** $\mathsf{lb} \leftarrow \mathsf{thr}$
7: $\quad$**end if**
8: **end while**
9: **return** $(\mathsf{thr}, \mathsf{ret\_off})$

future work the formalisation of this intuition and the analysis of false positives in the Skorokhod-approach. Potentially undesirable behaviour in $\mathcal{S}_{\mathsf{p}}$ cannot be hidden when we evaluate s_{rob}. Since the distributions in $\mathcal{S}_{\mathsf{p}}$ in J are now fixed, a small value of s_{rob} means that the perturbed behaviour did not go too far from the intended one, i.e., that the system was able to maintain its behaviour despite the perturbation. Similar considerations on the choice of intervals and the trade off between spatial and temporal discrepancies made for resilience apply to the evaluation of robustness.

3 The Algorithms

We present the binary search algorithm we use for the evaluation of the Skorokhod-like distance. Assume two evolution sequences $\mathcal{S}_1, \mathcal{S}_2$, a time step t, two time intervals $I = [\mathsf{l}, \mathsf{r}], I' = [\mathsf{l}', \mathsf{r}']$, a resolution σ, a rank function ρ, a ground distance m^{ρ}, and a time normalisation $\rho_{I \to I'}$. Algorithm 1 is a binary search algorithm that iteratively computes approximations to $\mathbf{Sk}_{I+t \to I'+t}(\mathcal{S}_1, \mathcal{S}_2)$, where $I + t = [t + \mathsf{l}, t + \mathsf{r}]$. Variables lb and ub are a lower bound and an upper bound, resp., to the distance we aim to compute and are initialised with the minimal and maximal values 0 and 1, resp. At each iteration the algorithm refines lb and ub by means of Algorithm 2, until their difference goes below σ. The interval $[\mathsf{lb}, \mathsf{ub}]$ is replaced by its left half if Algorithm 2 constructs a retiming function realising a Skorokhod-like distance below $\frac{(\mathsf{ub}+\mathsf{lb})}{2}$, or by its right half if the construction fails. To represent the retiming $\lambda : I + t \to I' + t$, Algorithm 2 uses the array $\mathsf{ret\_off}$: for each $i \in I + t$ we have $\mathsf{ret\_off}[i] = |\lambda(i) - i|$. Algorithm 2 attempts to construct λ left-to-right: each iteration of the outer loop attempts to assign a retiming offset to step after those for all points in $[0, \mathsf{step} - 1] + t + \mathsf{l}$ have been already assigned. The inner loop looks for an offset for step ensuring $\mathbf{Sk}_{I \to I'}(\mathcal{S}_1, \mathcal{S}_2) \leq \mathsf{thr} = \frac{(\mathsf{ub}+\mathsf{lb})}{2}$.

The values of Wasserstein distances are stored in a matrix to avoid double computations. Hence, the worst case complexity of our algorithm is $O(\log_2(\frac{1}{\sigma}) \cdot (|I| + |I'|) \cdot n\log(n))$, with $n\log(n)$ the cost of computing the Wasserstein distance over n samples. The complexity of the algorithm in [8], using our variables, is $O(2n \cdot |I'| \cdot m)$, where m is the dimension of the data states.

Algorithm 2. Refining Skorokhod

Input Evolution sequences $\mathcal{S}_1, \mathcal{S}_2$, distance threshold thr, step t, intervals $I = [\mathsf{l}, \mathsf{r}], I' = [\mathsf{l}', \mathsf{r}']$, rank function ρ, ground distance m^{ρ}, time normalisation $\rho_{I \to I'}$.

Output Boolean $\mathbf{Sk}_{I+t \to I'+t}(\mathcal{S}_1, \mathcal{S}_2) \leq \mathsf{thr}$, and the offsets of the retiming.

1: $\mathsf{ret\_off} \leftarrow [0, \dots, 0]$; $\mathsf{offset} \leftarrow \mathsf{l}' - \mathsf{l}$; $\mathsf{step} \leftarrow t + \mathsf{l}$;
2: **while** ($\mathsf{step} <= t + \mathsf{r} \wedge \mathsf{step} + \mathsf{offset} <= t + \mathsf{r}'$) **do**
3: $\quad$ $\mathsf{time\_distortion} \leftarrow \rho_{I \to I'} * |\mathsf{offset}|$
4: $\quad$ $\mathsf{spatial\_distance} \leftarrow \mathbf{W}(\mathrm{m}^{\rho})(\mathcal{S}_1^{\mathsf{step}}, \mathcal{S}_2^{\mathsf{step}+\mathsf{offset}})$
5: $\quad$ $\mu \leftarrow \max(\mathsf{time\_distortion}, \mathsf{spatial\_distance})$
6: $\quad$ **while** ($\mu > \mathsf{thr}$) **do**
7: $\quad\quad$ $\mathsf{offset} \leftarrow \mathsf{offset} + 1$
8: $\quad\quad$ $\mathsf{time\_distortion} \leftarrow \rho_{I \to I'} * |\mathsf{offset}|$
9: $\quad\quad$ **if** (($\mathsf{time\_distortion} > \mathsf{thr}$) $\vee$ ($\mathsf{step} + \mathsf{offset} > t + \mathsf{r}'$)) **then**
10: $\quad\quad\quad$ **return** (`False`, $\mathsf{ret\_off}$)
11: $\quad\quad$ **end if**
12: $\quad\quad$ $\mathsf{spatial\_distance} \leftarrow \mathbf{W}(\mathrm{m}^{\rho})(\mathcal{S}_1^{\mathsf{step}}, \mathcal{S}_2^{\mathsf{step}+\mathsf{offset}})$
13: $\quad\quad$ $\mu \leftarrow \max(\mathsf{time\_distortion}, \mathsf{spatial\_distance})$
14: $\quad$ **end while**
15: $\quad$ $\mathsf{ret\_off}[\mathsf{step}] \leftarrow |\mathsf{offset}|$; $\mathsf{step} \leftarrow \mathsf{step} + 1$; $\mathsf{offset} \leftarrow \max\{\mathsf{l}' - \mathsf{l}, \mathsf{offset} - 1\}$
16: **end while**
17: **return** (`True`, $\mathsf{ret\_off}$)

4 Case Study: The Repressilator

The repressilator is a gene regulatory network consisting of m genes that form a directed cycle of *negative interactions*: the activity of gene i (mod m) inhibits the activity of gene $i+1$ (mod m). Negative interactions result in oscillations in the levels of proteins produced by each gene. We refer to [4] for a full description of the model in STARK: we consider three genes G_i, each producing a protein Z_i. We simulate the effects of protein translation deregulation [13] on G_1 as a perturbation p that periodically reduces the amount of Z_1, thus also affecting the production of Z_2 and Z_3.

We want to analyse robustness and resilience of the repressilator against p. While we can expect the oscillations to go back to the nominal regime, the perturbation delays them with respect to the original ones, as shown in Fig. 1a for Z_2. Assuming that p is active in the interval $[0, 500]$ and letting $I = [500, 800], J = [0, 200]$, with RobTL we can test if, for every $i \in I$, the distance $[\![\mathtt{G}^{J} <^{\rho_{Z_2}}]\!]^{i}_{\mathcal{S}, \mathcal{S}_{\mathrm{p}}}$ is below a certain value. Here ρ_{Z_2} assigns to each data state the (normalised) level of Z_2 stored in it. The evaluation is reported as the solid line in Fig. 1b, giving that the system is robust with respect to the threshold 0.06. The dotted line in Fig. 1b corresponds to the evaluation of robustness with the new approach: for each $i \in I$ we compute $\mathbf{Sk}_{J+i \to J'+i}(\mathcal{S}_{\mathrm{p}}, \mathcal{S})$ with $J' = [0, 600]$. The dashed line in Fig. 1b depicts the pointwise evaluation of $\mathbf{Sk}_{J+i \to J'+i}(\mathcal{S}, \mathcal{S}_{\mathrm{p}})$, i.e., the resilience of the system. The code used to run experiments is available at https://github.com/the-stark-tool/STARK/blob/main/examples/repressilator/src/main/java/repressilator/Main_Skorokhod.java.

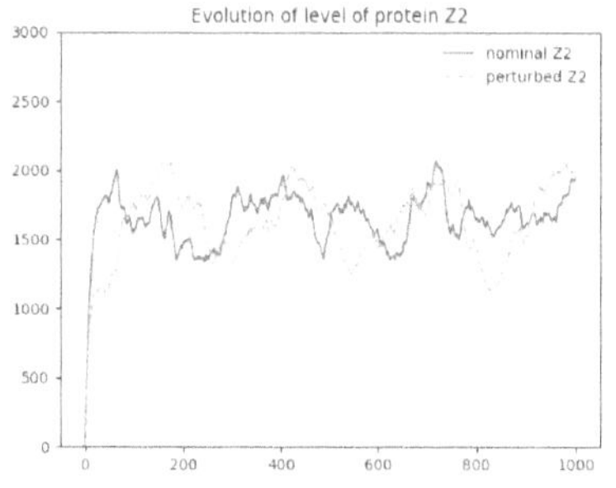

(a) Variation of Z_2 (solid=nominal, dashed=perturbed).

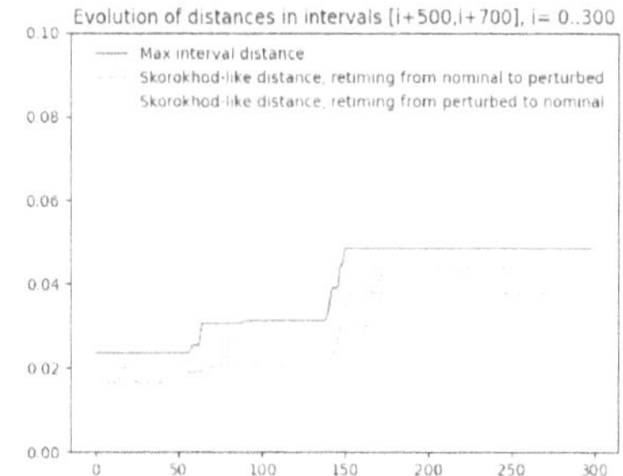

(b) $\mathtt{G}^{J}<^{\rho Z_2}$ (solid) and $\mathbf{Sk}_{J+i\to J'+i}$ distances (dashed=resilience, dotted=robustness).

Fig. 1. Analysis of the repressilator (perturbation active in the first 500 steps).

5 Evaluation of the Proposed Approach

Advantages. The addition of a Skorokhod-like distance to STARK allows us to refine and extend the analysis that we can carry out with the tool. Firstly, it paves the way to a more precise quantification of the system's robustness, as it allows to account for time distortions on behaviour that are induced by perturbations. Secondly, being able to quantify temporal distances between behaviours, on top of the spatial ones, enables the possibility to measure system's resilience. In both cases, the analysis is favoured by our choice to work with non-decreasing retimings, without imposing other constraints, such as surjectivity. This leaves a lot of freedom in finding the optimal matching of behaviours. Moreover, this choice allowed us to develop a binary search algorithm for the computation of distances that is computationally more efficient than the one in [8].

Limitations and Future Work. In this paper, we could only give an intuition on how to use our approach to evaluate robustness and resilience. A formalisation of this properties will be the first step for future work, including how to determine proper intervals for the retiming. Currently, the major limitation of our proposal is the risk of obtaining false positives: the minimisation over the retimings might hide some unwanted, hazarduous, behaviour of the perturbed system, thus giving an over optimistic quantification of robustness/resilience. Our main task will be to develop effective techniques to detect false positives and to study under which conditions we can prevent them.

Acknowledgements. This publication is part of the project *NODES* which has received funding from the MUR M4C2 1.5 of PNRR with grant agreement no. ECS00000036.

References

1. Abbas, H., Mittelmann, H.D., Fainekos, G.: Formal property verification in a conformance testing framework. In: Proceedings of MEMOCODE 2014, pp. 155–164. IEEE (2014). https://doi.org/10.1109/MEMCOD.2014.6961854

2. Billingsley, P.: Convergence of Probability Measures. Wiley (2013)
3. Castiglioni, V., Loreti, M., Tini, S.: A framework to measure the robustness of programs in the unpredictable environment. Log. Methods Comput. Sci. **19**(3) (2023). https://doi.org/10.46298/LMCS-19(3:2)2023
4. Castiglioni, V., Loreti, M., Tini, S.: Bio-STARK: a tool for the time-point robustness analysis of biological systems. In: Gori, R., Milazzo, P., Tribastone, M. (eds.) CMSB 2024. LNCS, vol. 14971, pp. 62–70. Springer, Cham (2024). https://doi.org/10.1007/978-3-031-71671-3_5
5. Castiglioni, V., Loreti, M., Tini, S.: RobTL: robustness temporal logic for CPS. In: Proceedings of CONCUR 2024. LIPIcs, vol. 311, pp. 15:1–15:23. Schloss Dagstuhl - Leibniz-Zentrum für Informatik (2024). https://doi.org/10.4230/LIPICS.CONCUR.2024.15
6. Castiglioni, V., Loreti, M., Tini, S.: Stark: a tool for the analysis of CPSs robustness. Sci. Comput. Program. **236**, 103134 (2024). https://doi.org/10.1016/j.scico.2024.103134
7. Davoren, J.M.: Epsilon-tubes and generalized skorokhod metrics for hybrid paths spaces. In: Majumdar, R., Tabuada, P. (eds.) HSCC 2009. LNCS, vol. 5469, pp. 135–149. Springer, Heidelberg (2009). https://doi.org/10.1007/978-3-642-00602-9_10
8. Deshmukh, J.V., Majumdar, R., Prabhu, V.S.: Quantifying conformance using the skorokhod metric. Formal Methods Syst. Des. **50**(2–3), 168–206 (2017). https://doi.org/10.1007/S10703-016-0261-8
9. Dimitrova, R., Gazda, M., Mousavi, M.R., Biewer, S., Hermanns, H.: Conformance-based doping detection for cyber-physical systems. In: Gotsman, A., Sokolova, A. (eds.) FORTE 2020. LNCS, vol. 12136, pp. 59–77. Springer, Cham (2020). https://doi.org/10.1007/978-3-030-50086-3_4
10. Elowitz, M.B., Leibler, S.: A synthetic oscillatory network of transcriptional regulators. Nature **403**, 335–338 (2000). https://doi.org/10.1038/35002125
11. Henzinger, T.A., Otop, J., Samanta, R.: Lipschitz robustness of timed I/O systems. In: Jobstmann, B., Leino, K.R.M. (eds.) VMCAI 2016. LNCS, vol. 9583, pp. 250–267. Springer, Heidelberg (2016). https://doi.org/10.1007/978-3-662-49122-5_12
12. Jaksic, S., Bartocci, E., Grosu, R., Nguyen, T., Nickovic, D.: Quantitative monitoring of STL with edit distance. Formal Methods Syst. Des. **53**(1), 83–112 (2018). https://doi.org/10.1007/S10703-018-0319-X
13. Jia, X., He, X., Huang, C., Li, J., Dong, Z., Liu, K.: Protein translation: biological processes and therapeutic strategies for human diseases. Signal Transduct. Target. Ther. **9**(44), 2786–2791 (2024). https://doi.org/10.1038/s41392-024-01749-9
14. Majumdar, R., Prabhu, V.S.: Computing distances between reach flowpipes. In: Abate, A., Fainekos, G. (eds.) Proceedings of HSCC 2016, pp. 267–276. ACM (2016). https://doi.org/10.1145/2883817.2883850
15. Skorokhod, A.V.: Limit theorems for stochastic processes. Theory Probab. Appl. **1**(3), 261–290 (1956). https://doi.org/10.1137/1101022
16. Vaserstein, L.N.: Markovian processes on countable space product describing large systems of automata. Probl. Peredachi Inf. **5**(3), 64–72 (1969)

RustMC: Automated Verification of Real-World Concurrent Rust

Oliver Pearce(✉), Julien Lange(✉), and Dan O'Keeffe(✉)

Royal Holloway, University of London, Egham, UK
oliver.pearce.2020@live.rhul.ac.uk,
{Julien.Lange,Daniel.OKeeffe}@rhul.ac.uk

Abstract. RustMC is a stateless model checker that targets push-button verification of unmodified concurrent Rust programs. As both Rust and C/C++ compile to LLVM IR, RustMC builds on GenMC which provides a verification framework for LLVM IR. This allows verification of Rust code and any foreign function dependencies. In this tool paper we present key implementation challenges, use-cases, and an empirical evaluation of RustMC. The challenges include intercepting threading operations, promoting memory intrinsics, and handling uninitialised accesses, all stemming from Rust's unique compilation strategy. Case studies adapted from real-world programs show RustMC finds concurrency bugs in unsafe Rust code, FFI calls to C/C++, and atomic operations. We evaluate our tool's functionality on the Loom model checker test suite and a set of production-level Rust concurrent data structures.

Keywords: Model Checking · Rust · LLVM

1 Introduction

Rust is a popular systems programming language that enforces memory and thread safety through its ownership and borrowing system. Values in Rust have a single owner and can be borrowed either mutably or immutably, with mutable borrowing preventing any concurrent borrows of the same value. These constraints effectively prevent data races in most safe Rust code, as threads cannot make concurrent unsynchronised memory accesses when any access is a write. While Rust's type system prevents many of the common memory safety issues found in other systems programming languages, verification of concurrent programs remains an ongoing challenge. Concurrency bugs occur in Rust for a range of reasons, including atomicity violations, "unsafe" Rust code and interactions between Rust and C/C++ foreign function interface (FFI) dependencies.

In this tool paper, we extend GenMC [17], a stateless model checker that systematically explores executions of concurrent C/C++ programs under weak

---

Artefacts available in https://doi.org/10.5281/zenodo.18806668.

Published by Springer Nature Switzerland AG 2026
L. Bocchi and B. Kulahcioglu Ozkan (Eds.): FORTE 2026, LNCS 16589, pp. 235–255, 2026.
https://doi.org/10.1007/978-3-032-28187-6_14

memory models at the LLVM IR level, to support the verification of multi-threaded Rust programs. By leveraging the LLVM compiler infrastructure's intermediate representation (IR) we derive verifiable LLVM IR modules from both Rust programs and their C/C++ dependencies. RustMC is, to the best of our knowledge, the only available framework capable of exhaustively exploring the state space of Rust programs and their dependencies, facilitating the detection of data races stemming from Rust, C/C++ and interactions between the languages. While our LLVM IR based approach allows us to verify mixed-language programs, relying on this low-level representation introduces challenges that impact on both RustMC's out-of-the-box support for real-world Rust code and the performance of verification. Specifically, transforming an IR module emitted by the Rust compiler into a verifiable representation requires significant changes to GenMC's compilation and transformation stages. Below we describe how we addressed these challenges and demonstrate the tool's applicability to real-world concurrent programs. The key contributions of this paper are:

1. We present RustMC, an extension of GenMC, the first model checker capable of verifying concurrent Rust programs and their FFI dependencies;
2. We develop novel LLVM transformations to handle Rust-specific challenges, including LLVM memory intrinsics, mixed-size accesses and uninitialised memory accesses, that arise from Rust's unique compilation strategy;
3. We demonstrate RustMC's effectiveness through examples adapted from real-world programs, showing its ability to detect data races in both pure Rust code and mixed-language programs that use C/C++ dependencies;
4. We evaluate RustMC's scalability and support for push-button verification of real-world Rust code. We evaluate our tool on two sets of examples. One consists of 72 tests adapted from the test suite of the Loom model checker [36], the other is based on tests from the 14 most popular crates providing concurrent data structures in Rust; and
5. We provide RustMC as an open-source tool that extends GenMC and enables the fully automated verification of concurrent Rust applications. Our artefact will consist of: the source code of RustMC, its documentation, and the datasets used in our evaluation. All are readily available on GitHub. A video demonstrating the tool is also provided [35].

2 Background

2.1 Concurrency Bugs in Rust

While Rust code provides strong safety guarantees, concurrency bugs can still occur. One potential source is seemingly safe Rust code that harbours data races due to unsafe operations in foreign function dependencies. For example, consider the simple Rust program shown in Fig. 1, which calls a C function `inc_C_counter()` from multiple threads. Rust's type system normally prevents concurrent access to shared data. However, the C function bypasses these safeguards and directly manipulates a global counter variable without synchronisation. Rust's borrow checker cannot verify memory safety guarantees across

```
// Rust code
extern "C" {fn inc_C_counter();}
#[test]
fn test_C_counter() {
        thread::spawn(|| {unsafe {inc_C_counter();}});
        thread::spawn(|| {unsafe {inc_C_counter();}});
}
```

```
// C dependency
int counter = 0;
void inc_C_counter() { counter++; }
```

Fig. 1. A data race caused by an external, non-thread-safe, C function.

language boundaries. RustMC successfully identifies the race condition automatically, detecting a data race in which one thread attempts to read the `counter` while another thread simultaneously writes to it. Verification is performed automatically and it is not required to rewrite code using a specific API, as is the case with the Loom model checker [36].

Even safe Rust code can experience atomicity violations when using atomic types, as these types permit shared access and modification across multiple threads [28]. Figure 2 presents code adapted from an atomicity violation bug reported in the `rand` crate [30] (also documented in a study of Rust concurrent programming bugs [40]). Function `is_getrand_available()` implements a common pattern to cache the result of an expensive system call (`getrandom`) in a thread-safe way without using a (more expensive) mutex.

Two `AtomicI64` variables are used to synchronise operations: `CHECKED` indicates whether `getrandom` has been called before and `AVAILABLE` denotes the availability of `getrandom`; both are first initialised to 0. At compile time or run time, the atomic operations at lines 8 and 9 may be re-ordered such that one thread loads `AVAILABLE` before it is set by another.

We show an example of an undesirable interleaving below, assuming threads `t1` and `t2` are concurrently executing `is_getrand_available()` in Fig. 2.

t1	t2	
`CHECKED.store(...)` (line 9)		
	`CHECKED.load(...)` (line 4)	(1)
	`AVAILABLE.load(...)` (line 11)	
`AVAILABLE.store(...)` (line 8)		

Here, `t1` encountered `CHECKED==false`, and sets both `CHECKED` and `AVAILABLE` to `true`. From `t2`'s point-of-view, if `t1` has set `CHECKED` before setting `AVAILABLE`, then the function incorrectly returns false for `t2`. To identify this bug, we must specify the property we are interested in with an assert (line 19). This assertion characterises the consistency of concurrent calls to this function (i.e., all threads should see the same results, for all interleavings). RustMC

```
1  static CHECKED: AtomicI64 = AtomicI64::new(0);
2  static AVAILABLE: AtomicI64 = AtomicI64::new(0);
3  fn is_getrand_available() -> i64 {
4      if (CHECKED.load(Ordering::Relaxed) == 0 ){
5          let mut buf: [u64; 0] = [];
6          let result = getrandom(&mut buf);
7          let available = if result == -1 {...} else { 1 };
8          AVAILABLE.store(available, Ordering::Relaxed);
9          CHECKED.store(1, Ordering::Relaxed);
10         available
11     } else { AVAILABLE.load(Ordering::Relaxed) }
12 }
13 fn main() {
14     let t1 = thread::spawn(||{is_getrand_available()});
15     let t2 = thread::spawn(||{is_getrand_available()});
16     let r1 = t1.join().unwrap();
17     let r2 = t2.join().unwrap();
18
19     assert_eq!(r1, r2);
20 }
```

Fig. 2. An atomicity violation in safe code, adapted from the Rand crate [14].

can detect the bug and reports a trace, see (1), violating atomicity. The `unsafe` keyword disables the Rust compiler's safety checks to provide developers with greater flexibility. This can lead to data races in Rust code without any FFI calls. We show further real-world examples of concurrency bugs brought about by the `unsafe` keyword in Appendix A and online [35].

2.2 GenMC: A Stateless Model Checker for C/C++

GenMC [17] supports verification under several weak memory models (e.g., RC11, IMM, LKMM) and represents program behaviours through execution graphs comprising events (nodes) that correspond to individual memory accesses. The tool's architecture consists of three main stages: first, it compiles source code into LLVM IR (e.g. using `clang`); second, it transforms this code to make it easier and faster to analyse, e.g., bounding infinite loops, eliminating dead allocations, etc.; and finally, it conducts verification by exploring program executions and checking for errors such as data races, assertion violations, and memory safety issues. Some of the latest development of the tool includes an optimal dynamic partial order reduction (DPOR) algorithm that explores all possible executions up to some equivalence relation while avoiding redundant explorations [15]. GenMC explores exactly one execution per equivalence class while maintaining polynomial memory requirements.

GenMC provides an ideal foundation for extending stateless model checking to Rust programs. Its integration with LLVM's intermediate representation creates a natural bridge for verifying Rust code, as both Rust and C/C++ compile to LLVM IR. This alignment enables RustMC to verify not only pure Rust programs but also their interactions with C/C++ dependencies. Moreover, GenMC's three-stage architecture provides a modular framework that RustMC can extend to handle Rust-specific challenges. As GenMC remains under active development, RustMC stands to benefit automatically from future enhancements to the underlying verification framework without requiring significant modifications to its Rust-specific components. Notably, support for mixed-size accesses was recently added as part of the Mixer extension to GenMC [23]. As we discuss in the next section, mixed-size access support is essential for push-button verification of many real-world Rust programs.

3 RustMC: Overview and Implementation Challenges

We next present RustMC, an extension to the GenMC framework for verifying Rust applications. Figure 3 gives an overview of the framework. As in GenMC, there are three stages: compilation, transformation and verification. RustMC also includes an automated test harness component (not shown) that enables a Rust crate's existing test suite to serve as input drivers for verification.

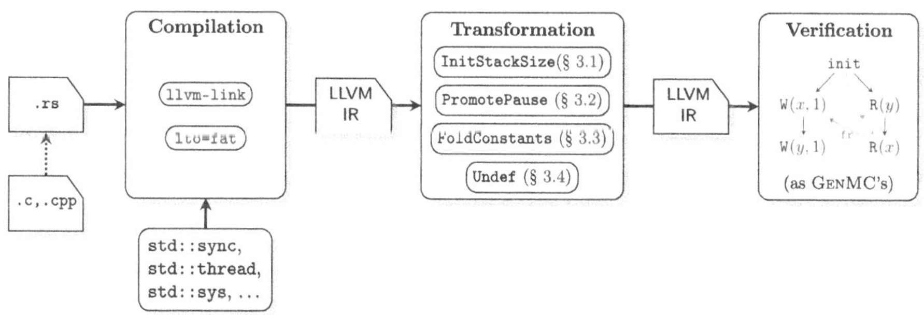

Fig. 3. Architecture of RustMC.

RustMC first compiles the application to LLVM IR, then the `llvm-link` tool [21] is used to link the IR file with the GenMC verification component. This allows for the interception and tracking of relevant threading events. If the application contains FFI calls to C/C++ code, the C IR is also linked. RustMC transforms the resulting IR using a series of LLVM passes to prepare it for verification. In comparison to GenMC, RustMC introduces additional passes that address implementation challenges relating to uninitialised memory accesses (see § 3.4), calls to external functions (see § 3.1) and unsupported LLVM intrinsics (see § 3.2).

Finally, RUSTMC feeds the transformed IR file to the verification component. This executes the GENMC stateless model checking algorithm to detect any data races or assertion violations across all potential thread interleavings.

3.1 Externally Linked Dependencies

To control a program's schedule, a model checker must intercept thread creation and synchronisation operations. In C/C++, these operations appear directly in a program's compiled IR, allowing GENMC to redefine the corresponding symbols (e.g. `pthread_create`) with its own internal wrapper functions (e.g. `__VERIFIER_thread_create`). However, for Rust applications, many standard library functions are externally linked. As a result, thread creation and synchronisation operations are not visible in the compiled IR.

A naive solution to this problem is to build the entire standard library alongside the application to expose threading calls. However, this approach has several downsides: first, the larger codebase significantly increases the engineering effort required to handle edge cases and unsupported LLVM behaviours; second, processing the much larger IR through each LLVM transformation pass becomes significantly slower; and third, the increased code complexity breaks LLVM optimisation passes that GENMC relies on.

Instead RUSTMC leverages the `lto=fat` compilation flag to perform link-time optimisation across the target crate and its dependencies, pulling standard library code into standalone LLVM IR modules [8]. This targeted approach keeps the IR size manageable and avoids most LLVM transformation issues. One issue is that the standard library's thread creation implementation queries environment variables and calls native threading internals to set a stack size for new threads. Since GENMC's interpreter does not model environment variables or the required native internals, calls to `thread::spawn` result in a segmentation fault. To mitigate this issue we use an LLVM pass to preinitialise the stack size of new threads to the default value for Rust on Linux.

3.2 Handling LLVM Intrinsics

LLVM supports a number of memory-related intrinsic functions such as those corresponding to the C standard library functions `memcpy()`, `memmove()`, and `memset()`. A call to one of these intrinsics may perform a series of byte-wise accesses. For example, `memcpy(ptr %dest, ptr %src, i64 24)` will copy 24 bytes from `%src` to `%dest`. In GENMC, a custom LLVM pass promotes any intrinsic calls with lengths evaluable at compile time into a series of typed loads and stores. This allows the verification component to handle them as individual accesses. Unpromotable memory intrinsics remain in the IR and trigger a runtime error if they are executed during verification. Rust's compilation strategy frequently produces intrinsics with lengths that cannot be resolved at compile time, necessitating a runtime fallback.

An IR-level implementation would require the use of integer types, as LLVM does not have a representation for raw memory values. This introduces two semantic issues. First, integer types do not carry provenance information, so provenance is lost during copies. This can cause alias analysis to miss pointer escapes, potentially affecting any transformation passes that reason about aliasing. Second, manual implementations of `memcpy` may over-propagate `poison`. For example, if a `memcpy` is implemented using an `i64` load and some bits within the `i64` are `poison`, the load returns poison for the entire `i64` [24]. By handling memory intrinsics inside the interpreter as direct byte-by-byte copies, RustMC avoids both problems.

This change is sound because the intrinsic implementations are only invoked at runtime by the interpreter, after the `IntrinsicLowering` pass has already converted intrinsic calls into external function calls. Passes earlier in the pipeline may rely on `@llvm.memcpy`'s intrinsic semantics, which guarantee that the source and destination are either equal or non-overlapping. This guarantee would be lost in any IR-level implementation since passes would observe an ordinary function call with no non-overlapping constraint. Note that GenMC's custom memory intrinsic promotion pass also runs after the `IntrinsicLowering` pass, preserving `memcpy` semantics for any prior passes which rely on alias analysis. The Mixer [23] extension to GenMC is used to support any subsequent non-bytewise accesses to memory written bytewise by the interpreter fallback. To reduce the performance overhead associated with mixed-size accesses we run the static promotion pass first, transforming as many intrinsics as possible into loads and stores which match the size of subsequent accesses.

In addition to memory intrinsics, we encountered calls to the `sse2.pause` intrinsic for optimising the performance of spin loops. As this intrinsic is not supported by GenMC's interpreter and does not affect verification we introduce a pass to remove any calls to it.

3.3 Aggregate Types

The Rust compiler emits many values of LLVM aggregate type (e.g. structs, arrays) and frequently uses them in patterns not supported by the verification component, presenting two problems.

First, the compiler can emit statically evaluable `extractvalue` instructions to extract an element from an aggregate. However, the interpreter does not support the direct conversion of constant aggregates into its internal value representation, which is common in IR derived from Rust programs. We transform these `extractvalue` instructions into constants with a custom `FoldInterpreterUnsupportedConstants` pass based on LLVM's `ConstantFoldExtractValueInstruction()` function. Figure 4 illustrates an example of this transformation for LLVM IR that extracts the second field from a constant struct with two `i64` fields. The pass transforms the IR to a simple store of the constant field value (`i64 10`).

Second, while shared globals are initialised using native LLVM functions, LLVM delegates the initialisation of thread-local globals to the client application. GenMC stores per-thread copies of thread-local globals in a dedicated hashmap and initialises them using the LLVM `getConstantValue()` function,

```
1 %1 = extractvalue { i64, i64 } { i64 0, i64 10 }, 1
2 store i64 %1, ptr %6, align 8
```

```
1 store i64 10, ptr %6
```

Fig. 4. FoldInterpreterUnsupportedConstants transformation of LLVM IR to extract elements from a constant struct (top) to a simple store (bottom).

which does not support aggregate types with concrete initialisers. The Rust compiler frequently emits thread-local globals of aggregate type, causing the interpreter to crash when initialising them. RustMC addresses this by decomposing thread-local globals into their constituent bytes during initialisation, reconstructing them on access. As only shared memory accesses are added to the event graph, this change does not affect the execution graphs produced during verification.

3.4 Undefined Values

LLVM supports undefined (`undef`) values to represent indeterminate values. Each time an `undef` value is used by an instruction a different bit pattern may be observed. Typically, `undef` models loading from uninitialised memory [18,22]. This is permitted as long as the `undef` value is not used in a subsequent operation that may trigger immediate undefined behaviour for some potential bit pattern [20]. For example, dividing any value by an `undef` value leads to undefined behaviour as the `undef` value could be 0. GenMC's model of memory accesses does not handle uninitialised loads (it requires that each read has a preceding write to take its value from). As loads from uninitialised memory have no preceding write the tool is unable to construct an execution graph.

```
1 pub fn foo() -> Result<(), i64> { Ok(()) }
```

```
1  define { i64, i64 } @foo() unnamed_addr #0 !dbg !7 {
2    %_0 = alloca [16 x i8], align 8 ; allocate 16 bytes
3    store i64 0, ptr %_0, align 8, !dbg !35 ; put 0 in 1st chunk
4    %0 = load i64, ptr %_0, align 8, !dbg !36 ; initialised read
5    %1 = getelementptr inbounds i8, ptr %_0, i64 8, !dbg !36
6    %2 = load i64, ptr %1, align 8, !dbg !36 ; uninitialised read
7    %3 = insertvalue { i64, i64 } poison, i64 %0, 0, !dbg !36
8    %4 = insertvalue { i64, i64 } %3, i64 %2, 1, !dbg !36
9    ret { i64, i64 } %4, !dbg !36
10 }
```

Fig. 5. Uninitialised read in Rust (top) and corresponding LLVM IR (bottom).

Figure 5 shows an uninitialised read arising from typical Rust code. The function foo() returns the Ok(T) variant of Result<T, E>. A Result<T, E> is stored in memory as a tagged union whose size is determined by its largest variant. When T is the zero-sized unit type (), the Ok() variant occupies less space than is allocated for the union. The remaining bytes are never written, yet must be loaded when Result<(),i64> is read. This occurs at line 6 in Fig. 5. Nothing is stored in the second 8-byte chunk of allocated memory, so the load yields undef. The function returns {0, undef} where 0 is the discriminant for the Ok() variant.

To handle uninitialised loads while meeting RustMC's verification requirements, we implement an LLVM pass that explicitly writes undefined values into each stack allocation. This approach allows us to verify programs containing uninitialised reads as RustMC interprets an explicit "store undef" as storing 0 to a memory location. Consequently each uninitialised read has a preceding write, as required. Interpreting accesses to uninitialised memory as 0 preserves program semantics provided there is no immediate undefined behaviour arising from uninitialised values taking non-zero bit patterns [20]. We consider this an acceptable trade-off for concurrency verification given the tool's focus on detecting data races and memory ordering issues rather than detecting all forms of undefined behaviour. Alternatives, such as exploring all possible undef values, would cause state explosion and make the verification of real-world code impractical. We note that RustMC's undefined value transformation currently only supports stack allocations. Extending it to handle undefined values in dynamic heap allocations using a similar approach should be possible, but is currently unsupported by the tool.

3.5 Soundness, Completeness and Optimality

As GenMC's soundness, completeness and optimality guarantees depend on preserving the semantics of a program under test, the LLVM transformations introduced by RustMC are designed to be semantics-preserving. Our undefined value handling explores all execution traces in which undef is consistently observed as 0 in programs that misuse uninitialised memory. For all other programs, all possible execution traces described by the LLVM semantics are explored.

While promoting memory intrinsics into sequences of typed loads and stores and handling any non-constant intrinsics with a custom internal implementation can increase the number of events in execution graphs—and consequently the number of potential interleavings—this does not compromise GenMC's optimality. The theoretical properties of GenMC's verification algorithm [15] are defined at the level of execution graphs and their exploration; RustMC inherits these properties directly as it reuses GenMC's verification component without modification. Thus, RustMC maintains the same formal guarantees as GenMC while extending support to Rust-specific compilation patterns.

We note that RustMC employs the Mixer algorithm of GenMC to handle mixed-size accesses. Although Mixer is parametric in its choice of memory model, the current implementation is restricted to the Release-Acquire (RA) fragment of RC11.

4 Evaluation

We evaluate RustMC through two complementary experiments that measure its correctness on established benchmarks and its applicability to production-level concurrent data structures.

The first experiment assesses our tool's bug-detection accuracy and practical efficiency on 72 concurrent tests [37] adapted from the Loom model checker test suite. The second experiment evaluates RustMC's support for real-world Rust language features by verifying test functions from 14 popular concurrency-focused crates.

Both experiments use functions marked with the `#[test]` attribute as self-contained verification harnesses. For each test we explore all concurrent behaviours and consider verification successful if RustMC's output matches the expected behaviour. A test's expected behaviour is considered to be a panic when annotated with the `#[should_panic]` attribute, or when its body exercises Rust's unwinding functionality. Because RustMC uses the `panic=abort` strategy, tests that rely on unwinding to recover from a panic will instead abort. We accept a panic outcome as a successful verification for these tests.

4.1 Experiment 1: RustMC and the Loom Test Suite

To evaluate RustMC's effectiveness on established benchmarks, we assessed its performance on 72 concurrent Rust tests adapted from the Loom model checker test suite [37]. These tests cover a range of concurrency primitives including atomics, mutexes, read-write locks, condition variables, thread-local storage, and `UnsafeCell<T>` (primitive for interior mutability in Rust) operations. This constitutes a demanding evaluation: the tests were designed for a production-level model checker operating at the Rust API level, while our research tool works at the lower LLVM IR abstraction, where the same patterns manifest with significantly greater implementation complexity.

For each test, we record whether RustMC's outcome (success, panic, or crash) matches the expected behaviour. We also measure resource consumption: the number of executions explored, maximum memory usage, and CPU time (broken down into the transformation and verification phases). This evaluation aims to measure RustMC's bug-detection accuracy (false negatives and false positives) and its practical efficiency on real-world concurrency scenarios.

Loom requires tests to be written using the Loom API, hence they require adaptation to be used by a push-button model checker like RustMC. Notably if one wants to model check program `P` with Loom, then one must wrap it around the construct `loom::model(|| { P })` which will tell Loom to explore all possible interleavings of `P`. All tests used in this experiment require this wrapper to

Table 1. RustMC verification results on tests adapted from Loom. Status: **S**: success, **P**: panic, **C**: crash. Expected: ✓: matches expected, ×: does not match. Executions: executions explored, Mem: max memory (MB), CPU: user time (s), P.Mem/P.CPU: Transformation pipeline max memory (MB) and user time (s). † indicates a test flagged with `#[ignore]` in the Loom test suite.

File	Test	Status	Expected	Executions	Mem	CPU	P.Mem	P.CPU
arc	basic_usage	S	✓	4	155.6	0.86	179.9	2.09
	sync_in_drop	S	✓	3	153.0	0.83		
	try_unwrap_succeeds	S	✓	1	145.8	0.51		
	try_unwrap_fails	S	✓	1	145.8	0.41		
	try_unwrap_multithreaded	C	–	–	148.0	0.48		
atomic	compare_and_swap_reads_old†	S	×	4	155.4	1.48	179.3	2.23
	fetch_add_atomic	S	✓	2	151.3	0.72		
atomic_int	xor	S	✓	1	136.2	0.47	169.8	1.93
	max	S	✓	1	136.6	0.37		
	min	S	✓	1	136.9	0.47		
	compare_exchange	S	✓	1	136.6	0.38		
	compare_exchange_weak†	S	✓	1	136.8	0.37		
	fetch_update	S	✓	1	137.0	0.34		
atomic_relaxed	compare_and_swap	S	✓	1	150.5	0.56	181.7	2.09
	check_ordering_valid	S	✓	5	157.6	1.09		
	check_ordering_invalid_1	P	✓	10	163.5	1.86		
	check_ordering_invalid_2	P	✓	10	163.0	1.85		
condvar	notify_one	C	–	–	147.9	0.57	179.8	2.12
	notify_all	C	–	–	152.4	1.13		
fence	fence_sw_base	S	✓	2	159.0	1.06	187.9	2.14
	fence_sw_collapsed_store	S	✓	2	159.2	1.00		
	fence_sw_collapsed_load	S	✓	2	159.4	0.88		
	sb_fences	P	×	2	158.8	0.95		
	fence_hazard_pointer	P	×	1	159.1	0.89		
	rwc_syncs	P	×	4	170.5	2.87		
	w_rwc	P	×	3	166.9	2.80		
futures	atomic_waker_valid	C	–	–	149.2	0.46	179.5	2.28
	spurious_poll	S	✓	2	151.4	0.73		
litmus	load_buffering†	S	✓	3	150.8	0.86	178.0	2.05
	store_buffering	S	✓	4	152.2	1.32		
mutex	mutex_enforces_mutual_exclusion	S	✓	1	151.5	0.57	182.0	2.31
	mutex_establishes_seq_cst	S	✓	15	163.3	2.02		
	mutex_into_inner	S	✓	1	151.6	0.76		
rwlock	rwlock_read_one	S	✓	1	152.8	0.59	183.0	2.55
	rwlock_read_two_write_one	S	✓	2	153.2	0.65		
	rwlock_write_three	S	✓	2	154.3	0.62		
	rwlock_write_then_try_write	S	✓	1	148.4	0.39		
	rwlock_write_then_try_read	S	✓	1	148.7	0.44		
	rwlock_read_then_try_write	S	✓	1	148.9	0.46		
	rwlock_try_read	S	✓	1	147.9	0.42		
	rwlock_write	S	✓	1	147.8	0.40		
	rwlock_try_write	S	✓	1	148.0	0.42		
	rwlock_into_inner	S	✓	1	151.8	0.56		
rwlock_r1	rwlock_two_writers	S	✓	24	176.2	11.43	179.2	2.09
smoke*	checks_fail	P	✓	0	170.0	5.74	179.8	2.22
spec	relaxed†	S	×	15	174.8	8.98	186.3	2.30
	acq_rel	S	✓	178	232.9	239.68		
	test_seq_cst†	S	✓	178	233.2	241.92		
thread_api	initial_thread	S	✓	1	192.7	0.61	261.0	3.44
	many_joins	S	✓	1	196.5	0.73		
	alt_join	S	✓	3	207.3	4.73		
	threads_have_unique_ids	C	–	–	202.9	3.00		
	thread_names	C	–	–	202.8	2.87		
	thread_stack_size	S	✓	1	234.5	58.80		
	park_unpark	S	✓	1	192.7	0.67		
thread_local	thread_local_test	S	✓	1	152.1	1.00	178.9	2.12
	nested_with	S	✓	1	143.9	0.36		
	drop_test	S	✓	1	151.6	1.03		
unsafe_cell	atomic_causality_success	S	✓	2	165.9	0.85	202.5	2.60
	atomic_causality_fail	P	✓	0	163.3	0.61		
	unsafe_cell_race_mut_mut_1	P	✓	0	163.5	0.61		
	unsafe_cell_race_mut_mut_2	P	✓	0	168.8	1.34		
	unsafe_cell_race_mut_immut_1	P	✓	0	163.8	0.65		
	unsafe_cell_race_mut_immut_2	P	✓	0	163.6	0.61		
	unsafe_cell_race_mut_immut_3	P	✓	0	168.3	0.95		
	unsafe_cell_race_mut_immut_4	P	✓	0	168.0	0.98		
	unsafe_cell_race_mut_immut_5	P	✓	0	168.9	0.99		
	unsafe_cell_ok_1	S	✓	1	163.8	0.62		
	unsafe_cell_ok_2	S	✓	1	163.8	0.70		
	unsafe_cell_ok_3	S	✓	1	167.0	0.90		
	unsafe_cell_access_after_sync	P	✓	5	169.7	1.13		
yield	yield_completes	S	✓	4	152.2	0.76	175.3	2.02

be removed. In addition, some Loom-specific calls must be re-interpreted (see comment on `spec` below).

Out of the 20 test files in the Loom repository, we rule out three as they either focus on higher-level concurrency issues or primitives we do not target (e.g., channels, memory leak, deadlocks) or aim at testing the Loom API itself. In the remaining 17 files, shown in the first column of Table 1, we additionally omit three further tests aimed at testing the Loom API. For all files, we run RustMC with the GenMC flag `-unroll=1` except for `smoke` where it is necessary to unroll to 3 to detect the bug (highlighted with $*$).

Table 1 gives the results of our experiment. Out of the 72 tests, our tool currently supports 66 tests, it crashes for the remaining 6 ($\approx$9.0%). Out of these 66 supported tests, 60 ($\approx$91.0%) returned the expected outcome. Out of the 6 misdiagnosed tests, two are not supported by Mixer's memory model, nor by Loom, i.e., Loom returns the wrong result too (they are flagged as `#[ignore]`) because it does not fully model `Ordering::Relaxed`. Similarly, the four unexpected panics in `fences` are due to sequentially-consistent fences which we do not support due to the current limitation of Mixer to the RA memory model. The 6 crashes are due to an external function with variable arguments (i.e., `syscall`). Resource consumption is reasonable, with an average memory footprint of 162.35 MB and mean CPU time of 8.75 s per test, though two tests in the `spec` file require significantly more resources (178 executions, 233 MB, 240 s). These tests involve 4 threads looping on a `load()` and invoking `thread::yield_now()` in the body of the loop. The original tests include a Loom preemption bound of one (i.e., `builder.preemption_bound = Some(1)`) which we approximated by bounding the loop with one.

4.2 Experiment 2: RustMC and Popular Crates

To evaluate RustMC's applicability to real-world concurrent Rust code, we conducted a characterisation study on tests from 14 popular crates in the Rust ecosystem. Our aim is to establish a baseline for push-button verification of real-world Rust code and identify areas for future improvement.

We selected crates by surveying those with the most downloads in the last 90 days from the concurrency category of `crates.io`. Our current focus is on user-facing concurrent data structures, and so we excluded crates that serve primarily as internal building blocks or rely on higher-level concurrency models (e.g., asynchronous runtimes, channels). While asynchronous runtimes are supported by our tool, we leave a systematic evaluation of async crates to future work. Figure 6 gives an overview of the number of tests available for each crate.

Our test-harness component automatically identifies all test functions in a given crate and invokes RustMC on them as targets for verification. Tests were filtered to remove those dependent on external testing frameworks including Loom and Proptest (External testing frameworks in Fig. 6). We also excluded macro-generated test cases (Macros in Fig. 6) as our test harness does not currently support using them as entry points. This filtering process is conservative: for example, tests removed due to Loom dependencies could potentially be adapted (as in Experiment 1), and macro-generated tests represent an engineering challenge rather than a fundamental limitation. All tests are run with the `-unroll=2` GenMC flag. Figure 7 presents verification results across the 14 crates, with tests categorised by outcome.

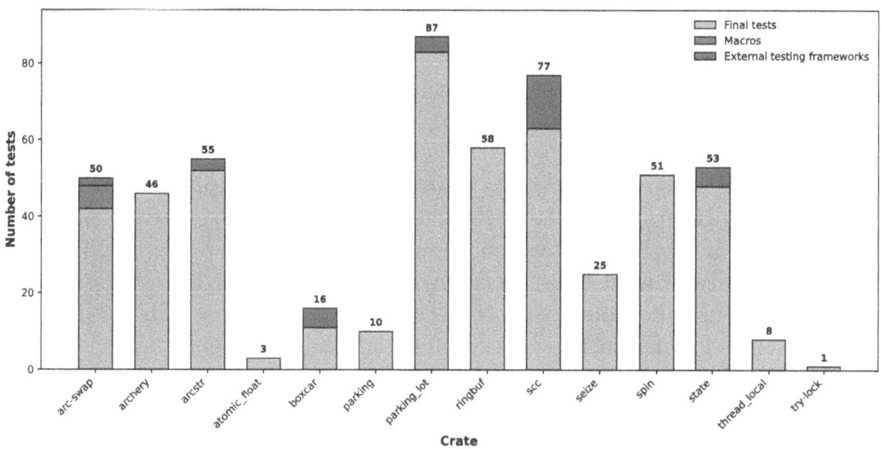

Fig. 6. Selection of tests from popular concurrency-related crates.

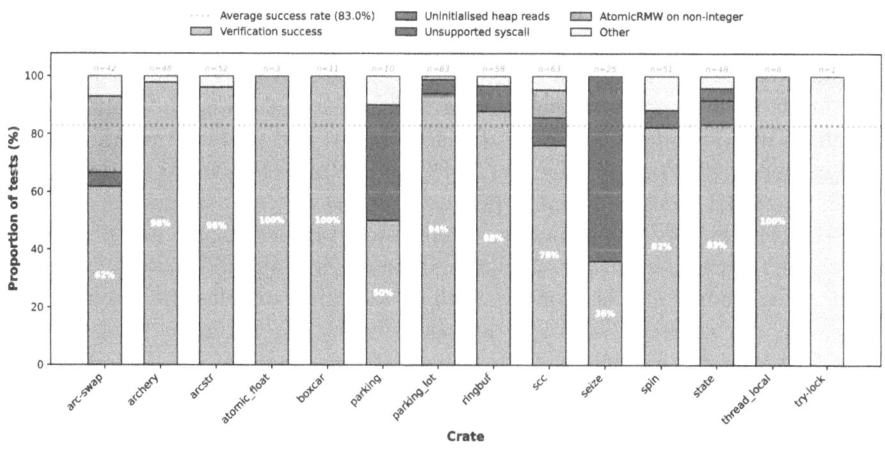

Fig. 7. Results of model-checking tests from popular concurrency-related crates.

RustMC achieved an 83.0% verification success rate over all tests in our dataset. This includes tests from production-grade concurrent data structures such as `archery` and `boxcar`, demonstrating the tool's ability to scale from synthetic benchmarks to complex, real-world concurrent Rust code. Tests that fail to verify fall into three primary categories:

- Uninitialised heap reads: Uninitialised reads from dynamically allocated memory, e.g., when using Rust's `MaybeUninit` type, which requires extending our undefined value handling from stack to heap allocations.
- Unimplemented syscalls: External functions with variable arguments which we do not currently support.
- AtomicRMW on non-integer: Atomic operations on pointers, which are not supported by the verification component.

The Other category in Fig. 7 notably includes (*i*) a few unsupported intrinsics we conservatively convert to runtime errors and (*ii*) four (>1h) timeouts due to unusually large tests [5–7, 39].

The varying success rates across crates (from near-complete verification in some to limited coverage in others) reflects the diversity of concurrent programming patterns in the Rust ecosystem. Some crates heavily utilise language features that align well with RustMC's current capabilities, while others employ patterns that push the boundaries of our LLVM-level analysis. The results provide a baseline for measuring future improvements and identify specific areas (particularly dynamic memory patterns and modelling common syscalls) where extending support would increase coverage of real-world code.

5 Related Work

Rust and its usage have been the focus of much research in the last decade. Notably, RustBelt [12] provides formal verification of Rust's type system and ownership model. Evans et al. [10] shows that while only 30% of Rust libraries explicitly use unsafe code, over half contain unsafe operations somewhere in their dependency chain that bypass Rust's static checks. Astrauskas et al. [3] shows that unsafe code appears frequently, particularly for language interoperability, though its unsafe code tends to be straightforward and well-contained.

Dynamic partial order reduction (DPOR) techniques have been successfully applied to model check concurrent programs across different languages and contexts [1,2,11]. For Rust specifically, several tools target concurrency bug detection, though with different approaches and tradeoffs compared to ours. Kani [34] is a bounded model checker for Rust which identifies undefined behaviour and verifies custom correctness properties provided by assertions or function contracts for sequential programs.

Miri [13] is part of the Rust compiler project and is advertised as "an undefined behavior detection tool for Rust". It works as an interpreter of Rust's mid-level IR. Miri is particularly effective at detecting undefined behaviours, but its inherently dynamic approach means that it cannot systematically analyse all potential interleavings of concurrent programs. Loom [36] is an adaptation of CDSChecker [25]. It explores interleavings of concurrent code under the C11 memory model using partial-order reduction techniques. In comparison to RustMC/GenMC, the CDSChecker algorithm is less efficient since its backtracking algorithms can explore both redundant and infeasible (prohibited by the memory model) executions [15,16]. Loom requires developers to port their code to use the Loom API, as opposed to the push-button approach of RustMC. Shuttle [4] is another concurrent code testing tool for Rust, developed at AWS. It is similar to (and inspired by) Loom but aims at better scalability at the cost of soundness. Shuttle uses a randomised scheduler [9] to guarantee good coverage. Lockbud [26,27] is a static bug detector for blocking bugs and potential atomicity violations in Rust. It identifies potential atomicity violations by detecting syntactical patterns commonly found in atomicity violation bugs. While this pattern-based approach can identify potential issues, RustMC's systematic exploration of thread interleavings allows it to definitively verify atomicity properties through assert statements, detecting actual violations rather than potential ones. Other work [19,38] explores verification techniques for Rust's FFI dependencies, but focuses primarily on memory management bugs rather than concurrency issues.

6 Conclusions

RustMC represents a significant step forward in verification of Rust code, and opens new possibilities for detecting subtle concurrency bugs in concurrent Rust programs and their FFI dependencies. Extending GenMC to handle Rust's compilation characteristics presented several technical challenges but its modular architecture allowed us to re-use the back-end verifier. Hence RustMC will automatically benefit from future improvements to GenMC's verification engine.

Looking ahead, RustMC provides a foundation for systematic analysis of real-world concurrent Rust programs, helping developers ensure their code is free from concurrency issues. Our future work will focus on applying RustMC to verify more concurrent code in Rust projects and their dependencies.

A Additional examples

A.1 Out of bounds accesses

Data races in Rust may also cause out of bounds accesses to allocated memory, resulting in an immediate unrecoverable `panic!` error [32]. Figure 8 gives an example of such a bug.

Variable `other_idx` is a clone of the `Arc` type used as a thread safe reference counter, i.e., `idx` and `other_idx` both contain references to the same value. Recall that atomics have interior mutability and are not subjected to restrictions on mutable aliasing. An ownership move is performed at line 6, and the thread which has been passed ownership of `other_idx` increments the variable by 10. At line 10, a bounds check is performed and if `idx` is smaller than the length of the allocated `vec`, then the position of `idx` in the allocated `vec` array is accessed. In an interleaving where `other_idx` is incremented after the bounds check at line 10, an out-of-bounds read occurs at line 13.[1] This leads to an immediate `panic!`

[1] Method `get_unchecked()` is an unsafe method that retrieves an element from a vector without performing any bounds checking, i.e., it is a potentially faster version of the regular `get()` method.

call which is detected by RustMC along with the interleaving responsible for the error.

A.2 Raw Pointers

In Rust, developers can use raw pointers to bypass the language's safety guarantees around aliasing and mutability when necessary [33]. In [26], Qin et al. show that sharing data between threads through raw pointers to shared memory is a prevalent source of concurrency bugs. Figure 9 illustrates a concrete example of such an issue. While raw pointers can be created in safe code as is seen at line

```
1  fn main() {
2      let data = vec![1, 2, 3, 4];
3      let idx = Arc::new(AtomicUsize::new(0));
4      let other_idx = idx.clone();
5
6      thread::spawn(move || {
7          other_idx.fetch_add(10, Ordering::SeqCst);
8      });
9
10     if idx.load(Ordering::SeqCst) < data.len() {
11         unsafe {
12             let i = idx.load(Ordering::SeqCst);
13             let x = *data.get_unchecked(i);
14         }
15     }
16 }
```

Fig. 8. A data race which leads to an unrecoverable `panic!` error, adapted from [31].

```
1  fn main() {
2      let mut x: i64 = 2;
3      let x_ptr = &mut x as *mut i64; // Pointer #1 to x
4
5      unsafe {
6        let x_ptr_2: &mut i64 = &mut *x_ptr; // Pointer #2 to x
7        let handle = thread::spawn(move || {
8              *x_ptr_2 = 5;
9          });
10       *x_ptr = 10;
11       handle.join().unwrap();
12     }
13     let y = x;
14 }
```

Fig. 9. A data race caused by the use of raw pointers for sharing data between threads.

3, dereferencing a raw pointer is always considered unsafe and must be marked as such. At line 6, `x_ptr` is dereferenced, creating a second mutable reference to the value held at `x`. Ownership of this reference is transferred to a new thread where the underlying value `x` is mutated. This is performed concurrently with another write to `x` at line 10.

Now `y` may be assigned different values (10 or 5) depending on the observed interleaving. RustMC is able to detect this as a non-atomic race and reports the conflicting write events at lines 8 and 10.

A.3 Data Race in Thread-safe Traits

We give another example that demonstrates how incorrect implementations of Rust's thread safety traits can lead to data races. The `Sync` trait, which marks types as safe to share between threads, requires careful implementation to maintain Rust's safety guarantees. This type of bug has occurred in practice, e.g., the `internment` crate contained a data race due to an unsafe implementation of `Sync` for its `Intern<T>` struct [29]. The implementation allowed the struct to be shared between threads even when instantiated with non-thread-safe types, potentially leading to memory corruption. To illustrate this class of bug, we create a minimal example where a struct containing a `Cell<i64>` incorrectly implements `Sync`. The `Cell` type provides interior mutability but is explicitly designed to be non-thread-safe, making this implementation unsound. Figure 10 shows how this type definition can lead to data races.

```
1  struct MyStruct { data: Cell<i64>, }
2
3  unsafe impl Send for MyStruct {}
4  unsafe impl Sync for MyStruct {}
5
6  impl MyStruct {
7      fn new(value: i64) -> Self {
8          MyStruct { data: Cell::new(value), }
9      }
10     fn increment(&self) {self.data.set(self.data.get() + 1);}
11 }
12
13 fn main() {
14     let foo = Arc::new(MyStruct::new(0));
15     let foo_clone1 = foo.clone();
16     let foo_clone2 = foo.clone();
17     let t1 = thread::spawn(move || {foo_clone1.increment();});
18     foo_clone2.increment();
19     t1.join().unwrap();
20     let final_value = foo.data.get();
21 }
```

Fig. 10. Data race in safe Rust code.

`MyStruct` contains a single field data which is a `Cell<i64>`, i.e., a type that provides interior mutability (data can be mutated even via an immutable reference). Lines 3 and 4 declare `MyStruct` as safe to send between threads (`Send`) and safe to share references across threads (`Sync`). As they appear in an `unsafe` block, the programmer is taking responsibility for thread safety. However, `MyStruct` implements the `increment()` method, which is clearly not thread-safe. To expose the issue, we provide a `main()` function which makes two concurrent calls to `increment()`. Line 14 wraps a new `MyStruct` in an `Arc` (Atomic Reference Counted), which allows safe sharing between threads. Lines 15 and 16 create new references to `foo`; hence both threads are modifying the same underlying data. When given Fig. 10 as input, RustMC correctly identifies the race. It detects a conflict between the unsynchronised accesses to `foo` made by the main thread at line 18 and the spawned thread at line 17.

References

1. Abdulla, P.A., Aronis, S., Atig, M.F., Jonsson, B., Leonardsson, C., Sagonas, K.: Stateless model checking for TSO and PSO. In: Baier, C., Tinelli, C. (eds.) Tools and Algorithms for the Construction and Analysis of Systems - 21st International Conference, TACAS 2015, Held as Part of the European Joint Conferences on Theory and Practice of Software, ETAPS 2015, London, UK, April 11-18, 2015.

Proceedings. LNCS, vol. 9035, pp. 353–367. Springer, Cham (2015). https://doi.org/10.1007/978-3-662-46681-0_28
2. Abdulla, P.A., Aronis, S., Jonsson, B., Sagonas, K.: Optimal dynamic partial order reduction. In: Jagannathan, S., Sewell, P. (eds.) The 41st Annual ACM SIGPLAN-SIGACT Symposium on Principles of Programming Languages, POPL '14, San Diego, CA, USA, 20–21 January 2014, pp. 373–384. ACM (2014). https://doi.org/10.1145/2535838.2535845
3. Astrauskas, V., Matheja, C., Poli, F., Müller, P., Summers, A.J.: How do programmers use unsafe Rust? Proc. ACM Program. Lang. **4**(OOPSLA), 136:1–136:27 (2020). https://doi.org/10.1145/3428204
4. AWS: Shuttle, a library for testing concurrent Rust code. https://github.com/awslabs/shuttle. Accessed 30 Jan 2024
5. Barretto, J.: Large test in `spin-rs` (mutex fair) (2025). https://github.com/zesterer/spin-rs/blob/91b8001beb553dfe382f65518eef9eb0f1c78602/src/mutex/fair.rs#L598
6. Barretto, J.: Large test in `spin-rs` (mutex spin) (2025). https://github.com/zesterer/spin-rs/blob/91b8001beb553dfe382f65518eef9eb0f1c78602/src/mutex/spin.rs#L454
7. Barretto, J.: Large test in `spin-rs` (mutex ticket) (2025). https://github.com/zesterer/spin-rs/blob/91b8001beb553dfe382f65518eef9eb0f1c78602/src/mutex/ticket.rs#L410
8. rustc book, T.: lto. https://doc.rust-lang.org/rustc/codegen-options/index.html#lto. Accessed 19 Feb 2026
9. Burckhardt, S., Kothari, P., Musuvathi, M., Nagarakatte, S.: A randomized scheduler with probabilistic guarantees of finding bugs. In: Hoe, J.C., Adve, V.S. (eds.) Proceedings of the 15th International Conference on Architectural Support for Programming Languages and Operating Systems, ASPLOS 2010, Pittsburgh, Pennsylvania, USA, 13–17 March 2010. pp. 167–178. ACM (2010). https://doi.org/10.1145/1736020.1736040
10. Evans, A.N., Campbell, B., Soffa, M.L.: Is Rust used safely by software developers? In: Rothermel, G., Bae, D. (eds.) ICSE '20: 42nd International Conference on Software Engineering, Seoul, South Korea, 27 June - 19 July, 2020. pp. 246–257. ACM (2020). https://doi.org/10.1145/3377811.3380413
11. Flanagan, C., Godefroid, P.: Dynamic partial-order reduction for model checking software. In: Palsberg, J., Abadi, M. (eds.) Proceedings of the 32nd ACM SIGPLAN-SIGACT Symposium on Principles of Programming Languages, POPL 2005, Long Beach, California, USA, January 12-14, 2005. pp. 110–121. ACM (2005). https://doi.org/10.1145/1040305.1040315
12. Jung, R., Jourdan, J., Krebbers, R., Dreyer, D.: Rustbelt: securing the foundations of the Rust programming language. Proc. ACM Program. Lang. **2**(POPL), 66:1–66:34 (2018). https://doi.org/10.1145/3158154
13. Jung, R., Kimock, B., Poveda, C., Muñoz, E.S., Scherer, O., Wang, Q.: Miri: practical undefined behavior detection for rust. Proc. ACM Program. Lang. **10**(POPL) (2026). https://doi.org/10.1145/3776690
14. klutzy: Fix race condition of atomics (2015). https://github.com/rust-random/rand/commit/e0e8263c25dc291f818cd20c034912de5ae05189. Accessed 30 Jan 2024
15. Kokologiannakis, M., Marmanis, I., Gladstein, V., Vafeiadis, V.: Truly stateless, optimal dynamic partial order reduction. Proc. ACM Program. Lang. **6**(POPL) (2022). https://doi.org/10.1145/3498711

16. Kokologiannakis, M., Raad, A., Vafeiadis, V.: Model checking for weakly consistent libraries. In: McKinley, K.S., Fisher, K. (eds.) Proceedings of the 40th ACM SIGPLAN Conference on Programming Language Design and Implementation, PLDI 2019, Phoenix, AZ, USA, June 22-26, 2019. pp. 96–110. ACM (2019). https://doi.org/10.1145/3314221.3314609
17. Kokologiannakis, M., Vafeiadis, V.: GenMC: a model checker for weak memory models. In: Silva, A., Leino, K.R.M. (eds.) Computer Aided Verification. CAV 2021. LNCS, vol. 12759, pp. 427–440. Springer, Cham (2021). https://doi.org/10.1007/978-3-030-81685-8_20
18. Lee, J., et al.: Taming undefined behavior in llvm. SIGPLAN Not. **52**(6), 633–647 (2017). https://doi.org/10.1145/3140587.3062343
19. Li, Z., Wang, J., Sun, M., Lui, J.C.S.: Detecting cross-language memory management issues in rust. In: Atluri, V., Pietro, R.D., Jensen, C.D., Meng, W. (eds.) Computer Security - ESORICS 2022 - 27th European Symposium on Research in Computer Security, Copenhagen, Denmark, 26–30 September 2022, Proceedings, Part III. LNCS, vol. 13556, pp. 680–700. Springer, Cham (2022). https://doi.org/10.1007/978-3-031-17143-7_33
20. LLVM: Llvm ir undefined behavior (ub) manual. https://llvm.org/docs/UndefinedBehavior.html. Accessed 30 Jan 2024
21. LLVM: llvm-link - llvm bitcode linker. https://llvm.org/docs/CommandGuide/llvm-link.html. Accessed 30 Jan 2024
22. LLVM: 'load' instruction. https://llvm.org/docs/LangRef.html#load-instruction. Accessed 30 Jan 2024
23. Marmanis, I., Kokologiannakis, M., Vafeiadis, V.: Model checking C/C++ with mixed-size accesses. Proc. ACM Program. Lang. **9**(POPL), 2232–2252 (2025). https://doi.org/10.1145/3704911
24. Mitenkov, G., Lopes, N., Lee, J.: [RFC] Introducing a byte type to LLVM. LLVM Developer Mailing List (2021). https://lists.llvm.org/pipermail/llvm-dev/2021-June/150883.html
25. Norris, B., Demsky, B.: A practical approach for model checking C/C++11 code. ACM Trans. Program. Lang. Syst. **38**(3), 10:1–10:51 (2016). https://doi.org/10.1145/2806886
26. Qin, B., et al.: Understanding and detecting real-world safety issues in Rust. IEEE Trans. Softw. Eng. **50**(6), 1306–1324 (2024). https://doi.org/10.1109/TSE.2024.3380393
27. Qin, B.: Lockbud: statically detect memory, concurrency bugs and possible panic locations for rust. https://github.com/BurtonQin/lockbud
28. Reference, T.R.: Interior mutability. https://doc.rust-lang.org/reference/interior-mutability.html. Accessed 30 Jan 2024
29. Roundy, D., Contributors, G.: Issue #20: Intern<t>: Data race allowed on t (2021). https://github.com/droundy/internment/issues/20. Accessed 30 Jan 2024
30. Rust-random maintainers: Rand. https://github.com/rust-random/rand. Accessed 30 Jan 2024
31. Rustonomicon, T.: Data races and race conditions. https://doc.rust-lang.org/nomicon/races.html. Accessed 30 Jan 2024
32. Klabnik, S., Nichols, C.: Url. https://doc.rust-lang.org/book/ch09-03-to-panic-or-not-to-panic.html. Accessed 30 Jan 2024
33. Klabnik, S., Nichols, C.: Raw pointers. https://doc.rust-lang.org/book/ch19-01-unsafe-rust.html?highlight=raw%20pointer#dereferencing-a-raw-pointer. Accessed 31 Jan 2024

34. Team, T.K.: The kani rust verifier (2025). https://github.com/model-checking/kani
35. The Authors: RustMC, url. https://github.com/Ollie-Pearce/rustmc
36. Tokio: Loom, concurrency permutation testing tool for Rust. https://github.com/tokio-rs/loom. Accessed 30 Jan 2024
37. Tokio: Loom, concurrency permutation testing tool for Rust. https://github.com/tokio-rs/loom/tree/master/tests
38. Toman, J., Pernsteiner, S., Torlak, E.: Crust: a bounded verifier for Rust (N). In: Cohen, M.B., Grunske, L., Whalen, M. (eds.) 30th IEEE/ACM International Conference on Automated Software Engineering, ASE 2015, Lincoln, NE, USA, 9–13 November 2015, pp. 75–80. IEEE Computer Society (2015). https://doi.org/10.1109/ASE.2015.77
39. Vaner, M.: Large test in `arc-swap` (2025). https://github.com/vorner/arc-swap/blob/19f0d661a27bb6312c6ba9e19e1453db19c30ab5/src/lib.rs#L1169
40. Yu, Z., Song, L., Zhang, Y.: Fearless concurrency? Understanding concurrent programming safety in real-world Rust software. CoRR **abs/1902.01906** (2019). http://arxiv.org/abs/1902.01906

AsmetaComp: A Tool for Runtime Contract Checking with I/O Abstract State Machines

Silvia Bonfanti[1], Angelo Gargantini[1], Elvinia Riccobene[2], and Patrizia Scandurra[1](✉)

[1] University of Bergamo, Bergamo, Italy
{silvia.bonfanti,angelo.gargantini,patrizia.scandurra}@unibg.it
[2] Università degli Studi di Milano, Milan, Italy
elvinia.riccobene@unimi.it

Abstract. Contract-based Design specifies components via *assume–guarantee* contracts, enabling modular development and verification. In state-based system modeling, it helps manage complexity through decomposition into analyzable sub-models coordinated by I/O events. However, its adoption is hindered by the lack of integrated languages and tools for the specification and verification of component contracts.

This paper presents AsmetaComp, a tool that supports Contract-based Design for systems specified using I/O Abstract State Machines (ASMs), a state-based formalism for modeling and analyzing discrete-event systems. Originally developed for compositional simulation of interacting I/O ASM models, AsmetaComp has been extended to support Contract-based Design by integrating assume–guarantee contracts with executable I/O ASM models and enabling automated runtime contract checking during compositional execution. A healthcare case study is used to illustrate the tool and evaluate its effectiveness in supporting modular reasoning and dynamic contract checking in safety-critical, state-based systems.

Keywords: Contract-based Design · Models composition · Runtime Contract Checking · Abstract State Machines

1 Introduction

Contract-based Design (CbD) [6,7,20,27] is a well-established paradigm for building reliable systems through the explicit specification of behavioral *contracts*. Contracts define assumptions on inputs, guarantees on outputs, and invariants preserved during execution, supporting assume/guarantee reasoning and modular verification. While Design-by-Contract (DbC) [32] introduced contracts at the programming level, CbD generalizes these principles to components and systems, enabling scalable and compositional design.

Artefacts available in https://doi.org/10.5281/zenodo.18678488.

Published by Springer Nature Switzerland AG 2026
L. Bocchi and B. Kulahcioglu Ozkan (Eds.): FORTE 2026, LNCS 16589, pp. 256–275, 2026.
https://doi.org/10.1007/978-3-032-28187-6_15

Despite its conceptual maturity, practical tool support for CbD in formal system modeling remains fragmented. Existing solutions either embed contracts within programming languages (e.g., Eiffel, JML, ACSL) or provide partial support within verification frameworks. However, seamlessly integrating contract specification, compositional modeling, and automated runtime checking in a unified environment is still a challenge [8,21,25].

In previous work [13,14], we introduced I/O Abstract State Machines (I/O ASMs) as a state-based formalism for modeling interacting components in discrete-event systems. We also developed `AsmetaComp`, a compositional simulation engine that orchestrates the execution of I/O ASM components through dedicated composition operators.

This paper presents a tool-supported contract-based framework built on top of I/O ASMs and their simulation engine [13,14]. Our contribution is threefold:

- We introduce a dedicated contract language for I/O ASMs, explicitly reflecting the assume/guarantee paradigm.
- We define inference rules for compositional operators, enabling systematic derivation of contracts for composed components.
- We extend the `AsmetaComp` engine to support automated runtime contract checking during compositional simulation.

This framework provides a unified environment in which component modeling, contract specification, and contract checking are seamlessly combined. Contracts are checked dynamically during orchestrated execution of models. Unlike traditional contract-based approaches that primarily rely on static compositional verification through model checking, our framework supports runtime validation under concrete execution scenarios. Rather than aiming at exhaustive state-space exploration, it complements static verification by enabling scalable, scenario-driven detection of contract violations in dynamically composed systems.

To show the tool applicability, we apply the framework to a healthcare system case study, illustrating how runtime contract monitoring supports correctness assurance and complexity management in safety-critical, state-based systems.

The paper is structured as follows. Section 2 relates our work within existing CbD frameworks. Section 3 introduces the case study. Section 4 provides background on I/O ASMs and their composition operators. Section 5 recalls component contracts in CbD and presents CbD for I/O ASMs as the underlying theory of the tool. Section 6 describes the `AsmetaComp` tool for CbD. Section 7 reports the validation results of the case study. Section 8 concludes the paper.

2 Related Work

We focus on tool-supported formal approaches to CbD, distinguishing between those aimed at contract verification and refinement, and those oriented toward simulation and runtime contract checking.

On CbD for Formal Compositional Verification and Refinement. Traditionally, CbD has been used to manage complexity and scalability in embedded system verification. Together with assume/guarantee reasoning, it mainly supports formal compositional verification and stepwise refinement from design to implementation. We highlight a few, inspiring contributions in this direction.

Cimatti et al. [20] propose a trace-based contract framework built upon HRELTL, an expressive specification language extending Linear Temporal Logic (LTL) to hybrid traces, together with the OCRA verification engine for assessing contract refinement. Their approach analyzes the verification conditions necessary to establish the correctness of contract refinement in a *top-down decomposition*, emphasizing the critical role of architectural connections in component composition. The notion of contract decomposition and refinement is also explored in [35], where contract patterns are translated into automata and contract refinement is defined in terms of trace-set inclusion. Related A/G (assume/guarantee) contract frameworks are based on variants of I/O automata, e.g., Interface Automata [29] and choreography automata [24]. AGREE provides A/G compositional reasoning for architecture models [22], while an information-flow–based tool for enforcing system-wide security properties is presented in [3]. Bocchi et al. [9] propose a Design-by-Contract framework for distributed multiparty interactions, based on global assertions, their projection onto endpoint assertions, and a compositional proof system for process verification. Their approach provides a rigorous formal basis for specifying and verifying multiparty protocols by enriching session types with logical predicates, thus mainly supporting reasoning at design time. All these frameworks operate at the design stage, abstracting away from component implementations.

Other approaches more closely tied to component implementations are the following. In [19], a compositional specification theory is proposed for components interacting via I/O synchronization. Specifications constrain the temporal ordering of interactions and support composability, assumption modeling, and runtime reasoning, using either operational models (I/O-labeled transition systems with inconsistency predicates) or trace-based declarative models. Inconsistency is captured over states or traces, refinement ensures safe substitutability, and operators such as parallel composition, conjunction, and quotient support incremental design. In [30], a methodology applies contract theory to embedded software design by instantiating contracts with component-level syntaxes and enabling formal reasoning via semantically parameterized abstractions. The approach is demonstrated on a realistic example using TLA (Temporal Logic of Actions) at the system level and ACSL pre/post-conditions for C components. More recently, [31] proposes a runtime verification framework that uses LTL to express contracts and complements static model checking by monitoring individual execution traces.

On Runtime Contract Checking. While formal verification remains the dominant application, newer research is broadening its scope toward compositional system design and analysis in different formalisms, and practical composition workflows with contract checking [37]. The work in [36], for example, introduces an approach for automatically checking semantic constraints by transforming Palladio architecture models into MontiArc, where constraint validation is performed using the A/G paradigm. By combining evaluation and soundness within a single framework, the method enhances architecture reliability and avoids redundant modeling across different formalisms. Our approach pursues a similar intent, i.e. to ensure the semantic soundness of compositions during composition. Our focus is not on proving global correctness properties exhaustively, but on enabling compositional runtime assurance through executable contract-aware models.

Formal approaches to CbD that rely on simulation/testing of models and runtime contract checking include CARE [4] with Uppaal model checker, runtime verification in Simulink [23], and a stochastic contract framework for real-time systems [33] (to name a few). These methods extend traditional A/G reasoning by validating contracts dynamically during execution, and share aspects with the synthesis/verification of runtime monitors ([4], [33]) and quantitative verification via statistical inference of properties [33]. Our compositional simulation approach shares the same intent of runtime checking, and like in [4] is a *bottom-up analysis*.

In line to support continuous assurance, we aim to use ASMs as runtime formal models [18], exploiting their feature of being executable besides being verifiable. Like runtime monitoring, runtime simulation identifies violations of A/G assertions only after they occur, recording the corresponding execution runs. Since these techniques analyze one run at a time, they scale efficiently and do not suffer from state-space explosion. However, unlike model checking, they cannot ensure the complete absence of constraint violations.

Channel-based coordination models for component composition have been proposed in the literature, including Reo [2] and BIP [5]. Reo is an exogenous coordination model in which complex *connectors* are built by composing simpler ones, with the emphasis placed on connectors rather than on the interacting entities themselves. BIP (*Behaviour-Interaction-Priority*) is a component-based framework for heterogeneous concurrent systems that separates component behavior from coordination. In BIP, systems are constructed by coordinating atomic components through *connectors*, which define interaction patterns, and *priorities*, which resolve conflicts among enabled interactions. It also supports validation of key safety properties and has been applied to real-time embedded systems, including industrial case studies such as robot controllers and satellite on-board software. Reo and BIP primarily focus on coordination and component interaction rather than providing an explicit CbD in the classical assume/guarantee sense. This is especially true for Reo, while contract-based reasoning has been investigated in connection with the BIP framework in subsequent works. For example, Quinton et al. address contract-based verification of hierarchical component systems using BIP glue operators [34], while later work studies contract-based reasoning for component systems with rich interactions, explicitly considering BIP as a representative framework [26].

3 Running Case Study

We illustrate the usage of AsmetaComp through a system example in the medical domain, modeled as a composition of I/O ASMs. Inspired by [14,15], the case study (shown in Fig. 1) is about a *Medicine Reminder and Monitoring (MRM) System* designed to control a smart medicine dispenser (a remotely controllable pillbox) for medicine administration. The (client side) system consists of two main sub-systems:

- *Electronic pill reminder and dispenser* (pillbox) with several compartments and slots per compartment;
- *Remote control mobile app* running on a smartphone, which monitors and configures the pillbox via local wireless (Bluetooth or Wi-Fi Direct).

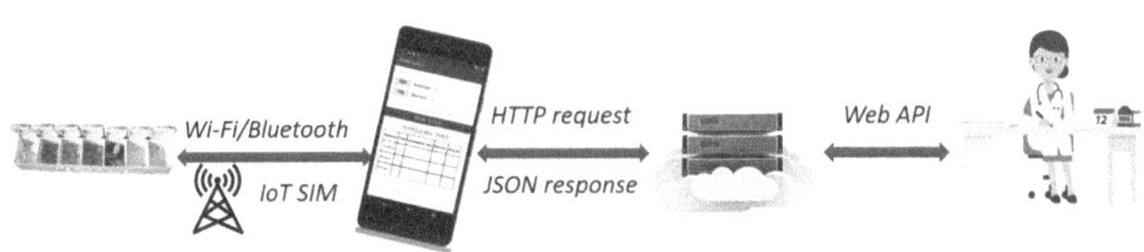

Fig. 1. MRM system: high-level interaction flow (taken from [15]).

A cloud-based information system provides persistent services for health records, prescriptions, and treatments entered by doctors through a web application. In this architecture, the smartphone acts as a *gateway* between the pillbox and the cloud, to synchronize patient data with the cloud using the smartphone's Internet connection (Wi-Fi or cellular). Our running example focuses only on the patient side system. The mobile app is responsible for checking the pillbox configuration after it is filled by the caregiver and connected to power, and for dynamically rescheduling pills to ensure safe drug intake. Unlike typical systems that only notify caregivers of missed doses, this solution automatically reschedules missed doses while ensuring no harmful drug interferences occur.

4 Background Concepts

This section introduces the formal method underlying the tool, along with the specification of components and their compositional execution semantics.

4.1 Abstract State Machines and the ASMETA Toolset

ASMs [16,17] extend Finite State Machines (FSMs) where unstructured FSM control states are replaced by first-order logic structures comprising domains of objects with functions defined on them, and state *transitions* are expressed by transition rules describing how function values saved into *locations*[1] change from one state to the next. Functions are *static* or *dynamic*. Dynamic functions can be *monitored* (input values), *controlled* (internal state), *out* (output values), or *derived* (computed in terms of other functions).

The basic unit of rule construction is the *update* rule of the form: ***if*** *condition* ***then*** *Updates* where *Updates* is a set of simultaneous assignments $f(t_1, \ldots, t_n) := v$, being f an n-ary dynamic function, t_i terms, and v the value of $f(t_1, \ldots, t_n)$ in the next state. Other transition rules *constructors* are used depending on the update structure they express: guarded updates (*if-then-else*), parallel updates (*par*), non-determinism (*choose*), unrestricted synchronous parallelism (*forall*).

An ASM model *run* is a finite or infinite sequence $S_0, S_1, \ldots, S_i, \ldots$ of states: starting from an initial state S_0, a *run step* from S_i to S_{i+1} consists of the execution of all the transition rules invoked from a *main rule*[2] and enabled to fire, and leads to simultaneous updates of a number of locations. The model execution fails if an inconsistent update occurs, when a location is assigned conflicting values, or if an invariant, expressed as a first-order logic formula that must hold in every state, is violated.

ASMETA (ASM mETAmodeling) [1,10] is a set of tools based on ASMs to support the specification, validation, and verification of systems' behavior. In this work, we rely on ASMETA, using it as a comprehensive toolset to specify ASM models and to analyze their correctness in a systematic manner.

An ASMETA model is specified in a `.asm` file using the textual language `AsmetaL`. Listing 1 shows a model excerpt, which is structured into five sections:

- `import`: Imports definitions from external modules, including the StandardLibrary which provides names for basic domains and functions for the operations over these domains (line 2).
- `signature`: Declares domains and functions modeling knowledge about the system (lines 3–21).
- `definitions`: Contains static functions, transition rules declaration, and invariants – first-order formulas that must hold in all states – (lines 22–38).
- `main rule`: Defines the entry point for computation at each run step. It may invoke other transition rules by name[3].
- `default init`: Initializes dynamic domains and controlled/out functions.

4.2 I/O Abstract State Machines

In [13,14], we defined an *I/O ASM* as an ASM with input/output interfaces, and orchestration operators enabling compositional simulation of I/O ASMs that interact via I/O events.

[1] An ASM location is a memory unit represented by a function together with specific argument values, identifying where a value is stored in a given state.

[2] According to the working definition of ASM model implemented in ASMETA.

[3] A named rule in the `definitions` section is defined as `r_rule(`*`params`*`)`, while it is invoked from another rule as `r_rule[`*`params`*`]`.

Definition 1 (I/O ASM). *An* I/O ASM *is an ASM m with a non-empty set I_m of input (or monitored) functions and a non-empty set O_m of output (or out) functions in its signature. We denote by (I_m, m, O_m) an I/O ASM, and by $curr\_state(m)$ the set of its locations values.*

Case Study. Figure 2 depicts several examples of I/O ASM for the MRM system in a black-box manner. The I/O interface, defined in terms of monitored and out ASM functions, represents the set of interaction ports (or points) with the environment or other ASMs, while the set of controlled locations represents the internal state of the I/O ASM. An excerpt of the ASM *ConfigurationMgr* has been already reported in Listing 1.

```
1   asm configurationMgr
2   import StandardLibrary
3   signature:
4    enum domain States = {INIT | NORMAL}
5    ...
6       //INPUT from Pillbox
7       monitored time_consumption: Compartment -> Seq(Natural)
8       monitored name: Compartment -> String
9       monitored drugIndex: Compartment -> Natural
10      monitored redLed: Compartment -> LedLights
11   //INPUT from prescription
12   monitored medicine_list: Seq(String)
13   monitored amount: String -> Natural
14   ...
15   controlled state: States
16   controlled prevRedLed: Compartment -> LedLights
17   ...
18      derived ledStatusUpdateOk: Compartment -> Boolean
19      static compartment1: Compartment
20      static compartment2: Compartment
21      ...
22  definitions:
23      function ledStatusUpdateOk($compartment in Compartment) =
24          ((prevRedLed($compartment) = OFF and redLed($compartment)= BLINKING) or
25          (prevRedLed($compartment) = BLINKING and redLed($compartment)= ON))

27      rule r_INIT =
28          par
29              forall $s in asSet(medicine_list) do extend Medicine with $m do id($m) := $s
30              state := NORMAL
31          endpar
32   //The only valid traces of a led light are the sequences: OFF, ON, BLINKING and BLINKING, OFF
33   invariant inv_A_redLed over redLed: ( forall $c in Compartment with not ledStatusUpdateOk($c) )
34   //Pills type consistency between the prescription and the compartments of the pillbox
35   invariant inv_A_medicineList over name(Compartment): ( forall $c in Compartment with (contains(
36    medicine_list,name($c)))) // compartments contain only prescribed pills
37   ...
38   main rule r_Main = if state = INIT then r_INIT[] else r_keepPrevLiths[] endif
39      default init s0:
40      function state = INIT
41      function medicine_list = ["fosamax","moment"] // Medicine prescription (e.g., from a JSON file)
42      ...
```

Listing 1. Excerpt of an ASM model in `AsmetaL` from the MRM running example.

4.3 Compositional Execution of I/O ASMs

I/O ASMs can be connected and interact *by binding* [13,14] input and out functions with the same name and type. The resulting *assembly* of I/O ASM models can be then executed according to a *composition formula* denoting an orchestration schema for the co-simulation of the composed I/O ASMs. A composition formula uses the composition operators defined in [13,14]. Formally, a (recursive) composition formula of I/O ASMs is defined as follows:

Definition 2 (I/O ASM composition formula). *A composition formula c over an assembly A of I/O ASMs is: a single I/O ASM m of A or $c_1 \mid c_2$ or $c_1 <|> c_2$ or $c_1 <\|> c_2$ or $c_1 \| c_2$ where c_1 and c_2 are composition formulas and $\{|, <|>, <\|>, \|\}$ are composition operators.*

Table 1 reports the basic binary composition operators over two I/O ASMs m_1 and m_2 (the basic cases of composition formula in Definition 2 when operands are I/O ASMs), and informally recalls their execution semantics. More details on the simulation mechanism of an I/O ASM assembly can be found in [13,14].

Table 1. I/O ASM composition operators (from [14]).

Operator name	Symbol	Semantics description
(Simplex) pipe or sequence	$m_1 \mid m_2$	First execute m_1, then use the output of m_1 as input to execute m_2.
Half-duplex bidirectional pipe	$m_1 <|> m_2$	First execute m_1, subsequently use the output of m_1 as input to execute m_2; then, return the output of m_2 as input to m_1 for its next future execution (and not the current one).
Full-duplex bidirectional pipe	$m_1 <\|> m_2$	First execute both m_1 and m_2 simultaneously, then return the outputs of m_1 to m_2 and the outputs of m_2 to m_1 for their next execution.
Synchronous parallel split (or fork-join)	$m_1 \| m_2$	Execute both m_1 and m_2 separately on their inputs, then return the union of their outputs.

Case Study. Figure 2 shows the I/O ASM assembly (the architecture) of the MRM system. To ensure patient safety, the mobile app includes two key components:

- *ConfigurationMgr*, which checks the actual pillbox configuration against the medicine prescription;
- *Rescheduler*, which manages critical situations by applying corrective actions on the time scheduling for medicine intake when possible.

The user manually fills the pillbox compartments' slots (one medicine type per compartment) according to the prescription. A patient's prescription contains medicine details like: name, amount, minimum time separation between drugs, time schedule, and retry intervals for missed doses. This data are used to initialize the configuration manager and the rescheduler. When it is time to take a medicine, the pillbox sends a notification message to the caregiver/patient through the corresponding compartment, which lights up and unlocks. The patient confirms intake by opening and closing the compartment. If the medicine is not taken within 10 min, the compartment's LED flashes for another 10 min

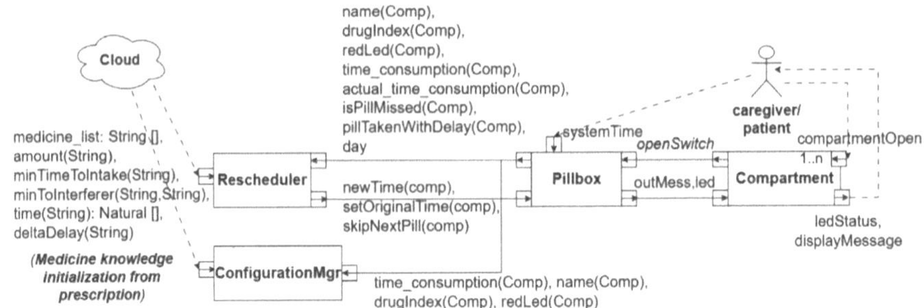

Fig. 2. MRM I/O ASM assembly.

before the dose is marked as missed. Runtime knowledge, including the current pillbox configuration, the state of each compartment, the actual intake time of a pill, etc., is constantly monitored by the Pillbox and sent in a targeted way to the configuration manager and the rescheduler according to their supervisioning goal.

Once all of the components have been initialized, the MRM assembly can be executed using the composition formula:

$$((PB <|> (CM \parallel RES)) <|> (C_1 \parallel \ldots \parallel C_n))$$

where PB is the *Pillbox* component, CM is the *ConfigurationMgr*, RES is the *Rescheduler*, and $C_1 \ldots C_n$ are different compartments of the pill dispenser. Intuitively, the pillbox operates first, and its intended actions are then supervised by the *ConfigurationMgr*—which verifies the pillbox configuration against the prescription—and by the *Rescheduler*, which may adjust the medication schedule if needed, before the final confirmation and actuation of the compartments.

5 Underlying Theory: CbD for Compositional I/O ASMs

In CbD [6,7,20,27], a system architecture is defined by means of components, which encompass both implementations and contracts. An implementation is an instantiation of a component. A contract is a description of the expected interaction of the component with the environment (i.e., other components). A contract specifies the expected behavior of a component by defining the *assumptions* A that must be satisfied by the environment and the *guarantees* G satisfied by the component in response. Thus, we can denote the contract of a component c as the pair (A, G), and, following the Hoare-style notation [28], we express contract satisfaction as the triple $\{A\}c\{G\}$ meaning that, if the component implementation c is executed from a state where A holds (the pre-state) and its execution terminates, then G will hold in the resulting state (the post-state).

Following this assume-guarantee paradigm, we define the contract of an I/O ASM, which, in our framework, models a component behavior (i.e., the implementation). In our underlying theory, we take into consideration that the externally observable part of a component model is the set of I/O location values, which change along an ASM run (see Sect. 4.1)[4].

Definition 3 (Contract of an I/O ASM). *The contract ctr_m for an* I/O ASM (I_m, m, O_m) *is the pair* $ctr_m = (A_m, G_m)$ *where assumptions* A_m *are assertions (i.e., first-order logic formulas) over* I_m *and guarantees* $\{G_m\}$ *are assertions (i.e., first-order logic formulas) over* O_m.

Case study. Listing 1 reports two of the assumptions in A_{MRM} of the MRM component: the first one, `inv_A_redLed` (see line 33), checks the valid sequence of led lights in the compartment of the MRM system; the second one, `inv_A_medicineList` (see line 36), verifies that the medicine loaded in each compartment corresponds to those prescribed by the doctor (see the ASMETA model of the *ConfigurationMgr* in the replication package [11] for the complete list of the MRM component's assumptions).

We now define the condition for an I/O ASM to satisfy its contract.

Definition 4 (Contract satisfaction of an I/O ASM). *We say that an I/O ASM m satisfies a contract* $ctr_m = (A_m, G_m)$ *iff every time m is executed from a current state where the assumptions* A_m *hold and its execution step terminates, then the guarantees* G_m *will hold in the resulting next state. In this case, we can write:* $\{A_m\}\ m\ \{G_m\}$.

To deal with the composition of contracts for I/O ASMs and ensure the correctness of an I/O ASM composition formula (so called *compositional correctness*) w.r.t. a contract, we define how contract composition is expressed and computed for the basic composition operators of I/O ASMs. For this purpose, we introduce inference rules defining how to derive the composition of the contracts from the sub-component's contracts and suitable logical constraints.

To express these inference rules, we use the following notation:

$$\frac{\{A_{c_1}\}c_1\{G_{c_1}\},\ \{A_{c_2}\}c_2\{G_{c_2}\}\ldots\{A_{c_n}\}c_n\{G_{c_n}\}\ ,l_1\ldots l_n}{\{A_c\}c = \bigotimes(c_1,\cdots,c_n)\{G_c\}}$$

where $\bigotimes(c_1,\cdots,c_n)$ is the composite model c of the n component models $c_1,\cdots,c_n$ according to a composition formula c (see Definition 2 in Sect. 4). The rule states that if the components $c_1,\ldots,c_n$ satisfy their contracts and the logical assertions $l_1\ldots l_n$ hold, then we can derive the contract for the composed model c with assumption A_c and guarantee G_c.

Note that every composition rule holds modulo invariants, i.e., assuming that the state invariants of an I/O ASM are always preserved.

The definition of the contract for each compositional operator is given below.

[4] This notion is similar to the notion of *trace* introduced in the contract framework presented in [20].

Definition 5 (Contract of composition $c_1 \mid c_2$). *The contract of composition $c_1 \mid c_2$ is defined as:*

$$\frac{\{A_{c_1}\}\ c_1\ \{G_{c_1}\}, \{A_{c_2}\}\ c_2\ \{G_{c_2}\}, G_{c_1} \Rightarrow A_{c_2}}{\{A_{c_1}\}\ c_1 \mid c_2\ \{G_{c_2}\}}$$

thus: $A_{c_1|c_2} \equiv A_{c_1}$ and $G_{c_1|c_2} \equiv G_{c_2}$.

Definition 6 (Contract of composition $c_1 || c_2$). *The contract of composition $c_1 \parallel c_2$ is defined as:*

$$\frac{\{A_{c_1}\}\ c_1\ \{G_{c_1}\}, \{A_{c_2}\}\ c_2\ \{G_{c_2}\}}{\{A_{c_1} \wedge A_{c_2}\}\ c_1 \parallel c_2\ \{G_{c_1} \wedge G_{c_2}\}}$$

thus: $A_{c_1||c_2} \equiv A_{c_1} \wedge A_{c_2}$ and $G_{c_1||c_2} \equiv G_{c_1} \wedge G_{c_2}$.

Definition 7 (Contract composition $c_1 <|> c_2$). *The contract of composition $c_1 <|> c_2$ is defined as:*

$$\frac{\{A_{c_1}\}\ c_1\ \{G_{c_1}\}, \{A_{c_2}\}\ c_2\ \{G_{c_2}\}, G_{c_1} \Rightarrow A_{c_2}, G_{c_2} \Rightarrow A'_{c_1}}{\{A_{c_1}\}\ c_1 <|> c_2\ \{A'_{c_1}\}}$$

where A'_{c_1} is the evaluation of the assumptions of component c_1 after executing c_2; thus: $A_{c_1<|>c_2} \equiv A_{c_1}$ and $G_{c_1<|>c_2} \equiv A'_{c_1}$.

Definition 8 (Contract of composition $c_1 <||> c_2$). *The contract of composition $c_1 <||> c_2$ is defined as:*

$$\frac{\{A_{c_1}\}\ c_1\ \{G_{c_1}\}, \{A_{c_2}\}\ c_2\ \{G_{c_2}\}, G_{c_1} \Rightarrow A'_{c_2}, G_{c_2} \Rightarrow A'_{c_1}}{\{A_{c_1} \wedge A_{c_2}\}\ c_1 <||> c_2\ \{A'_{c_1} \wedge A'_{c_2}\}}$$

where A'_{c_1} is the evaluation of the assumptions of component c_1 after executing c_2, and A'_{c_2} is the evaluation of the assumptions of component c_2 after executing c_1; thus: $A_{c_1<||>c_2} \equiv A_{c_1} \wedge A_{c_2}$ and $G_{c_1<||>c_2} \equiv A'_{c_1} \wedge A'_{c_2}$.

These inference rules are sound; formal proofs are omitted, as the paper focuses on the tool[5]. Besides the rules presented above, classical rules that strengthen the assumption A and/or weaken the guarantee G [28] can be used.

Case study. As an example of contract composition, let us consider the parallel composition $CM \parallel RES$ in the MRM system. The contract of this composition, denoted as $ctr_{CM||RES}$, is obtained by combining the assumptions A and guarantees G of the two specifications CM and RES according to Definition 6. Given the following contracts for CM and RES[6]:

- $ctr_{CM} = (A_{CM}, G_{CM})$, where A_{CM}={`inv_A_redLed`, `inv_A_medicineList`, `inv_A_compName`, `inv_A_CompSize`, `inv_A_CompMed`, `inv_A_timeConsumption`}, G_{CM}=true

[5] The proof of the definitions' soundness is available as additional material associated with this paper at [12].

[6] The complete ASMETA models of CM and RES are in the replication package [11].

- $ctr_{RES} = (A_{RES}, G_{RES})$, where A_{RES}={`inv_A_actual_time`}, G_{RES}={`inv_G_newTime`, `inv_G_skipNextPill`}

the contract of the composition $CM \mid\mid RES$ is:
$ctr_{CM||RES} = (A_{CM||RES}, G_{CM||RES})$, where $A_{CM||RES} = A_{CM} \wedge A_{RES}$ ={`inv_A_redLed`, `inv_A_medicineList`, `inv_A_comp_Name`,`inv_A_CompSize`, `inv_A_CompMed`, `inv_A_time Consumption`,`inv_A_actual_time`} and $G_{CM||RES} = G_{CM} \wedge G_{RES}$ ={`inv_G_newTime`, `inv_G_skipNextPill`}.

6 The AsmetaComp tool for Runtime Contract Checking

The inference approach for deriving and checking composed contracts presented in the previous section has been implemented by extending the ASMETA tool `AsmetaComp` [14]. This section presents the AsmetaComp architecture, the notations for contract definition and composition, the mechanism for runtime contract checking, and a summary of the tool features and its limitations.

A replication package containing the `AsmetaComp` tool (a Java archive file), all MRM ASMETA models, and composition scripts for validation scenarios reproducibility are available online at [11]. A demo video of the tool is also available online at: https://foselab.unibg.it/asmeta/videos/AsmetaComp@FORTE26.mp4.

6.1 Overview and Component Architecture

For contract checking, `AsmetaComp` can be invoked via a Java CLI program (see Fig. 3) that reads from a script a sequence of commands for setting (*setup*) and running (*run*) the composition formula(s) for I/O ASMs. I/O ASMs are ASMETA models that are written in the `AsmetaL` textual notation, and enriched with A/G contracts. They are executed in a compositional manner, with the contracts being validated inline on the models themselves. The output of the compositional simulation is an ASM run that is recorded on the standard console.

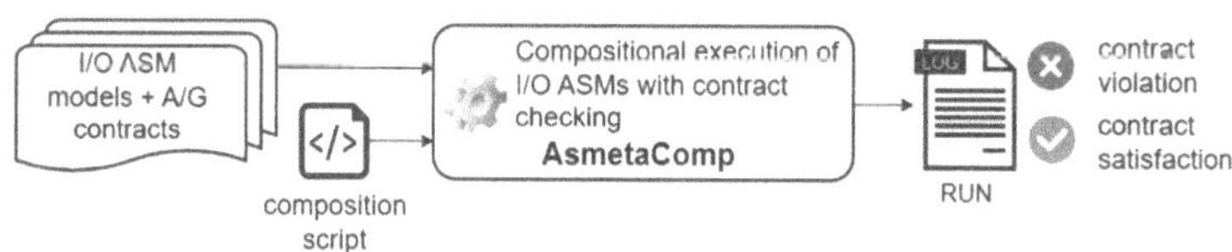

Fig. 3. `AsmetaComp` and artifacts.

The core component of `AsmetaComp` is `CompositionManager`, which implements the interface `IModelComposition` to simulate a composition—represented by the abstract class `Composition`—of ASMETA models (see Fig. 4). It may throw exceptions during the compositional simulation in case a model execution fails (the exception class `CompositionException`) or an A/G contract is violated (the class `CBDException`). The methods `eval()` of `Composition` and `run()` of `IModelComposition` have been appropriately overloaded to enable (through a boolean flag) runtime contract checking. Details on the class hierarchy representing the entity types involved in the composition of I/O ASMs, where the abstract class `Composition` serves as the root node, and on the compositional simulation algorithm over these entities are in [14].

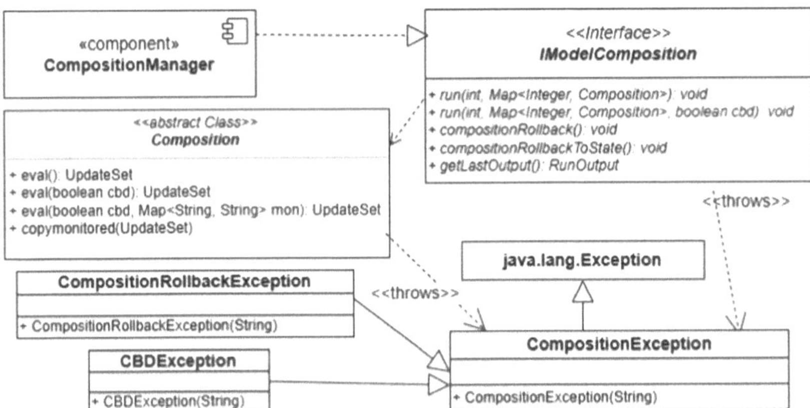

Fig. 4. `AsmetaComp` class diagram: blue elements are extensions for contract checking. (Color figure online)

6.2 Contract Definition and Composition

As *assertion language* to define contracts we adopt the `AsmetaL` textual notation. Contracts and components are therefore specified in a unified way using the same modeling notation. Specifically, contracts are defined in terms of *state invariants* of an I/O ASM model. The variables that are used in the contracts are locations local to the owning I/O ASM. Concretely, *assumptions* A are state invariants over *input locations* of the owning I/O ASM, while *guarantees* G are state invariants over *output locations* of the I/O ASM. At each model execution step, `AsmetaS`, the model simulator in ASMETA, checks for the state invariants over the input locations, and over the output locations before updating them according to the ASM transition rules. A failure of the A invariants means the environment misuses the model, a failure of the invariant G means that the model operates incorrectly.

To compose and run I/O ASMs, `AsmetaComp` provides a lightweight *scripting language*, executed via a Java-based CLI (see Fig. 3). A composition script contains *setup* and *run* commands to, respectively, define and execute I/O ASM composition formulae. An example of composition script for the MRM system is reported in Listing 2. Note that ASM models can be closed (all input locations are bound to output locations of other models) or open (some input locations are unbounded or, in other words, are bound to an abstract environment). For open models, the key–value pairs within curly braces in a *run* command provide an explicit initialization for unbound input locations, thus all models before running a composition are closed. For example, in Listing 2 (see line 11), before executing the composed system, initialization runs are performed. The scheduling subsystem is initialized (see line 8), while each compartment is set to closed, its LED is switched off, and a unique identifier (`myID`) is assigned (see lines 9– 10). The next commands advance the fully composed system (`pillbox_comp`). In each run (from line 11), both compartments remain closed, and the global clock `systemTime` (simulated time, in minutes) is assigned a value. The chosen time stamps correspond to moments of interest for observing scheduling and dispensing behaviors. Running the system at these discrete times allows systematic evaluation of the timed interactions among all of the components.

```
1  setup CM as Pillbox_CBD/configurationMgr.asm
2  setup RES as Pillbox_CBD/rescheduler.asm
3  setup C1 as Pillbox_CBD/compartment.asm
4  setup C2 as Pillbox_CBD/compartment.asm
5  setup PB as Pillbox_CBD/pillbox.asm
6  setup setup_comp as ( CM || RES )
7  setup pillbox_comp as ( ( PB <|> ( CM || RES ) ) <|> ( C1 || C2 ) )
8  run(setup_comp, {pillboxSystemTime=0;day=0;isPillMissed(compartment1)=false;pillTakenWithDelay(
       compartment1)=false;isPillMissed(compartment2)=false;pillTakenWithDelay(compartment2)=false;
       redLed(compartment1)=OFF;redLed(compartment2)=OFF;name(compartment1)="fosamax";name(
       compartment2)="moment";time_consumption(compartment1)=[360];time_consumption(compartment2)
       =[730,1140];actual_time_consumption(compartment1)=[0];actual_time_consumption(compartment2)
       =[0,0];drugIndex(compartment1)=0;drugIndex(compartment2)=0})
9  run(C1, {compartmentOpen(1)=false;outMess(1)="";led(1)=OFF;myID=1})
10 run(C2, {myID=2;compartmentOpen(2)=false;outMess(2)="";led(2)=OFF})
11 run(pillbox_comp, {compartmentOpen(1)=false;compartmentOpen(2)=false;systemTime=10n})
12 run(pillbox_comp, {compartmentOpen(1)=false;compartmentOpen(2)=false;systemTime=361n})
13 run(pillbox_comp, {compartmentOpen(1)=false;compartmentOpen(2)=false;systemTime=365n}) ...
```

Listing 2. Composition script

6.3 Runtime Contract Checking Mechanism

During the execution of an I/O ASM composition, `AsmetaComp` leverages the *invariant checking* mechanism of the `AsmetaS` simulator to check the A/G assertions of the whole composition. Indeed, during the execution of a composition operator in the I/O ASM composition, `AsmetaComp` checks for the validation of the components' contract and the further assertions required in the premises of the inference rule of the contract composition operator (see definitions of the inference rules in Sect. 5), so guaranteeing the contract of the resulting composition before proceeding. On the atomic components, the contract satisfaction is performed as previously explained on the single model. In case of contract violation, `AsmetaComp` throws an exception, which keeps track of the violated A/G assertion. This violation is recorded in the output console; the composite model execution fails, but models are rolled-back to their previous state.

6.4 Tool Features and Limitations

Overall, `AsmetaComp` offers an executable environment that integrates modeling, composition, and runtime contract verification, providing native support for Contract-based Design with I/O ASMs and the following ***key functionalities***:

- **Unified Modeling and Contracts.** The tool supports specifying both component behavior and A/G contracts within a unified modeling environment, using a contract language aligned with I/O ASM semantics.
- **Compositional Execution.** Independent components modeled as I/O ASMs can be composed using dedicated operators. The execution engine orchestrates their interaction according to the defined composition semantics.
- **Inference Support for Composed Contracts.** The framework provides inference rules that allow the systematic derivation of contracts for composed components from the contracts of their constituents.
- **Automated Runtime Contract Checking.** During compositional simulation, contracts are automatically checked, enabling early detection of assumption violations and guarantee breaches as components interact.

Despite its capabilities, the current implementation exhibits ***limitations*** primarily related to *scalability* and the *user-friendly output interface*. Broader empirical validation is required to assess scalability and usability in large-scale industrial case studies. In addition, improving the output interface would facilitate clearer reporting of contract violations, execution traces, and verification results in a more accessible and interpretable format. These aspects will be addressed as future improvements of our tool.

7 Validation

This section presents the scenario-based experimental validation of AsmetaComp on the MRM case study, framed around the following research question:

RQ—Can `AsmetaComp` *check assume/guarantee (A/G) contracts during the compositional simulation of I/O ASMs?*

Table 2. MRM model size metrics (#m: monitored, #c: controlled, #d: derived, #o: out, #s: static, #r: rule constructors, #rd: rule declarations, #ct: contracts)

MRM model	#m	#c	#d	#o	#s	#r	#rd	#ct
pillbox.asm	7	3	3	12	4	135	13	5
configurationMgr.asm	4	9	1	0	2	13	4	6
compartment.asm	4	2	0	3	0	9	1	6
knowledge.asm	0	1	8	0	0	0	0	0
rescheduler.asm	9	9	1	5	2	48	5	3

Models and Validation Scenarios. To provide an indication of the complexity of the MRM system model, Table 2 lists the sub-models along with their size metrics, including the number of functions (by type), rule constructors, rule declarations, and contracts. It is a medium-size modular system model with a contract mainly consisting of functional assertions (adherence to functional requirements), interaction assertions (for correct sequencing of outputs, e.g. valid led light color transitions), safety assertions (to avoid unsafe states, e.g., no invalid medicine intake), and temporal assertions (e.g., scheduling of pill intakes). We introduce here four scenarios (see Table 3): two that result in contract violations (*WP* and *PO*) and two that do not (*CS1* and *CS2*). In *CS1*, a pill (e.g., pill "fosamax" in the first compartment) is missed and it is expected that it cannot be rescheduled because the minimum required interval before the next pill (e.g., "moment" in the second compartment) is not satisfied. The second non-violation scenario *CS2* models the situation in which the "fosamax" dose is taken on time, while the "moment" dose is rescheduled and subsequently taken at the new time. Other scenarios are in the online replication package.

In scenario *WP*, we set the second pillbox's compartment to "pantoprazole" instead of the prescribed "moment". This setting should result in a violation of the safety assertion `inv_A_medicineList` for the *ConfigurationMgr* (see Listing 1, line 36), which checks consistency between the prescribed pills and those contained in the pillbox. In scenario *PO*, we set the assumption time for the "fosamax" pill in the first compartment in a way that causes a dose overlap with the next pill ("moment" in the second compartment) in case of rescheduling. We simulate the patient not taking the "fosamax"

Table 3. Validation Scenarios

Scenario	Error	Expected violated assertion	Description
CS1	none	–	A pill is missed, and not rescheduled since it interferes with the next pill.
CS2	none	–	The first pill is taken on time, and the second is rescheduled and taken at the new time.
WP	Wrong pill	`inv_A_medicineList`	The patient loads an incorrect pill in the second compartment.
PO	Pill overlap	`inv_A_timeConsumption`	The rescheduler sets a new time consumption that violates the minimum interval before the next pill.

pill by keeping the `compartmentOpen(1)` to false. When the *Rescheduler* intervenes to reschedule the missed "fosamax" pill, the temporal assertion **`inv_A_timeConsumption`** (see line 67 of the ASMETA model *ConfigurationMgr* in the replication package [11]) is violated, which ensures that any two potentially interacting doses, either across compartments or within the same compartment, are scheduled with a time gap of at least the minimum safe interval specified by **`minToInterferer`**.

Validation Results. We report here the execution of scenarios WP and PO, which lead to contract violations; the others are available in the online repository.

```
1  Composition setup for alias: PB -> ASM pillbox: {}
2  {RES=ASM reschedulerNonOptimal: {}, PB=ASM pillbox: {}, setup_comp= ( ASM configurationMgr: {} ||
       ASM reschedulerNonOptimal: {} ) , CM=ASM configurationMgr: {}, C1=ASM compartment: {}, C2=
       ASM compartment: {}} ...
3  RUN STEP 1
4  Running composition: setup_comp with input: {name(compartment2)="moment", name(compartment1)="
       fosamax", ...} ...
5  RUN STEP 4
6  Running composition: pillbox_comp with input: {compartmentOpen(2)=false, compartmentOpen(1)=false, ...}
7  Monitored locations pillbox: {compartmentOpen(2)=false, compartmentOpen(1)=false, ...}
8  Out locations: pillbox: {name(compartment2)=pantoprazole , name(compartment1)=fosamax, ...}
9  Monitored locations configurationMgr: {name(compartment1)="fosamax", name(compartment2)=
       "pantoprazole", ...}
10 Error in composition pillbox_comp: Assumption violation over inv_A_medicineList
11 Composition script interrupted due to contract violation.
```

Listing 3. Composition contract violation: wrong pill

```
1 Composition setup for alias: PB −> ASM pillbox: {}
2 {RES=ASM reschedulerNonOptimal: {}, PB=ASM pillbox: {}, setup_comp= ( ASM configurationMgr: {} ||
      ASM reschedulerNonOptimal: {} ) , CM=ASM configurationMgr: {}, C1=ASM compartment: {}, C2=
      ASM compartment: {}} ...
3 RUN STEP 10
4 Running composition: pillbox_comp with input: {compartmentOpen(2)=false, compartmentOpen(1)=false,
      systemTime=753n}
5 Monitored locations pillbox: {systemTime=753n, openSwitch(1)=false, openSwitch(2)=false,
      setNewTime(compartment1)=true, displayMessage(1)="fosamax missed", displayMessage(2)="Take
      moment in 10 minutes"}
6 Out locations pillbox: {led(1)=OFF, led(2)=OFF, outMess(1)=fosamax rescheduled, outMess(2)=moment
      missed, redLed(compartment1)=OFF, redLed(compartment2)=OFF,
      time_consumption(compartment1)=[420], time_consumption(compartment2)=[730,1140], name(
      compartment1)=fosamax, name(compartment2)=moment, pillboxSystemTime=753}
7 Monitored locations configurationMgr: {minToInterferer(fosamax,moment)=360,
      time_consumption(compartment1)=[420], time_consumption(compartment2)=[730,1140],... }
8 Error in composition pillbox_comp: Assumption violation over inv_A_timeConsumption
9 Composition script interrupted due to contract violation.
```

Listing 4. Composition contract violation: time overlap with the next medicine

Listing 3 shows the execution of scenario *WP* in which, the patient placed "pantoprazole" in the second compartment (see the prompted pill names at line 8), which does not match the prescribed medicines (see the prompted pill names at line 4).

Listing 4 shows the execution of scenario *PO*: the rescheduler updates the administration time of "fosamax" pill to 420 (see line 6) because the patient missed the dose. However, this adjustment fails to respect the minimum required interval before the subsequent dose —"moment", scheduled at 730—since the time difference is less than 360 (see line 7).

8 Conclusion

This paper presented AsmetaComp, a tool for Contract-based Design and runtime contract checking of I/O ASM models. Future work includes improving the tool output features and applying it to further industrial case studies.

References

1. ASMETA (ASM mETAmodeling) toolset. https://asmeta.github.io/
2. Arbab, F.: Reo: a channel-based coordination model for component composition. Math. Struct. Comput. Sci. **14**(3), 329–366 (2004). https://doi.org/10.1017/S0960129504004153
3. Bartocci, E., Ferrère, T., Henzinger, T.A., Nickovic, D., da Costa, A.O.: Information-flow interfaces. In: Johnsen, E.B., Wimmer, M. (eds.) Fundamental Approaches to Software Engineering. FASE 2022. LNCS, vol. 13241, pp. 3–22. Springer, Cham (2022). https://doi.org/10.1007/978-3-030-99429-7_1
4. Basile, D., ter Beek, M.H.: A runtime environment for contract automata. In: Chechik, M., Katoen, J.P., Leucker, M. (eds.) Formal Methods. FM 2023. LNCS, vol. 14000, pp. 550–567. Springer, Cham (2023). https://doi.org/10.1007/978-3-031-27481-7_31
5. Basu, A., Combaz, J., Nguyen, T.H., Jaber, M., Sifakis, J., Bensalem, S., Bozga, M.: Rigorous component-based system design using the BIP framework . IEEE Software **28**(03), 41–48 (2011). https://doi.org/10.1109/MS.2011.27, https://doi.ieeecomputersociety.org/10.1109/MS.2011.27

6. Benveniste, A., Caillaud, B., Ferrari, A., Mangeruca, L., Passerone, R., Sofronis, C.: Multiple viewpoint contract-based specification and design. In: de Boer, F.S., Bonsangue, M.M., Graf, S., de Roever, W.P. (eds.) Formal Methods for Components and Objects. FMCO 2007. LNCS, vol. 5382, pp. 200–225. Springer, Berlin, Heidelberg (2008). https://doi.org/10.1007/978-3-540-92188-2_9
7. Benveniste, A., et al.: Contracts for system design. Found. Trends® Electron. Des. Autom. **12**(2-3), 124–400 (2018). https://doi.org/10.1561/1000000053, http://dx.doi.org/10.1561/1000000053
8. Bicarregui, J., Fitzgerald, J., Larsen, P.G., Woodcock, J.: Industrial practice in formal methods: a review. In: Misra, J., Nipkow, T., Sekerinski, E. (eds.) FM 2006: Formal Methods. FM 2006. LNCS, vol. 4156, pp. 182–195. Springer, Berlin, Heidelberg (2006). https://doi.org/10.1007/11813040_14
9. Bocchi, L., Honda, K., Tuosto, E., Yoshida, N.: A theory of design-by-contract for distributed multiparty interactions. In: Gastin, P., Laroussinie, F. (eds.) CONCUR 2010 - Concurrency Theory, pp. 162–176. Springer, Berlin, Heidelberg (2010). https://doi.org/10.1007/978-3-642-15375-4_12
10. Bombarda, A., Bonfanti, S., Gargantini, A., Riccobene, E., Scandurra, P.: ASMETA tool set for rigorous system design. In: Platzer, A., Rozier, K.Y., Pradella, M., Rossi, M. (eds.) Formal Methods. FM 2024. LNCS, vol. 14934, pp. 492–517. Springer, Cham (2024). https://doi.org/10.1007/978-3-031-71177-0_28
11. Bonfanti, S., Gargantini, A., Riccobene, E., Scandurra, P.: Accompanying tool artifact for the paper “AsmetaComp: a tool for Runtime Contract Checking with I/O Abstract State Machines” (2026). https://doi.org/10.5281/zenodo.18678488
12. Bonfanti, S., Gargantini, A., Riccobene, E., Scandurra, P.: AsmetaComp: a Tool for Runtime Contract Checking with I/O Abstract State Machines (2026). https://github.com/asmeta/asmeta_based_applications/tree/main/MRM_CBD
13. Bonfanti, S., Gargantini, A., Riccobene, E., Scandurra, P.: Compositional simulation of Abstract State Machines for safety critical systems. In: Tapia Tarifa, S.L., Proença, J. (eds.) Formal Aspects of Component Software. FACS 2022. LNCS, vol. 13712, pp. 3–19. Springer, Cham (2022). https://doi.org/10.1007/978-3-031-20872-0_1
14. Bonfanti, S., Gargantini, A., Riccobene, E., Scandurra, P.: A compositional simulation framework for abstract state machine models of discrete event systems. Form. Aspects Comput. (2024)
15. Bonfanti, S., Riccobene, E., Scandurra, P.: A runtime safety enforcement approach by monitoring and adaptation. In: Biffl, S., Navarro, E., Löwe, W., Sirjani, M., Mirandola, R., Weyns, D. (eds.) Software Architecture, pp. 20–36. Springer, Cham (2021). https://doi.org/10.1007/978-3-030-86044-8_2
16. Börger, E., Raschke, A.: Modeling Companion for Software Practitioners. Springer, Berlin, Heidelberg (2018). https://doi.org/10.1007/978-3-662-56641-1
17. Börger, E., Stärk, R.: Abstract State Machines: A Method for High-Level System Design and Analysis. Springer, Cham (2003). https://doi.org/10.1007/978-3-642-18216-7
18. Calinescu, R., Kikuchi, S.: Formal methods @ runtime. In: Calinescu, R., Jackson, E. (eds.) Foundations of Computer Software. Modeling, Development, and Verification of Adaptive Systems. LNCS, vol. 6662, pp. 122–135. Springer, Berlin, Heidelberg (2011). https://doi.org/10.1007/978-3-642-21292-5_7
19. Chen, T., Chilton, C., Jonsson, B., Kwiatkowska, M.: A compositional specification theory for component behaviours. In: Seidl, H. (ed.) Programming Languages and Systems, pp. 148–168. Springer, Berlin, Heidelberg (2012). https://doi.org/10.1007/978-3-642-28869-2_8

20. Cimatti, A., Tonetta, S.: Contracts-refinement proof system for component-based embedded systems. Sci. Comput. Program. **97**, 333–348 (2015). https://doi.org/10.1016/j.scico.2014.06.011, https://www.sciencedirect.com/science/article/pii/S0167642314002901, object-Oriented Programming and Systems (OOPS 2010) Modeling and Analysis of Compositional Software (papers from EUROMICRO SEAA'12)
21. Cimatti, Alessandro, E.G.H.P., Rozier, K.Y.: Software contracts meet system contracts (2026). https://www.dagstuhl.de/26031, dagstuhl Seminar 26031, January 11–16, 2026
22. Cofer, D., Gacek, A., Miller, S., Whalen, M.W., LaValley, B., Sha, L.: Compositional verification of architectural models. In: Goodloe, A.E., Person, S. (eds.) NASA Formal Methods, pp. 126–140. Springer, Berlin, Heidelberg (2012). https://doi.org/10.1007/978-3-642-28891-3_13
23. Ferrante, O., Passerone, R., Ferrari, A., Mangeruca, L., Sofronis, C.: BCl: a compositional contract language for embedded systems. In: Proceedings of the 2014 IEEE Emerging Technology and Factory Automation (ETFA), pp. 1–6 (2014). https://doi.org/10.1109/ETFA.2014.7005353
24. Gheri, L., Lanese, I., Sayers, N., Tuosto, E., Yoshida, N.: Design-by-contract for flexible multiparty session protocols. In: Ali, K., Vitek, J. (eds.) 36th European Conference on Object-Oriented Programming, ECOOP 2022, Berlin, Germany, June 6-10, 2022. LIPIcs, vol. 222, pp. 8:1–8:28. Schloss Dagstuhl - Leibniz-Zentrum für Informatik (2022). https://doi.org/10.4230/LIPICS.ECOOP.2022.8
25. Gleirscher, M., Marmsoler, D.: Formal methods: oversold? Underused? A survey. arXiv preprint arXiv:1812.08815 (2018). https://arxiv.org/abs/1812.08815
26. Graf, S., Passerone, R., Quinton, S.: Contract-based reasoning for component systems with rich interactions. In: Sangiovanni-Vincentelli, A., Zeng, H., Di Natale, M., Marwedel, P. (eds.) Embedded Systems Development: From Functional Models to Implementations, vol. 20, pp. 139–154. Springer, Cham (2014). https://doi.org/10.1007/978-1-4614-3879-3_8
27. Gurov, D., Hähnle, R., Huisman, M., Reger, G., Lidström, C.: Principles of contract languages (Dagstuhl Seminar 22451). Dagstuhl Reports **12**(11), 1–27 (2023). https://doi.org/10.4230/DagRep.12.11.1, https://drops.dagstuhl.de/entities/document/10.4230/DagRep.12.11.1
28. Hoare, C.A.R.: An axiomatic basis for computer programming. Commun. ACM **12**(10), 576–580 (1969). https://doi.org/10.1145/363235.363259
29. Incer, I., Benveniste, A., Sangiovanni-Vincentelli, A., Seshia, S.A.: From Interface Automata to Hypercontracts, pp. 477–493. Springer Nature Switzerland, Cham (2022). https://doi.org/10.1007/978-3-031-22337-2_23
30. Lidström, C., Gurov, D.: Contract based embedded software design. In: David, C., Sun, M. (eds.) Theoretical Aspects of Software Engineering. TASE 2023. LNCS, vol 13931, pp. 77–94. Springer Nature Switzerland, Cham (2023). https://doi.org/10.1007/978-3-031-35257-7_5
31. Lu, X., Tian, C., Gu, B., Yu, B., Chen, C., Duan, Z.: A contract-based framework for formal verification of embedded software. In: Bourke, T., Chen, L., Goharshady, A. (eds.) Dependable Software Engineering. Theories, Tools, and Applications. SETTA 2024. LNCS, vol. 15469, pp. 180–196. Springer, Singapore (2025). https://doi.org/10.1007/978-981-96-0602-3_10
32. Meyer, B.: Applying 'design by contract'. Computer **25**(10), 40–51 (1992). https://doi.org/10.1109/2.161279

33. Nandi, C., Monot, A., Oriol, M.: Stochastic contracts for runtime checking of component-based real-time systems. In: Proceedings of the 18th International ACM SIGSOFT Symposium on Component-Based Software Engineering, pp. 111–116. CBSE '15, Association for Computing Machinery, New York, NY, USA (2015). https://doi.org/10.1145/2737166.2737173
34. Quinton, S., Graf, S.: Contract-based verification of hierarchical systems of components. In: Proceedings of the 6th IEEE International Conference on Software Engineering and Formal Methods (SEFM 2008), pp. 377–381. IEEE Computer Society (2008). https://doi.org/10.1109/SEFM.2008.28
35. Stierand, I., et al.: Using contract-based component specifications for virtual integration testing and architecture design. In: Proceedings of the DATE Conference (2010)
36. Taghavi, B., et al.: Modeling the composition of analysis components and automatic constraint checking for semantic soundness. J. Syst. Softw. **231**, 112637 (2026). https://doi.org/10.1016/j.jss.2025.112637, https://www.sciencedirect.com/science/article/pii/S0164121225003061
37. Talcott, C.L., et al.: Composition of languages, models, and analyses. In: Heinrich, R., Durán, F., Talcott, C.L., Zschaler, S. (eds.) Composing Model-Based Analysis Tools, pp. 45–70. Springer, Cham (2021). https://doi.org/10.1007/978-3-030-81915-6_4

Author Index

Published by Springer Nature Switzerland AG 2026
L. Bocchi and B. Kulahcioglu Ozkan (Eds.): FORTE 2026, LNCS 16589, pp. 277–278, 2026.
https://doi.org/10.1007/978-3-032-28187-6

Zeitfracht Medien GmbH
Ferdinand-Jühlke-Straße 7
99095 Erfurt, Deutschland
produktsicherheit@kolibri360.de